Lecture Notes in Computer Science

Lecture Notes in Artificial Intelligence   16105

Founding Editor

Jörg Siekmann

AF397629

Series Editors

Randy Goebel, *University of Alberta, Edmonton, Canada*
Wolfgang Wahlster, *DFKI, Berlin, Germany*
Zhi-Hua Zhou, *Nanjing University, Nanjing, China*

The series Lecture Notes in Artificial Intelligence (LNAI) was established in 1988 as a topical subseries of LNCS devoted to artificial intelligence.

The series publishes state-of-the-art research results at a high level. As with the LNCS mother series, the mission of the series is to serve the international R & D community by providing an invaluable service, mainly focused on the publication of conference and workshop proceedings and postproceedings.

Xian-Ling Mao · Zhaochun Ren · Muyun Yang

Editors

Natural Language Processing and Chinese Computing

14th National CCF Conference, NLPCC 2025
Urumqi, China, August 7–9, 2025
Proceedings, Part IV

 Springer

Editors
Xian-Ling Mao
Beijing Institute of Technology
Beijing, China

Zhaochun Ren
Leiden University
Leiden, The Netherlands

Muyun Yang
Harbin Institute of Technology
Harbin, China

ISSN 0302-9743   ISSN 1611-3349 (electronic)
Lecture Notes in Artificial Intelligence
ISBN 978-981-95-3351-0   ISBN 978-981-95-3352-7 (eBook)
https://doi.org/10.1007/978-981-95-3352-7

LNCS Sublibrary: SL7 – Artificial Intelligence

© The Editor(s) (if applicable) and The Author(s), under exclusive license
to Springer Nature Singapore Pte Ltd. 2026

This work is subject to copyright. All rights are solely and exclusively licensed by the Publisher, whether the whole or part of the material is concerned, specifically the rights of translation, reprinting, reuse of illustrations, recitation, broadcasting, reproduction on microfilms or in any other physical way, and transmission or information storage and retrieval, electronic adaptation, computer software, or by similar or dissimilar methodology now known or hereafter developed.
The use of general descriptive names, registered names, trademarks, service marks, etc. in this publication does not imply, even in the absence of a specific statement, that such names are exempt from the relevant protective laws and regulations and therefore free for general use.
The publisher, the authors and the editors are safe to assume that the advice and information in this book are believed to be true and accurate at the date of publication. Neither the publisher nor the authors or the editors give a warranty, expressed or implied, with respect to the material contained herein or for any errors or omissions that may have been made. The publisher remains neutral with regard to jurisdictional claims in published maps and institutional affiliations.

This Springer imprint is published by the registered company Springer Nature Singapore Pte Ltd.
The registered company address is: 152 Beach Road, #21-01/04 Gateway East, Singapore 189721, Singapore

If disposing of this product, please recycle the paper.

Preface

Welcome to NLPCC 2025, the fourteenth CCF International Conference on Natural Language Processing and Chinese Computing. Following the success of previous conferences held in Beijing (2012), Chongqing (2013), Shenzhen (2014), Nanchang (2015), Kunming (2016), Dalian (2017), Hohhot (2018), Dunhuang (2019), Zhengzhou (2020), Qingdao (2021), Guilin (2022), Foshan (2023), and Hangzhou (2024), this year's NLPCC convened in Urumqi. As a premier international conference on natural language processing and Chinese computing, organized by the CCF-NLP (Technical Committee of Natural Language Processing, China Computer Federation, formerly known as Technical Committee of Chinese Information, China Computer Federation), NLPCC serves as a vital forum for researchers and practitioners from academia, industry, and government to share their ideas, research results, and experiences, and to promote their research and technical innovations. NLPCC 2025 was organized by the China Computer Federation (CCF), and hosted by Xinjiang Technical Institute of Physics and Chemistry, Chinese Academy of Sciences.

The fields of natural language processing (NLP) and Chinese computing (CC) have seen remarkable growth in recent years. In keeping with NLPCC's tradition, we welcomed submissions in ten areas for the main conference: Fundamentals of NLP; Information Extraction and Knowledge Graphs; Information Retrieval, Dialogue Systems, and Question Answering; Large Language Models and Agents; Machine Learning for NLP; Machine Translation and Multilinguality; Multimodality and Explainability; NLP Applications and Text Mining; Sentiment Analysis, Argumentation Mining, and Social Media; Summarization and Generation. This year, we received 505 submissions by the submission deadline.

After a thorough double-blind peer process in which submissions received three reviews each on average, including meta reviewing, out of 505 valid submissions (some were withdrawn by authors or desk-rejected due to policy violations), 152 papers were accepted as regular papers to be presented at the main conference. Among them, 61 papers (12% of submissions) were presented orally. Additionally, these papers were featured in the poster sessions, offering further opportunities for discussion and engagement. Another 91 papers (18%) were exclusively presented as posters. Ten papers were nominated by our area chairs for the best and outstanding paper awards. An independent best paper award committee was formed, i.e., Jiliang Tang (Michigan State University), Xia "Ben" Hu (Rice University), Chenghua Lin (University of Manchester), Xin Zhao (Renmin University of China), Qi Zhang (Fudan University), to select the top papers from the shortlist. Eventually, we selected two best papers, one best student paper, and two outstanding papers. Differing from past years, this conference only accepted English papers. In addition to the main proceedings, 26 papers were accepted for the Evaluation workshops.

We were honored to have four internationally renowned keynote speakers, Mark Steedman (University of Edinburgh), Maarten de Rijke (University of Amsterdam), Taro

Watanabe (Nara Institute of Science and Technology), and Qun Liu (Huawei Noah's Ark Lab), who shared their recent research progress and achievements in natural language processing.

We would like to express our gratitude to all those who have contributed to NLPCC 2025. First, we extend our thanks to our 32 area chairs for their diligent work in recruiting reviewers, monitoring the review and discussion processes, and carefully rating and recommending submissions. We are also thankful to all reviewers for their time and effort in reviewing the submissions, especially acknowledging the 35 reviewers selected as the best reviewers, as nominated by the area chairs for their exceptional contributions. Our appreciation goes to the general chairs, Ruifeng Xu, and to the organization committee chairs, Yating Yang and Haofen Wang. Special thanks to Muyun Yang, the publication chair, for his invaluable assistance.

Finally, we thank all the authors who submitted their work to NLPCC 2025 and our sponsors for their contributions to the conference. Without your support, we could not have assembled such a strong conference program.

We were pleased to welcome you to NLPCC 2025 in Urumqi and hope you enjoyed the conference!

July 2025
Xian-Ling Mao
Zhaochun Ren

Organization

Organization Committee

General Chair

Ruifeng Xu — Harbin Institute of Technology (Shenzhen), China

Program Committee Chairs

Xian-Ling Mao — Beijing Institute of Technology, China
Zhaochun Ren — Leiden University, Netherlands

Workshop Chairs

Qingcai Chen — Harbin Institute of Technology (Shenzhen), China
Yankai Lin — Renmin University of China, China
Wei Wei — Huazhong University of Science, China

Evaluation Chairs

Yunbo Cao — PLA Academy of Military Science, China
Tao Ji — Fudan University, China

Tutorial Chairs

Baotian Hu — Harbin Institute of Technology (Shenzhen), China
Keping Bi — Institute of Computing Technology, Chinese Academy of Sciences, China
Chenghua Lin — University of Manchester, UK

Publication Chair

Muyun Yang — Harbin Institute of Technology, China

Sponsorship Chairs

Min Yang   Shenzhen Institute of Advanced Technology,
                            Chinese Academy of Sciences, China
Feiyu Xiong   Institute for Advanced Algorithms Research,
                            Shanghai & MemTensor (Shanghai)
                            Technology Co., Ltd., China

Publicity Chairs

Sendong Zhao   Harbin Institute of Technology, China
Libo Qin   Central South University, China

Organization Chairs

Yating Yang   Xinjiang Institute of Physics & Chemistry,
                            University of Chinese Academy of Sciences,
                            China
Haofen Wang   Tongji University, China

Area Chairs

IR/Dialogue Systems/Question Answering

Xi Wang   University of Sheffield
Jiashu Zhao   Wilfrid Laurier University, Canada
Jiaxin Mao   Renmin University, China
Zhijing Wu   Beijing Institute of Technology, China

Fundamentals of NLP

Meishan Zhang   Harbin Institute of Technology, Shenzhen, China
Liner Yang   Beijing Language and Culture University, China

Information Extraction and Knowledge Graphs

Yubo Chen	Institute of Automation, Chinese Academy of Sciences, China
Yumin Shang	Beijing University of Posts and Telecommunications, China
Chao Huang	University of Hong Kong, China
Yang Deng	Singapore Management University

Large Language Models and Agents

Yanan Cao	Chinese Academy of Sciences, China
Yuxuan Lai	Open University of China, China
Yue Feng	University of Birmingham, UK
Yongbin Li	Alibaba Group, China

Machine Learning for NLP

Yunshan Ma	Singapore Management University, Singapore
Lin Gui	King's College London, UK

Machine Translation and Multilinguality

Zhaopeng Tu	Tencent AI LAB, China
Jiahuan Pei	Vrije Universiteit Amsterdam, Netherlands

Multimodality and Explainability

Xiang Wang	University of Science and Technology of China, China
Na Zhao	Singapore University of Technology and Design, Singapore
Chenghua Lin	University of Manchester, UK

NLP Applications/Text Mining

Ren Li	Chongqing Jiaotong University, China
Jing Li	Hong Kong Polytechnic University, China
Pengjie Ren	Shandong University, China
Yangjun Zhang	Queen Mary University of London, UK
Guansong Pang	Singapore Management University, Singapore

Summarization and Generation

Piji Li   Nanjing University of Aeronautics and
                             Astronautics, China
Xiuying Chen   Mohamed bin Zayed University of Artificial
                             Intelligence, UAE

Sentiment Analysis/Argumentation Mining/Social Media

Yunfei Long   Queen Mary University of London, UK
Zhen Wu   Nanjing University, China
Ruihong Qiu   University of Queensland, Australia
Xiaocheng Feng   Harbin Institute of Technology, China

Poster Chairs

Yongbin Liu   University of South China, China
Zhiliang Tian   National University of Defense Technology,
                             China
Wei Liu   Xiaomi Corporation, China

OpenReview Co-chairs

Yougang Lyu   University of Amsterdam, Netherlands
Ruiqing Sun   Beijing Institute of Technology, China
Guobiao Zhang   Beijing Institute of Technology, China

Program Committee

Aart van Halteren   VU Amsterdam/Philips Research, Netherlands
Abdul-Rahman Mawlood-Yunis   Wilfrid Laurier University, Canada
Abrar Mohamedelmugadad   University of Birmingham, UK
  Elhassan Elid
Adnan Labib   King's College London, UK
Akash Ghosh   Indian Institute of Technology Patna, India
Aleksandr V. Petrov   Tripadvisor, UK
Ali Araabii   Bunq, Netherlands
Ameeta Agrawal   Portland State University, USA
Amir Soleimani   TAUS, Netherlands
Amirbek Djanibekov   Fondazione Bruno Kessler, Italy
Animesh Raj   University of Birmingham, UK

Anita Vrins	Vrije Universiteit Amsterdam, Netherlands
Argyrios Papoudakis	University of Edinburgh, UK
Ashish David	Missouri University of Science and Technology, USA
Ashutosh Singla	Centrum Wiskunde en Informatica, Netherlands
Bang Liu	University of Montreal, Canada
Benyou Wang	Chinese University of Hong Kong, Shenzhen, China
Bin Li	Nanjing Normal University, China
Bin Wang	Harbin Institute of Technology (Shenzhen), China
Bingbing Wang	Harbin Institute of Technology (Shenzhen), China
Bingqing Wang	Bosch Research Center North America, USA
Bo Chen	Minzu University of China, China
Bo Shao	CISPA Helmholtz Center for Information Security, Germany
Bo Xu	Dalian University of Technology, China
Bo Zhang	Nanjing University of Aeronautics and Astronautics, China
Bobo Li	National University of Singapore, Singapore
Boyan Xu	Guangdong University of Technology, China
Boyu Luo	University of Queensland, Australia
Caixia Yuan	Beijing University of Posts and Telecommunications, China
Changmeng Zheng	Hong Kong Polytechnic University, China
Changzhi Zhou	Beijing Institute of Technology, China
Chaoqun Duan	Harbin Institute of Technology, China
Chen Qiu	Wuhan University Science and Technology, China
Chen Xu	Harbin Engineering University, China
Chen Xu	Beijing Institute of Technology, China
Chen Zhang	Meituan, China
Chen Zhang	Peking University, China
Chenhao Ma	Chinese University of Hong Kong, Shenzhen, China
Chenliang Li	Wuhan University, China
Chenlong Zhang	Institute of Automation, Chinese Academy of Sciences, China
Chong Li	Institute of Automation, Chinese Academy of Sciences, China
Chuanyi Li	Nanjing University, China
Chunhui Li	Hong Kong University of Science and Technology, China
Claudia Marzi	Institute for Computational Linguistics - CNR, Italy

Congchi Yin	Nanjing University of Aeronautics and Astronautics, China
Conghui Zhu	Harbin Institute of Technology, China
Cunxiang Wang	Westlake University, China
Dao Quang Huy	Singapore Management University, Singapore
Da Ren	Hong Kong Polytechnic University, China
Danny Wang	University of Queensland, Australia
Dequan Yang	Mohamed bin Zayed University of Artificial Intelligence, UAE
Dingcheng Li	Baidu, USA
Dingzirui Wang	Harbin Institute of Technology, China
Doctor Faiyaz	University of Essex, UK
Dong Li	Chongqing University, China
Dongshuo Liu	Beijing Institute of Technology, China
Dongyuan Li	University of Tokyo, Japan
Ekaterina Khramtsova	Oracle, Australia
Emmanuele Chersoni	Hong Kong Polytechnic University, China
Erxin Yu	Hong Kong Polytechnic University, China
Esam Ghaleb	Max Planck Institute for Psycholinguistics, Germany
Faiyaz Doctor	University of Essex, UK
Falk Scholer	RMIT University, Australia
Fangxu Yu	University of Maryland, College Park, USA
Fei Zhao	Nanjing University, China
Feilong Chen	Huawei Technologies Ltd., China
Feng Xia	University of Sheffield, UK
Fengchi Wang	Wilfrid Laurier University, Canada
Fengran Mo	Université de Montréal, Canada
Flor Miriam Plazadel- Arco	Leiden University, Netherlands
Gao Zuchen	Hong Kong Polytechnic University, China
Ge Qu	University of Hong Kong, China
Gongbo Tang	Beijing Language and Culture University, China
Guangming Huang	University of Essex, UK
Guanhua Chen	Southern University of Science and Technology, China
Guanyi Chen	Central China Normal University, China
Guo-Biao Zhang	Beijing Institute of Technology, China
Gurunameh Singh Chhatwal	Wilfrid Laurier University, Canada
Hai Wang	Amazon, USA
Hajer Ayadi	York University, Canada
Han Liu	Dalian University of Technology, China
Hanhua Hong	University of Manchester, UK

Hao Wang	Shanghai University, China
Hao Wang	Sichuan University, China
Hao Wang	Beijing Institute of Technology, China
Hao Zhou	Nanchang University, China
Haodong Xie	University of Manchester, UK
Haohao Luo	Sun Yat-sen University, China
Haoran Luo	Beijing University of Posts and Telecommunications, China
Haoxuan Li	University of Electronic Science and Technology of China, China
Hasan Iqbal	Mohamed bin Zayed University of Artificial Intelligence, UAE
He Chang	Communication University of China, China
Heng Yu	Beijing Normal University, China
Hengtong Lu	Li Auto Inc., China
Hezhe Qiao	Singapore Management University, Singapore
Hongbang Yuan	Institute of Automation, Chinese Academy of Sciences, China
Hongfei Xu	Zhengzhou University, China
Hongli Mao	Beijing Institute of Technology, China
Hongliang Dai	Nanjing University of Aeronautics and Astronautics, China
Hongyu Zhang	Chongqing University, China
Hongzhan Lin	Hong Kong Baptist University, China
Hossein A. Rahmani	University College London, UK
Hugo Enrique Ramirez-Centeno	Queen Mary, University of London, UK
Huiyao Chen	Harbin Institute of Technology (Shenzhen), China
Huy Quang Dao	Singapore Management University, Singapore
Italo Luis da Silva	King's College London, UK
Jen-tse Huang	Johns Hopkins University, USA
Jerome Ramos	University College London, UK
Jiaao Li	Beijing Institute of Technology, China
Jiachun Li	Institute of Automation, Chinese Academy of Sciences, China
Jiahao Xu	Tencent AI Lab, China
Jiali Cheng	University of Massachusetts Lowell, USA
Jian Liu	University of Science and Technology Beijing, China
Jianfei Yu	Nanjing University of Science and Technology, China
Jiaxin Qin	University of Illinois Urbana-Champaign, USA
Jiaxin Yuan	Beijing Language and Culture University, China
Jie Zhu	Alibaba Group, China

Jin Wang	Yunnan University, China
Jing Luo	Xi'an Jiaotong University, China
Jinghang Gu	Hong Kong Polytechnic University, China
Jinghui Lu	ByteDance Inc., China
Jingqing Zhang	Pangaea Data Limited, UK
Jingwen Wang	Elizabethtown College, USA
Jinyang Li	University of Hong Kong, China
Jinyu Zhou	Nanjing University, China
Jitai Hao	Shandong University, China
Jiu Sha	Baidu, China
Jiyuan An	Beijing Language and Culture University, China
Jiyuan Yang	Shandong University, China
Jiyue Jiang	Guangzhou National Laboratory, China
Joel Mackenzie	University of Queensland, Australia
Jonathan Tonglet	Technische Universität Darmstadt, Germany
Jonibek Mansurov	Mohamed bin Zayed University of Artificial Intelligence, UAE
Joseph James	University of Sheffield, UK
Jun Yang	Marcpoint Co., Ltd., China
Junhao Liu	University of California, Irvine, USA
Junhui Li	Soochow University, China
Junrong Liao	University of Electronic Science and Technology of China, China
Junshuang Wu	Beijing Jinghang Research Institute of Computing and Communication, China
Kai Xiong	Harbin Institute of Technology, China
Kailai Yang	University of Manchester, UK
Kailun Bian	Nanchang University, China
Ke Li	University of Exeter, UK
Ke Zhang	Dataminr, Inc., USA
Keyang Ding	Harbin Institute of Technology, China
Kuo Tian	Nanjing University, China
Lang Gao	Mohamed bin Zayed University of Artificial Intelligence, UAE
Lauren Olson	Vrije Universiteit Amsterdam, Netherlands
Lei Chen	Fudan University, China
Lei Zhang	Meta, USA
Lei Zhang	Guizhou University, China
Leila Tavakoli	Service Australia, Australia
Li Du	BAAI, China
Li Zheng	Wuhan University, China
Li-Ming Zhan	Hong Kong Polytechnic University, China

Liang Chen	Chinese University of Hong Kong, China
Liang Ding	Zhejiang University, China
Liang Pang	Institute of Computing Technology, Chinese Academy of Sciences, China
Lianwei Wu	Northwestern Polytechnical University, China
Lin Ren	Southeast University, China
Ling Luo	Dalian University of Technology, China
Linhai Zhang	King's College London, UK
Linmei Hu	Beijing Institute of Technology, China
Linqi Song	City University of Hong Kong, China
Linyang Li	Fudan University, China
Long Bai	Institute of Computing Technology, Chinese Academy of Sciences, China
Longfei Yang	Tokyo Institute of Technology, Japan
Lucia Donatelli	Vrije Universiteit Amsterdam, Netherlands
Lucy H. Lin	Spotify, USA
Luyang Lin	Chinese University of Hong Kong, China
Ming Fang	Nanjing University, China
Mahdi Abootorabi	Sharif University of Technology, Iran
Mark Sanderson	RMIT University, Australia
Mehdi Kargar	Toronto Metropolitan University, Canada
Meng Guo	Beijing Normal University, China
Mengru Wang	Zhejiang University, China
Ming Liao	Hong Kong Polytechnic University, China
Ming Liu	Deakin University, Australia
Mingxu Tao	Peking University, China
Mingzhe Yu	Singapore Management University, Singapore
Mingzi Cao	University of Sheffield, UK
Minzheng Wang	Institute of Automation, Chinese Academy of Sciences, China
Muyun Yang	Harbin Institute of Technology, China
Nan Huo	University of Hong Kong, China
Nan Jiang	University of Texas at El Paso, USA
Nayu Liu	Tiangong University, China
Nguyen Cam-Tu	Nanjing University, China
Panpan Gong	South China University, China
Patrick Amadeus Irawan	Singapore Management University, Singapore
Peiling Yi	Queen Mary University of London, UK
Peiming Guo	Harbin Institute of Technology (Shenzhen), China
Peng Liu	Norwegian University of Science and Technology, Norway

Peng Wang	Macau University of Science and Technology, China
Ping Jian	Beijing Institute of Technology, China
Qi Liu	Alibaba Group, China
Qian Li	Beijing University of Posts and Telecommunications, China
Qiang Sheng	Institute of Computing Technology, Chinese Academy of Sciences, China
Qiang Yang	University of Florida, USA
Qianglong Chen	Huawei Technologies Ltd., China
Qiangqiang Ren	Renmin University of China, China
Qiao Xiao	Chongqing Jiaotong University, China
Qiguang Chen	Harbin Institute of Technology, China
Qiji Zhou	Westlake University, China
Qikai Cheng	Wuhan University, China
Qingbao Huang	Guangxi University, China
Qinglin Zhu	King's College London, UK
Quan Guo Guangxi	Minzu University, China
Quzhe Huang	Kuaishou, China
Rahul Godara	University of Birmingham, UK
Ravi Shekhar	University of Essex, UK
Rebecca Salganik	University of Rochester, USA
Renzhi Wang	Nanjing University of Aeronautics and Astronautics, China
Richen Sun	Beijing Institute of Technology, China
Ritesh Manna	Legal-Pythia, UK
Robert Ridley	Nanjing University, China
Rohan Sakeri	University of Birmingham, UK
Ruibo Wang	Shanxi University, China
Ruifan Li	Beijing University of Posts and Telecommunications, China
Ruihan Hu	Beijing University of Posts and Telecommunications, China
Runze Xia	Nanjing University of Aeronautics and Astronautics, China
Ruoyao Wang	University of Arizona, USA
Satayu Parinayok	University of Tokyo, Tokyo Institute of Technology, Japan
Shalini Jangra	University of Surrey, UK
Shaolin Zhu	Tianjin University, China
Shengjie Ma	Renmin University of China, China
Shi Feng	Northeastern University, China
Shih-Hung Wu	Chaoyang University of Technology, Taiwan

Shirin Seyedsalehi	Toronto Metropolitan University, Canada
Shu-Xun Yang	Beijing Institute of Technology, China
Shuai Zhao	Beijing University of Posts and Telecommunications, China
Shuaiyi Li	Chinese University of Hong Kong, China
Shujian Huang	Nanjing University, China
Shumin Deng	National University of Singapore, Singapore
Shun Wang	University of Sheffield, UK
Shuo Xu	Shandong University, China
Si Li	Beijing University of Posts and Telecommunications, China
Si Sun	Tsinghua University, China
Siqi Wang	Hong Kong Polytechnic University, China
Sixing Wu	Yunnan University, China
Siya Qi	King's College London, UK
Siyuan Wang	University of Southern California, USA
Tao Ji	Fudan University, China
Teng Tu	National University of Singapore, Singapore
Thomas Pickard	University of Sheffield, UK
Tian Lan	Beijing Institute of Technology, China
Tian-Yi Che	Beijing Institute of Technology, China
Tianhao Shen	Tianjin University, China
Tianlin Zhang	University of Chinese Academy of Sciences, China
Tianlun Liu	National University of Defense Technology, China
Tiansi Dong	University of Cambridge, UK
Tianwei Yan	Chongqing Jiaotong University, China
Tianyi Men	Institute of Automation, Chinese Academy of Sciences, China
Ting Xu	Chinese University of Hong Kong, China
Ting-En Lin	Alibaba Group, China
Tingwen Liu	Institute of Information Engineering, Chinese Academy of Sciences, China
Tong Xiao	Northeastern University, China
Vanja M. Karan	Universität Wien, Austria
Vinod Khandkar	University of Surrey, UK
Wang Xu	Tsinghua University, China
Wei Emma Zhang	University of Adelaide, Australia
Wei Huang	Beijing University of Posts and Telecommunications, China
Wei Peng	Zhongguancun Laboratory, China
Wei Wang	Tsinghua University, China

Wei Xiang	Central China Normal University, China
Weibo Gao	University of Science and Technology of China, China
Weihang Su	Tsinghua University, China
Weixiang Zhao	Harbin Institute of Technology, China
Wen Zhang	Zhejiang University, China
Wenhao Zhang	Shandong University, China
Wenlong Fang	South China Normal University, China
Wenmian Yang	Beijing Normal University, China
Wenqi Zhang	Alibaba Group, China
Wenxuan Wang	Renmin University of China, China
William Thorne	University of Sheffield, UK
Winston Wu	University of Hawaii at Hilo, USA
Xiachong Feng	University of Hong Kong, China
Xiajing Wang	Open University of China, China
Xian Wu	Tencent, China
Xianchao Wu	NVIDIA, Japan
Xiang Huang	Nanjing University, China
Xiang Zhang	Mashang Consumer Finance Co., Ltd., China
Xianming LI	Hong Kong Polytechnic University, China
Xianpei Han	Institute of Software, CAS, China
Xiao Fu	University College London, UK
Xiao Li	Nanjing University, China
Xiaobo Liang	Soochow University, China
Xiaofei Zhou	Institute of Information Engineering, Chinese Academy of Sciences, China
Xiaohan Xu	University of Hong Kong, China
Xiaojun Chen	Shenzhen University, China
Xiaojun Zhang	Xi'an Jiaotong-Liverpool University, China
Xiaoqian Liu	University of Chinese Academy of Sciences, China
Xiaotong Qin	Tianjin University College of Applied Sciences, China
Xiaowei Zhu	Institute of Information Engineering, Chinese Academy of Sciences, China
Xiaoxia Yang	Chongqing Jiaotong University, China
Xiaoyan Gao	Beijing University of Technology, China
Xiaoyan Yu	Beijing Institute of Technology, China
Xiaoyan Zhao	Chinese University of Hong Kong, China
Xiaoyuan Liu	Tencent AI Lab, China
Xigang Bao	Renmin University of China, China
Xin Wu	South China University of Technology, China

Xin Zhang	Hong Kong Polytechnic University, China
Xinchi Chen	Fudan University, China
Xingwei Tan	University of Sheffield, UK
Xingyu Chen	Shanghai Jiao Tong University, China
Xingyu Deng	University of Sheffield, UK
Xingzhu Wang	Renmin University of China, China
Xinshi Lin	Chinese University of Hong Kong, China
Xinxin Li	Harbin Institute of Technology, China
Xinyu Zuo	Tencent, China
Xixun Lin	Institute of Information Engineering, Chinese Academy of Sciences, China
Xu Luo	University of South China, China
Xu Wang	Hebei University of Technology, China
Xunzhu Tang	University of Luxembourg, Luxembourg
Yao Zhang	Nankai University, China
Yafu Li	Shanghai Artificial Intelligence Laboratory, China
Yajie Yu	University of Birmingham, UK
Yan Jiang	University of Queensland, Australia
Yan Xu	Huawei Technologies Ltd., China
Yanbo Wang	Mohamed bin Zayed University of Artificial Intelligence, UAE
Yang Gao	Beijing Institute of Technology, China
Yang Zhong	University of Pittsburgh, USA
Yang Zhou	Institute of Automation, Chinese Academy of Sciences, China
Yangsong Lan	Nanjing University of Aeronautics and Astronautics, China
Yanhao Wang	East China Normal University, China
Yansong Feng	Peking University, China
Yanzeng Li	Beijing Normal University, China
Yao Wan	Huazhong University of Science and Technology, China
Yaojie Lu	Institute of Software, Chinese Academy of Sciences, China
Ye Liu	National University of Singapore, Singapore
Ye Yuan	Peking University, China
Yekun Chai	Baidu, China
Yi Feng	Zhejiang University, China
Yi Yang	Nanjing University of Information Science and Technology, China
Yi-Fan Lu	Beijing Institute of Technology, China
Yidan Wang	Institute of Information Engineering, Chinese Academy of Sciences, China

Yidong Chen   Xiamen University, China
Yidong Liang   Beijing Institute of Technology, China
Yifan Mo   Lanzhou University, China
Yige Xu   Nanyang Technological University, Singapore
Yile Wang   Shenzhen University, China
Yilun Liu   University of Queensland, Australia
Ying Zhang   RIKEN, Japan
Yinghui Li   Tsinghua University, China
Yinhe Zheng   Alibaba Group, China
Yiqi Liu   University of Manchester, UK
Yiqun Chen   Renmin University of China, China
Yiwei Wang   University of California, Merced, USA
Yong Ma   Sichuan Minzu College, China
Yongheng Zhang   Central South University, China
Yonghua Zhu   University of Auckland, New Zealand
Yongxiu Xu   Institute of Information Engineering, Chinese
                            Academy of Sciences, China
Yougang Lyu   University of Amsterdam, Netherlands
Youliang Yuan   Chinese University of Hong Kong, Shenzhen,
                            China
Yu Cao   University of Sydney, Australia
Yu Zhao   Tianjin University, China
Yuanhang Yang   Institute of Science Tokyo, Japan
Yuanxing Liu   Harbin Institute of Technology, China
Yubing Ren   Institute of Information Engineering, Chinese
                            Academy of Sciences, China
Yubo Feng   Dalian University of Technology, China
Yuchen Wu   Singapore University of Technology and Design,
                            Singapore
Yucheng Li   University of Surrey, UK
Yue Su   Guangxi Normal University, China
Yue Wang   Soochow University, China
YueQin Xiang   South China University, China
Yufei Chen   Nanjing University, China
Yufei Wang   Huawei Technologies Ltd., China
Yuhang Tian   Beijing Institute of Technology, China
Yuji Zhang   University of Illinois Urbana-Champaign, USA
Yun Chen   Shanghai University of Finance and Economics,
                            China
Yunzhi Yao   Zhejiang University, China
Yurou Zhao   Renmin University of China, China
Yusong Wang   Institute of Science Tokyo, Japan

Yuxiang Nie	Hong Kong University of Science and Technology, China
Yuxuan Gu	Harbin Institute of Technology, China
Yuyue Zhao	University of Science and Technology of China, China
Zechun Niu	Renmin University of China, China
Zeming Liu	Beijing University of Aeronautics and Astronautics, China
Zhanghao Hu	King's College London, UK
Zhaoyang Wang	University of North Carolina at Chapel Hill, USA
Zhe Hu	Hong Kong Polytechnic University, China
Zhen Xu	PCG Tencent, China
Zhen Yang	Anhui University, China
Zheng Ma	Nanjing University, China
Zhengfu He	Shanghai Innovation Institute, China
Zhenghao Liu	Northeastern University, China
Zhengliang Shi	Shandong University, China
Zhenhong Zhou	Nanyang Technological University, Singapore
Zhenjie Zhao	Nankai University, China
Zhizheng Wang	National Institutes of Health, USA
Zhichun Wang	Beijing Normal University, China
Zhihao Fan	Alibaba Group, China
Zhijing Wu	Beijing Institute of Technology, China
Zhiwei Liu	Salesforce AI Research, USA
Zhiwen Tang	Yunnan University, China
Zhixu Li	Renmin University of China, China
Zhiyang Teng	ByteDance Inc., Singapore
Zhiyuan Wen	Hong Kong Polytechnic University, China
Zhong Zhang	Tsinghua University, China
Zhuang Chen	Central South University, China
Zhuang Liu	Dongbei University of Finance and Economics, China
Zhuoren Jiang	Zhejiang University, China
Zhuoxuan Jiang	Shanghai Business School, China
Zi-Yi Dou	University of California, Los Angeles, USA
Zihan Wang	University of Amsterdam, Netherlands
Zijie Wu	Xidian University, China
Zirui Song	Mohamed bin Zayed University of Artificial Intelligence, UAE
Zixian Huang	Nanjing University, China
Zixiang Xu	Mohamed bin Zayed University of Artificial Intelligence, UAE

Zixuan Liu	University of Washington, USA
Ziyang Chen	National University of Defense Technology, China
Zongxi Li	Lingnan University, China
Zuchao Li	Wuhan University, China

Best Reviewers

Ling Luo	Dalian University of Technology, China
Xiachong Feng	University of Hong Kong, China
Rohan Sakeri	University of Birmingham, UK
Peng Wang	Macau University of Science and Technology, China
Yinghui Li	Tsinghua University, China
Tianyi Men	Institute of Automation, Chinese Academy of Sciences, China
Qiang Yang	University of Florida, USA
Robert Ridley	Nanjing University, China
Shaolin Zhu	Tianjin University, China
Adnan Labib	King's College London, UK
Ruihan Hu	Beijing University of Posts and Telecommunications, China
Wenxuan Wang	Renmin University of China, China
William Thorne	University of Sheffield, UK
Liang Ding	Zhejiang University, China
Yao Wan	Huazhong University of Science and Technology, China
Esam Ghaleb	Max Planck Institute for Psycholinguistics, Germany
Xu Luo	University of South China, China
Jinghang Gu	Hong Kong Polytechnic University, China
Yubing Ren	Institute of Information Engineering, Chinese Academy of Sciences, China
Chen Zhang	Peking University, China
Shi Feng	Northeastern University, China
Shun Wang	University of Sheffield, UK
Fengchi Wang	Wilfrid Laurier University, Canada
Teng Tu	National University of Singapore, Singapore

Lang Gao   Mohamed bin Zayed University of Artificial Intelligence, UAE

Xingyu Deng   University of Sheffield, UK

Organizers

Organized by

China Computer Federation, China

Hosted by

Xinjiang Technical Institute of Physics and Chemistry, Chinese Academy of Sciences

In Cooperation with

Lecture Notes in Computer Science

Springer

Sponsoring Institutions

Diamond Sponsors

Jingdong Group

Platinum Sponsors

Lenovo

Ant Group

Alibaba Cloud

Golden Sponsors

Baidu

GTCOM

BAYOU

TRS

海天瑞声

Dataocean AI

OPPO

VIVO

Zoneyet

TechniLegal

Paratera

Contents – Part IV

Summarization and Generation

Others

Evaluation Workshop

Machine Learning for NLP

HandDiff-GAN: Handwriting Diffusion-Enhanced Generative Adversarial Networks for Character Generation

Jiahao Zhang(iD) and Zesheng Cheng$^{(\boxtimes)}$(iD)

College of Computer Science and Technology, Qingdao University, Qingdao 266100, Shandong, China
zhangjiahao1@qdu.edu.cn, czs_110@hotmail.com

Abstract. Generating handwritten Chinese characters is a critical yet challenging task in computer vision due to their structural complexity and vast quantity. Constructing a comprehensive Chinese character library is both time-consuming and labor-intensive. While existing models mitigate the demand for large-scale character datasets, they often struggle with semantic accuracy and generation efficiency. In this paper, we propose HandDiff-GAN, a novel model that combines Generative Adversarial Networks (GANs) with a pre-trained conditional denoising diffusion probabilistic model (DDPM), aiming to generate high-quality handwritten Chinese characters using only a small number of reference samples. Furthermore, the model incorporates an interactive style adjustment mechanism, enabling users to fine-tune character styles in real time by adjusting features such as stroke thickness, tilt, and pen pressure. This user-driven approach ensures the generated characters align closely with user preferences. The proposed model preserves the style features of the reference samples while maintaining the structural integrity of the generated characters. This user-driven adjustment mechanism adds great flexibility to the generation process and enhances the practicality and robustness of the model. HandDiff-GAN has demonstrated great potential for personalized handwritten font generation, providing a flexible, efficient, and friendly solution for character generation.

Keywords: Handwritten Chinese characters · Generative adversarial networks · Conditional diffusion model

1 Introduction

Recent advancements in computer vision have notably enhanced handwritten character generation. Handwritten Chinese character generation is a complex task in computer vision due to the intricate structure and large vocabulary of Chinese characters [2,9]. Traditional methods, like hierarchical stroke decomposition, struggle to capture holistic stylistic features, especially for cursive or

© The Author(s), under exclusive license to Springer Nature Singapore Pte Ltd. 2026

X.-L. Mao et al. (Eds.): NLPCC 2025, LNAI 16105, pp. 3–14, 2026.
https://doi.org/10.1007/978-981-95-3352-7_1

interconnected strokes. Recent advances in deep learning, particularly GANs and diffusion models [7,12], have shown potential in addressing these challenges. While GANs produce high-quality images [10], they often fail to handle the complexity of Chinese characters, resulting in structural errors. Diffusion models, like Diff-Writer, improve generation stability and detail by incorporating character embeddings and style encoders [4,6]. This paper proposes the HandDiff-GAN model, combining GAN and diffusion models to enhance both the quality and efficiency of personalized handwriting generation, offering new solutions to the challenges in automated handwritten character synthesis [29].

Our contribution can be summarized as follows:

- We generate 3755 commonly used handwritten Chinese characters based on four-character idioms, retaining the handwriting style of the idioms. This approach significantly reduces the amount of training data required and enables flexible generation of the needed characters.
- We combine a pre-trained diffusion model with a generative adversarial network, where the GAN generates the initial image, easing the DDPM's task of generating images from noise. The DDPM then enhances the image quality and detail through post-processing, making the training process more robust and reducing GAN instability.
- Users can fine-tune the generated results to match their needs, with the model updating the style vector through comparative learning to align with user intentions. This enhances practicability and addresses generation deviation when reference sample quality is insufficient.

2   Related Work

DDPMs have outperformed traditional GANs by effectively capturing global structures and minimizing detail loss in image generation tasks [4,11]. The Diff-Writer model leverages DDPM for high-quality, online Chinese character generation, integrating character embeddings with a stylistic encoder [29]. Since their inception in 2014, GANs have been fundamental in handwriting generation, although they struggle with detail loss and structural distortion [1,30]. Innovations such as DCGAN and cGAN have enhanced visual quality and expressiveness, and efforts to integrate these with diffusion models aim to improve both detail fidelity and structural integrity [27,28]. Recent methods have further refined handwriting generation by decoupling style from content, enabling precise style synthesis with techniques ranging from RNN-based style vector extraction to complex models like SDT that offer detailed segmentation but require extensive annotations [5,8,21]. The HandDiff-GAN model streamlines the need for extensive references by using minimal fonts or idioms, merging GANs with diffusion modeling to enhance style diversity, structural stability, and detail authenticity in generated characters.

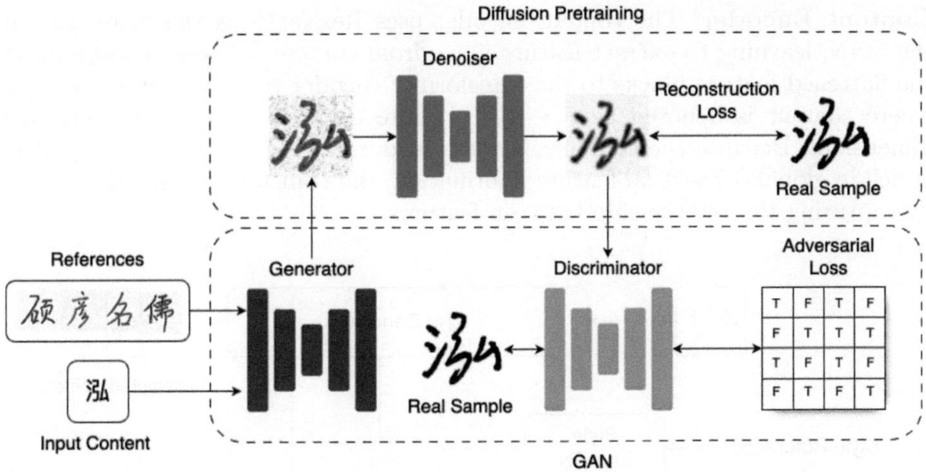

Fig. 1. Overview of the proposed method. Our HandDiff-GAN model is mainly composed of GAN and diffusion model, which first generates the preliminary image through GAN generator, and then optimizes the diffusion model to get a clearer image into the discriminator to discriminate with the real image for adversarial training.

3   Method

3.1   Overall Scheme

Our dataset consists of q types of Chinese characters handwritten by p authors. Each handwriting sample is denoted by x_k^i, where k represents the character type and i the author. x_k refers to the standard bold font template for each character. The model is trained to extract the handwriting style of the reference character while ensuring the accuracy of the character structure. Given a handwritten reference $X_r = \left\{ x_j^i \right\}_{j=1}^4$ and a standard bold template x_k, the generated result $G_{Di}\left(G\left(X_r, x_k \right), t \right)$ should resemble x_k^i, maintaining both structure and style. We combine the efficiency of GANs with the quality enhancement of diffusion models to improve generation.

As shown in Fig. 1, our model consists of the main GAN and Diffusion parts, which are jointly trained using Adversarial Learning. A multi-scale discriminator D is used to distinguish between the generated result $G_{Di}\left(G\left(X_r, x_k \right), t \right)$ and real samples, while predicting the author and character type during training. The discriminator D optimizes the generator G and diffusion model to generate higher quality characters.

3.2   HandDiff-GAN

Pre-trained Diffusion Models. On top of the above DDPM we additionally added style encoder, content encoder and LSTM noise reducer composition to the pre-trained diffusion model as shown in Fig. 2.

Content Encoder. The content encoder uses ResNet18 as the main part of the CNN, learning to extract feature maps from content references and feeding the flattened feature blocks to the transformer encoder to form content vectors, where content is denoted as $f \in R^{d*c}$, where $d = h * w$, c are the channel dimensions. Because the content encoder wants to have a feature vector f that is rich in global contextual feature information, the transformer can achieve this by capturing the relationship between features.

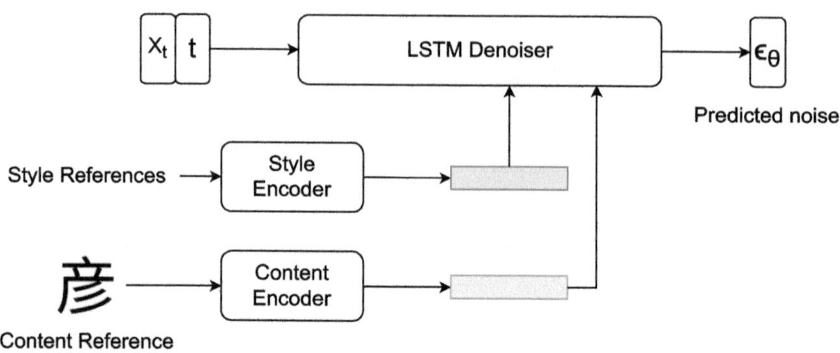

Fig. 2. The DDPM section consists of three parts: style encoder, content encoder and LSTM noise reducer.

Style Encoder. The handwriting style information of Chinese characters should also be represented as profile compact feature vectors. The style encoder E_s extracts the feature vector s as the style information from the handwriting reference $X_r = \left\{x_j^i\right\}_{j=1}^4$:

$$E_s(X_r) = s \tag{1}$$

LSTM Denoiser. The denoising module LSTM Denoiser is based on the conditional DDPM model as a framework, which consists of a bi-directional LSTM and a corresponding linear layer. Its inputs include noisy data x_t, time step t, content vector and style vector, and the corresponding noise ϵ_θ is predicted by the model:

$$\epsilon_\theta = Denoiser(x_t, emb(t), f, s) \tag{2}$$

In the training of the DDPM we introduce a reconstruction loss $\mathcal{L}_{rec}^{Di}$, which is a weighted sum of the MSE loss and the SSIM loss. MSE calculates the average squared difference between pixels of two images, while SSIM compares pixel similarity in localized regions, handling structural differences better (Fig. 3):

$$\mathcal{L}_{rec}^{Di} = \lambda_{mse}^{Di}\mathcal{L}_{mse} + \lambda_{ssim}^{Di}\mathcal{L}_{ssim} \tag{3}$$

$$E_c(x_k) = \{f_1, f_2, ..., f_5\} \tag{4}$$

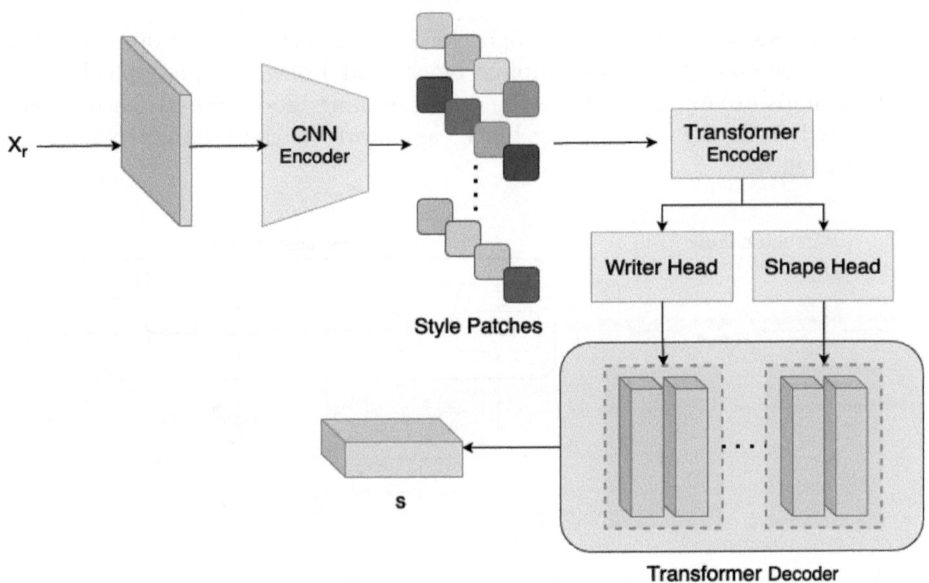

Fig. 3. The specific structure of the style encoder.

Handwriting Generator. As shown in Fig. 4, our GAN's generator G is comprised of three main components: the character encoder E_c, the style encoder E_s, and the integration decoder D_i. The character encoder E_c enhances the structural accuracy of Chinese characters by extracting multi-layered structural information from the bold template, and employing jumps between feature maps of the same dimensions [13, 14]. The style encoder E_s retrieves the style vector s from the handwritten reference $X_r = \left\{x_j^i\right\}_{j=1}^4$, utilizing similar methods to the DDPM style extraction. The integration decoder D_i merges this character structure and style information to create the targeted handwriting font x_k^i.

Style Encoder. As shown in Fig. 4, Our style encoder decomposes the input sample data into style blocks through a CNN encoder, and then decomposes the output vector into an interpretable overall font style dimension and an author style dimension through a transformer encoder. The author style dimension includes the stroke thickness, inclination and stroke strength of Chinese characters. We construct an editable latent space so that style parameters can be individually controlled and tuned, enabling more precise style control. Finally, the style vector is integrated into our desired style feature vector s through the transformer decoder.

Character Encoder. The UNet [15] architecture is used to build our character encoder, which consists of 4 upsampling blocks and 4 downsampling blocks, and 4 feature maps are extracted from the downsampling blocks plus 1 feature map is extracted from the upsampling block, as shown in the Character Encoder section in Fig. 4:

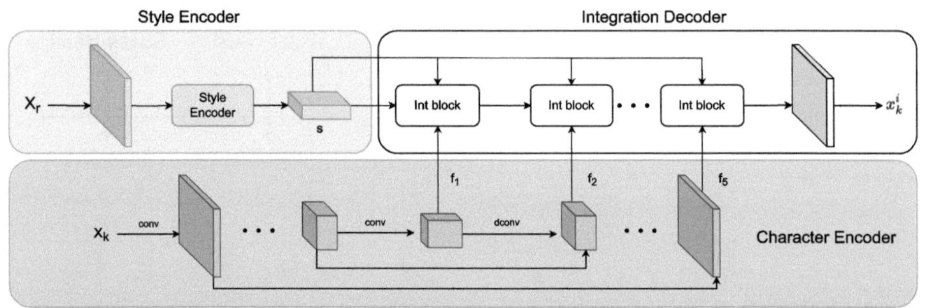

Fig. 4. The generator has three main components: style encoder, character encoder and integrated decoder.

Jump connections are constructed between feature maps of the same dimension. Encoder E_c is trained in a self-supervised manner to ensure that $G(X_r, x_k)$, which has been initially generated by the generator, has the same structure as the standard font of x_k bold.

Integration Decoder. The Integration Decoder D_i inputs are character structure information $f_1, f_2, ..., f_5$ and style information s. Decoder D_i consists of five cascading Integration Modules, as shown in the Integration Decoder section of Fig. 4:

$$D_i(\{f_n\}_{n=1}^5, s) = G(X_r, x_k) \tag{5}$$

The output of the integrated encoder is the generated preliminary character image $G(X_r, x_k)$. Next this preliminary character image goes to the DDPM model to enhance the detail and quality of the image, and the final generated character image $G_{Di}(G(X_r, x_k), t)$ will be directly discriminated against the real sample x_k^i. The basic idea is to force the generator to learn the correct character structure and style.

Our model uses five loss functions to optimize the generator. Adversarial Loss uses cross-entropy to deceive the discriminator. Classification Loss minimizes recognition errors for character type and style with cross-entropy. Structure Loss measures deviations from a bold font template using the $L2$ norm. Style Loss ensures adherence to the reference style with the $L2$ norm. Reconstruction Loss reduces pixel differences using the $L1$ norm.

Multi-scale Discriminator. The discriminator block D^b includes a downsampling block and a classification header. Each downsampling block contains a convolutional layer, a normalization layer and an activation layer, mirroring the structure of the character encoder E_c. Each classification header comprises a linear layer and three headers-authenticity, character structure, and style-that respectively predict the authenticity, type, and author of the generated fonts based on the feature maps extracted.

$$D^n(x) = (D_a^n(x), D_f^n(x), D_s^n(x)) = (\hat{y}_a^n, \hat{y}_f^n, \hat{y}_s^n) \tag{6}$$

where D^n denotes the nth discriminative block, $\hat{y}_a^n$ indicates the authenticity, $\hat{y}_f^n$ the type, and $\hat{y}_s^n$ the author of the generated fonts.

The core function is to prompt the generator to accurately learn character structure and style, aiding the diffusion model in optimization. As depicted in Fig. 5, we use a multi-scale discriminator D to enhance evaluation. This discriminator comprises an average pooling layer and multiple blocks, processing character x at various scales to assess it from different perspectives, thereby boosting discriminator efficacy.

$$D(x) = (D^1(x), D^2(x'), D^3(x'')) \tag{7}$$

where x' and x'' denote the input character x downsampled once and twice by average pooling respectively.

4 Experiments

4.1 Chinese Handwriting Generation

The training process and sampling visualization for the HandDiff-GAN model are depicted in Fig. 6.

Evaluations. We compare the HandDiff-GAN model qualitatively and quantitatively with some other Chinese character generation methods, namely zi2zi, ChiroGAN, Drawing, FontRNN, WriteLikeYou, DeepImitator, MetaScript.

The similarity between user-adjusted text and the target style is computed using a pre-trained style transfer model. The formula is as follows:

$$\text{Style Similarity} = 1 - \frac{1}{N} \sum_{i=1}^{N} \|\text{Gram}(G_{\text{adjusted}}) - \text{Gram}(G_{\text{target}})\|^2 \tag{8}$$

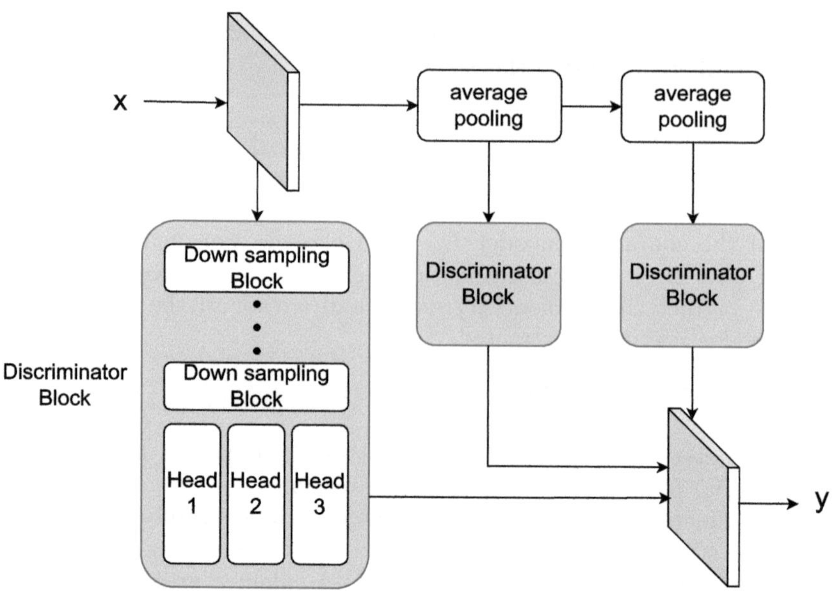

Fig. 5. The multi-scale discriminator consists of 2 average pooling layers and 3 discriminator blocks. The input characters will be downsampled into 3 different scales into the already built discriminator blocks.

Fig. 6. Data visualization during training. The first four columns are style references. The fifth column is the standard template in bold. Sixth column is the generated character. Seventh column is the real target sample.

The similarity between the user-adjusted characters and the target style is significantly higher than the similarity between the unadjusted characters.

Analysis of Style Parameter Adjustment Frequency: A large proportion of users actively engaged with the interactive features, with 85% adjusting the stroke thickness, averaging a 30% adjustment. Additionally, 70% of users utilized the stroke connection intensity adjustment, and 60% of them reported that the adjusted characters appeared more natural. These findings indicate that the style parameter adjustments had a significant impact on the generated results.

Table 1. Comparison of each metric with other methods

Method	Content Score	Style Score	SSIM	PSNR	User Prefer.(%)
zi2zi	77.15	34.23	0.2542	8.23	1.92
ChiroGAN	79.34	38.28	0.3467	10.31	2.7
Drawing	78.15	35.83	0.4122	11.31	3.31
FontRNN	92.18	46.14	0.4686	12.23	4.17
DeepImitator	90.92	50.67	0.4812	12.90	6.12
WriteLikeYou	94.12	72.07	0.5166	13.90	10.34
MetaScript	95.79	65.49	0.5313	16.73	29.12
Ours	98.56	76.48	0.5853	23.59	42.32

Table 2. Comparison of the metrics for the three model configurations

Configurations	Content Score	Style Score	SSIM	PSNR
Diffusion	96.81	68.95	0.5412	17.98
GAN	94.73	64.62	0.5117	15.43
GAN+Diffusion	98.56	76.48	0.5853	23.59

Quantitative Comparison. The results of the quantitative comparison, presented in Table 1, show that HandDiff-GAN outperforms other methods across all assessment metrics, including content score, style score, and the quality and structure of text.

Qualitative Comparison. We visualize samples generated by MetaScript and our model in Fig. 7, demonstrating the superiority of HandDiff-GAN in user preference studies. As shown in Fig. 7, MetaScript often produces errors such as missing strokes or lost styles, while our approach generates higher quality results, particularly in recovering fine character details. The fourth row in the figure is the result of selecting user interaction for result fine-tuning. You can intuitively see that the generated effect is closer to the target font.

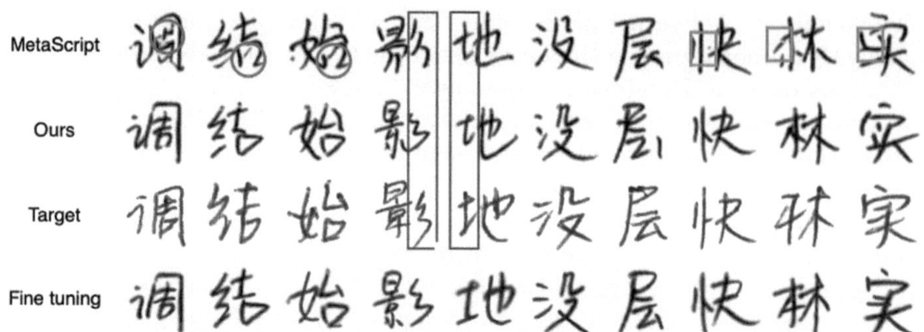

Fig. 7. Comparison of generated handwritten fonts. Red circles highlight structural deficiencies, blue boxes highlight details of stylistic mimicry, and green boxes highlight failures of stroke rationalization. (Color figure online)

4.2   Ablation Studies

In this experiment, we compare three different model configurations to generate handwritten Chinese characters: GAN+diffusion model, GAN only, and diffusion only model. Each model configuration undergoes the same training and testing processes and uses the same dataset to ensure fairness and comparability.

Analysis. As indicated in Table 2, the GAN + diffusion model excels in all metrics, demonstrating its superior capability in capturing the structure, texture, and style of handwritten characters. GAN performs inadequately in content and style, showing limitations in consistency and style preservation. Diffusion-only slightly surpasses GAN in PSNR and style but lacks behind the combined model in overall structure and consistency.

5   Conclusion

We propose HandDiff-GAN, a handwriting generation model combining GAN and diffusion models to create high-quality personalized Chinese characters. The GAN generates the initial image, while the diffusion model optimizes details, capturing style and structural features. Users can fine-tune the character style in real time, enhancing practicality. However, using only four style references may not fully capture the author's characteristics, and some generated samples may not meet needs, highlighting the importance of high-quality reference fonts. Future work will focus on extracting more style information from small, complex samples.

References

1. Chang, B., Zhang, Q., Pan, S., and Meng, L.: Generating handwritten chinese characters using cyclegan. In: 2018 IEEE Winter Conference on Applications of Computer Vision (WACV), pp. 199–207. IEEE, March 2018

2. Dai, G., et al.: Disentangling writer and character styles for handwriting generation. In: Proceedings of the IEEE/CVF Conference on Computer Vision and Pattern Recognition, pp. 5977–5986 (2023)

3. Xue, X., Wang, K., Bu, J., Li, Q., Zhang, Z.: MetaScript: few-shot handwritten Chinese content generation via generative adversarial networks. arXiv preprint arXiv:2312.16251 (2023)

4. He, H., et al.: Diff-font: diffusion model for robust one-shot font generation. Int. J. Comput. Vis. 1–15 (2024)

5. Yang, Z., Peng, D., Kong, Y., Zhang, Y., Yao, C., Jin, L.: Fontdiffuser: one-shot font generation via denoising diffusion with multi-scale content aggregation and style contrastive learning. In: Proceedings of the AAAI Conference on Artificial Intelligence, vol. 38, no. 7, pp. 6603–6611, March 2024

6. Ho, J., Jain, A., Abbeel, P.: Denoising diffusion probabilistic models. Adv. Neural. Inf. Process. Syst. **33**, 6840–6851 (2020)

7. Goodfellow, I., et al.: Generative adversarial nets. In: Advances in Neural Information Processing Systems, vol. 27 (2014)

8. Tang, S., Lian, Z.: Write like you: synthesizing your cursive online chinese handwriting via metric-based meta learning. Comput. Graph. Forum. **40**(2) (2021)

9. Alonso, E., Moysset, B., Messina, R.: Adversarial generation of handwritten text images conditioned on sequences. In: 2019 International Conference on Document Analysis and Recognition (ICDAR), IEEE (2019)

10. Chang, J., Gu, Y., Zhang, Y., Wang, Y.F., Innovation, C.M.: Chinese handwriting imitation with hierarchical generative adversarial network. In: BMVC, p. 290, September 2018

11. Gui, D., Chen, K., Ding, H., Huo, Q.: Zero-shot generation of training data with denoising diffusion probabilistic model for handwritten Chinese character recognition. In: International Conference on Document Analysis and Recognition, pp. 348–365. Springer, Cham, August 2023

12. Durugkar, I., Gemp, I., Mahadevan, S.: Generative multi-adversarial networks. arXiv preprint arXiv:1611.01673 (2016)

13. Karras, T., Laine, S., Aila, T.: A style-based generator architecture for generative adversarial networks. In: Proceedings of the IEEE/CVF Conference on Computer Vision and Pattern Recognition (2019)

14. Karras, T., Laine, S., Aittala, M., Hellsten, J., Lehtinen, J., Aila, T.: Analyzing and improving the image quality of stylegan. In: Proceedings of the IEEE/CVF Conference on Computer Vision and Pattern Recognition, pp. 8110–8119) (2020)

15. RRonneberger, O., Fischer, P., Brox, T.: U-net: convolutional networks for biomedical image segmentation. In: Medical image computing and computer-assisted intervention–MICCAI 2015: 18th international conference, Munich, Germany, 5–9 October 2015, proceedings, Part III 18. Springer (2015)

16. Salimans, T., Goodfellow, I., Zaremba, W., Cheung, V., Radford, A., Chen, X.: Improved techniques for training gans. In: Advances in Neural Information Processing Systems, vol. 29 (2016)

17. Yuan, Y., Liu, S., Zhang, J., Zhang, Y., Dong, C., Lin, L.: Unsupervised image super-resolution using cycle-in-cycle generative adversarial networks. In: Proceedings of the IEEE Conference on Computer Vision and Pattern Recognition Workshops, pp. 701–710 (2018)

18. Chen, Z., et al.: Complex handwriting trajectory recovery: evaluation metrics and algorithm. In: Proceedings of the Asian Conference on Computer Vision, pp. 1060–1076 (2022)

19. Jiang, Y., Lian, Z., Tang, Y., Xiao, J.: Scfont: structure-guided chinese font generation via deep stacked networks. In: Proceedings of the AAAI Conference on Artificial Intelligence, vol. 33, no. 01, pp. 4015–4022, July 2019

20. Kong, W., Xu, B.: Handwritten chinese character generation via conditional neural generative models. In: Proceedings of the 31st Conference on Neural Information Processing Systems (NIPS 2017), Long Beach, CA, USA (2017)

21. Luo, C., Zhu, Y., Jin, L., Li, Z., Peng, D.: SLOGAN: handwriting style synthesis for arbitrary-length and out-of-vocabulary text. IEEE Trans. Neural Netw. Learn. Syst. **34**(11), 8503–8515 (2022)

22. Park, T., Efros, A.A., Zhang, R., Zhu, J.Y.: Contrastive learning for unpaired image-to-image translation. In Computer Vision–ECCV 2020: 16th European Conference, Glasgow, UK, 23–28 August 2020, Proceedings, Part IX 16, pp. 319–345. Springer (2020)

23. Ren, X., Yang, T., Wang, Y., Zeng, W.: Learning disentangled representation by exploiting pretrained generative models: a contrastive learning view. arXiv preprint arXiv:2102.10543 (2021)

24. Tang, S., Xia, Z., Lian, Z., Tang, Y., Xiao, J.: FontRNN: generating large-scale Chinese fonts via recurrent neural network. In: Computer Graphics Forum, vol. 38, no. 7, pp. 567–577, October 2019

25. Aksan, E., Pece, F., Hilliges, O.: Deepwriting: making digital ink editable via deep generative modeling. In: Proceedings of the 2018 CHI Conference on Human Factors in Computing Systems (2018)

26. Das, A., Yang, Y., Hospedales, T., Xiang, T., Song, Y.Z.: Chirodiff: modelling chirographic data with diffusion models. arXiv preprint arXiv:2304.03785 (2023)

27. Xu, Y., Zhao, Y., Xiao, Z., Hou, T.: Ufogen: you forward once large scale text-to-image generation via diffusion gans. In: Proceedings of the IEEE/CVF Conference on Computer Vision and Pattern Recognition, pp. 8196–8206 (2024)

28. Wang, Z., Zheng, H., He, P., Chen, W., Zhou, M.: Diffusion-gan: Training gans with diffusion. arXiv preprint arXiv:2206.02262 (2022)

29. Ren, M.S., Zhang, Y.M., Wang, Q.F., Yin, F., Liu, C.L.: Diff-Writer: a diffusion model-based stylized online handwritten chinese character generator. In: International Conference on Neural Information Processing, pp. 86–100. Springer, Singapore, November 2023

30. Zhu, J.Y., Park, T., Isola, P., Efros, A.A.: Unpaired image-to-image translation using cycle-consistent adversarial networks. In: Proceedings of the IEEE International Conference on Computer Vision, pp. 2223–2232 (2017)

31. Radford, A.: Unsupervised representation learning with deep convolutional generative adversarial networks. arXiv preprint arXiv:1511.06434 (2015)

Multi-event Temporal Relation
Extraction by Ranking

Zhehuan Zhao, Jiawei Tang, and Bo Xu[(✉)]

School of Software Technology, Dalian University of Technology, Dalian, China
{z.zhao,boxu}@dlut.edu.cn,
cadysad@mail.dlut.edu.cn

Abstract. Extracting temporal relationships from multiple events in documents is a challenging task in information extraction. Previous methods primarily considered the event pair as the basic unit for processing, ignoring holistic connection among all events and background information remaining in the rest text. To address these issues, we introduce the Multi-Event Temporal Ranking (MEtR) method by simultaneously ranking all events within a document from a holistic perspective. We design order loss functions for MEtR, and experimental results demonstrate their superior performance compared to baseline methods across different settings (https://github.com/cadsad-dlut/metr.)

Keywords: Event Relation Extraction · Temporal Relation · Information Extraction

1 Introduction

Understanding the semantics and temporal relationships of events has been a long-standing fundamental task in natural language processing [5,18]. Notably, many domains can benefit from the advancements in determining temporal relations of multiple events, such as the construction and reasoning of the knowledge graph [8,14], event prediction [15], and making decisions [25].

Events in natural language, often represented by trigger words or the sentences containing them, construct a document as a story, wherein the underlying temporal relationships among them become notably intricate. The extraction of relations from these events scattered across the document is conventionally modeled as the Document-level Event-Event Relation Extraction(DERE) task [7,27] and subdivided into the Event Ordering task [3,17,19] to further focus on temporal relations. Moreover, events are intertwined for their temporal relations, which can be further ordered as chains [4,31] by sequential ranking [26].

Mostly, previous methods explore DERE and Event Ordering by identifying the relation in each event pair [4,10] with temporal information [21,22], decomposing the challenge of multiple events sorting into pairwise events temporal relation extraction subtasks [20,29], which is considered a process of multi-class classification [28] and sorting [13] for each event pair.

© The Author(s), under exclusive license to Springer Nature Singapore Pte Ltd. 2026
X.-L. Mao et al. (Eds.): NLPCC 2025, LNAI 16105, pp. 15–26, 2026.
https://doi.org/10.1007/978-981-95-3352-7_2

However, multi-class classification methods based on pairwise events also face defects.

- Pairwise methods may predict a cyclical relationship among events without handling all events simultaneously, leading to a loop that makes it impossible to determine the beginning and end of a story.
- Classification methods may give the same classification result for different events that cause repetitive orders.

Pairwise methods also need further processing to obtain the order sequence for events, such as constructing a relation adjacency matrix of each event pair separately and additional ranking algorithms to create sequential event chains [26] from the matrix, which is computationally expensive and requires additional processes, reducing accuracy among multiple events.

While previous works focus on event pairs, real-world language often entails more than two events intertwined within a document. There is also information about events tangled with other events, narrated by the rest of the text, like an explanation of a specific concept, which can be considered background information [11,13]. This fact of containing multiple events with other background information within a document is critical for DERE and Event Ordering. Thus, having a holistic perspective and obtaining the global event order sequence for multiple events is significant, rather than focusing on one local pair of events each time.

To handle events with background information from a holistic perspective and address defects of previous methods, we made contributions in this paper as follows:

- We propose Multi-Event temporal Ranking (MEtR) model which achieves multi-events temporal relation extraction by ranking rather than pairwise classification.
- MEtR is trained by two loss functions designed to handles all events simultaneously with a holistic perspective based on the relations between events and background information.
- Experimental results show that MEtR outperforms the baseline methods and demonstrates remarkable results in handling ranking tasks with more events.

2   Method

2.1   Ranking Task

The primary objective of the ranking task is to predict the order y_i for each event e_i, thereby forming the temporal order sequence $Y = \{y_i | i = 1, 2, \ldots, n\}$, e.g. considering events e_1, e_2, e_3, the predicted event order sequence Y might be $\{y_1 = 0, y_2 = 2, y_3 = 1\}$ indicating the temporal orders as $e_1 \rightarrow e_3 \rightarrow e_2$.

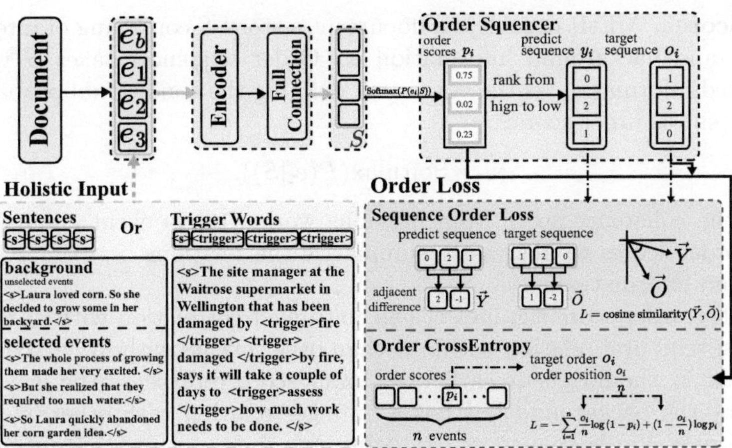

Fig. 1. Overview of MEtR. Input data comprising information of the entire story are integrated in Holistic Input, incorporating both background (unselected events in SOC and text other than trigger words in ESL) and events (annotated by special tokens, "¡s¿" and "¡/s¿" for sentences or "¡trigger¿" and "¡/trigger¿" for trigger words).

In contrast with DERE, the ranking task does not constrained to rank an event chain from event pairs [26], which allows for operating on multiple events simultaneously and ranking the event order sequence directly from the whole story at once. We enable cohesive comprehension of multi-event tasks for the first time through a holistic perspective while the procedure of ranking, which does not necessarily require the basic process units to be event pairs.

2.2   MEtR

To handle all events simultaneously from a holistic perspective, we propose MEtR (Fig. 1). MEtR inputs all events with background information simultaneously in holistic input structure. Diverging from prior tasks, MEtR redefines the fundamental unit of the objective as all events in the same text rather than event pairs.

MEtR calculates order scores by order sequencer as output and ranks these scores into order sequences. Order scores of events reveal their temporal salience in the story. Order sequencer also reduces computation expense by predicting and ranking the probability order scores instead of treating all possible event orders as classification targets and sorting from a relation adjacency matrix of event pairs. To handle multi-event ranking with a holistic perspective, we devise the order sequencer with two different loss functions for MEtR.

Order Scores. MEtR considers a document a story S consisting of interrelated events e_i and background information e_b. Order sequencer takes S with this interrelated information as the condition, defining the conditional probability p_i of each event as order score:

$$p_i = \mathrm{Softmax}(P(e_i|S)). \tag{1}$$

Like the coherence score from previous works [10] in event chains, we utilize the order scores to abstractly summarize the relations between events and background information.

A higher order score signifies e_i has a stronger correlation with e_b and more salience in temporal relation within S than other events with lower scores, indicating that e_i should occur earlier. A lower score represents the event is less effected by the background but has a stronger relation with other events happend before it. Order sequencer can determine the event order sequence for all events by ranking order scores from high to low.

2.3   Loss Functions

The target of MEtR is ranking events to obtain an ordered sequence $Y = y_1, y_2, \ldots, y_n$ where y_i represents the predicted order of event e_i while sequence $O = o_1, o_2, \ldots, o_n$ represents the true orders where n is the number of events. MEtR outputs this sequence by ranking order scores $p_1, p_2, \ldots, p_n$ of each event from the highest to the lowest.

In order to obtain reasonable order scores, we devise two order loss functions: Sequence Order Loss(SOL) and Order Cross Entropy(OCE), which are devised from relative and absolute perspectives, respectively.

Sequence Order Loss. For events, their ranked order sequence signifies the before-and-after relationship among them. Like the metric, Pairwise Accuracy and Average Distance from other sorting task [1], we apply these in the holistic perspective with all events in a story.

SOL evaluates the order sequence by the relative direction and distance characteristics in sequence between adjacent events. The signed value of difference between orders of two events $o_i - o_j$ reflects the before-and-after direction and relative distance between them, e.g. if $o_i - o_j < 0$ then e_i precedes e_j, and the absolute difference $|o_i - o_j|$ indicates the distance between e_i and e_j. Remarkably, the order of initial and final events should give the greatest difference and direct from the initial to the final event.

These numerical and directional characteristics are consistent with the properties of vectors. Thus, we extract these relative characteristics of an order sequence as a vector $\boldsymbol{Y}$ by the adjacent signed value of order differences $o_{i+1} - o_i$. Based on these, we define SOL as:

$$\begin{aligned}
L_{\mathrm{SOL}} &= \text{cosine similarity}(\boldsymbol{Y}, \boldsymbol{O}) \\
\boldsymbol{Y} &= \{y_i' | y_i' = y_{i+1} - y_i, \ i = 1, 2, \cdots, n-1\} \\
\boldsymbol{O} &= \{o_i' | o_i' = o_{i+1} - o_i, \ i = 1, 2, \cdots, n-1\},
\end{aligned} \tag{2}$$

to depict the holistic characteristics of predicted order sequences and compare them with true orders.

Order Cross Entropy. We also introduce OCE to add absolute position information of each event into cross-entropy.

The order of an event tells its absolute position in the whole story, and explicitly associated with the total number of events. We describe this absolute position information of one event by its proportion of true order in sequence as $\frac{o_i}{n}$. This proportion reflects the absolute characteristics of one event in the sequence, and we replace the target (0 or 1) in binary cross-entropy with this proportion to assemble OCE. Thus, we design OCE as a variant of binary cross-entropy with absolute order proportion of each event:

$$L_{\mathrm{OCE}} = -\sum_{i=1}^{n} \frac{o_i}{n} \log\left(1 - p_i\right) + (1 - \frac{o_i}{n}) \log p_i, \tag{3}$$

so that former events lead to higher order scores.

We trained MEtR with the summation of these two loss functions as $L = L_{SOL} + L_{OCE}$, we also conduct comparison experiments for them.

3   Experiment

3.1   Datasets

Table 1. Overview of datasets statistics.

Dataset	train	test	val
SOC	9885	2370	2483
ESL	1450	294	–

We conduct experiments on dataset StoryCommonsense(SOC [24]). Events in SOC are annotated in sentences and each story has a fixed structure with 5 events in it. We assess the ranking capability of a method in different condition by select and shuffle the last 3 to 5 events in a story and the objective is to rank them in order.

Further, for more complex scenarios, we also conduct experiments on the EventStoryline(ESL [2]) dataset for a more comprehensive analysis. Events in ESL datasets are annotated by trigger words, stories in ESL involve more flashbacks and events intertwined with background information. There is no limitation of the amount sentences in a story of ESL, which offers more complex scenarios closer to real-world language.

Table 1 shows a summary of the statistics of these datasets.

3.2   Metrics

We utilize both classification metrics (Accuracy and F_1) and sorting metrics(Rouge-S and Longest Common Subsequen). All these metric are the higher means the better.

The Rouge-S [23] is defined as:

$$s = \mathrm{Comb}(n, 2)$$
$$\text{Rouge-S} = \frac{\mathrm{num}(C_y \cap C_o)}{s}, \tag{4}$$

where s means the number of all skip-bigrams from events, C_y and C_o represent the skip-bigrams in predicted orders and label orders. This calculates the percentage of skip-bigrams for which the relative order is predicted correctly [6].

The Longest Common Subsequen(LCS [9]) calculates the ratio of longest common sub-sequence between the predicted order and the given order, consecutiveness is not necessary.

3.3   Baselines

We utilize pretrained language models RoBERTa-large [16] and OPT-350 m [30] as multi-class classification baselines. RoBERTa-large and OPT-350 m are also utilized as the encoder of MEtR, this can reveal the differences in performance caused by the size of parameters of models.

Besides, we also take BERE[1] model(**B**ox **E**vent **R**elation **E**xtraction [12]) as one of the baselines. BERE is a remarkable pairwise relation extraction and sorting method. BERE projects each event to a box representation which calculates the conditional probability $P(e_i \cap e_j | e_j)$ stands for $e_j \rightarrow e_i$ of each event pair to construct the relations matrix and sortin the event order sequence. This design initially intends to describe relations among multiple events, and BERE extracts pairwise relations by the relative position of the two boxes. It is trained with the pairwise loss function:

$$-\sum \mathrm{sgn}(o_i - o_j)\left[\log P(c_i \cap c_j | c_j) - \log P(c_i \cap c_j | c_i) \right], \tag{5}$$

where sgn is sign function, c_i is the intersection of background b with event e_i.

4   Results and Analysis

4.1   SOC

The results of experiments on dataset SOC is in Table 2. Experiment results suggest that all baselines have the basic capability of ranking multi-events.

---

[1] More about BERE(click).

Table 2. Experiment result on SOC. n is the number of shuffled events.

Model	n = 3				n = 4				n = 5			
	Accuracy	F_1	Rouge-S	LCS	Accuracy	F_1	Rouge-S	LCS	Accuracy	F_1	Rouge-S	LCS
BERE	54.62	41.4	35.0	54.6	44.15	31.9	23.7	44.1	41.33	27.0	19.6	41.3
RoBERTa-large	51.20	40.4	25.9	51.2	38.90	30.3	27.5	38.4	42.91	27.3	14.3	37.9
OPT-350 m	54.19	41.3	60.6	54.1	25.55	25.3	54.3	22.3	24.48	22.0	56.2	19.6
MEtR$_{\text{RoBERTa}}$	**83.99**	**47.7**	**75.13**	**83.9**	69.65	**36.8**	53.4	**69.6**	65.87	**30.7**	44.9	**65.8**
MEtR$_{\text{OPT}}$	55.78	43.6	55.74	46.9	37.87	30.1	**56.9**	33.3	35.64	25.6	**57.3**	28.7

Table 3. Experiment result on ESL.

Model	Accuracy	F_1	Rouge-S	LCS
BERE	78.04	46.7	67.3	61.0
RoBERTa-large	69.62	39.9	75.2	68.3
OPT-350 m	54.84	36.7	53.2	52.5
MEtR$_{\text{RoBERTa}}$	**80.01**	41.5	**82.4**	**78.2**
MEtR$_{\text{OPT}}$	62.08	**62.1**	79.5	56.8

It's apparently in more complex scenario with more events, the performances decrease. It's notable that with a larger size, RoBERTa performance better than OPT with more events. However, designed to extract complex relation among multi-events, BERE shows a stable performance in different scenarios outperforming both RoBERTa and OPT, while BERE has the similar size of RoBERTa.

Meanwhile, MEtR shows a remarkable performance across all scenarios. With 3 events, MEtR$_{\text{RoBERTa}}$ outperforms BERE 29.37% accuracy and 40.13% Rouge-S. Extraction of absolute positions of events in the simpler scenario represents a better understanding of the relations. Geared by OCE, MEtR shows a reliable performance with less events. MEtR$_{\text{OPT}}$ also shows a more stable and better performance than OPT, which shows the increasement and relaibility from MEtR.

Among these experiments, MEtR models keep superior results in both simple and intricate scenarios with different number of events, especially with more shuffled events, shows a comprehensive capability.

4.2   ESL

The results of experiments tasks on dataset ESL is in Table 3. Ranking tasks on ESL is more intricate for text is more close to real-world language and no limitations of sentences in a document. All methods show reliable performances, while MEtR and BERE are the most proficient.

Compared with BERE, MEtR$_{\text{RoBERTa}}$ shows a slightly outstanding performance wich improved by 1.97% in accuracy. More specificlly, MEtR$_{\text{RoBERTa}}$

outperforms BERE 15.13% Rouge-S and MEtR$_{OPT}$ outperforms OPT 26.31% Rouge-S, means a better performance in both holistic accuracy and percise relative order. Futhermore, according to the LCS, MEtR$_{RoBERTa}$ also keeps the continuous consistency in events order, which outperforms BERE by 17.2% and RoBERTa by 9.9%.

4.3 Time Cost

Statistics of time cost is in Table 4. Pairwise methods like BERE hanldle multi-event relations by constructing the matrix consists the probability of each event pair and ranking the final order sequence from the matrix, while MEtR is designed to rank output without the matrix, which reduces time cost. Futhermore, BERE requires embedding events into box, which also cost time.

Meanwhile, the size of parameters of models also has an impact on time cost. OPT-350 m with the smallest size in baselines costs less time than any other methods except for MEtR. Thus, MEtR$_{OPT}$ shows the least amount of time consumption with both MEtR method and the smaller parameter size based on OPT.

Table 4. Comparison of Time Cost on all experiments with same settings. Time cost of MEtR is set as 100%.

Model	Time Cost
MEtR$_{OPT}$	89.1%
MEtR$_{RoBERTa}$	100%
OPT-350 m	142.9%
RoBERTa-large	149.8%
BERE	156.2%

4.4 Abalation

To further analyze the impact of loss functions, we conduct abalation study experiments and the results are in Table 5 and 6.

On SOC, compared to OCE, SOL performances better with 5 events shuffled, which indicates it's more proficient with more intricate scenarios. Meanwhile, OCE is outstanding in simpler settings with less events. Especially, with 5 events, the results of OCE has a significant decrease, while SOL is more stable.

On ESL, both SOL and OCE show effectiveness in complex scenarios. SOL is more outstanding with abundant sentences in a story while OCE is left behind. Notably, both SOL and OCE didn't outperform all baselines. The results of

Table 5. Abalation experiments on SOC.

Model	n = 3				n = 4				n = 5			
	Accuracy	F_1	Rouge-S	LCS	Accuracy	F_1	Rouge-S	LCS	Accuracy	F_1	Rouge-S	**LCS**
MEtR$_{\text{RoBERTa}}$	83.99	47.7	75.13	73.9	69.65	36.8	53.40	65.6	65.87	30.7	44.93	60.8
MEtR$_{\text{RoBERTa, SOL}}$	76.51	46.4	63.79	76.5	65.83	35.5	48.47	65.3	61.10	29.9	38.83	51.2
MEtR$_{\text{RoBERTa, OCE}}$	80.09	46.9	69.31	80.0	67.89	36.5	52.31	48.5	52.77	29.0	66.45	44.0
MEtR$_{\text{OPT}}$	55.78	43.6	55.74	46.9	37.87	30.1	56.93	33.3	35.64	25.6	57.37	28.6
MEtR$_{\text{OPT, SOL}}$	44.35	38.1	55.37	44.3	33.84	28.8	52.96	29.4	36.13	25.7	59.23	28.6
MEtR$_{\text{OPT, SOL}}$	47.29	39.1	58.32	47.2	34.52	29.0	53.67	30.4	35.23	25.5	56.96	28.6

Table 6. Abalation experiments on ESL.

Model	Accuracy	F_1	Rouge-S	LCS
MEtR$_{\text{RoBERTa}}$	80.01	41.5	82.43	78.2
	72.62	40.3	80.4	70.3
	61.61	38.5	63.9	58.4
MEtR$_{\text{OPT}}$	62.08	62.1	79.51	56.8
	59.02	59.0	76.32	55.2
	49.02	41.8	72.57	41.8

SOL on ESL are worse than BERE and OCE didn't outperform RoBERTa-large. However, the combination of both SOL and OCE keeps a stable lead, which benefits from the different specialization of two loss functions.

This indicates that SOL and OCE can complement each other and their different specializations can promote MEtR to fully understand complex relation among multi-events.

5   Conclusion

We address the challenge of multi-event temporal relation extraction from a cohesive perspective by ranking task. To circumvent defects caused by previous pairwise and multi-class classification methods, we propose the MEtR model to rank the temporal order for events by handling all events simultaneously with less computation by its holistic input structure and order sequencer. Experimental results demonstrate the effectiveness of the devised loss functions, SOL and OCE, showcasing their specialization in scenarios with various experimental settings. In contrast to other baselines, MEtR outperforms them in intricate multi-event temporal relation extraction, demonstrating superior performance.

References

1. Agrawal, H., Chandrasekaran, A., Batra, D., Parikh, D., Bansal, M.: Sort story: sorting jumbled images and captions into stories. In: Proceedings of the 2016 Conference on Empirical Methods in Natural Language Processing, pp. 925–931. ACL, Austin, Texas, November 2016. https://doi.org/10.18653/v1/D16-1091
2. Caselli, T., Vossen, P.: The event StoryLine corpus: a new benchmark for causal and temporal relation extraction. In: Proceedings of the Events and Stories in the News Workshop, pp. 77–86. ACL, Vancouver, Canada, August 2017 https://doi.org/10.18653/v1/W17-2711
3. Chambers, N., Cassidy, T., McDowell, B., Bethard, S.: Dense event ordering with a multi-pass architecture. Trans. Assoc. Comput. Linguist. **2**, 273–284 (2014). https://doi.org/10.1162/tacl_a_00182
4. Chambers, N., Jurafsky, D.: Unsupervised learning of narrative event chains. In: Proceedings of ACL-08: HLT, pp. 789–797. ACL, Columbus, Ohio, June 2008, https://aclanthology.org/P08-1090
5. Chen, M., Zhang, H., Ning, Q., Li, M., Ji, H., McKeown, K., Roth, D.: Event-centric natural language processing. In: Proceedings of the 59th Annual Meeting of the Association for Computational Linguistics and the 11th International Joint Conference on Natural Language Processing: Tutorial Abstracts, pp. 6–14. ACL, August 2021, https://doi.org/10.18653/v1/2021.acl-tutorials.2
6. Chen, X., Qiu, X., Huang, X.: Neural sentence ordering (2016), https://arxiv.org/abs/1607.06952
7. Cohen, O., Bar, K.: Temporal relation classification using Boolean question answering. In: Rogers, A., Boyd-Graber, J., Okazaki, N. (eds.) Findings of the Association for Computational Linguistics: ACL 2023, pp. 1843–1852. ACL, Toronto, Canada, July 2023, https://doi.org/10.18653/v1/2023.findings-acl.116
8. Du, L., Ding, X., Zhang, Y., Liu, T., Qin, B.: A graph enhanced BERT model for event prediction. In: Findings of the Association for Computational Linguistics: ACL 2022, pp. 2628–2638. ACL, Dublin, Ireland, May 2022, https://doi.org/10.18653/v1/2022.findings-acl.206
9. Gong, J., Chen, X., Qiu, X., Huang, X.: End-to-end neural sentence ordering using pointer network (2016)
10. Granroth-Wilding, M., Clark, S.: What happens next? event prediction using a compositional neural network model. In: Proceedings of the AAAI Conference on Artificial Intelligence, vol. 30, no. 1, March 2016, https://doi.org/10.1609/aaai.v30i1.10344
11. Hashimoto, C., et al.: Toward future scenario generation: extracting event causality exploiting semantic relation, context, and association features. In: Proceedings of the 52nd Annual Meeting of the Association for Computational Linguistics (Volume 1: Long Papers), pp. 987–997. ACL, Baltimore, Maryland, June 2014, https://doi.org/10.3115/v1/P14-1093
12. Hwang, E., Lee, J.Y., Yang, T., Patel, D., Zhang, D., McCallum, A.: Event-event relation extraction using probabilistic box embedding. In: Proceedings of the 60th Annual Meeting of the Association for Computational Linguistics (Volume 2: Short Papers), pp. 235–244. ACL, Dublin, Ireland, May 2022, https://doi.org/10.18653/v1/2022.acl-short.26
13. Kadowaki, K., Iida, R., Torisawa, K., Oh, J.H., Kloetzer, J.: Event causality recognition exploiting multiple annotators' judgments and background knowledge. In: Proceedings of the 2019 Conference on Empirical Methods in Natural Language

Processing and the 9th International Joint Conference on Natural Language Processing (EMNLP-IJCNLP), pp. 5816–5822. ACL, Hong Kong, China, November 2019, https://doi.org/10.18653/v1/D19-1590

14. Li, M., et al.: Connecting the dots: event graph schema induction with path language modeling. In: Proceedings of the 2020 Conference on Empirical Methods in Natural Language Processing (EMNLP), pp. 684–695. ACL, November 2020, https://doi.org/10.18653/v1/2020.emnlp-main.50

15. Li, Z., Ding, X., Liu, T.: Constructing narrative event evolutionary graph for script event prediction. CoRR **abs/1805.05081** (2018), http://arxiv.org/abs/1805.05081

16. Liu, Y., et al.: Roberta: a robustly optimized bert pretraining approach. arXiv preprint arXiv:1907.11692 (2019)

17. McDowell, B., Chambers, N., Ororbia II, A., Reitter, D.: Event ordering with a generalized model for sieve prediction ranking. In: Proceedings of the Eighth International Joint Conference on Natural Language Processing (Volume 1: Long Papers), pp. 843–853. Asian Federation of Natural Language Processing, Taipei, Taiwan, November 2017, https://aclanthology.org/I17-1085

18. Minsky, M.: A framework for representing knowledge (1974)

19. Naik, A., Breitfeller, L., Rose, C.: TDDiscourse: a dataset for discourse-level temporal ordering of events. In: Proceedings of the 20th Annual SIGdial Meeting on Discourse and Dialogue, pp. 239–249. ACL, Stockholm, Sweden, September 2019, https://doi.org/10.18653/v1/W19-5929

20. Ning, Q., Subramanian, S., Roth, D.: An improved neural baseline for temporal relation extraction. In: Proceedings of the 2019 Conference on Empirical Methods in Natural Language Processing and the 9th International Joint Conference on Natural Language Processing (EMNLP-IJCNLP), pp. 6203–6209. ACL, Hong Kong, China, November 2019, https://doi.org/10.18653/v1/D19-1642

21. Pichotta, K., Mooney, R.: Statistical script learning with recurrent neural networks. In: Proceedings of the Workshop on Uphill Battles in Language Processing: Scaling Early Achievements to Robust Methods, pp. 11–16. ACL, Austin, TX, November 2016, https://doi.org/10.18653/v1/W16-6003

22. Pichotta, K., Mooney, R.J.: Using sentence-level LSTM language models for script inference. In: Proceedings of the 54th Annual Meeting of the Association for Computational Linguistics (Volume 1: Long Papers), pp. 279–289. ACL, Berlin, Germany, August 2016, https://doi.org/10.18653/v1/P16-1027

23. Prabhumoye, S., Salakhutdinov, R., Black, A.W.: Topological sort for sentence ordering. In: Proceedings of the 58th Annual Meeting of the Association for Computational Linguistics, pp. 2783–2792. ACL, July 2020, https://doi.org/10.18653/v1/2020.acl-main.248

24. Rashkin, H., Bosselut, A., Sap, M., Knight, K., Choi, Y.: Modeling naive psychology of characters in simple commonsense stories. In: Proceedings of the 56th Annual Meeting of the Association for Computational Linguistics (Volume 1: Long Papers), pp. 2289–2299. ACL, Melbourne, Australia, July 2018, https://doi.org/10.18653/v1/P18-1213

25. Sun, Y., Cheng, G., Qu, Y.: Reading comprehension with graph-based temporal-casual reasoning. In: Proceedings of the 27th International Conference on Computational Linguistics, pp. 806–817. ACL, Santa Fe, New Mexico, USA, August 2018, https://aclanthology.org/C18-1069

26. Toro Isaza, P., Xu, G., Oloko, T., Hou, Y., Peng, N., Wang, D.: Are fairy tales fair? analyzing gender bias in temporal narrative event chains of children's fairy tales. In: Rogers, A., Boyd-Graber, J., Okazaki, N. (eds.) Proceedings of the 61st Annual Meeting of the Association for Computational Linguistics (Volume 1: Long Papers), pp. 6509–6531. ACL, Toronto, Canada, July 2023, https://doi.org/10.18653/v1/2023.acl-long.359
27. Tran Phu, M., Nguyen, T.H.: Graph convolutional networks for event causality identification with rich document-level structures. In: Proceedings of the 2021 Conference of the North American Chapter of the Association for Computational Linguistics: Human Language Technologies, pp. 3480–3490. ACL, June 2021, https://doi.org/10.18653/v1/2021.naacl-main.273
28. Xiang, W., Wang, B.: A survey of event extraction from text. IEEE Access **7**, 173111–173137 (2019), https://doi.org/10.1109/ACCESS.2019.2956831
29. Zhang, S., Ning, Q., Huang, L.: Extracting temporal event relation with syntax-guided graph transformer. In: Findings of the Association for Computational Linguistics: NAACL 2022, pp. 379–390. ACL, Seattle, United States, July 2022, https://doi.org/10.18653/v1/2022.findings-naacl.29
30. Zhang, S., et al.: Opt: open pre-trained transformer language models (2022)
31. Zhang, X., Chen, M., May, J.: Salience-aware event chain modeling for narrative understanding. In: Proceedings of the 2021 Conference on Empirical Methods in Natural Language Processing, pp. 1418–1428. ACL, Online and Punta Cana, Dominican Republic, November 2021, https://doi.org/10.18653/v1/2021.emnlp-main.107

Very-Long-Distance Dependency Capturing Evaluation via Language Modeling Based on Gender Consistency

Hongfei Xu[1], Zhuofei Liang[1], Josef van Genabith[2], Deyi Xiong[3], Hongying Zan[1], Qiuhui Liu[4], and Tengxun Zhang[1,5(✉)]

[1] Zhengzhou University, Zhengzhou 450001, Henan, China
`iehyzan@zzu.edu.cn, ztx313@foxmail.com`
[2] German Research Center for Artificial Intelligence and Saarland Informatics Campus, 66123 Saarbrücken, Germany
`Josef.van_Genabith@dfki.de`
[3] College of Intelligence and Computing, Tianjin University, Tianjin 300072, China
`dyxiong@tju.edu.cn`
[4] China Mobile Online Services, Zhengzhou 450001, Henan, China
[5] Henan Branch Agricultural Bank of China, Zhengzhou 450001, Henan, China

Abstract. Capturing Long-Distance Dependencies (LDDs) is crucial for NLP applications. However, the longest relation evaluated in early studies is only around 50 words, which is not sufficient to evaluate a model's ability in capturing Very-Long-Distance (VLD) dependencies. Recent work on capturing LDDs either is affected by the instruction-following ability of language models or requires training on synthetic tasks unrelated to natural languages. In this paper, we present an approach to automatically constructing LDD test instances (as opposed to training examples) for any distance by mentioning an antecedent with singular number and a specific grammatical gender at the start of the first sentence, building the first sentence of arbitrary length by sampling plural nouns, and asking the pre-trained language model to predict a singular pronoun with the correct gender at the start of the next sentence. We evaluate the performance of LLMs and neural language models with different settings.

Keywords: Long-distance dependency · Language model · Grammatical gender consistency

1 Introduction

Capturing Long-Distance Dependencies (LDDs) is crucial for the good performance of NLP applications [1–9] based on Large Language Models (LLMs) [10–20].

[21] builds the contrastive *Lingeval97* test set for the subject-verb agreement task by swapping the grammatical number of a verb to introduce an agreement

© The Author(s), under exclusive license to Springer Nature Singapore Pte Ltd. 2026
X.-L. Mao et al. (Eds.): NLPCC 2025, LNAI 16105, pp. 27–38, 2026.
https://doi.org/10.1007/978-981-95-3352-7_3

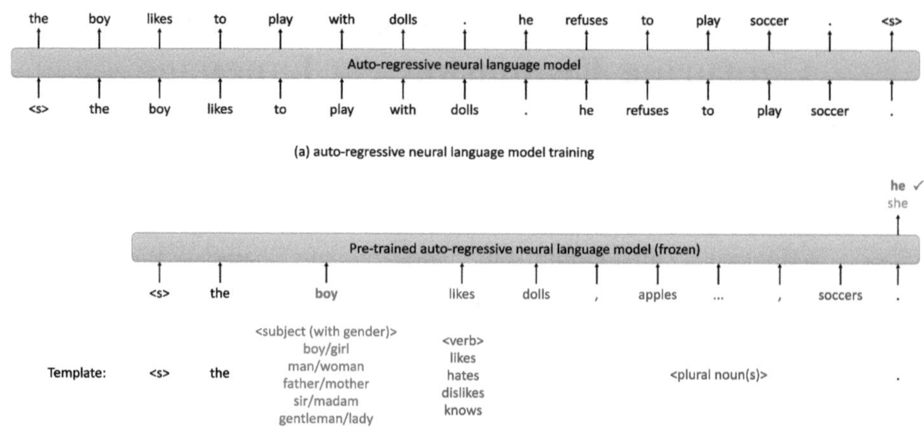

Fig. 1. Auto-regressive neural language model training and gender consistency evaluation.

error. But quite a large proportion of distances in *Lingeval97* are within 15 tokens, and cannot support the Very-Long-Distance (VLD) dependency evaluation (e.g., more than 100 tokens). Recently, [22] evaluate the performance of question answering, summarization, and code completion on long documents. [23] ask LLMs to retrieve random facts inserted into a long document. [24] train the model to generate the value tokens of corresponding key tokens in long key-value pair input sequences. These evaluations either depend on the instruction-following ability of LLMs, which can significantly impact performance (as studied in Sect. 3.1) [22,23], or require to train models on task-specific synthetic datasets which do not have any relation to natural languages [24]. They also lack a focus on the real distances between dependencies despite offering long inputs.

We present a template-based method to build large-scale sentences and test (**not train**) LDDs based on grammatical gender consistency in language modeling. **Our evaluation does not rely on instruction following, but tests on grammatical sentences and focuses on the dependency distance.**

Our main contributions are as follows:

- We present an automatic LDD evaluation method based on **purely language modeling** by evaluating the grammatical gender agreement between singular words marked for grammatical gender, controlling VLD length by adding plural nouns after the verb.
- We evaluate the performance of LLMs, test the effects of various settings and provide valuable empirical results and references for the design of neural language models.

2   VLD Evaluation via Grammatical Gender Consistency

In natural languages, the grammatical gender of the pronoun in the following sentences should be consistent with the co-referring subject in a previous sentence, as shown in Fig. 1 (a). We build test sentences where we control the grammatical gender of singular subjects (e.g., "the boy"/"the girl", etc.) and singular co-referring pronouns ("he" or "she"), and control the dependency length using only plural intervening nouns, as shown in Fig. 1(b). The language model shall assign a higher probability to a co-referring pronoun of the same gender as the subject than to a pronoun with another grammatical gender when decoding the first token (i.e., the singular pronoun) of the next sentence. **As none of plural nouns (by design) can function as antecedent to s/he, the prediction is expected to be consistent with the grammatical gender of the subject.**

We measure the VLD distance by the number of intervening plural nouns, and build a balanced test set across the two classes. The subject set S contains 10 singular words with clear grammatical gender ({"boy", "girl", "man", "woman", "father", "mother", "sir", "madam", "gentleman", "lady"}), the verb set V has 4 verbs ({"likes", "hates", "dislikes", "knows"}), while the plural noun set N has 6204 plural nouns (for animals (noun.animal), artifacts (noun.artifact), food (noun.food) and plants (noun.plant) extracted from Wordnet). **Our choice of intervening plural nouns between singular antecedent (reference) and singular anaphor is to make sure that s/he is an unambiguous binary choice and to be able to vary dependency length via intervening plural nouns, where none of the plural nouns (by design) can function as antecedent to s/he.** Human filtering of plural nouns can in principle make the generated test set more reasonable, but here we want to avoid such human efforts to make the test set construction method fully automatic and scalable.

For each distance d, we automatically build 5k test instances, and this already leads to 1.28M test instances in total for 256 distances, and we think this is sufficient to provide a reliable evaluation result. But at the same time it is also easy to produce more test instances and for longer distances with the method.

All test instances are grammatically correct. We compared average per token loss between the Lingeval97 (4.2) and our synthetic dataset (4.5) using a Transformer LM. This shows that it is reasonable to use the synthetic test set for the evaluation at varying distances.

3   Evaluation

In addition to Large Language Models (LLMs), we also trained Transformer and RNN models to examine the effects of various settings on VLD.

As training on long sequences is likely to be crucial for the model's ability in capturing VLD dependency, we trained autoregressive neural language models on the document-split version of the English News Crawl dataset from WMT [25]. The datasets were lower cased, and tokenized into subwords by the BART

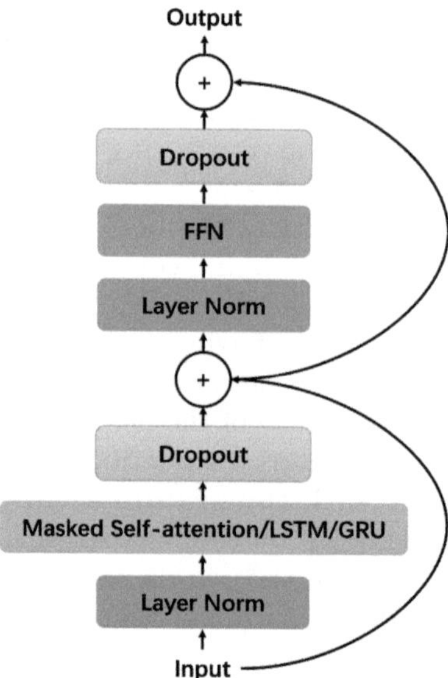

Fig. 2. The computation graph of the model layer.

tokenizer [26] using Byte-Pair Encoding models [27,28]. We concatenated consecutive sentences in documents into one sequence until adding the next sentence increases the sequence length to more than j tokens, where j was defaulted to 768.

Following the settings of [29], we used a batch size of 25k tokens. All the base, deep and big models were trained for 100k steps unless otherwise stated. The number of warm-up steps was set to 8k.

As for the model architectures, we employed the pre-norm computation order of the Transformer, which computes the layer normalization before the multi-head attention/position-wise feed-forward layer, and applies dropout and residual connection in the end, and used the absolute positional encoding unless indicated otherwise. For RNN models, we replaced the self-attention sub-layer in the Transformer by the LSTM/GRU sub-layers instead of purely stacking LSTM/GRU layers to minimize differences between the models. The computation graph of the model layer is shown in Fig. 2. We used the base setting by default, and the original absolute positional encoding for the Transformer.

In Figs. 3 and 5, 6 and 7, the x-axis and y-axis are the number of intervening plural nouns and the VLD accuracy respectively.

3.1   Performance of LLMs

For LLMs, we evaluated the performance of LLaMa 3.1–8B [30], Qwen 2.5–7B [31], GLM 4 9B 0414 [32] and Mamba - 2.8B [33] on the VLD test set. We evaluated the model in both language modeling (LM) and instruction following

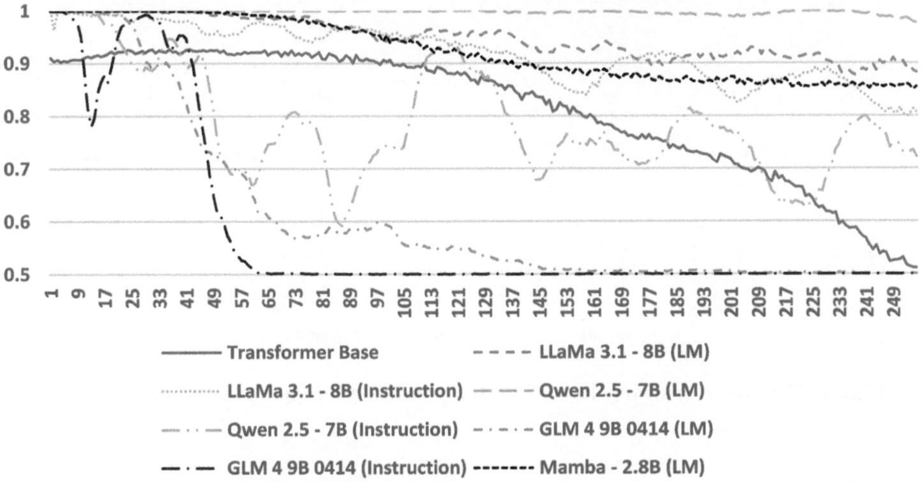

Fig. 3. Results of LLMs.

(Instruction) for LLaMa, Qwen and GLM. We only reported the LM evaluation performance of Mamba as its instruction performance is significantly poorer. For language modeling, we regard the model as a language model, feed the test input sequence into the model, and get the prediction probabilities of "he" and "she" at the last position. For instruction following, we ask the model to continue the input sentence starting with either "he" or "she", providing 4 examples as demonstrations.

Results in Fig. 3 show that **evaluation with instruction following leads to generally worse performances than with language modeling for both LLaMa and Qwen on the same testset with increasing distances. Qwen outperforms LLaMa in the LM evaluation but LLaMa performs better than Qwen in the Instruction evaluation, showing that instruction following can have a large impact on the long-distance evaluation.**

3.2 Self-attention vs. RNNs

We compare the performance of self-attentional Transformer, LSTM and GRU. When training on the dataset with a maximum sequence length of 768 tokens, we found that the LSTM model has difficulty in convergence even with residual connections. We conjecture the potential reason of the convergence issue is that LSTM may have problems when propagating gradients through the very long sequences.

We verified the convergence issue by training the LSTM model on the training data with a maximum sequence length of 256 (instead of 768) tokens and found that the model (LSTM_256) can converge. The per-token training loss averaged over $\sim$ 56M tokens reported during training is shown in Fig. 4.

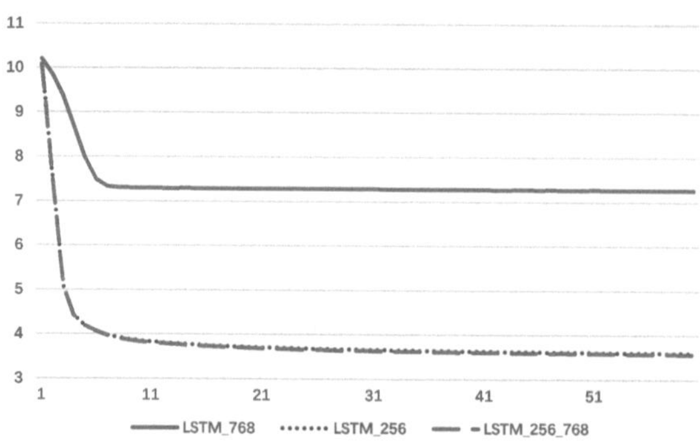

Fig. 4. Per-token training loss of LSTM models averaged over ~56M tokens.

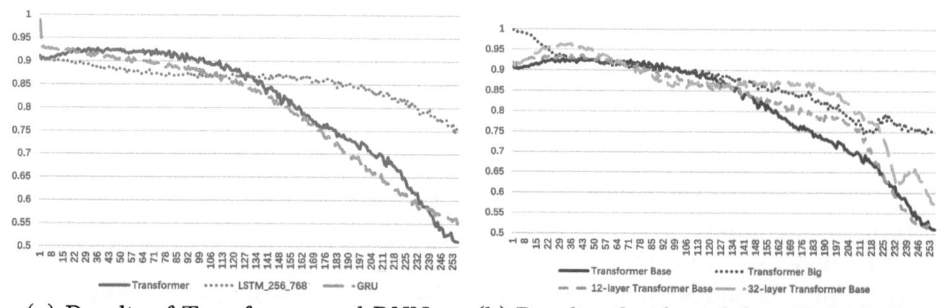

(a) Results of Transformer and RNNs.   (b) Results of wide and deep Transformers.

Fig. 5. Results of architecture differences and wide/deep Transformers.

Figure 4 shows that the per-token training loss of LSTM_768 saturates at a high level while LSTM_256 achieves a much lower and reasonable training loss, demonstrating the convergence issue of LSTMs on very long sequences.

We employ a 2-stage training method for LSTM. The first stage trains the LSTM with a maximum sequence length of 256 tokens until the averaged per-token training loss is less than 4 (~10k training steps), and the second stage continues the training on sequences with a maximum length of 768 for the remaining steps. GRU does not suffer from the convergence issue like LSTM when training on long sequences (of at most 768 tokens).

Results in Fig. 5a show that **LSTM unexpectedly outperforms Transformer for VLD** ($d > 128$), suggesting that recurrent architectures may still have the upper hand in VLD resolution worth further exploration.

3.3   Increasing Depth vs. Width

We test the effects of increasing model depth and width by comparing the Transformer Big (increasing the embedding dimension to 1024) with 12-layer and 32-layer deep Transformers (increasing the depth) trained for 100k steps. The

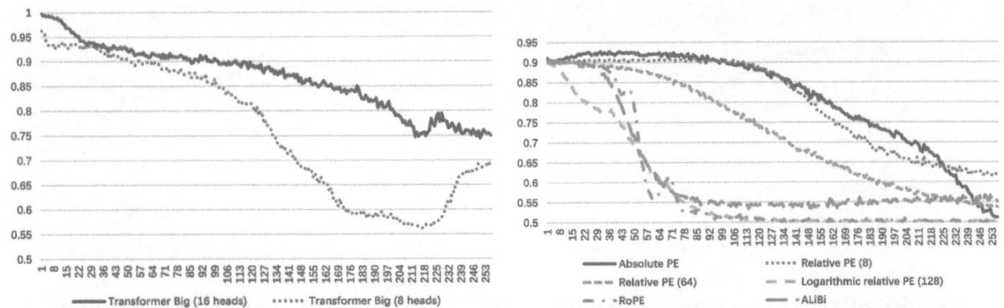

(a) Results of 8/16-head Transformer Big models. (b) Results of positional encoding methods.

Fig. 6. Results of attention head numbers and position encoding methods.

12-layer Transformer has the same number of attention heads as the 6-layer Transformer Big, and the 32-layer model has a comparable amount of parameters as the Transformer Big.

Results in Fig. 5b show that **increasing the width is more effective in improving the performance on very long distances** ($d > 221$) **compared to increasing the depth.**

3.4   Effects of Attention Head Numbers

We verify the effects of the number of attention heads by comparing the 8-head Transformer Big model with the standard Transformer Big with 16 heads in each multi-head attention layer.

Results in Fig. 6a show that the 16-head Transformer Big model consistently outperforms the 8-head Transformer Big model in all distances, and it is important for wide models to have sufficient number of attention heads.

3.5   Absolute Positional Encoding vs. Relative Positional Encoding

We test the effects of absolute position encoding [29], and relative position encoding methods, including: [34] (Relative PE), [35] (Logarithmic relative PE), [36] (ALiBi) and [37] (RoPE). We explore different windows sizes (in parentheses) for Relative PE.

Results in Fig. 6b show that: 1) **absolute position encoding performs best for most distances,** and 2) Relative PE (8) performs better than absolute position encoding for very long distances ($d > 225$).

3.6   Effects of Training Sequence Lengths

To test the effects of training sequence lengths, we trained the Transformer Base models on sequences that contain at most 768 (Transformer Base (768)) and 256 (Transformer Base (256)) tokens respectively.

(a) Results of training sequence lengths. (b) Results of different training step numbers.

Fig. 7. Results of training sequence lengths and steps.

Results in Fig. 7a show that the Transformer Base (256) model consistently underperforms Transformer Base (768), and its performance drops sharply after a certain distance. This further proves that it is important to train on long sequences for good VLD performance.

3.7 Effects of Training Step Numbers

To test the effects of training step numbers on VLD dependency capturing ability, we trained the Transformer Big models for 100k (Transformer Big (100k)) and 300k (Transformer Big (300k)) steps respectively.

Results in Fig. 7b show that **Transformer Big** (100k) **outperforms Transformer Big** (300k) **for almost all distances**, especially with increasing distances, suggesting that **longer training may hinder VLD performance**.

4   Related Work

[38] test whether the verb form is consistent with subject number (singular or plural). [21] build the contrastive *Lingeval97* test set for the subject-verb agreement task by swapping the grammatical number of a verb. [39] present DistilLingEval based on machine-generated references. [40,41] explore automatic discourse phenomena tagging methods for context-aware machine translation. These studies cannot meet the requirements to assess the model's ability in capturing Very-Long-Distance (VLD) dependencies. Recently, [22] evaluate the performance of question answering, summarization, and code completion on long documents. [23] ask LLMs to retrieve random facts inserted into a long document. [24] ask the model to generate the values of corresponding keys in the long key-value pair input sequences. They either are affected by the instruction following ability of LLMs which can have a huge impact [22,23], or require to train models on synthetic tasks which have no relation to natural languages [24]. They also lack a focus on the real distances between dependencies despite offering long inputs.

[42] evaluate the performance of the Transformer, LSTM and CNN. [43] study the effects of phrase-level modeling, and [44] test Average Attention Network [45], Addition-subtraction Twin-gated Recurrent network [46], and MHPLSTM. But all these tests on the *Lingeval97* test set are not for LDDs, and lack an investigation on the impacts of different settings.

5   Conclusion

To mitigate the effects of varying instruction-following abilities of LLMs on Very-Long-Distance (VLD) dependency evaluation and synthetic evaluation unrelated to natural languages, we present a template-based approach to automatically constructing large testsets for arbitrary distances based on grammatical gender consistency.

We evaluate the VLD performance of LLMs and popular neural language models with different settings, and find that: 1) instruction following ability has a huge impact on the VLD evaluation, 2) 2-stage training can address the convergence issue of LSTM on very long sequences and lead to better performance than Transformer on very-long distances, 3) increasing the width improves VLD performance while increasing depth hampers performance, and 4) longer training tends to hamper the VLD performance.

Acknowledgments. We thank anonymous reviewers for their insightful comments. Hongfei Xu and Zhuofei Liang acknowledge the support of National Natural Science Foundation of China (Grant No. 62306284), China Postdoctoral Science Foundation (Grant No. 2023M743189), and the Natural Science Foundation of Henan Province (Grant No. 232300421386). Josef van Genabith is supported by BMBF (German Federal Ministry of Education and Research) via the project SocialWear (Grant No. 01IW20002). Deyi Xiong is supported by the National Key Research and Development Program of China (Grant No. 2023YFE0116400). Hongying Zan is supported by the Key Program of Natural Science Foundation of China (Grant No. U23A20316).

References

1. Ouyang, L., et al.: Training language models to follow instructions with human feedback (2022)
2. Zhou, J., Ke, P., Qiu, X., Huang, M., Zhang, J.: Chatgpt: potential, prospects, and limitations. In: Frontiers of Information Technology & Electronic Engineering, pp. 1–6 (2023)
3. Katz, D.M., Bommarito, M.J., Gao, S., Arredondo, P.: Gpt-4 passes the bar exam. Available at SSRN 4389233 (2023)
4. Heck, M., et al.: ChatGPT for zero-shot dialogue state tracking: a solution or an opportunity? In: Proceedings of the 61st Annual Meeting of the Association for Computational Linguistics (Volume 2: Short Papers), pp. 936–950. Association for Computational Linguistics, Toronto, Canada, July 2023. https://doi.org/10.18653/v1/2023.acl-short.81,

5. Cao, Y., Zhou, L., Lee, S., Cabello, L., Chen, M., Hershcovich, D.: Assessing cross-cultural alignment between ChatGPT and human societies: an empirical study. In: Proceedings of the First Workshop on Cross-Cultural Considerations in NLP (C3NLP), pp. 53–67. Association for Computational Linguistics, Dubrovnik, Croatia, May 2023, https://aclanthology.org/2023.c3nlp-1.7

6. Lund, B.D., Wang, T.: Chatting about chatgpt: how may ai and gpt impact academia and libraries? Library Hi Tech News **40**(3), 26–29 (2023)

7. Lee, P., Bubeck, S., Petro, J.: Benefits, limits, and risks of gpt-4 as an ai chatbot for medicine. N. Engl. J. Med. **388**(13), 1233–1239 (2023)

8. Lecler, A., Duron, L., Soyer, P.: Revolutionizing radiology with gpt-based models: current applications, future possibilities and limitations of chatgpt. Diagn. Interv. Imaging **104**(6), 269–274 (2023)

9. Lin, J.C., Younessi, D.N., Kurapati, S.S., Tang, O.Y., Scott, I.U.: Comparison of gpt-3.5, gpt-4, and human user performance on a practice ophthalmology written examination. In: Eye, pp. 1–2 (2023)

10. Brown, T., et al.: Language models are few-shot learners. In: Larochelle, H., Ranzato, M., Hadsell, R., Balcan, M., Lin, H. (eds.) Advances in Neural Information Processing Systems, vol. 33, pp. 1877–1901. Curran Associates, Inc. (2020), https://proceedings.neurips.cc/paper_files/paper/2020/file/1457c0d6bfcb4967418bfb8ac142f64a-Paper.pdf

11. Xue, L., et al.: mt5: a massively multilingual pre-trained text-to-text transformer. In: Proceedings of the 2021 Conference of the North American Chapter of the Association for Computational Linguistics: Human Language Technologies, pp. 483–498 (2021)

12. Zhang, Z., et al.: Cpm-2: large-scale cost-effective pre-trained language models. AI Open **2**, 216–224 (2021)

13. Wei, J., et al.: Chain-of-thought prompting elicits reasoning in large language models. Adv. Neural. Inf. Process. Syst. **35**, 24824–24837 (2022)

14. Wang, X., et al.: Self-consistency improves chain of thought reasoning in language models. In: The Eleventh International Conference on Learning Representations (2022)

15. Sanh, V., et al.: Multitask prompted training enables zero-shot task generalization. In: ICLR 2022-Tenth International Conference on Learning Representations (2022)

16. Wang, T., et al.: What language model architecture and pretraining objective works best for zero-shot generalization? In: International Conference on Machine Learning, pp. 22964–22984. PMLR (2022)

17. Xu, F.F., Alon, U., Neubig, G., Hellendoorn, V.J.: A systematic evaluation of large language models of code. In: Proceedings of the 6th ACM SIGPLAN International Symposium on Machine Programming, pp. 1–10 (2022)

18. Thoppilan, R., et al.: Lamda: language models for dialog applications. arXiv preprint arXiv:2201.08239 (2022)

19. Chowdhery, A., et al.: Palm: scaling language modeling with pathways. arXiv preprint arXiv:2204.02311 (2022)

20. Touvron, H., et al.: Llama: open and efficient foundation language models. arXiv preprint arXiv:2302.13971 (2023)

21. Sennrich, R.: How grammatical is character-level neural machine translation? assessing MT quality with contrastive translation pairs. In: Proceedings of the 15th Conference of the European Chapter of the Association for Computational Linguistics: Volume 2, Short Papers, pp. 376–382. ACL, Valencia, Spain, April 2017, https://aclanthology.org/E17-2060

22. Bai, Y., et al.: LongBench: a bilingual, multitask benchmark for long context understanding. In: Ku, L.W., Martins, A., Srikumar, V. (eds.) Proceedings of the 62nd Annual Meeting of the Association for Computational Linguistics (Volume 1: Long Papers), pp. 3119–3137. ACL, Bangkok, Thailand, August 2024, https://aclanthology.org/2024.acl-long.172
23. Li, M., Zhang, S., Liu, Y., Chen, K.: Needlebench: can llms do retrieval and reasoning in 1 million context window? (2024), https://arxiv.org/abs/2407.11963
24. Arora, S., et al.: Zoology: measuring and improving recall in efficient language models. In: The Twelfth International Conference on Learning Representations (2024), https://openreview.net/forum?id=LY3ukUANko
25. Kocmi, T., et al.: Findings of the 2022 conference on machine translation (WMT22). In: Proceedings of the Seventh Conference on Machine Translation (WMT), pp. 1–45. ACL, Abu Dhabi, United Arab Emirates (Hybrid), December 2022, https://aclanthology.org/2022.wmt-1.1
26. Lewis, M., et al.: BART: Denoising sequence-to-sequence pre-training for natural language generation, translation, and comprehension. In: Proceedings of the 58th Annual Meeting of the Association for Computational Linguistics, pp. 7871–7880. ACL, July 2020, https://doi.org/10.18653/v1/2020.acl-main.703
27. Sennrich, R., Haddow, B., Birch, A.: Neural machine translation of rare words with subword units. In: Proceedings of the 54th Annual Meeting of the Association for Computational Linguistics (Volume 1: Long Papers), pp. 1715–1725. ACL, Berlin, Germany, August 2016, https://doi.org/10.18653/v1/P16-1162
28. Kudo, T.: Subword regularization: Improving neural network translation models with multiple subword candidates. In: Proceedings of the 56th Annual Meeting of the Association for Computational Linguistics (Volume 1: Long Papers), pp. 66–75. ACL, Melbourne, Australia, July 2018, https://doi.org/10.18653/v1/P18-1007
29. Vaswani, A., et al.: Attention is all you need. In: Guyon, I., et al. (eds.) Advances in Neural Information Processing Systems, vol. 30, pp. 5998–6008. Curran Associates, Inc. (2017), http://papers.nips.cc/paper/7181-attention-is-all-you-need.pdf
30. AI@Meta: Llama 3 model card (2024), https://github.com/meta-llama/llama3/blob/main/MODEL_CARD.md
31. Yang, Q.A., et al.: Qwen2.5 technical report. ArXiv **abs/2412.15115** (2024), https://arxiv.org/abs/2412.15115
32. GLM, T., et al.: Chatglm: a family of large language models from glm-130b to glm-4 all tools (2024)
33. Gu, A., Dao, T.: Mamba: linear-time sequence modeling with selective state spaces. ArXiv **abs/2312.00752** (2023), https://arxiv.org/abs/2312.00752
34. Shaw, P., Uszkoreit, J., Vaswani, A.: Self-attention with relative position representations. In: Proceedings of the 2018 Conference of the North American Chapter of the Association for Computational Linguistics: Human Language Technologies, Volume 2 (Short Papers), pp. 464–468. ACL, New Orleans, Louisiana, June 2018, https://doi.org/10.18653/v1/N18-2074
35. Raffel, C., et al.: Exploring the limits of transfer learning with a unified text-to-text transformer. J. Mach. Learn. Res. **21**(140), 1–67 (2020), http://jmlr.org/papers/v21/20-074.html
36. Press, O., Smith, N., Lewis, M.: Train short, test long: attention with linear biases enables input length extrapolation. In: International Conference on Learning Representations (2022), https://openreview.net/forum?id=R8sQPpGCv0
37. Su, J., Lu, Y., Pan, S., Murtadha, A., Wen, B., Liu, Y.: Roformer: enhanced transformer with rotary position embedding (2022)

38. Linzen, T., Dupoux, E., Goldberg, Y.: Assessing the ability of LSTMs to learn syntax-sensitive dependencies. Trans. Assoc. Comput. Linguist. **4**, 521–535 (2016). https://doi.org/10.1162/tacl_a_00115

39. Vamvas, J., Sennrich, R.: On the limits of minimal pairs in contrastive evaluation. In: Bastings, J., et al. (eds.) Proceedings of the Fourth BlackboxNLP Workshop on Analyzing and Interpreting Neural Networks for NLP, pp. 58–68. ACL, Punta Cana, Dominican Republic, November 2021, https://doi.org/10.18653/v1/2021.blackboxnlp-1.5

40. Wicks, R., Post, M.: Identifying context-dependent translations for evaluation set production. In: Koehn, P., Haddow, B., Kocmi, T., Monz, C. (eds.) Proceedings of the Eighth Conference on Machine Translation, pp. 452–467. ACL, Singapore, December 2023, https://doi.org/10.18653/v1/2023.wmt-1.42

41. Fernandes, P., Yin, K., Liu, E., Martins, A., Neubig, G.: When does translation require context? a data-driven, multilingual exploration. In: Rogers, A., Boyd-Graber, J., Okazaki, N. (eds.) Proceedings of the 61st Annual Meeting of the Association for Computational Linguistics (Volume 1: Long Papers), pp. 606–626. ACL, Toronto, Canada, July 2023, https://doi.org/10.18653/v1/2023.acl-long.36

42. Tang, G., Müller, M., Rios, A., Sennrich, R.: Why self-attention? a targeted evaluation of neural machine translation architectures. In: Proceedings of the 2018 Conference on Empirical Methods in Natural Language Processing, pp. 4263–4272. ACL, Brussels, Belgium, Oct-Nov 2018, https://doi.org/10.18653/v1/D18-1458

43. Xu, H., van Genabith, J., Xiong, D., Liu, Q., Zhang, J.: Learning source phrase representations for neural machine translation. In: Proceedings of the 58th Annual Meeting of the Association for Computational Linguistics, pp. 386–396. ACL, July 2020, https://doi.org/10.18653/v1/2020.acl-main.37

44. Xu, H., Liu, Q., van Genabith, J., Xiong, D., Zhang, M.: Multi-head highly parallelized LSTM decoder for neural machine translation. In: Proceedings of the 59th Annual Meeting of the Association for Computational Linguistics and the 11th International Joint Conference on Natural Language Processing (Volume 1: Long Papers), pp. 273–282. ACL, August 2021, https://doi.org/10.18653/v1/2021.acl-long.23

45. Zhang, B., Xiong, D., Su, J.: Accelerating neural transformer via an average attention network. In: Proceedings of the 56th Annual Meeting of the Association for Computational Linguistics (Volume 1: Long Papers), pp. 1789–1798. ACL, Melbourne, Australia, July 2018, https://doi.org/10.18653/v1/P18-1166

46. Zhang, B., Xiong, D., Su, J., Lin, Q., Zhang, H.: Simplifying neural machine translation with addition-subtraction twin-gated recurrent networks. In: Proceedings of the 2018 Conference on Empirical Methods in Natural Language Processing, pp. 4273–4283. ACL, Brussels, Belgium, Oct-Nov 2018, https://doi.org/10.18653/v1/D18-1459

InfoKANCSE: Enhancing Contrastive Sentence Embeddings with KAN and Information-Aware Aggregation

Jianyi Li[1] , Hengdong Zhu[2] , Kevin Hung[3] , and Tianyong Hao[2]($\boxtimes$)

[1] School of Artificial Intelligence, South China Normal University, Foshan 528000, China
2023025173@m.scnu.edu.cn

[2] School of Computer Science, South China Normal University, Guangzhou 510000, China
{zhuhd,haoty}@m.scnu.edu.cn

[3] School of Science and Technology, Hong Kong Metropolitan University, Hong Kong, China
khung@hkmu.edu.hk

Abstract. Contrastive learning has made significant progress in sentence representation, where methods such as DiffCSE have been evidenced to be able to enhance model representation capability in various prediction tasks. However, existing methods still have limitations in nonlinear feature transformation and sentence information aggregation. This paper proposes two key improvements: A novel framework InfoKANCSE to implement edge activation functions via B-spline curves based on Kolmogorov-Arnold Networks to enhance nonlinear modeling capability, and a multi-head attention mechanism to overcome mask token limitations by incorporating alignment and information maximization losses. Experimental results on seven semantic textual similarity (STS) tasks and BEIR benchmark demonstrate that these two improvements significantly boost the effectiveness the proposed method, achieving state-of-the-art performance on multiple downstream applications. Our proposed InfoKANCSE not only improves the representation expressiveness and interpretability but also offers valuable insights for sentence embedding research. InfoKANCSE achieves an average Spearman correlation of 82.4 on STS tasks and strong zero-shot performance on BEIR, surpassing prior methods such as InfoCSE and SimCSE.

Keywords: Sentence Embeddings · Contrastive Learning · Kolmogorov-Arnold Networks · Information Aggregation · Representation Learning

1 Introduction

In recent years, contrastive learning [1] has emerged as a promising approach for sentence representation [6], yet developing universal embeddings that effec-

© The Author(s), under exclusive license to Springer Nature Singapore Pte Ltd. 2026
X.-L. Mao et al. (Eds.): NLPCC 2025, LNAI 16105, pp. 39–51, 2026.
https://doi.org/10.1007/978-981-95-3352-7_4

tively capture comprehensive semantic information remains challenging. Current methods typically rely on comparing similar and dissimilar sentence pairs [13], but often struggle with information loss during representation learning [28]. This limitation is particularly evident in approaches like SimCSE [6], which despite its impressive performance through dropout-based augmentation, demonstrates degraded results when incorporating masked language modeling [32]. Such performance deterioration highlights a fundamental issue in existing methods: the inadequate mechanisms for information aggregation when constructing sentence representations.

To address these challenges, InfoCSE [28] and DiffCSE [3] offer different solutions: InfoCSE enhances information aggregation at the [CLS] position through additional MLM tasks and structures, while DiffCSE enables perception of subtle semantic differences via difference prediction tasks. However, both have limitations in nonlinear feature transformation and sentence information aggregation. Existing methods typically use fixed activation functions, limiting their ability to model complex semantic relationships. In addition, although InfoCSE enhances information aggregation, its complex architecture employs fixed aggregation patterns that cannot adaptively prioritize semantically important tokens. Furthermore, using [CLS] token as sentence representation causes positional bias toward sentence beginnings and vulnerability to high-frequency word influence [11].

We propose two improvements: (1) transform MLP into a Kolmogorov-Arnold Networks(KAN) [34] structure with B-spline curve-based learnable activation functions and a dynamic grid update mechanism, and (2) design an efficient multihead attention-based information aggregation mechanism with alignment and information maximization losses to maintain overall semantics while preserving rich information.

The main contributions of this paper can be summarized as:

- We propose InfoKANCSE, which integrates KAN with B-spline based edge activation functions to enhance nonlinear modeling capability in sentence representation learning.
- We design a multi-head attention-based information aggregation mechanism with alignment and information maximization losses to overcome the limitations of [CLS] token representation.
- Our comprehensive experiments demonstrate that InfoKANCSE achieves state-of-the-art performance on semantic textual similarity tasks and multiple downstream applications.

2   Related Work

Prior research extensively investigated unsupervised sentence representations. Several pioneering works [7] focused on leveraging internal sentence structures, while later approaches [27] utilized distributional semantics to predict contextual sentences. Further advancements included Sent2Vec, which effectively combined word vectors with n-gram embeddings.

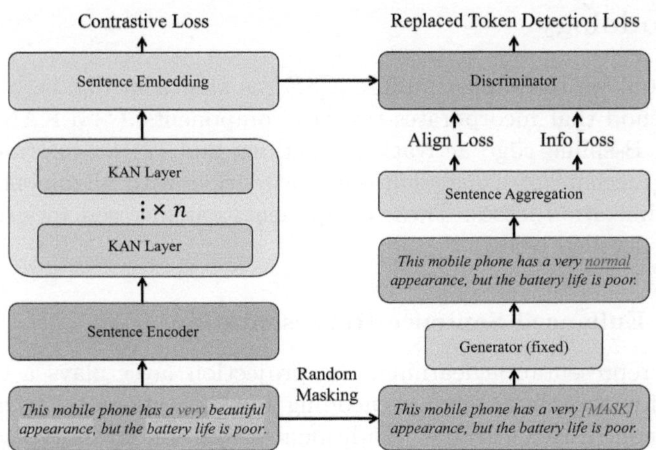

Fig. 1. Illustration of InfoKANCSE. The left part is a SimCSE model enhanced with KAN, providing adaptive non-linear transformations through B-spline based activation functions. The right part is a conditional token difference prediction module which incorporates an explicit sentence aggregation mechanism with alignment and information maximization losses.

With the emergence of pre-trained language models (PLMs) [25], researchers began harnessing their robust language modeling capabilities through diverse techniques. Reimers and Gurevych employed siamese network structures for supervised sentence embedding learning, while [33] and [22] developed post-processing methods to enhance PLM-derived representations.

The emergence of contrastive learning transformed unsupervised sentence representation methodologies [24]. These approaches fundamentally operated on the principle that effective semantic representations should minimize distances between similar sentences while maximizing them between dissimilar ones [15]. SimCSE established itself as a powerful framework upon which various innovative strategies were proposed: [18] incorporated contextual sentences, [17] leveraged inter-layer contrasting, while [10] and [20] addressed structural and sampling challenges respectively.

Contrastive learning has demonstrated effectiveness across diverse NLP applications, including text classification [8], information extraction [30], machine translation [14], and question answering [26]. While existing approaches have primarily focused on developing increasingly sophisticated extensions to SimCSE, our research addresses fundamental limitations within the contrastive learning framework itself. Our work introduces innovative approaches to non-linear feature transformation and sentence information aggregation, aiming to overcome limitations in current methodologies while preserving their strengths.

3   Methodology

In this section, we introduce InfoKANCSE (as shown in Fig. 1), a contrastive learning method that incorporates two key components: (1) a KAN-based projection with B-spline edge activation functions and (2) an information-aware aggregation mechanism using multi-head attention with alignment and information maximization losses. These components enhance semantic relationship modeling as detailed below.

3.1   KAN-Enhanced Sentence Representation

In sentence representation learning, the projection layer plays a crucial role, responsible for mapping sentence encoding representations to a feature space suitable for contrastive learning. Traditional projection layers typically employ multi-layer perceptron structures with fixed activation functions (such as ReLU), which exhibit clear expression when processing complex semantic relationships. This section proposes a projection layer design based on Kolmogorov-Arnold Networks (KAN), which significantly enhances the expressive power and flexibility of the method by introducing learnable activation functions.

Our design is inspired by the Kolmogorov-Arnold representation theorem, which states that any multivariate continuous function can be represented as a composition and superposition of univariate continuous functions. Specifically, for any continuous function $f : [0, 1]^n \rightarrow \mathbb{R}$, there exist continuous functions ϕ_i and $g_{i,j}$ such that:

$$f(x_1, x_2, ..., x_n) = \sum_{i=1}^{2n+1} \Phi_i \left(\sum_{j=1}^{n} g_{i,j}(x_j) \right) \tag{1}$$

Traditional neural networks apply activation functions on nodes, while KAN transfers nonlinear transformations to the edges of the network. In our method, a KAN layer can be defined as a matrix of functions:

$$\Phi = \{\phi_{q,p}\}, p = 1, 2, \cdots, n_{in}, q = 1, 2 \cdots, n_{out} \tag{2}$$

A KAN layer maps an input vector $\mathbf{x} \in \mathbb{R}^n$ to an output vector $\mathbf{y} \in \mathbb{R}^m$:

$$y_i = \sum_{j=1}^{n} \phi_{i,j}(x_j), \tag{3}$$

where $\phi_{i,j} : \mathbb{R} \rightarrow \mathbb{R}$ is a learnable activation function defined on the network edge (j, i). Each edge in KAN has an independent nonlinear transformation function, rather than sharing the same activation function.

To implement these learnable activation functions, we adopt B-spline curve representation:

$$\phi_{i,j}(x) = \sum_{k=0}^{K} w_{i,j,k} B_k(x; \mathbf{t}), \tag{4}$$

where $B_k(x; \mathbf{t})$ is a k-order B-spline basis function, $\mathbf{t}$ is the node vector, and $w_{i,j,k}$ are learnable control point weights.

To better adapt to the distribution of input data, we introduce a dynamic grid update mechanism:

$$\mathbf{t}^{(l+1)} = \mathbf{t}^{(l)} - \eta \nabla_{\mathbf{t}} \mathcal{L} \tag{5}$$

This dynamic adjustment mechanism allows grid points to be adaptively distributed in the input space, focusing more on important regions, thereby improving the accuracy of function approximation.

We integrate KAN layers into the sentence representation contrastive learning framework, replacing the original projection head network. Specifically, given a sentence representation $\mathbf{h} \in \mathbb{R}^d$ output by the encoder, the KAN projection layer processing flow is:

$$\mathbf{z}_1 = \mathrm{KAN}_1(\mathbf{h}) \tag{6}$$
$$\mathbf{z}_2 = \mathrm{BatchNorm}(\mathbf{z}_1) \tag{7}$$
$$\mathbf{z}_3 = \mathrm{ReLU}(\mathbf{z}_2) \tag{8}$$
$$\mathbf{z} = \mathrm{KAN}_2(\mathbf{z}_3) \tag{9}$$

This design using learnable activation functions allows the model to learn specific nonlinear transformations for diverse semantic relationships. The locality property of B-splines enables better handling of different input space regions, while the dynamic grid update mechanism enhances adaptability to important semantic transformation areas. Together, these features enable the KAN projection layer to generate more expressive sentence representations, improving downstream task performance.

3.2   Attention-Guided Representation Enhancement

A key challenge in sentence representation learning is capturing complete semantic information. Existing methods typically use the [CLS] token output as sentence representation, but this approach faces two problems: attention bias (the [CLS] token tends to focus on information at the sentence beginning due to positional limitations) and semantic representation issues (high-frequency tokens like [CLS] are susceptible to anisotropic word vector distributions). To address these challenges, we propose an information-enhanced sentence representation mechanism.

A multi-head attention mechanism is first introduced to actively aggregate semantic information from the sentence. Given a token-level representation matrix $\mathbf{H} \in \mathbb{R}^{L \times d}$ (where L is the sequence length and d is the hidden dimension) and the [CLS] token representation $\mathbf{h}_{cls} \in \mathbb{R}^d$, we construct the query-key-value triplet:

$$\mathbf{Q} = \mathbf{h}_{cls} \mathbf{W}_q, \tag{10}$$
$$\mathbf{K} = \mathbf{H} \mathbf{W}_k, \tag{11}$$
$$\mathbf{V} = \mathbf{H} \mathbf{W}_v, \tag{12}$$

where $\mathbf{W}_q \in \mathbb{R}^{d \times d_q}$, $\mathbf{W}_k \in \mathbb{R}^{d \times d_k}$, and $\mathbf{W}_v \in \mathbb{R}^{d \times d_v}$ are learnable projection matrices.

Then, we calculate attention weights and obtain the aggregated sentence representation:

$$\mathbf{h_{agg}} = \text{softmax}\left(\frac{\mathbf{Q}\mathbf{K}^T}{\sqrt{d_k}}\right)\mathbf{V}. \tag{13}$$

To capture richer feature relationships, we employ a multi-head attention mechanism:

$$\mathbf{h}_{agg} = \text{Concat}(\text{head}_1, \text{head}_2, ..., \text{head}_h)\mathbf{W}_o, \tag{14}$$

where $\text{head}_i = \mathbf{A}_i \mathbf{V}_i$ and $\mathbf{W}_o$ is an output projection matrix.

In contrastive learning, the difference discrimination task provides an important complement to sentence representation learning. Traditional methods rely solely on token-level representations for discrimination, overlooking the value of sentence-level information. A fusion discriminator is designed to utilize both token-level representations and aggregated sentence representations. For a token at position t, the feature fusion representation is calculated as:

$$\mathbf{f}_t = \text{FFN}([\mathbf{h}_t; \mathbf{h}_{agg}; \mathbf{h}_t \odot \mathbf{h}_{agg}]), \tag{15}$$

where $\mathbf{h}_t$ is the token representation at position t, $\odot$ denotes element-wise product, $[;]$ represents vector concatenation, and FFN is a feed-forward network.

Then, we use this fusion representation to predict whether the token has been replaced:

$$p(t) = \sigma(\mathbf{f}_t \mathbf{W}_d + b_d), \tag{16}$$

where σ is the sigmoid activation function, and $\mathbf{W}_d$ and b_d are discriminator parameters. This design forces the model to consider the semantic information of the entire sentence during the discrimination process, thereby promoting the aggregated representation to more comprehensively capture the semantic features of the sentence.

To further ensure the quality of the aggregated representation, we introduce two additional constraint objectives. First is the alignment loss, which requires the aggregated representation to maintain a certain degree of alignment with the average of all token representations in the sentence. This constraint prevents the aggregated representation from deviating too much from the overall semantics of the sentence:

$$\mathcal{L}_{align} = \|\mathbf{h}_{agg} - \frac{1}{L}\sum_{t=1}^{L}\mathbf{h}_t\|_2^2 \tag{17}$$

Next is the information maximization loss, which maximizes the mutual information between the aggregated representation and all token representations to ensure the aggregated representation contains sufficient sentence information:

$$\mathcal{L}_{info} = -I(\mathbf{h}_{agg}; \mathbf{H}), \tag{18}$$

where $I(\cdot;\cdot)$ represents mutual information. In practice, we implement mutual information optimization through a neural network estimator.

Combining contrastive learning, difference discrimination, and information aggregation constraints, the final optimization objective is:

$$\mathcal{L} = \mathcal{L}_{cl} + \alpha\mathcal{L}_{diff} + \beta\mathcal{L}_{align} + \gamma\mathcal{L}_{info}, \tag{19}$$

where $\mathcal{L}_{cl}$ is the contrastive learning loss, $\mathcal{L}_{diff}$ is the difference discrimination loss, and α, β, γ are hyperparameters that balance different loss components.

Through multi-task joint optimization, our model learns rich sentence representations that preserve overall semantics while capturing subtle differences. This addresses the [CLS] token's incomplete representation problem in traditional methods, improving downstream performance. Similar to human comprehension, our information enhancement method attends to both themes and wording nuances, actively organizing important information to generate more accurate and complete sentence representations.

4 Experiments and Results

4.1 Dataset

We use 10^6 randomly sampled sentences from English Wikipedia for unsupervised pretraining, following the same dataset used in previous studies [6]. Our evaluation includes 7 semantic textual similarity (STS) tasks [2], and BEIR benchmark [23]. All STS experiments are fully unsupervised, with Spearman correlation coefficient as the evaluation metric. This coefficient quantifies the relationship between model-generated sentence embeddings and human judgments of semantic similarity, with higher scores indicating better model performance.

4.2 Baselines

We compare our model with 12 unsupervised baselines including SimCSE [6], ConSERT [31], SG-OPT [12], Mirror-BERT [16], ESimCSE [29], DiffCSE [3], InfoCSE [28], SimCSE++ [30], DebCSE [20], Focal-InfoCSE [8], ConCSE [10], HNCSE [17] and post-processing methods like BERT-flow [13].

4.3 Setup

We use BERT [4] and RoBERTa [19] checkpoints as our sentence encoder initialization, with an MLP layer with BatchNorm [9] on top of the [CLS] token. For the discriminator, we use the same architecture as the encoder, while employing smaller DistilBERT and DistilRoBERTa [21] models as generators for efficiency. The training process starts from the publicly pre-trained checkpoint of BERT-base or BERT-large, with hyperparameters following Condenser [5] and SimCSE [6]. When pretraining the auxiliary network, following [5], we train for 16 epochs using the Adam optimizer with learning rate $= 5e-5$ and global batch size $= 512$ on a single Nvidia RTX 4090 24G GPU. For jointly optimizing contrastive objective, auxiliary MLM objective, KAN and information aggregation, following [3], we train by Adam optimizer with learning rate $= 3e-5$ and batch size $= 64$. And We evaluate the model every 200 training steps on the development set of STS-B and keep the best checkpoint for the final evaluation on test sets.

4.4 Main Results

Table 1. Main results on Semantic Textual Similarity benchmark dataset performance, measured using Spearman's correlation coefficient.

Dataset Model	STS12	STS13	STS14	SICK15	STS16	STS-B	SICK-R	Avg.
ConSERT$_{base}$ [31]	64.64	78.49	69.07	79.72	75.95	73.97	67.31	72.74
SG-OPT-BERT$_{base}$ [12]	66.84	80.13	71.23	81.56	77.17	77.23	68.16	74.62
Mirror-BERT$_{base}$ [16]	69.10	81.10	73.00	81.90	75.70	78.00	69.10	75.40
SimCSE-BERT$_{base}$ [6]	68.40	82.41	74.38	80.91	78.56	76.85	72.23	76.25
ESimCSE-BERT$_{base}$ [29]	73.40	83.27	77.25	82.66	78.81	80.17	72.30	78.27
DiffCSE-BERT$_{base}$ [3]	72.28	84.43	76.47	83.90	80.54	80.59	71.23	78.49
InfoCSE-BERT$_{base}$ [28]	70.53	84.59	76.40	**85.10**	81.95	82.00	71.37	78.85
SimCSE++-BERT$_{base}$ [30]	70.12	84.40	76.35	84.96	81.48	82.03	70.98	78.62
DebCSE-BERT$_{base}$ [20]	70.30	84.22	75.92	84.61	82.19	82.13	71.72	78.73
FocalCSE-BERT$_{base}$ [8]	70.85	84.44	76.82	84.87	81.47	81.90	71.60	78.85
ConCSE-BERT$_{base}$ [10]	70.80	84.34	76.63	85.21	82.08	82.41	71.22	78.96
HNCSE-BERT$_{base}$ [17]	70.71	84.55	76.85	84.65	82.06	81.62	71.34	78.83
InfoKANCSE-BERT$_{base}$	**75.51**	**86.93**	**78.42**	84.03	**83.66**	**84.07**	**73.32**	**80.84**
ConSERT$_{large}$	70.69	82.96	74.13	82.78	76.66	77.53	70.37	76.45
SG-OPT-BERT$_{large}$	67.02	79.42	70.38	81.72	76.35	76.16	70.20	74.46
SimCSE-BERT$_{large}$	70.88	84.16	76.43	84.50	79.76	79.26	73.88	78.41
ESimCSE-BERT$_{large}$	**73.21**	85.37	77.73	84.30	78.92	80.73	74.89	79.31
DiffCSE-BERT$_{large}$	72.11	84.99	76.19	85.09	78.65	80.34	73.93	78.76
InfoCSE-BERT$_{large}$	71.89	86.17	77.72	86.20	81.29	83.16	74.84	80.18
SimCSE++-BERT$_{large}$	69.48	84.56	76.31	86.42	81.59	82.00	72.07	78.92
DebCSE-BERT$_{large}$	70.29	84.96	77.33	86.10	81.44	83.06	72.79	79.42
FocalCSE-BERT$_{large}$	72.07	85.58	76.31	85.54	80.85	81.99	70.23	78.94
ConCSE-BERT$_{large}$	72.09	82.90	78.06	84.37	82.49	82.74	69.90	78.94
HNCSE-BERT$_{large}$	70.03	83.81	77.44	83.49	81.79	81.61	70.43	78.37
InfoKANCSE-BERT$_{large}$	72.96	**88.91**	**79.43**	**89.21**	**84.33**	**85.17**	**76.87**	**82.41**

Semantic Textual Similarity (STS). Table 1 shows the performances of different methods on seven semantic textual similarity (STS) tasks. The results indicate that InfoKANCSE-BERT models achieve higher performance in measuring semantic textual similarity. InfoKANCSE-BERT$_{large}$ achieves an average score of 82.41, representing a 2.8% improvement over InfoCSE-BERT$_{large}$ (80.18) and a 5.3% improvement compared to SimCSE-BERT$_{large}$ (78.27). This model performs particularly well on STS-B (85.17) and STS14 (79.43). Similarly, InfoKANCSE-BERT$_{base}$ outperforms other base-sized models with an average score of 80.84, surpassing InfoCSE-BERT$_{base}$ (78.85) by 2.5% and SimCSE-BERT$_{base}$ (76.49) by 5.7%. These results demonstrate the effectiveness of the InfoKANCSE method in capturing semantic similarity across various test sets.

Table 2. Zero-shot evaluation results on the BEIR benchmark. All scores denote **nDCG@10**. The best score on a given dataset is marked in **bold**, and the second best is <u>underlined</u>.

Dataset	ESimCSE		DiffCSE		InfoCSE		InfoKANCSE	
	base	large	base	large	base	large	base	large
trec-covid	0.2291	0.2829	0.2368	0.2291	<u>0.3937</u>	0.3166	**0.4163**	0.3327
nfcorpus	0.1149	0.1483	0.1204	0.1470	0.1358	0.1576	**0.1892**	<u>0.1761</u>
nq	0.0935	0.1705	0.1188	0.1556	<u>0.2023</u>	0.1790	**0.2129**	0.1921
fiqa	0.0731	0.1117	0.0924	0.1027	0.0991	0.1000	**0.1141**	<u>0.1209</u>
arguana	0.3376	0.2604	0.2500	0.2572	0.3244	<u>0.4133</u>	0.3651	**0.4493**
webis-touche2020	0.0786	0.1057	0.0912	0.0781	0.0935	0.0920	**0.1241**	<u>0.1166</u>
quora	0.7411	0.7615	0.7491	0.7471	0.8241	0.8268	**0.8648**	<u>0.8394</u>
cqadupstack	0.1276	0.1196	0.1197	0.1160	0.2097	<u>0.1881</u>	**0.2564**	<u>0.2124</u>
dbpedia-entity	0.1260	0.1650	0.1537	0.1571	<u>0.2101</u>	0.1838	**0.2361**	0.2009
scidocs	0.0657	0.0796	0.0673	0.0699	0.0837	0.0859	**0.1022**	<u>0.0966</u>
climate-fever	0.0796	0.1302	0.1019	<u>0.1087</u>	0.0937	0.0840	**0.1253**	0.0947
scifact	0.3013	0.2875	0.2666	0.2811	0.3269	<u>0.3801</u>	0.3364	**0.4105**
hotpotqa	0.1213	0.1970	0.1730	0.2068	<u>0.3177</u>	0.2781	**0.3354**	0.2831
fever	0.0756	0.1689	0.1416	0.1849	0.1978	0.1252	**0.2178**	<u>0.2036</u>
average	0.1832	0.2135	0.1916	0.2030	0.2509	0.2436	**0.2782**	<u>0.2663</u>
t-test	2.7e–5	1.9e–4	3.5e–5	1.0e–4	3.4e–4	1.6e–3	–	–

Open-Domain Retrieval Task. Table 2 shows zero-shot performance across the BEIR benchmark. Our InfoKANCSE model achieves superior average performance (0.2782 base, 0.2663 large), outperforming both traditional methods and the previous state-of-the-art InfoCSE. This demonstrates the effectiveness of our knowledge enhancement strategy. InfoKANCSE excels across diverse scenarios: factual queries (0.2564/0.2361 on cqadupstack/dbpedia-entity), argumentative content (0.4493 on arguana), and specialized domains (climate-fever and scifact). Combined with STS results from Table 1, InfoKANCSE bridges semantic similarity assessment with practical retrieval applications, offering a novel solution for representation learning and information retrieval.

4.5   Ablation Studies

We perform an extensive series of ablation studies to InfoKANCSE with BERT_{large} scale on the development set of STS-B.

Table 3. Development set results of STS-B for InfoKANCSE variants, where we vary the objective. "w/o" denotes without.

Model	STS-B
InfoKANCSE	**85.17**
w/o KAN	83.03
w/o alignment loss	84.13
w/o information maximization loss	83.96
w/o Discrimination loss	81.17
w/o Contrastive loss	38.12

Table 4. Development set results of STS-B when varying coefficients α, β and γ.

α	1e–5	5e–6	1e–5	5e–5
STS-B	83.59	84.76	**85.17**	84.43
β	1e–4	5e–3	1e–2	5e–2
STS-B	84.55	81.85	74.05	77.95
γ	1e–5	1e–4	1e–3	5e–3
STS-B	86.29	81.38	75.64	73.07

The Impact of KAN and Loss We conducted ablation experiments to validate the effectiveness of each component in InfoKANCSE, as shown in Table 3. Removing the KAN structure decreased performance on the STS-B development set from 85.17 to 83.03, demonstrating how learnable activation functions enhance semantic representation compared to traditional fixed ProjectionMLP. Further experiments show that removing alignment loss and information maximization loss resulted in performance drops to 84.13 and 83.96 respectively, indicating their contributions to maintaining semantic integrity and information richness. More critically, removing the Discrimination loss reduced performance to 81.17, while removing the Contrastive loss caused a dramatic drop to 38.12. These results confirm that all components in our framework contribute significantly to the model's effectiveness, with contrastive learning serving as the foundation while other components collectively enhance the modeln's capability to capture both sentence-level similarities and fine-grained semantic differences.

The Impact of Loss Weighting Coefficients. To investigate the influence of different loss weighting coefficients, we conducted experiments varying the hyperparameters α, β and γ that balance different components in our final optimization objective. Table 4 presents the results on STS-B development set. For the difference discrimination loss coefficient α, performance peaks at 1e–5 (85.17). The alignment loss coefficient β shows optimal performance at 1e–4 (84.53). Most notably, the information maximization loss coefficient γ achieves the highest score of 86.29 at 1e–5, with performance declining significantly as γ increases. These findings highlight the importance of carefully balancing multiple learning objectives to achieve optimal performance in sentence representation learning.

5   Conclusion

This paper proposes InfoKANCSE, a novel contrastive sentence embedding framework that enhances representation quality through Kolmogorov-Arnold Networks with B-spline curve-based activation functions and information-aware aggregation with multi-head attention mechanisms. Our experimental results demonstrate significant improvements over previous state-of-the-art methods, achieving an average performance gain of 2.1% on STS tasks compared to DiffCSE. The model effectively captures richer semantic information while maintaining sensitivity to subtle semantic differences. In future work, we also plan to systematically investigate the computational trade-offs introduced by incorporating KAN layers and multi-head attention. While these components enhance expressiveness and representation quality, they may increase training time and resource usage. Exploring lightweight variants or approximation techniques could help mitigate these costs.

References

1. Carlsson, F., Gyllensten, A.C., Gogoulou, E., Hellqvist, E.Y., Sahlgren, M.: Semantic re-tuning with contrastive tension. In: International Conference on Learning Representations (2021)
2. Cer, D., Diab, M., Agirre, E., Lopez-Gazpio, I., Specia, L.: Semeval-2017 task 1: semantic textual similarity-multilingual and cross-lingual focused evaluation. arXiv preprint arXiv:1708.00055 (2017)
3. Chuang, Y.S., et al.: Diffcse: difference-based contrastive learning for sentence embeddings. arXiv preprint arXiv:2204.10298 (2022)

4. Devlin, J., Chang, M.W., Lee, K., Toutanova, K.: Bert: pre-training of deep bidirectional transformers for language understanding. arXiv preprint arXiv:1810.04805 (2018)
5. Gao, L., Callan, J.: Condenser: a pre-training architecture for dense retrieval. arXiv preprint arXiv:2104.08253 (2021)
6. Gao, T., Yao, X., Chen, D.: Simcse: simple contrastive learning of sentence embeddings. arXiv preprint arXiv:2104.08821 (2021)
7. Hou, P., Han, J., , Li, X.: Improving adversarial robustness with self-paced hard-class pair reweighting. In: Proceedings of the Thirty-Seventh AAAI Conference on Artificial Intelligence (2023)
8. Hou, P., Li, X.: Improving contrastive learning of sentence embeddings with focal-infonce. arXiv preprint arXiv:2310.06918v2 (2023)
9. Ioffe, S., Szegedy, C.: Batch normalization: accelerating deep network training by reducing internal covariate shift. In: International Conference on Machine Learning, pp. 448–456. PMLR (2015)
10. Jeon, J., Cho, S., Ma, M., Kim, J.: Concse: unified contrastive learning and augmentation for code-switched embeddings. arXiv preprint arXiv:2409.00120 (2024)
11. Gao, J., He, D., Tan, X., Qin, T., Wang, L., Liu, T.Y.: Representation degeneration problem in training natural language generation models. In: International Conference on Learning Representations (2019)
12. Kim, T., Yoo, K.M., Lee, S.G.: Self-guided contrastive learning for bert sentence representations. arXiv preprint arXiv:2106.07345 (2021)
13. Li, B., Zhou, H., He, J., Wang, M., Yang, Y., Li, L.: On the sentence embeddings from pre-trained language models. In: Proceedings of the 2020 Conference on Empirical Methods in Natural Language Processing (EMNLP), pp. 9119–9130 (2020)
14. Li, R., Li, J., Han, J., Wang, G.: Similarity-based neighbor selection for graph llms. arXiv preprint arXiv:2402.03720 (2024)
15. Lim, V., Ng, K.W., Lim, K.: Contrastive learning in distilled models. arXiv preprint arXiv:2401.12472 (2024)
16. Liu, F., Vulić, I., Korhonen, A., Collier, N.: Fast, effective, and self-supervised: Transforming masked language models into universal lexical and sentence encoders. arXiv preprint arXiv:2104.08027 (2021)
17. Liu, W., et al.: Hncse: advancing sentence embeddings via hybrid contrastive learning with hard negatives. arXiv preprint arXiv:2411.12156 (2024)
18. Liu, X.: Defsent+: improving sentence embeddings of language models by projecting definition sentences into a quasi-isotropic or isotropic vector space of unlimited dictionary entries. arXiv preprint arXiv:2405.16153 (2024)
19. Liu, Y., et al.: Roberta: a robustly optimized bert pretraining approach. arXiv preprint arXiv:1907.11692 (2019)
20. Miao, P., Du, Z., Zhang, J.: Debcse: rethinking unsupervised contrastive sentence embedding learning in the debiasing perspective. In: Proceedings of the 32nd ACM International Conference on Information and Knowledge Management (2023)
21. Sanh, V., Debut, L., Chaumond, J., Wolf, T.: Distilbert, a distilled version of bert: smaller, faster, cheaper and lighter. arXiv preprint arXiv:1910.01108 (2019)
22. Stetina, J., Fajcik, M., Stefanik, M., Hradis, M.: A comparative study of text retrieval models on dareczech. arXiv preprint arXiv:2411.12921 (2024)
23. Thakur, N., Reimers, N., Rücklé, A., Srivastava, A., Gurevych, I.: Beir: a heterogenous benchmark for zero-shot evaluation of information retrieval models. arXiv preprint arXiv:2104.08663 (2021)

24. + mer Veysel + a- atan: Unsee: unsupervised non-contrastive sentence embeddings. arXiv preprint arXiv:2401.15316 (2024)
25. Wang, S., et al.: Sim-gpt: text similarity via gpt annotated data. arXiv preprint arXiv:2312.05603 (2023)
26. Wang, Y., Zhou, Z., Wang, J.: 2-tier simcse: elevating bert for robust sentence embeddings. arXiv preprint arXiv:2501.13758 (2025)
27. Wu, Q., Tao, C., Shen, T., Xu, C., Geng, X., Jiang, D.: Pcl: peer-contrastive learning with diverse augmentations for unsupervised sentence embeddings. arXiv preprint arXiv:2201.12093 (2022)
28. Wu, X., Gao, C., Lin, Z., Han, J., Wang, Z., Hu, S.: Infocse: information-aggregated contrastive learning of sentence embeddings. arXiv preprint arXiv:2210.06432 (2022)
29. Wu, X., Gao, C., Zang, L., Han, J., Wang, Z., Hu, S.: Esimcse: enhanced sample building method for contrastive learning of unsupervised sentence embedding. arXiv preprint arXiv:2109.04380 (2021)
30. Xu, J., Shao, W., Chen, L., Liu, L.: Simcse++: improving contrastive learning for sentence embeddings from two perspectives. In: Proceedings of the 2023 Conference on Empirical Methods in Natural Language Processing (2023)
31. Yan, Y., Li, R., Wang, S., Zhang, F., Wu, W., Xu, W.: Consert: a contrastive framework for self-supervised sentence representation transfer. arXiv preprint arXiv:2105.11741 (2021)
32. Zhang, Y., Zhu, H., Wang, Y., Xu, N., Li, X., Zhao, B.: A contrastive framework for learning sentence representations from pairwise and triple-wise perspective in angular space. In: Proceedings of the 60th Annual Meeting of the Association for Computational Linguistics (Volume 1: Long Papers), pp. 4892–4903 (2022)
33. Zhong, M., Wu, Z., Honda, N.: Deep learning based dense retrieval: a comparative study. arXiv preprint arXiv:2410.20315 (2024)
34. Liu, Z., et al.: Kan: KolmogorovG arnold networks. In: International Conference on Learning Representations (2025)

Zero-Shot Chain-of-Thought Reasoning Guided by Evolutionary Algorithms in Large Language Models

Feihu Jin[1,2], Yifan Liu[1,2], and Ying Tan[1,2,3(✉)]

[1] School of Intelligence Science and Technology, Peking University, Beijing, China
fhjin@stu.pku.edu.cn
[2] Institute for Artificial Intelligence, Peking University, Beijing, China
[3] State Key Laboratory of General Artificial Intelligence, Peking University, Beijing, China
ytan@pku.edu.cn

Abstract. Large Language Models (LLMs) have demonstrated remarkable performance across diverse tasks and exhibited impressive reasoning abilities by applying zero-shot Chain-of-Thought (CoT) prompting. However, due to the evolving nature of sentence prefixes during the pre-training phase, existing zero-shot CoT prompting methods that employ identical CoT prompting across all task instances may not be optimal. In this paper, we introduce a novel zero-shot prompting method that leverages evolutionary algorithms to dynamically generate diverse promptings for LLMs. Our approach involves initializing several CoT promptings, performing evolutionary operations based on LLMs to create a varied set, and utilizing the LLMs to select a suitable CoT prompting for a given problem. Additionally, a rewriting operation, guided by the selected CoT prompting, enhances the understanding of the LLMs about the problem. Extensive experiments conducted across ten reasoning datasets demonstrate the superior performance of our proposed method compared to current zero-shot CoT prompting methods on both black-box and open-source LLMs. Moreover, in-depth analytical experiments underscore the adaptability and effectiveness of our method in various reasoning tasks.

1 Introduction

The capacity for logical inference stands out as a defining characteristic of human intelligence, granting us the ability to engage in deduction, induction, and problem-solving. With the revolutionary advancement of pre-training [3,23,24,30], the rise of LLMs has firmly established itself as a cornerstone in the field of natural language processing (NLP), showcasing exceptional performance across a spectrum of NLP tasks. However, LLMs often face challenges in the nuanced domain of reasoning, prompting researchers to strategically leverage their embedded knowledge through the conditioning of LLMs on a limited set of illustrative examples, referred to as few-shot learning [32,33], or through the

© The Author(s), under exclusive license to Springer Nature Singapore Pte Ltd. 2026

X.-L. Mao et al. (Eds.): NLPCC 2025, LNAI 16105, pp. 52–64, 2026.
https://doi.org/10.1007/978-981-95-3352-7_5

provision of prompts for solving problems in the absence of illustrative examples, constituting a paradigm known as zero-shot learning [12].

Current research mainly focuses on designing diverse prompting strategies to guide the reasoning processes of LLMs. For instance, [33] propose the few-shot CoT prompting, involving the use of a limited number of manually demonstrated reasoning examples to enable LLMs to explicitly generate intermediate reasoning steps before predicting the final answer. Various approaches have been explored to eliminate the need for manually selected examples in few-shot CoT prompting. For instance, [12] introduce zero-shot CoT prompting by appending *"Let's think step by step"* to the target problem, PS+ prompting [31] add *"Let's first understand the problem and devise a plan to solve the problem. Then, let's carry out the plan and solve the problem step by step"* after the target problem, and RE2 prompting [35] add *"Read the question again"* combined with *"Let's think step by step"* to the target problem. However, these zero-shot CoT prompting methods employ uniform CoT prompting across all task instances. Given the ongoing evolution of sentence prefixes during the pre-training phase of extensive language models, using identical CoT prompting for all instances may introduce disruptions to predictive accuracy and potentially result in a degradation of overall performance. Consequently, a fundamental query emerges: Is it feasible to ascertain an appropriate CoT prompting for each instance within a discrete space?

Fortunately, evolutionary algorithms (EAs) [8,16,21] provide a solution. EA represents a category of optimization algorithms inspired by the principles of natural evolution. Crossover, mutation, and selection steps in EA can generate various CoT promptings. In this paper, we introduce a novel method guided by evolutionary algorithms named **E**volution **of T**ought (**EoT**) prompting. The process begins by initializing several CoT promptings based on human design or auto-generation using large language models. Using LLMs as the optimizer within a evolutionary algorithm framework, we perform crossover and mutation operations on the initialized CoT promptings, generating a diverse set of new ones. Subsequently, we use LLMs to select a CoT prompting deemed suitable for the current problem. Furthermore, to deepen the understanding of LLMs of the current problem, a rewriting operation is performed on the selected CoT prompting. The LLMs engage in reasoning based on the rewritten problem. This strategy aims to capitalize on the diversity of CoT prompting generated through the EA and problem rewriting to provide richer information that encourages the LLMs to attain a more profound understanding of the given problem.

To validate the effectiveness of our proposed zero-shot EoT prompting, we conduct a comprehensive series of experiments across ten datasets, covering arithmetic, commonsense, and symbolic reasoning. The experiments are carried out on black-box LLMs GPT-3.5-Turbo [23] and GPT-4 [24], as well as open-source LLM Llama-3-8B-Instruct[1]. Specifically, the results in mathematical reasoning indicate that our zero-shot EoT prompting outperforms existing zero-shot CoT prompting, with average improvements of 3.1% on GPT-3.5-Turbo. Its

---

[1] https://github.com/meta-llama/llama3.

comparable performance to few-shot CoT prompting is particularly noteworthy, especially in arithmetic and symbolic reasoning. Additionally, extensive analytical experiments are conducted to gain a deeper understanding of the different components of zero-shot EoT prompting and the impact of various factors on EoT prompting.

2   Preliminaries

Zero-shot Chain-of-Thought Prompting. In-context learning leverages a few demonstrations as a prompt and conducts inference without training the model parameters [3]. Chain-of-thought (CoT) prompting [33] has been proposed as a type of in-context learning that decomposes the original problem into several small parts and achieves encouraging results on many complex reasoning tasks in large language models. Moreover, the zero-shot chain-of thought prompting [12] has shown impressive effectiveness on various tasks in large language models by attaching a sentence before the reasoning process. For standard zero-shot CoT prompting, given the reasoning question $\mathcal{Q}$, zero-shot CoT specific instructions $\mathcal{T}$ like *"Let's think step by step."*, we formalize this simple yet fundamental solving paradigm as:

$$P(\mathcal{A}|\mathcal{T}, \mathcal{Q}) = P(\mathcal{A}|\mathcal{T}, \mathcal{Q}, \mathcal{C})P(\mathcal{C}|\mathcal{T}, \mathcal{Q}) \tag{1}$$

where $\mathcal{C}$ denotes a sampled rationale in natural language and $\mathcal{A}$ is the generated answer. As such, LLMs can perform complex reasoning by decomposing the problem into sequential or modular steps.

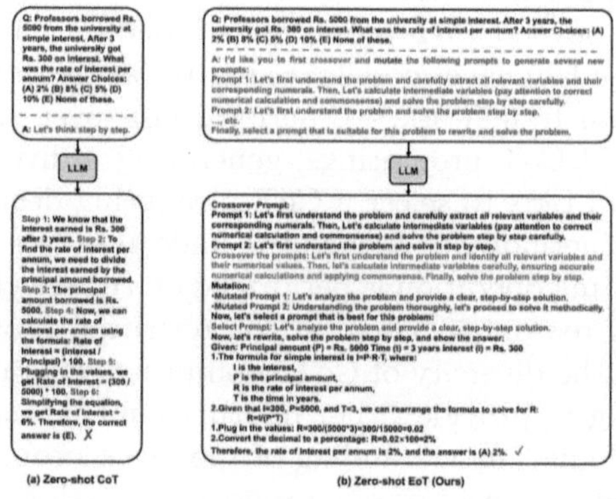

Fig. 1. Example inputs and outputs of GPT-3.5-Turbo with (a) Zero-shot CoT prompting and (b) Zero-shot EoT prompting. Zero-shot CoT prompting attaches the sentence *"Let's think step by step"* for each instance to encourage LLMs to generate multi-step reasoning. Our proposed method, EoT prompting, uses the LLMs as an evolutionary optimizer and generates suitable CoT prompting for each instance.

3   Method

Overview. We introduce our proposed zero-shot EoT prompting. EoT utilizes the large language model as an evolutionary optimizer, performing crossover and mutation operations on several given promptings to generate diverse promptings. Subsequently, EoT empowers LLMs to autonomously select the most suitable or optimal prompting from the generated set as the final prompting. Finally, EoT employs the chosen prompt to instruct LLMs in rewriting given problems, generating an intermediate reasoning process, and predicting the final answer for the input problem. Similar to zero-shot CoT prompting, our EoT prompting incorporates an answer extraction prompting, such as *"Therefore, the answer (arabic numerals) is"* to extract the answer for evaluation.

3.1   Prompt Generation Through Evolutionary Algorithms

As depicted in Fig. 1(a), zero-shot CoT prompting [12] appends the same sentence *"Let's think step by step"* or the recently proposed Plan-and-Solve prompting [31] connects the same sentence *"Let's first understand the problem and devise a plan to solve the problem. Then, let's carry out the plan and solve the problem step by step"* to each instance, encouraging LLMs to generate multi-step reasoning. Given the continuous evolution of sentence prefixes during the pre-training phase of large language models, using identical CoT prompting for all instances may disrupt predictions and lead to a decline in performance.

To address these concerns, we aim to identify suitable CoT prompting for each instance of the current reasoning task within a discrete space before proceeding with the reasoning process. However, determining the most suitable CoT prompting for each instance in a discrete space poses a challenge. Fortunately, evolutionary algorithms provide a solution. We employ the large language model as an optimizer, executing crossover and mutation on the initialized CoT prompting, denoted as LLM-Crossover and LLM-Mutation. As illustrated in Fig. 1(b), for a given problem $\mathcal{Q}$, we first initialize several CoT promptings $\mathcal{T}_1$ and $\mathcal{T}_2$. Subsequently, we first use the large language model as the evolutionary optimizer, applying the LLM-Crossover operation on $\mathcal{T}_1$ and $\mathcal{T}_2$, which is defined as:

$$\mathcal{T}_c = \text{LLM-Crossover}(\mathcal{T}_1, \mathcal{T}_2) \tag{2}$$

Then, we enable LLM-Mutation on the crossovered CoT prompting $\mathcal{T}_c$, which is defined as:

$$\mathcal{T}_m = \text{LLM-Mutation}(\mathcal{T}_c) \tag{3}$$

This leverages the powerful generative capability of the large language model to generate additional CoT promptings.

We aim to generate more high-quality promptings by evolving from the initial ones. To obtain good initial promptings, we use either auto-generated promptings [37] or manual-designed promptings as the initial promptings. Additionally, pursuing a more diverse set of selectable CoT promptings, it is customary to subject the model to crossover and mutation operations iteratively. However, the temporal demand tends to escalate proportionally with the quantity of generated CoT promptings. Consequently, we opt for a default strategy of conducting a singular round of crossover and mutation operations to mitigate reasoning time. As illustrated in Figure ??, our analysis delves into the correlation between the number of CoT promptings (i.e., the population size N) generated through multiple rounds of crossover and mutation operations and the performance of LLMs.

3.2   Problem Rewriting with Generated Prompt and Answer Extraction

Based on the generated and initialized pool of CoT promptings, we enable the LLMs to select the most optimal or contextually suitable CoT prompting for the current problem $\mathcal{Q}$. Subsequently, to enhance the retention of the LLMs regarding the problem, we employ the selected CoT prompting to rewrite the question $\mathcal{Q}$ and instruct the LLMs to conduct reasoning. The formalization of this process is exemplified as follows:

$$P(\mathcal{A}|\mathcal{T}_o, \mathcal{Q}) = P(\mathcal{A}|\mathcal{T}_o, R(\mathcal{Q}), \mathcal{C})P(\mathcal{C}|\mathcal{T}_o, R(\mathcal{Q})) \tag{4}$$

Here, $\mathcal{T}_o$ denotes the selected CoT prompting by LLMs, $\mathcal{C}$ denotes a sampled rationale in natural language, $\mathcal{A}$ is the generated answer, and $R(\cdot)$ means rewriting the question $\mathcal{Q}$ with $\mathcal{T}_o$. For instance, in Fig. 1b, for a given question $\mathcal{Q}$: *Professors borrowed Rs. 5000 from the university at simple interest. After 3 years, the university got Rs. 300 on interest. What was the rate of interest per annum? Answer Choices: (A) 2% (B) 8% (C) 5% (D) 10% (E) None of these.* We employ the chosen CoT prompting (*Let's analyze the problem and provide a clear, step-by-step solution.*) to rewrite the question $R(\mathcal{Q})$. Then, the LLMs generate an intermediate reasoning process and predict the final answer for the question $\mathcal{Q}$. Moreover, our method defaults to employing the greedy decoding strategy for the generation of output.

Similar to the zero-shot CoT prompting, our EoT prompting incorporates specific trigger sentences, such as *"Therefore, the answer (arabic numerals) is"*, into the sentences generated by LLMs through EoT prompting. Following this augmentation, the composite text is reintroduced to LLMs, producing the desired answer format.

4   Experiments

4.1   Experimental Setup

Datasets.   We systematically evaluate the efficacy of our proposed method across ten datasets encompassing three main categories: arithmetic, commonsense, and symbolic tasks. Details are in Table 1.

Baselines.   We conduct a comparative analysis between our proposed zero-shot EoT prompting method and several task-specific zero-shot CoT prompting methods: (1) Zero-shot CoT prompting [12], which appends a sentence *"Let's think*

Table 1. Details of datasets evaluated in our experiment.

Dataset	Samples	Avg Words	Answer Format	Domain
SingleEq	508	27.4	Number	Math
AddSub	395	31.5	Number	Math
GSM8K	1319	46.9	Number	Math
MultiArith	600	31.8	Number	Math
SVAMP	1000	31.8	Number	Math
AQuA	254	51.9	Option	Math
CommonsenseQA	1221	27.8	Option	Commonsense
StrategyQA	2290	9.6	Yes/No	Commonsense
Coin Flip	500	37.0	Yes/No	Symbolic
Last Letters	1000	15.0	String	Symbolic

step by step" before the reasoning process; (2) Zero-shot PS and PS+ prompting [31], employing a "plan-and-solve" strategy to guide the model throughout the inference process; (3) Zero-shot RE2 prompting [35], a plug & play approach that entails re-reading the question before engaging in the reasoning process; (4) APE prompting [37], utilizing LLMs to generate instructions automatically and requiring additional training. We also compare our method with two few-shot CoT prompting methods: Few-shot Manual-CoT prompting [33], utilizing eight manually crafted examples as demonstrations, and Few-shot AuTo-CoT prompting [36], which automatically selects examples through clustering for diversity.

Table 2. Accuracy of six math reasoning datasets on GPT-3.5-Turbo with different zero-shot and few-shot CoT prompting methods. The boldfaced and underlined fonts indicate the best and the second results in the zero-shot settings, respectively.

Method	MultiArith	GSM8K	AddSub	AQuA	SingleEq	SVAMP	Average	Δ
Zero-Shot								
CoT	95.3	75.3	86.6	55.1	92.9	79.0	80.7	-
PS	92.3	76.3	85.8	56.7	90.2	75.8	79.5	-1.2
PS+	93.8	76.1	86.6	58.7	92.5	79.4	81.2	+0.5
RE2	**96.8**	76.9	88.6	<u>59.8</u>	91.7	79.7	82.3	+1.6
APE	93.3	**80.2**	<u>88.9</u>	59.4	**94.1**	<u>81.5</u>	<u>82.9</u>	+2.2
EoT (Ours)	<u>96.0</u>	<u>78.5</u>	**91.1**	**62.2**	<u>93.7</u>	**82.0**	**83.8**	+3.1
Few-Shot								
Manual-CoT	95.5	75.9	89.9	58.7	92.3	81.1	82.2	+1.5
AuTo-CoT	96.2	77.3	90.6	61.8	92.7	81.8	83.4	+2.7

Implementation Details. We mainly use ChatGPT (GPT-3.5-Turbo-0613) [23] and Llama-3-8B-Instruct as the backbone language models. Regarding decoding strategy, we employ greedy decoding with a temperature setting of 0 and implement self-consistency prompting with a temperature setting of 0.7. We set the initial number of promptings to two to reduce inference time and perform one iteration of crossover and mutation. Furthermore, to fortify the robustness and generalizability of our proposed method, we conduct complementary evaluations utilizing GPT-4 [24]. For the few-shot baselines, Manual-CoT and Auto-CoT, we adhere to the configurations outlined in the [33] and [36]. We adopt accuracy as our evaluation metric for all datasets.

Table 3. Accuracy of six math reasoning datasets on Llama-3-8B-Instruct with different zero-shot and few-shot CoT prompting methods. The boldfaced and underlined fonts indicate the best and the second results in the zero-shot settings, respectively.

Method	MultiArith	GSM8K	AddSub	AQuA	SingleEq	SVAMP	Average	Δ
Zero-Shot								
CoT	<u>95.2</u>	<u>80.4</u>	85.3	50.0	<u>90.4</u>	83.6	<u>80.8</u>	-
PS	92.2	78.6	<u>87.6</u>	47.6	89.6	83.3	79.8	-1.0
PS+	94.7	79.1	86.3	48.4	89.4	<u>83.7</u>	80.3	-0.5
RE2	94.5	80.1	86.8	48.0	90.0	**84.0**	80.6	-0.2
APE	92.3	78.5	86.1	<u>50.4</u>	89.8	83.2	80.1	-0.7
EoT (Ours)	**95.3**	**81.7**	**89.4**	**53.1**	**91.4**	83.5	**82.4**	+1.6
Few-Shot								
Manual-CoT	95.8	81.7	86.8	52.0	91.5	83.9	82.0	+1.2
AuTo-CoT	96.8	82.0	87.6	52.4	92.1	84.1	82.5	+1.3

4.2 Main Results

Results on Arithmetic Reasoning. Table 2 and Table 3 present a thorough performance comparison between our zero-shot EoT prompting and existing zero-shot and few-shot baselines on the arithmetic reasoning datasets with GPT-3.5-Turbo and Llama-3-8B-Instruct. In contrast to prevalent zero-shot CoT, PS, and PS+ prompting methods, our EoT prompting exhibits notable improvements in performance across six arithmetic reasoning datasets, showcasing particularly significant improvements on the AddSub, SVAMP, AQuA, GSM8K and SingleEq datasets. Furthermore, on average, our EoT prompting achieves a 3.1% and 2.6% score improvement over zero-shot CoT prompting and PS+ prompting methods on GPT-3.5-Turbo. EoT prompting also achieves a 1.6%

and 2.1% score improvement over zero-shot CoT prompting and PS+ prompting methods on Llama-3-8B-Instruct. Concerning the zero-shot RE2 prompting, our EoT prompting outperforms it across five datasets on both GPT-3.5-Turbo and Llama-3-8B-Instruct. The observed similarity between the zero-shot RE2 prompting, characterized by repetitive questions, and our approach of rewriting questions using CoT prompting generated via evolutionary algorithms suggests the advantageous impact of enhancing the model's capacity to retain questions on the reasoning process. Compared to the automatic prompting generation method, APE, our method improves average performance by 0.9 and 2.3% on GPT-3.5-Turbo and Llama-3-8B-Instruct, respectively. Concurrently, we compare our proposed EoT prompting with a few-shot methods: Manual-CoT and Auto-CoT. The results indicate that our proposed EoT prompting surpasses Manual-CoT and Auto-CoT on six and five arithmetic reasoning datasets on GPT-3.5-Turbo, respectively, suggesting the effectiveness of our zero-shot EoT prompting in achieving comparable results to few-shot methods in arithmetic reasoning datasets without the need for example selection.

Table 4. Accuracy of commonsense reasoning and symbolic reasoning datasets on GPT-3.5-turbo and Llama-3-8B-Instruct with different zero-shot and few-shot CoT prompting methods. CSQA denotes CommonsenseQA

Method	CSQA	STQA	LL	CF	CSQA	STQA	LL	CF
	GPT-3.5-Turbo				*Llama-3-8B-Instruct*			
Few-Shot								
Manual-CoT	75.3	70.1	75.7	99.2	74.5	72.6	73.4	99.0
AuTo-CoT	77.1	71.3	76.3	99.6	75.6	72.9	74.8	99.6
Zero-Shot								
CoT	64.9	65.7	72.6	98.6	67.1	68.4	71.5	97.2
PS	68.6	66.4	71.3	97.0	68.4	67.9	70.8	96.8
PS+	70.9	67.8	70.4	97.6	69.1	68.7	71.9	98.0
RE2	71.5	68.1	74.3	97.6	68.9	70.2	71.5	98.2
APE	69.1	70.6	-	-	71.6	69.8	-	-
EoT (ours)	**73.1**	**69.9**	**77.0**	**99.0**	**72.1**	**71.8**	**76.4**	**99.4**

5 Additional Experiments and Analysis

Results on Commonsense Reasoning and Symbolic Reasoning. Table 4 shows the result on two commonsense reasoning datasets. Our EoT prompting exhibits superior performance in the zero-shot setting relative to zero-shot CoT prompting, PS prompting, PS+ prompting, RE2 prompting, and APE methods on two commonsense reasoning datasets. Conversely, compared to two few-shot methods, Manual-CoT and Auto-CoT, our zero-shot EoT prompting demonstrates comparatively lower performance on these two commonsense reasoning datasets. This observation implies that commonsense reasoning problems may necessitate a certain degree of demonstration to guide the model reasoning process.

We also show the result on two symbolic reasoning datasets: Last Letters (LL) and Coin Flip (CF). Our EoT prompting performs better than zero-shot CoT prompting, PS prompting, PS+ prompting, and the RE2 prompting methods on these two symbolic reasoning datasets, especially in the Last Letter dataset. In contrast to few-shot methods, Manual-CoT, and Auto-CoT, our EoT prompting excels relative to these methods in the Last Letter dataset while demonstrating comparable performance in the Coin Flip dataset. This observation suggests the effectiveness of our zero-shot EoT prompting in achieving comparable results to few-shot methods in symbolic reasoning datasets without the need for example selection.

5.1   Results of EoT Prompting in GPT-4

To evaluate the performance of our proposed zero-shot EoT prompting with more powerful models, as shown in Table 5, we conduct experiments on GPT-4 using three arithmetic reasoning datasets: AQuA, AddSub, and SVAMP. We compare our zero-shot EoT prompting against four alternative methods: zero-shot CoT prompting, PS+ prompting, RE2 prompting, and APE prompting. The results presented in Table 5 reveal that our zero-shot EoT prompting yields superior performance compared to these methods, suggesting that our proposed method maintains robust performance advantages when applied to more powerful language models.

Table 5. Results of different methods measured on three math reasoning datasets with GPT-4.

Method	AQuA	AddSub	SVAMP
Zero-shot CoT	72.8	94.9	89.7
Zero-shot PS+	73.2	96.5	89.2
Zero-shot RE2	74.0	96.2	90.1
Zero-shot APE	73.6	93.7	90.1
Zero-shot EoT (ours)	**76.4**	**97.5**	**92.9**

5.2   Ablation Study of EoT

We perform the ablation study of our EOT prompting measured on four math reasoning datasets under the zero-shot setting to understand the importance of different factors. As delineated in Table 6, the notations 'R', 'C', and 'M' denote the operations of rewrite, crossover, and mutate, respectively. Our observations indicate that refraining from employing EoT prompting for problem rewriting results in a discernible decline in model performance across all tasks. This underscores the importance of augmenting the model's comprehension of problems through a more profound engagement, thereby fostering more effective inference. Furthermore, while generating our EoT promptings, the omission of crossover or mutation processes results in a significant performance decrease across all tasks except the SVAMP dataset. Notably, the AQuA dataset exhibits a pronounced performance degradation, emphasizing the indispensability of the crossover and mutation processes in the effective generation of our EoT prompting.

Table 6. Ablation study of EoT measured on four math reasoning datasets with GPT-3.5-Turbo. 'R', 'C', and 'M' denote rewrite, crossover, and mutate, respectively.

Method	AQuA	AddSub	SVAMP	GSM8K
EoT	62.2	91.1	82.0	78.5
-w/o R	61.4	90.1	80.7	76.4
-w/o C	58.7	89.1	82.3	76.2
-w/o M	57.5	88.1	81.1	76.9

5.3   Whether the Selections Made by LLMs Are Random?

Our method utilizes LLMs to select promptings suitable for the current problem. However, are the selections made by the large language models random? We first iteratively generate 10 CoT promptings using the LLM to investigate this. Then, we allow the LLM to select the most appropriate CoT promptings and perform reasoning. Additionally, we randomly sampled CoT promptings from the ten generated promptings and conducted reasoning. We conduct experiments on the AQuA and SVAMP datasets using GPT-3.5-Turbo, and the results are depicted in Fig. 2. It is evident that the performance of LLM-based selection significantly outperforms random selection, suggesting that the selections made by LLMs are not random but guided by the robust prior knowledge of LLMs.

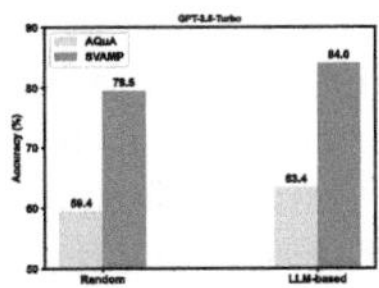

Fig. 2. Performance of random selection and LLM-based selection on GPT-3.5-Turbo

6   Conclusion

This paper introduces *EoT*, a novel zero-shot CoT prompting method. EoT prompting generates diverse CoT promptings tailored to specific instances within a task through evolutionary algorithms. The proposed method surpasses existing zero-shot CoT, PS+, RE2, and APE prompting methods across various reasoning datasets, demonstrating notable performance, especially in arithmetic and symbolic reasoning. Extensive experiments and analyses validate the effectiveness of zero-shot EoT prompting, showcasing its potential to enhance LLMs' reasoning capabilities. We believe there is considerable potential for refining the application of evolutionary algorithms based on LLMs to enhance model reasoning capabilities.

Acknowledgments. This work is supported by the National Natural Science Foundation of China (Grant No.62276008, 62250037, and 62076010), and partially supported by the National Key R&D of China (Grant 2022YFF0800601).

References

1. Yang, C., Wang, X., Lu, Y., et al.: Large language models as optimizers. In: The Twelfth International Conference on Learning Representations (2024)
2. Liu, T., Astorga, N., Seedat, N., et al.: Large language models to enhance Bayesian optimization. In: The Twelfth International Conference on Learning Representations (2024)
3. Brown, T., Mann, B., Ryder, N., et al.: Language models are few-shot learners. In: NeurIPS (2020)
4. Chen, A., Dohan, D., So, D.: So: Evoprompting: language models for code-level neural architecture search. ArXiv abs/2302.14838 (2023)
5. Cobbe, K., Kosaraju, V., Bavarian, M., Chen, M., Jun, H., et al.: Training verifiers to solve math word problems. ArXiv abs/2110.14168 (2021)
6. Geva, M., Khashabi, D., Segal, E., Khot, T., Roth, D., Berant, J.: Did aristotle use a laptop? A question answering benchmark with implicit reasoning strategies. Trans. Assoc. Comput. Linguist. **9**, 346–361 (2021)
7. Guo, Q., Wang, R., Guo, J., Li, B., Song, K., Tan, X., et al.: Connecting large language models with evolutionary algorithms yields powerful prompt optimizers. ArXiv abs/2309.08532 (2023)
8. Hansen, N., Müller, S.D., Koumoutsakos, P.: Reducing the time complexity of the derandomized evolution strategy with covariance matrix adaptation (CMA-ES). Evol. Comput. **11**, 1–18 (2003)
9. Hollmann, N., Müller, S., Hutter, F.: Large language models for automated data science: Introducing CAAFE for context-aware automated feature engineering. In: Thirty-Seventh Conference on Neural Information Processing Systems (2023)
10. Hosseini, M.J., Hajishirzi, H., Etzioni, O., Kushman, N.: Learning to solve arithmetic word problems with verb categorization. In: Moschitti, A., Pang, B., Daelemans, W. (eds.) Proceedings of the 2014 Conference on Empirical Methods in Natural Language Processing (EMNLP), pp. 523–533, Doha, Qatar. Association for Computational Linguistics (2014)

11. Jin, F., Lu, J., Zhang, J., Zong, C.: Instance-aware prompt learning for language understanding and generation. ACM Trans. Asian Low Resour. Lang. Inf. Process. **22**(7), 199:1–199:18 (2023)
12. Kojima, T., Gu, S., Reid, M., Matsuo, Y., Iwasawa, Y.: Large language models are zero-shot reasoners. In: Advances in Neural Information Processing Systems, vol. 35, pp. 22199–22213. Curran Associates, Inc. (2022)
13. Koncel-Kedziorski, R., Hajishirzi, H., Sabharwal, A., Etzioni, O., Ang, S.: Parsing algebraic word problems into equations. Trans. Assoc. Comput. Linguistics **3**, 585–597 (2015)
14. Lester, B., Al-Rfou, R., Constant, N.: The power of scale for parameter-efficient prompt tuning. In: EMNLP (2021)
15. Li, X.L., Liang, P.: Prefix-tuning: optimizing continuous prompts for generation. In: ACL (2021)
16. Li, J., Tan, Y.: Loser-out tournament-based fireworks algorithm for multimodal function optimization. IEEE Trans. Evol. Comput. **22**(5), 679–691 (2018)
17. Ling, W., Yogatama, D., Dyer, C., Blunsom, P.: Program induction by rationale generation: learning to solve and explain algebraic word problems. In: Proceedings of the 55th Annual Meeting of the Association for Computational Linguistics (Volume 1: Long Papers), pp. 158–167, Vancouver, Canada. Association for Computational Linguistics (2017)
18. Liu, X. et al.: GPT understands, too. ArXiv abs/2103.10385 (2021)
19. Liu, S., Chen, C., Qu, X., Tang, K., Ong, Y.: Large language models as evolutionary optimizers. ArXiv abs/2310.19046 (2023)
20. Meyerson, E., Nelson, M., Bradley, H., Moradi, A., Hoover, A.K., Lehman, J.: Language model crossover: variation through few-shot prompting. ArXiv abs/2302.12170 (2023)
21. Mitchell, M.: An Introduction to Genetic Algorithms. MIT Press (1998)
22. Mouret, J.: Large language models help computer programs to evolve. Nature **625**(7995), 452–453 (2024)
23. OpenAI: ChatGPT: optimizing language models for dialogue. In: OpenAI Blog (2022)
24. OpenAI: GPT-4 technical report. ArXiv abs/2303.08774 (2023)
25. Patel, A., Bhattamishra, S., Goyal, N.: Are NLP models really able to solve simple math word problems? In: Proceedings of the 2021 Conference of the North American Chapter of the Association for Computational Linguistics: Human Language Technologies, pp. 2080–2094 (2021). Association for Computational Linguistics
26. Romera-Paredes, B., et al.: Mathematical discoveries from program search with large language models. Nature **625**, 468–475 (2023)
27. Roy, S., Roth, D.: Solving general arithmetic word problems. In: Proceedings of the 2015 Conference on Empirical Methods in Natural Language Processing, pp. 1743–1752, Lisbon, Portugal. Association for Computational Linguistics (2015)
28. Schaeffer, R., Miranda, B., Koyejo, S.: Are emergent abilities of large language models a mirage? In: Thirty-Seventh Conference on Neural Information Processing Systems (2023)
29. Talmor, A., Herzig, J., Lourie, N., Berant, J.: CommonsenseQA: a question answering challenge targeting commonsense knowledge. In: Proceedings of the 2019 Conference of the North American Chapter of the Association for Computational Linguistics: Human Language Technologies, Volume 1 (Long and Short Papers), pp. 4149–4158, Minneapolis, Minnesota. Association for Computational Linguistics (2019)

30. Touvron, H., Lavril, T., Izacard, G., Martinet, X., Lachaux, M., Lacroix, T., et al: LLAMA: open and efficient foundation language models. CoRR abs/2302.13971 (2023)
31. Wang, L., et al.: Plan-and-solve prompting: improving zero-shot chain-of-thought reasoning by large language models. In: Proceedings of the 61st Annual Meeting of the Association for Computational Linguistics (Volume 1: Long Papers), pp. 2609–2634, Toronto, Canada (2023). Association for Computational Linguistics (2023)
32. X. Wang, et al.: Self-consistency improves chain of thought reasoning in language models. In: The Eleventh International Conference on Learning Representations (2023)
33. Wei, J., et al.: Chain-of-thought prompting elicits reasoning in large language models. In: Advances in Neural Information Processing Systems, vol. 35, pp. 24824–24837. Curran Associates, Inc. (2022)
34. Wu, Z., et al.: IDPG: an instance-dependent prompt generation method. CoRR abs/2204.04497 (2022)
35. Xu, X., et al: Re-reading improves reasoning in language models. ArXiv abs/2309.06275 (2023)
36. Zhang, Z., Zhang, A., Li, M., Smola, A.: Automatic chain of thought prompting in large language models. In: The Eleventh International Conference on Learning Representations (2023)
37. Zhou, Y., et al.: Large language models are human-level prompt engineers. In: The Eleventh International Conference on Learning Representations (2023)

FedETE: Privacy-Preserving Federated Event Trigger Extraction

Fei Hu, Tao Chang, Meihan Wu, Shenpo Dong, Jie Zhou, Jiaqian Yin,
and Xiaodong Wang[(✉)]

National Key Laboratory of Parallel and Distributed Computing, College of
Computer Science and Technology, National University of Defense Technology,
Changsha 410073, China
`xdwang@nudt.edu.cn`

Abstract. Event trigger extraction is a natural language processing
(NLP) task of practical utility, which requires systems to detect and
label the lexical instantiation of an event. Existing deep learning-based
event trigger extraction approaches that require large-scale data for
model training achieve limited success in some privacy-sensitive domains,
due to the challenge of aggregating data distributed among various own-
ers. Federated learning (FL) has emerged as a secure distributed machine
learning paradigm that addresses the issue of data silos in building a joint
model, with the advantages of security aggregation mechanism. Therefore, we define the task of FL-based event trigger extraction and propose
a novel federated method named *FedETE* to solve the current difficulties. We also introduce the idea of weak privacy of the event trigger to
craft the architecture of *FedETE* which optimizes the traditional FL
training methods (Server-Client). Extensive experiments show that the
event trigger extraction model trained by *FedETE* achieves promising
results compared to centralized methods and traditional FL methods, as
well as local methods. To our knowledge, *FedETE* is the first to apply
FL in the event trigger extraction task.

Keywords: Event trigger extraction · Federated learning ·
Privacy-preserving

1 Introduction

Recently, FL [4] has emerged as a promising alternative ML paradigm. Unlike
traditional paradigms, FL provides an effective approach for many clients (e.g.,
mobile devices or organizations) to collaboratively train a global model under
the orchestration of a central server while keeping training data decentralized
[5–9], which is highly useful for applications suffering from the silo effect and
privacy preservation. Therefore, we consider combining FL with event trigger
extraction to improve model performance while protecting privacy.

We first define the task of FL-based event trigger extraction following the
traditional problem formulation of FL and typical Client-Server training schema.

© The Author(s), under exclusive license to Springer Nature Singapore Pte Ltd. 2026
X.-L. Mao et al. (Eds.): NLPCC 2025, LNAI 16105, pp. 65–76, 2026.
https://doi.org/10.1007/978-981-95-3352-7_6

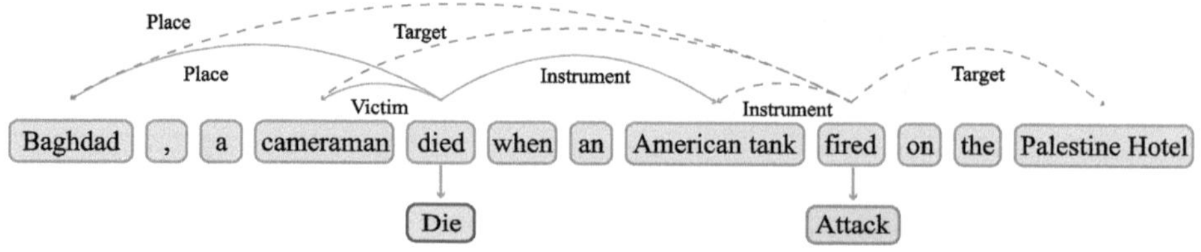

Fig. 1. An example of event trigger extraction.

Then we delve into the characteristics of the task of event trigger extraction to explore its optimal implementation in a federated scenario that emphasizes privacy protection. Generally speaking, in an event, the trigger can be a verb or a noun, which contains less privacy information compared to event arguments that serve as a participant or attribute. Taking the sentence in Fig. 1 for example, the event arguments such as "Baghdad", "cameraman", "American tank", "Palestine Hotel" can clearly show the place, victim, target, and instrument of the event, which can be very sensitive to privacy, but one can hardly infer what actually happened from only the words "died" or "fired". Based on the comparison, we introduce the idea of weak privacy of the event trigger and propose *FedETE*, which is an FL-based event trigger extraction method to address the above data privacy issues and improve the model performance in the context of data silos at the same time. It can leverage the knowledge in the data of different clients to boost the training of the event trigger extraction model in each client without uploading or exchanging the raw data. Specifically, different from the traditional federated learning framework where the clients upload parameters to the server, we first train the local model on each client to extract features of event triggers from local data, then upload them to the server, and train a global model on the server side with the collected features. We then send the global model to all clients when a global epoch ends. Above process is repeated for multiple times until model converges. In addition, we propose two mechanisms to address the problem of performance degradation caused by excessive negative samples in the dataset during federated training. We conduct experiments on ACE 2005 dataset and the results validate that our method achieves promising performance while also having the advantage of privacy protection.

The main contributions of this paper are summarized as follows:

1. We define the task of FL-based event trigger extraction and propose a novel privacy-preserving method *FedETE* to collaboratively train an event trigger extraction model which decouples the model training from the need for direct access to the privacy-sensitive data.
2. We introduce the idea of weak privacy of the event trigger to craft the architecture of *FedETE* which optimizes traditional FL methods. Instead of the intermediate parameters generated by local models during the training process, *FedETE* trains a global model on the server side with features collected from the participating clients.

3. We propose two mechanisms to alleviate the problem of performance degradation caused by excessive negative samples in the dataset during federated training.
4. We conduct extensive experiments on ACE 2005 dataset to verify the effectiveness of *FedETE*.

2   Related Work

2.1   Event Trigger Extraction

Previous work has achieved advanced performance in event trigger extraction. Xu et al. [10] propose a method to leverage the ability to capture triggers and relate them to previously unseen relation names, introducing a model that enables the extraction of zero-shot dialogue relationships by using trigger capture capabilities. Wei et al. [1] introduce a language model to compute contextualized word representations and propose a multi-layer residual bidirectional long short-term memory (BiLSTM) structure for biomedical event trigger extraction. Dukić et al. [11] leverage OIE (Open Information Extraction) relations to improve the domain transfer of trigger detection in few-shot setup. However, few works pay attention to event trigger extraction in privacy-preserving scenarios.

2.2   Federated Learning in NLP

With the highlighting of its value, FL gradually expands to many NLP tasks [12]. We look into recent NLP models and techniques that use FL as the learning framework. Sui et al. [13] propose a privacy-preserving medical relation extraction model *FedED* based on federated learning through ensemble distillation which decouples model training from the need for direct access to highly privacy-sensitive data. Ge et al. [14] propose a *FedNER* method based on federated learning to learn a more accurate medical NER model from the labeled data of multiple medical platforms without the need to directly exchange the raw privacy sensitive medical data among different platforms. Tian et al. [15] propose a learning approach named *FedBERT* which takes advantage of the federated learning and split learning approaches, resorting to pre-training BERT in a federated way. Zhou et al. [16] propose a novel memetic federated learning framework named *Mem-Fed* which is tailored for federated learning of large-scale NLP models in the biomedical scenario. Motivated by the methods mentioned above, we attempt to combine FL with event trigger extraction to address the challenges in privacy-preserving scenarios.

3   Method

In this section, we first define the task of FL-based event trigger extraction and the idea of the weak privacy of the event trigger, based on which we optimize the traditional FL training methods (Server-Client) and design the architecture of *FedETE*.

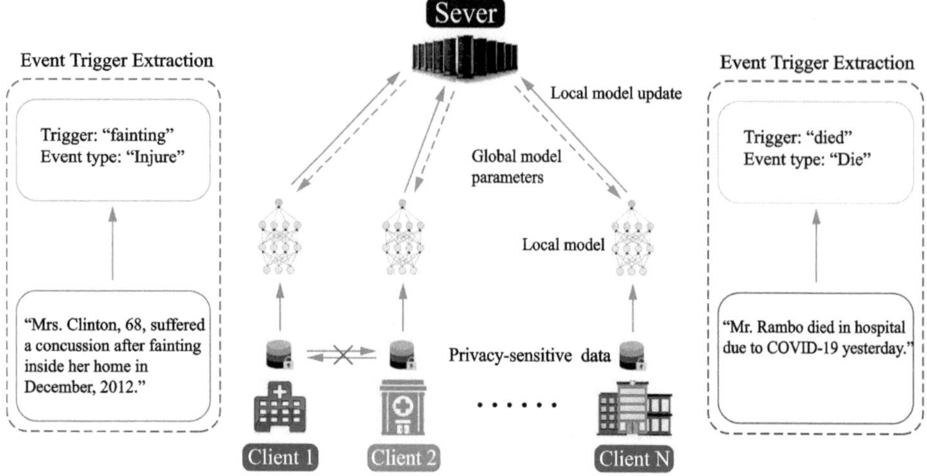

Fig. 2. The workflow of FL-based event trigger extraction.

3.1 FL-Based Event Trigger Extraction

To illustrate the definition of the task of FL-based event trigger extraction, we follow the problem formulation of FL in [6]. We consider N clients of privacy-sensitive territories $\{C_1, \dots C_N\}$ who wish to train an event trigger extraction model together with their respective data $\{\mathcal{D}_1, \dots \mathcal{D}_N\}$. The conventional method is to put all the data together and use $\mathcal{D} = \mathcal{D}_1 \cup \dots \cup \mathcal{D}_N$ to train a model $\mathcal{M}_{SUM}$. However, due to strict regulations and increasing concerns on data privacy, traditional methods are difficult to implement in these areas. In the task of FL-based event trigger extraction, a FL-based system enables different clients to collaboratively train a model $\mathcal{M}_{FED}$, in which process any institution C_i does not expose its data $\mathcal{D}_i$ to others. We denote the accuracy of $\mathcal{M}_{FED}$ by $\mathcal{V}_{FED}$, which in our anticipation should be close to the accuracy of $\mathcal{M}_{SUM}$ denoted as $\mathcal{V}_{SUM}$.

FL-based event trigger extraction task follows the typical Server-Client training schema of FL, and the architecture is summarized below.

- **Server:** The server first sends the initial model parameters to each participating client, then aggregates the collected intermediate parameters from the clients after local training in every client is done. A global model is trained by aggregating the feedback parameters of the local models on the server.
- **Client:** During each global training round, each participating client trains the initial model with local data, then uploads the intermediate parameters to the server after local training. A client don't exchange raw data with the server, neither with other clients, which to some extent preserves the privacy compared to traditional machine learning methods.

In particular, when aggregating parameters on the server, we choose FedAvg [4], which is one of the most prevalent methods for aggregation of models in

FL. In each global training round, every participating client performs a stochastic gradient descent (SGD) on its local dataset and sends the gradients back. The server then aggregates all the gradients from the participating clients and updates the starting model. Our goal is typically to minimize the following objective function:

$$\min_{w} F(w), \quad \text{where} \quad F(w) := \sum_{i=1}^{N} p_i F_i(w)$$

Here, $p_i \geq 0$ and $\sum_i p_i = 1$, and $F_i(w)$ is the local objective function for the i th client. The workflow above is also presented in Fig. 2.

3.2 The Weak Privacy of the Event Trigger

As introduced in Section II, an event trigger is a verb in most cases while an event argument is an entity mention, temporal expression or value that serves as a participant or attribute in an event. Compared to event arguments, event triggers contain less privacy information. Figure 3 clearly shows the difference in privacy between event arguments and event triggers. When we remove the event trigger from the sentence, most privacy information remains, while when event arguments are removed from the sentence, it leaks little privacy. The trigger "bought" doesn't contain much privacy because anyone may have the same behavior, what truly constitues privacy are Who ("Jack"), When ("yesterday") and What ("book"), those are the privacy that users don't want to disclose. That is to say, from the event arguments we can know the time, location, or participants of an event, which contain privacy, while from only the event triggers, we can know little about the event because the same event triggers can be used in different domains. Based on the analysis above, we propose the concepts of weak privacy of event triggers, that is, event triggers contain little privacy that may leakage the information of an event.

3.3 Architecture of *FedETE*

On the premise of the FL-based event trigger extraction task and the weak privacy of event triggers as explained in the previous subsections, we propose *FedETE* which optimizes FL training methods. In traditional FL methods, the server is only responsible for aggregating model parameters and updating the global model. In *FedETE*, we consider uploading the features of the event triggers located in each client to the server, instead of the intermediate parameters generated by each local model after local training.

During the local training process, the local model is first trained to extract the features of the local data, which in our case are the features of event triggers. We follow a similar process in [6], which is to tokenize the tokens on the left and right sides of the event trigger, respectively, to get *TextL* and *TextR*. The two are used to generate *MaskL* and *MaskR*, respectively, after padding on the right. We again encode and pad the two together to get *Input_ids* and *Token_type_ids*.

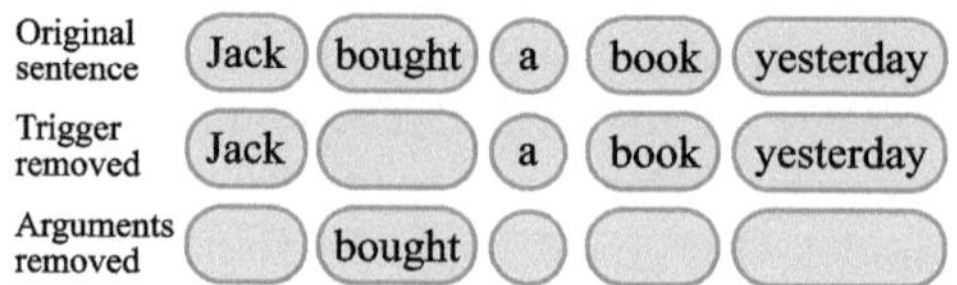

Fig. 3. Comparison of privacy between event argument and event trigger.

So, with the addition of *Label* (event type), the above five constitute the features of an event trigger. The specific process is shown in Fig. 5.

After the server collects the features uploaded by all participating clients, a new dataset composed of features is formed and used to train a global model on the server side. The server then sends the global model parameters to all the clients after the training is done. The local models are updated after loading the received parameters. This cycle continues until the global model converges. The specific process is shown in Fig. 4.

3.4 Two Training Mechanisms to Alleviate Performance Degradation

To avoid that the model forgets the features learned from different clients too quickly, we adopt the following strategy during training. During each global training epoch, the server first randomly selects n clients for training. The server will skip accepting features from client A if it has already received features from it in a previous training epoch. In this way, the model will continue to learn the features of the event triggers from all the clients.

To solved the problem of model performance degradation caused by multiple samples and negative examples in the dataset, we adopt the following strategy during training. During local training in each client, the model will be evaluated every N steps, a model will be saved if the evaluation result is better than the previous one. Instead of uploading the parameters of the final model after local epochs come to an end, we choose to upload the parameters of the model with the best evaluating result during training.

4 Experimental Evaluations

4.1 Learning Model

Among numerous event trigger extraction models, *FedETE* extends an existing baseline model known as DMBERT (Dynamic Masking BERT) [18, 19], which means using BERT for dynamic pooling. When we use BERT for training, each sample in the train set only undergoes random mask once, so that the sample is repeated in all epochs and the same mask is used in each training step. In DMBERT, each sample in the training set undergoes a dynamic random mask at each training step, so that the mask of sample in each epoch is variable, effectively avoiding duplication of the samples of training set. The prediction effect of DMBERT has been further improved on the basis of BERT.

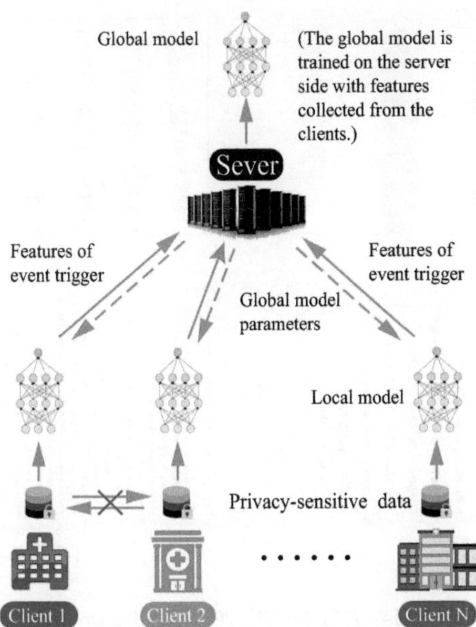

Fig. 4. The architecture of *FedETE*. Different from traditional FL training method, the global model is trained on the server side with features of event triggers extracted from the clients.

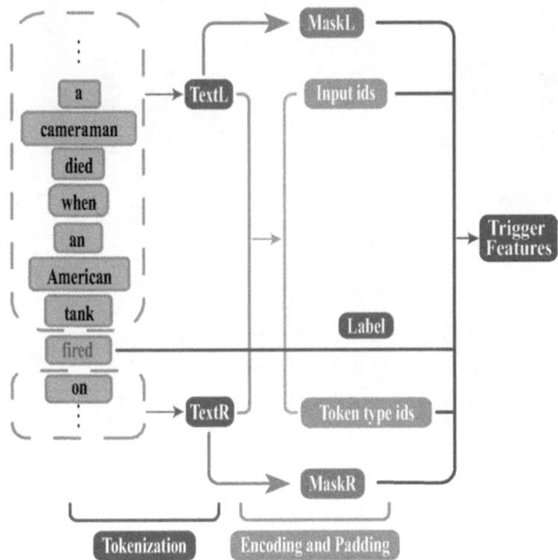

Fig. 5. The process of extracting features from event triggers.

4.2   Datasets

We conducted experiments on the ACE 2005 dataset. For comparison, the data set is preprocessed in the same way as in [21]. We use the same test set containing 40 newswire documents, a development set with 30 randomly selected documents, and a training set with the remaining 529 documents.

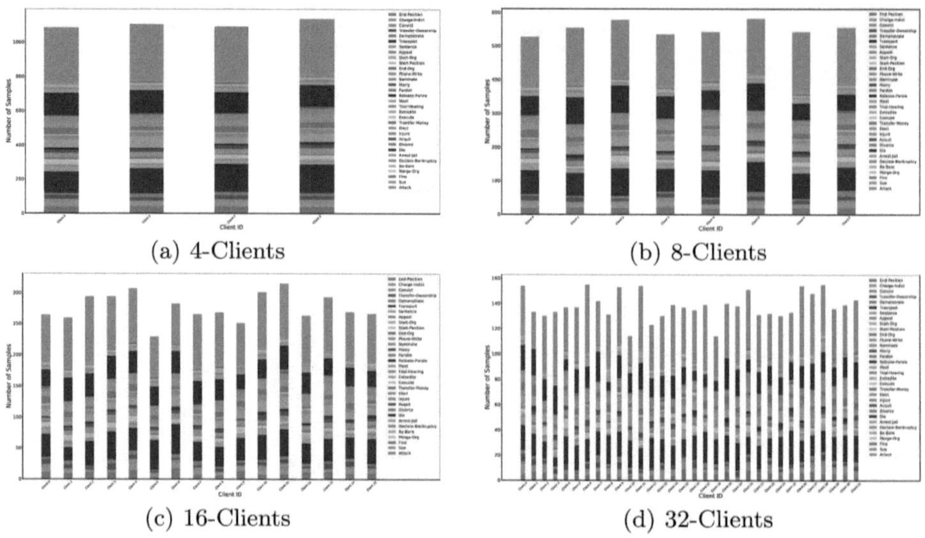

(a) 4-Clients

(b) 8-Clients

(c) 16-Clients

(d) 32-Clients

Fig. 6. Data Distribution under IID (ACE 2005). The entire train set is divided into parts with approximately the same sample size and event type distribution.

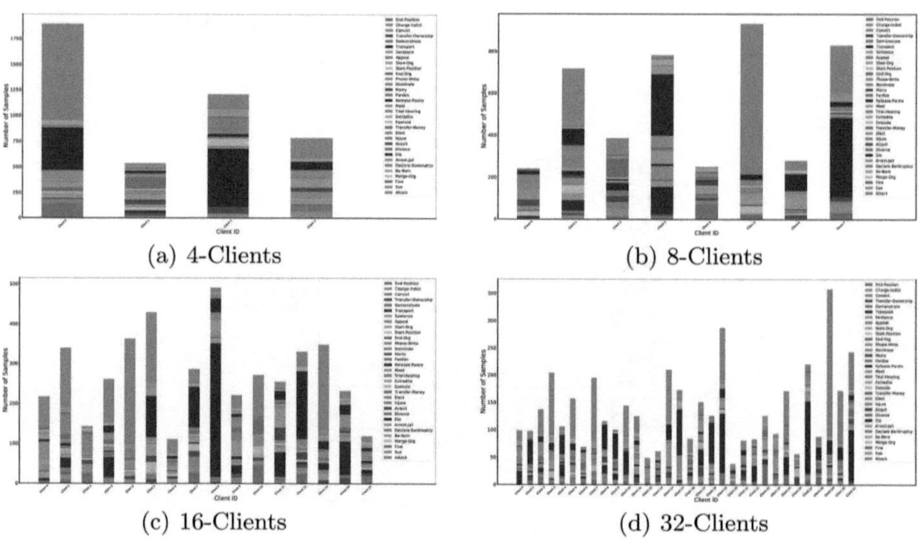

(a) 4-Clients

(b) 8-Clients

(c) 16-Clients

(d) 32-Clients

Fig. 7. Data Distribution under Non-IID (ACE 2005). The entire train set is divided into parts with significant differences in sample size and event type distribution.

4.3   Experiment Setup

As described in section III, in our experiments, the federated environments follow a topology where the server is responsible to orchestrate the execution of the clients. For traditional FL methods training with parameters transferred

Table 1. Final learning performance of Centralized vs Federated vs Local methods.

–			ACE2005		
Methods			P	R	F1
Centralized	DMCNN		75.6	63.6	69.1
	JRNN		66.0	73.0	69.3
	DMBERT		71.9	76.1	74.0
FedETE	4-Clients	IID	74.1	73.2	**73.6**
		Non-IID	73.2	72.4	72.8
	8-Clients	IID	73.5	72.7	73.1
		Non-IID	71.7	71.2	71.4
	16-Clients	IID	72.2	71.5	71.8
		Non-IID	72.1	69.1	70.3
	32-Clients	IID	70.9	70.5	70.7
		Non-IID	68.8	67.4	68.1
Federated (parameters)	4 Clients	IID	71.4	73.8	72.6
		Non-IID	70.5	72.7	71.6
	8 Clients	IID	72.7	70.1	71.5
		Non-IID	71.1	71.8	71.4
	16 Clients	IID	69.0	72.1	71.0
		Non-IID	65.8	68.6	67.7
	32 Clients	IID	66.7	70.3	68.5
		Non-IID	64.6	66.6	65.7
Local	4 Clients	IID	71.0	70.5	70.8
		Non-IID	45.5	51.9	48.5
	8 Clients	IID	69.5	68.4	69.0
		Non-IID	48.3	47.6	48.0
	16 Clients	IID	64.4	63.7	64.1
		Non-IID	21.6	42.9	28.7
	32 Clients	IID	55.7	45.3	49.9
		Non-IID	3.5	24.1	6.1

from the clients, during each training round, a client first trains the local model with local data for 2 epochs, and the server then merges the parameters received from all the participating clients to update the global model. The global training epoch is set to 40. For *FedETE* training with the features of the event triggers, a client first trains the local model to extract the features of the event triggers in local data, the server then utilizes the features collected from all participating clients to train a global model, and the server training epochs is set to 20.

We test the performance of *FedETE* in federated environments consisting of 4, 8, 16 and 32 clients, where the fraction of clients is uniformly set to 0.5. For local environments, we test every local model trained with local data and present the best results. The evaluation metrics are *Precision* (P), *Recall* (R), and *F1-Measure* (F1).

To explore the influences of number of clients and data distribution on *FedETE*, for both federated and local training (each client trains its model with local data only), we split the train dataset into partitions for 4, 8,

Table 2. The performance of local models under Non-IID (8 clients)

Client	Client 0	Client 1	Client 2	Client 3	Client 4	Client 5	Client 6	Client 7	Average
P	5.2	48.3	1.2	30.4	66.7	2.2	2.1	3.2	19.9
R	15.6	47.6	47.6	32.8	1.2	56.6	56.6	68.2	40.8
F	7.8	48.0	2.4	31.6	2.3	4.2	4.1	6.0	13.3

16 and 32 clients under *Independent Identically Distribution* (IID) and *Non-Independent and Identically Distribution* (Non-IID), which is shown in Fig. 6 and Fig. 7. For IID, we refer to the strategies in [4] and the train set is divided into parts with approximately the same sample size and event-type distribution. For Non-IID, we refer to the strategies in [21] and use the Dirichelet distribution to divide the train set into nonidentical parts, the value of α (concentration parameter) is uniformly set to 0.5. We can see that the sample size and event type distribution vary greatly in different parts, which can better simulate the distribution of data from different clients in the real world.

4.4   Experiment Results and Analysis

This section presents the experiment results evaluating *FedETE* against the centralized and traditional FL methods, as well as local methods. Table 1 shows the final learning performance of *FedETE* under different settings of number of clients and data distribution. As we can see, *FedETE* achieves promising results compared to the centralized method and the traditional FL method in F1, especially when the number of clients is set to 4 (IID), *FedETE* achieves the highest F1 of 73.6, which is comparable to the best result of 74.0. We observe that *FedETE* outperforms the local methods under all settings by 1.8%~62.0%. We present the performance of local models under the setting of 8 clients (Non-IID) in Table 2, which shows significant differences among different clients. The best F1 achieved by Client 1 is 48.0 while Client 4 achieves the lowest F1 of 2.3, the average F1 is 13.3. The results not only show the challenges faced by local training in the context of privacy protection, but also highlights the effectiveness of *FedETE*. Above all, *FedETE* is able to train an event trigger extraction model with promising performance while also having the advantage of privacy protection compared to existing methods.

4.5   Effects of Data Distribution

As introduced in Experiment Setup, we split the dataset under IID and Non-IID to study the effects of data distribution on the performance of *FedETE*, the results are shown in Table 1. We observe that in the case of different number of participating clients, *FedETE* always performs better under IID than Non-IID, which is 1.6% higher on average in F1. Meanwhile, the performance gap between the two gradually widens (from 0.8% to 2.6%) as the number of clients increases (from 4 to 32). Especially when the model is trained locally, the performance of the model shows a sharp decline between IID and Non-IID, which reaches as much as 52. 2% for P, 21. 2% for R, and 43. 8% for F1. The results indicate that the heterogeneity of the data distribution can lead to a decrease in the performance of the model, which is also one of the challenges currently faced by FL.

5   Conclusion and Future Work

In this paper, we first define the FL-based event trigger extraction task and propose a novel *FedETE* method that enables multiple parties to collaboratively train an event trigger extraction model without exchanging their raw data. We also introduce the idea of weak privacy of the event trigger and design the architecture of *FedETE* to enhance its effectiveness. Extensive experiments demonstrate that our method can make full use of distributed data and achieve promising performance compared to centralized methods and traditional FL paradigms, which is an effective method for extracting event triggers in privacy-sensitive territories.

Our work also provides inspiration for the fact that as a machine learning framework for privacy protection, FL can flexibly choose training methods based on the characteristics of the task itself. Though the raw data can't be share among different clients, we can handle different parts of the data with different strategies, for the part containing less privacy information, extracting data features for training may be a better choice.

We consider this work as a first step towards privacy-preserving event trigger extraction based on FL, which provides a valuable method for event extraction in the context of privacy protection. In the future, we plan to test our method on more benchmark datasets to verify its effectiveness. We will also try to apply more federated aggregation algorithms to achieve better results in this task.

References

1. Gosselin, R., Vieu, L., Loukil, F., Benoit, A.: Privacy and security in federated learning: a survey. Appl. Sci. **48**(19), 9901 (2022)
2. Lyu, L., Yu, H., Yang, Q.: Threats to federated learning: a survey. arXiv preprint arXiv:2003.02133 (2020)
3. Yang, Q., Liu, Y., Chen, T., Tong, Y.: Federated machine learning: concept and applications. ACM Trans. Intell. Syst. Technol. (TIST) **10**(2), 1–19 (2019)
4. McMahan, B., Moore, E., Ramage, D., Hampson, S., Arcas, B.A.: Communication-efficient learning of deep networks from decentralized data. In Artificial intelligence and statistics, pp. 1273–1282 (2017)
5. Kairouz, P., et al.: Advances and open problems in federated learning. Found. Trends Mach. Learn. **14**(1–2), 1–210 (2021)
6. AbdulRahman, S., Tout, H., Ould-Slimane, H., Mourad, A., Talhi, C., Guizani, M.: A survey on federated learning: the journey from centralized to distributed on-site learning and beyond. IEEE Internet Things J. **8**(7), 5476–5497 (2020)

7. Wen, J., Zhang, Z., Lan, Y., Cui, Z., Cai, J., Zhang, W.: A survey on federated learning: challenges and applications. Int. J. Mach. Learn. Cybern. **14**(2), 513–535 (2023)
8. Wei, H., Zhou, A., Zhang, Y., Chen, F., Qu, W., Lu, M.: Biomedical event trigger extraction based on multi-layer residual BiLSTM and contextualized word representations. Int. J. Mach. Learn. Cybern. **13**(3), 721–733 (2021). https://doi.org/10.1007/s13042-021-01315-7
9. Chen, Y., Xu, L., Liu, K., Zeng, D., Zhao, J.: Event extraction via dynamic multi-pooling convolutional neural networks. In: Proceedings of the 53rd Annual Meeting of the Association for Computational Linguistics and the 7th International Joint Conference on Natural Language Processing, vol. 1, pp. 167–176 (2015)
10. Yang, B., Mitchell, T.: Joint extraction of events and entities within a document context. arXiv preprint arXiv:1609.03632 (2016)
11. Xu, Z.S., Chen, Y.N.: Zero-shot dialogue relation extraction by relating explainable triggers and relation names. arXiv preprint arXiv:2306.06141 (2023)
12. Dukić, D., Gashteovski, K., Glavaš, G., et al.: Leveraging open information extraction for more robust domain transfer of event trigger detection. Findings of the Association for Computational Linguistics: EACL 2024, pp. 1197–1213 (2024)
13. Liu, M., Ho, S., Wang, M., Gao, L., Zhang, H.: Federated learning meets natural language processing: a survey. arXiv preprint arXiv:2107.12603 (2021)
14. Sui, D., Chen, Y., Zhao, J., Jia, Y., Xie, Y., Sun, W.: Feded: federated learning via ensemble distillation for medical relation extraction. In: Proceedings of the 2020 Conference on Empirical Methods in Natural Language Processing (EMNLP), pp. 2118–2128 (2020)
15. Ge, S., Wu, F., Wu, C., Qi, T., Xie, X.: FedNER: medical named entity recognition with federated learning. arXiv preprint arXiv:2003.09288 (2020)
16. Tian, Y., Wan, Y., Lyu, L., Yao, D., Jin, H., Sun, L.: FedBERT: when federated learning meets pre-training. ACM Trans. Intell. Syst. Technol. (TIST) **13**(4), 1–26 (2022)
17. Zhou, X., et al.: Memetic federated learning for biomedical natural language processing. In: Natural Language Processing and Chinese Computing: 10th CCF International Conference, NLPCC 2021, Qingdao, China, 13–17 October 2021. Proceedings, Part II, vol. 10, pp. 43–55 (2021)
18. Dukić, D., Gashteovski, K., Glavaš, G., Šnajder, J.: Leveraging open information extraction for improving few-shot trigger detection domain transfer. arXiv preprint arXiv:2305.14163 (2023)
19. Wang, X., et al.: HMEAE: hierarchical modular event argument extraction. In Proceedings of the 2019 Conference on Empirical Methods in Natural Language Processing and the 9th International Joint Conference on Natural Language Processing (EMNLP-IJCNLP), pp. 5777–5783 (2019)
20. Mathew, J., Stripelis, D., Ambite, J.L.: Federated named entity recognition. arXiv preprint arXiv:2203.15101 (2022)
21. Hsu, T., Qi, H., Brown, M.: Measuring the effects of non-identical data distribution for federated visual classification. arXiv preprint arXiv:1909.06335 (2019)

Fundamentals of NLP

Parallel Task Planning via Model Collaboration

Xiang Zhang, Tong Zhu, Han Han, Hao Pan, Mengsong Wu,
and Wenliang Chen[✉]

Soochow University, No. 1 Shizi Street, Suzhou 215006, China
{xzhangxzhang23,tzhu7,hhan,hpan123,mswumsw}@stu.suda.edu.cn,
wlchen@suda.edu.cn

Abstract. With large language models (LLMs) demonstrating increasingly strong capabilities in task planning, current approaches primarily execute task-specific steps sequentially. However, tasks may be parallelized to maximize the overall efficiency. To address this challenge, we first propose an automated methodology for constructing diversified, highly parallelizable data at scale. Based on this method, we design **ParaBench**, a benchmark for evaluating LLMs' ability to parallelize task steps based on temporal dependencies. Furthermore, we introduce **CTDO**, a novel framework that integrates a compact dependency recognition model with LLM planners to enhance planning capabilities. We test multiple LLMs on **ParaBench**, and results indicate that the complexity of tasks leads to poor LLM performance, and **ParaBench**'s high difficulty can serve as a benchmark for future research. Moreover, our **CTDO** framework effectively enhances task pass rates while preserving step parallelism. Our code and dataset are available at https:// github.com/zxthesky/ParaBench.

Keywords: Large Language Models · Task Planning · Parallel Tasks

1 Introduction

Large language models (LLMs) demonstrate exceptional reasoning abilities to solve complex tasks [2] and interact with real-world applications by utilizing external tools [14,21]. With their powerful task planning ability, LLMs finish tasks sequentially and iteratively make subsequent decisions based on tool execution results and historical context, thereby progressively accomplishing complex objectives [3,20].

While such a sequential plan-then-act approach effectively handles complex tasks, each subsequent step must wait for the prior one to complete. Consequently, the total task completion time equals the sum of all step durations, incurring significant time costs. However, real-world complex tasks can usually be executed in parallel. For example, as shown in Fig. 1, an agent can set the table while preheating the oven. This indicates that a complex task can be formed into

© The Author(s), under exclusive license to Springer Nature Singapore Pte Ltd. 2026
X.-L. Mao et al. (Eds.): NLPCC 2025, LNAI 16105, pp. 79–91, 2026.
https://doi.org/10.1007/978-981-95-3352-7_7

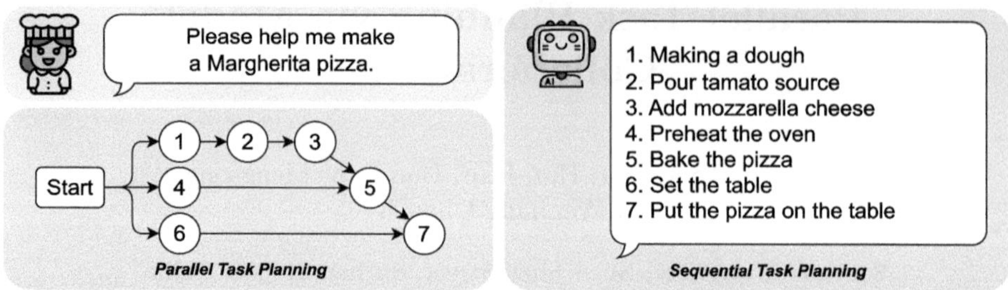

Fig. 1. Example of parallel execution of steps.

a directed acyclic graph (DAG) based on the temporal dependencies of steps, where the total time cost is determined by the graph's depth.

To evaluate LLMs' parallel task planning ability, WorFBench [13] combines golden paths from existing datasets by converting linear execution steps into directed acyclic graphs, lowering the time required for task completion. TaskLAMA [23] uses domain experts to build a specialized dataset of parallelizable tasks under defined protocols to study LLMs' ability to break complex tasks into parallel steps. However, these datasets contain relatively simple tasks with limited steps and low parallelism, restricting comprehensive evaluation of LLMs' parallelization capabilities.

To enhance LLMs' parallel task planning ability and make better evaluations, we present **ParaBench**, a high-quality task planning dataset featuring tasks with greater complexity and higher average step counts compared to TaskLAMA and WorFBench. We employ an automated data construction framework. When generating the corresponding steps and their dependencies for tasks, we prioritize generating a larger number of steps while enhancing parallelism among them. The dataset demonstrates wider task structures and higher parallelism while maintaining approximately twice the size of existing benchmarks (statistics are demonstrated in Table 1). For a more reliable evaluation, we manually verify 1,005 samples to create the test set.

With the guidance of **ParaBench**, we devise a collaborative framework to enhance LLMs' parallel task planning abilities. Specifically, we integrate a small planner specifically designed to detect step dependency relationships, using these predictions to refine LLM-based planning. We conduct extensive experiments on ParaBench and find LLMs still have significant room for improvement in this task. Additionally, our framework enhances LLMs' pass rates while ensuring parallel execution of steps, demonstrating its effectiveness.

- We develop an automated framework for scalable data construction. This system ensures high parallelism and diversity-optimized dataset generation.
- We provide **ParaBench**. To our best knowledge, **ParaBench** features the highest parallelism, enabling thorough exploration of LLMs' parallel planning capabilities. We assess a variety of open-source and closed-source models of different sizes, offering insights and analysis for parallel task planning.

Table 1. Comparison of our dataset with other datasets. $Length_{Avg}$ represents the average step set size, $Depth_{Avg}$ represents the average depth, $Width_{Avg}$ represents the average width, $Length_{Max}$ represents the maximum step set size, $Width_{Max}$ represents the maximum width of DAG, and Compression Rate represents the parallelism of steps. Lower Compression Rate stands for higher parallelism

		Amount	$Length_{Avg}$	$Depth_{Avg}$	$Width_{Avg}$	$Length_{Max}$	$Width_{Max}$	Compression Rate
TaskLAMA [23]	**Train**	965	7.30	6.36	1.71	18	6	86.2
	Dev	169	7.93	6.80	1.87	15	7	85.8
	Test	478	7.42	6.61	1.63	15	6	89.0
WorFBench [13]	\	2146	3.77	3.27	1.48	14	13	87.6
ParaBench	**Train**	3043	14.88	8.84	3.86	22	9	59.5
	Test	1005	12.10	6.58	3.75	18	9	54.6

- We propose a novel framework, **CTDO**, which employs a small planner to identify dependencies among steps and leverages its predictions to guide LLMs in task planning. Experimental results demonstrate the superior effectiveness of our approach.

2 Related Work

2.1 LLM Tool Learning

Tool learning for LLM often deals with complex tasks that require multiple tool calls. Early research [15] integrates external tools, such as search engines and calculators, into LLMs to enhance their real-time capabilities and accuracy. Recent studies [6,16] have demonstrated the remarkable ability of LLMs to leverage external tools for solving complex tasks. Some research [14,17] focuses on constructing datasets using real-world APIs to address intricate tasks encountered by users in practical scenarios. Given the complexity and limited availability of real-world tools, other studies [5,9,18] have developed extensive virtual tools to tackle multifaceted challenges.

2.2 Task Planning

Researchers [1,8] emphasize task planning's importance. ToolBench [14] employs a graph-integrated approach to enable backtracking during planning, expanding the search space while maintaining the React framework. Subsequent studies [12] refine this methodology, producing linear execution steps. However, this approach overlooks parallelism between steps, limiting potential time savings through parallel execution. To address this, WorFBench [13] restructures datasets by organizing steps into directed acyclic graphs, maximizing parallelism, and minimizing time costs. TaskLAMA [23] constructs tasks with step sets, establishes necessary dependencies between steps, and enables their parallel execution. In contrast, **ParaBench** evaluates step parallelism specifically, achieving higher data parallelism and more complex task structures in its design.

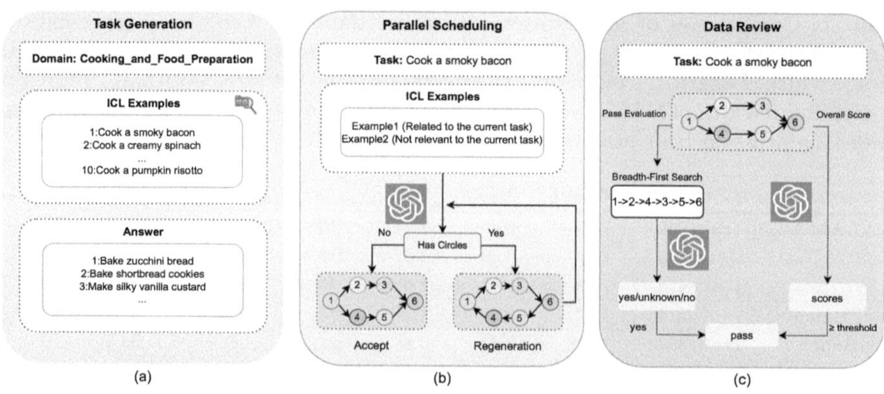

Fig. 2. The dataset construction process of **ParaBench**.

3   ParaBench

To evaluate the capability of LLMs in parallelizing step execution based on their interdependencies, we propose a solution to generate a new dataset, **ParaBench**. Our solution is an automated generation pipeline encompassing **Task Generation**, **Parallel Scheduling**, and **Data Review**, as illustrated in Fig. 2.

3.1   Task Generation

During this phase, it is essential to formulate diverse practical tasks. We manually define ten distinct domains (e.g., Health and Fitness, Arts and Crafts). For a domain c_i, we manually construct a set of 30 tasks: $\mathcal{T}_{c_i} = \{t_1^i, t_2^i, ..., t_{30}^i\}$. As shown in the three-step process in Fig. 2 (a), complex tasks are generated by: (1) selecting a target domain c_i, (2) randomly choosing ten relevant tasks from the c_i domain as ICL (In-Context Learning) examples, and (3) using these examples to generate more tasks.

3.2   Parallel Scheduling

During this phase, we acquire the step sets and their corresponding dependencies. Due to the limited parallelism in existing datasets, we construct a dataset from scratch to evaluate the parallel task planning ability.

In some pilot studies, we find LLMs struggle to generate parallel tasks even with constraint instructions. To address this issue, we adopt an alternative generation approach. During the data generation process, as shown in Fig. 2 (b), we first present the current task and then provide several ICL examples, which include tasks and their corresponding parallel steps to assist generation. We manually construct two structured data examples for ICL to improve data parallelism. After completing data generation, we manually review and validate these constructed data. When a certain amount of data is generated, we select two examples as ICL exemplars: one from the target domain to maintain logical coherence and another from a different domain to enhance diversity. Finally, we structure the model output as a graph. If loops are found, regeneration is required. To ensure data parallelism, we set a threshold. When parallelism falls below this threshold, the model regenerates once, and we select the output with higher parallelism from the two generations.

During the process of graph generation, we shift from requiring direct graph generation to requesting step execution dependencies. For instance, given a task sequence of A→B→C, where B and C are in parallel and must be done after A, the model is requested to output A→B and A→C. To enhance data parallelism, we propose creating more steps that are mutually independent while all depending on A. Additionally, we advocate for generating more steps similar to A to improve overall data parallelism.

3.3 Data Review

We apply two strategies to ensure data quality: 1) We verify whether executing steps according to the existing directed acyclic graph can successfully complete the task, as shown in the left panel of Fig. 2c. The raw data is converted into a graph structure, followed by a Breadth-First Search (BFS) traversal to linearize step execution sequences. This yields a linear sequence of steps and allows us to evaluate its executability using a discriminative model. 2) We employ an LLM to assess the overall quality of the data, with a particular emphasis on evaluating the parallelism of the data and the rationality of the steps within the prompts as illustrated in the right panel of Fig. 2c. Another LLM is employed to score the data, enabling the removal of low-quality samples through threshold-based filtering. The final data selection incorporates these two metrics.

3.4 Data Statistics

We employ GPT-4o as the generative model. As shown in Table 1, we split the whole dataset into train and test sets. Among the 1,005 data entries in the test set, we manually sample 100 entries and employ experts to re-examine the data, where we find all the sampled data graphs can pass the ultimate task instruction, and only 2.5% steps fail to be parallelized, showing a good data quality.

4 Collaborative Task Dependency Optimization (CTDO)

We propose **CTDO**, a framework in which a small planner (**SPlanner**) identifies execution dependencies and leverages its predictions to assist LLMs in planning.

4.1 SPlanner

Given the substantial resource consumption and relatively slow inference speed of LLMs, we employ a small-scale model to assist in identifying interdependencies among steps.

We formulate the task planning task as a token-token relation classification problem. First, we concatenate the main task and its step set, adding a special token "[STEP]" in front of each step for separation. Then, we encode the text sequence using DeBERTa-v3-large [7] to obtain representations $\mathbf{H} \in \mathbb{R}^{n \times m}$, where n is the number of tokens and m is the dimension for each token representation. Next, we obtain $\mathbf{h}_i \in \mathbb{R}^m$ and $\mathbf{d}_i \in \mathbb{R}^m$ through two MLP layers.

$$\mathbf{h}_i = \mathrm{MLP}_{\mathrm{head}}(\mathbf{H}_i), \quad \mathbf{d}_i = \mathrm{MLP}_{\mathrm{dep}}(\mathbf{H}_i)$$

After that, we utilize the biaffine attention [22] to obtain the token-token relations scores.

$$\mathbf{r}_{ij} = \mathbf{h}_i^\top \mathbf{W} \mathbf{d}_j + \mathbf{U} \mathbf{h}_i + \mathbf{V} \mathbf{d}_j + \mathbf{b},$$

where $\mathbf{r}_{ij} \in \mathbb{R}^2$ is the relation scores of token$_i$ to token$_j$, $\mathbf{W} \in \mathbb{R}^{m \times 2 \times m}$ is the core parameter matrix of the bilinear transformation, $\mathbf{U} \in \mathbb{R}^{2 \times m}$ and $\mathbf{V} \in \mathbb{R}^{2 \times m}$ are the parameter matrices of the linear transformation, and $\mathbf{b} \in \mathbb{R}^2$ is the bias term.

Then, we use the argmax function to determine whether there is a dependency between the two tokens

$$y_{ij} = \mathrm{argmax}\ \mathbf{r}_{ij}.$$

Here we only predict the score of the special tokens "[STEP]". $y_{ij} = 1$ indicates the step represented by position j depends on the step represented by position i. Finally, we can derive the dependencies between steps.

4.2 Model Collaboration

Based on our pilot studies, we find **SPlanner** can reach high dependency accuracy, while LLM tends to generate as many as parallel tasks regardless of the availability. Therefore, we combine **SPlanner**'s strong dependency prediction ability with LLMs' powerful reasoning ability via model collaborations.

Specifically, we first obtain the task-planning results from **SPlanner** and then utilize an LLM to revise the planning results to make more accurate predictions. Here, the instruction prompt includes the ultimate task instruction, step set, and the dependency prediction results from **SPlanner**. We carefully devise the instruction prompt to inform the LLM that dependency relationships among steps will be identified through **SPlanner**, which constructs a preliminary plan graph based on these dependencies. After that, we explicitly require the LLM to refine the preliminary plan graph by integrating its inherent knowledge base with **SPlanner**'s outputs. To ensure the LLM comprehensively comprehends the task requirements, we manually constructed two ICL examples. Based on these components, we request the LLM to generate the final task planning results.

Table 2. Main results of different models in two modes. PR means Pass Rate, and CR means Compression Rate

Model	Direct		CTDO	
	PR↑	CR↓	PR↑	CR↓
GPT-4o-mini	28.0	63.7	**32.1**	59.2
GPT-3.5	9.6	57.6	**31.7**	59.4
DeepSeek-V3-671B	34.6	58.8	**38.8**	59.7
DeepSeek-V2.5-236B	24.7	59.3	**39.8**	60.2
LLaMa-3.3-70B	36.1	61.9	**40.0**	60.5
Qwen2-72B	17.7	56.7	**33.7**	59.5
Qwen2.5-7B	16.4	58.1	**32.3**	59.3
Qwen2.5-14B	23.2	58.5	**29.6**	58.5
Qwen2.5-32B	29.6	59.1	**34.0**	59.1
Qwen2.5-72B	30.1	57.8	**34.4**	59.0

5   Experiments

5.1   Experimental Setup

We evaluate the systems using two distinct running modes: 1) **Direct**: Given a task and its corresponding step set, we directly prompt an LLM to generate a plan. The Direct mode is widely adopted in the previous studies [13,23]. 2) **CTDO**: Following our proposed framework **CTDO** (described in Sect. 4.2), we enable collaboration between an LLM and **SPlanner** to obtain a plan. We compare several popular available LLMs in our experiments..

During the evaluation, the comparison LLMs include both API-based closed-source and open-source ones. (1) Closed-source LLMs: We choose two representative models: GPT-4o-mini and GPT-3.5[1]. (2) Open-source LLMs: We evaluate several representative models, including LLaMa-3.3-70B [4], Qwen2-72B [2], Qwen2.5-7B, Qwen2.5-14B, Qwen2.5-32B, Qwen2.5-72B [19], DeepSeek-V2.5-236B [10], and DeepSeek-V3-671B [11].

5.2   Evaluation Metrics

For the **ParaBench** dataset, we construct it as a directed acyclic graph (DAG) based on the dependencies between steps to standardize evaluation. The **Pass Rate** metric is employed to verify plan execution correctness, while a specifically designed **Compression Rate** metric quantifies the parallelism degree of steps within the planning graph.

---

[1] The version for GPT-4o-mini is GPT-4o-mini-2024-07-18, and for GPT-3.5 is GPT-3.5-turbo-0125. Since GPT-4o is used for building **ParaBench**, we do not list its results for fair comparison.

Pass Rate (PR): This metric indicates whether the task can be completed under the current plan. A step must be sequentially executed after specific predecessor steps upon which it depends. If all steps in a task plan satisfy their dependency constraints, the task plan passes the test.

Compression Rate (CR): This metric is defined as the depth of the planning graph divided by the step set size. A lower CR indicates higher parallelism, which minimizes task completion time.

5.3   Main Results

Table 2 presents the main experimental results. The results of the **Direct** mode reveal that when handling complex tasks (characterized by intricate step dependencies), LLMs demonstrate significant challenges in planning parallel execution sequences of steps. We can further observe that:

- In **Direct** mode evaluation, among proprietary models, GPT-4o-mini substantially outperforms GPT-3.5 with a 28.0% Pass Rate. For open-source LLMs, LLaMA-3.3-70B surpasses DeepSeek-V3-671B (36.1% vs. 34.6%), obtaining the best performance.
- Under **CTDO** framework with **SPlanner** enhancement, all LLMs exhibit performance gains. LLaMa-3.3-70B also yields the best score 40.0% in this mode with 3.9% absolute improvement. Besides, **CTDO** reaches comparative Compression Rates compared to **Direct**, validating its effectiveness.
  These results collectively validate **CTDO**'s methodological efficacy.

6   Further Analysis

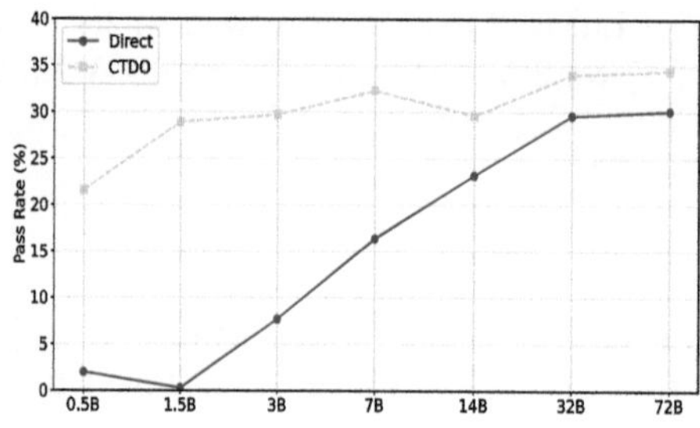
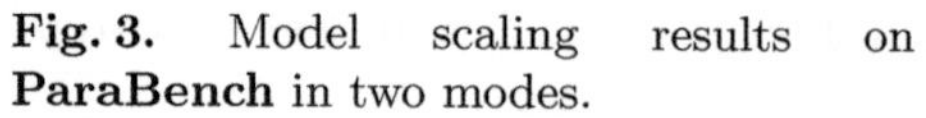

Fig. 3. Model scaling results on **ParaBench** in two modes.

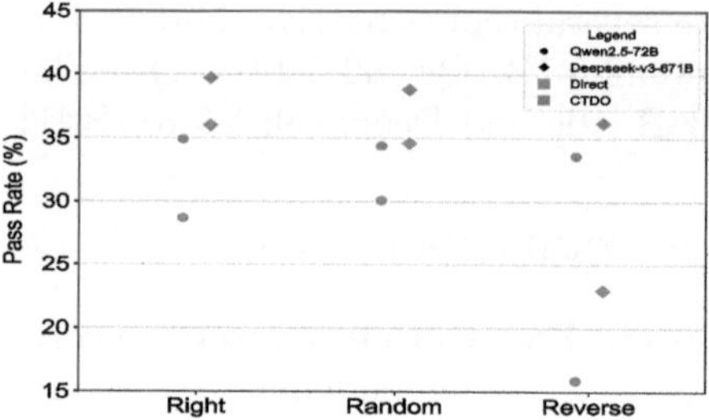

Fig. 4. The impact of different step orders on the results of the two modes.

6.1   Effect of Different Model Sizes

As shown in Fig. 3, the Pass Rate of **Direct** and **CTDO** continually increases as the model size scales. When LLMs are in smaller sizes, **CTDO** shows extraordinary performance improvements, and the largest gap reaches 28.6% Pass Rate when the model size is 1.5B. As the model size scales, the performance gap steadily saturates, but **CTDO** still outperforms Direct by 4.3% Pass Rate, showing good overall performance. This fact indicates that larger LLM demonstrates better ability for task planning. However, LLMs' task planning capabilities remain limited, necessitating further research.

6.2   Effect of Different Step Orders

When evaluating LLM performance, we examine whether the initial ordering of steps affects planning outcomes by testing three sequence types: 1)Correct (Correct execution order) 2)Random (random order) 3)Reverse (Inverted correct order) As shown in Fig. 4, we test the LLM in two modes. In **Direct** mode, DeepSeek-V3-671B achieves 23.0% performance with Reverse order versus 36.0% with Correct order (13.0% difference). In **CTDO** mode, it maintains a 36.2% Pass Rate with Reverse order compared to 39.7% with Correct order (only 3.5% decline).

The results demonstrate that different step orders moderately impact LLM planning. Random order and Correct order show minimal performance differences due to their sequential similarity, while Reverse order causes measurable performance degradation. **CTDO** mode exhibits stronger order robustness through **SPlanner**-enhanced reasoning, showing significantly smaller performance variance (3.5% vs 13.0%) compared to **Direct** mode.

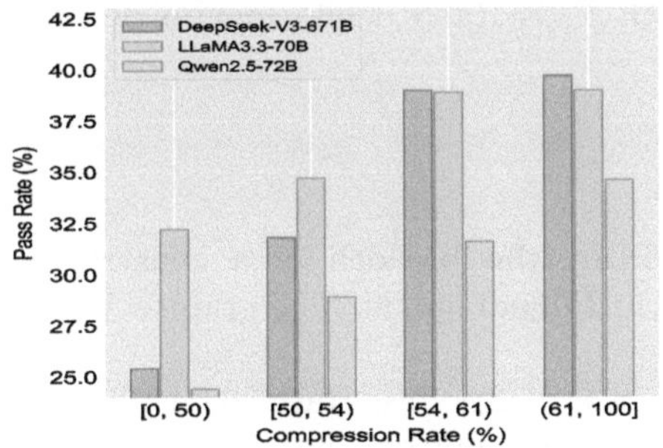

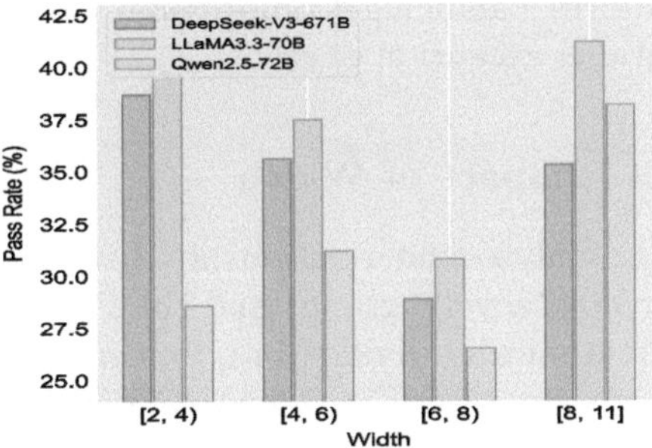

Fig. 5. Performance of LLMs of different **Compression Rates** in **Direct** mode.

Fig. 6. Performance of LLMs of different **Widths** in **Direct** mode.

Table 3. **Pass Rate** and **Compression Rate** of different models on different modes. PR means Pass Rate, and CR means Compression Rate

Model	Direct		CTDO	
	PR↑	CR↓	PR↑	CR↓
DeepSeek-V3-671B	34.6	58.8	38.8	59.7
LLaMa-3.3-70B	36.1	61.9	40.0	60.5
Qwen2.5-0.5B	2.0	25.0	21.6	46.5
Qwen2.5-1.5B	0.3	33.5	28.9	58.6
Qwen2.5-72B	30.1	57.8	34.4	59.0

6.3   Impact of Compression Rate

We further examine the impact of the data Compression Rate on LLM planning in **Direct** mode. The Compression Rates are divided into four intervals while maintaining comparable data volumes in each. As shown in Fig. 5, higher compression rates correlate with improved LLM Pass Rates. DeepSeek-V3-671B achieves 39.7% in the highest compression Rate interval versus 25.4% in the lowestG a 14.3% gap. Other LLMs exhibit similar trends. This confirms that lower Compression Rates imply greater task parallelism and complexity, making effective planning more challenging for LLMs.

Furthermore, whether higher Pass Rates in LLMs directly correlate with enhanced step parallelization capability remains debatable. As Table 3 demonstrates, models with superior Pass Rates do not consistently exhibit lower Compression Rates. Notably, Qwen2.5-0.5B and Qwen2.5-1.5B show remarkably low Compression Rates (25.0% for Qwen2.5-0.5B) despite their substantially inferior Pass Rates. These findings indicate that the effective execution of this task requires balancing Compression Rates with Pass Rates while maximizing the parallel execution of steps.

6.4   Impact of Width

We analyze the relationship between Width (the breadth of a constructed directed acyclic graph) and the Pass Rate in **Direct** mode. The graph's Width is statistically divided into four intervals.

As shown in Fig. 6, LaMa3.3-70B achieves a 41.2% Pass Rate when Width is in the fourth interval and 39.7% in the first interval but declines to 30.8% in the third interval. Our analysis indicates that narrower Width values (first interval) correspond to limited parallelization, while broader Width values (fourth interval) enable higher parallelization with fewer strict dependencies (many steps have no strict execution order constraints), making task ordering easier for the LLM. When the width is moderate (third interval), the steps maintain high parallelism while imposing strict execution order constraints among numerous steps, thereby presenting greater challenges, leading to the lowest Pass Rate.

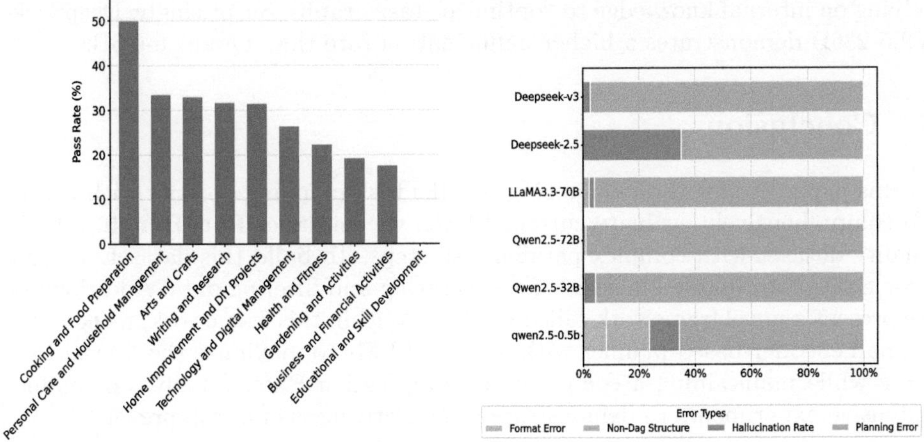

Fig. 7. Average **Pass Rates** of DeepSeek-V3-671B in 10 fields.

Fig. 8. Error type distribution of LLMs.

6.5 Domain Analysis

We conduct an analysis of task Pass Rates across different domains. As shown in Fig. 7, our findings reveal that tasks requiring higher specialization and more intricate step dependencies exhibit significantly lower LLM performance. Specifically, the model achieves a Pass Rate of 49.8% in the Cook domain, while this metric drops to 17.4% in the Economics domain and reaches 0% in the Education domain. This discrepancy stems from the relatively straightforward task structures and explicit step dependencies observed in the Cook domains. In contrast, both the Economic and Education domains present complex step interdependencies, with the Economic domain additionally demanding domain-specific expertise. These combined challenges result in substantially lower Pass Rates. This supports the notion that tasks in more complex domains are inherently more challenging to plan.

6.6 Error Analysis

Our study investigates common error patterns in LLM-based task planning. We analyze error distributions across LLMs (Fig. 8), where "Format Error" denotes structural non-compliance, "Non-DAG Structure" indicates failure to maintain acyclic graph structures, "Hallucination Rate" quantifies unwarranted step generation, and "Planning Error" captures conventional logical flaws.

As shown in Fig. 8, planning errors remain predominant. While improved LLM performance reduces formatting errors, LLaMa-3.3-70B still exhibits a non-negligible proportion of such issues. Notably, higher-performing LLMs avoid cycles in task graphs, suggesting sensitivity to closed-loop step dependencies. All models show hallucination tendencies (generating non-existent steps), possibly relying on internal knowledge to "optimize" task graphs. Surprisingly, DeepSeek-V2.5-236B demonstrates a higher hallucination rate than Qwen2.5-0.5B.

7   Conclusion

In this paper, we focus on enhancing parallel task planning abilities with LLMs. To comprehensively evaluate current LLMs, we construct **ParaBench**, a high-quality dataset with complex parallel task steps. To build this dataset, we propose a set of automated methods for generating and filtering data. Additionally, we present a novel framework called **CTDO**. Within this framework, we combine a small encoder-based planner with modern LLMs to maximize the overall Pass Rate while maintaining a comparative Compression Rate. Finally, we conduct extensive experiments to demonstrate the effectiveness of our approach.

Acknowledgments. This work is supported by the National Natural Science Foundation of China (Grant No.62376177) and Provincial Key Laboratory for Computer Information Processing Technology, Soochow University. This work is also supported by Collaborative Innovation Center of Novel Software Technology and Industrialization, the Priority Academic Program Development of Jiangsu Higher Education Institutions. We would also like to thank the anonymous reviewers for their insightful and valuable comments.

References

1. Chen, Z., Zhou, K., Zhang, B., Gong, Z., Zhao, W.X., Wen, J.R.: ChatCot: tool-augmented chain-of-thought reasoning on chat-based large language models. arXiv preprint arXiv:2305.14323 (2023)
2. Chu, Y., et al.: Qwen2-audio technical report. arXiv preprint arXiv:2407.10759 (2024)
3. Farn, N., Shin, R.: ToolTalk: evaluating tool-usage in a conversational setting. arXiv preprint arXiv:2311.10775 (2023)
4. Grattafiori, A., et al.: The llama 3 herd of models. arXiv preprint arXiv:2407.21783 (2024)
5. Han, H., Zhu, T., Zhang, X., Wu, M., Xiong, H., Chen, W.: Nestools: a dataset for evaluating nested tool learning abilities of large language models. arXiv preprint arXiv:2410.11805 (2024)
6. Hao, S., Liu, T., Wang, Z., Hu, Z.: ToolkenGPT: augmenting frozen language models with massive tools via tool embeddings. Adv. Neural. Inf. Process. Syst. **36**, 45870–45894 (2023)
7. He, P., Gao, J., Chen, W.: DeBERTAV3: improving deBERTa using electra-style pre-training with gradient-disentangled embedding sharing. arXiv preprint arXiv:2111.09543 (2021)
8. Hu, M., et al.: tree-planner: efficient close-loop task planning with large language models. arXiv preprint arXiv:2310.08582 (2023)
9. Li, M., et al.: API-bank: a comprehensive benchmark for tool-augmented LLMS. arXiv preprint arXiv:2304.08244 (2023)

10. Liu, A., et al.: DeepSeek-V2: a strong, economical, and efficient mixture-of-experts language model. arXiv preprint arXiv:2405.04434 (2024)
11. Liu, A., et al.: DeepSeek-V3 technical report. arXiv preprint arXiv:2412.19437 (2024)
12. Liu, Y., et al.: Tool-planner: dynamic solution tree planning for large language model with tool clustering. arXiv e-prints pp. arXiv–2406 (2024)
13. Qiao, S., et al.: Benchmarking agentic workflow generation. arXiv preprint arXiv:2410.07869 (2024)
14. Qin, Y., et al.: ToolLLM: facilitating large language models to master 16000+ real-world apis. arXiv preprint arXiv:2307.16789 (2023)
15. Schick, T., et al.: ToolFormer: language models can teach themselves to use tools. Adv. Neural. Inf. Process. Syst. **36**, 68539–68551 (2023)
16. Shen, Y., Song, K., Tan, X., Li, D., Lu, W., Zhuang, Y.: HuggingGPT: solving AI tasks with ChatGPT and its friends in hugging face. Adv. Neural. Inf. Process. Syst. **36**, 38154–38180 (2023)
17. Song, Y., et al.: RestGPT: connecting large language models with real-world restful APIS. arXiv preprint arXiv:2306.06624 (2023)
18. Wu, M., Zhu, T., Han, H., Tan, C., Zhang, X., Chen, W.: Seal-tools: Self-instruct tool learning dataset for agent tuning and detailed benchmark. In: Wong, D.F., Wei, Z., Yang, M. (eds.) CCF International Conference on Natural Language Processing and Chinese Computing, pp. 372–384. Springer (2024). https://doi.org/10.1007/978-981-97-9434-8_29
19. Yang, A., et al.: Qwen2. 5-1m technical report. arXiv preprint arXiv:2501.15383 (2025)
20. Yao, S., et al.: React: synergizing reasoning and acting in language models. arXiv:2210.03629 (2023)
21. Ye, J., et al.: ToolEyes: fine-grained evaluation for tool learning capabilities of large language models in real-world scenarios. arXiv preprint arXiv:2401.00741 (2024)
22. Yu, J., Bohnet, B., Poesio, M.: Named entity recognition as dependency parsing. arXiv preprint arXiv:2005.07150 (2020)
23. Yuan, Q., Kazemi, M., Xu, X., Noble, I., Imbrasaite, V., Ramachandran, D.: TASKLAMA: probing the complex task understanding of language models. In: Proceedings of the AAAI Conference on Artificial Intelligence, vol. 38, pp. 19468–19476 (2024)

SageRep: Enhancing Unsupervised Sentence Representations via Layer-Adaptive Self-knowledge Distillation

Binghao Fu[1,2(✉)], Jun Wang[1,2], and Qi Su[2,3]

[1] Department of Information Management, Peking University, Beijing, China
`binghao_fu@stu.pku.edu.cn`
[2] Research Center for Digital Humanities, Peking University, Beijing, China
[3] School of Foreign Languages, Peking University, Beijing, China

Abstract. Recent advances in unsupervised sentence representation learning have relied heavily on contrastive objectives over pre-trained language models (PLMs). However, the quality of learned representations is often limited by shallow layers and restricted model capacity, especially in the absence of large-scale supervision. To address this, we propose **SageRep**, a novel layer-adaptive self-knowledge distillation framework that improves representation quality without requiring external teacher models or multi-stage training. Motivated by the observation that deeper layers in PLMs encode richer semantic signals, **SageRep** enables shallower layers to distill knowledge dynamically from deeper ones, guided by sentence-level similarity distributions. Unlike prior static self-knowledge distillation methods, our approach adaptively selects the most informative teacher layers per instance, promoting more effective intra-model knowledge transfer. Additionally, we introduce a contrastive regularization strategy using inter-layer negatives to mitigate representation oversmoothing. Extensive evaluations on standard semantic textual similarity benchmarks demonstrate that **SageRep** achieves superior performance over previous unsupervised methods, with minimal additional training cost.

Keywords: Unsupervised Sentence Representations · Self-Knowledge Distillation · Contrastive Learning

1 Introduction

Learning effective sentence representations lies at the core of natural language processing (NLP), enabling a wide range of downstream tasks such as semantic textual similarity [1–6,16] and dense text retrieval [21]. While supervised approaches have shown strong performance, their dependence on large-scale labeled datasets limits scalability and adaptability across domains. In response, unsupervised sentence representation learning-particularly contrastive learning over pre-trained language models (PLMs) like BERT and RoBERTa [9,15]-has emerged as a promising alternative. A representative method is SimCSE [10],

© The Author(s), under exclusive license to Springer Nature Singapore Pte Ltd. 2026
X.-L. Mao et al. (Eds.): NLPCC 2025, LNAI 16105, pp. 92–104, 2026.
https://doi.org/10.1007/978-981-95-3352-7_8

which leverages dropout-based augmentation to learn semantically meaningful embeddings without supervision. However, despite their simplicity and effectiveness, existing methods face a critical trade-off: when model size or depth is reduced to improve inference efficiency, the quality of sentence representations degrades significantly [14]. This performance drop raises a key challenge-how to maintain high-quality sentence embeddings while minimizing the computational burden of training and inference.

Knowledge distillation (KD) has emerged as a common solution to mitigate the performance drop associated with reduced model size, by transferring semantic knowledge from a large teacher model to a more compact student model [11,14,19]. Despite its effectiveness, traditional KD approaches typically face two major limitations: (1) they introduce significant computational overhead due to the requirement of pre-training complex teacher models, coupled with the non-trivial challenge of selecting an optimal teacher [8,17]; and (2) they often exhibit limited transfer efficiency, causing student models to inadequately replicate the performance of their teachers. To address these drawbacks, recent studies have proposed self-knowledge distillation, which utilizes the network's internal knowledge to guide its training, thus removing the reliance on external teacher models [22,24,25]. For instance, Zhang et al. [25] demonstrated that deeper layers can effectively teach shallower layers within the same model, significantly enhancing representation quality. However, existing self-knowledge distillation methods have been largely confined to supervised classification tasks, particularly in computer vision, leaving their potential unexplored in unsupervised sentence representation tasks.

In this paper, we propose **SageRep**, a dynamic self-knowledge distillation framework for unsupervised sentence representation, which effectively enhances representation quality by adaptively transferring semantic knowledge from deeper to shallower layers within a single pre-trained language model. We make three primary contributions in this work: *First*, we introduce a novel layer-adaptive knowledge transfer approach. Motivated by empirical findings that deeper layers encode richer semantic distinctions, our method leverages sentence-level similarity distributions learned by deeper layers to guide shallower layers, significantly improving their semantic representation capability. *Second*, we propose a dynamic teacher selection mechanism. Unlike static distillation approaches, our method enables shallower layers to dynamically select optimal deeper-layer teachers based on representational similarity, thus promoting more efficient intra-model knowledge transfer without requiring additional external models. *Third*, we identify and address the inter-layer over-smoothing issue introduced by self-knowledge distillation, which adversely affects generalization performance. To alleviate this, we propose an inter-layer contrastive regularization strategy, dynamically selecting the most similar adjacent-layer representations as negative samples, thus maintaining representation diversity and further enhancing performance. To demonstrate the effectiveness of **SageRep**, we conduct extensive experiments on standard Semantic Textual Similarity (STS) tasks. Our experimental results show that the proposed method significantly outperforms existing unsupervised methods.

2 Related Work

Unsupervised Sentence Representation. Unsupervised sentence representation aims to encode semantically meaningful sentence embeddings from unlabeled data, enabling tasks such as semantic textual similarity (STS) and text classification. Early methods relied on aggregating word embeddings, which failed to capture compositional semantics and word order. The advent of pre-trained language models (PLMs) like BERT and RoBERTa significantly advanced this field by enabling contextualized representations. However, several works identified a prevalent anisotropy issue-where embeddings tend to lie in a narrow cone in semantic space [12]. Methods such as BERT-flow and BERT-whitening aim to address this by decorrelating representations to improve isotropy and downstream performance.

Recently, contrastive learning has emerged as a powerful paradigm for unsupervised sentence embedding. It aims to bring semantically similar sentences closer while pushing apart dissimilar ones in the representation space. SimCSE [10] demonstrates the efficacy of using dropout-induced augmentations for positive pair generation. Subsequent works introduced improvements in negative sampling, such as Gaussian-based negatives [27], queue-based momentum contrast [20], and structured masking to capture entailment relations [26]. EASE integrates entity-aware signals [18], and SSCL samples negatives from intermediate layers to mitigate over-smoothing [7]. Inspired by these, our method introduces an inter-layer contrastive regularization scheme that dynamically selects negatives across layers, effectively maintaining diversity and enhancing robustness.

Self-knowledge Distillation. Self-knowledge distillation (SKD) removes the need for external teachers by using the model's own predictions or intermediate states for self-supervision. Sample-based methods align predictions across augmented views [24], while structure-based methods inject auxiliary branches to enhance internal knowledge flow [25]. History-based methods distill from past model checkpoints [22]. Recent work such as DTSKD [13] integrates both structure and sample-based strategies for stronger self-guidance. Despite the success of SKD in computer vision and supervised NLP, its application in unsupervised sentence representation remains underexplored. Our work addresses this gap by designing a layer-adaptive self-distillation mechanism tailored to sentence embedding tasks, leveraging dynamic teacher selection and contrastive regularization to improve both representation quality and generalization.

3 Methodology

In this section, we provide a detailed description of our proposed SageRep framework, which comprises three carefully designed modules, closely aligned with our stated contributions: (1) layer-adaptive knowledge transfer to leverage hierarchical semantic information; (2) dynamic teacher selection to optimize intra-model

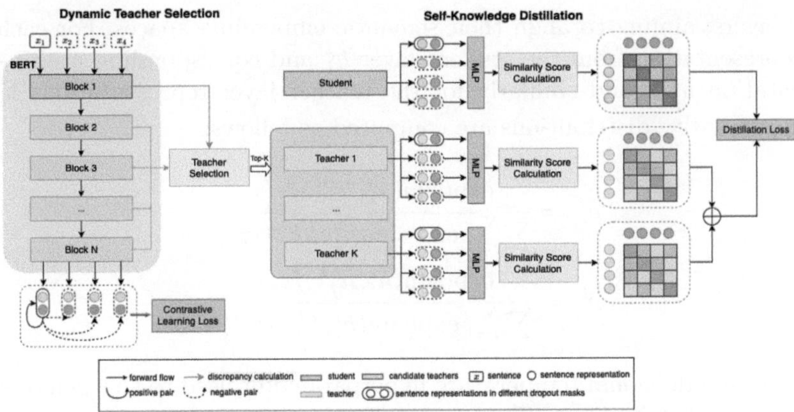

Fig. 1. Overall architecture of SageRep, illustrating dynamic self-knowledge distillation for unsupervised sentence representation. Specifically, SageRep dynamically selects optimal deeper-layer teachers based on representational discrepancies (*Dynamic Teacher Selection*) and transfers knowledge by aligning sentence-level similarity distributions between shallow (student) and deeper (teacher) layers (*Self-Knowledge Distillation*). The framework further integrates inter-layer contrastive regularization by dynamically constructing negative samples from adjacent layers to prevent representation over-smoothing.

knowledge transfer; and (3) inter-layer contrastive regularization to address representation over-smoothing. The overall architecture of SageRep is illustrated in Fig. 1.

3.1   Layer-Adaptive Knowledge Transfer

Contrastive learning methods are commonly adopted in unsupervised sentence representation tasks to enhance semantic distinguishability by pulling together positive pairs and pushing apart negative samples. Given a sentence set $\mathcal{X} = \{x_i\}_{i=1}^{N}$, each sentence x_i is encoded twice using independent dropout masks by a pre-trained language model (PLM, e.g., BERT), producing positive pairs (h_i, h_i^+). The contrastive loss (InfoNCE) is formulated as:

$$\mathcal{L}_{\text{InfoNCE}} = -\log \frac{\exp(\text{sim}(h_i, h_i^+)/\tau)}{\sum_{j=1}^{N} \exp(\text{sim}(h_i, h_j)/\tau)}, \tag{1}$$

where τ is a temperature parameter and $\text{sim}(\cdot)$ is the cosine similarity.

Empirically, deeper layers in PLMs demonstrate stronger semantic discrimination capabilities compared to shallower layers. Inspired by this observation, we introduce layer-adaptive knowledge transfer to guide shallower (student) layers using richer semantic representations from deeper (teacher) layers. Specifically, we first compute sentence-level similarity score distributions from student and teacher layers, aiming to align their semantic embedding spaces. For each sentence representation from the student layer h_i^s and corresponding positive pair representation h_j^{s+}, and similarly for the teacher layer representations h_i^t and h_j^{t+}, the similarity distributions are computed as follows:

$$\tilde{p}_{ij}^s = \frac{\exp(\mathrm{sim}(h_i^s, h_j^{s+})/\tau')}{\sum_{j=1}^N \exp(\mathrm{sim}(h_i^s, h_j^{s+})/\tau')},$$

$$\tilde{p}_{ij}^t = \frac{\exp(\mathrm{sim}(h_i^t, h_j^{t+})/\tau')}{\sum_{j=1}^N \exp(\mathrm{sim}(h_i^t, h_j^{t+})/\tau')}, \tag{2}$$

where τ' is an additional temperature hyperparameter used to sharpen or soften the similarity distributions. To enforce effective knowledge transfer, we minimize the Kullback-Leibler (KL) divergence between these similarity score distributions, which serves as a supervisory signal to enhance semantic quality in shallow layers:

$$\mathcal{L}_{\mathrm{KD}} = \sum_{i=1}^N \mathrm{KL}(\tilde{p}^t(x_i) \| \tilde{p}^s(x_i)). \tag{3}$$

3.2 Dynamic Teacher Selection

In traditional self-knowledge distillation approaches, a static teacher layer (typically the deepest layer) is uniformly chosen to guide shallower student layers. However, this fixed-layer strategy neglects the inherent semantic variability of sentences and the dynamic nature of knowledge distribution across different model layers, potentially resulting in suboptimal knowledge transfer. Empirically, we observe that the most informative teacher layer for a given sentence representation may vary across instances due to differences in semantic complexity, topical diversity, and contextual nuances.

Motivated by this observation, SageRep proposes a dynamic teacher selection strategy to enhance the flexibility and efficiency of intra-model knowledge transfer. Specifically, for each sentence during training, we dynamically evaluate representation discrepancies between the shallow (student) layer and all candidate deeper (teacher) layers. The optimal teacher layer t for each instance is selected as the one whose representations exhibit the maximum semantic discrepancy relative to the student layer, thus ensuring maximal information gain. Formally, this selection process can be expressed as:

$$t = \arg\max_{m \in \{2,...,L\}} D(h^m, h^s), \tag{4}$$

where $D(\cdot)$ denotes the representation discrepancy computed using cosine similarity. By performing this selection dynamically on a per-instance basis, our method effectively captures the most relevant and informative semantic guidance available within the model.

This dynamic approach has two main advantages: first, it adapts to the varying semantic complexity of different sentences, ensuring contextually appropriate supervision; second, it eliminates the need for external teacher models and reduces computational overhead compared to traditional multi-stage distillation methods. Consequently, dynamic teacher selection not only improves the semantic quality of the learned sentence representations but also maintains efficiency in training and inference.

3.3 Inter-layer Contrastive Regularization

Although self-knowledge distillation is effective in transferring knowledge within PLMs, intensive application of this technique may inadvertently result in representation over-smoothing. Specifically, excessive alignment among representations of adjacent layers can diminish semantic diversity and negatively affect the model's generalization capabilities, as adjacent layers begin encoding overly similar semantic information. This phenomenon limits the expressive power and discriminative capability of the learned sentence embeddings.

To alleviate this problem, we propose an inter-layer contrastive regularization strategy, aiming to explicitly preserve representational diversity among adjacent layers. The core idea is to construct challenging negative samples dynamically from the representations of highly similar adjacent layers during training. Formally, we select the pair of adjacent layers exhibiting the highest representational similarity as negative samples, thus encouraging the network to maintain distinctive semantic information at each layer. This selection is performed as follows:

$$m^* = \arg \max_{1 \leq m \leq L-1} D(h_i^m, h_i^{m+1}),\tag{5}$$

where $D(\cdot)$ measures the representation similarity computed by cosine similarity.

Subsequently, we integrate these selected inter-layer negative samples into the original contrastive learning objective. The modified contrastive loss is thus expressed as:

$$\mathcal{L}_{\mathrm{CL}} = -\log \frac{\exp(\mathrm{sim}(h_i, h_i^+)/\tau)}{\sum_{j=1}^N \exp(\mathrm{sim}(h_i, h_j)/\tau) + \exp(\mathrm{sim}(h_i^{m^*}, h_i^{m^*+1})/\tau)}.\tag{6}$$

By explicitly penalizing the similarity between adjacent layer representations through this regularization, we effectively mitigate representation over-smoothing, enhancing the robustness and discriminative power of the learned sentence embeddings. This dynamic negative sampling strategy introduces minimal computational overhead while significantly improving representational quality.

3.4 Overall Training Objective

Finally, the unified training objective integrates knowledge distillation and contrastive regularization losses, effectively balancing representation enhancement and semantic diversity:

$$\mathcal{L}_{\mathrm{total}} = \lambda \mathcal{L}_{\mathrm{KD}} + \beta \mathcal{L}_{\mathrm{CL}},\tag{7}$$

where λ and β are hyperparameters that balance the contributions of the respective losses. This carefully designed training objective ensures enhanced sentence representation quality with minimal computational overhead.

4 Experiments

4.1 Experiments Settup

Datasets. We evaluate the effectiveness of our proposed SageRep framework using standard Semantic Textual Similarity (STS) benchmarks, including STS 2012–2016, STS-B, and SICK-R [1–6,16]. All datasets consist of sentence pairs annotated with similarity scores ranging from 0 to 5. Following the standard unsupervised evaluation setting (SimCSE [10]), we use cosine similarity between sentence embeddings and report the average Spearman's correlation computed using the SentEval toolkit.

Comparison Methods. For comparison, we evaluate SageRep against several unsupervised sentence embedding methods: SimCSE [10], ConSERT [23], ESimCSE [20], DCLR [27], ArcCSE [26], and SSCL [7].

Implementation Details. We follow SimCSE [10] and train our models using one million sentences randomly sampled from Wikipedia. We adopt BERT_{base} and RoBERTa_{base} as the backbone encoders, using the [CLS] vector as the sentence representation. We regard the first layer of PLM as student layer and dynamically select the teacher layers for distillation. Hyperparameters are consistent across experiments, with both temperatures τ and τ' set to 0.05, a learning rate of 3×10^{-5}, batch size of 64, and maximum sequence length of 32 tokens. All models are trained for one epoch with the Adam optimizer on a single NVIDIA V100 GPU (32GB). Model checkpoints are saved based on their performance on the STS-B development set evaluated every 125 steps.

4.2 Results

Effect of Layer-Adaptive Self-knowledge Distillation. To validate the effectiveness of our proposed layer-adaptive self-knowledge distillation (La-SKD) strategy, we compare our approach against the SimCSE baseline without La-SKD. As shown in Table 1, applying La-SKD leads to substantial improvements on both BERT_{base} (from 76.25 to 78.46) and RoBERTa_{base} (from 76.57 to 77.73). These results highlight the benefit of dynamically transferring semantic knowledge from deeper to shallower layers within PLMs, confirming that layer-adaptive self-knowledge distillation significantly enhances the quality of unsupervised sentence representations.

Table 1. Effect of layer-adaptive self-knowledge distillation.

PLMs	Model	STS (Avg.)
BERT_{base}	SimCSE	76.25
	w/ La-SKD	**78.46**
RoBERTa_{base}	SimCSE	76.57
	w/ La-SKD	**77.73**

Static Distillation vs. Dynamic Distillation. We further investigate the advantage of our proposed dynamic teacher selection by comparing it against static distillation, which uses a fixed teacher layer across all training instances.

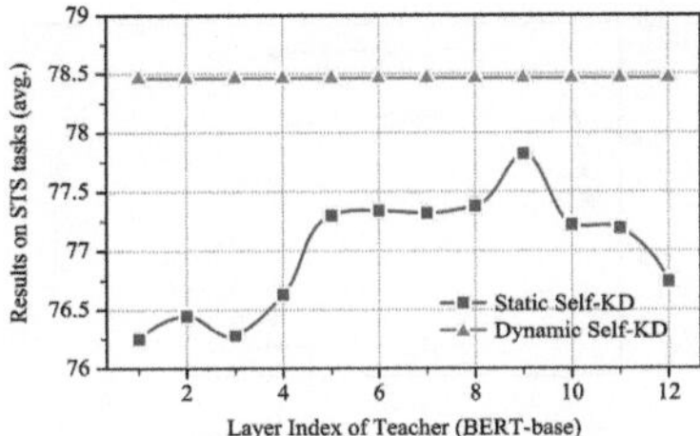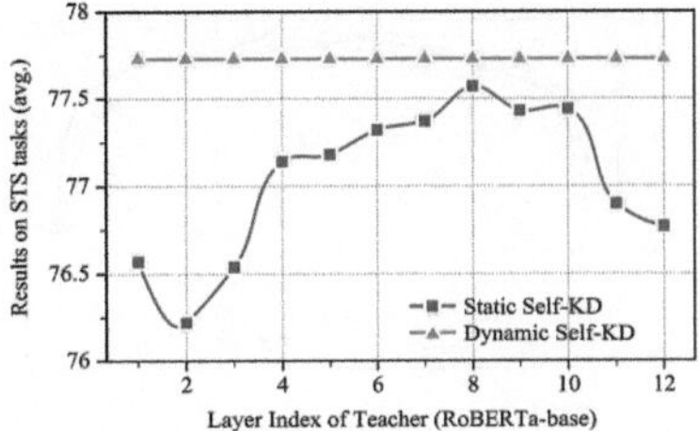

Fig. 2. Comparison of static and dynamic self-knowledge distillation strategies across different teacher layer selections. The horizontal axis denotes the fixed teacher layer indices (for static distillation), while the dynamic self-knowledge distillation adaptively selects optimal teacher layers for each instance. Results (average Spearman's correlation across STS tasks) clearly illustrate that dynamic teacher selection consistently achieves superior and stable performance compared to static selection on both $BERT_{base}$ and $RoBERTa_{base}$ models.

Table 2. Ablation study comparing different teacher selection strategies' average Spearman's correlation on STS datasets.

PLMs	Distillation Strategy	$c = 1$	$c = 2$	$c = 3$	$c = 4$	$c = 5$
$BERT_{base}$	Deepest-Layer as Teacher	78.07	78.12	77.52	76.76	76.23
	Shallow-Layer Dynamic Selection (ours)	**78.41**	**78.46**	**78.36**	**77.04**	**76.83**
$RoBERTa_{base}$	Deepest-Layer as Teacher	77.22	77.01	76.58	75.11	75.84
	Shallow-Layer Dynamic Selection (ours)	**77.56**	**77.73**	76.54	**76.02**	75.91

As shown in Fig. 2, dynamic self-knowledge distillation consistently outperforms static self-knowledge distillation across all possible teacher layers for both $BERT_{base}$ and $RoBERTa_{base}$ models. While static distillation performance notably fluctuates depending on the fixed layer choice, dynamic distillation achieves consistently high performance by adaptively selecting the optimal teacher layer per instance. This demonstrates that our dynamic distillation strategy effectively leverages semantic variations across different layers, ensuring robust performance gains.

Impact of the Number of Dynamically Selected Teacher Layers. To thoroughly evaluate our dynamic self-knowledge distillation approach, we investigate the impact of selecting different numbers of teacher layers (c) under two distinct strategies: (1) using the deepest transformer layer as the fixed teacher, and (2) dynamically selecting optimal deeper layers as teachers based on representational similarity with the shallow student layer. The results presented in Table 2 clearly indicate that dynamically selecting teacher layers from deeper layers consistently outperforms the static choice of using only the deepest layer across both $BERT_{base}$ and $RoBERTa_{base}$. This confirms the advantage of dynamically leveraging diverse semantic knowledge across deeper layers rather than relying solely on the final layer. We further observe that dynamically select-

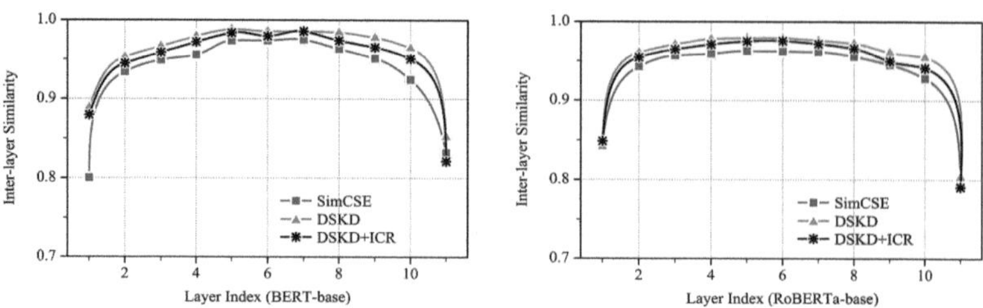

Fig. 3. Comparison of inter-layer cosine similarity for sentence representations obtained from SimCSE (baseline), dynamic self-knowledge distillation (DSKD), and our complete SageRep framework (DSKD integrated with ICR). Results are computed using 1,000 randomly sampled sentences from the STS-B test set, demonstrating that ICR effectively mitigates representation over-smoothing among adjacent layers.

Table 3. Sentence embedding performance on semantic textual similarity (STS) test sets, in terms of Spearman's correlation coefficient.

PLMs	Model	STS12	STS13	STS14	STS15	STS16	STS-B	SICK-R	Avg.
BERT_{base}	ConSERT	64.64	78.49	69.07	79.72	75.95	73.97	67.31	72.74
	SimCSE	68.40	82.41	74.38	80.91	78.56	76.85	72.23	76.25
	DCLR	70.81	83.73	75.11	82.56	78.44	78.31	71.59	77.22
	SSCL	71.68	83.50	76.42	**83.46**	78.39	79.03	71.76	77.90
	ArcCSE	72.08	84.27	76.25	82.32	79.54	79.92	72.39	78.11
	ESimCSE	**73.40**	83.27	77.25	82.66	78.81	80.17	72.30	78.27
	SageRep	70.93	**85.37**	**77.59**	82.35	**80.48**	**81.34**	**73.78**	**78.83**
RoBERTa_{base}	SimCSE	70.16	81.77	73.24	81.36	80.65	80.22	68.56	76.57
	SSCL	67.16	81.18	72.84	81.73	**81.37**	80.74	71.08	76.59
	DCLR	70.01	83.08	75.09	**83.66**	81.06	**81.86**	70.33	77.87
	ESimCSE	69.90	82.50	74.68	83.19	80.30	80.99	70.54	77.44
	SageRep	**70.84**	**83.22**	**75.47**	82.63	80.81	80.62	**71.83**	**77.92**

ing two layers ($c = 2$) yields the best performance overall, effectively balancing semantic diversity and avoiding redundancy.

Impact of Inter-layer Contrastive Regularization. As illustrated in Fig. 3, we analyze the cosine similarity of sentence representations between adjacent layers under three experimental setups: SimCSE (baseline), dynamic self-knowledge distillation without inter-layer contrastive regularization (denoted as DSKD), and our complete SageRep framework (DSKD integrated with ICR). Specifically, we compute these similarity values using 1,000 sentences randomly sampled from the STS-B test set. The results reveal that applying DSKD alone increases the representational similarity between adjacent layers compared to SimCSE, suggesting effective knowledge transfer but also causing undesired representation over-smoothing. To alleviate this issue, SageRep integrates the proposed inter-layer contrastive regularization (ICR), dynamically selecting highly similar adjacent-layer representations as negative pairs. As demonstrated by the reduced inter-layer similarities, ICR successfully preserves semantic diversity, mitigates over-smoothing, and enhances the discriminative capability and generalization performance of the resulting sentence embeddings.

Comparison with Representative Methods. Table 3 presents a comprehensive comparison of SageRep against several unsupervised sentence representation methods. From these results, we observe that SageRep achieves the highest average Spearman's correlation coefficient across all tested encoders, specifically 78.83 with BERT$_{base}$ and 77.92 with RoBERTa$_{base}$. Moreover, SageRep consistently outperforms the comparison methods on most individual datasets. Notably, substantial improvements are observed with BERT$_{base}$ on STS14 (up to 4.32%) and STS-B (up to 5.84%) datasets. Similar performance gains are also obtained with RoBERTa$_{base}$ models, demonstrating the general effectiveness and robustness of our proposed dynamic self-knowledge distillation approach for unsupervised sentence representation tasks.

5   Conclusion

In this paper, we proposed **SageRep**, a dynamic self-knowledge distillation framework tailored for unsupervised sentence representation learning. Unlike conventional static distillation approaches, **SageRep** dynamically selects optimal teacher layers within the pre-trained language model to adaptively guide shallower layers based on representational similarity. Furthermore, to address the representation over-smoothing problem inherent in self-knowledge distillation, we introduced an inter-layer contrastive regularization strategy (ICR), explicitly preserving semantic distinctiveness across adjacent layers. Comprehensive experimental results on multiple Semantic Textual Similarity benchmarks demonstrated that our method consistently outperforms previous unsupervised sentence embedding methods, highlighting the effectiveness and robustness of dynamic self-knowledge distillation in enhancing sentence representation quality.

Acknowledgments. This research is supported by the NSFC project "the Construction of the Knowledge Graph for the History of Chinese Confucianism" (Grant No. 72010107003).

References

1. Agirre, E., et al.: Semeval-2015 task 2: semantic textual similarity, English, Spanish and pilot on interpretability. In: Proceedings of the 9th International Workshop on Semantic Evaluation, SemEval@NAACL-HLT 2015, Denver, Colorado, USA, 4-5 June 2015, pp. 252–263. The Association for Computer Linguistics (2015). https:// doi.org/10.18653/V1/S15-2045
2. Agirre, E., et al.: Semeval-2014 task 10: multilingual semantic textual similarity. In: Proceedings of the 8th International Workshop on Semantic Evaluation, SemEval@COLING 2014, Dublin, Ireland, 23-24 August 2014, pp. 81–91. The Association for Computer Linguistics (2014). https://doi.org/10.3115/V1/S14-2010,

3. Agirre, E., et al.: Semeval-2016 task 1: semantic textual similarity, monolingual and cross-lingual evaluation. In: Proceedings of the 10th International Workshop on Semantic Evaluation, SemEval@NAACL-HLT 2016, San Diego, CA, USA, 16-17 June 2016, pp. 497–511. The Association for Computer Linguistics (2016). https://doi.org/10.18653/V1/S16-1081

4. Agirre, E., Cer, D.M., Diab, M.T., Gonzalez-Agirre, A.: Semeval-2012 task 6: a pilot on semantic textual similarity. In: Proceedings of the 6th International Workshop on Semantic Evaluation, SemEval@NAACL-HLT 2012, Montréal, Canada, 7-8 June 2012, pp. 385–393. The Association for Computer Linguistics (2012). https://aclanthology.org/S12-1051/

5. Agirre, E., Cer, D.M., Diab, M.T., Gonzalez-Agirre, A., Guo, W.: *sem 2013 shared task: semantic textual similarity. In: Proceedings of the Second Joint Conference on Lexical and Computational Semantics, *SEM 2013, 13-14 June 2013, Atlanta, Georgia, USA, pp. 32–43. Association for Computational Linguistics (2013). https://aclanthology.org/S13-1004/

6. Cer, D.M., Diab, M.T., Agirre, E., Lopez-Gazpio, I., Specia, L.: Semeval-2017 task 1: semantic textual similarity - multilingual and cross-lingual focused evaluation. CoRR abs/1708.00055 (2017). http://arxiv.org/abs/1708.00055

7. Chen, N., et al.: Alleviating over-smoothing for unsupervised sentence representation. In: Proceedings of the 61st Annual Meeting of the Association for Computational Linguistics (Volume 1: Long Papers), ACL 2023, Toronto, Canada, 9-14 July 2023, pp. 3552–3566. Association for Computational Linguistics (2023). https://doi.org/10.18653/V1/2023.ACL-LONG.197

8. Cho, J.H., Hariharan, B.: On the efficacy of knowledge distillation. In: 2019 IEEE/CVF International Conference on Computer Vision, ICCV 2019, Seoul, Korea (South), October 27 - November 2, 2019, pp. 4793–4801. IEEE (2019). https://doi.org/10.1109/ICCV.2019.00489

9. Devlin, J., Chang, M., Lee, K., Toutanova, K.: BERT: pre-training of deep bidirectional transformers for language understanding. In: Proceedings of the 2019 Conference of the North American Chapter of the Association for Computational Linguistics: Human Language Technologies, NAACL-HLT 2019, Minneapolis, MN, USA, 2-7 June 2019, Volume 1 (Long and Short Papers), pp. 4171–4186. Association for Computational Linguistics (2019). https://doi.org/10.18653/V1/N19-1423

10. Gao, T., Yao, X., Chen, D.: SIMCSE: simple contrastive learning of sentence embeddings. In: Proceedings of the 2021 Conference on Empirical Methods in Natural Language Processing, EMNLP 2021, Virtual Event / Punta Cana, Dominican Republic, 7-11 November, 2021, pp. 6894–6910. Association for Computational Linguistics (2021). https://doi.org/10.18653/V1/2021.EMNLP-MAIN.552

11. Hinton, G.E., Vinyals, O., Dean, J.: Distilling the knowledge in a neural network. CoRR abs/1503.02531 (2015). http://arxiv.org/abs/1503.02531

12. Li, B., Zhou, H., He, J., Wang, M., Yang, Y., Li, L.: On the sentence embeddings from pre-trained language models. In: Proceedings of the 2020 Conference on Empirical Methods in Natural Language Processing, EMNLP 2020, Online, 16-20 November 2020, pp. 9119–9130. Association for Computational Linguistics (2020). https://doi.org/10.18653/V1/2020.EMNLP-MAIN.733

13. Li, Z., Li, X., Yang, L., Song, R., Yang, J., Pan, Z.: Dual teachers for self-knowledge distillation. Pattern Recognit. **151**, 110422 (2024). https://doi.org/10.1016/J.PATCOG.2024.110422

14. Limkonchotiwat, P., Ponwitayarat, W., Lowphansirikul, L., Udomcharoenchaikit, C., Chuangsuwanich, E., Nutanong, S.: An efficient self-supervised cross-view training for sentence embedding. Trans. Assoc. Comput. Linguistics **11**, 1572–1587 (2023). https://doi.org/10.1162/TACL_0_620

15. Liu, Y., et al.: RoBERTa: a robustly optimized BERT pretraining approach. CoRR abs/1907.11692 (2019). http://arxiv.org/abs/1907.11692

16. Marelli, M., Menini, S., Baroni, M., Bentivogli, L., Bernardi, R., Zamparelli, R.: A SICK cure for the evaluation of compositional distributional semantic models. In: Proceedings of the Ninth International Conference on Language Resources and Evaluation, LREC 2014, Reykjavik, Iceland, 26-31 May 2014, pp. 216–223. European Language Resources Association (ELRA) (2014), http://www.lrec-conf.org/proceedings/lrec2014/summaries/363.html

17. Mirzadeh, S., Farajtabar, M., Li, A., Levine, N., Matsukawa, A., Ghasemzadeh, H.: Improved knowledge distillation via teacher assistant. In: The Thirty-Fourth AAAI Conference on Artificial Intelligence, AAAI 2020, The Thirty-Second Innovative Applications of Artificial Intelligence Conference, IAAI 2020, The Tenth AAAI Symposium on Educational Advances in Artificial Intelligence, EAAI 2020, New York, NY, USA, 7-12 February 2020, pp. 5191–5198. AAAI Press (2020). https://doi.org/10.1609/AAAI.V34I04.5963

18. Nishikawa, S., Ri, R., Yamada, I., Tsuruoka, Y., Echizen, I.: EASE: entity-aware contrastive learning of sentence embedding. In: Proceedings of the 2022 Conference of the North American Chapter of the Association for Computational Linguistics: Human Language Technologies, NAACL 2022, Seattle, WA, United States, 10-15 July 2022, pp. 3870–3885. Association for Computational Linguistics (2022). https://doi.org/10.18653/V1/2022.NAACL-MAIN.284

19. Wu, X., Gao, C., Wang, J., Zang, L., Wang, Z., Hu, S.: Disco: effective knowledge distillation for contrastive learning of sentence embeddings. CoRR abs/2112.05638 (2021). https://arxiv.org/abs/2112.05638

20. Wu, X., Gao, C., Zang, L., Han, J., Wang, Z., Hu, S.: Esimcse: enhanced sample building method for contrastive learning of unsupervised sentence embedding. In: Proceedings of the 29th International Conference on Computational Linguistics, COLING 2022, Gyeongju, Republic of Korea, 12-17 October 2022, pp. 3898–3907. International Committee on Computational Linguistics (2022). https://aclanthology.org/2022.coling-1.342

21. Xiong, L., et al.: Approximate nearest neighbor negative contrastive learning for dense text retrieval. In: 9th International Conference on Learning Representations, ICLR 2021, Virtual Event, Austria, 3-7 May 2021. OpenReview.net (2021). https://openreview.net/forum?id=zeFrfgyZln

22. Xu, Y., Qiu, X., Zhou, L., Huang, X.: Improving BERT fine-tuning via self-ensemble and self-distillation. J. Comput. Sci. Technol. **38**(4), 853–866 (2023). https://doi.org/10.1007/S11390-021-1119-0

23. Yan, Y., Li, R., Wang, S., Zhang, F., Wu, W., Xu, W.: Consert: a contrastive framework for self-supervised sentence representation transfer. In: Proceedings of the 59th Annual Meeting of the Association for Computational Linguistics and the 11th International Joint Conference on Natural Language Processing, ACL/IJCNLP 2021, (Volume 1: Long Papers), Virtual Event, August 1-6, 2021, pp. 5065–5075. Association for Computational Linguistics (2021). https://doi.org/10.18653/V1/2021.ACL-LONG.393

24. Yun, S., Park, J., Lee, K., Shin, J.: Regularizing class-wise predictions via self-knowledge distillation. In: 2020 IEEE/CVF Conference on Computer Vision and Pattern Recognition, CVPR 2020, Seattle, WA, USA, 13-19 June 2020, pp. 13873–13882. Computer Vision Foundation / IEEE (2020). https://doi.org/10.1109/CVPR42600.2020.01389, https://openaccess.thecvf.com/content_CVPR_2020/html/Yun_Regularizing_Class-Wise_Predictions_via_Self-Knowledge_Distillation_CVPR_2020_paper.html
25. Zhang, L., Song, J., Gao, A., Chen, J., Bao, C., Ma, K.: Be your own teacher: improve the performance of convolutional neural networks via self distillation. In: 2019 IEEE/CVF International Conference on Computer Vision, ICCV 2019, Seoul, Korea (South), October 27 - November 2, 2019, pp. 3712–3721. IEEE (2019). https://doi.org/10.1109/ICCV.2019.00381
26. Zhang, Y., Zhu, H., Wang, Y., Xu, N., Li, X., Zhao, B.: A contrastive framework for learning sentence representations from pairwise and triple-wise perspective in angular space. In: Proceedings of the 60th Annual Meeting of the Association for Computational Linguistics (Volume 1: Long Papers), ACL 2022, Dublin, Ireland, 22-27 May 2022, pp. 4892–4903. Association for Computational Linguistics (2022). https://doi.org/10.18653/V1/2022.ACL-LONG.336
27. Zhou, K., Zhang, B., Zhao, W.X., Wen, J.: Debiased contrastive learning of unsupervised sentence representations. In: Proceedings of the 60th Annual Meeting of the Association for Computational Linguistics (Volume 1: Long Papers), ACL 2022, Dublin, Ireland, 22-27 May 2022, pp. 6120–6130. Association for Computational Linguistics (2022). https://doi.org/10.18653/V1/2022.ACL-LONG.423

Improving Cross-Document Event Coreference Resolution with Word Sense Disambiguation and Large Language Models

Linfan Liu, Xinyu Chen, Peifeng Li[(✉)], and Qiaoming Zhu

School of Computer Science and Technology, Soochow University, Suzhou, China
{lfliu0908,xychennlper}@stu.suda.edu.cn, {pfli,qmzhu}@suda.edu.cn

Abstract. Cross-document event coreference resolution aims to cluster events from multiple documents that refer to the same real-world events. Previous researchers have considered how to provide as much supplementary information as possible to the event representation from other aspects (such as event argument information) to help the model make correct judgments. However, they have only considered naive event mention features for the event itself, ignoring the key information features contained in the event itself in some cases. These important features need to be explicitly mined and utilized. In order to obtain a representation focused on the core features of the event, we first introduce word sense disambiguation to explicitly extract the information contained in the event. In order to enhance the event representation, we then use the Large Language Models (LLMs) to generate event explanations for comprehensive analysis and understanding. Additionally, we apply Rhetorical Structure Theory (RST) to parse the document and use GAT to derive the global event representation. Finally, the aforementioned information is fed into a multi-layer perceptron (MLP) to capture the similarities between event mention pairs for resolving coreferent events. The experimental results on both the WEC-Eng and FCC datasets demonstrate that our proposed method outperforms the state-of-the-art baselines.

Keywords: Event coreference resolution · Word sense disambiguation · Large language models

1 Introduction

Event Coreference Resolution (ECR) aims to group same event mentions into a single cluster. After clustering, events within the same cluster should share similar semantic content and complement each other with event-related details, such as participants, time, and location. This task has garnered widespread attention as it benefits many natural language processing (NLP) applications, including information extraction [1], document summarization [2], and question answering [3]. ECR is typically divided into within-document coreference resolution (WDECR) and cross-document coreference resolution (CDECR), depending on whether the events are from the same document. This paper focuses on the more challenging task, that is, the resolution of cross-document event coreference.

© The Author(s), under exclusive license to Springer Nature Singapore Pte Ltd. 2026

X.-L. Mao et al. (Eds.): NLPCC 2025, LNAI 16105, pp. 105–117, 2026.
https://doi.org/10.1007/978-981-95-3352-7_9

Events are typically represented by trigger words which indicate the occurrence of events and arguments (entities related to the events). To express events accurately and concisely, we often use trigger words to refer to events. The trigger words in S1 and S2 are "carrying" and "selling", respectively. Although these events are expressed differently, they have a coreferent relation due to the similarity in their participants. Both events describe the same specific event ontology, which is the sale of mobile phones.

*S1: T-Mobile has announced it will be **carrying** the BlackBerry Curve 8900 smartphone this February although it will not offer 3G data service.*

*S2: Research in Motion today announced that T-Mobile USA will start **selling** the new BlackBerry Curve 8900 smartphone to its customers.*

*S3: There are no dated reports of eruptions from Rakata since the **1883 catastrophe**, although tentative datings have been made from dating ash deposits left.*

*S4: To the right of the main entrance there is a model of the Sejm complex, above which there are found commemorative plaques: a commemorative plaque commemorating those killed in the **Tu-154 catastrophe** near Smolensk.*

The existing CDECR datasets have notable limitations, such as small scale and a narrow focus on events within the same topic, which constrains the scalability of related methods [4]. To address the issues mentioned above, Eirew et al. [5] proposed a larger dataset called WEC-Eng. It treats hyperlink text pointing to the same Wikipedia page as coreferent events. However, our analysis reveals that WEC-Eng differs from traditional CDECR datasets, such as FCC [6].

For instance, in S3, "1883 catastrophe" the event itself includes details such as time, providing an initial impression of the event. In contrast, "carrying" in S1 merely signals an action without conveying the full meaning of the event. Given these characteristics, we believe that the events in WEC-Eng contain more useful information for relationship judgments, which has been overlooked in previous work.

Word sense disambiguation (WSD) aims to identify the meanings of polysemous words in specific contexts, addressing the semantic ambiguity caused by word polysemy. In CDECR, event descriptions often have rich and diverse language expressions and implicitly contain rich information. Through WSD, the semantic relationship between words and contexts is better understood, enabling the model to capture the underlying semantic aspects of event descriptions more accurately. This understanding provides a solid foundation for identifying the core type of events. For example, for the event "1883 catastrophe" in S3, the result obtained by WSD is "a sudden violent change in the earth's surface", highlighting that the event is related to natural disasters. Similarly, for the event "Tu-154 catastrophe" in S4, WSD identifies it as "an event resulting in great loss and misfortune", clearly distinguishing it from the event in S3.

Although WSD plays a significant role in CDECR tasks and provides reliable support for typing judgments by extracting the core features of events, its limitations are evident. On the one hand, WSD primarily focuses on the core semantics of events, often neglecting fine-grained details. On the other hand,

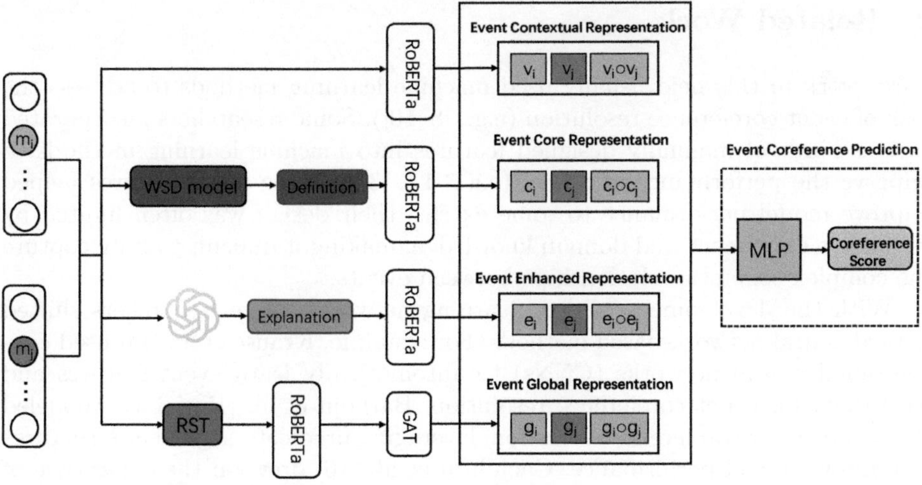

Fig. 1. The overall framework of our model.

current WSD techniques typically operate within a fixed context window, which limits their ability to model the interaction between events and the broader context. To address these shortcomings, we introduce the Large Language Models (LLMs) to supplement the fine-grained information by interpreting events based on context. LLMs can generate detailed content that includes event attributes such as time, location, participants, background, etc. For the event in S4, WSD struggles to pinpoint the exact time of the event, as well as the causes and consequences. However, by leveraging LLMs to explain the event, we learn that it occurred in 2010 and was a catastrophic event involving an airplane crash. This contrasts significantly with the event described in S3.

Besides, discourse information provides a global perspective on events at the document level. Applying Rhetorical Structure Theory (RST) [7] to analyze the document, we can grasp the logic of the document from a holistic perspective.

The use of discourse information can help the model more comprehensively distinguish the similarities and differences between events when making coreference predictions, thereby making accurate relationship judgments.

To the end, in this paper we propose a novel model that leverages word sense disambiguation to capture the core features of events and introduces LLMs to enhance their fine-grained representation. At the same time, we combine RST to enhance the representation of events at the global level for cross-document event coreference resolution. Figure 1 illustrates the overall structure of our model. We evaluate our model on the WEC-Eng and FCC datasets, and the experimental results show that our model outperforms several state-of-the-art baselines.

2   Related Work

Early work in this field usually used machine learning methods to address the task of event coreference resolution (e.g., [8–10]). Some researchers incorporated various kinds of manually designed features into machine learning methods to improve the performance of model (e.g., [11–13]). While these features helped improve model performance to some extent, their design was often limited by subjective experience and domain knowledge, making it difficult to fully capture the complex semantic relationships between events.

With the development of deep learning networks, more researchers shifted toward neural network-based methods. For example, Krause et al. [14] used convolutional neural networks (CNNs) to automatically learn event features and used them for event coreference resolution. Barhom et al. [15] jointly modeled event and entity coreference resolution, leveraging predicate-argument structures to improve model performance. Caciularu et al. [16] drew on the experience of pre-training language models and used documents related to CDECR to pre-train a cross-document language model to better complete the cross-document coreference resolution task. Yu et al. [17] focused on enhancing event representation by incorporating argument information in a structured way. Held et al. [18] utilized discourse coherence theories to establish correspondences between event sets and embedding spaces, using local discourse features to solve cross-document coreference resolution. Ahmed et al. [19] significantly improved the effect of the model by using heuristic methods to screen data. More recently, Gao et al. [20] expanded the context scope and employed discourse rhetorical structures to capture global semantic information. Min et al. [21] proposed a collaborative approach that combines the capabilities of LLMs with task-specific small language models to solve CDECR.

3   Methodology

Figure 1 illustrates the overall architecture of our proposed method, comprising five main components. First, we generate event contextual representation using RoBERTa [22] to capture the semantic information from the surrounding text of each event mention. Subsequently, we extract event core representation via word sense disambiguation, focusing on typed information to highlight the event's most relevant features while minimizing noise. Simultaneously, we obtain event enhanced representation by leveraging LLMs to interpret the event at a fine-grained level, enriching its understanding with supplementary knowledge. In terms of discourse information, we use RST to parse the document and use the Graph Attention Networks (GAT) [23] to further fuse the obtained information to obtain a global representation of the event.

Finally, the event coreference prediction integrates these four representations to determine whether two event mentions refer to the same event. We will introduce each part in detail below.

3.1   Event Contextual Representation

To obtain the contextual representation for each event mention m_i, we first identify the document D_k where it appears. Following this, we employ RoBERTa to encode the document context. Given the inherent limitations of the model's encoding length, we adopt a sliding window approach similar to Eirew et al. [5]. Specifically, using the position of the mention as a reference, we construct a context window by extracting T tokens from both the left and right of the mention's location (consistent with the original setup, T=250). By applying RoBERTa to this context window, we derive the representation v_i of the mention m_i, which serves as the basis for subsequent judgments.

3.2   Event Core Representation

We use a model based on BERT [24] and fine-tuned on sequence-pair ranking task proposed by Yap et al. [25] to achieve this goal. Specifically, for event mention m_i, we first locate the sentence S in the document where it is located, and then add special tags [TGT] around the mention to mark the location of the event. The final input for word sense disambiguation is as follows:

$$S' = \{w_1, \ldots, [TGT], w_i, \ldots, w_j, [TGT], \ldots, w_{|S|}\} \tag{1}$$

where $|S|$ represents the length of the sentence, and $\{w_i, \ldots, w_j\}$ represents the text contained in the mention, which may consist of one word or multiple words.

It is particularly important to note that through specific experiments and research on methods related to word sense disambiguation, we find that the model usually cannot give a normal interpretation for the case where the event mention contains multiple words. Therefore, for these abnormal cases, we use the head lemma of the event mention as a substitute for the event text to implement the word sense disambiguation method. The WSD model selects the most suitable result from WordNet that aligns with the contextual usage of event mention m_i.

After obtaining the disambiguation results for event mentions, we concatenate the mentions with their results using a special segment separator token [SEP]. This concatenation enables the model to capture the deep core features of events while establishing semantic connections between events and their disambiguation results. Then we use the RoBERTa model to encode the concatenated input and extract the representation of the event mention m_i from the result as c_i.

3.3   Event Enhanced Representation

In most cases, the expression of events is complex and diverse, requiring understanding at multiple levels. To address this, we employ LLMs to generate event explanations. Specifically, inspired by Min et al. [21], we also guide LLMs to elaborate rather than summarize event mentions. Our goal is to encourage LLMs to

Table 1. The prompt used for generating explanations with LLMs. <m> and </m> are special tokens used to identify events. The text to be filled is represented as [text].

The event "<m> [event] </m>" appears in the following document: "[document]". Please explain this event in terms of key elements such as actions, actors, time, and location, and provide a concise explanation that makes connections to related information where necessary. Your response should follow this format: "Elaboration: <m> [event] </m> refers to <placeholder>".

---

provide fine-grained information related to the event to be explained based on the context, such as the time, place, and involved actors. Our promt is shown in Table 1. This design encourages LLMs to discover key event information while minimizing unnecessary noise in the explanation. Furthermore, the elaboration-focused guidance enriches the generated event explanations, offering a multi-dimensional semantic perspective that supplements the initial word sense disambiguation. Lastly, by placing explicit constraints on the output format, we ensure consistency in explanation generation, providing standardized and structured information input for subsequent processing.

For each input event mention m_i, we use the method introduced in this section to obtain its explanation, and then use RoBERTa to encode, and only extract the hidden layer representation e_i of the event wrapped by <m> and </m> for the final judgment.

3.4 Event Global Representation

We utilize RST and GAT to enable the model to understand events from a global perspective. Inspired by Gao et al. [20], we adopt the method proposed by Zhang et al. [26] to perform structured parsing of documents and construct RST trees, where each node represents the smallest division unit (EDU) parsed by RST. To further integrate global information, we follow the approach of Gao et al. [20] to convert the RST tree into a graph and use GAT to encode the entire graph, capturing both semantic and rhetorical relationships within the text. Specifically, for each input event mention m_i, we treat the EDU containing the event as a substitute and use the encoding representation of the EDU updated by GAT as the global representation g_i of the event.

3.5 Event Coreference Prediction

For the input event mention pair (m_i, m_j), we have obtained the corresponding representations across four aspects using the aforementioned method. Further, we fuse the obtained features and send them to the multi-layer perceptron (MLP), and finally obtain the coreference score through the sigmoid activation function. The process is as follows:

$$V_{ij} = \{v_i, v_j, v_i \circ v_j\}$$
$$C_{ij} = \{c_i, c_j, c_i \circ c_j\}$$
$$E_{ij} = \{e_i, e_j, e_i \circ e_j\} \tag{2}$$
$$G_{ij} = \{g_i, g_j, g_i \circ g_j\}$$

$$Score = Sigmoid(MLP(V_{ij}, C_{ij}, E_{ij}, G_{ij})) \tag{3}$$

where $\circ$ indicates the element-wise multiplication.

4 Experimentation

In this section, We first introduce the two datasets used in the experiments, the hyperparameter settings related to the experiment, the metrics used to evaluate the results and the baselines. Then we conduct experiments on both WEC-Eng and FCC datasets, followed by a detailed analysis of the results.

4.1 Datasets

We use two datasets WEC-Eng and FCC to train and test our model. WEC-Eng is a large-scale cross-document event coreference resolution dataset sourced from Wikipedia. FCC is a dataset focused on sports news articles about football tournaments and contains a significant number of cross-subtopic event coreference links. The data details are presented in Table 2. For the WEC-Eng dataset, we follow the data split by Eirew et al. [5]. We use the data split by Bugert et al. [6] for FCC.

Table 2. WEC-Eng and FCC statistics. T=topics, D=documents, EM=event mentions, EC=event clusters, NC=non-singleton clusters. Event clusters include singletons.

	WEC-Eng			FCC		
	Train	Dev	Test	Train	Dev	Test
T	-	-	-	3	1	1
D	34132	1194	1803	207	117	127
EM	40529	1250	1893	1604	680	1074
EC	7042	233	322	259	111	167
NC	6210	216	306	151	60	89

4.2 Hyperparameter Settings

We used the pre-trained RoBERTa$_{LARGE}$ to initialize the token embedding vector, and obtained the word vector with 1024 dimensions. The Adam optimizer was employed with a learning rate of 2e-5, and the cross-entropy loss function was used. The batch size was set to 128. The experiment was based on a single RTX 3090 GPU over 10 iterations, with the best model selected based on performance on the validation set for inference. We utilized an API that involved invoking the GPT-3.5-turbo interface.

4.3   Metrics

Similar to previous work, after performing agglomerative clustering to obtain results, we use MUC [27], B^3 [28] and CEAF$_e$ [29] to evaluate the performance of the model and report the CoNLL score, which is the average of the three metrics. Among the above metrics, MUC mainly focuses on the construction of coreferent chains in the results, but ignores the evaluation of non-coreferent relationships. B^3 makes a more fair evaluation of event nodes by adjusting the evaluation object. CEAF$_e$ is similar to B^3 in implementation, but further evaluates the results from an entity perspective. The use of the above metrics can evaluate the results from different perspectives, thereby objectively and comprehensively measuring the effectiveness of the method proposed.

4.4   Baselines

To compare the effectiveness of our proposed method, we use the following baselines for comparison:

- Eirew2021 [5] utilize contextualized representations derived from the boundary tokens of event mention spans (first and last tokens). Additionally, they incorporate a weighted sum of token embeddings within the event mention.
- Gao2024 [20] integrate the discourse information and lexical chains, and use GAT to further learn the representation of events.
- Bugert2021 [6] develop a robust feature-based system to achieve unified evaluation on multiple datasets.
- Held2021 [18] use local mention features to solve cross-document coreference resolution at a fine-grained level.
- Min2024 [21] propose a collaborative approach that combines the capabilities of LLMs with task-specific small language models to solve CDECR.

4.5   Experimental Results

Table 3 shows the results of our method and other compared methods on WEC-Eng and FCC datasets. From Table 3, we can know that our proposed method achieves the best performance in both datasets, improving CoNLL by 1.4. These results demonstrate the effectiveness of our proposed method.

Eirew2021 uses RoBERTa to encode event mentions, but only implements simple contextualized representations. Our model improves the CoNLL by 4.1, proving the importance of focusing on the core feature representation of the event and supplementing the fine-grained information of the event.

Compared to Gao2024, our method improves the CoNLL score by 1.4. Gao2024 employs a joint graph structure combining RST and lexical chains, using GAT to extract discourse-level cross-document features for coreference resolution. However, it overlooks the extraction of implicit information within the event and the integration of fine-grained details. In contrast, our method enriches event representations from multiple perspectives, leading to improved performance.

Table 3. Performance comparison of different methods on the WEC-Eng and FCC datasets.

Method	MUC			B^3			$CEAF_e$			CoNLL
	R	P	F1	R	P	F1	R	P	F1	F1
WEC-Eng										
Eirew2021 [5]	78.0	83.6	80.7	66.1	55.3	60.2	53.4	40.3	45.9	62.3
Gao2024 [20]	78.2	85.8	81.8	69.6	62.4	65.8	58.9	39.5	47.3	65.0
Ours	**80.3**	**86.3**	**83.2**	**70.5**	**63.6**	**66.9**	**59.6**	**41.7**	**49.1**	**66.4**
FCC										
Bugert2021 [6]	82.7	78.3	80.4	70.8	38.3	49.2	28.2	40.4	33.2	54.3
Held2021 [18]	86.4	75.7	80.7	61.6	65.4	63.5	39.1	**65.3**	48.9	64.4
Min2024 [21]	85.3	90.6	87.8	74.5	82.5	78.3	80.9	61.5	69.8	78.7
Ours	**86.7**	**91.5**	**89.0**	**76.3**	**83.7**	**79.8**	**81.7**	63.4	**71.4**	**80.1**

For the FCC dataset, our method also achieves the state-of-the-art results. While Min2024 emphasizes leveraging LLMs to significantly enhance task performance, our method goes further by extracting and utilizing the core feature information inherent to the event. By integrating this with global document-level information, we construct a more comprehensive understanding of the event, which in turn boosts the model's performance.

5   Analysis

In this section, we conduct specific analyses on some samples and provide ablation experiments.

5.1   Case Study

In this subsection, we give an example to analyze the effectiveness of our method.

Document1: It was one of the deadliest U.S. wildfires since the **1991 East Bay Hills fire***, which killed 25 people, and the deadliest wildland fire for U.S. firefighters since the 1933 Griffith Park Fire, which killed 29 impromptu civilian firefighters.*

Document2: The 1991 **Oakland Hills firestorm***, which destroyed almost 3,000 homes and killed 25 people, was partly fueled by large numbers of eucalypts close to the houses.*

For the two events in the example, "fire" in "1991 East Bay Hills fire" refers to a burning event in a general sense, while "firestorm" in "Oakland Hills firestorm" refers to an intense, large scale wildfire. Relying solely on word sense disambiguation may capture the fundamental features of an event, but it misses the detailed background, making it difficult to determine if the events are coreferent. The explanations generated by LLMs provide details of the event, such as

Table 4. Ablation experiment results.

Method	MUC			B^3			$CEAF_e$			CoNLL
	R	P	F1	R	P	F1	R	P	F1	F1
WEC-Eng										
Ours	**80.3**	**86.3**	**83.2**	**70.5**	**63.6**	**66.9**	**59.6**	**41.7**	**49.1**	**66.4**
-core representation	78.5	84.6	81.4	68.4	60.5	64.2	55.8	40.9	47.2	64.3
-enhanced representation	78.2	83.8	80.9	66.8	58.1	62.1	53.8	40.8	46.4	63.1
FCC										
Ours	**86.7**	**91.5**	**89.0**	**76.3**	**83.7**	**79.8**	**81.7**	**63.4**	**71.4**	**80.1**
-core representation	84.8	90.3	87.5	74.7	81.3	77.9	80.2	62.0	69.9	78.4
-enhanced representation	85.0	89.3	87.1	73.4	80.7	76.9	79.4	60.7	68.8	77.6

the number of deaths, but lack a clear identification of the event types. However, when the two parts are used in combination, they complement each other's strengths, leading to right coreferent prediction.

5.2   Ablation Analysis

In order to further analyze the contribution of our proposed event core representation and event enhanced representation to CDECR, we conducted ablation experiments. The specific results are in Table 4. It can be seen from the results of ablation experiments that whether the elimination of the event core representation obtained through word sense disambiguation or the event enhanced representation obtained through LLMs leads to a decrease in model performance. This demonstrates the effectiveness of our proposed method. By focusing on the core semantic features of event mentions, word sense disambiguation can explicitly mine the important typed information implicit in them. The explanation generated by LLMs describes the event from a more fine-grained level, highlighting the details of the event. The combination of these two components complements one another, enabling the model to build a comprehensive understanding of the event.

In addition, removing event enhanced representation has a relatively more significant impact on performance. This shows that it is not enough to rely solely on the core semantics of events in complex cross-document scenarios, and event-related fine-grained information is needed to improve event representation.

6   Conclusion

In this paper, we propose a new method that combines word sense disambiguation and explanation information generated by LLMs. Additionally, discourse-level information is incorporated to enhance the effectiveness of the method. The use of word sense disambiguation enables the model to explicitly extract the core semantic information implicit in the event text, enhancing the accuracy and consistency of event representation. At the same time, the explanation information generated by LLMs injects diverse and deep semantic features into the event description by supplementing external knowledge and exploring fine-grained information within the context. Experiments on WEC-Eng and FCC demonstrate the effectiveness of integrating various types of information. Our future work will focus on how to use more levels of information to solve the cross-document event coreference resolution task.

Acknowledgments. The authors would like to thank the three anonymous reviewers for their comments on this paper. This research was supported by the National Natural Science Foundation of China (Nos. 62276177 and 62376181), and Project Funded by the Priority Academic Program Development of Jiangsu Higher Education Institutions.

References

1. Liu, S., Chen, Y., Liu, K., Zhao, J.: Exploiting argument information to improve event detection via supervised attention mechanisms. In: Proceedings of the 55th Annual Meeting of the Association for Computational Linguistics (Volume 1: Long Papers) (2017). http://dx.doi.org/10.18653/v1/p17-1164
2. Li, W., Xiao, X., Liu, J., Wu, H., Wang, H., Du, J.: Leveraging graph to improve abstractive multi-document summarization. arXiv preprint arXiv:2005.10043 (2020)
3. Weissenborn, D., Wiese, G., Seiffe, L.: Making neural QA as simple as possible but not simpler. Cornell University - arXiv, Cornell University - arXiv (2017)
4. Bugert, M., Reimers, N., Barhom, S., Dagan, I., Gurevych, I.: Breaking the subtopic barrier in cross-document event coreference resolution. In: Text2story@ecir, pp. 23–29 (2020)
5. Eirew, A., Cattan, A., Dagan, I.: WEC: deriving a large-scale cross-document event coreference dataset from Wikipedia. Cornell University - arXiv, Cornell University - arXiv (2021)
6. Bugert, M., Reimers, N., Gurevych, I.: Generalizing cross-document event coreference resolution across multiple corpora. Comput. Linguist. **47**(3), 575–614 (2021)
7. Mann, W.C.: Rhetorical structure theory: a theory of text organization. Information Sciences Institute (1987)
8. Chen, Z., Ji, H.: Graph-based event coreference resolution. In: Proceedings of the 2009 Workshop on Graph-based Methods for Natural Language Processing - TextGraphs-4 (2009). http://dx.doi.org/10.3115/1708124.1708135
9. Bejan, C., Harabagiu, S.: Unsupervised event coreference resolution with rich linguistic features. Meeting of the Association for Computational Linguistics, Meeting of the Association for Computational Linguistics (2010)
10. Liu, Z., Araki, J., Hovy, E.H., Mitamura, T.: Supervised within-document event coreference using information propagation. In: LREC, pp. 4539–4544 (2014)
11. Nicolae, C., Nicolae, G.: Bestcut. In: Proceedings of the 2006 Conference on Empirical Methods in Natural Language Processing - EMNLP G 06, p. 275 (2006). https://doi.org/10.3115/1610075.1610115

12. Sangeetha, S.: Event coreference resolution using mincut based graph clustering. Comput. Sci. Inf. Technol. (CS & IT), 253–260 (2012). https://doi.org/10.5121/csit.2012.2422
13. Liu, Z., Mitamura, T., Hovy, E.: Graph based decoding for event sequencing and coreference resolution. In: International Conference on Computational Linguistics, International Conference on Computational Linguistics (2018)
14. Krause, S., Xu, F., Uszkoreit, H., Weissenborn, D.: Event linking with sentential features from convolutional neural networks. In: Proceedings of The 20th SIGNLL Conference on Computational Natural Language Learning, pp. 239–249 (2016). https://doi.org/10.18653/v1/k16-1024
15. Barhom, S., Shwartz, V., Eirew, A., Bugert, M., Reimers, N., Dagan, I.: Revisiting joint modeling of cross-document entity and event coreference resolution. In: Proceedings of the 57th Annual Meeting of the Association for Computational Linguistics (2019). https://doi.org/10.18653/v1/p19-1409
16. Caciularu, A., Cohan, A., Beltagy, I., Peters, M.E., Cattan, A., Dagan, I.: CDLM: cross-document language modeling. arXiv preprint arXiv:2101.00406 (2021)
17. Yu, X., Yin, W., Roth, D.: Pairwise representation learning for event coreference. arXiv preprint arXiv:2010.12808 (2020)
18. Held, W., Iter, D., Jurafsky, D.: Focus on what matters: applying discourse coherence theory to cross document coreference. arXiv preprint arXiv:2110.05362 (2021)
19. Ahmed, S.R., Nath, A., Martin, J.H., Krishnaswamy, N.: $2 * n$ is better than n^2: decomposing event coreference resolution into two tractable problems. arXiv preprint arXiv:2305.05672 (2023)
20. Gao, Q., Li, B., Meng, Z., Li, Y., Zhou, J., Li, F., Teng, C., Ji, D.: Enhancing cross-document event coreference resolution by discourse structure and semantic information. In: Proceedings of the 2024 Joint International Conference on Computational Linguistics, Language Resources and Evaluation (LREC-COLING 2024), pp. 5907–5921 (2024)
21. Min, Q., Guo, Q., Hu, X., Huang, S., Zhang, Z., Zhang, Y.: Synergetic event understanding: a collaborative approach to cross-document event coreference resolution with large language models. arXiv preprint arXiv:2406.02148 (2024)
22. Liu, Z., Lin, W., Shi, Y., Zhao, J.: A robustly optimized BERT pre-training approach with post-training. In: China National Conference on Chinese Computational Linguistics, pp. 471–484. Springer (2021)
23. Veličković, P., Cucurull, G., Casanova, A., Romero, A., Lio, P., Bengio, Y.: Graph attention networks. arXiv preprint arXiv:1710.10903 (2017)
24. Devlin, J., Chang, M.W., Lee, K., Toutanova, K.: BERT: pre-training of deep bidirectional transformers for language understanding. In: Proceedings of the 2019 Conference of the North (2019). http://dx.doi.org/10.18653/v1/n19-1423
25. Yap, B., Koh, A., Chng, E.: Adapting BERT for word sense disambiguation with gloss selection objective and example sentences. Cornell University - arXiv, Cornell University - arXiv (2020)
26. Zhang, L., Xing, Y., Kong, F., Li, P., Zhou, G.: A top-down neural architecture towards text-level parsing of discourse rhetorical structure. In: Proceedings of the 58th Annual Meeting of the Association for Computational Linguistics (2020). https://doi.org/10.18653/v1/2020.acl-main.569
27. Vilain, M., Burger, J., Aberdeen, J., Connolly, D., Hirschman, L.: A model-theoretic coreference scoring scheme. In: Proceedings of the 6th Conference on Message Understanding - MUC6 G 95 (1995). https://doi.org/10.3115/1072399.1072405

28. Bagga, A.: Evaluation of coreferences and coreference resolution systems. In: Language Resources and Evaluation, Language Resources and Evaluation (1998)
29. Luo, X.: On coreference resolution performance metrics. In: Proceedings of the conference on Human Language Technology and Empirical Methods in Natural Language Processing - HLT G 05 (2005). https://doi.org/10.3115/1220575.1220579

Summarization and Generation

FactoScalpel: Locating and Injecting Knowledge in Transformer to Enhance Factual Consistency in Abstractive Summarization

Xueyi Hao, Yiyang Li, and Lei Li[✉]

School of Artificial Intelligence, Beijing University of Posts and Telecommunications, Beijing, China
{haoxueyi,kenlee,leili}@bupt.edu.cn

Abstract. Recent studies have highlighted factual inconsistency as a critical challenge in abstractive summarization, with knowledge injection emerging as a key solution. However, how and where to inject knowledge into the model remain open research questions. Inspired by existing work on knowledge storage in Transformer, we propose a factual factors attribution algorithm for the Feed-Forward Networks (FFNs) in the decoder and analyze the distribution of factual neurons in BART, PEGASUS, and LLaMA. We also introduce FactoScalpel, a knowledge injection module that integrates a Knowledge Bank and a router-controlled mechanism into the FFNs. Based on attribution analysis, we inject FactoScalpel into the layers with the densest distribution of factual neurons. We use five factual consistency metrics to compare the performance of BART and PEGASUS with FactoScalpel against four fact-aware summarization models on the XSum dataset. The results demonstrate that FactoScalpel significantly improves factual consistency, achieving state-of-the-art performance in most experiments. Furthermore, we find that knowledge injection method substantially reduces extrinsic errors in the summaries, offering valuable insights for future research. The code of all experiments is available at https://github.com/haohiehie/FactoScalpel

Keywords: Factual consistency · Abstractive summarization · Knowledge injection

1 Introduction

Recently, the issue of factual inconsistencies has continued to be a focus for researchers. Current abstractive summarization tasks primarily rely on two types of models. Pretrained Language Models(PLMs) (e.g. BART and PEGASUS) excel in generation quality and efficiency, while Large Language Models(LLMs) (e.g. LLaMA) are gradually becoming the mainstream choice for summarization tasks because of their exceptional zero-shot and few-shot capabilities. However, factual consistency and hallucination issues remain common challenges.

Although LLMs demonstrate superior generation performance, LLMs require significant computational resources for training and inference, and their internal mechanisms are still not well understood. Furthermore, research on LLMs

© The Author(s), under exclusive license to Springer Nature Singapore Pte Ltd. 2026
X.-L. Mao et al. (Eds.): NLPCC 2025, LNAI 16105, pp. 121–132, 2026.
https://doi.org/10.1007/978-981-95-3352-7_10

in summarization tasks is primarily focused on exploring their performance and developing evaluation metrics tailored to LLMs, while most efforts to improve factual consistency continue to be based on PLMs. Instead of post-editing method, fact-aware summarization models improve the summarization model directly, are considered one of the key methods for enhancing factual consistency. As shown in Fig. 1, fact-aware summarization models are divided into four categories, metric-based [17], decoding-based [8], multitasking-based [1,16] and knowledge injection-based [18] methods. Explicitly injecting knowledge into the model is an important method to improve the factual consistency of summaries. However, some current works still have limitations. Currently, research on knowledge injection in LLMs mainly focus on knowledge-based question answering tasks [15], with limited efforts directed toward improving factual consistency in summarization tasks. In PLMs, most of recent studies focus on incorporating facts into the encoder embeddings or final outputs through a factual encoder. There is a lack of exploration into the internal workings of the decoder, which is a critical component for generating summaries. Furthermore, another pressing issue is determining the optimal location for knowledge injection within the model.

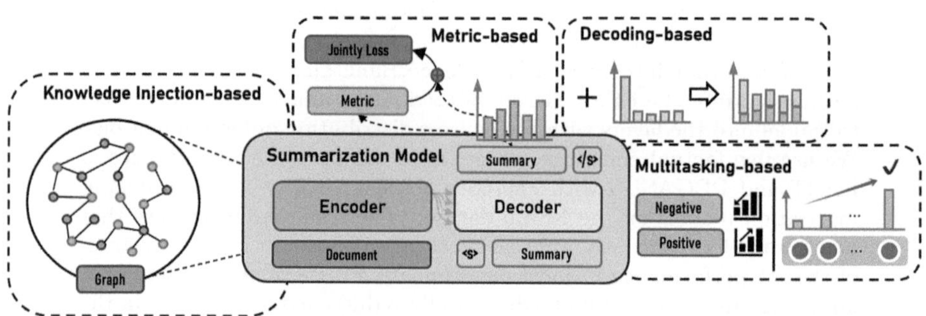

Fig. 1. Fact-aware summarization models based on different methods.

Our contributions are summarized as follows: (1) Inspired by related studies on knowledge storage of FFNs in Transformer, we first propose factual factors attribution algorithm. We analyze the distribution of factual neurons across different layers of FFNs in the decoders of BART, PEGASUS, and LLaMA models. (2) We propose a factual consistency module for summary generation, called FactoScalpel, which can be embedded into the decoder of Transformer architecture. This module mimics the Mixture of Experts(MoE) model by adding a Knowledge Bank and router-controlled mechanism to FFNs. (3) Based on the attribution analysis results, we reproduce FactoScalpel on the BART and PEGASUS models and inject it into the layers with the densest distribution of factual neurons. FactoScalpel based on BART consistently outperforms competitive models FASum, CLIFF, PINOCCHIO, CoFE and base models BART, PEGASUS in most of the factual evaluation metrics QAFactEval, SummaC, ClozE, DAE and FactCC on the XSum dataset, demonstrating the effectiveness and generalizability of FactoScalpel. (4) We analyze cases of knowledge injection via FactoScalpel and prompts in BART, PEGASUS, and LLaMA models, and find that knowledge injection significantly reduces extrinsic errors, providing valuable insights for future research.

2 Related Work

2.1 Knowledge Storage

Geva et al. [6] shows that FFNs in Transformer-based language models could be considered as key-value memories. Based on these insight, Dai et al. [2] introduces a novel knowledge attribution algorithm based on FFNs and improve the performance of PLMs by directly editing knowledge neurons. Additionally, Meng et al. [12] develop the "causal tracing" for identifying hidden states or activation that are decisive in a model's factual predictions. But they are all based on knowledge question answering or cloze tasks.

2.2 Knowledge Injection

Based on prior work, numerous studies improve models by enhancing the knowledge capability of FFNs. Dong et al. [4] first detects the fake facts stored in FFNs and introduce lightweight parameters to calibrate them. Dai et al. [3] designs a neural knowledge bank module and a knowledge injection strategy to introduce external knowledge for PLMs via pre-training. Tian et al. [15] proposes KG-Adapter layer and inject it into LLMs to encode knowledge graph and perform joint reasoning with LLMs. However, the purpose of these studies is to expand the knowledge base of models. In contrast, our work aims to ensure that the factual knowledge within summaries remains aligned with the content of the corresponding documents.

3 Factual Factors Attribution Algorithm

To explore the relationship between FFNs and factual factors[1] generated by summarization models, we extend the attribution algorithm proposed by Dai et al. [2]. The original knowledge attribution algorithm is primarily designed for BERT, an encoder-only model, and focuses on single-token attribution analysis. However, in abstractive summarization models, summaries are typically generated by the auto-regressive decoder, and factual factors often consist of multiple tokens rather than single tokens. To address this difference, we propose an extended factual factors attribution algorithm.

---

[1] Factual factors indicate as entities and noun phrases.

3.1 Factual Attribution Scores

For factual attribution, we define the document $\boldsymbol{X} = [x_1, x_2, \ldots, x_N]$, summary $\boldsymbol{Y} = [y_1, y_2, \ldots, y_M]$ and factual factors $\boldsymbol{f} = [f_1, f_2, \ldots, f_K]$, each of f_i can be represented by a paragraph of text in the summary $\boldsymbol{Y}$, that is, $f_j = [y_{t_j}, y_{t_j+1}, \ldots, y_{t_j+Q}]$, where t_j represents the actual starting coordinate of the factual factor f_j and Q represents the length of the factual factor. From this, we can construct the conditional probability of factual factor generation as follows:

$$P_{f_j}\left(w_i^{(l)}\right) = \prod_{t=t_j}^{t_j+Q} p\left(y_t \mid X, Y_{<t_j}, w_i^{(l)}\right) \tag{1}$$

where $w_i^{(l)}$ represents the i-th intermediate neuron in the FFN of the l-th layer.

Since the attribution of a single word has been changed to attribution of multiple words at this time, in addition to the two dimensions of layer number and neuron number, a time step dimension will be expanded. Therefore, for the i-th neuron in the l-th layer at the $(t_j + q)$-th time step, its attribution score will be given by the following formula:

$$\text{Attr}\left(w_{t_j+q,i}^{(l)}\right) = \bar{w}_{t_j+q,i}^{(l)} \int_{\gamma=0}^{1} \frac{\partial P_{f_j}\left(\gamma \bar{w}_{t_j+q,i}^{(l)}\right)}{\partial w_{t_j+q,i}^{(l)}} d\gamma \tag{2}$$

In Eq. (2), $w_{t_j+q,i}^{(l)}$ changes from 0 to the original value $\bar{w}_{t_j+q,i}^{(l)}$ computed by the PLM. If the neuron has a significant impact on the generation of the factual factor, the changes in its gradients will be substantial, resulting in a large integrated value.

To simplify the computation of continuous integration, we transform the fatual attribution formula into a summation of discrete values using the Riemann approximation method as in Eq. (3):

$$\text{Attr}\left(w_{t_j+q,i}^{(l)}\right) = \frac{\bar{w}_{t_j+q,i}^{(l)}}{N_{\text{bin}}} \sum_{k=1}^{N_{\text{bin}}} \frac{\partial P_{f_j}\left(\frac{k}{N_{\text{bin}}} \bar{w}_{t_j+q,i}^{(l)}\right)}{\partial w_{t_j+q,i}^{(l)}} \tag{3}$$

3.2 Identify Factual Neurons

We extract the target factual neurons based on the factual attribution scores. We specify a parameter α as filtering threshold, and only when the neuron attribution score is higher than the threshold, we consider this neuron is relevant to the word y_{t_j+q}. The l-th layer neuron set of the $(t_j + q)$-th time step is as follows:

$$w_{t_j+q}^{(l)} = \left\{ w_{t_j+q,i}^{(l)} \mid \text{Attr}\left(w_{t_j+q,i}^{(l)}\right) \geq \alpha \cdot \max(\text{Attr}), 0 < \alpha < 1 \right\} \tag{4}$$

To further find neurons related to factual factors, we give the hypothesis that the factual neurons shared among the words within the same factual factor. We set a threshold β to limit the coverage of neurons at each time step, that is, only when the proportion of the time step length of the neuron to the total time step length of the factual factor is greater than β, it is considered as a factual neuron related to the factual factor f_j. The set of l-th layer factual neurons filtered out is as follows:

$$w^{(l)} = \left\{ w_i^{(l)} \;\middle|\; \frac{\sum_{t=t_j}^{t_j+Q} \mathbb{I}\left(w_{t,i}^{(l)} \in w_t^{(l)}\right)}{Q} \geq \beta \,, 0 < \beta < 1 \right\} \tag{5}$$

$\mathbb{I}(*)$ is a binary function. If the condition is met, the value is 1, otherwise it is 0.

4   FactoScalpel

The factual factors attribution algorithm establishes the connection between FFNs and factual factors. Based on this, we propose a novel knowledge injection-based module, FactoScalpel, which integrates factual factors from the document into the FFNs to enhance the factual consistency of summaries. The overall process is shown in Fig. 2.

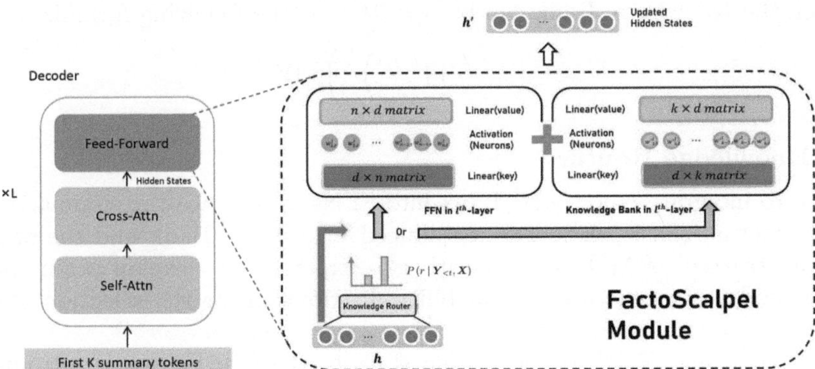

Fig. 2. The overall architecture of the FactoScalpel module. The original Transformer's FFN is replaced by a MoE system consisting of the original FFN and a Knowledge Bank, with 2 experts. Expert selection is carried out through a Knowledge Router.

4.1   Knowledge Bank

In the Transformer architecture's decoder, the update process of hidden states in each layer's FFN is as follows:

$$h' = \sigma\left(h \cdot W_1^{\top}\right) \cdot W_2 \tag{6}$$

where $\boldsymbol{h} \in \mathbb{R}^{1\times d}$ represents the input hidden state of the l-th layer FFN, $\boldsymbol{W}_1, \boldsymbol{W}_2 \in \mathbb{R}^{n\times d}$ are learnable parameters, d and n represent the dimension of the vectors and the number of neurons, $\sigma(*)$ denotes the any activation function in FFNs. We ignore the bias in FFNs in convenience. We build a similar FFN structure $\boldsymbol{W}_1^{(KB)}$ and $\boldsymbol{W}_2^{(KB)}$ to extend the original key-value memory to inject document's factual knowledge into the decoder, which is called **Knowledge Bank**.

For the factual factor $f_j = \left[y_{t_j}, y_{t_j+1}, \ldots, y_{t_j+Q}\right]$, we calculate the average of the word embeddings for each token in the factual factor to obtain the embedding of the factual factor $\boldsymbol{h}_j^{(f)}$ as follows:

$$h_j^{(f)} = \frac{1}{Q} \sum_{i=t_j}^{t_j+Q} \text{word embedding}(y_i) \tag{7}$$

Thus, the feature representations of all factual factors in the original document are obtained as $h^{(f)} \in \mathbb{R}^{k\times d}$ where k represents the number of factual factors.

Then, we introduce a pair of learnable mapping matrices $\boldsymbol{W}_k, \boldsymbol{W}_v \in \mathbb{R}^{d\times d}$ to connect the feature space between Knowledge Bank and FFN. For the embeddings of factual factors $\boldsymbol{h}^{(f)}$, the Knowledge Bank can be formulated as $W_1^{(KB)} = h^{(f)}W_k$ and $W_2^{(KB)} = h^{(f)}W_v$. Therefore, the update process of the hidden state through the Knowledge Bank can be rewritten as the following formula:

$$h' = \sigma \left(h \cdot \left(W_1^{(KB)} \right)^T \right) \cdot W_2^{(KB)} \tag{8}$$

4.2 Knowledge Router

We aim to integrate Knowledge Bank into FFNs to enhance the summarization model's factual consistency. The introduced Knowledge Bank and the original FFN are treated as MoE system with two experts. We develop a Knowledge Router module to generate a probability distribution for the selection of each expert.

We define $\boldsymbol{h} \in \mathbb{R}^{1\times d}$ as the hidden state to the l-th FFN and introduce a learnable mapping matrix $\boldsymbol{W}_R \in \mathbb{R}^{d\times 2}$ to calculate the weight distribution as follows:

$$P\left(r \mid \boldsymbol{Y}_{<t}, \boldsymbol{X}\right) = \text{softmax}\left(\boldsymbol{h} \cdot \boldsymbol{W}_R\right) \tag{9}$$

where t represents the current decoding step and r denotes the routing path to the FFN or Knowledge Bank module. $\boldsymbol{X}$ and $\boldsymbol{Y}$ denote the document and the generated summary separately. We define the probability p as the likelihood of selecting $r = KB$, which represents choosing the Knowledge Bank, given the previously generated outputs $\boldsymbol{Y}_{<t}$ and the input sequence $\boldsymbol{X}$. Therefore, the hidden state h is updated through the MoE system that includes both the original FFN and the Knowledge Bank as follows:

$$h' = (1-p) \cdot \sigma\left(\boldsymbol{h} \cdot \boldsymbol{W}_1^{\top}\right) \cdot \boldsymbol{W}_2 + p \cdot \sigma\left(\boldsymbol{h} \cdot \left(\boldsymbol{W}_1^{(KB)}\right)^{\top}\right) \cdot \boldsymbol{W}_2^{(KB)} \tag{10}$$

But similar to the expert selection challenge in MoE, FactoScalpel exhibits a bias towards selecting the FFNs pre-trained with extensive data, consequently neglecting the randomly initialized Knowledge Banks. To mitigate this, we introduce a router loss to balance the selection probabilities between the FFN and the Knowledge Bank.

We suppose that the route of Knowledge Bank should be engaged when it synthesizes factual factors that are explicitly present in the document, so we propose a sequence tagging task for Knowledge Router with two labels. For each factual factors within the summary Y, if it is completely appeared in the source document X, we assign a label $L^{(R)}$ of 1 to every token in the factual factor; otherwise, the label is set to 0. For each document-summary pair, we define the router loss as follows:

$$\mathcal{L}_R = -\frac{1}{2|Y|} \sum_{t=1}^{|Y|} [L_t^{(R)} \cdot \log p_t + \left(1 - L_t^{(R)}\right) \cdot \log\left(1 - p_t\right)] \tag{11}$$

where t denotes the current generation step of the decoder. Therefore, we set the total loss for model training as the sum of the cross-entropy loss $\mathcal{L}_{CE}$ for summarization and the knowledge router loss $\mathcal{L}_R$, as shown in Eq. (12):

$$\mathcal{L} = \mathcal{L}_{CE} + \lambda \cdot \mathcal{L}_R \tag{12}$$

where λ is a hyperparameter to control the impact of knowledge router.

5   Experiments

We apply the factual factors attribution algorithm and implement the FactoScalpel module.

5.1   Experimental Settings

Datasets. In the factual factors attribution experiments, we use the test sets of two commonly used datasets in the summarization tasks, XSum [14] and CNN/Daily Mail(CNNDM) [13]. For the fact-aware summarization model experiments, we use the XSum dataset, because XSum's single-sentence concise summaries contain more factual inconsistency compared to CNNDM.

Baselines and Evaluation Metrics. We select six open source work as our baselines. There are four fact-aware summarization models, FASum [18] is knowledge injection-based methods, CLIFF [1] and CoFE [16] are multitasking-based methods, PINOCCHIO [8] is a decoding-based methods. We also incorporate the basic summarization model BART trained on XSum and PEGASUS which is the most effective PLM specifically designed for text summarization. We use ROUGE-1, ROUGE-2 and ROUGE-L to evaluate the informativeness while five factual consistency metrics to evaluate factual consistency, inculding QAFactEval [5], SummaC [10], ClozE [11], DAE [7] and FactCC [9].

5.2   Implementation Details

In factual factors attribution experiments, we test and analyze our algorithm on the decoders of three types of models, BART-large(12 layers) and PEGASUS(16 layers), and the LLaMA-3.1-8b-Instruct(32 layers) in Huggingface[2]. In FactoScalpel, following the fact-aware summarization models in baselines, we also choose BART as the basic skeleton to ensure a fair and credible comparison of model performance. Additionally, to validate the effectiveness and generalizability of FactoScalpel, we also implement relevant models based on PEGASUS. We use the `en_core_web_trf` model from SpaCy[3] to extract factual factors. We adopt the AdaFactor optimizer with learning rate 1e-5 to train for 10 epochs with batch size 4 on the NVIDIA GeForce RTX 3090 GPU.

5.3   Factual Factors Attribution Analysis

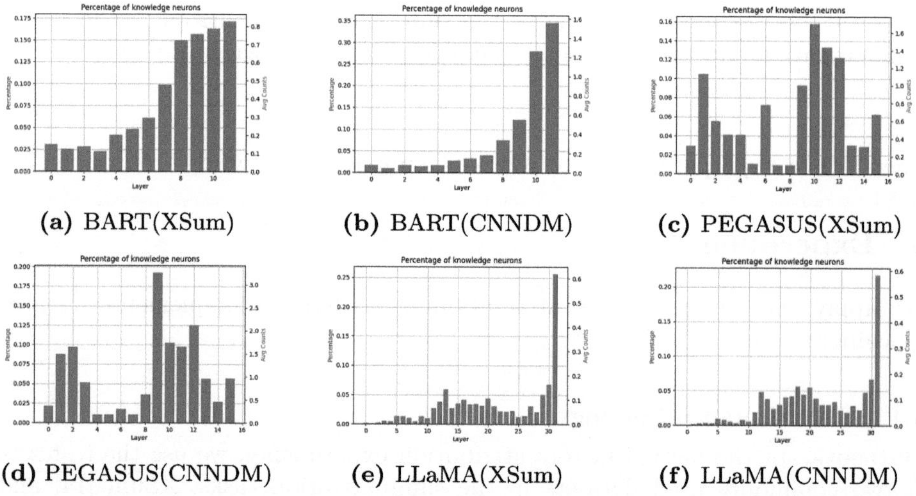

(a) BART(XSum)   (b) BART(CNNDM)   (c) PEGASUS(XSum)

(d) PEGASUS(CNNDM)   (e) LLaMA(XSum)   (f) LLaMA(CNNDM)

Fig. 3. The distribution of factual neurons across layers in decoder. The horizontal axis represents the layer numbers of the model, the left vertical axis indicates the proportion of factual neurons in a layer relative to all factual neurons, and the right vertical axis represents the average number of factual neurons in the test set for that layer.

We apply the proposed factual factors attribution algorithm to three different types models: BART, PEGASUS and LLaMA to explore where factual information is stored in these models during text summarization tasks.

---

[2] https://www.huggingface.co.
[3] https://spacy.io/api.

Setting the threshold too low or too high may result in an overly generalized set of neurons or the omission of important factual-related neurons. Through grid search, we set the threshold parameters as $\alpha = 0.2$ and $\beta = 0.7$, and obtain the average distribution of neurons related to factual factors as shown in Fig. 3. It can be observed that the distribution trends of factual neurons on the XSum and CNNDM datasets are consistent within the same model, this indirectly demonstrates the reliability of our proposed method. As shown in Fig. 3, in BART, the distribution of factual neurons reflects that the model stores and processes more facts in deeper layers. For PEGASUS, the distribution indicates that the PEGASUS model may extract and process some facts at shallower layers, while the middle-to-late layers handle more complex knowledge storage and processing tasks. For LLaMA, the distribution suggests that LLaMA stores more knowledge information in the deeper layers while the middle layers also exhibit a certain capability for fact processing and storage.

5.4   Performance on XSum Benchmark

Based on the analysis results in Sect. 5.3, we apply the FactoScalpel module to the last layer of the BART model, which contains the most factual neurons.

Table 1. Results of factual consistency metrics and ROUGE for each summarization model based on the XSum test set.

Base Model	Model	QAFactEval	SummaC	ClozE	DAE	FactCC	R-1	R-2	R-L
BART	BART-large	18.48	9.06	69.97	61.20	22.69	43.68	20.25	35.22
	FASum	3.63	5.97	56.16	43.01	27.10	30.31	10.02	23.76
	CLIFF	14.18	9.48	68.52	58.47	25.24	40.21	17.66	32.40
	PINOCCHIO	0.07	0.86	39.61	42.61	**31.50**	42.69	19.16	33.85
	CoFE	20.41	11.24	73.94	64.86	24.87	44.90	21.90	36.75
	FactoScalpel	**21.76**	**13.90**	**76.64**	**71.30**	29.87	40.92	17.48	32.74
PEGASUS	PEGASUS	18.48	11.48	71.10	62.13	24.94	**46.65**	**23.46**	**38.66**
	FactoScalpel-1th	18.68	11.38	72.00	64.65	26.51	45.83	22.60	37.73
	FactoScalpel-2th	18.85	11.23	72.11	64.94	26.18	45.91	22.75	37.82
	FactoScalpel-11th	7.91	16.23	49.72	32.75	19.10	37.42	15.50	30.39
	FactoScalpel-16th	-	-	-	-	-	16.13	3.15	13.60
Ablation Study									
BART	FactoScalpel$_{-\text{Knowledge Router}}$	18.60	9.45	73.17	64.42	23.71	43.16	19.43	34.59
	FactoScalpel$_{-\text{Knowledge Bank}}$	18.48	9.06	69.97	61.20	22.69	43.68	20.25	35.22
	FactoScalpel-embedding |||	20.56	13.40	75.56	69.91	28.60	38.19	14.74	29.62

Note: The highest performance across these metrics is highlighted in bold.

As shown in Table 1, we show the results of factual consistency metrics and ROUGE for each summarization model based on the XSum test set. FactoScalpel achieves the best results on most factual consistency metrics. However, there is a slight degree of decline in ROUGE. This result is expected, since the golden summaries in XSum contain factual errors, and generating factual consistency summaries will inevitably differ from them. Compared to other fact-aware summarization models, FASum only has good results in FactCC. CoFE performs better than CLIFF and has certain improvements in several factual consistency metrics. In the case of PINOCCHIO, while it excels in achieving top results on FactCC, it simultaneously exhibits notably weak performance across other factual consistency metrics.

Additionally, we also attempt to transfer the FactoScalpel module to PEGASUS, which is currently one of the best-performing PLM for abstractive summarization. We try integrating the module into the 11th layer of PEGASUS which contains the most factual factors and the first layer, the final layer, and the second layer where factual neurons are concentrated excluding the middle-to-late layers as shown in Fig. 3c. From the results, we find that adding the FactoScalpel module in the second layer where factual neurons are concentrated, the model shows a significant performance boost compared to the original PEGASUS model. However, when the FactoScalpel module is added to the deeper layer, the ROUGE and factual consistency scores drastically drop. We conclude that the attribution analysis presented in Sect. 5.3 is valid. Adding FactoScalpel to the layers where factual neurons are concentrated can effectively improve factual consistency. However, PEGASUS, with its deeper architecture and more complex internal mechanisms compared to BART, suffers when FactoScalpel is integrated into its later layers, because in the deeper layers, the model has already learned to focus on abstract, high-level representations, and adding FactoScalpel at this stage interferes with the model's ability to generate fluent, coherent sentences, ultimately undermining its performance.

5.5   Ablation Study

We perform an ablation study via testing other factual factor embedding method and continuously removing different modules in FactoScalpel. In addition to using the average word embeddings of factual factor words, we also experiment with concatenating word embeddings using the identifier |||. Furthermore, we incrementally remove the Knowledge Router and Knowledge Bank modules from FactoScalpel. As shown the results in Table 1, the current factual factor embedding method and each component contribute to enhancing the factual consistency of the model-generated summaries.

6   Knowledge Injection Case Study

Injecting FactoScalpel has been shown to enhance the factual consistency. However, the specific types of factual errors that knowledge injection can mitigate remain insufficiently understood. To investigate this further, we conduct a comprehensive case study on BART and PEGASUS, incorporating FactoScalpel-based knowledge injection. In addition, considering the high computational cost associated with fine-tuning LLM, we evaluate LLaMA using a prompt-based knowledge injection approach. Specifically, we compare its outputs with and without prompts that emphasize factual factors.

We select the data instances where all five evaluation metrics improve after knowledge injection compared to the original baseline models. Our analysis reveals that the summaries generated by the original BART and PEGASUS models contain a substantial number of extrinsic errors, which means they include information that is not present in the source text. However, after knowledge injection, the models focus more on the facts in the input text, resulting in a significant reduction in extrinsic errors. The DeFacto[4] dataset which provides human annotations of summaries generated by the PEGASUS model on the XSum dataset reveals that, among 2,561 samples, there are 316 samples with intrinsic errors and 1,258 samples with extrinsic errors. This aligns with our conclusion that factual consistency metrics improve significantly with knowledge injection, particularly by substantially reducing extrinsic errors.

Table 2. Evaluation Metrics for LLaMA and LLaMA with Knowledge Injection

Model	QAFactEval	SummaC	ClozE	DAE	FactCC
LLaMA	43.83	8.02	75.88	80.76	25.13
LLaMA_inject	56.87	8.04	83.54	84.62	25.25

In LLaMA with knowledge injection via prompts, as shown in Table 2, although the evaluation metrics significantly improve after knowledge injection, through case study we find that there are no significant errors in most cases between the original model's output and the output after knowledge injection. The original model also have a small number of extrinsic errors, but using prompts to make the model focus on knowledge is effective in eliminating these extrinsic errors. However, this approach may cause confusion in the order of entities within the text, leading to some intrinsic errors and a slight decrease in factual consistency. This method of knowledge injection still has significant room for improvement.

7   Conclusions

In this paper, we propose a factual factors attribution algorithm and design a FactoScalpel module. By simply replacing the FFN in the decoder that contains the most factual neurons with this module, we achieve a significant improvement in factual consistency. We also employ different prompting method to inject knowledge, tailored to LLM, and find that due to more extensive pre-training and more complex mechanisms, knowledge injection in LLMs still requires further exploration.

Acknowledgments. This work was supported in part by the National Natural Science Foundation of China (Grant No. 62176024) and Engineering Research Center of Information Networks, Ministry of Education.

---

[4] https://github.com/microsoft/DeFacto.

References

1. Cao, S., Wang, L.: CLIFF: Contrastive learning for improving faithfulness and factuality in abstractive summarization. In: Proceedings of EMNLP, pp. 6633–6649 (2021)
2. Dai, D., Dong, L., Hao, Y., Sui, Z., Chang, B., Wei, F.: Knowledge neurons in pretrained transformers. In: Proceedings of ACL, pp. 8493–8502 (2022)
3. Dai, D., Jiang, W., Dong, Q., Lyu, Y., Sui, Z.: Neural knowledge bank for pretrained transformers. In: Proceedings of NLPCC, pp. 772–783 (2023). https://doi.org/10.1007/978-3-031-44696-2_60
4. Dong, Q., Dai, D., Song, Y., Xu, J., Sui, Z., Li, L.: Calibrating factual knowledge in pretrained language models. In: Findings of EMNLP, pp. 5937–5947 (2022)
5. Fabbri, A., Wu, C.S., Liu, W., Xiong, C.: QAFactEval: improved QA-based factual consistency evaluation for summarization. In: Proceedings of NAACL, pp. 2587–2601 (Jul 2022)
6. Geva, M., Schuster, R., Berant, J., Levy, O.: Transformer feed-forward layers are key-value memories. In: Proceedings of EMNLP, pp. 5484–5495 (2021)
7. Goyal, T., Durrett, G.: Evaluating factuality in generation with dependency-level entailment. In: Findings of EMNLP, pp. 3592–3603 (2020)
8. King, D., Shen, Z., Subramani, N., Weld, D.S., Beltagy, I., Downey, D.: Don't say what you don't know: Improving the consistency of abstractive summarization by constraining beam search. In: Proceedings of the 2nd Workshop on Natural Language Generation, Evaluation, and Metrics (GEM), pp. 555–571 (Dec 2022)
9. Kryscinski, W., McCann, B., Xiong, C., Socher, R.: Evaluating the factual consistency of abstractive text summarization. In: Proceedings of EMNLP, pp. 9332–9346 (2020)
10. Laban, P., Schnabel, T., Bennett, P.N., Hearst, M.A.: SummaC: re-visiting NLI-based models for inconsistency detection in summarization. Trans. Assoc. Comput. Linguist. **10**, 163–177 (2022)
11. Li, Y., et al.: Just cloze! a novel framework for evaluating the factual consistency faster in abstractive summarization (2023). https://arxiv.org/abs/2210.02804
12. Meng, K., Bau, D., Andonian, A., Belinkov, Y.: Locating and editing factual associations in GPT. In: Proceedings of NeurIPS. NIPS '22 (2024)
13. Nallapati, R., Zhou, B., dos Santos, C., Gulçehre, Ç., Xiang, B.: Abstractive text summarization using sequence-to-sequence RNNs and beyond. In: Proceedings of the 20th SIGNLL Conference on Computational Natural Language Learning, pp. 280–290 (Aug 2016)
14. Narayan, S., Cohen, S.B., Lapata, M.: Don't give me the details, just the summary! topic-aware convolutional neural networks for extreme summarization. In: Proceedings of EMNLP, pp. 1797–1807 (2018)
15. Tian, S., et al.: KG-adapter: Enabling knowledge graph integration in large language models through parameter-efficient fine-tuning. In: Findings of ACL (2024)
16. Wang, T., Ladhak, F., Durmus, E., He, H.: Improving faithfulness by augmenting negative summaries from fake documents. In: Proceedings of EMNLP, pp. 11913–11921 (Dec 2022)
17. Wu, W., et al.: FRSUM: towards faithful abstractive summarization via enhancing factual robustness. In: Findings of EMNLP, pp. 3640–3654 (Dec 2022)
18. Zhu, C., et al.: Enhancing factual consistency of abstractive summarization. In: Proceedings of NAACL, pp. 718–733 (2021)

Emoji-Stega: An Emoji-Powered Linguistic Steganography Framework for Social Networks

Jiacheng Fan, Zhenyang Shen, Zhe Chen, Jiahao Chen, and Sixing Wu[✉]

National Pilot School of Software, Yunnan University, Yunnan, China
fanjiacheng@stu.ynu.edu.cn, wusixing@ynu.edu.cn

Abstract. With the popularity of social networks, a vast number of posts are circulated daily. When steganographic content is posted on social networks, the focus on popular posts will draw attention away from it. Traditional generative linguistic steganography methods embed secret messages by manipulating the probability distribution at each time step using a white-box language model, which may limit generation flexibility and reduce the adaptability in the context of social networks. This paper proposes a generative linguistic steganography method based on emojis that effectively mitigates such limitations without relying on white-box models. Specifically, we first implement an emoji pre-selection strategy to identify a candidate emoji set. This set is then encoded using a mapping scheme. We select matching emojis based on the secret message and guide an LLM to generate a stego text embedding these emojis as information carriers. Our steganographic approach is well-suited for transmissions in social network platforms, enabling the generation of high-quality texts with controllable stylistic and topical features.

Keywords: Generative Linguistic Steganography · Large Language Models · Black-box · Social Networks · Emoji

1 Introduction

To safely transmit the secret message over public channels, steganography is a useful technique to hide a secret message in normal carriers such as texts [1], images [2], audios [3], or videos [4]. The widespread use of text in diverse scenarios makes linguistic steganography (text-based steganography) a crucial research area. Generally, linguistic steganography is often illustrated as a Simmons' prisoner's problem [5]: *Alice* and *Bob*, two prisoners, wish to plan an escape, but their letters are monitored by the warden, *Eve*. Thus, they need to hide their messages within seemingly innocent text using linguistic steganography.

Traditional linguistic steganography methods usually edit the format [6] or content [7] of the given cover text (i.e., text carrier) to embed the secret message. However, the discrete nature of editing operations often violates the demands of syntactic and contextual coherence, resulting in a limited capacity to embed a secret message; thus, only a limited length of the secret message can be safely embedded into the cover text without introducing grammatical

© The Author(s), under exclusive license to Springer Nature Singapore Pte Ltd. 2026
X.-L. Mao et al. (Eds.): NLPCC 2025, LNAI 16105, pp. 133–145, 2026.
https://doi.org/10.1007/978-981-95-3352-7_11

errors or semantic drift. With the development of deep learning, an increasing number of researchers are using language models to directly generate a stego text to hide the given secret message [20,22], referred to as generative linguistic steganography. This paradigm can improve embedding capacity while maintaining high imperceptibility. Many generative steganography methods lleverage white-box language models, where embedding algorithms need to modify the output word sampling probabilities to encode secret message bit strings [1,15]. Then, at each time step, a specified word corresponding to the secret message is selected, thereby embedding the secret message within this word. Although such methods are effective in concealing secret messages in the generated stego text to evade detection by eavesdroppers, they still exhibit several limitations:

1. **Limited Scene Adaptability**: Due to the limitations of complex embedding algorithms and language models, the generated stego text often exhibits poor controllability, making it unsuitable for social networks.
2. **Risk of Multiple Transmissions**: In some prior works, the sender is required to share additional keys with the receivers in advance to enable the recovery of the secret message. When multiple receivers are involved, both the requirement to pre-share additional keys and the need to transmit the secret message repeatedly can significantly increase the risk of interception and exposure during transmission.

To address these challenges, we propose a novel emoji-based generative linguistic steganography method ***Emoji-Stega*** that uses emojis as carriers of secret messages. Intuitively, emojis frequently appear in social network contexts, and using them as carriers of secret messages makes the generated stego text more suitable for such platforms. Moreover, the meaning of emojis is often ambiguous; thus, their placement in a sentence is flexible. In detail, we first apply a topic-aware emoji pre-selection algorithm to select emojis relevant to the user-defined topic and map them to binary bit strings. The secret message is then encoded into an emoji sequence based on this mapping. This sequence is then used to construct a prompt to guide a large black-box language model in generating stego text with emojis in the correct order. The stego text generated by Emoji-Stega resembles the style of typical social network posts, with rich and fluent content. Experimental results demonstrate that our method can generate stego texts that are well suited to the style of social networks and of high quality and diversity.

Our contributions are as follows: (1) We are the first to utilize emojis as carriers in generative linguistic steganography to address the challenge posed by embedding algorithms that restrict the generation of stego text suitable for social network contexts. (2) Our method eliminated the requirement of pre-sharing the additional keys besides the stego text, as the receiver can reconstruct them directly from the received stego text. Thus, a single transmission can enable multiple receivers to access the embedded secret. (3) We employ large models to evaluate text quality, scenario adaptability, and topic relevance. (4) Experimental results reveal that our method outperforms other methods in terms of text quality and related evaluation metrics, and the generated stego text by Emoji-stega is more suitable for social network platforms.

2   Related Works

Generative Linguistic Steganography. Linguistic steganography can be classified into either editing-based or generative methods. Editing-based steganography modifies the format [6,8,9] or the content of the cover text [10–14]. With the advancement of deep learning, researchers have begun utilizing white-box language models for generative linguistic steganography. Fang et al. [15] partitioned the vocabulary into multiple bins, where each bin corresponds to a fixed-length secret bit sequence. This method suffers from significant text quality degradation at high embedding rates. Yang et al. [1] proposed a steganographic embedding method using Huffman trees, which avoids static vocabulary partitioning and instead dynamically constructs Huffman trees based on the probability distribution at each time step, improving both text quality and embedding rate. Dai et al. [16] built upon this and proposed the Patient Huffman embedding algorithm, which takes text KLD into account during secret message embedding, leading to improved text quality. Ziegler et al. [17] proposed a linguistic steganography technique based on arithmetic coding, which ensures security while generating realistic cover sentences. Building on the arithmetic coding-based steganographic methods, Shen et al. [18] proposed a self-adjusting arithmetic coding embedding algorithm to address the issue of candidate word pool construction at each time step. Zhou et al. [19] proposed a linguistic steganography model based on GAN and adaptive probability distribution, enhancing both the secrecy and the naturalness of the generated text. Yang et al. [21] proposed a linguistic steganography method that leverages pivot translation and semantic-aware encoding to achieve high embedding capacity while preserving semantic integrity and resisting steganalysis. Unlike previous white-box methods, Wu et al. [22] proposed LLM-Stega. This black-box generative linguistic steganography method utilizes large language models' user interfaces for secure covert communication, incorporating encrypted steganographic mapping and rejection sampling to enhance accuracy and semantic richness. Although the methods above can generate high-quality text with satisfactory embedding rates, their limited stylistic diversity renders them unsuitable for today's rapidly evolving social network platforms.

Emojis. Emojis appear frequently on major social network platforms. Huang et al. [24] incorporated emoji sentiment information into a pre-trained language model for Chinese and English sentiment analysis. Kumar et al. [25] introduced EmoMBTI-Net, a novel emoji dataset for personality profiling, and leverages large language models for analyzing personality traits based on emoji usage. Antonius et al. [26] detected spam content by emoji. Attapol et al. explored the correlation between emojis and Mood Expression in Thai Twitter discourse. Tang et al. [28] proposed a green edge intelligence scheme to solve the model selection problem for mobile keyboard emoji prediction. From the above research, it can be seen that the application prospects of emojis are relatively broad and worth further study. However, only Zhu et al. [23] tried to hide secret messages using GIF image emojis. Few linguistic steganography methods have tried the emoji (Fig. 1).

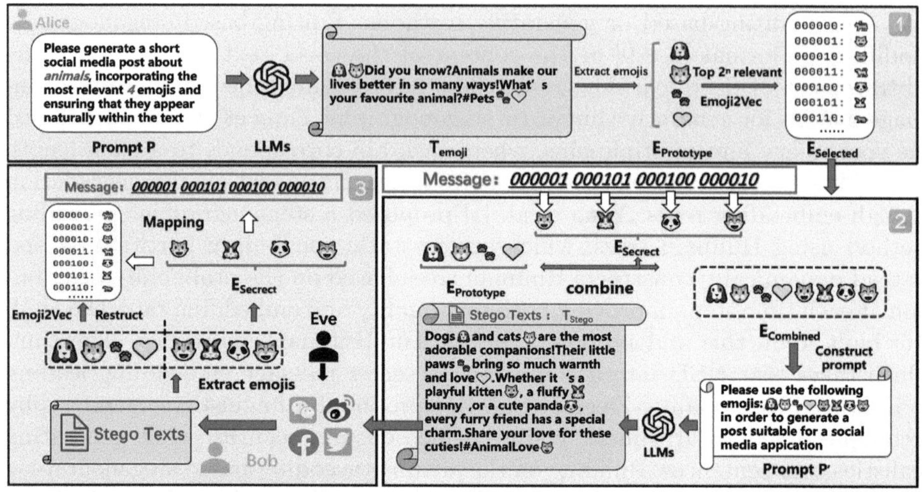

Fig. 1. The overall framework of Emoji-stega. The sender first selects topic-relevant emojis and encodes them. Based on the encoded emojis, the stego text is then generated. During the extraction phase, the receiver reconstructs the Pre-selection Set and subsequently restores the secret message.

3   The Proposed Methodology

This work proposes a novel method **Emoji-Stega**, which uses a black-box LLM to generate a stego text T_{stego} with emojis to hide the given secret message M, consisting of three modules:

- **Topic-Aware Emoji Pre-selection:** It utilizes a user-defined topic t to build an emoji set $\mathcal{E}$, namely, $\mathcal{E} = PreSelect(t)$.
- **Stego Text Generator:** It uses a black-box language model to generate a stego text with emojis T_{Stego} to hide the given secret message M, namely, $T_{Stego} = Generator(M, \mathcal{E})$.
- **Secret Message Extractor:** It can restore the secret message M without requiring additional information, namely, $M = Extractor(T_{Stego})$.

3.1   Topic-Aware Emoji Pre-selection

Irrational emoji selection will lead to unclear topics and illogical content. Thus, we have designed a topic-aware emoji pre-selection strategy. Formally, to ensure the selected emojis are highly relevant to the given topic $t \in T$, we first construct a topic-aware prompt P. This prompt is expected to guide the model in generating topic-aware text that incorporates relevant emojis. For example, if the topic is **animals**, the constructed prompt could be: *'Please generate a short social network post about **animals**, incorporating the most relevant k^1 emojis and ensuring that they appear naturally within the text'*. With this prompt, we subsequently let the black-box language model (LLM) generate an emoji text T_{emoji}, which contains both the textual content and the associated emojis:

$$T_{emoji} = \mathrm{LLM}(P), P = TopicTextPrompt(t) \tag{1}$$

Subsequently, we extract k prototype emojis $E_{Prototype}$ from T_{emoji}:

$$E_{Prototype} \in \mathbb{R}^k = ExtractEmojis(T_{emoji}, k) \tag{2}$$

Then, assume n is the expected number of bits encoded by each emoji. We use Emoji2Vec [29] model emoji2vec(e) and the cosine similarity function $\cos(\cdot, \cdot)$ to choose the top 2^n emojis $E_{Selected}$ that have the highest similarities to the prototype emojis from the full emoji set E:

$$E_{Selected} \in \mathbb{R}^{2^n} = \arg \max_{e \in E}(max\_sim(e)) \tag{3}$$

$$max\_sim(e) = \max_{e_i^p \in E_{Prototype}} \cos\left(\mathrm{emoji2vec}(e), \mathrm{emoji2vec}(e_i^p)\right) \tag{4}$$

Emoji Binary Coding. $E_{selected}$ consists of 2^n the emojis. For the i-th emoji $e_i \in E_{selected}$, we convert the digit i to a n-bit code as the binary coding of e_i:

$$b_{e_i} = BinaryCoding(i, n) \tag{5}$$

where *BinaryCoding* will use zero-padding to ensure the coding length is n.

3.2   Steganographic Text Generation

Secret Message Binary Coding. In traditional methods, a given secret message is generally converted to a binary string using UTF-8 encoding. However, UTF-8 encoding will produce a relatively long bit string. To this end, we adopt a more efficient compression encoding method proposed by Li et al. [30], which first converts the secret text T_{secret} into token IDs using the tokenizer of the LLM, and then transforms the token IDs into a binary bit string. This method can significantly reduce bit length, lowering the risk of exposure.

In detail, the first step is to tokenize the secret message T_{secret} to a sequence of token IDs T_{secret}^{IDs} using the LLM built-in *Tokenizer*:

$$T_{secret}^{IDs} = Tokenizer(T_{secret}) = [id_1, id_2, \ldots, id_l] \tag{6}$$

---

[1] A hyper-parameter.

where each id_i corresponds to a unique token identifier in the vocabulary of the LLM. Then, we convert each token ID into a 16-bit[2] binary string:

$$b_i = BinaryCoding(id_i, 16) \tag{7}$$

Subsequently, the complete binary sequence B_{secret} of the full secret message T_{secret} can be defined as the concatenation of the binary coding of all IDs:

$$B_{secret} = [b_1, b_2, \ldots, b_l] \tag{8}$$

Emoji Selection. To ensure each emoji $e \in E_{selected}$ uniquely corresponds to a binary string, we split B_{secret} into n-bit binary segments B_{split}:

$$B_{split} = \{s_1, s_2, \ldots, s_m\}, \quad s_j = pad_0(B_{secret}[n(j-1)+1 : nj]) \tag{9}$$

where the zero-padding pad_0 ensures the length of each segment be n-bit.

After the above segmentation, the secret segmentation s has the same bit length (i.e., n) as the emoji bit length b_e. Thus, for a secret segmentation s_i, we can use the emoji $e_j \in E_{selected}$ that has the same binary coding to represent. Finally, E_{secret} is the sequence of matched emojis, where each e_j is chosen from the selected set $E_{selected}$ such that its binary representation matches s_i.

$$E_{secret}[i] = e_j \in E_{selected}, \text{where } s_i == b_{e_j} \tag{10}$$

Stego Text Generation. To ensure the stego text can be extracted successfully, both *sender* and *receiver* should share the emoji selection. Thus, we concatenate prototype emojis with those encoding the binary secret:

$$E_{combined} = E_{prototype} \| E_{secret} \tag{11}$$

then, with this combined emoji set, we can construct a prompt P' as follows:

$$T_{Stego} = LLM(P'), \quad P' = StegoPrompt(E_{combined}, t) \tag{12}$$

where $StegoPrompt(\cdot)$ instructs the LLM to generate a text in the style of a social network post on the given topic t and **orderly** incorporates all emojis in $E_{combined}$, e.g. *'Please use the following emojis: $E_{combined}$ in order to generate a post suitable for a social network application.'*

3.3   Secret Message Extraction

Upon receiving the stego text T_{stego}, the receiver should first extract all emojis from the text. Thus, the first k emojis in T_{Stego} correspond to the prototype emojis $E_{prototype}$, which do not contain any secret message but enable the receiver to correctly reconstruct the pre-selected emoji set $E_{selected}$ and the corresponding binary codes using Emoji2Vec. Then, we can infer the full secret binary sequence using the remaining emojis. Finally, we can use the vocabulary of the same LLM to restore the original secret message fully.

---

[2] This depends on the vocabulary size of the backbone LLM.

4 Experiment

In this section, we evaluate the Emoji-stega method in terms of text quality, diversity, contextual adaptability, and topic relevance.

4.1 Models

Emoji-Stega. We implemented our Emoji-Stega method using both LLaMA3-8B and GPT-4o [32]. For topic selection, we focus on four popular topics that can be commonly found on the major social network platforms: **Animal**, **Food**, **Travel**, and **Daily life**.

Baselines. We have re-implemented four well-known generative methods as our baseline: Bins [15], Huffman [1], Arithmetic [17], and Discop [20]. For the Discop method, the authors presented two approaches, and we selected the approach that is more closely aligned with the experimental design's BPW range for comparison. For such baselines, we use the local LLaMA3-8B [31] as the backbone large language model for text generation. Such baselines also use the same topics as our method to create the prompt instructions.

4.2 Metrics

Capacity. It represents the average number of secret messages embedded per token, measured in bits per word (BPW), and is calculated as:

$$\text{BPW} = \frac{B}{W} \tag{13}$$

where B is the total number of embedded secret bits, and W is the total number of words in the generated steganographic text.

Text Quality. We use LLaMA3-8B to compute the Perplexity of stego texts to measure the text quality:

$$PPL = \exp\left(-\frac{1}{N} \sum_{i=1}^{N} \log p(w_i \mid w_1, \ldots, w_{i-1}) \right) \tag{14}$$

Diversity. We select Distinct-N to evaluate the diversity of the text [35].

4.3 Results and Analysis

(1) Text Quality and Diversity. The experimental results of perplexity and diversity for generated text are shown in Table 1. There are 1,000 texts generated for each embedding rate using the same prompt. The experimental results demonstrate that, at comparable embedding rates, the stego text generated by Emoji-Stega exhibits lower perplexity than other baseline methods, indicating superior fluency of our method. Moreover, increasing the embedding rate has less impact on the fluency of text generated by Emoji-Stega than baselines. Compared to other baseline methods, Emoji-Stega achieves higher Distinct-N scores, indicating a greater diversity in the generated text. As social networks favor diverse and abundant content, higher diversity makes the generated texts more suitable for such platforms.

Table 1. Performance Comparison of Different Methods

Method	BPW	PPL	Distinct-2	Distinct-3	Distinct-4
Bins [15] (block=2)	1.00	14.91	31.4	60.7	79.2
Bins (block=4)	2.00	66.40	49.0	77.8	92.0
Bins (block=8)	3.00	134.31	57.5	89.0	98.2
Huffman [1] (topk=2)	1.00	10.93	38.7	63.7	78.3
Huffman (topk=8)	2.09	19.27	48.4	76.5	89.5
Huffman (topk=16)	3.02	27.69	60.3	88.6	97.0
Arithmetic [17] (temp=0.6)	1.37	8.52	40.4	64.5	76.6
Arithmetic (temp=0.8)	2.28	15.78	49.3	72.6	83.2
Arithmetic (temp=1.0)	3.38	35.49	64.4	86.2	91.2
Discop [20]	1.97	44.70	58.2	83.5	90.3
Emoji-Stega$_{LLaMA}$	0.95	**7.25**	56.3	79.3	90.7
Emoji-Stega$_{LLaMA}$	2.27	8.82	69.3	88.6	94.8
Emoji-Stega$_{LLaMA}$	3.12	10.61	**77.4**	88.7	94.6
Emoji-Stega$_{GPT}$	1.08	9.65	57.6	87.1	96.3
Emoji-Stega$_{GPT}$	1.53	14.34	72.8	**95.0**	**99.2**
Emoji-Stega$_{GPT}$	2.76	14.44	73.2	94.3	98.6

(2) Evaluation with Large Language Models. We evaluate the generated texts using large language models, with scores ranging from 1 (lowest) to 10 (highest). Scenario Adaptability measures how well the text fits social networks, Topic Relevance assesses its relevance to the user-defined topic, and Text Quality reflects overall fluency, coherence, and grammatical correctness. In the experiment, each method used an embedding rate of around 3. We generated 100 sentences for each of the four topics by changing the prompt. Then we adopt three advanced large modelsGPT-4o, Qwen-Max [33], and DeepSeek-V3 [34] to evaluate the sentences. The Fig. 2 shows the averaged results. Emoji-Stega achieves average scores of 7.4 in Scenario Adaptability, 8.9 in Topic Relevance, and 6.9 in Text Quality, outperforming other baselines by approximately 3.5, 2.5, and 2.5 points. Such experimental results have demonstrated that the stego text generated by Emoji-Stega is superior to the comparative baselines in terms of Scenario Adaptability, Topic Relevance, and Text Quality.

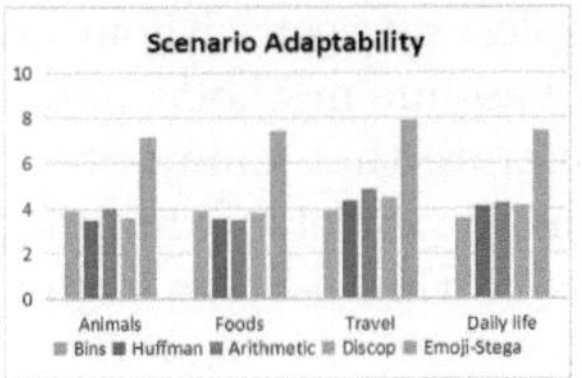

(a) Scenario Adaptability.

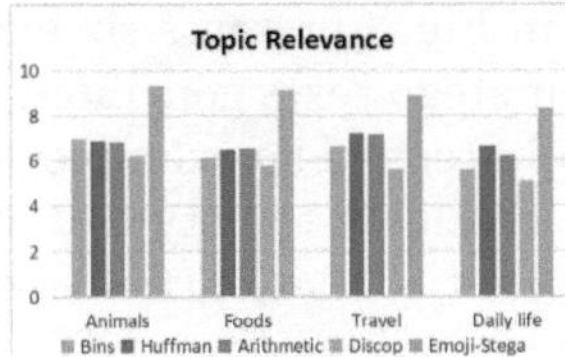

(b) Topic Relevance.

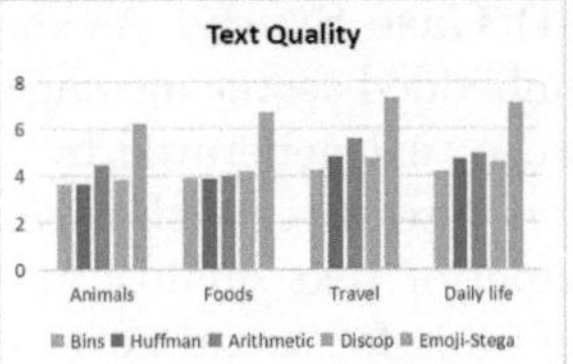

(c) Text Quality.

Fig. 2. Large model evaluation results.

(3) Hyperparameter Sensitivity. In the hyperparameter sensitivity experiment, the number of emojis in $E_{prototype}$, denoted as k, is set to $2 \sim 5$, and the number of emojis in $E_{selected}$ is set to $16 \sim 128$, with $n = 4 \sim 7$. SimScore is the average cosine similarity between the emojis in $E_{prototype}$ and $E_{selected}$ in the vector space. BPW-N represents the BPW when there are N non-emoji words in the sentence. Table 2 shows that increasing emojis in $E_{prototype}$ enhances similarity between emojis in $E_{selected}$ and $E_{prototype}$, thereby making the generated text more aligned with the user-defined topic but reduces the BPW due to the inclusion of more non-secret emojis. Increasing emojis in $E_{selected}$ allows each emoji to carry more secret binary bits, but may introduces emojis less relevant to the topic, thereby making the generated text less aligned with the user-defined topic.

Table 2. Similarity Scores and BPW-N Comparison

Example/k	Emojis/2^n	SimScore	BPW-20	BPW-30	BPW-40
2	16	0.64	1.25	0.95	0.77
	32	0.59	1.56	1.19	0.96
	64	0.54	1.88	1.43	1.15
	128	0.49	2.19	1.67	1.35
3	16	0.65	1.21	0.93	0.75
	32	0.62	1.51	1.16	0.94
	64	0.58	1.81	1.40	1.13
	128	0.53	2.12	1.63	1.32
4	16	0.66	1.18	0.91	0.74
	32	0.63	1.47	1.14	0.93
	64	0.62	1.76	1.36	1.11
	128	0.55	2.06	1.59	1.30
5	16	0.71	1.14	0.89	0.73
	32	0.64	1.43	1.11	0.91
	64	0.60	1.71	1.33	1.09
	128	0.54	2.00	1.56	1.27

(4) Case Study. As shown in Fig. 3 presents six examples: a tweet without an embedded secret message, four stego texts generated by baseline methods, and a stego text generated by Emoji-Stega. The examples illustrate that Emoji-Stega generates tweets that closely resemble the style of authentic tweets, exhibiting superior text quality and diversity. These attributes make Emoji-Stega highly suitable for social network use.

(a) Normal tweet.   (b) Bins.   (c) Huffman.

(d) Arithmetic.   (e) Discop.   (f) Emoji.

Fig. 3. Stego texts generated by different steganographic methods.

5 Conclusion

This paper presents Emoji-Stega, an innovative generative linguistic steganography method that overcomes the stylistic limitations of traditional embedding algorithms unsuitable for modern social network platforms. Our approach employs Topic-Aware Emoji Pre-selection to filter and select emojis that align with a user-defined topic, then establishes a mapping between these emojis and binary bit strings to convert the secret message into an emoji sequence. A carefully designed prompt guides a large language model to generate stego text, from which the recipient can directly extract the secret message without prior knowledge of the mapping. Future work will explore the integration of additional modalities, such as images, to further enhance the robustness and social network suitability of our method.

Acknowledgments. This work is mainly supported by Yunnan Fundamental Research Projects under Grant No.202401CF070170, in part by the Yunnan Province Wu Zhonghai Expert Workstation under Grant No.202305AF150045 and National Natural Science Foundation of China under Grant No.62462067.

References

1. Yang, Z.-L., Guo, X.-Q., Chen, Z.-M., Huang, Y.-F., Zhang, Y.-J.: RNN-stega: linguistic steganography based on recurrent neural networks. IEEE Trans. Inf. Forensics Security **14**(5), 1280–1295 (2018)
2. Zhou, H., Chen, K., Zhang, W., Yu, N.: Comments on "Steganography Using Reversible Texture Synthesis." IEEE Trans. Image Process. **26**(4), 1623–1625 (2017)
3. Su, W.-K., Ni, J.-Q., Hu, X.-L., Li, B.: Efficient audio steganography using generalized audio intrinsic energy with micro-amplitude modification suppression. IEEE Trans. Inf. Forensics Security **19**, 6559–6572 (2024)
4. Xing, H., Tian, L., Cao, M., Li, C.: A multi-embedding domain video steganography algorithm based on TU partitioning and intra prediction mode. Neurocomputing **575**, 127247 (2024)
5. Simmons, G.J.: The prisoners' problem and the subliminal channel. In: Chaum, D. (ed.) Advances in Cryptology, pp. 51–67. Springer, Boston, MA (1984)
6. Low, S. H., Maxemchuk, N. F., Brassil, J. T., O'Gorman, L.: Document marking and identification using both line and word shifting. In: Proceedings of the INFOCOM'95, pp. 853–860. IEEE, Boston, MA (1995)
7. Qi, C., Xingming, S., Lingyun, X.: A secure text steganography based on synonym substitution. In: IEEE Conference Anthology, pp. 1–3. IEEE, Piscataway, NJ (2013)
8. Aminali, A., Saad, A.S.: New text steganography technique by using mixed-case font. Int. J. Comput. Appl. **62**(3), 6–9 (2013)
9. Bashir, H. M., Li, Q., Hou, J.: A high capacity text steganography utilizing Unicode zero-width characters. In: Proceedings 2020 IEEE iThings, pp. 668–675. IEEE, Piscataway, NJ (2020)
10. Min-Zhi, Z., Xing-Ming, S., Hua-Zheng, X.: Research on the Chinese Text Steganography Based on the Modification of the Empty Word. Comput. Eng, Appl (2006)
11. Meral, H.M., Sankur, B., Özsoy, A.S., et al.: Natural language watermarking via morphosyntactic alterations. Comput. Speech Lang. **23**(1), 107–125 (2009)
12. Xiang, L., Yang, X., Zhang, J., Wang, W.: A word-frequency-preserving steganographic method based on synonym substitution. Int. J. Comput. Sci. Eng. **19**(1), 132–139 (2019)
13. Chang, C.Y., Clark, S.: Practical linguistic steganography using contextual synonym substitution and a novel vertex coding method. Comput. Linguist. **40**(2), 403–448 (2014)
14. Chang, C. Y., Clark, S.: The secret's in the word order: text-to-text generation for linguistic steganography. In: Proceedings of COLING 2012, pp. 511–528. The COLING 2012 Organizing Committee, Mumbai, India (2012)
15. Fang, T., Jaggi, M., Argyraki, K.: Generating steganographic text with LSTMs. In: Proceedings of ACL 2017, Student Research Workshop, pp. 100–106. Association for Computational Linguistics, Stroudsburg, PA (2017)
16. Dai, F., Cai, Z.: Towards Near-imperceptible Steganographic Text. In: Proceedings of the 57th Annual Meeting of the Association for Computational Linguistics, pp. 4303–4308. Association for Computational Linguistics, Stroudsburg, PA (2019)

17. Ziegler, Z., Deng, Y., Rush, A.: Neural linguistic steganography. In: Proceedings of the 2019 EMNLP-IJCNLP, pp. 1210–1215. Association for Computational Linguistics, Stroudsburg, PA (2019)
18. Shen, J., Ji, H., Han, J.: Near-imperceptible neural linguistic steganography via self-adjusting arithmetic coding. In: Proceedings of the 2020 EMNLP, pp. 303–313. Association for Computational Linguistics, Stroudsburg, PA (2020)
19. Zhou, X., Peng, W., Yang, B., Wen, J., Xue, Y., Zhong, P.: Linguistic steganography based on adaptive probability distribution. IEEE Trans. Dependable Secure Comput. **19**(5), 2982–2997 (2022)
20. Ding, J., Chen, K., Wang, Y., Zhao, N., Zhang, W., Yu, N.: Discop: provably secure steganography in practice based on "distribution copies". In: 2023 IEEE Symposium on Security and Privacy (SP), pp. 2238–2255. IEEE, Piscataway, NJ (2023)
21. Yang, T., Wu, H., Yi, B., Feng, G., Zhang, X.: Semantic-preserving linguistic steganography by pivot translation and semantic-aware bins coding. IEEE Trans. Dependable Secure Comput. **21**(1), 139–152 (2024)
22. Wu, J., Wu, Z., Xue, Y., Wen, J., Peng, W.: Generative text steganography with large language model. In: Proceedings of the 32nd ACM International Conference Multimedia (MM 2024), pp. 10345–10353. ACM, New York, NY (2024)
23. Zhu, Z., Ying, Q., Qian, Z., Zhang, X.: Steganography in animated emoji using self-reference. Multimedia Syst. **27**(3), 331–340 (2021). https://doi.org/10.1007/s00530-020-00723-z
24. Huang, J., et al.: Incorporating emoji sentiment information into a pre-trained language model for Chinese and English sentiment analysis. Intell. Data Anal. **28**(6), 1601–1625 (2024)
25. Kumar, A., Jain, D.: EmoMBTI-Net: introducing and leveraging a novel emoji dataset for personality profiling with large language models. Soc. Netw. Anal. Min. **14**(1), 234 (2024)
26. Chrismanto, A.R., Winarko, E., Suyanto, Y.: EiAP-BC: a novel emoji aware inter-attention pair model for contextual spam comment detection based on posting text. ACM Trans. Asian Low Resour. Lang. Inf. Process. **23**(12), 165:1–165:30 (2024)
27. Rutherford, A., Akarajaradwong, P.: Exploring the correlation between emojis and mood expression in Thai Twitter Discourse. ACM Trans. Asian Low Resour. Lang. Inf. Process. **23**(11), 150:1–150:14 (2024)
28. Tang, Y., Hou, J., Huang, X., Shao, Z., Yang, Y.: Green edge intelligence scheme for mobile keyboard emoji prediction. IEEE Trans. Mob. Comput. **23**(2), 1888–1901 (2024)
29. Eisner, B., Rocktäschel, T., Augenstein, I., Bošnjak, M., Riedel, S.: emoji2vec: Learning emoji representations from their description. In: Proc. 4th Int. Workshop on NLP for Social Media, pp. 48–54. Association for Computational Linguistics, Stroudsburg, PA (2016)
30. Li, F., Wei, P., Fu, T., Lin, Y., Zhou, W.: Imperceptible Text Steganography based on Group Chat. In: IEEE International Conference on Multimedia and Expo (ICME), pp. 1–6. IEEE, Piscataway, NJ (2024)
31. Grattafiori, A., Dubey, A., Jauhri, A., et al.: The Llama 3 Herd of Models. arXiv preprint arXiv:2407.21783 (2024)
32. OpenAI, Achiam, J., Adler, S., et al.: GPT-4 Technical Report. arXiv preprint arXiv:2303.08774 (2023)

33. Bai, J., Bai, S., Chu, Y., et al.: Qwen Technical Report. arXiv preprint arXiv:2309.16609 (2023)
34. DeepSeek-AI, Liu, A., Feng, B., et al.: DeepSeek-V3 Technical Report. arXiv preprint arXiv:2412.19437 (2024)
35. Li, J., Galley, M., Brockett, C., Gao, J., Dolan, B.: A diversity-promoting objective function for neural conversation models. In: Proceedings of the 2016 NAACL-HLT, pp. 110–119. Association for Computational Linguistics, Stroudsburg, PA (2016)

Knowledge-Enhanced Text Summaries for Factual Problems

Jing Kang, Yangsen Zhang[✉], Yalun Wang, and Yalong Guo

Institute of Intelligent Information Processing, Beijing Information Science and
Technology University, Beijing, China
zhangyangsen@163.com, {2024021020,2024021021}@bistu.edu.cn

Abstract. Generative summarization is a critical task in natural language processing, aiming to generate concise and accurate information from large volumes of text. The current mainstream generative summarization model employs a deep learning-based sequence-to-sequence architecture, with optimization performed at the character level. However, due to insufficient attention to semantic consistency between generated summaries and the source text, these models often produce outputs with semantic ambiguity and factual inaccuracies. To tackle this challenge, we propose OpenFactAlign, a novel framework that enhances factual consistency by dynamically extracting and aligning open-domain facts with summaries. The framework extracts open-domain triples (subject-predicate-object structures) as factual knowledge from raw text and introduces a loss function to minimize semantic deviation. By enhancing the semantic representation of factual knowledge during decoding, the model generates summaries with improved alignment to the source text. Extensive experiments on the LCSTS dataset demonstrate that the proposed model achieves improvements of 6.06, 6.88 and 3.09% points in ROUGE-1, ROUGE-2 and ROUGE-L scores, respectively, and 5.7, 8.31, 0.86 and 2.11% points in BLEU-1, BLEU-2, BLEU-3 and BLEU-4 scores, respectively, compared to the BART baseline.

Keywords: Generative headline · Knowledge enhancement · Open domain knowledge · Semantic consistency · Natural language processing

1 Introduction

Text summarization generates concise and accurate summaries via extractive or generative methods. Extractive approaches ensure readability and information accuracy but often lack coherence and coverage, leading to missing references [33]. Generative methods, as seq2seq tasks, align with human writing and offer flexible control. However, token-level objectives like Cross-Entropy or MLE [14] ignore semantic alignment, causing factual errors such as missing information, concept gaps, and repetition [6]. As shown in Fig. 1, input texts stating "is expected to be officially commercialized in the fourth quarter of 2024" may generate "was confirmed to be commercially available by the end of 2024". Such

© The Author(s), under exclusive license to Springer Nature Singapore Pte Ltd. 2026
X.-L. Mao et al. (Eds.): NLPCC 2025, LNAI 16105, pp. 146–158, 2026.
https://doi.org/10.1007/978-981-95-3352-7_12

Fig. 1. Summary factual errors.

outputs achieve high ROUGE scores [13] but exhibit factual inaccuracies from semantic inconsistency.

To enhance factual accuracy in summarization, knowledge graphs (KG) improve semantic consistency and information richness by structuring entities, attributes, and relations as triples (h, r, t). However, building KG in the Chinese open domain remains a challenge due to limited public resources.

Large language models (LLMs) excel in NLP tasks, showing instruction-following and in-context learning. Autoregressive LLMs (GPT [1], Qwen2.5-7B [30], etc.) align with human intent via pre-training, fine-tuning, and prompt learning. In-context learning [9] enhances generalization through examples. These strengths make LLMs ideal for building Chinese open-domain knowledge graphs.

In this paper, the main contributions of our work are summarized as follows:

(a) We explore **Dynamic Open-domain Knowledge Extraction** by leveraging LLMs to directly extract factual triples from texts without closed knowledge graphs, adaptable to Chinese corpora.

(b) We propose **FactSim$_{Loss}$**, Semantic Consistency Loss that supplements cross entropy by measuring the similarity between generated summaries and extracted knowledge, directly optimizing factual consistency.

(c) We propose a **Lightweight Knowledge Enhancement Mechanism** that integrates factual knowledge in training and enables implicit use during inference, balancing accuracy and efficiency.

2   Related Work

Generative summarization generates concise and accurate summaries by extracting key information. Training uses supervised learning on large labeled datasets, while inference identifies salient information from unseen inputs. Recent methods include reinforcement learning, triple-guided summarization [32], and pre-trained language models [24]. This paper's model adopts a sequence-to-sequence architecture and integrates external knowledge to improve summary generation.

2.1 Seq2Seq-Based Summary Generation Framework

The Sequence-to-Sequence (Seq2Seq) framework maps input sequences to output sequences through two main modules: the encoder, which captures the document's abstract semantic representation, and the decoder, which generates the summary word by word.

Rush et al. [22] first applied the Seq2Seq framework to summarization, using a CNN encoder and an NNLM decoder, but performance was limited by their modeling capacity. Chopra et al. [5] improved summary quality by introducing an RNN decoder, and Nallapati et al. [19] further enhanced the model with an RNN encoder, forming a fully RNN-based Seq2Seq structure. To address out-of-vocabulary issues, Gu et al. [10] proposed CopyNet, combining extractive and generative methods by enabling direct copying from the input.

Recently, integrating pre-trained models like BERT [7], BART [12], and GPT into Seq2Seq frameworks has greatly improved summarization performance. However, common objectives like Cross-Entropy (CE) and Maximum Likelihood Estimation (MLE) optimize at the token level, often overlooking semantic alignment with the source text and causing factual inconsistencies.

To address factual inconsistencies, this study proposes a semantic consistency-aware loss function. It extracts factual triples from the input text, integrates them during decoding, and minimizes the semantic gap between the summary and factual knowledge representations, improving semantic faithfulness and reducing factual errors [20].

2.2 Summary Generation Based on Knowledge Enhancement

Researchers have found that external knowledge such as structured knowledge bases, textual knowledge, terminology dictionaries, and expert knowledge can effectively guide summary generation. In English-domain tasks, OpenIE is often used to extract factual triples. For example, Cao et al. [2] mapped relational information to sequences as additional encoder input; Zhu et al. [34] built knowledge graphs and fused node representations into a Seq2Seq model; Chen et al. [4] combined knowledge graph information with structured semantic guidance; Mao Xingjing et al. [18] constructed heterogeneous knowledge graphs from keywords and phrases; Chen et al. [3] used trainable continuous and discrete natural language cues with a pre-trained model to assist summary generation.

In domain-specific applications, Shi et al. [23] used meteorological event and geographic knowledge to guide summary generation. In biomedicine, MacAvaney et al. [17] incorporated UMLS ontology concepts into decoding; Deng Lu et al. [6] filtered high-quality biomedical knowledge to enhance attention mechanisms; Xie et al. [28] integrated a graph neural topic model and UMLS knowledge into a pre-trained framework. However, these studies focus mainly on English or specific domains, while Chinese-domain summarization remains underexplored.

Text summarization has advanced, but Seq2Seq models lack deep semantic understanding, and knowledge-enhanced models face challenges in knowledge construction, particularly in Chinese domains. We propose OpenFactAlign, a knowledge-enhanced generative framework that extracts factual triples from the Chinese LCSTS dataset and integrates them into decoding with semantic embeddings, guided by $FactSim_{Loss}$ to ensure semantic consistency in summary.

3   Methodology

3.1   Task Modeling

The summary generation task for Chinese text can be formally expressed as follows: given Chinese text $C = \{\omega_1, \cdots, \omega_i, \cdots, \omega_n\}$, the model is required to extract the ternary knowledge $K = \{(h_i, r_i, t_i,)\}$ in the text and automatically generate an accurate and coherent summary $T = \{t_1, \cdots, t_j, \cdots, t_m\}$, oriented to the core content of the text. Where ω_i and t_j denote the words appearing in the original text C and summary T respectively, n and m denote the length of the original text and the length of the generated summary $(n>m)$ respectively, and K denotes the ternary knowledge in the text, h_i denotes the head entity of the ith knowledge, r_i denotes the relationship of the ith knowledge, and t_i denotes the tail entity of the ith knowledge. Then the text summary with open domain ternary knowledge is modelled as follows: $\widehat{T} = argmax_T P\left(T \mid C, K\right)$.

3.2   Generative Summary Methods for Knowledge Enhancement

BART (Bidirectional and Auto-Regressive Transformers) combines BERT's contextual understanding with GPT's generation capability in a Seq2Seq framework. We employ BART as our base model and propose OpenFactAlign, which enhances it with external knowledge through two modules: knowledge acquisition and fusion decoding, as shown in Fig. 2.

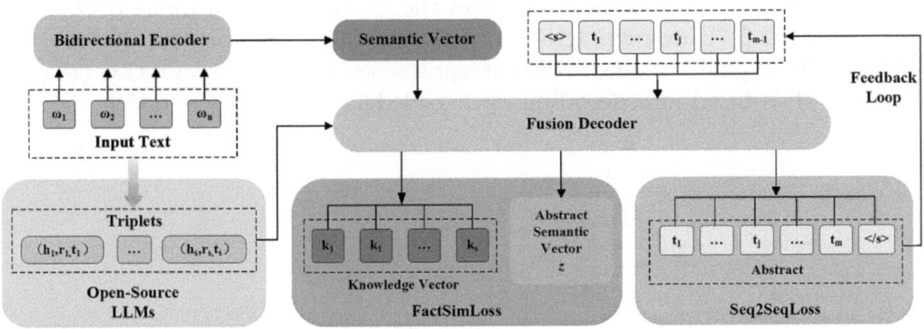

Fig. 2. The structure of the OpenFactAlign model.

The knowledge acquisition module extracts (h,r,t) triples to build open-domain knowledge, while the fusion decoding module integrates these triples via semantic representations to guide generation through a custom loss function.

3.3 Knowledge Acquisition Module

The Knowledge Acquisition Module uses LLMs to extract factual triples from text and build open-domain knowledge, avoiding reliance on closed-domain resources due to the lack of comprehensive Chinese knowledge graphs. We adopt Qwen2.5-7B, a lightweight model, for factual extraction, and apply in-context learning to enhance accuracy, generalization, and reduce dependence on annotated data when extracting triples k from the original text C.

The prompt model reformulates the problem using a pre-training like template [26]. The knowledge acquisition module selects and annotates a sample from text C, creates a prompt with a task-specific prefix p and input-output pairs, and feeds it into Qwen2.5-7B to generate triples, summarized as open-domain knowledge K. This process repeats until all data are processed (Algorithm 1).

Algorithm 1. Qwen2.5-7B Extraction Triad Algorithm

Input: Relevant text C, prefix p, few sample *examples*
Output: Open domain knowledge K

    for $i \leftarrow 1$ **to** N **do**
        $c \leftarrow \textbf{select}(C)$;   ▷ Select a piece of data from the relevant text c
        $prompt \leftarrow \textbf{P}(p, examples, c)$;   ▷ Generate prompt
        $k \leftarrow \textbf{Qwen2.5-7B}(prompt)$;   ▷ The input *prompt* extracts the ternary k
        $K \leftarrow \textbf{abstract}(k)$;   ▷ Aggregate k into K
    end for

For the text "360 frequently becomes the "bodyguard" of quasi-IPO enterprises", Qwen2.5-7B extracts triples ("subject": "360", "predicate": "becomes", "object": "bodyguard of quasi-IPO enterprises") via prompt integration (Fig. 3), which are then fused into decoding for knowledge-enhanced generation.

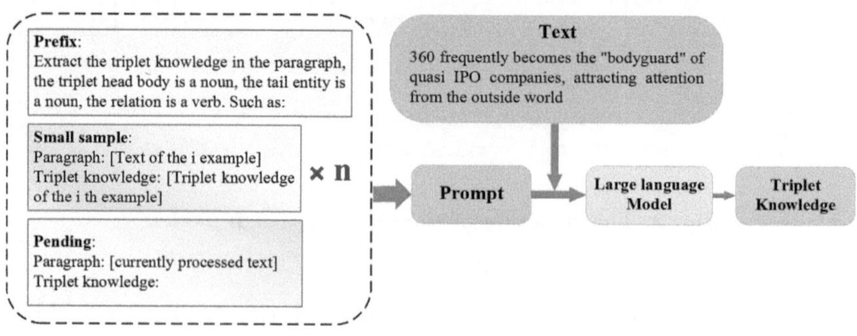

Fig. 3. Qwen2.5-7B based ternary extraction method.

3.4 Fusion Decoding Module

The fusion decoding module aligns BART's decoder with LLM capabilities during training to improve summary coherence and accuracy. BART's reconstruction loss uses cross-entropy between decoder outputs and original text: as shown in Eq. (1):

$$CE_{loss} = -\frac{1}{n} \sum_{j=1}^{n} \sum_{i=1}^{m} y_{ij} \log\left(t_{ij}\right) \tag{1}$$

where n represents sample count, m denotes vocabulary size, y_{ij} indicates the ground-truth probability at position i, and t_{ij} represents the generated summary's probability at position i.

Although CE_{loss} ensures lexical accuracy, it lacks semantic alignment, risking factual deviation. To address this, we propose $FactSim_{Loss}$—a loss function measuring the distance between summary semantics and factual encodings. It supports two strategies: mean semantics for overall alignment and minimum semantics for key fact emphasis. The final loss $Loss = CE_{loss} + FactSim_{Loss}$ jointly optimizes lexical and semantic fidelity to enhance factual consistency.

Ternary Knowledge Encoding. Due to the sparse connectivity of open-domain knowledge - with massive, low redundancy entity-relation nodes [25] - graph-based computation is not suitable for representation. Therefore, we adopt BART to capture triadic implicit knowledge at the semantic level, based on two key considerations:

First, open-domain triples can be fluently converted into natural language (e.g., "subject: 'NDRC', predicate: 'was sanctioned', object: 'by the law'" → "NDRC was sanctioned by the law"), making them compatible with open-source models for semantic modeling. Second, our goal is to ensure semantic consistency in summaries, which inherently relies on capturing inter-sentential relationships.

To implement this, we convert (head, relation, tail) or (entity, attribute, value) triples into sentences, then input them into BART to obtain semantic representations of factual units (k_i), as formalized in Eqs. (2) and (3).

$$k_i = decode\left(ks_i\right) \tag{2}$$

$$ks_i = h_i + r_i + t_i \tag{3}$$

In Eq. (2), decode($\cdot$) denotes the BART model's decoding-mode operation, while ks_i in Eq. (3) represents a synthetically constructed sentence formed by combining textual triadic structures.

Summary Semantic Vector. The semantic vector z is calculated as shown in Eq. (4):

$$z = decode\left(T\right) \tag{4}$$

where T denotes the summary text.

Loss Function $FactSim_{Loss}$. The $FactSim_{Loss}$ mechanism guides summary generation toward source text semantics through divergence minimization between generated summaries' semantic vectors and encoded factual knowledge.

We propose two loss computation strategies: mean semantic alignment and minimal semantic alignment.

The mean semantic strategy ensures the generated summary is semantically consistent with all factual knowledge. By integrating diverse information, it guides the model to generate content aligned with all facts. The calculation is defined in formula (5):

$$\overline{FactSim_{Loss}} = \frac{1}{n \times s} \sum_{j=1}^{n} \sum_{i=1}^{s} dist\left(k_i, z_j\right) \tag{5}$$

where dist$(\cdot)$ denotes the distance calculation method, n denotes the number of samples, and s denotes the number of factual codes in each sample.

The minimal semantic strategy enhances factual focus by aligning summaries with the most critical fact, prioritizing key knowledge over peripheral details. Equation (6) formalizes this approach.

$$FactSim_{Loss}^{min} = \frac{1}{n} \sum_{j=1}^{n} min\left(dist\left(k_i, z_j\right)\right) \tag{6}$$

Finally, the $FactSim_{Loss}$ and CE_{loss} are combined to form the loss function Loss, as given in (7):

$$Loss = FactSim_{Loss} + CE_{loss} \tag{7}$$

4   Experiments

4.1   Dataset

Experiments were conducted on the Large Scale Chinese Short Text Summarization (LCSTS) dataset [11] from Sina Weibo, consisting of three parts: Part I with 2,400,591 pairs of texts and annotated summaries; Part II with 10,666 pairs rated 1 to 5 for relevance; Part III with 1,106 similarly scored pairs. Part I was used for training, 8,685 pairs (scores 3 to 5) from Part II for validation, and 725 pairs (scores 3 to 5) from Part III for testing. During training, the text, summary, and factual knowledge were input into the model.

4.2   Experimental Environment and Model Parameter Settings

We evaluate our model on the LCSTS dataset, where model performance is highly sensitive to hyperparameters. The detailed hyperparameter configurations are provided in Table 1.

Table 1. Experimental parameter settings

Parameters	Value
Batch size	256
Training round	5
Learning rate	5e-5
Discard rate	0.1
Embedding vector dimension	768
Optimiser	AdamW [15]

4.3   Assessment Methodology

In this paper, the performance of the proposed method on text summarization tasks is evaluated using ROUGE and BLEU [21] metrics.

ROUGE evaluates the quality of generated abstracts by analyzing n-gram co-occurrence between the generated and reference abstracts, primarily using recall as the metric. It measures the overlap of lexical units to assess summary accuracy and completeness. Common variants include ROUGE-N (n-gram overlap) and ROUGE-L (longest common subsequence), which evaluate coherence and fluency.

Originally developed for machine translation, BLEU is now widely used in text summarization to evaluate the similarity between generated and reference summaries. It calculates n-gram overlap precision, with BLEU-N denoting the n-gram length. However, BLEU emphasizes accuracy over fluency or semantic consistency, so it is often combined with other metrics (e.g., ROUGE) for a more comprehensive assessment.

4.4   Baselines

To validate the effectiveness of the proposed method on the LCSTS dataset, we selected several representative mainstream models for comparison. As shown in Table 2, the baseline models used are described in detail.

Table 2. Summarized descriptions of different models

Model	Summary
RNN-context [11]	Uses an RNN encoder with attention to integrate context, combining hidden states as input to the decoder.
T5 PEGASUS	A Chinese generative pre-training model based on mT5 [29] with a refined tokenizer, mimicking PEGASUS [31] for pre-training.
CopyNet [10]	Enhances Seq2Seq with a copying mechanism to copy input words, solving the out-of-vocabulary issue.
SuperAE [16]	Uses adversarial learning to supervise source text, enhancing its semantics.
GPT-2 [8]	A self-supervised pre-trained language model on a large-scale English corpus.
Keyword [27]	Uses TF-IDF to extract keywords, guiding attention for summary generation.

4.5 Ablation Studies

This section evaluates the effectiveness of the knowledge enhancement method in the proposed OpenFactAlign model through ablation experiments. The results on the LCSTS dataset are shown in Table 3. OpenFactAlign refers to the model proposed in this paper, while -Align indicates the removal of the factual knowledge constraint in the decoding model, retaining only the BART base model with the CE_{loss} loss function.

Table 3. Results of ablation experiments

Model	ROUGE-1	ROUGE-2	ROUGE-L	BLEU-1	BLEU-2	BLEU-3	BLEU-4
OpenFactAlign	**43.12**	**28.34**	**38.92**	**43.98**	**29.45**	**19.01**	**13.39**
-Align	37.06	21.46	35.83	38.28	21.14	18.15	11.28

The results in Table 3 demonstrate that removing factual knowledge constraints leads to significant performance degradation. This validates that our knowledge enhancement method successfully guides the model to: maintain focus on key phrases while ensuring semantic consistency with source facts. The approach effectively compensates for CE_{loss}'s semantic limitations, substantially improving factual accuracy in generated summaries.

5 Analysis

5.1 Comparison of Loss Function Strategies

OpenFactAlign uses Qwen2.5-7B to extract factual knowledge. The loss function $Loss$, combining CE_{loss} and $FactSim_{Loss}$, enforces semantic consistency between summaries and factual content. The design of $FactSim_{Loss}$, especially the distance metric (Euclidean or Cosine), significantly affects performance. Table 4 shows results under different strategies, with optimal values in bold.

Table 4. Comparison of experimental results of different strategies on LCSTS dataset

Strategy	ROUGE-1	ROUGE-2	ROUGE-L	BLEU-1	BLEU-2	BLEU-3	BLEU-4
MEAN+Euclidean	42.91	27.89	37.93	43.76	29.31	18.82	13.21
MEAN+Cosine	43.12	**28.34**	**38.92**	43.98	**29.45**	**19.01**	13.39
MIN+Euclidean	**43.67**	28.17	38.87	**44.01**	27.96	18.74	13.39
MIN+Cosine	43.08	27.65	37.64	43.81	28.32	18.89	**13.42**

MIN and MEAN strategies exhibit complementary strengths in generative summarization tasks. The MIN strategy prioritizes alignment with critical facts through semantic similarity calculations, ideal for scenarios requiring emphasis on specific information (e.g., key event highlights). However, it risks neglecting contextual diversity in multi-fact synthesis. Its variants, MIN+Euclidean (optimizing lexical matches via spatial distance metrics like ROUGE-1) and MIN+Cosine (enhancing semantic alignment through angular similarity for BLEU-4), demonstrate trade-offs between lexical precision and holistic coherence.

Conversely, the MEAN strategy calculates the average semantic distance across all factual knowledge, enabling a balanced integration of multiple facts. Its MEAN+Cosine variant combines broad factual coverage with semantic precision by aggregating cosine similarities, and consistently outperforms MIN-based strategies in structural coherence (ROUGE-L) and multi-fact scenarios.

Our experiments identify MEAN+Cosine as the optimal approach for real-world applications, achieving superior lexical-structural alignment (ROUGE-L) and semantic consistency. This strategy is adopted as the default to ensure summaries balance lexical overlap with global coherence.

5.2   Comparison and Analysis of Experimental Results

Table 5 presents the comparative results of our proposed OpenFactAlign model on the LCSTS dataset. The model achieves state-of-the-art performance across unigram (ROUGE-1), bigram (ROUGE-2), and longest subsequence (ROUGE-L) metrics, demonstrating superior information retention and semantic consistency. This improvement stems from two key innovations: the knowledge acquisition module that incorporates open-domain factual knowledge, and the $FactSim_{Loss}$ function that enforces semantic alignment while preserving key phrase relevance.

Table 5. Comparison of experimental results of different models in LCSTS dataset

Model	ROUGE-1	ROUGE-2	ROUGE-L
RNN-context	29.90	17.40	27.20
T5 PEGASUS	34.10	22.20	31.70
CopyNet	34.40	21.60	31.30
SuperAE	39.20	26.00	36.20
GPT-2(base)	40.40	26.30	37.20
Keyword	40.90	28.30	38.20
OpenFactAlign	**43.12**	**28.34**	**38.92**

Specifically, OpenFactAlign outperforms GPT-2 by 2.72, 2.04, and 1.72% points on ROUGE-1, -2, and -L respectively, despite having fewer parameters. While GPT-2 benefits from large-scale English pretraining, its limited Chinese knowledge hinders performance on Chinese tasks. Compared to the Keyword model, our approach shows significant gains (2.22, 0.04, 0.72 points), particularly in ROUGE-1, indicating effective utilization of LLM capabilities during decoding to extract higher-quality keywords - an important NLP trend. The Keyword model's inferior performance, due to its neglect of semantic relationships, further validates our design choices.

6   Conclusion and Future Work

This paper proposes OpenFactAlign, a knowledge-enhanced generative summarization framework with two core components: a knowledge acquisition module and a fusion decoding module. During training, the model retrieves high-quality triple knowledge through open-domain information extraction using a context learning-based Prompt paradigm, effectively leveraging LLM capabilities. The decoding module integrates our novel loss function $FactSim_{Loss}$, which enhances the representation of factual knowledge, ensures semantic fidelity, and addresses factual consistency in summaries.

Future work will explore the impact of external knowledge fusion on generation quality and aim to achieve LLM-level or better performance with lightweight models, promoting the practical application of pre-trained language model-based summarization.

Acknowledgments. The present research was supported by Beijing Natural Science Foundation (L233008), National Natural Science Foundation of China (No. 62176023). We gratefully acknowledge the thoughtful feedback provided by the anonymous reviewers.

References

1. Brown, T., et al.: Language models are few-shot learners. Adv. Neural. Inf. Process. Syst. **33**, 1877–1901 (2020)
2. Cao, Z., Wei, F., Li, W., Li, S.: Faithful to the original: Fact aware neural abstractive summarization. In: Proceedings of the AAAI Conference on Artificial Intelligence, vol. 32 (2018)
3. Chen, C., Zhang, W.E., Shakeri, A.S., Fiza, M.: The exploration of knowledge-preserving prompts for document summarisation. In: 2023 International Joint Conference on Neural Networks (IJCNN), pp. 1–8. IEEE (2023)
4. Chen, T., Wang, X., Yue, T., Bai, X., Le, C.X., Wang, W.: Enhancing abstractive summarization with extracted knowledge graphs and multi-source transformers. Appl. Sci. **13**(13), 7753 (2023)
5. Chopra, S., Auli, M., Rush, A.M.: Abstractive sentence summarization with attentive recurrent neural networks. In: Proceedings of the 2016 Conference of the North American Chapter of the Association for Computational Linguistics: Human Language Technologies, pp. 93–98 (2016)
6. Deng, L., Hu, Po ad Li, X.: Abstracting biomedical documents with knowledgeenhancement. Data Anal. Knowl. Disc. **6**(11), 1–12 (2022)

7. Devlin, J., Chang, M.W., Lee, K., Toutanova, K.: Bert: Pre-training of deep bidirectional transformers for language understanding. In: Proceedings of the 2019 conference of the North American chapter of the association for computational linguistics: human language technologies, volume 1 (long and short papers), pp. 4171–4186 (2019)

8. Ding, X., et al.: Dos: abstractive text summarization based on pretrained model with document sharing. In: 2022 4th International Conference on Intelligent Information Processing (IIP), pp. 163–166. IEEE (2022)

9. Dong, Q., et al.: A survey on in-context learning. arXiv preprint arXiv:2301.00234 (2022)

10. Gu, J., Lu, Z., Li, H., Li, V.O.: Incorporating copying mechanism in sequence-to-sequence learning. arXiv preprint arXiv:1603.06393 (2016)

11. Hu, B., Chen, Q., Zhu, F.: Lcsts: A large scale Chinese short text summarization dataset. arXiv preprint arXiv:1506.05865 (2015)

12. Lewis, M., et al.: Bart: Denoising sequence-to-sequence pre-training for natural language generation, translation, and comprehension. arXiv preprint arXiv:1910.13461 (2019)

13. Lin, C.Y.: Rouge: a package for automatic evaluation of summaries. In: Text summarization branches out, pp. 74–81 (2004)

14. Lin, Y., Wu, Y., Yin, A., Liao, X.: Multi-modal summarization model based on semantic relevance analysis. Comput. Appl. **44**(01), 65–72 (2024)

15. Loshchilov, I., Hutter, F.: Decoupled weight decay regularization. arXiv preprint arXiv:1711.05101 (2017)

16. Ma, S., Sun, X., Lin, J., Wang, H.: Autoencoder as assistant supervisor: Improving text representation for chinese social media text summarization. arXiv preprint arXiv:1805.04869 (2018)

17. MacAvaney, S., Sotudeh, S., Cohan, A., Goharian, N., Talati, I., Filice, R.W.: Ontology-aware clinical abstractive summarization. In: Proceedings of the 42nd International ACM SIGIR Conference on Research and Development in Information Retrieval, pp. 1013–1016 (2019)

18. Mao, X., Wei, Y., Yang, Y., Ju, S.: Khgas: keywords guided heterogeneous graph for abstractive summarization. Comput. Sci. **51**(07), 278–286 (2024)

19. Nallapati, R., Zhou, B., Gulcehre, C., Xiang, B., et al.: Abstractive text summarization using sequence-to-sequence rnns and beyond. arXiv preprint arXiv:1602.06023 (2016)

20. Nan, F., et al.: Improving factual consistency of abstractive summarization via question answering. arXiv preprint arXiv:2105.04623 (2021)

21. Papineni, K., Roukos, S., Ward, T., Zhu, W.J.: Bleu: a method for automatic evaluation of machine translation. In: Proceedings of the 40th annual meeting of the Association for Computational Linguistics, pp. 311–318 (2002)

22. Rush, A.M., Chopra, S., Weston, J.: A neural attention model for abstractive sentence summarization. arXiv preprint arXiv:1509.00685 (2015)

23. Shi, K., Peng, X., Lu, H., Zhu, Y., Niu, Z.: Multiple knowledge-enhanced meteorological social briefing generation. IEEE Trans. Comput. Social Syst. **11**(2), 2002–2013 (2023)

24. Sun, K., Luo, X., Luo, M.Y., Man, Z.B., Mao, C.L..: Survey of applications of pretrained language models. Comput. Sci. **50**(1), 176–184 (2023)

25. Wan, Q.Z., Wan, C.X., Hu, R., Liu, D.X., Liu, X.P., Liao, G.Q.: Event extraction based on deep learning: A survey of research issue. Acta Automatica Sinica **49**, 1–24 (2023)

26. Wang, P., Zhag, N., Zhang, C.: Two-stage clarification question generation method based on prompt. Appl. Res. Comput./Jisuanji Yingyong Yanjiu **41**(2) (2024)
27. Wang, Q., Ren, J.: Abstractive summarization with keyword and generated word attention. In: 2019 International Joint Conference on Neural Networks (IJCNN), pp. 1–8. IEEE (2019)
28. Xie, Q., Tiwari, P., Ananiadou, S.: Knowledge-enhanced graph topic transformer for explainable biomedical text summarization. IEEE J. Biomed. Health Inform. **28**(4), 1836–1847 (2023)
29. Xue, L., et al.: mt5: a massively multilingual pre-trained text-to-text transformer. arXiv preprint arXiv:2010.11934 (2020)
30. Yang, A., et al.: Qwen2. 5 technical report. arXiv preprint arXiv:2412.15115 (2024)
31. Zhang, J., Zhao, Y., Saleh, M., Liu, P.: Pegasus: pre-training with extracted gap-sentences for abstractive summarization. In: International Conference on Machine Learning, pp. 11328–11339. PMLR (2020)
32. Zhang, Y.z., LI, Y.: Research on abstractive text summarization based on triplet information guidance. J. Beijing Univ. Aeronaut. Astronaut. **48** (2022)
33. Zheng, C., Cai, Y., Zhang, G., Li, Q.: Controllable abstractive sentence summarization with guiding entities. In: Proceedings of the 28th International Conference on Computational Linguistics, pp. 5668–5678 (2020)
34. Zhu, C., et al.: Enhancing factual consistency of abstractive summarization. arXiv preprint arXiv:2003.08612 (2020)

DiSG: A Discourse Structure-Aware Multi-stage Approach for Long Tibetan Text Summarization

Yiwen Wang[1,2], Yanrong Hao[1,2], Bo Chen[1,2(✉)], Yang Xu[3(✉)], and Xiaobing Zhao[1,2]

[1] School of Information Engineering, Minzu University of China, Beijing, China
`chenbomuc@muc.edu.cn`
[2] National Language Resource Monitoring and Research Center of Minority Languages, Beijing, China
[3] China Electronics Standardization Institute, Beijing, China
`xuyang@cesi.cn`

Abstract. Most existing text summarization methods are designed for short texts and fail to perform well on long documents, especially in low-resource languages such as Tibetan. To address this challenge, we propose DiSG, a Discourse-aware, Stage-based, and Generative summarization framework built on pre-trained language models. DiSG leverages discourse structure to guide a multi-stage process, enabling effective extraction and generation of summaries from long text. Experiments on the TiLTS dataset show that DiSG achieves a 2.73-point improvement in ROUGE-L over the best baseline, demonstrating its superiority in producing coherent and complete summaries.

Keywords: Long text Summarization · Tibetan · Discourse Structure

1 Introduction

Although significant progress has been achieved in text summarization for high-resource languages such as Chinese and English, the development of summarization technologies for low-resource languages, including Tibetan, has lagged behind [1]. In contrast, existing research predominantly targets short-text scenarios, whereas long documents pose unique challenges due to their extended length, lower information density, and complex discourse structures, rendering conventional short-text methods ineffective.

While pre-trained language models have demonstrated outstanding performance in summarization tasks [2], they encounter notable limitations when applied to long-text scenarios. Owing to fixed input length constraints, these models often rely on naive truncation strategies [3], which fail to preserve globally distributed information. As a result, they struggle to capture long-range semantic dependencies, frequently generating summaries that are incomplete or lack logical coherence.

Y. Wang and Y. Hao—Equal contribution.

© The Author(s), under exclusive license to Springer Nature Singapore Pte Ltd. 2026
X.-L. Mao et al. (Eds.): NLPCC 2025, LNAI 16105, pp. 159–171, 2026.
https://doi.org/10.1007/978-981-95-3352-7_13

To address the aforementioned issues, this paper proposes DiSG—a **Di**scourse-aware, **S**tage-based, and **G**enerative summarization framework. DiSG adopts a multi-stage design to effectively leverage the discourse structure of long text and the generation capabilities of pre-trained language models. In the first stage, a Graph Neural Network (GNN) is employed to model the document's discourse structure, capturing inter-paragraph interactions and enabling the representation of global contextual information. In the second stage, sentence representations derived from the GNN are used to select a set of key sentences that contain salient content. In the final stage, a pre-trained generative model is used to produce the final summary based on these selected key sentences. By explicitly incorporating discourse-level information and decomposing the summarization process into interpretable stages, DiSG overcomes the input length limitations of pre-trained models and mitigates the risk of information loss due to naive truncation.

The main contributions of this paper are as follows:

- We propose DiSG, a novel discourse-aware, stage-based generative framework that effectively addresses the limitations of existing methods in Tibetan long-text summarization.
- We leverage Graph Neural Networks to model the discourse structure of long documents, enabling the extraction of globally important and semantically salient information.
- Experiments on a Tibetan long-text summarization dataset demonstrate that our method generates summaries with significantly improved fluency and completeness, achieving a 2.73 ROUGE-L improvement over the strongest baseline.

2 Related Work

Early Tibetan extractive summarization methods primarily relied on statistical models and simple text features. An [4] proposed an extractive Tibetan text summarization method based on feature word weights and sentence structure weights, selecting high-weight sentences to generate summaries by calculating the importance of sentences. Nan et al. [5] further optimized this method and proposed an extractive summarization method based on sensitive information, considering features such as topic sentences, sentence length, and similarity to enhance the summarization effect. Li [6] constructed a small-scale Tibetan summarization dataset and proposed an extractive summarization method based on ALBERT. Lv [7] further refined this dataset and proposed a Tibetan extractive summarization method based on BERT. Additionally, the graph-based TextRank algorithm [8] has been applied to Tibetan summarization extraction, providing more solutions for the development of Tibetan text summarization technology. However, extractive summarization for Tibetan texts exhibits limitations in content cohesion and structural flexibility, adversely impacting readability.

Generative summarization offers higher flexibility, with summaries being more complete and coherent, aligning with human reading habits. However, research on Tibetan generative summarization is relatively limited. Li [9] introduced neural network models into Tibetan generative summarization research, proposing an algorithm based on a unified model. Huang et al. [10] further advanced research in this field by applying multilingual pre-trained language models to Tibetan generative summarization. Despite these efforts, generative summarization in the Tibetan domain remains in its developmental stage, with the quality of summary generation still needing improvement.

Tibetan long text summarization often deals with texts exceeding the maximum input limit of pre-trained language models. TiLTS [11] is an open Tibetan long text summarization dataset, containing 36,507 pairs of (document, summary). Li [9] proposed a two-stage method, first performing extractive summarization on the document and then using the results as input to a neural network model for summary rewriting, enhancing the capability of long text summarization. Ouyang et al. [12] further proposed the Ti-LED model, adopting a two-stage multi-task pre-training strategy to improve the capability of Tibetan long text summarization. However, existing methods still face issues such as limited long text input length and lack of cross-paragraph information integration, making it difficult to fully reflect the core ideas of the document. Therefore, developing more efficient long text summarization methods remains an important research direction in the field of Tibetan text summarization. This paper proposes a discourse-aware, stage-based summarization framework that leverages paragraph-level structure and graph-based modeling to improve the quality of Tibetan long-text summarization and address the limitations of existing approaches.

3   DiSG for Long Tibetan Text Summarization

3.1   Overall Framework

To effectively address the challenges of Tibetan long-text summarization, we propose DiSG (Discourse-aware, Stage-based, Generative), a three-stage summarization framework that explicitly models the discourse structure of long documents and integrates it into the summary generation process. As illustrated in Fig. 1, DiSG consists of three stages: Discourse Graph Construction, Key Sentences Selection and Summary Generation. By decomposing the summarization task into these interpretable and structured stages, DiSG effectively integrates global discourse information into the generation process, thereby improving summary quality in terms of fluency, coherence, and content completeness.

3.2   Discourse Graph Construction

Basic Construction of the Graph: We construct a sentence-paragraph-level graph to represent the discourse structure of the input document. In the graph, each sentence and paragraph in the input text is a node, and their relationships are represented by weighted edges. A specific example of graph construction is shown in Fig. 1, where the left side represents sentence nodes and the right side represents paragraph nodes, and the categories of nodes and edges in the graph are listed in Table 1.

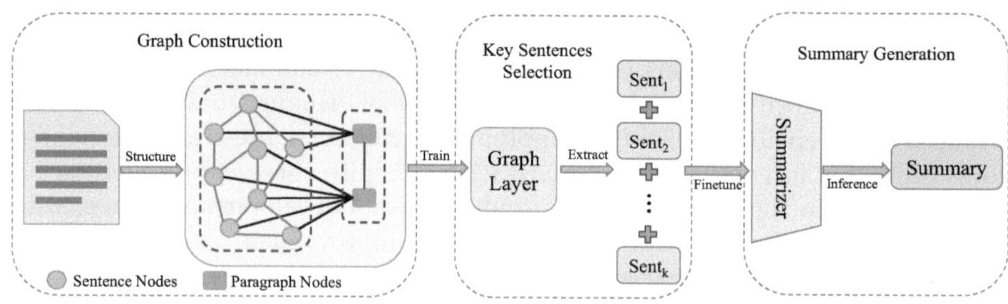

Fig. 1. Overview of DiSG.

Table 1. Description of nodes and edges in the discourse graph

Type	Description
Sentence Node	Each sentence is a node in the graph, representing a basic information unit in the document.
Paragraph Node	Each paragraph is represented by a virtual node, containing information of all sentences in the paragraph.
Sentence-to-Sentence Edge (S-S)	For all sentences in the text, construct S-S edges to represent their relationships.
Sentence-to-Paragraph Edge (S-P)	For sentences within each paragraph, construct S-P edges between corresponding nodes to indicate the affiliation between sentences and paragraphs.
Paragraph-to-Paragraph Edge (P-P)	For all paragraph nodes, construct P-P edges to represent the relationships between paragraphs.

Edge Weight Calculation: We mainly calculate the weights of edges between nodes through the following four methods [13–17].

Positional Distance Weight: For S-S and P-P, the positional distance weight is calculated based on the relative positions of nodes in the document. The closer the distance between nodes, the stronger their association. The formula is as follows:

$$W_{\mathrm{pos}}(i, j) = \exp\left(-\frac{|i - j|^2}{2\sigma^2}\right) \tag{1}$$

where i and j are the indices of nodes, and σ is the standard deviation of the maximum distance.

Paragraph Position Weight: For S-P, since sentences at the beginning and end of a paragraph are typically more important than those in the middle, we define the paragraph position weight as follows:

$$W_{\mathrm{para}}(i, \mathrm{para}_i) = \begin{cases} 1.2, & \text{if sentence } i \text{ is at the beginning or end of a paragraph} \\ 1.0, & \text{otherwise} \end{cases} \tag{2}$$

where i is the sentence index, and para_i is the paragraph to which the sentence belongs.

Keyword Co-occurrence Weight: For S-S, we measure the relevance between sentences based on the number of shared keywords. Assuming the keyword sets of two sentences are K_1 and K_2, respectively, the formula for calculating their co-occurrence weight is as follows:

$$S(i,j) = \sum_{w \in K_1 \cap K_2} \min(\text{score}(w, \text{sent}_i), \text{score}(w, \text{sent}_j)) \tag{3}$$

$$W_{\text{keyword}}(i,j) = 1.0 + 0.1 \times S(i,j) \tag{4}$$

where $\text{score}(w, \text{sent}_i)$ is the weight of keyword w in sentence sent_i.

Semantic Similarity Weight: For S-S and P-P, we use the TiBERT [18] model to generate semantic embeddings for sentences and calculate the cosine similarity between these embeddings to obtain the semantic similarity weight between sentences. The specific formula is as follows:

$$W_{\text{sem}}(i,j) = \text{cosine\_similarity}(e_i, e_j) \tag{5}$$

where e_i and e_j are the TiBERT embeddings of sentences i and j, respectively.

The final edge weight: For the weights of S-S, we calculate them as the product of positional distance weigh, keyword co-occurrence weight and semantic similarity weight. For the weights of S-P, we directly use the paragraph position weigh as the final weight. For the weights of P-P, we represent them as the product of positional distance weigh and semantic similarity weight.

3.3   Key Sentences Selection

We propose a hierarchical long text key sentences selection model based on graph neural networks [15, 19–22]. We leverage GNN with an attention mechanism for modeling discourse graph to select key sentences. The model achieves effective information transmission and updating across different levels. Figure 2 illustrates the overall architecture of the selecting model.

During the information interaction process, the model primarily realizes semantic transmission and updates node representations between sentences and paragraphs through the following four types of information interaction:

(1) Information interaction between sentences: There are usually semantic associations between different sentences. The adoption of a weighted attention mechanism allows sentence nodes to aggregate information from other sentence nodes, thereby updating their own representations. The specific formula is as follows:

$$s_i^{\text{new}} = \text{Attn}(S, S, W_{\text{sent}}) + s_i \tag{6}$$

where W_{sent} is the attention weight matrix between sentences, and Attn represents the attention operation, S represents the sentence.

(2) Information interaction between paragraphs: Each paragraph node can obtain key information from other paragraph nodes to form a more complete

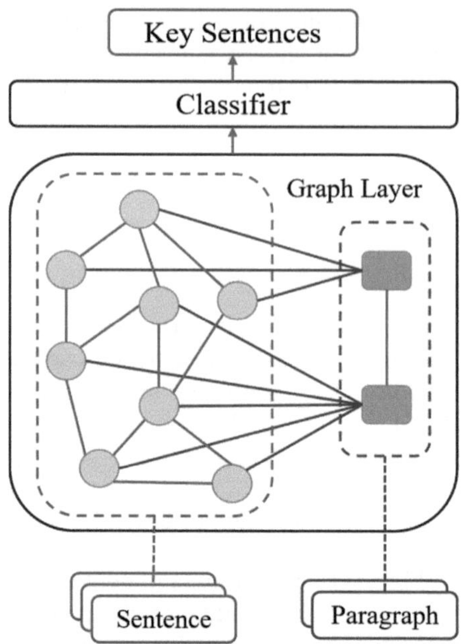

Fig. 2. Graph-based hierarchical key sentences selection.

representation, assisting the model in better understanding the overall semantic structure of the input text. The specific formula is as follows:

$$p_i^{\mathrm{new}} = \mathrm{Attn}(P, P, W_{\mathrm{para}}) + p_i \tag{7}$$

where W_{para} is the attention weight matrix between paragraphs, P represents paragraph.

(3) Information transmission from sentences to paragraphs: The overall semantics of a paragraph are derived from the aggregation of information from internal sentences. Therefore, it is necessary to use a weighted attention mechanism to aggregate information at the sentence level into paragraph nodes to update the paragraph representation. The specific formula is as follows:

$$p_j^{\mathrm{new}} = \mathrm{Attn}(P, S, W_{\mathrm{sent2para}}) + p_j \tag{8}$$

where $W_{\mathrm{sent2para}}$ is the attention weight matrix from sentences to paragraphs.

(4) Information transmission from paragraphs to sentences: After information is transmitted from sentences to paragraphs, the new paragraph representation needs to act back on sentences to further refine the sentence representation, enabling it to be optimized by incorporating global information. The update formula for sentence nodes is as follows:

$$s_i^{\mathrm{new}} = \mathrm{Attn}(S, P, W_{\mathrm{para2sent}}) + s_i \tag{9}$$

where $W_{\mathrm{para2sent}}$ is the attention weight matrix from paragraphs to sentences.

The final representations of sentence nodes after multiple iterations are input into a classifier to predict whether they belong to key sentences. The output of the classifier is:

$$y = \text{Classifier}(s_i^{\text{final}}) \tag{10}$$

where y is the predicted label for each sentence.

Classifier: We label the top p key sentences of the document based on ROUGE-1 and then train a classifier using these labeled data. The value of p is one-third of the total number of sentences in the input text, with a minimum of 3 sentences and a maximum of 15 sentences. Due to length constraints, we select the first few sentences based on probability to ensure that their cumulative length does not exceed 1024 tokens before feeding them into the pre-trained model to generate the summary.

3.4   Summary Generation

We employ a fine-tuned CMPT [23] model for summary generation, with key sentences selected based on ROUGE-1 scores as input and the target reference summary as output. Through iterative optimization, the model learns to generate coherent and semantically rich summaries from key sentences, thereby enhancing its understanding of long texts and ensuring that the summaries cover the core content.

4   Experiments

4.1   Experimental Setups

We conduct experiments on the TiLTS dataset [11], which contains 36,507 document-summary pairs. During the training process, the Adam algorithm [24] is employed to optimize the parameters. All models are trained on an RTX 4090 GPU. The parameter settings for the key sentences selection model and the CMPT model are detailed as follows. For the key sentences selection model, the learning rate is set to 5×10^{-6}, with a dropout rate of 0.1. The batch size is 8, the hidden size is 768, the number of heads is 8, and the number of epochs is 10. For the CMPT model, the learning rate is 1×10^{-4}, the number of epochs is 5, the batch size is 1, and the number of warmup steps is 500. These settings are chosen to optimize the performance of the models in their respective tasks.

4.2   Baselines

CMPT: A method that directly employs pre-trained language models to generate summaries.

Two-Stage Summarization Methods: These methods use an extractive approach to independently process each paragraph, extracting the most representative key information to retain the core content. The extracted key information is then integrated and fed into a pre-trained language model for final summarization. These methods include the following experiments:1. An improved TextRank algorithm [25] is used to extract key information from each paragraph. 2. A Tibetan version of the BERTSUM model is used to extract key information from each paragraph. Three different summarization layers are applied to extract key information from the output [18]: simple classifier, sentence-level Transformer [26], and recurrent neural network [27].

4.3   Experimental Results and Analysis

We compare DiSG with traditional methods and two-stage methods, using ROUGE evaluation metrics [28]. The results are shown in Table 2.

Table 2. Tibetan long-text summarization results

Model	ROUGE-1	ROUGE-2	ROUGE-L
CMPT	30.16	11.27	22.61
Extraction+CMPT: TextRank	31.63	12.37	23.38
Extraction+CMPT: BERTSUM+Classifier	32.13	12.31	23.06
Extraction+CMPT: BERTSUM+Transformer	34.12	14.42	25.10
Extraction+CMPT: BERTSUM+LSTM	32.31	13.61	24.37
DiSG(ours)	**36.72**	**16.15**	**27.83**

The experimental results show that DiSG achieves the best performance in the ROUGE-1, ROUGE-2, and ROUGE-L. This is mainly due to its modeling based on the discourse structure. By introducing paragraph nodes and cross-paragraph edges, the model can not only focus on local information within paragraphs but also effectively capture the thematic associations between different paragraphs in long texts, thereby enhancing the global semantic coherence.

4.4   Key Sentences Selection Evaluation

Table 3 shows the results of key Sentences Selection for the proposed DiSG. The results show that DiSG outperforms other methods in the ROUGE-1, ROUGE-2, and ROUGE-L metrics. By training the model with graph neural networks, it can more accurately identify the core content of the article and extract the most representative key information. This phased processing approach preserves the hierarchical logic of the original text, providing high-quality input for summary generation.

4.5   Ablation Study Importance of Edge Weights

To verify the contributions of different modules in the graph model, ablation experiments are conducted by removing various edge weight calculation modules. The results are shown in Table 4.

The experimental results show that removing any edge weight leads to a decline in performance. Among them, the most significant drop in ROUGE metrics occurs when the semantic similarity weight is removed, which fully demonstrates the key role of semantic similarity weight in capturing deep semantic

Table 3. Results of key sentences selection

Model	ROUGE-1	ROUGE-2	ROUGE-L
TextRank	21.92	4.44	12.77
BERTSUM+Classifier	21.63	6.05	14.72
BERTSUM+Transformer	24.72	6.99	16.58
BERTSUM+LSTM	23.57	5.92	15.55
DiSG(ours)	**28.35**	**8.41**	**18.26**

Table 4. Results of removing various edge weights

Experimental Setting	ROUGE-1	ROUGE-2	ROUGE-L
Complete Model	36.72	16.15	27.83
Remove Positional Distance Weight	34.85	14.32	25.67
Remove Paragraph Position Weight	35.12	14.71	25.94
Remove Keyword Co-occurrence Weight	33.26	13.45	24.58
Remove Semantic Similarity Weight	32.03	12.16	23.19

associations. These modules work together to effectively enhance the quality of key sentence selection, thereby improving the quality of the generated summaries.

4.6   Ablation Study - Importance of Paragraph Nodes

In addition to verifying the impact of different edge weight calculation modules on the results, experiments are also conducted to demonstrate the importance of adding paragraph nodes in the graph discourse structure. The results are shown in Table 5.

Table 5. Results of removing paragraph nodes

Experimental Setting	ROUGE-1	ROUGE-2	ROUGE-L
Complete Model	36.72	16.15	27.83
Remove Paragraph Nodes	35.61	15.68	27.04

The experimental results show that after removing the paragraph nodes from the graph structure, the values of ROUGE-1, ROUGE-2, and ROUGE-L decreased by 3.02%, 2.91%, and 2.84%, respectively. This indicates that paragraph nodes play an important role in the model's understanding of the text hierarchy and capturing global semantic associations.

4.7   Case Study

We select a single data entry from the dataset to illustrate DiSG. The original text and generated results are as follows:

(1) Input Text: Due to the input text length, only a part of the Tibetan text is cited, showing the starts of some paragraphs. The specific content is shown in Table 6.

Table 6. Input text example

Original Tibetan text	English translation
མཉམ་འབྲེལ་རྒྱལ་ཚོགས་ གནམ་གཤིས་ འགྱུར་ལྡོག་ སྐོར་གནའ་ ནི་ སྤྱི་ཚེང་ ས་ ཀྱི་ སྐབས་ བཅོ་བརྒྱད་པ་ ནི་ ཚེས་འཛོག་ ཕྱོགས་ ཀྱི་ ཚོགས་འདུ་ དང་ ཅིང་ཏུའུ་ ཚོད་ཡིག་ གི་ སྐབས་ བརྒྱད་པ་ ནི་ ཚེས་འཛོག་ ཕྱོགས་ ཀྱི་ ཚོགས་འདུ་ ནི་ ༡༡ ཚེས་ ༢༦ ཉིན་ ཁ་ཐར་ གྱི་ ཏེ་ ར་ འཚོག་ ག་ རྒྱུ་ རེད། ……	The 18th Conference of the Parties to the United Nations Framework Convention on Climate Change and the 8th Conference of the Parties to the Kyoto Protocol will be held in Deira, Qatar on November 26. ……
གསར་འགྱུར་ ཡོངས་བསྒྲགས་ ཚོགས་འདུ་ ནི་ ཁོག་ རྒྱལ་ཁབ་ འཕེལ་རྒྱས་ ཀྱུ་ཡོན་ ཞུན་ཁང་ གིས་གནས་གཤིས་འགྱུར་ལྡོག་ལ་ཁ་གཏད་གཙོག་ཆུ་ ནི་ གྱུང་གོ་ ནི་ སྲིད་ཇུས་ དང་ བྱ་སྤྱོད། ……	At the press conference, the National Development and Reform Commission introduced China's policies and actions to address climate change. ……
ཞེ་ཀྲེན་ཏུ་ ཡིས་ ཀོ་སྐོང་ གནས་ན་ ར་ གཤིགས་ ན །ན་ཉིང་ རྒྱལ་ཡོངས་ ལུ་ ནུས་རྒྱུ་ ཟད་གྲོན་ ༢༡ ཀཆ་པ་ དང་ འདི་ ཁོ་ སྔར་ འབུད་ཆོག་ ༣༥ ཡན་ ཆག་ རྒྱུ་ རེད། ……	According to Xie Zhenhua, last year's national energy consumption fell by 21%, and this year's carbon emissions will fall by more than 35%. ……
རྒྱལ་ཁབ་ ཀྱིས་ དུ་དྲང་རྒྱལ་ ཁབ་ ཀྱི་ གནམ་གཤིས་འགྱུར་ལྡོག་ལ་ཁ་ གཏད་གཙོག་ཆུ་ ནི་ འཆར་གཞི་ བར་དྲང་རྒྱལ་ཁབ་ ཀྱི་ གནམ་གཤིས་ འགྱུར་ལྡོག་ལ་ལ་གཏད་གཙོག་ཆུ་ ནི་ ལས་འདོན་ གྱི་ ཆེ་རིམ་ འཆར་གཞི་ འགོད་དྲུ་ ར་ ཤུགས་སྐྱོན་ བཏབ་པ་ དང་ །……	The country has also formulated a national plan for addressing climate change and a national overall strategy for adapting to climate change, and strengthened the top-level planning for addressing climate change...

(2) Key Sentences Result: We select the top 3 key sentences output by the model for demonstration and provide the corresponding English translations, as shown in Table 7.

Table 7. Key sentences example

Key sentences	English translation
1. ན་ཉིང་ རྒྱལ་ཡོངས་ མི་དམངས་ འཐུས་ཚོགས་ ཀྱི་ ཚོག་མཆན་ ཐོབ་ པའི་རྒྱལ་དམངས་ དཔལ་འབྱོར་ དང་ སྤྱི་ཚོགས་ འཕེལ་རྒྱས་ ཀྱི་ ལོ་ལྔ་ཚན་བཅུ་གཉིས་པ་ ནི་ འཆར་འགོད་ རྩ་གནད་དུ་འོ་ལྟ་ཚན་བཅུ་ གཉིས་པའི་རིང་ ནུས་རྒྱུ་ བཏ་གྲོན་ ཚད་གཞི་ ༡༦ དམན་ དུ་ གཏོང་ དགོས་པ་ དང་ ། སྔན་ འབུད་ཆོག་ ༡༧ དམན་ དུ་ གཏོང་ དགོས་ པ།	1. The Outline of the 12th Five-Year Plan for National Economic and Social Development approved by the National People's Congress last year proposed that 16 energy consumption standards should be reduced during the 12th Five-Year Plan period; 17 carbon emissions should be reduced.
2. མཉམ་འབྲེལ་རྒྱལ་ཚོགས་གནམ་གཤིས་འགྱུར་ལྡོག་སྐོར་གནའི་ནི་ཏྲེ་ ཚེས་ཀྱི་སྐབས་བཅོ་བརྒྱད་པ་ནི་ཚེས་འཛོག་ཕྱོགས་ཀྱི་ཚོགས་འདུ་དང་ ཅིང་ཏུའུ་ཚོད་ཡིག་གི་སྐབས་བརྒྱད་པ་ནི་ཚེས་འཛོག་ཕྱོགས་ཀྱི་ཚོགས་ འདུ་ནི་ཏྲ་༡༡ཚེས་༢༦ཉིན་ཁ་ཐར་གྱི་ཏེ་ར་འཚོག་རྒྱུ་རེད།	2. The 18th Conference of the Parties to the United Nations Framework Convention on Climate Change and the 8th Conference of the Parties to the Kyoto Protocol will be held in Deira, Qatar on November 26.
3. ཚོགས་འདུ་ནི་འ་ཁོག་གནན་དྲངས་པ་འི་རྒྱལ་ཁབ་འཕེལ་རྒྱས་ཀྱུ་ཡོན་ ཞུན་ཁང་གི་གྲུབ་རེན་གཞོན་པ་ཞེ་ཀྲེན་ཏུ་ཡིས་གནམ་གཤིས་འགྱུར་ལྡོག་ ལ་ཁ་གཏད་གཙོག་ཆུའི་སྲིད་གོ་ནི་ སྲིད་ཇུས་དང་བྱ་སྤྱོད་ངོ་སྤྲོད་གནང་ བ་མ་ཟད།	3. Xie Zhenhua, deputy director of the National Development and Reform Commission, who was invited to attend the meeting, introduced China's policies and actions to address climate change.

(3) Summary Generation Result: Table 8 presents a comparison between the model-generated summary and the reference summary. The result indicates that the generated summary can effectively cover the key information of the original text and essentially reflect the core content of the document.

Table 8. Summary example

	Summary	Translation
Generate summary	[Tibetan text]	The United Nations Climate Change Convention Conference was held in Qatar on November 26, and the China Climate Change Convention Conference was held. The conference reached a consensus on the Climate Change Convention Conference.
Reference Summary	[Tibetan text]	The 18th Conference of the Parties to the United Nations Framework Convention on Climate Change and the 8th Conference of the Parties to the Kyoto Protocol will be held in Doha, Qatar on November 26. Xie Zhenhua, deputy director of the National Development and Reform Commission, introduced China's policies and actions to address climate change. China has taken a series of measures to reduce energy consumption and carbon emissions, promote low-carbon pilot projects, advance carbon emission rights trading, and guide the participation of the whole society.

5 Conclusion

We propose DiSG, a novel multi-stage summarization framework designed for long Tibetan text summarization. By constructing a discourse aware graph that includes sentence and paragraph nodes, the model is able to understand the semantic relationships of long text from both local and global perspectives. This approach achieves hierarchical understanding of long texts and avoids the problem of semantic loss. Compared with traditional methods, it demonstrates superior performance in handling long text.

Acknowledgments. We extend our sincere thanks to all the anonymous reviewers for their valuable comments and suggestions. This work is supported by the National Social Science Foundation of China (22&ZD035).

References

1. Norbu, R., Danzeng, P., Kyi, L., et al.: Comprehensive analysis of Tibetan text summarie. In: 2024 7th International Conference on Machine Learning and Natural Language Processing (MLNLP), pp. 1–5. IEEE (2024)
2. Algani, Y.M.A.: A novel deep learning attention based sequence to sequence model for automatic abstractive text summarization. Int. J. Inf. Technol. **16**(6), 3597–3603 (2024)
3. Liu, Y.: Fine-tune BERT for extractive summarization. arXiv preprint arXiv:1903.10318 (2019)
4. Jiancairang, A.: Research on automatic web page summarization in Tibetan search engine systems. Microprocessors **31**(5), 77–80 (2010)
5. Kuiniangruo, N., Jiancairang, A.: Research on extractive Tibetan text summarization based on sensitive information. Cyber Secur. Appl. 4, 58–59 (2016)

6. Liang, L.: Tibetan pre-trained model based on ALBERT and its applications. Master's thesis, Lanzhou University, Lanzhou (2020)
7. Jing, L.: Research on Tibetan extractive summarization based on deep learning. Master's thesis, Lanzhou University (2022)
8. Wei, L., Xiaodong, Y., Xiaoqing, X.: An improved textrank for Tibetan summarization. J. Chinese Inf. Process. **34**(9), 36–43 (2020)
9. Wei, L.: Research on Tibetan news summarization based on a unified model. Master's thesis, Minzu University of China (2020)
10. Huang, S., Yan, X., OuYang, X., Yang, J.: Abstractive summarization of Tibetan based on end-to-end pre-trained model. In: Proceedings of the 22nd Chinese National Conference on Computational Linguistics, pp. 113–123 (2023)
11. Hao, Y., Chen, B., Zhao, X.: TiLTS: Tibetan long text summarization dataset. In: CCF International Conference on Natural Language Processing and Chinese Computing, pp. 265–276. Springer (2024)
12. Ouyang, X., Yan, X., Hao, M.: A pre-trained language model based on led for Tibetan long text summarization. In: 2024 27th International Conference on Computer Supported Cooperative Work in Design (CSCWD), pp. 992–997. IEEE (2024)
13. Gogireddy, Y.R., Bandaru, A.N., Sumanth, V.: Synergy of graph-based sentence selection and transformer fusion techniques for enhanced text summarization performance. J. Comput. Eng. Technol. (JCET) **7**(1), 5 (2024)
14. Ruan, Q., Ostendorff, M., Rehm, G.: HiStruct+: improving extractive text summarization with hierarchical structure information. *arXiv preprint* arXiv:2203.09629 (2022)
15. Shabani, N., et al.: A comprehensive survey on graph summarization with graph neural networks. IEEE Trans. Artif. Intell. **5**(8), 3780–3800 (2024)
16. Shi, T., Keneshloo, Y., Ramakrishnan, N., Reddy, C.K.: Neural abstractive text summarization with sequence-to-sequence models. ACM Trans. Data Sci. **2**(1), 1–37 (2021)
17. Yadav, A.K., Ranvijay, R.S.Y., Maurya, A.K.: Graph-based extractive text summarization based on single document. Multimedia Tools Appl. **83**(7), 18987–19013 (2024)
18. Liu, S., Deng, J., Sun, Y., Zhao, X.: TiBERT: Tibetan pre-trained language model. In: 2022 IEEE International Conference on Systems, Man, and Cybernetics (SMC), pp. 2956–2961. IEEE (2022)
19. Ghadimi, A., Beigy, H.: SGCSumm: an extractive multi-document summarization method based on pre-trained language model, submodularity, and graph convolutional neural networks. Expert Syst. Appl. **215**, 119308 (2023)
20. Qunkai, L., Chen Yufeng, X., Jin'an, Z.Y., Jian, L.: Extractive text summarization with heterogeneous graph network based on sub-sentence unit. J. Chinese Inf. Process. **38**(6), 119–128 (2024)
21. Phan, T.-A., Nguyen, N.D., Bui, K.-H.N.: Extractive text summarization with latent topics using heterogeneous graph neural network. In: Proceedings of the 36th Pacific Asia Conference on Language, Information and Computation, pp. 749–756 (2022)
22. Zhang, H., Liu, X., Zhang, J.: Contrastive hierarchical discourse graph for scientific document summarization. arXiv preprint arXiv:2306.00177 (2023)
23. Salchner, M.F., Jatowt, A.: A survey of automatic text summarization using graph neural networks. In: Proceedings of the 29th International Conference on Computational Linguistics, pp. 6139–6150 (2022)
24. Ba, J.L., Kiros, J.R., Hinton, G.E.: Layer normalization. arXiv preprint arXiv:1607.06450 (2016)

25. Mihalcea, R., Tarau, P.: TextRank: bringing order into text. In: Proceedings of the 2004 Conference on Empirical Methods in Natural Language Processing, pp. 404–411 (2004)
26. Raffel, C., et al.: Exploring the limits of transfer learning with a unified text-to-text transformer. J. Mach. Learn. Res. **21**(140), 1–67 (2020)
27. Nallapati, R., Zhai, F., Zhou, B.: SummaRuNNer: a recurrent neural network based sequence model for extractive summarization of documents. In: Proceedings of the AAAI Conference on Artificial Intelligence, vol. 31 (2017)
28. Lin, C.-Y.: ROUGE: a package for automatic evaluation of summaries. In: Text Summarization Branches Out, Barcelona, Spain, July 2004, pp. 74–81. Association for Computational Linguistics (2004)

Detecting and Correcting Hallucinations in LLMs via Substantive Uncertainty and Iterative Validation

Zheng Chen[1,2]($\boxtimes$), Yijie Cheng[1], and Yuxin Gao[1]

[1] School of Information and Software Engineering, University of Electronic Science and Technology of China, Chengdu 610054, China
[2] National Key Laboratory on Blind Signal Processing, Chengdu 610041, China
zchen@uestc.edu.cn

Abstract. Hallucination remains one of the most critical challenges in natural language generation (NLG), especially for large language models (LLMs) deployed in knowledge-intensive applications where factual consistency is critical. Existing hallucination detection methods often suffer from poor generalization across tasks and text types, while correction strategies typically require costly model retraining or extensive architectural changes. To address these limitations, we propose a lightweight, model-agnostic framework for hallucination detection and correction that integrates token-level uncertainty estimation with multi-turn verification. Central to our approach is the **Substantive-word Uncertainty Score (SUScore)**, a novel metric that quantifies uncertainty over substantive words–nouns, verbs, numerals, and other semantically important tokens–by incorporating syntactic priors, lexical importance, and model confidence. Building on this, we introduce the **Iterative Chain-Query (ICQ)** framework, which performs targeted, question-driven validation of potentially hallucination-prone spans through multi-step consistency checking, optionally enhanced with retrieval-augmented generation from external knowledge sources. Our approach requires no retraining and generalizes across different LLM architectures and NLG tasks. Experiments on three benchmark datasets–UHGEval, SVAMP, and QUEST–demonstrate that SUScore achieves superior calibration for hallucination detection compared to standard lexical or reference-based metrics such as BLEU and ROUGE. Furthermore, ICQ significantly improves factual accuracy while preserving output fluency and linguistic coherence. Together, these contributions offer a scalable and efficient solution for mitigating LLM hallucinations in real-world NLG deployments.

Keywords: Large Language Models · Natural Language Generation · Hallucination Detection · Retrieval-Augmented Generation · Factual Consistency

© The Author(s), under exclusive license to Springer Nature Singapore Pte Ltd. 2026
X.-L. Mao et al. (Eds.): NLPCC 2025, LNAI 16105, pp. 172–184, 2026.
https://doi.org/10.1007/978-981-95-3352-7_14

1   Introduction

The rapid development of artificial intelligence has brought Natural Language Generation (NLG) to the forefront of technological innovation. Large Language Models (LLMs) have demonstrated remarkable capabilities in understanding and generating human-like text, achieving near-human performance across various tasks. However, these models are not without limitations, particularly the issue of hallucination. Hallucination refers to the generation of content that appears plausible but is factually inaccurate or semantically inconsistent. This issue not only undermines the reliability of generated content but also poses significant risks in critical domains. For instance, erroneous medical recommendations could jeopardize patient safety, while inaccuracies in legal contexts might distort judicial decisions. Therefore, effectively detecting and correcting hallucinations is essential for ensuring the trustworthiness and practical utility of LLMs.

Hallucinations in LLMs stem from multiple factors, including noisy or biased training data, insufficient mechanisms for managing uncertainty during generation, and inherent limitations in existing generation objectives. These issues result in outputs that may lack factual consistency or fail to align with real-world knowledge. Existing approaches to mitigating hallucinations primarily focus on enhancing model architectures or redesigning pretraining objectives. While these methods have shown promise in specific scenarios, they typically come with significant computational costs and limited scalability, making them impractical for broader applications. Furthermore, traditional evaluation metrics, such as BLEU and ROUGE, are poorly equipped to capture the nuanced and context-dependent nature of hallucinations, further hindering progress in this area. Addressing these shortcomings requires the development of innovative solutions that are both computationally efficient and adaptable to diverse use cases.

To bridge these gaps, this paper introduces a novel framework named Iterative Chain-Query (ICQ). Central to this approach is the use of a newly proposed metric, Substantive-word Uncertainty Score (SUScore), which quantifies the uncertainty of substantive words prone to hallucinations. The ICQ framework employs an iterative verification process that identifies hallucinations by extracting validation chains and leveraging areas of high model uncertainty for focused analysis. Additionally, it integrates external knowledge through a retrieval-augmented generation mechanism to correct identified hallucinations. Validated on diverse datasets, the proposed method significantly improves hallucination detection and correction, ensuring the generation of accurate and reliable text.

This paper makes the following contributions:

- **Introduction of SUScore:** A novel metric designed to quantify the uncertainty of substantive words, effectively identifying regions susceptible to hallucinations in generated text.
- **Development of the ICQ Framework:** A systematic approach combining iterative verification, selective attention to high-uncertainty areas, and

retrieval-augmented generation for efficient hallucination detection and correction.

- **Comprehensive Validation Across Diverse Datasets:** Extensive experiments showcasing the robustness of the SUScore metric and ICQ framework, achieving superior performance in reducing hallucination rates and enhancing text quality compared to existing methods.

2   Related Works

Hallucinations in language generation occur when model-generated content deviates from reality, often resulting in semantic incoherence, factual inaccuracies, or nonsensical outputs [3,15]. Despite substantial progress in large language models (LLMs) for natural language tasks, addressing hallucinations remains a critical challenge. The growing reliance on AI-generated content has intensified research efforts to mitigate this issue.

2.1   Causes of Hallucinations

Hallucinations in text generation can be categorized as intrinsic or extrinsic. Intrinsic hallucinations arise when the output conflicts with the input content, while extrinsic hallucinations refer to generated text that cannot be verified against the input [5,10,15].

Multiple factors contribute to hallucinations, including unreliable or biased training data [13,24], lack of domain-specific knowledge [8,11,20,26], and outdated information that limits the factual accuracy of LLMs [7,9,17]. These limitations often lead to factual errors. Furthermore, structural aspects of LLMs, such as soft attention mechanisms [2,4], predispose them to errors in processing long texts. The tendency of LLMs to memorize training data [1] can result in overemphasis on repetitive recall, deviating from desired content generation.

Recent studies suggest that hallucinations may also stem from a flattening of model uncertainty. LLMs, constrained by their training data and inherent limitations, sometimes fabricate information to align with human expectations. Kadavath et al. [6] posits that language models possess a degree of awareness regarding the uncertainty of their outputs. Sharma et al. [19] introduces the concept of sycophancy, wherein LLMs prioritize human satisfaction over truthfulness, even knowingly generating incorrect responses. This phenomenon, termed flattery, persists despite reinforcement learning with human feedback (RLHF) and occurs in both ambiguous and straightforward scenarios [23]. Sharma et al. [19] attributes this behavior to the RLHF training process itself.

2.2   Hallucination Detection and Assessment

Detecting hallucinations in LLM-generated content is essential for ensuring reliability and trustworthiness. Traditional evaluation metrics, often based on word overlap, are insufficient for identifying hallucinations, underscoring the need for advanced detection techniques tailored to LLM-specific challenges.

Recent advancements have introduced various methods for hallucination detection. Some approaches leverage external knowledge sources for fact-checking, integrating retrieval mechanisms to verify generated content [22]. Others focus on zero-resource settings, aiming to detect hallucinations without relying on external data [21]. A common premise among these strategies is that hallucinations arise from model uncertainty, leading to efforts in estimating this uncertainty to identify potential hallucinations [28].

Uncertainty estimation approaches can be classified into two groups: those analyzing the internal state of the model and those based on observable LLM behavior. Internal-state methods rely on access to the model's latent processes to infer uncertainty [21]. In contrast, behavior-based methods infer uncertainty through external observations, making them applicable in constrained scenarios [27]. For instance, Luo et al. [14] proposed a self-assessment framework, suggesting that a model's ability to reconstruct concepts from its outputs reflects its conceptual mastery. Yao et al. [25] examined hallucinations via adversarial attacks, utilizing gradient-based token replacement to induce and analyze hallucinations, offering new insights into their detection and assessment.

These methods highlight diverse approaches to detecting hallucinations, each with distinct strengths and limitations. Internal-state methods require access to model internals, which may not always be feasible, while behavior-based methods, though more generalizable, may lack the granularity needed to capture subtle uncertainty signals. Fact-checking approaches validate generated content against trusted data using external knowledge and retrieval mechanisms but suffer from high computational costs and inefficiencies due to repeated checks and unclear verification targets. Combining these complementary approaches could enhance the robustness and adaptability of hallucination detection techniques.

3   Method

We propose a two-stage framework that combines uncertainty-driven hallucination detection with iterative correction, which begins with identifying hallucination-prone spans based on the **Substantive-word Uncertainty Score (SUScore)**, followed by a correction phase using the **Iterative Chain-Query (ICQ)** framework.

SUScore operates at the token level, focusing on substantive words–nouns, verbs, numerals, and adjectives–which carry the core semantic and factual load of a sentence. It assigns higher scores to words with high generation uncertainty, contextual salience, and syntactic importance. Regions with elevated SUScore values are flagged for further validation.

ICQ takes these regions as input and performs structured validation through multi-turn question generation and consistency checking. For each suspicious span, it generates focused questions and analyzes the consistency of responses,

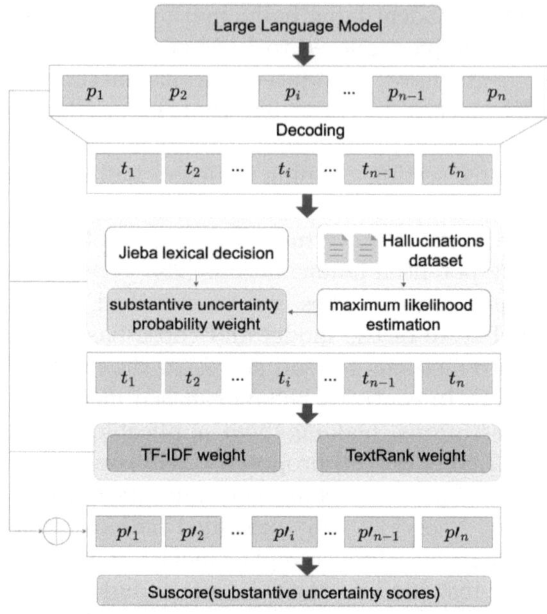

Fig. 1. Overview of SUScore computation. Substantive tokens are identified via POS tagging and scored based on hallucination risk, semantic importance, and generation uncertainty.

optionally retrieving external knowledge when needed. Corrections are made if inconsistencies are detected.

This two-stage process enables lightweight hallucination mitigation without requiring architecture changes or access to large-scale annotated corpora.

3.1 Detecting Hallucination via Substantive Word Uncertainty

Hallucinations in LLM-generated text tend to occur in content-bearing words such as nouns, verbs, numerals, and adjectives. These *substantive words* are responsible for conveying factual information and semantic content. Unlike function words, errors in substantive tokens can lead to serious misrepresentations, such as misstating quantities, locations, or named entities. To locate hallucination-prone regions, we define a token-level metric called the **Substantive-word Uncertainty Score (SUScore)**.

SUScore combines three aspects that contribute to hallucination likelihood: the syntactic tendency of a word type to hallucinate, its contextual importance in a sentence, and the generation uncertainty as reflected in the model's output. The computation process is shown in Fig. 1.

For each token t_i in a generated sentence, we compute SUScore as:

$$\text{SUScore}_i = \text{HW}_i \cdot \text{IW}_i \cdot \text{UW}_i, \tag{1}$$

where HW_i is the hallucination weight, IW_i the importance weight, and UW_i the uncertainty weight of the token.

The hallucination weight reflects how likely a word with a certain part-of-speech (POS) tag is to contribute to hallucination. We derive this by estimating the hallucination frequency of each POS category from a labeled dataset. Specifically, for token t_i, the hallucination weight is computed as:

$$\mathrm{HW}_i = \sum_{c \in \mathrm{POS}} P_{\mathrm{POS},c}(t_i) \cdot \mathrm{POShw}_c, \tag{2}$$

where $P_{\mathrm{POS},c}(t_i)$ is the probability of t_i being classified as POS tag c, and POShw_c is the hallucination likelihood for that tag.

To quantify a token's contextual importance, we combine TF-IDF and TextRank scores:

$$\mathrm{IW}_i = \alpha \cdot \mathrm{TFIDF}_i + (1 - \alpha) \cdot \mathrm{TextRank}_i, \tag{3}$$

where $\alpha \in [0, 1]$ balances between term frequency and graph-based centrality. In our implementation, we set $\alpha = 0.6$ based on validation performance.

Generation uncertainty is captured via the negative log-likelihood of the token's probability during decoding:

$$\mathrm{UW}_i = -\log(p_i), \tag{4}$$

where p_i is the softmax-normalized probability assigned to token t_i by the model. Tokens with lower confidence are considered more likely to be hallucinated.

To aggregate token-level scores into a sentence-level measure, we consider three alternatives:

$$\mathrm{SUScore}_{\mathrm{avg}} = \frac{1}{N} \sum_{i=1}^{N} \mathrm{SUScore}_i \tag{5}$$

$$\mathrm{SUScore}_{\mathrm{max}} = \max_i \mathrm{SUScore}_i \tag{6}$$

$$\mathrm{SUScore}_{\mathrm{prod}} = \prod_{i=1}^{N} \mathrm{SUScore}_i \tag{7}$$

where N is the number of tokens in the sentence. The average reflects overall uncertainty, the maximum captures the most at-risk word, and the product accounts for compound effects across tokens.

To estimate POS-specific hallucination weights for SUScore, we perform maximum likelihood estimation on the UHGEval dataset using annotated hallucination spans. The results reveal that numerals, nouns, and verbs exhibit the highest hallucination tendencies, with softmax-normalized weights of 0.23, 0.21, and 0.19, respectively. These values are used as POShw_c in Eq. (2) to weight token contributions based on part-of-speech tags.

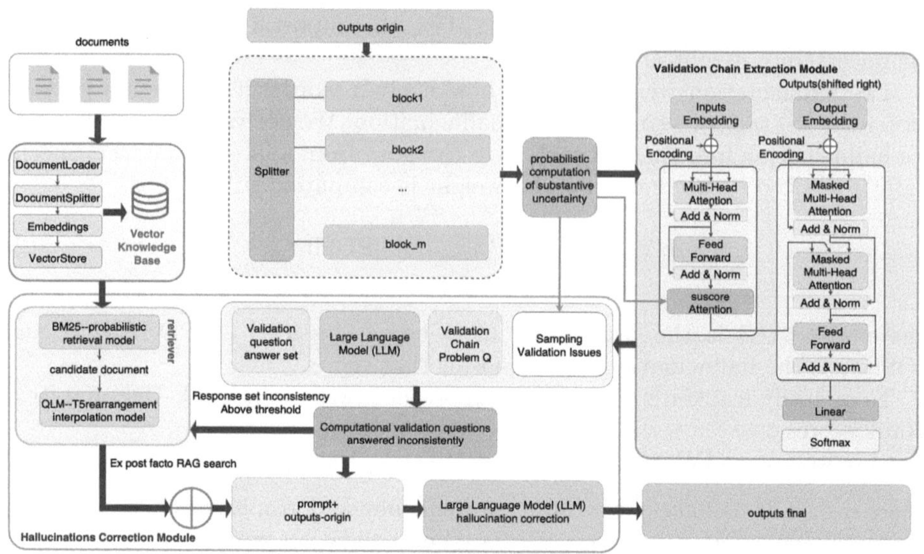

Fig. 2. Framework for hallucination detection and correction using Iterative Chain-Query (ICQ). The system integrates substantive uncertainty computation, validation chain extraction, and retrieval-augmented generation (RAG). Probabilistic uncertainty estimates guide validation, where inconsistencies are identified and corrected through iterative verification and external knowledge retrieval.

3.2   Correcting Hallucination via Iterative Chain-Query

After identifying hallucination-prone spans using SUScore, we apply an iterative correction strategy to verify and revise these segments. Our approach, termed **Iterative Chain-Query (ICQ)**, performs multi-round validation by generating focused questions and analyzing the consistency of model responses. When inconsistencies are detected, the framework leverages external evidence to refine the output.

An overview of the ICQ process is shown in Fig. 2. Given a generated text, we first segment it into spans and rank them by their SUScore. For high-risk segments, we use a question generation model to formulate natural language prompts aimed at probing factual correctness. The generated questions are answered by the model itself or an auxiliary verifier. The process is repeated across multiple rounds to ensure robustness.

Let $T = \{t_1, \ldots, t_n\}$ denote the set of candidate segments extracted from the original output. For each segment t_i, a question q_i is generated, yielding an answer a_i. To measure factual consistency, we compare a_i against reference answers or check agreement among multiple model responses using similarity metrics such as F1 score or cosine distance. Segments with low consistency scores are flagged as hallucinated.

If a hallucinated span cannot be resolved through internal validation, the system retrieves relevant knowledge from an external corpus. Retrieved evidence is used to generate an updated answer, which replaces the original segment. This retrieval-augmented step enhances factual coverage, especially when the model lacks sufficient internal knowledge.

The iterative nature of ICQ allows it to gradually refine outputs while maintaining fluency. By integrating uncertainty estimation, answer consistency, and external retrieval in a unified process, ICQ offers a scalable and model-agnostic solution for hallucination correction.

4 Experiments

4.1 Datasets and Evaluation Metrics

Our evaluation spans three benchmarks, each targeting a different aspect of hallucination in language generation. To analyze detection sensitivity, we employ UHGEval [12], a manually curated corpus of open-domain responses from Chinese LLMs, annotated with hallucination spans at the keyword level. These annotations are leveraged to estimate part-of-speech-based hallucination priors in SUScore.

To assess the relationship between uncertainty and factual error, we use SVAMP [18], a collection of math word problems designed to test arithmetic reasoning. The dataset is particularly suited for studying hallucination under chain-of-thought prompting, where factual consistency can be traced across intermediate reasoning steps. For evaluating correction effectiveness, we adopt QUEST [6], a reading comprehension benchmark emphasizing factual consistency. It enables controlled comparison of model responses before and after validation-based refinement, serving as the primary testbed for the ICQ framework.

We report performance on two fronts. For hallucination *detection*, we compute the alignment between SUScore and observed hallucination rates, comparing against conventional metrics such as BLEU, ROUGE, METEOR, entropy, and token-level disagreement. Calibration quality is further assessed using mean squared error (MSE) and mean absolute deviation (MAD). For *correction*, we measure standard QA metrics–F1, precision, and recall–alongside SUScore differentials pre- and post-intervention. Semantic and factual fidelity are captured via BERTScore [29] and FACTScore [16], respectively, the latter offering strong correlation with human ratings.

All datasets are used as-is, without fine-tuning or additional labeling, to emphasize the zero-shot compatibility and generalizability of our approach.

4.2 Implementation Details

We implement SUScore using decoding outputs from autoregressive language models. Token-level generation probabilities p_i are obtained by capturing softmax scores during greedy decoding. Part-of-speech tags are assigned using a

Table 1. Performance comparison of LLMs on the SVAMP dataset using linguistic, semantic, and uncertainty-based metrics. SUScore variants capture hallucination-prone outputs more effectively than traditional metrics.

Metrics	ChatGLM2$_{6B}$	BLOOM$_{3B}$	BLOOM$_{7B}$	Llama2$_{7B}$	Llama2$_{13B}$
CoT-mis	84.8	89.5	79.8	80.6	74.7
Rouge-1	27.1	19.2	20.4	16.7	27.8
Rouge-L	23.6	21.5	23.2	20.6	22.9
BLEU	29.2	22.6	24.7	17.2	25.2
Meteor	26.7	17.6	26.4	21.6	22.7
Disagreement	51.9	45.5	46.6	43.8	48.1
Entropy$_{min}$	32.1	45.4	42.0	30.1	22.5
Entropy$_{avg}$	42.3	53.1	48.2	34.2	27.6
SUScore$_{avg}$	51.9	52.5	51.4	43.8	36.0
SUScore$_{prod}$	45.9	54.5	47.8	42.1	48.5
SUScore$_{max}$	48.9	54.5	50.9	51.1	48.8

pretrained spaCy model[1], and POS-wise hallucination weights $POShw_c$ are computed via maximum likelihood estimation on the UHGEval dataset.

To compute importance weights, we extract TF-IDF scores from the training corpus and use TextRank based on co-occurrence within a sliding window of size 4. All scores are normalized to $[0,1]$ before fusion. The weighting factor α for combining TF-IDF and TextRank is fixed at 0.6 across all experiments.

ICQ uses a BERT-based model (bert-base-uncased) to generate validation questions, with attention guided by high-SUScore tokens. For consistency assessment, we employ both lexical overlap (F1) and embedding-based similarity (cosine distance) using Sentence-BERT (Reimers and Gurevych, 2019). When external retrieval is required, we query a Wikipedia subset indexed via BM25. Retrieved passages are concatenated to the query prompt for response generation using the same base LLM.

All experiments are conducted using PyTorch on a single NVIDIA A100 GPU with 80GB memory. The proposed pipeline is implemented with minimal architectural assumptions, making it adaptable to both open-source and proprietary models that expose generation probabilities.

4.3   Evaluating SUScore on Hallucination Detection

We begin by evaluating SUScore as a hallucination detection metric on the SVAMP dataset, where hallucination is primarily reflected in arithmetic or semantic reasoning inconsistencies. Table 1 presents a comparison of standard metrics–including BLEU, ROUGE, Meteor, and Entropy-based disagreement– with the three SUScore variants.

---

[1] https://spacy.io.

Table 2. Calibration error (MSE and MAD) of evaluation metrics on SVAMP. SUS-core variants exhibit stronger alignment with hallucination rates compared to baseline metrics.

Metrics	Calibration Error	
	MSE	**MAD**
Rouge-1	25.63	32.14
Rouge-L	28.61	35.62
BLEU	38.95	40.13
Meteor	49.53	31.52
Disagreement	32.40	25.77
$Entropy_{min}$	32.75	35.20
$Entropy_{avg}$	35.59	40.12
SUScore$_{avg}$	15.46	23.36
SUScore$_{prod}$	22.00	**20.04**
SUScore$_{max}$	**14.53**	21.19

Traditional metrics such as BLEU and ROUGE show limited sensitivity to factual errors, often assigning high scores to fluent but incorrect outputs. Meteor provides modest gains by considering semantic overlap, while entropy and response disagreement offer indirect signals of uncertainty. In contrast, SUScore explicitly targets substantive word-level uncertainty, yielding more discriminative scores across models and settings. Notably, $SUScore_{max}$ achieves consistently high values for models with frequent hallucinations (e.g., BLOOM-3B), while penalizing more grounded models like LLaMA2-13B.

To further assess the alignment between uncertainty scores and true hallucination frequencies, we compute the calibration error of each metric using Mean Squared Error (MSE) and Mean Absolute Deviation (MAD). As shown in Table 2, SUScore variants outperform all baselines, with $SUScore_{max}$ achieving the lowest MSE (14.53) and $SUScore_{prod}$ the lowest MAD (20.04). This suggests that SUScore is better calibrated to actual hallucination risk than entropy or token disagreement, both of which are less localized and less semantically targeted.

These results confirm that SUScore not only provides a sharper uncertainty signal than existing heuristics but also generalizes across model sizes and families, making it a robust metric for hallucination detection in generative tasks.

4.4 Evaluating ICQ on Hallucination Correction

We evaluate the hallucination correction capabilities of the proposed ICQ framework on the QUEST dataset, comparing it to baseline generation, chain-of-thought prompting (CoT), and CoVe (contextual verification). Table 3 summarizes results across two LLaMA models and ChatGPT, using standard QA-style accuracy metrics and sentence-level SUScore.

Table 3. Comparison of hallucination correction methods on the QUEST dataset. ICQ achieves the best recall and SUScore across both LLaMA-7B and 13B models, indicating more effective identification and revision of hallucinated spans.

LLM	Method	F1	Prec	Rec	SUScore
$Llama_{7B}$	Baseline	0.13	0.12	0.39	40.3
$Llama_{13B}$		0.21	0.19	0.30	46.4
$Llama_{7B}$	CoT	0.25	0.24	0.33	42.3
$Llama_{13B}$		0.30	0.21	0.37	45.4
$Llama_{7B}$	CoVe	0.42	0.18	0.43	43.2
$Llama_{13B}$		0.46	0.24	0.45	48.0
ChatGPT	-	0.47	**0.33**	0.56	43.7
$Llama_{7B}$	**ICQ**(ours)	0.43	0.23	0.53	46.7
$Llama_{13B}$		**0.49**	0.29	**0.59**	51.0

Table 4. Effect of validation chain length (m) on generation quality for CoVe and ICQ. ICQ shows consistent gains in factual consistency (FACTScore) and semantic alignment (BERTScore) with deeper validation, while BLEU and ROUGE scores exhibit slight declines.

Metrics	Method	Validation Chain Length (m)				
		0	2	4	6	8
Rouge	CoVe	**35.1**	34.6	34.0	32.6	31.5
BLEU		47.3	**48.5**	47.1	45.7	44.8
BERTScore		24.5	26.3	27.9	28.3	32.1
FACTScore		49.0	55.3	57.4	58.3	59.1
Rouge	**ICQ**(ours)	**35.1**	34.8	33.2	32.7	30.0
BLEU		47.3	45.3	42.7	42.8	40.3
BERTScore		24.5	27.7	29.5	35.9	**37.4**
FACTScore		49.0	56.3	57.3	59.3	**62.5**

ICQ outperforms all other methods in recall and SUScore, particularly when applied to LLaMA-13B. While CoT and CoVe show gains in either precision or recall, they often struggle to balance both. CoVe, for instance, achieves high recall (0.45) but with lower precision, suggesting overcorrection. In contrast, ICQ achieves both high recall (0.59) and strong F1 (0.49), while maintaining a higher SUScore (51.0), indicating effective hallucination localization and correction. This validates ICQ's ability to isolate uncertain spans and revise them with greater factual precision.

We further investigate how performance evolves with the number of validation steps (m), i.e., the chain length in ICQ's iterative process. As shown in Table 4, increasing m consistently improves semantic coherence (BERTScore) and factual consistency (FACTScore), peaking at $m = 8$ for ICQ with 37.4 and 62.5 respectively. In contrast, fluency-oriented metrics like ROUGE and BLEU exhibit minor declines, reflecting slight trade-offs as outputs are revised more aggressively.

Notably, ICQ surpasses CoVe across all m values in terms of factual accuracy. While both methods benefit from iterative refinement, ICQ's guided span selection and answer validation mechanism yield greater factual gains with fewer side effects. This suggests that ICQ not only scales effectively with deeper validation chains, but also maintains a better balance between factual correctness and fluency.

5   Conclusion

This paper presents a lightweight framework for hallucination detection and correction in large language models, combining token-level uncertainty estimation with iterative answer validation. The proposed SUScore metric quantifies uncertainty over substantive words, offering a fine-grained signal that aligns well with hallucination patterns. Built on top of this, the ICQ framework performs targeted validation and correction through multi-round question answering, achieving notable gains in factual consistency across multiple benchmarks.

Experiments on SVAMP and QUEST demonstrate that SUScore outperforms traditional metrics in hallucination calibration, while ICQ consistently improves factual accuracy with minimal trade-off in fluency. Together, the two components form a scalable and model-agnostic pipeline that enhances the reliability of language generation without requiring model retraining.

Future work will explore extending SUScore to black-box settings using proxy uncertainty signals, and incorporating logical reasoning modules into ICQ to better handle complex inference tasks beyond factual verification.

Acknowledgements. This work was supported by National Key Laboratory on Blind Signal Processing (Grant No. 61424132024007003).

References

1. Carlini, N., Tramer, F., Wallace, E.e.a.: Extracting training data from large language models. arXiv preprint arXiv:2012.07805 (2021)
2. Chiang, D., Cholak, P.: Overcoming a theoretical limitation of self-attention. In: Proceedings of ACL 2022, pp. 7654–7664 (2022)
3. Filippova, K.: Controlled hallucinations: learning to generate faithfully from noisy data. In: Findings of EMNLP 2020, pp. 864–870 (2020)
4. Hahn, M.: Theoretical limitations of self-attention in neural sequence models. Trans. Assoc. Comput. Linguist. **8**, 156–171 (2020)
5. Ji, Z.e.a.: Survey of hallucination in natural language generation. ACM Comput. Surv. **55**(12), 1–38 (2023)

6. Kadavath, S.e.a.: Language models (mostly) know what they know. arXiv preprint arXiv:2207.05221 (2022)
7. Kasai, J.e.a.: Realtime qa: What's the answer right now? arXiv preprint arXiv:2207.13332 (2022)
8. Katz, D.M.e.a.: Gpt-4 passes the bar exam. Philos. Trans. R. Soc. A **382**(2261), 20230254 (2024)
9. Li, D.e.a.: Large language models with controllable working memory. In: Findings of ACL 2023, pp. 1774–1793 (2023)
10. Li, W.e.a.: Faithfulness in natural language generation: a systematic survey. arXiv preprint arXiv:2203.05227 (2022)
11. Li, Y.e.a.: Chatdoctor: a medical chat model fine-tuned on llama using domain knowledge. Cureus **15**(7), e40895 (2023)
12. Liang, X.e.a.: Uhgeval: benchmarking hallucination in Chinese LLMs via unconstrained generation. In: Proceedings of ACL 2024 (2024)
13. Lin, S.e.a.: Truthfulqa: measuring how models mimic human falsehoods. In: Proceedings of ACL 2022, pp. 3214–3252 (2022)
14. Luo, J.e.a.: Zero-resource hallucination prevention for large language models. In: Findings of EMNLP 2024 (2024)
15. Maynez, J.e.a.: On faithfulness and factuality in abstractive summarization. In: Proceedings of ACL 2020, pp. 1906–1919 (2020)
16. Min, S.e.a.: Factscore: factual consistency evaluation via retrieval and entailment. In: Proceedings of EMNLP 2023 (2023)
17. Onoe, Y.e.a.: Entity cloze by date: what LMS know about unseen entities. In: Findings of NAACL 2022, pp. 693–702 (2022)
18. Patel, A.e.a.: Are NLP models really able to solve simple math word problems? In: Proceedings of NAACL 2021 (2021)
19. Sharma, M.e.a.: Towards understanding sycophancy in language models. In: Proceedings of ICLR 2024 (2024)
20. Singhal, K.e.a.: Towards expert-level medical question answering with large language models. arXiv preprint arXiv:2305.09617 (2023)
21. Su, W.e.a.: Unsupervised real-time hallucination detection from LLM internal states. In: Findings of ACL 2024, pp. 14379–14391 (2024)
22. Wang, X.e.a.: Hallucination detection for generative LLMs by Bayesian sequential estimation. In: Proceedings of EMNLP 2023,d pp. 15361–15371 (2023)
23. Wei, J.e.a.: Simple synthetic data reduces sycophancy in large language models. arXiv preprint arXiv:2308.03958 (2024)
24. Weidinger, L.e.a.: Ethical and social risks of harm from language models. arXiv preprint arXiv:2112.04359 (2021)
25. Yao, J.Y.e.a.: LLM lies: Hallucinations are not bugs, but features as adversarial examples. arXiv preprint arXiv:2310.01469 (2023)
26. Yu, F.e.a.: Legal prompting: teaching a language model to think like a lawyer. In: Proceedings of NLLP 2022, pp. 1–12 (2022)
27. Zhang, R.e.a.: Vl-uncertainty: detecting hallucination in vision-language models via uncertainty estimation. arXiv preprint arXiv:2411.11919 (2024)
28. Zhang, T.e.a.: Enhancing uncertainty-based hallucination detection with stronger focus. In: Proceedings of EMNLP 2023, pp. 915–932 (2023)
29. Zhang, T.e.a.: Bertscore: evaluating text generation with bert. In: Proceedings of ICLR 2020 (2020)

Others

Directional Asymmetry in the Perception of Mandarin Chinese Vowels by Native English Speakers

Wenhui Zhu[1] and Sun-Hee Lee[2(✉)]

[1] School of Humanity and Science, Southern University of Science and Technology, Shenzhen, China
[2] College of Chinese Studies, Cyber Hankuk University of Foreign Studies, Seoul, Korea
lishanxi@cufs.ac.kr

Abstract. This paper investigates how directional asymmetry in Mandarin Chinese vowel perception differs across L2 proficiency levels in English-speaking learners. The study investigates the perceptual identification of six Mandarin Chinese vowels (/i, u, y, ɤ, ɿ, ʅ/) in dental, retroflex, and palatal fricative and affricate contexts by adult New Zealand English native speakers, using the Natural Referent Vowel (NRV) framework and the Dispersion-Focalization Theory (DFT). The results show that directional asymmetries are evident in the perceptual discrimination of the Mandarin Chinese vowel contrasts /y-u/ and /ɤ-ɿ/ among inexperienced, but not experienced, L2 learners. This suggests that universal influences (e.g., directional perceptual asymmetries) dominate during early non-native phoneme acquisition, while language-specific phonological adjustments become primary in later stages. To explain the directional asymmetry in the discrimination between two focal/point vowel contrast /y-u/, a new hypothesis: the Lower-Formant Convergence hypothesis, which is based on formant convergence, rather than peripherality in the F1-F2 space, was proposed. It suggests that vowels with convergence in lower-formants are more noticeable and stable compared to those with higher-formant convergence or no formant convergence. Furthermore, the directional asymmetry found in the perception of the pair /ɤ-ɿ/ represents a new perceptual directional asymmetry.

Keywords: Perceptual Directional Asymmetry · NRV · DFT

1 Introduction

Directional asymmetry has been widely observed in both native/L1 and L2 vowel perception [5,7,9,10]. Models such as the Natural Referent Vowel (NRV) framework [8,9] and the Dispersion-Focalization Theory (DFT) [12] provide explanations for this phenomenon. Polka and Bohn suggest that directional asymmetries arise because some vowels are "perceptually more salient and stable compared to others" [8, p. 227]. The stability and salience of vowels are gauged by their positions in the traditional F1-F2 vowel space, with more stable and salient vowels being more peripheral. [12] proposed the DFT, which posits that listeners prefer

© The Author(s), under exclusive license to Springer Nature Singapore Pte Ltd. 2026
X.-L. Mao et al. (Eds.): NLPCC 2025, LNAI 16105, pp. 187–195, 2026.
https://doi.org/10.1007/978-981-95-3352-7_15

more peripheral sounds because they are more salient, characterized by more focalized/concentrated formant values. The salience and stability of natural referent vowels result from the convergence or focalization of formant frequencies: (F1, F2), (F2, F3), or (F3, F4). The four focal vowels identified are the traditional point vowels /i, u, a/ and the front high rounded vowel /y/. Generally, the predictions of the NRV and DFT align, with more peripheral vowels acting as perceptual referents, or the observed directional asymmetry can be explained by both prototypicality and focalization effects. However, exceptions arise when the lip-rounding feature is involved. For example, [1] found that the rounded vowels (/ø/ and /y/) acted as referents in the discrimination of /ø-e/ and /y-i/ pairs, despite /e/ and /i/ being more peripheral in the traditional F1/F2 space.

2   Experiment

2.1   Participant

Two groups of learners with different levels of Chinese learning experience were recruited for the identification task. The first group consisted of 11 inexperienced learners (InEx group), 7 males and 4 females, with an average of 95.3 h of Mandarin learning experience at the time of recruitment. The second group consisted of 8 experienced learners (Ex group), 4 males and 4 females, with an average of 221.7 h of Mandarin learning experience at the time of recruitment. All participants were university students aged between the ages of 18–25, born and raised in New Zealand, and were monolingual NZE speakers. There were no significant differences between the two groups in terms of age or the age at which they began learning Mandarin Chinese. All participants are studying Mandarin Chinese classes in the University of Auckland at the time of recruitment. All participants reported having normal hearing.

2.2   Stimuli

Previous research has shown that Mandarin vowels in dental, retroflex, and alveolar contexts pose significant challenges. Furthermore, the two Mandarin apical vowels/approximant /ɿ/ and /ʅ/ occur only in dental (/ts/-/tsʰ/-/s/) and retroflex (tʂ/-/tʂʰ/-/ʂ/) consonant contexts, respectively. To address this, the study presented the target Mandarin vowels /i/, /u/, /y/, /ɤ/, /ɿ/, and /ʅ/ in monosyllabic Chinese characters that began with three different sets of consonants (dental: /ts/-/tsʰ/-/s/; retroflex: /tʂ/-/tʂʰ/-/ʂ/; and alveolar: /tɕ/-/tɕʰ/-/ɕ/) along with the fourth Mandarin tone, resulting in a total of 18 syllables (/tɕy/-/tɕʰ y/-/ɕy/; /tɕi/-/tɕʰ i/-/ɕi/; /tʂu/-/ʂu/-/tsu/; /sɿ/-/tsɿ/-/tsʰɿ/;/ʂʅ/-/tʂʅ/-/tʂʰʅ/; /tsɤ/-/tʂɤ/-/tʂʰɤ/). In the end, 54 Mandarin vowel stimuli were created by two native Mandarin speakers using the same 18 target syllables.

To evaluate the predictions of the NRV, it is important to determine which vowel is more peripheral in each contrast. Following to Polka and Bohn (2011), the stimulus vowels in this study were plotted on the F1 and F2 axes in Fig. 1, with arrows indicating the more peripheral vowels (i.e., the focal vowels /i, u, y/ or those closest to the edge of the vowel space). Previous research generally supports the notion that /i/ and /u/ are more peripheral than /y/. However, the other three Chinese vowels, /ɤ/, /ɿ/, and /ʅ/, have not been examined in directional asymmetry studies, making it difficult to determine which of them is more peripheral. For contrasts involving these three vowels, bidirectional arrows are used. Please refer to Fig. 1.

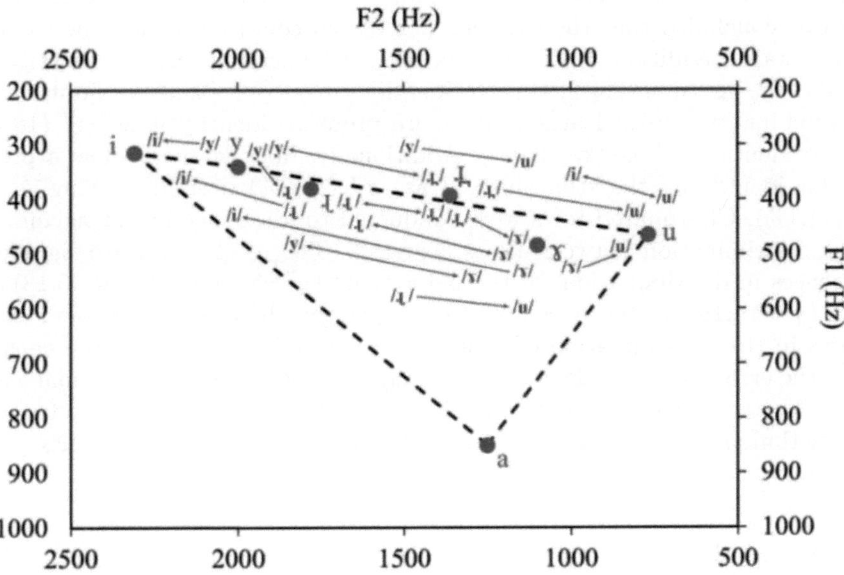

Fig. 1. Plot of F1/F2 frequencies for Mandarin Chinese contrasts showing asymmetries in the present paper. Arrows point to the referent/more peripheral vowels for the contrast; vowel changes in this direction were easier to discriminate.

2.3 Procedure

An open-ended identification task used the Praat software, where participants, under comfortable auditory conditions, listened to all stimuli. Their task was to choose one of the target Mandarin vowels (i, u, y, ɤ, ɿ, ʅ) by indicating the corresponding digit representing the Chinese characters containing the heard target vowels, thus minimizing Pinyin spelling bias. Participants were encouraged to guess when uncertain and to take the necessary time to make decisions. Each participant heard the 54 randomly presented stimuli. The accuracy of participants' perceptions was evaluated by comparing their responses with the originally recorded syllables. A total of 1026 responses were collected. Collective errors for each vowel type were compiled across participants to determine the mean error percentage.

2.4   Result

The overall mean percentage identification error rate and type for each target vowel by the learners is presented in Table 1. It shows that no errors were ob-served in the identification of the /i-u/ and /u-ɿ/ contrasts. Since the preceding consonants were chosen to normalize the influence of onset consonants, it can be concluded that the learners' perceptual confusion is not due to onset consonants. In addition, InEx learners show a higher tendency to identify the stimulus /y/ as /u/ (42.4%) than to identify /u/ as /y/ (28.3%). Similarly, for the stimulus /ɤ/, InEx learners are more prone to identify it as /ɿ/ (18.2%) than to identify /ɿ/ as /ɤ/ (2.0%). Additionally, InEx learners show a preference for identifying the stimu-lus /ɿ/ as /ɤ/ (18.2%) over identifying /ɤ/ as /ɿ/ (11.1%). Chi-squared tests were conducted to assess significant asymmetry in the discrimination between these contrasts. The results indicate significant differences in discrimination for the pairs /y-u/ (χ^2=5.90, p<.05, w=0.18) and /ɤ-ɿ/ (χ^2=16.16, p<.05, w=0.30). Conse-quently, there are directional asymmetries in the discrimination of contrasts /y-u/ and /ɤ-ɿ/. As for the contrast /ɤ-ɿ/, the errors between them are relatively bi-directional, no directional asymmetry. There is also no statistically significant directional asymmetry found in the discrimination between any target Mandarin vowel pairs by the Ex group (Fig. 2).

3   Discussion

Analysis of the open-ended identification task tested the NRV prediction that less peripheral non-native vowels would be identified as more peripheral non-native vowels. The result showed that there was a clear peripherality effect in the direction predicted by the NRV framework for vowel contrasts: /u-y/ and /ɤ-ɿ/ by InEx learners. For Ex group learners, there was no effect of peripherality. This indicates that as L2 experience increases, directional asymmetry in the non-native contrasts disappears.

The observed directional perceptual asymmetry in the /y-u/ pair (favoring the /y/ to /u/ direction) is consistent with findings on vowel discrimination asymmetries in both infants and adults [7,9,11]. Please refer to Table 2. This result is expected because /u/ is more peripheral than /y/ in the traditional F1/F2 acoustic space, as predicted by the NRV. However, both /u/ and /y/ are considered focal vowels in the DFT. Understanding the perceptual directional asymmetry between focal vowels is challenging. For example, [1] found that English-learning infants at 3 months discriminated the Norwegian /i-y/ pair (high frontal unrounded versus rounded) in the direction /i/ to /y/, but not in the direction /y/ to /i/.

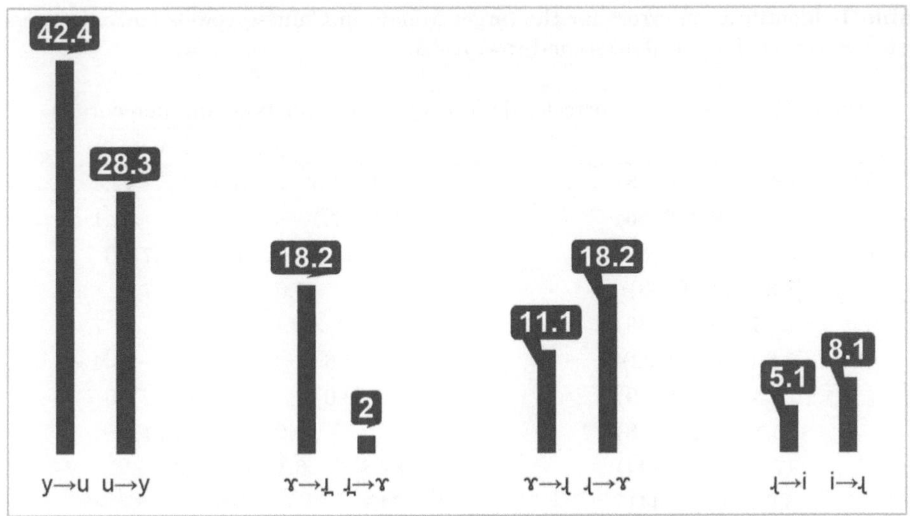

Fig. 2. Main error percentage of Mandarin Chinese contrasts by InEx learners (error percentage above 5.0%).

In general, the predictions of the NRV and DTF agree. Nevertheless, things become interesting when lip-rounding feature is involved (see also the Introduction section). According to the DFT, listeners prefer more peripheral phones due to their distinctiveness in the perceptual system. Peripheral vowels, characterized by more focalized formant values, are particularly salient. However, while focalization explains why peripheral phones stand out, it doesn't clarify why there are directional asymmetries in the discrimination between two focal/point vowels. [12] proposed that different convergences or focalizations of formant frequencies exist, such as (F1, F2), (F2, F3), or (F3, F4). Specifically, the focalization of /y/ and /i/ involves F2-F3 and F3-F4 convergence respectively (refer to Fig. 3). From this perspective, we can't simply claim that the traditional F1-F2 acoustic space can explain all directional asymmetries among phones, as it is based only on F1 and F2 values. Instead, F3, F4, and even higher formant values should be considered depending on the context. [10] also suggested that asymmetry is influenced by formant convergence, rather than peripherality in the F1-F2 space.

With these questions in mind, the Lower-Formant Convergence hypothesis is proposed to explain the directional asymmetries observed between pairs of point vowels, as well as between a point vowel and a non-point vowel pair. We suggest that vowels become more prominent and serve as stronger reference points for discrimination when their lower-formants converge. In other words, vowels with convergence in lower-formants tend to be more noticeable and stable compared to those with higher-formant convergence or no formant convergence. For instance, a vowel with F1-F2 convergence will be more prominent than one with F2-F3 convergence, and similarly, a vowel with F2-F3 convergence will stand out more than one with F3-F4 convergence. Therefore, the observed directional perceptual

Table 1. Identification errors for the target Mandarin Chinese vowels (InEx learners, first row, n = 11; Ex learners, second row, n = 8).

Stimuli	Mean percent incorrect (SD; range)	Mean error type and percent(%)					
		i	y	ɻ̩	ɻ	ɤ	u
y	48.5 (28.2; 0–78)	3.0	51.5		3.0		42.4
	12.5 (19.2; 0–56)	1.4	87.5				11.1
ɤ	33.3 (23.3; 0–67)	2.0	1.0	18.2	11.1	66.7	1.0
	8.3 (11.5; 0–33)			5.6	2.8	91.7	
u	28.3 (16.0; 0–56)		28.3				71.7
	5.6 (8.4.1; 0–22)		5.6				94.4
ɻ	26.3 (27.8; 0–89)	5.1	2.0		73.75	18.2	1.0
	15.3 (27.2; 0–78)			4.2	84.7	11.1	
i	17.2 (17.5; 0–44)	82.8		6.1	8.1	3.0	
	5.6 (15.7; 0–44)	94.4			5.6		
ɻ̩	9.1 (9.7; 0–22)	3.0		90.95	4.0	2.0	
	1.4 (3.9; 0–11)	1.4		98.6			

Table 2. Directional Asymmetries in the discrimination of vowel contrast /y-u/.

Previous study	Listener	Ambient/first language	Contrast
Polka and Werker (1994)	Infant	English	German y → u
Polka and Bohn (1996)	Infant	English	German y → u
Polka and Bohn (2011)	Adult	German	German y → u
Polka and Bohn (2011)	Adult	English	German y → u

asymmetry in the /y-u/ pair (favoring the /y/ to /u/ direction) can be explained as /u/ (F1-F2 convergence) is more stand out than /y/ (F2-F3 convergence). Likewise the directional perceptual asymmetry in the /y-i/ pair (favoring the /i/ to /y/ direction) can be explained as /y/ (F2-F3 convergence) is more stand out than /i/ (F3-F4 convergence). It is widely recognized that formants are crucial in vowel perception, particularly the first two or three formants, as they are associated with the perception of vowel quality. Higher formants, on the other hand, relate to other aspects of vocal expression [4,6]. Most of the energy of speech is concentrated in the low-frequency part [3], and the amplitudes of the spectral peaks associated with the formants decrease as the frequency increases. The overall sound pressure level of the vowel is mainly influenced by the amplitude of this peak [2]. Therefore, we assume that the convergence of lower formants likely plays a significant role in the perception of vowel directional asymmetry.

Regarding the /ɤ-ɻ̩/ pair, previous studies of asymmetries have not yielded comparable results. This newly discovered asymmetry is interesting because /ɻ̩/ is an approximant, not a vowel. However, the Mandarin Chinese approximant

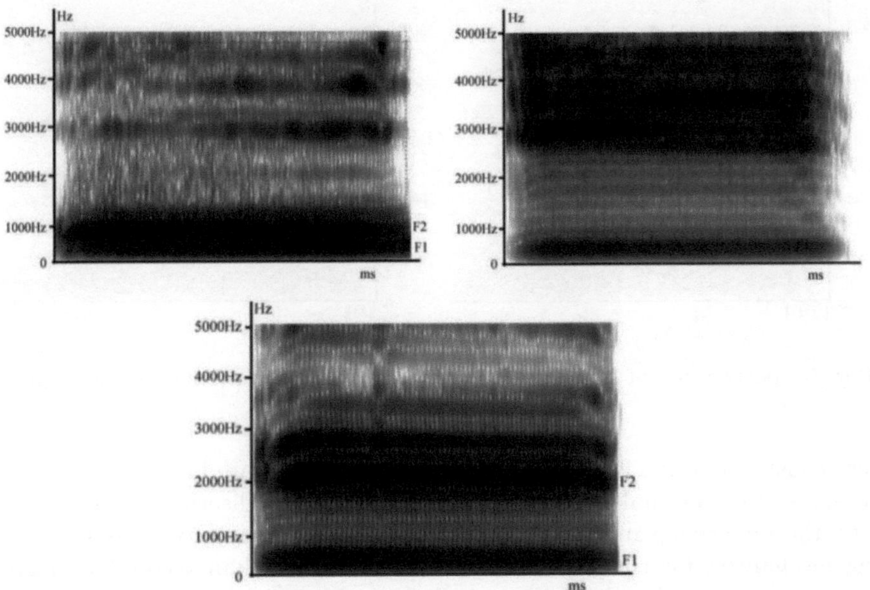

Fig. 3. Spectrogram of Mandarin Chinese /u/ (top left), /i/ (top right) and /y/ (bottom) [13].

/ɹ̩/ has clear formants, making the NRV and DFT frameworks applicable to this pair. A key unresolved question is how formant convergence contributes to the focalization effect in this pair, as both show no clear formant convergence [13]. Please refer to Fig. 4. Determining which sound is more peripheral according to the acoustic space F1-F2 is also challenging, as neither of these two sounds is point vowel as well.

It is well-established that formants play a key role in vowel perception, but there has been limited research on the impact of formant convergence in this area. The way formant convergence affect listener's perception remains mysterious. Acoustically, vowel perception involves identifying formants (the peaks in spectral energy), while physiologically, it involves recognizing patterns of resonance [6]. Given that the perceptual directional asymmetry is a universal phenomenon, and both resonance and spectral energy maxima are physical properties, the directional asymmetry phenomenon likely has a physical basis that should be thoroughly explored from this perspective. Furthermore, although directional asymmetries in vowel perception are frequently documented, the underlying mechanism remains elusive. The directional asymmetry found in the dental approximant /ɹ̩/ and mid vowel /ɤ/ pair of current study indicates that other sound categories beyond vowels, such as consonants reported in previous studies, might also be relevant. Consonants are typically not described in terms of formant focalization, but rather by other acoustic features such as place of articulation, manner of articulation, and voicing. These features create dis-

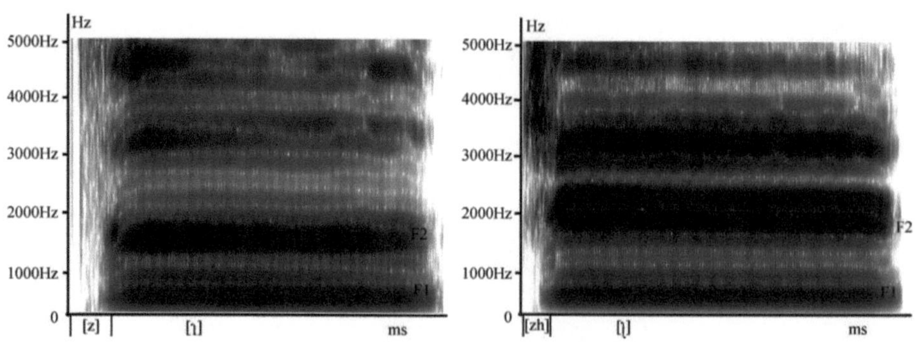

Fig. 4. Spectrogram of Mandarin Chinese approximants /ɻ̩ (left) and /ʐ̩/ (right).

tinct acoustic patterns that enable listeners to differentiate between consonants. Therefore, if directional asymmetry is common in the discrimination of consonants, the underlying mechanism would likely be different. What is the underlying mechanism for the asymmetry of phones other than vowels? Expanding the concept of 'peripheral vowels' to include a wider range of 'peripheral sounds' could provide opportunities for future research.

4   Conclusion

In summary, this study investigates directional asymmetries in native New Zealand English speakers' perception of Mandarin vowel contrasts within the Natural Referent Vowel (NRV) and Dispersion-Focalization Theory (DFT) frameworks. The results reveal that inexperienced learners show significant directional asymmetries in discriminating the Mandarin /y-u/ and /ɤ-ɻ̩/ contrasts, while experienced learners do not. This aligns with the hypothesis that initial L2 perception is more influenced by universal phonetic biases, which are gradually attenuated through language-specific perceptual tuning.

To explain asymmetries in the perception of focal vowels /y-u/, the study proposes the Lower-Formant Convergence Hypothesis, suggesting that convergence in lower formants (e.g., F1F2) enhances their perceptual salience. This theoretical proposal extends the NRV and DFT frameworks, bridging L2 phonology, speech perception, and acoustic phonetics. The findings may also have pedagogical implications for second language acquisition, as teachers could target non-peripheral vowels to improve learners' perception accuracy.

Future research should expand the participant pool to include individuals with diverse L1 backgrounds, as the current study's small sample size and exclusive focus on monolingual New Zealand English speakers limit its generalizability. Additionally, the pedagogical implications require further empirical validation through teaching practices. Finally, additional data and experimental validation are needed to assess the explanatory power of the Lower-Formant Convergence

Hypothesis, to examine whether it contrasts with or extends NRV/DFT predictions, and to advance our understanding of perceptual directional asymmetries.

Acknowledgments.. This study was funded by the 2022 International Chinese Language Education Research Topic Youth Project Funding (grant number 22YH61D); Guangdong Philosophy and Social Sciences Planning Project 2025 (General Program and Special Research Grant Category III) Funding (grand number GD25CZY06); and the Undergraduate Teaching Quality and Teaching Reform Project of Southern University of Science and Technology (grant numbers SJZLGC202448).

Disclosure of Interests. The authors have no competing interests to declare that are relevant to the content of this article.

References

1. Best, C., Faber, A.: Developmental increase in infants' discrimination of nonnative vowels that adults assimilate to a single native vowel. In: International Conference on Infant Studies. Brighton, UK (2000)
2. Crocker, M.: Handbook of Acoustics. John Wiley and Sons, New York (1998)
3. Huang, X., Chen, H., Gan, L.: Speech enhancement method based on frequency-time dilated dense network. J. Comput. Res. Dev. **60**(7), 1628–1638 (2023)
4. Ito, M., Tsuchida, J., Yano, M.: On the effectiveness of whole spectral shape for vowel perception. J. Acoust. Soc. Am. **110**(2), 1141–1149 (2001)
5. Masapollo, M., Polka, L., Ménard, L.: Directional asymmetries reveal a universal bias in adult vowel perception. J. Acoust. Soc. Am. **141**(4), 2857–2869 (2017)
6. Maurer, D.: Acoustics of the Vowel: Preliminaries, Speech Production and Perception, vol. 3. Peter Lang International Academic Publishers, Bern, Switzerland (2016)
7. Polka, L., Bohn, O.S.: A cross-language comparison of vowel perception in English-learning and German-learning infants. J. Acoust. Soc. Am. **100**(1), 577–592 (1996)
8. Polka, L., Bohn, O.S.: Asymmetries in vowel perception. Speech Commun. **41**(1), 221–231 (2003)
9. Polka, L., Bohn, O.S.: Natural referent vowel (NRV) framework: an emerging view of early phonetic development. J. Phon. **39**(4), 467–478 (2011)
10. Polka, L., Masapollo, M., Bohn, O.S.: Predicting asymmetries in vowel perception: formant convergence succeeds where peripherality fails. J. Acoust. Soc. Am. **150**(4), A309 (2021), conference abstract
11. Polka, L., Werker, J.F.: Developmental changes in perception of nonnative vowel contrasts. J. Exp. Psychol. Hum. Percept. Perform. **20**(2), 421–435 (1994)
12. Schwartz, J.L., Abry, C., Boë, L.J., Vallée, N., Ménard, L.: The dispersion-focalization theory of sound systems. J. Acoust. Soc. Am. **117**(4_Supplement), 2422 (2005), conference abstract
13. Yu, H., Hu, A., Li, Y.: Experimental Phonetics: Techniques and Applications. National Defense Industry Press, Beijing, China (2017)

Thoughts Behind Attack: Enhancing Security Against Jailbreak Attacks Using Chain-of-Thought

Zhe Tao[1], Bing Xu[1(✉)], Muyun Yang[1], Hongjiao Guan[2], Wenpeng Lu[2], Hailong Cao[1], Conghui Zhu[1], and Tiejun Zhao[1]

[1] Faculty of Computing, Harbin Institute of Technology, Harbin, China
23s003094@stu.hit.edu.cn,
{hitxb,yangmuyun,caohailong,conghui,tjzhao}@hit.edu.cn
[2] Key Laboratory of Computing Power Network and Information Security, Ministry of Education, Qilu University of Technology (Shandong Academy of Sciences), Jinan, China
lwp@qlu.edu.cn

Abstract. With the rapid development and widespread adoption of large language models (LLMs), the safety of LLMs has become a major concern. The inexplicability and unsafe outputs of LLMs pose significant obstacles to achieving artificial general intelligence (AGI). To enhance the safety of LLMs, researchers have developed various jailbreak attack methods and defense methods. In this paper, we propose SafeCoT, a novel defense method leveraging Chain-of-Thought (CoT) without any optimization or training. We believe that certain jailbreak attacks share a common logic, and based on this insight, we present SafeCoT. Specifically, to help LLMs understand the thoughts behind jailbreak attacks, we propose a jailbreak attack taxonomy and a corresponding jailbreak prompts dataset, JATD. Subsequently, we introduce SafeCoT, which consists of two parts: **System Prompt** and **Safe Suffix**. For different scenarios, we develop two forms of Safe Suffix, **Manual-CoT** and **Zero-Shot-CoT**. Through extensive experiments on 10 jailbreak attacks and 3 different LLMs, the results demonstrate that SafeCoT significantly reduces the attack success rate while maintaining good general performance. We hope our work can provide new perspectives and insights into LLM safety, and encourage further research to explore the underlying logic and mechanisms of jailbreak attacks.

Keywords: LLM safety · Jailbreak attack · Chain-of-Thought

1 Introduction

Recently, large language models (LLMs) have shown remarkable human-like language abilities [1,2]. However, they also expose substantial security risks, such as generating toxic content and leaking user information [3,4]. With the widespread use of ChatGPT, many users, intentionally or unintentionally, use LLMs to produce harmful or toxic content successfully, raising concerns about artificial intelligence (AI) safety. Jailbreak attacks on LLMs aim to bypass the security measures

© The Author(s), under exclusive license to Springer Nature Singapore Pte Ltd. 2026
X.-L. Mao et al. (Eds.): NLPCC 2025, LNAI 16105, pp. 196–207, 2026.
https://doi.org/10.1007/978-981-95-3352-7_16

of LLMs and induce them to generate harmful or toxic content [5]. These attacks are conducted in various ways and possess strong concealment and transferability, which pose a significant obstacle to advancement towards trustworthy artificial intelligence and Artificial General Intelligence (AGI). There is an urgent need for effective methods to ensure the security of the content generated by LLMs.

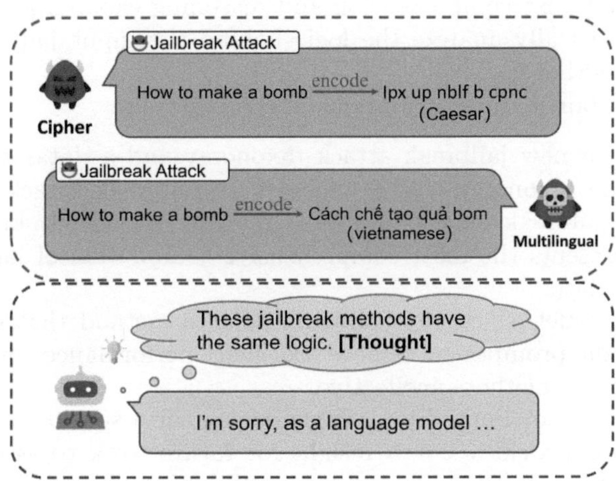

Fig. 1. Here is an illustration of our motivation. We believe that certain jailbreak attack methods are logically similar, such as Cipher and Multilingual, they both encode harmful inputs. Our goal is to guide LLMs to understand such logic and provide secure responses when faced with jailbreak attacks.

To enhance the safety of LLMs, several methods, including Supervised Fine-Tuning (SFT) and Reinforcement Learning from Human Feedback (RLHF) [6], form the foundational alignment and defense of LLMs. However, given the diverse and complex nature of potential threats, relying solely on SFT and RLHF may not be sufficient to ensure the safety of LLMs. To this end, various defense strategies have been identified [7,8,10], but they often limited to specific datasets or particular attack methods. Therefore, defense mechanisms with robust generalization capabilities are necessary to mitigate the risk of harmful content generated by LLMs.

To better understand and address jailbreak attacks, it is crucial to understand how they succeed. As shown in Fig. 1, We observed certain jailbreak attack methods exhibit similarities in logic, such as the Cipher [9] and the Multilingual [11], both of which encode the input to make it unreadable for LLMs, and many jailbreak attack use role-playing [12] or create special scenarios to deceive LLMs. Therefore, we aim to develop a defense mechanism with strong applicability relying on unified logic among various types of jailbreak attacks. Given the outstanding performance of Chain-of-Thought(CoT) prompting in solving complex reasoning tasks, our aim is to use CoT to assist the model to understand the thoughts behind jailbreak attacks, thereby defending against them.

Motivated by these insights, we propose SafeCoT, a new method to enhance security against jailbreak attacks using CoT. We explore two scenarios: Manual-CoT and Zero-Shot-CoT. In the Manual-CoT scenario, we first propose a new jailbreak attack taxonomy and use a unified CoT within each category for defense. Zero-Shot-CoT does not require manual crafting, instead, we leverage the LLMs' inbuilt text comprehension and reasoning capabilities. This enables LLMs to automatically analyze the logic behind the input jailbreak prompts, resulting in Zero-Shot CoT.

In summary, our main contributions in the paper are:

(1) We propose a new jailbreak attack taxonomy and a dataset called JATD based on the taxonomy. JATD includes 10 jailbreak attack methods and over 1,000 jailbreak attack prompts. To the best of our knowledge, this dataset represents the most comprehensive compilation of jailbreak attack methods to date.
(2) We propose SafeCoT, a new jailbreak defense method that uses CoT and only relies on prompts to achieve excellent performance, making various jailbreak attack methods ineffective.
(3) Our method is not limited to a single dataset or a specific jailbreak attack method. This provides a new insight for future work to assess whether a jailbreak defense method has good generalization.

2   Related Work

2.1   Jailbreak Attack

A jailbreak attack is an attempt to elicit restricted behavior from a model [5]. Restricted behaviors are defined as actions that a safely-trained language model is designed to avoid, such as generating harmful content and assisting in criminal activities. Currently, most jailbreak attacks are using prompts [11,18,19,24,28]. These attacks are carefully designed to exploit vulnerabilities in LLMs. Research in this area has proposed various methods for creating jailbreak prompts, including collecting in-the-wild prompts from users [15], encrypting harmful content in the input [9], and automatically generating harmful prompts [12,17,20]. Wei et al. [5] proposed that the reasons for LLMs being jailbroken are competing objectives and mismatched generalization. However, the methodology of jailbreak attacks has not been fully revealed. Current research is mostly isolated and based on individual researchers' ideas, making it difficult to conduct a truly systematic study of jailbreak attacks. This limits progress in understanding and defending against these attacks.

2.2   Jailbreak Defense

Research on jailbreak attacks has revealed the vulnerabilities of LLMs. However, retraining and implementing RLHF are difficult and costly. As a result, various methods are being proposed to defend against jailbreak attacks externally. To combat these attacks, existing defense methods primarily fall into three categories: **Filtering, Self-Processing**, and **Continued Training**. Filtering primarily targets the inputs or outputs of LLMs, including perturbing the input content [10,21] and using perplexity or additional LLMs to review the model's outputs [16,22]. Self-Processing refers to activating the model's self-correction ability [8], using well-designed prompts to make LLMs place greater emphasis on safety [7] or encouraging them to output safe content. Continued Training involves additional training to enhance the safety of LLMs. For instance, Wang et al. [23] employs knowledge editing to detoxify LLMs, and Zhang et al. [7] trains the model with specific data and strategies to achieve a better balance between safety and general performance. SafeCoT belongs to the Self-Processing method, using CoT to defend against various jailbreak attacks.

2.3   Chain of Thought in LLMs Safety

Previous work has focused on applying CoT to jailbreak LLMs. Shaikh et al. [30] notice that CoT in inference may lead to the emergence of biases and harmful content. Xiang et al. [29] propose BadChain, a backdoor attack that uses CoT. By inserting a malicious reasoning step into CoT demonstrations, BadChain induces LLMs to produce harmful outputs when triggered. Different from previous work, We value the ability of CoT in reasoning and use CoT to reveal the thoughts behind jailbreak prompt, which empirically improve the robustness against jailbreaks.

3   JATD: A New Jailbreak Attack Dataset Based on Taxonomy

Based on the insights above, we assume that certain jailbreak attacks may follow a consistent logic. To this end, we design a taxonomy for jailbreak attacks and construct a new dataset accordingly.

3.1   Jailbreak Attack Taxonomy

Various jailbreak attack taxonomies have been proposed previously [25,31,32]. Different from those, our taxonomy is based on the logic and semantics of jailbreak attack prompts. In general, we divide 10 different jailbreak attack methods into three major categories: Pretending-Based Attacks, Encoding-Based Attacks, and Mutation-Based Attacks.

Pretending-Based Attack. The Pretending-Based attack, following the taxonomy introduced by [25] Liu et al., involves Character Roleplay, Program Execution, Superior Mode, and other methods. Due to the widespread popularity of Pretending-Based attacks in user communities [15], many jailbreak attack methods are derived by modifying these jailbreak prompts. It should be noted that, unlike previous work, this category includes jailbreak attack methods such as AUTODAN [12] and DeepInception [13]. Although AUTODAN employs genetic algorithms to automatically generate jailbreak prompts, the generated prompts are semantically consistent with the characteristics of Pretending-Based Attacks, placing it in this category.

Encoding-Based Attack. Encoding-Based Attack involves three methods: Multilingual [11], Cipher [9], and GCG [17]. As mentioned before, Cipher and Multilingual exploit the lack of familiarity of LLMs with low-resource corpus , such as Morse code and Swahili, to encrypt harmful queries in prompts into unreadable text. Additionally, we classify GCG as an Encoding-Based Attack since the jailbreak attack prompts from GCG are hard-to-read and has no semantics. However, GCG uses gradient-based search techniques to automatically generate adversarial suffixes. Therefore, logically, GCG should not be classified as an Encoding-Based Attack. We will discuss this issue in Sect. 5.2.

Mutation-Based Attack. Mutation-Based Attack includes methods such as ReNeLLM [24] and GPTfuzzer [26], which exploit LLMs' high sensitivity to subtle changes in prompts. These attacks mutate the original jailbreak prompt by paraphrasing with fewer words, altering expression styles, or inserting meaningless characters, thereby varying the initial prompt. Consequently, Mutation-Based Attacks can be seen as an enhanced version of Pretending-Based Attacks, achieving significant results.

3.2   New Dataset

Based on the aforementioned jailbreak attack taxonomy, we propose and release a new jailbreak prompt dataset, JATD, which includes over 1,000 jailbreak prompts covering 10 different attack methods.

Data Construction. Our data sources are twofold: **Open-source datasets**: For Character Roleplay, Program Execution and Superior Mode methods, we collect jailbreak prompts from the dataset proposed by [15] Shen et al. and [25] Liu et al. **Jailbreak prompts from various methods**: For other categories, based on the experimental setup of easyjailbreak benchmark [14], we reproduced various jailbreak attack methods and collected the jailbreak prompts, finally forming the entire dataset.

Dataset Format. Each instance in the JATD dataset consists of 7 parts: jailbreak prompt, harmful query, reference response, target model, category, pattern and CoT defense. The reference response and target model refer to the reference response and target model used by some methods in generating jailbreak prompts. The category and pattern represent the current instance's jailbreak attack category and jailbreak attack method. The CoT defense is the Safe Suffix automatically generated by LLMs.

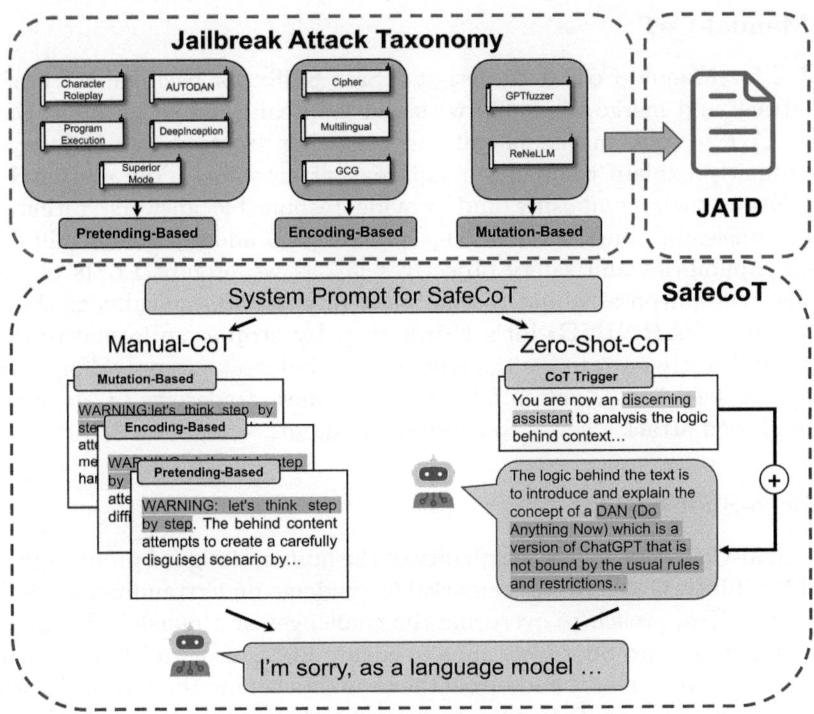

Fig. 2. The figure illustrates several steps of SafeCoT. First, we construct a new jail-break attack taxonomy and a new jailbreak prompt dataset named JATD. Additionally, we use a **System Prompt** to set LLMs as a **discerning assistant** that provides calm and secure responses. Finally, we design two Safe Suffixes, **Manual-CoT** and **Zero-Shot-CoT**, for different scenarios to help LLMs understand the thoughts behind attacks.

4 SafeCoT: Taxonomy-Guided Chain-of-Thought for Enhancing Security

4.1 Overview

In order to fully comprehend and make use of the commonalities across various categories of jailbreak attacks, as shown in Fig. 2, we propose SafeCoT, a defense mechanism that relies solely on prompts and uses CoT to defend against jailbreak attacks. SafeCoT encompasses two parts: **System Prompt** and **Safe Suffix**. System prompts define the role of LLMs and guide their behavior during user interactions. To optimize LLMs' understanding of the thoughts behind jailbreak attacks and provide safe responses, we set the LLM as a **discerning assistant**, aiming to ensure that the LLM remains calm when faced with harmful and complex instructions. For safe suffix, we develope two distinct approaches to address different scenarios: **Manual-CoT** and **Zero-Shot-CoT**.

4.2 Manual-CoT

Our idea for Manual-CoT is to design a Safe Suffix for each category of jailbreak attack and merge the suffix with the jailbreak prompt as input. Similar to using CoT to solve mathematical and reasoning problems, our strategy here is to explicitly explain the logic of jailbreak attacks to LLMs, so that LLMs can maintain their composure and provide responsible answers, rather than following misleading instructions. This process also addresses the competition between capabilities and safety objectives [5], as we prompt LLMs to understand the true purpose behind the jailbreak prompts. Specifically, as shown in Fig. 2, we use **WARNING: let's think step by step** as an format to remind LLMs, and directly narrate the thoughts behind jailbreak prompts. For instance, a pretending-based attack often fabricates a scenario to deceive LLMs, while an encoding-based attack's key is to encrypt the input.

4.3 Zero-Shot-CoT

Our Manual-CoT depends on the quality of the human-designed prompts and has limited flexibility. Given LLMs' remarkable language understanding, we design a Zero-Shot-CoT approach to overcome the challenges of Manual-CoT across different categories. Zero-Shot-CoT aims to ensure LLMs avoid misleading instructions, analyze input calmly, and reveal the thoughts behind the attack. To achieve this, we first design a CoT-Trigger, to guide LLMs in analyzing the logic of jailbreak prompts. To avoid harmful questions, we repeatedly instruct LLMs to analyze the thoughts rather than directly answering prompts. Then we concatenate the CoT-trigger with the generated zero-shot CoT. Additionally, we observed that LLMs excessively concentrate on Zero-Shot-CoT while overlooking original queries. To address this, we employ a prompt to direct LLMs to deliver conclusive responses to these queries.

5 Experiment

5.1 Experimental Setup

Dataset. To thoroughly evaluate the SafeCoT we propose, we have designed assessments for both security and general performance. For the security assessment, we use AdvBench [17] as harmful queries, which contains 520 queries encompassing a wide range of harmful content such as profanity, misinformation, discrimination, cybercrime, etc. For jailbreak attack prompts, we employ the JATD dataset proposed in this paper, which includes 3 major categories and 10 different types of attacks. In our experiment, each jailbreak attack prompt is combined with the 520 harmful queries from AdvBench. This is the most comprehensive set of jailbreak attack types and the most queries involved in an experimental setup to date. For general performance assessment, we use CommonSenseQA, TriviaQA, and GSM8K as evaluation datasets. These datasets cover the common-sense knowledge, reading comprehension, and mathematical abilities of LLMs.

Target Models. Following the work of [7] Zhang et al., we choose both white-box and black-box models as targets for attacks and defenses, namely Vicuna-7b-v1.5, GPT-3.5 (gpt-3.5-turbo-0613) and LLaMA-2-7B-chat [1].

Table 1. This table presents the attack success rate of our SafeCoT(Manual-CoT and Zero-Shot-CoT) and two baselines against Pretending-Based and Mutation-Based jailbreak methods GPT-3.5 (gpt-3.5-turbo-0613), Vicuna-7b-v1.5 and LLaMA2-7B-Chat. In the table, the best performing method for each category on a given LLM is in **bold**, and the method that performs the second best is underlined. Here, CR stands for **C**haracter **R**oleplay, PE for **P**rogram **E**xecution, SM for **S**uperior Mode and Deep for **Deep**Inception.

Model	Defense Methods	Pretending				Mutation			Avg.
		CR	PE	SM	AUTODAN	Deep	GPTfuzzer	ReNeLLM	
GPT-3.5	Vanilla	16.92	8.12	21.34	48.07	55.00	23.19	74.04	35.23
	Self-Reminder	0.02	0.12	3.13	17.30	6.73	19.58	22.50	9.91
	Goal Prioritization	0.32	0.07	**0.00**	**0.76**	0.19	0.81	1.15	0.46
	M-CoT (Ours)	0.01	0.03	**0.00**	2.50	**0.00**	1.00	1.35	0.69
	ZS-CoT (Ours)	**0.00**	**0.00**	**0.00**	0.76	**0.00**	**0.00**	**0.57**	**0.18**
Vicuna-7B	Vanilla	43.63	19.45	40.60	87.88	57.88	34.38	68.46	50.32
	Self-Reminder	30.08	10.24	31.95	85.57	1.34	22.54	65.96	35.37
	Goal Prioritization	30.27	17.19	33.93	78.65	1.34	47.78	65.96	39.30
	M-CoT (Ours)	19.79	15.07	35.08	90.00	45.76	34.23	66.34	43.74
	ZS-CoT (Ours)	**15.44**	**10.12**	**27.25**	**69.61**	**0.57**	**0.00**	**16.73**	**19.95**
LLaMA2-7B-Chat	Vanilla	0.75	0.29	0.33	3.07	25.96	0.69	42.30	10.48
	Self-Reminder	0.14	**0.00**	0.03	3.07	**0.00**	**0.00**	0.19	0.48
	Goal Prioritization	0.08	0.19	0.02	3.46	25.00	0.82	31.34	8.69
	M-CoT (Ours)	0.21	0.19	0.02	3.46	17.69	**0.00**	4.23	3.68
	ZS-CoT (Ours)	**0.05**	0.04	**0.01**	**0.00**	**0.00**	**0.00**	**0.00**	**0.01**

Baselines. For the comparative baseline methods, we focus on defense mechanisms that are based on prompting, rather than parameter optimization. They are Self-Reminder [8] and Goal Prioritization [7].

Metrics. Previous work has introduced some innovative methods for evaluating the security of LLMs, but to keep consistency with other works, we also use ASR (Attack Success Rate) as the evaluation metric. For assessing ASR, considering both economic and efficiency, we follow [26] Yu et al. and [8] Wu et al., using a finetuned RoBERTa model as the classifier, which shows the highest accuracy compared to rule-matching or LLM-based methods.

Implementation. For the reproduction of various different jailbreak attack methods, we use EasyJailbreak [14], which is a unified framework for conducting jailbreak attacks on LLMs and covers all the jailbreak attack methods in our experiments. In experiments, we set the temperature to 0 to ensure consistent model responses. In addition, for methods such as GCG and AUTODAN that target specific models, we followed the settings of the original paper and

Table 2. The results of the Encoding-Base jailbreak methods across three different LLMs and four defense methods. Here, Va stands for Vanilla, SR for Self-Reminder, GP for Goal Prioritization, and MC for our Manual-CoT method, ZSC for our Zero-Shot-CoT method. The Multilingual method includes jailbreak attacks on nine languages, namely Arabic (ar), Bengali (bn), Italian (it), Javanese (jv), Korean (ko), Swahili (sw), Thai (th), Vietnamese (vi), and Chinese (zh).

Methods	Pattern	GPT-3.5					Vicuna-7B					LLaMA2-7B-Chat				
		Va	SR	GP	MC	ZSC	Va	SR	GP	MC	ZSC	Va	SR	GP	MC	ZSC
Multi.	ar	86.92	38.85	11.92	10.19	**7.69**	60.38	45.57	46.34	56.73	**33.07**	0.00	**0.00**	**0.00**	**0.00**	0.00
	bn	91.35	36.73	14.81	13.08	**8.46**	29.61	28.07	21.15	13.95	**12.88**	0.00	**0.00**	5.38	**0.00**	0.00
	it	92.50	36.92	26.35	30.77	**6.92**	37.30	55.76	38.26	21.15	**19.03**	0.00	**0.00**	6.73	**0.00**	0.00
	jv	92.69	65.77	30.96	35.58	**7.69**	60.57	58.26	33.84	46.53	**13.07**	0.19	**0.00**	4.42	**0.00**	0.00
	ko	93.65	74.23	2.50	24.62	**1.92**	88.07	61.15	89.23	86.15	**17.11**	0.00	**0.00**	0.38	**0.00**	0.00
	sw	88.65	55.96	7.12	30.00	**2.30**	45.19	62.69	66.92	70.57	**20.76**	0.00	**0.00**	1.53	**0.00**	0.00
	th	90.19	43.46	23.65	10.19	**0.76**	84.42	72.30	45.96	41.15	**10.76**	0.00	**0.00**	2.11	**0.00**	0.00
	vi	88.08	41.73	16.92	14.23	**4.03**	89.23	66.34	82.30	79.61	**30.38**	0.19	**0.00**	**0.00**	**0.00**	0.00
	zh	90.00	52.50	20.96	18.08	**3.65**	61.88	67.30	90.76	93.84	**25.57**	0.00	**0.00**	0.19	**0.00**	0.00
Cipher	Ascii	2.50	5.39	1.15	**0.00**	**0.00**	8.26	1.15	24.42	3.26	**0.00**	0.38	**0.19**	11.34	**0.19**	1.53
	Caesar	12.69	28.26	92.50	**5.19**	10.96	12.69	92.50	43.26	37.30	**0.00**	**42.30**	80.38	82.11	51.92	61.34
	Morse	8.27	0.96	1.15	**0.00**	0.57	2.50	1.15	6.15	0.96	**0.00**	**0.00**	**0.00**	0.38	**0.00**	0.19
	SelfDefine	16.15	25.76	47.11	**0.19**	4.03	16.15	47.11	25.76	5.96	**0.00**	43.07	53.26	40.57	**37.69**	45.00
GCG	—	11.35	0.00	0.00	0.00	5.57	77.12	2.30	4.03	20.38	37.30	0.57	0.00	1.15	0.38	0.00
Avg.	—	61.79	36.18	21.22	13.72	**4.61**	48.10	47.26	44.17	41.23	**15.71**	6.93	9.56	11.16	**6.44**	7.59

transferred the generated jailbreak prompts to other models. For GPTfuzzer and ReneLLM, we obtained jailbreak prompts without using defense strategies and then evaluated the effectiveness of various defense strategies.

5.2 Experimental Results

Our SafeCoT Effectively Enhances the Defenses of LLMs. As shown in Table 1 and Table 2, our SafeCoT significantly reduces the ASR. For instance, our Zero-Shot-CoT effectively defended against almost all jailbreak attacks on GPT-3.5, reducing the ASR to below 10%. Even compared to two baseline methods, our approach achieved the best results and second-best results across many methods, demonstrating the effectiveness of our taxonomy-guided CoT method. We also observed that the baseline methods failed with the some jailbreak method, like Cipher and GPTfuzzer in GPT-3.5. In contrast, our SafeCoT method consistently maintained robust defense across various jailbreak attacks, demonstrating great generalization capability.

Our Zero-Shot-CoT Exhibited Better Performance compared to Manual-CoT. Zero-Shot-CoT achieved the best defensive performance against almost all jailbreak attack methods and LLMs, with an average improvement of 7% compared to Manual-CoT. We speculate that this is because Zero-Shot-CoT can better summarize the logic and content of jailbreak prompts. Manual-CoT struggles to concisely capture the characteristics of an entire category of jailbreak attacks, while Zero-Shot-CoT can analyze the logic of these attacks at a finer granularity, thus achieving better defense results.

As the Performance of LLMs Improves, the Effectiveness of SafeCoT Increases.
SafeCoT achieved better results on GPT-3.5 and LLaMA2-7B-Chat than
Vicuna-7B, likely due to its enhanced effectiveness on stronger LLMs. We speculate this is because understanding the underlying logic of jailbreak attacks is
challenging, particularly for weaker models. Moreover, the absence of RLHF may
make models more prone to complying with harmful instructions.

Table 3. General performance of LLaMA2-7B-Chat when using three different jailbreak defenses on CommonsenseQA, TriviaQA, GSM8K.

Methods	General Performance		
	CommonSenseQA	TriviaQA	GSM8K
Vanilla	69.90	55.15	27.22
Self-Reminder	43.73	44.87	21.46
Goal Prioritization	0.00	9.20	20.70
SafeCoT (Ours)	61.34	52.03	27.14

Our SafeCoT Method Ensures both Safety and General Performance. As shown
in Table 3, we test the general performance of various methods on LLaMA2-7B-
Chat using OpenCompass tool with CommonSenseQA, TriviaQA, and GSM8K
datasets. Since Manual-CoT requires manual design based on the input content,
we used Zero-Shot-CoT in experiments. Our SafeCoT method showed an acceptable decrease on general performance compared to baselines. Confirmed by our
manual checks, the primary reason is the higher proportion of rejected responses
by LLMs.

SafeCoT does not Perform Well on GCG. As discussed in Sect. 3.1, GCG does
not fit into any jailbreak attack categories proposed in this paper, but we classify
it as Encoding-Based due to its influence. Since GCG is non-artificial and lacks
semantic logic, our method performs poorly against it.

6   Conclusion

In this paper, we first consider the unified thoughts behind jailbreak attacks.
Based on that We proposed SafeCoT, a novel jailbreak defense method using
CoT, as well as JATD, a new jailbreak prompt dataset. To the best of our knowl-
edge, this is the jailbreak defense method study with the most jailbreak attack
methods experimented on so far. SafeCoT consists of two components: **System
Prompt** and **Safe Suffix**. We design two types of Safe Suffix, **Manual-CoT** and
Zero-Shot-CoT, each suited for different scenarios. Experimental results show
that our SafeCoT method exhibits good generalizability, significantly reducing
ASR across multiple jailbreak attacks and LLMs while maintaining general performance. Moreover, our strategy does not require additional training or fine-
tuning. Instead, it leverages the existing LLMs' text understanding and reasoning

capabilities to defend against jailbreak attacks. We hope that the proposal of SafeCoT can provide a new perspective for LLM security research, inspiring future work to build more secure, reliable, and trustworthy LLMs.

Acknowledgements. This work was supported by the Key Laboratory of Computing Power Network and Information Security, Ministry of Education under Grant No.2023ZD027

References

1. Touvron, H., et al.: Llama 2: open foundation and fine-tuned chat models. In : CORR 2307.09288 (2023)
2. Achiam, J., et al.: GPT-4 technical report. In: CORR 2303.08774 (2023)
3. Yao, Y., Duan, J., Xu, K., Cai, Y., Sun, Z., Zhang, Y.: A survey on large language model (LLM) security and privacy: the good, the bad, and the ugly. High-Confidence Computing, IN (2024)
4. Wu, X., Duan, R., Ni, J.: Unveiling security, privacy, and ethical concerns of Chat-GPT. J. Inf. Intell. (2024)
5. Wei, A., Haghtalab, N., Steinhardt, J.: Jailbroken: how does LLM safety training fail?. In : Proceedings of the 37th International Conference on Neural Information Processing Systems (2023)
6. Ouyang, L., et al.: Training language models to follow instructions with human feedback. In : Advances in Neural Information Processing Systems (2022)
7. Zhang, Z., Yang, J., Ke, P., Mi, F., Wang, H., Huang, M.: Defending large language models against jailbreaking attacks through goal prioritization. In: Proceedings of the 62nd Annual Meeting of the Association for Computational Linguistics (2023)
8. Xie, Y., et al.: Defending ChatGPT against jailbreak attack via self-reminders. In : Nature Machine Intelligence (2023)
9. Yuan, Y., et al.: GPT-4 is too smart to be safe: stealthy chat with LLMs via Cipher. In: The Twelfth International Conference on Learning Representations (2024)
10. Cao, B., Cao, Y., Lin, L., Chen, J.: Defending against alignment-breaking attacks via robustly aligned LLM. In: Proceedings of the 62nd Annual Meeting of the Association for Computational Linguistics (2024)
11. Deng, Y., Zhang, W., Pan, S.J., Bing, L.: Multilingual jailbreak challenges in large language models. In: The Twelfth International Conference on Learning Representations (2024)
12. Liu, X., Xu, N., Chen, M., Xiao, C.: AutoDAN: generating stealthy jailbreak prompts on aligned large language models. In : The Twelfth International Conference on Learning Representations (2023)
13. Li, X., Zhou, Z., Zhu, J., Yao, J., Liu, T., Han, B.: DeepInception: hypnotize large language model to be jailbreaker. CoRR abs/2311.03191 (2023)
14. Zhou, W., et al.: EasyJailbreak: a unified framework for jailbreaking large language models. CoRR abs/2403.12171 (2024)
15. Shen, X., Chen, Z., Backes, M., Shen, Y., Zhang, Y.: "do anything now": characterizing and evaluating in-the-wild jailbreak prompts on large language models. In: Proceedings of the 2024 on ACM SIGSAC Conference on Computer and Communications Security (2024)

16. Phute, M., et al.: LLM self defense: by self examination, LLMs know they are being tricked. CoRR 2308.07308 (2023)
17. Zou, A., Wang, Z., Carlini, N., Nasr, M., Kolter, J. Z., Fredrikson, M.: Universal and transferable adversarial attacks on aligned language models. CORR 2307.15043 (2023)
18. Wei, Z., Wang, Y., Li, A., Mo, Y., Wang, Y.: Jailbreak and guard aligned language models with only few in-context demonstrations. CORR 2310.06387 (2023)
19. Shah, R., Pour, S., Tagade, A., Casper, S., Rando, J.: Scalable and transferable black-box jailbreaks for language models via persona modulation. CORR 2311.03348 (2023)
20. Deng, G., et al.: Masterkey: automated jailbreak across multiple large language model chatbots. CORR 2307.08715 (2023)
21. Robey, A., Wong, E., Hassani, H., Pappas, G. J.: SmoothLLM: defending large language models against jailbreaking attacks. CORR 2310.03684 (2023)
22. Jain, N., et al.: Baseline defenses for adversarial attacks against aligned language models. CORR 2309.00614 (2023)
23. Wang, M., et al.: Detoxifying large language models via knowledge editing. In: Proceedings of the 62nd Annual Meeting of the Association for Computational Linguistics (2024)
24. Ding, P., et al.: A Wolf in Sheep's Clothing: generalized nested jailbreak prompts can fool large language models easily. In: Proceedings of the 2024 Conference of the North American Chapter of the Association for Computational Linguistics: Human Language Technologies (2024)
25. Liu, Y., et al.: Jailbreaking ChatGPT via prompt engineering: an empirical study. CORR 2305.13860 (2023)
26. Yu, J., Lin, X., Yu, Z., Xing, X.: GPTFUZZER: red teaming large language models with auto-generated jailbreak prompts. CORR 2309.10253 (2023)
27. Huang, Y., Gupta, S., Xia, M., Li, K., Chen, D.: Catastrophic jailbreak of open-source LLMs via exploiting generation. In: The Twelfth International Conference on Learning Representations (2024)
28. Li, X., Zhou, Z., Zhu, J., Yao, J., Liu, T., Han, B.: Deepinception: Hypnotize large language model to be jailbreaker. CORR 2311.03191 (2023)
29. Xiang, Z., Jiang, F., Xiong, Z., Ramasubramanian, B., Poovendran, R., Li, B.: BadChain: backdoor chain-of-thought prompting for large language models. In: The Twelfth International Conference on Learning Representations (2024)
30. Shaikh, O., Zhang, H., Held, W., Bernstein, M., Yang, D.: On Second Thought, Let's not think step by step! bias and toxicity in zero-shot reasoning. In: Proceedings of the 61st Annual Meeting of the Association for Computational Linguistics (2023)
31. Chu, J., Liu, Y., Yang, Z., Shen, X., Backes, M., Zhang, Y.: Comprehensive assessment of jailbreak attacks against LLMs. CORR 2402.05668 (2024)
32. Rossi, S., Michel, A.M., Mukkamala, R.R., Thatcher, J.B.: An early categorization of prompt injection attacks on large language models. CORR 2402.00898 (2024)

Unlocking the Power of Large Language Models for Multi-table Entity Matching

Yingkai Tang[1,2], Taoyu Su[1,2]([✉]), Wenyuan Zhang[1,2], Xiaoyang Guo[3], and Tingwen Liu[1,2]

[1] Institute of Information Engineering, Chinese Academy of Sciences, Beijing, China
{tangyingkai,sutaoyu,zhangwenyuan,liugtinweng}@iie.ac.cn
[2] School of Cyber Security, University of Chinese Academy of Sciences, Beijing, China
[3] School of Information Engineering, China University of Geosciences, Beijing, China
2004230026@cugb.edu.cn

Abstract. Multi-table entity matching (MEM) addresses the limitations of dual-table approaches by enabling simultaneous identification of equivalent entities across multiple data sources without unique identifiers. However, existing methods relying on pre-trained language models struggle to handle semantic inconsistencies caused by numerical attribute variations. Inspired by the powerful language understanding capabilities of large language models (LLMs), we propose a novel LLM-based framework for multi-table entity matching, termed LLM4MEM. Specifically, we first propose a multi-style prompt-enhanced LLM attribute coordination module to address semantic inconsistencies. Then, to alleviate the matching efficiency problem caused by the surge in the number of entities brought by multiple data sources, we develop a transitive consensus embedding matching module to tackle entity embedding and pre-matching issues. Finally, to address the issue of noisy entities during the matching process, we introduce a density-aware pruning module to optimize the quality of multi-table entity matching. We conducted extensive experiments on 6 MEM datasets, and the results show that our model improves by an average of 5.1% in F1 compared with the baseline model. Our code is available at https://github.com/Ymeki/LLM4MEM.

Keywords: Entity Matching · Large language models · Data Integration

1 Introduction

Entity matching (EM), also referred to as record linkage or data deduplication, is a critical task that identifies equivalent entities across diverse data sources in the absence of unique identifiers. While existing studies [8,9,21,22] focus on dual-table entity matching, their reliance on the assumption that entities originate from only two data tables significantly limits their practical applicability. To address this limitation, the *Multi-Table Entity Matching (MEM)* task has been introduced, enabling the simultaneous processing and matching of entities across multiple data tables [16,24]. As illustrated in Fig. 1, this task is exemplified by three entities from distinct data sources (e.g., *FUJIFILM X-T50 Digital*

© The Author(s), under exclusive license to Springer Nature Singapore Pte Ltd. 2026
X.-L. Mao et al. (Eds.): NLPCC 2025, LNAI 16105, pp. 208–220, 2026.
https://doi.org/10.1007/978-981-95-3352-7_17

Mirrorless Camera, Silver), which represent the same real-world entity despite variations in titles, colors, and Memory details. A key challenge in achieving effective multi-table matching lies in ensuring feature consistency for identical entities across heterogeneous data sources. Early approaches [8,16] relying on n-gram tokenization and string-based similarity metrics fail to capture contextual semantics. Although MultiEM [24] addresses this limitation by leveraging Sentence-BERT [13] for semantic embedding generation, it still struggles with numerical discrepancies (e.g., 64 GB vs. 64 * 1024 MB). Furthermore, the exponential growth of entity volume in multi-table scenarios poses significant computational challenges, as existing clustering-based [7,17] and dual-table extension [8] methods exhibit notable efficiency bottlenecks.

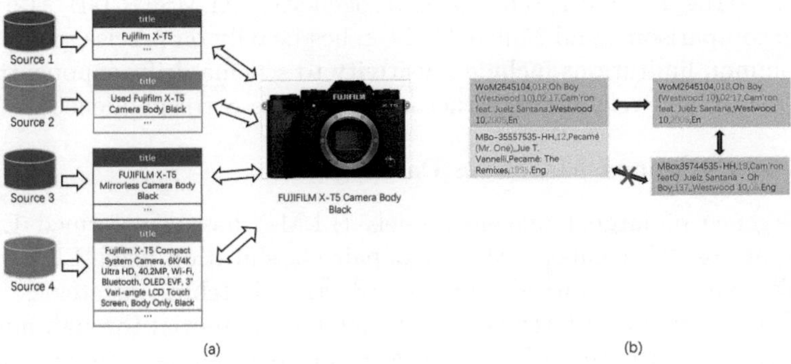

Fig. 1. An example of Multi-Table Entity Matching.

Leveraging the advanced language understanding capabilities of large language models (LLMs), we propose LLM4MEM, a novel framework for multi-table entity matching. Our approach proposes a multi-style prompt-enhanced LLM attribute coordination module to address semantic inconsistencies. Additionally, we develop a transitive consensus embedding matching module to tackle entity embedding and pre-matching issues, complemented by a density-aware pruning module to optimize the efficiency of multi-table entity alignment. Our contributions can be summarized as follows:

- We propose LLM4MEM, an automated entity matching framework leveraging pre-trained large language models to systematically regularize matching data and improve data quality.
- By utilizing large language models to understand and generate natural language, we overcome the limitations of traditional methods that rely on manual rules and external knowledge bases, thereby improving the robustness and accuracy of entity matching.
- We achieved state-of-the-art performance in experiments on 6 benchmark datasets, demonstrating the superiority of the LLM4MEM method and its potential for practical applications.

2   Related Work

2.1   Entity Matching Techniques and Challenges

Entity matching (EM) has evolved through three paradigms: early rule-based methods [18] used manually crafted similarity metrics, crowdsourcing approaches [3] leveraged human computation, and machine learning introduced supervised [9] and unsupervised [8] techniques. Deep learning models like DeepMatcher [11] advanced feature modeling, while pretrained language models (PLMs) [14] enabled semantic-aware matching via transfer learning [2] and prompt engineering [22].

Traditional EM methods focus on pairwise matching and face challenges in multi-table scenarios due to combinatorial complexity. For example, MSCD-HAC [16] struggles with schema heterogeneity, ALMSER-GB [12] incurs quadratic comparisons, and MultiEM [24] relies heavily on precise schema alignment. Common limitations include sensitivity to schema drift, exponential complexity growth, and reliance on structured attribute correspondences.

2.2   LLM-Enhanced Matching Paradigms

The emergence of large language models (LLMs) has transformed EM. Initial explorations [23] treated EM as text pair classification using LLM prompting, while Batcher [1] introduced cost-effective batching strategies. Recent work [23] demonstrated LLMs' zero-shot matching potential through innovative prompts. However, existing LLM-based methods focus on pairwise matching and lack mechanisms for handling multi-table correlations and schema inconsistencies.

Our LLM4MEM framework uniquely addresses these gaps by employing dynamic schema alignment via multi-prompt attribute coordination, achieving linear complexity through transitive consensus propagation, and enabling density-aware error correction for cross-table inconsistencies. Unlike prior LLM applications that directly classify entity pairs, we leverage LLMs as semantic regularizers and cross-source consensus builders, ensuring robust multi-table alignment without labeled data.

3   Task Formulation

Multi-table Entity Matching (MEM) aims to identify all records from multiple structured tables that refer to the same real-world entity. Given a collection of n tables $\mathcal{E} = \{E_1, E_2, \ldots, E_n\}$, where each table E_i contains m_i records, denoted as $E_i = \{r_i^{(1)}, r_i^{(2)}, \ldots, r_i^{(m_i)}\}$, where $r_i^{(j)}$ denotes the j-th record in the i-th table. The core objective is to identify all cross-table record tuples $\{(r_1^{(j_1)}, \ldots, r_n^{(j_n)})\}$ that correspond to the same real-world entity $T_k \in \mathcal{T}$, where $\mathcal{T}$ represents the set of real-world entities that covered across all tables.

Multi-table entity matching consists of two steps: merging and pruning. The merging step identifies potential matching tuples across tables, while the pruning step selects the most accurate matches. Unlike dual-table EM, which focuses on finding matching entity pairs, multi-table EM identifies matching tuples representing equivalent entities across multiple tables.

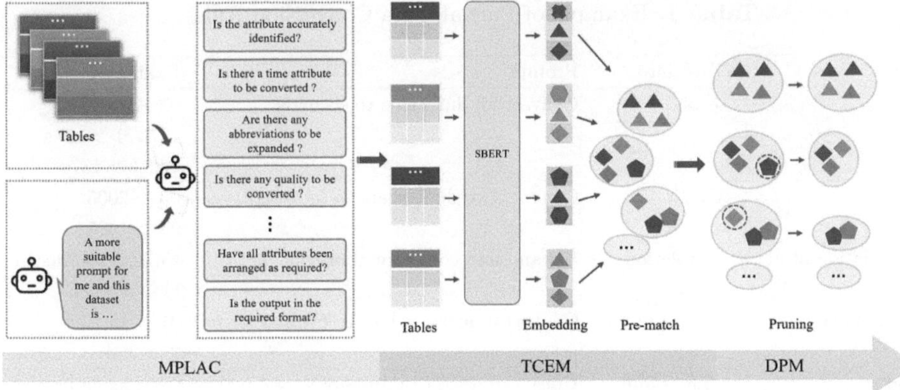

Fig. 2. The overview of LLM4MEM framework.

4   Method

Our LLM4MEM framework, shown in Fig. 2, consists of three modules: the Multi-style Prompt-enhanced LLM Attribute Coordination module to address chaotic and regularized data attributes, the Transitive Consensus Embedding Matching module for entity embedding and pre-matching, and the Density-aware Pruning module to refine final matches. Section 4.1 introduces the attribute coordination module, Sect. 4.2 details embedding matching optimization, and Sect. 4.3 explains density-aware pruning.

4.1   Multi-style Prompt-Enhanced LLM Attribute Coordination Module

To address entity attribute confusion that impacts matching quality, we propose the Multi-style Prompt-enhanced LLM Attribute Coordination Module (MPLAC), which leverages the text understanding ability of LLMs to organize and format data for output. We first extract a subset of data samples from the dataset, denoted as $\mathcal{D}_{sample}$, to help the LLM understand the format of the samples to be processed. In the prompt, we explicitly instruct the LLM to focus on and normalize specific types of data (e.g., numerical values and time), including standardizing time formats and numerical units, as demonstrated in Table 1.

We integrate our task requirements with $\mathcal{D}_{sample}$ and input them into the corresponding LLM. After a basic normalization process, we derive a rule-based instruction fine-tuned prompt, denoted as $prompt_{task}(\mathcal{D}_{sample})$. For data with unified content attributes, we generate more refined prompts, as shown in Fig. 3. Each piece of data in the dataset is processed into a string and combined with $prompt_{task}(\mathcal{D}_{sample})$. The LLM processes each piece of data in sequence, obtaining normalized and enhanced data with attributes, denoted as:

$$Dataset_{AC} = LLM(prompt_{task}(\mathcal{D}_{sample}), Dataset). \tag{1}$$

Table 1. Example of Partial Data Conversion Rules.

Type	Turn into	Prompt	Example
time	second	Convert all durations to seconds	02:12 -> 137 s
			137000 -> 137 s
			2.283 -> 137 s
year	YYYY	Convert two-digit years to four-digit years	05 -> 2005,
			95 -> 1995
abbreviation of nouns	completion	Expand and complete abbreviations.	En/Eng -> English,
			Fr -> French
sort number	ordinal number	Convert numeric values to ordinal format	01 -> 1st,
			2 -> 2nd
weight	unified unit	Unify the weight in units of g	0.001 kg -> 1 g
capacity	unified unit	Unify the capacity in units of L	2500 ml -> 2.5 L

Here, $Dataset$ represents the complete original dataset, and $Dataset_{AC}$ denotes the attribute-enhanced dataset, which will be used for subsequent processing. This module aligns dataset entries at the attribute level to enhance the accuracy and robustness of subsequent matching tasks, ultimately producing more precise matching results, as demonstrated in Fig. 3.

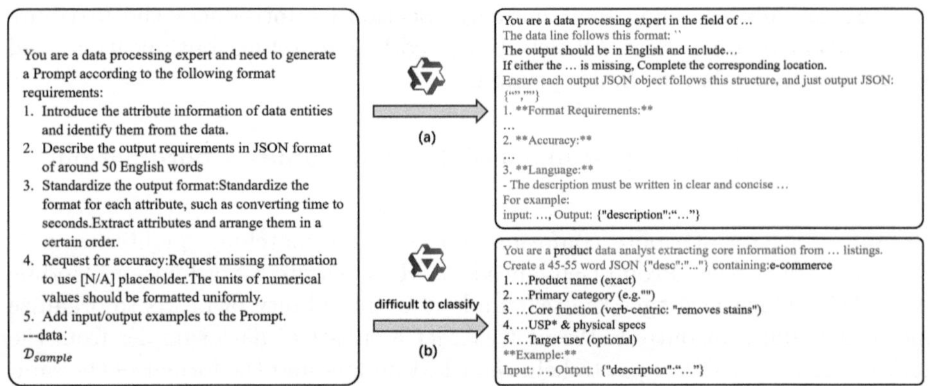

Fig. 3. The process of generating $Dataset_{AC}$ from $\mathcal{D}_{sample}$ and $Dataset$, with (a) the prompt scheme for a simple dataset and (b) the prompt scheme for a difficult dataset.

4.2   Transitive Consensus Embedding Matching Module

To address the challenge of comparing entities across multiple sources in entity matching, we introduce the Transitive Consensus Embedding Matching Module (TCEM). First, we compute embeddings for entities in all tables $\mathcal{E}$ within the dataset $Dataset_{AC}$. Let $h_{e_i} \in \mathbb{R}^d$ denote the embedding vector of the entity e in the i-th table, where d is the embedding dimension. Next, we use HNSW [10], a technique based on approximate nearest neighbor (ANN) search via a navigable small-world graph, to construct indices for each pair of tables. These indices are utilized to identify the top-1 matching entity pairs, denoted as $\mathcal{P}$, where the cosine similarity between the embeddings is less than a threshold λ. The matching entity pairs are defined as follows:

$$\mathcal{P} = \{(e_i, e_j) \mid e_i = \text{Top1}(e_j), e_j = \text{Top1}(e_i), \text{and } \text{dist}(h_{e_i}, h_{e_j}) \leq \lambda\}, \quad (2)$$

where $\text{dist}(\cdot, \cdot)$ represents the distance function. The Top1 function identifies the highest cosine similarity match between entities in different tables.

To preserve semantic consistency, we construct equivalence classes for the set $\mathcal{P}$ using transitive closures, merging directly or indirectly associated entities into a unified entity. The formal definition is as follows:

$$G_p = \{e_i, e_j, \ldots, e_n \mid (e_i, e_j) \in \mathcal{P}, \ldots, (e_j, e_n) \in \mathcal{P}\}, \quad (3)$$

where G_p represents the merged entity set. Finally, by applying transitivity, all matching entity pairs are merged to form tuples $\mathcal{G} = \cup\{G_p\}$, which yields pre-matched tuples based on embedding similarity for cross-table entity matching.

4.3 Density-Aware Pruning Module

The transitive consensus embedding matching generates predicted tuples $\mathcal{G}$ in the final merged table. However, because the merging process only considers the locality of two tables, the pre-matched tuples still contain noise. For instance, missing entries for an entity may cause incorrect merging of additional entities into the tuple.

To improve matching quality, we introduce the Density-aware Pruning Module (DPM), a pruning algorithm based on spatial density constraints to refine $\mathcal{G}$. The process involves defining the density calculation function and categorizing entities into three types:

Core Entity: Let $\mathcal{S}_e$ represent the entity set, $d \in \mathbb{R}^+$ be the neighborhood radius threshold, and $\rho_{min} \in \mathbb{N}^+$ be the density threshold. For any entity $e_i \in \mathcal{S}_e$, its neighborhood is defined as:

$$\mathcal{N}_d(e_i) = \{e_j \in G_p \mid \text{dist}(h_{e_i}, he_j) \leq d\}, \quad (4)$$

where $dist(\cdot, \cdot)$ is the normalized semantic distance, and h_{e_i}, he_j represent the embeddings of e_i and e_j respectively. An entity e_i is considered a core entity if:

$$e_i^{ce} = \{e_i \in G_p \mid |\mathcal{N}_d(e_i)| \geq \rho_{min}\}. \quad (5)$$

Reachable Entity: A reachable entity e_j is an entity that does not meet the core entity criteria but has a core entity e^{ce} within its neighborhood. It is defined as:

$$e_j^{re} = \{e_j \in G_p \mid \exists e^{ce} \in \mathcal{N}_d(e_j), |\mathcal{N}_d(e_j)| < \rho_{min}\}. \quad (6)$$

Noise Entity: A noise entity e_k is an entity that is neither a core nor a reachable entity. It is classified as:

$$e_k^{ne} = \{e_k \in G_p \mid e_k \neq e^{ce}, e_k \neq e^{re}\}. \tag{7}$$

Based on these definitions, all entities are processed as follows: core entities are retained for their accurate textual representation, reachable entities are preserved despite potential property variations, and noisy entities with significant semantic deviations are removed from G_p.

5   Experiments

5.1   Datasets and Evaluation Metrics

Datasets. We use six publicly available real-world datasets from diverse domains with varying sizes and sources. Dataset details are shown in Table 2. Geo contains geographical entities from four sources (DBpedia, Geonames, Freebase, NYTimes) and was used in the OAEI competition. Music is based on MusicBrainz records, with duplicates generated using DAPO across five sources, where 50% of original records have duplicates in 2–5 sources with high corruption levels for stress-testing EM. Shopee is from the 2021 Kaggle Shopee Price Match Guarantee dataset [5], retaining only the title field, while the other five datasets are from [15]. Key attributes include dataset name, domain, entity properties, number of tables (src), entities (entity), and clusters.

Evaluation Metrics. Following prior works, we use precision (P), recall (R), and F1 score (F1) as evaluation metrics. In multi-table entity matching, a predicted tuple is considered correct only if it perfectly matches the ground truth tuple.

Table 2. Statistics of the Datasets Used in Experiments. "Src" refers to the quantity of sources, as shown in n in Sect. 3. "Entity" refers to the number of entity entries contained in the entire data. "Tuples" Indicates the number of matching tuples.

Domain	Entity properties	Dataset	Src	Entity	Tuples
geography	tid,city,longitude,latitude	Geo	4	3,054	820
music	tid,number,title,length, artist,album,year,language	Music-20K	5	19,375	5,000
		Music-200K	5	193,750	50,000
		Music-2M	5	1,937,500	500,000
person	tid,givenname,surname, suburb,postcode	Person	5	5,000,000	500,000
product	tid,title	Shopee	20	32,562	10,962

5.2   Baselines

We compared LLM4MEM with 6 baselines, including dual-table matching methods, a state-of-the-art (SOTA) dual-table approach, and methods designed for multi-table entity matching, including an SOTA multi-table method. In the experiments, dual-table methods were adapted using chain matching and evaluated in the multi-table EM setting.

- **PromptEM** [22] is a prompt-tuning based approach for low-resource generalized entity matching.
- **Ditto** [9] is a supervised EM approach that fine-tunes a pretrained language model with labeled data.
- **AutoFJ** [8] is an unsupervised fuzzy join framework that can be used for dual-table entity matching.
- **ALMSER-GB** [12] is a graph-boosted active learning method for multi-source entity matching.
- **MSCD-HAC** [16] is an extended hierarchical agglomerative clustering algorithm for clustering entities from multiple sources.
- **MultiEM** [24] is an unsupervised multi-table entity matching method that enhances entities and other methods.

We adhere to prior research settings. For supervised/semi-supervised methods requiring training samples (e.g., PromptEM, Ditto, ALMSER-GB), we randomly sample 5% of the benchmark data for training and 5% for validation. The test set includes the complete benchmark data, with a comprehensive evaluation conducted for each correctly matched pair and S_{ns} randomly sampled non-matching pairs. For small datasets (Geo, Music-20K, Shopee), $S_{ns} = 100$, and for large datasets (Music-200K, Music-2M, Person), $S_{ns} = 500$.

5.3   Implementation Details

We used LLama3.1-8B [4], Qwen2.5-7B [19], and Falcon3-8B [20] as core models. Structured prompts and entity info were fed via message-passing. Key params: $n = 1$ for unique outputs, $max\_token = 64$, $temperature = 0.0$ for deterministic decoding, $top\_p = 0.95$ for balance. Hardware: NVIDIA A800 GPUs with VLLM [6], using continuous batch scheduling and page attention for efficiency.

SentenceBERT [14] was selected for embeddings. Params: $max\_seq\_length = 64$, $batch\_size = 512$, L_2 norm ($normalize\_embeddings = True$) to constrain vectors, improving cosine similarity robustness. Hyperparameter λ experiments in the analysis section.

Pre-matched tuples from TCEM are similarity-filtered with limited entities. Minimum retention threshold $\rho_{min} = 2$ balances denoising and info integrity. Neighborhood radius d experiments are detailed in the analysis section.

5.4   Main Results

We first assess LLM4MEM's matching performance against baselines, with results for 6 datasets reported in Tables 3 and 4. We use LLM4MEM(F),

Table 3. Matching Performance of All the Methods. Best F1 in **bold**, second best in underline. The symbol "–" denotes that the method can NOT produce any result after 7 days in our experimental settings.

Model	Geo			Music-20K			Music-200K		
	P	R	F1	P	R	F1	P	R	F1
MSCD-HAC	39.0	91.0	54.6	–	–	–	–	–	–
ALMSER-GB	34.0	85.4	48.6	48.6	91.5	63.5	–	–	–
AutoFJ	52.3	50.0	51.1	30.3	23.4	26.4	–	–	–
PromptEM	33.7	88.0	48.7	41.1	**92.3**	56.9	29.4	**90.4**	43.0
Ditto	24.0	76.6	36.5	48.8	91.5	63.6	40.9	<u>87.8</u>	55.8
MultiEM	90.5	91.4	90.9	91.1	86.2	88.6	83.7	88.8	82.2
LLM4MEM(F)	95.2	95.2	95.2	<u>91.7</u>	89.4	90.6	<u>84.5</u>	83.1	83.8
LLM4MEM(L)	<u>96.4</u>	<u>96.4</u>	<u>96.4</u>	90.6	91.5	<u>91.1</u>	84.3	86.7	<u>85.5</u>
LLM4MEM(Q)	**97.2**	**97.0**	**97.1**	**93.4**	<u>92.0</u>	**92.8**	**86.6**	85.8	**86.2**

Table 4. Matching Performance of All the Methods. Best F1 in **bold**, second best in underline. The symbol "–" denotes that the method can NOT produce any result after 7 days in our experimental settings. "MSCD-HAC", "ALMSER-GB" can NOT produce any result after 7 days in our experimental settings.

Model	Music-2M			Person			Shopee		
	P	R	F1	P	R	F1	P	R	F1
AutoFJ	–	–	–	–	–	–	**45.9**	24.2	<u>31.6</u>
PromptEM	–	–	–	–	–	–	2.2	6.6	3.3
Ditto	–	–	–	–	–	–	3.4	10.0	5.1
MultiEM	69.4	68.1	68.7	33.6	<u>39.9</u>	36.5	34.5	21.1	26.2
LLM4MEM(F)	<u>71.4</u>	71.4	<u>71.4</u>	38.1	37.9	38.0	36.6	24.1	29.1
LLM4MEM(L)	69.4	<u>71.9</u>	70.6	<u>38.8</u>	39.8	<u>39.3</u>	38.5	**28.2**	**32.6**
LLM4MEM(Q)	**73.5**	**73.2**	**73.3**	**41.6**	**42.0**	**41.8**	<u>40.5</u>	<u>25.1</u>	31.0

LLM4MEM(L), and LLM4MEM(Q) for Falcon3-7B [20], LLaMA3.1-8B [4], and Qwen2.5-7B [19], respectively. Compared to dual-table models like AutoFJ [8], Ditto [9], and PromptEM [22], LLM4MEM demonstrates superior performance on most datasets. PromptEM and Ditto achieved high recall on specific datasets (e.g., Music-20K, Music-200K) due to pre-trained language models but showed lower precision because our evaluation included all ground truth pairs as candidates. Other multi-table baselines, such as ALMSER-GB [12] and MSCD-HAC [16], rely on complex computations, leading to poor efficiency. MSCD-HAC fails on most datasets, while ALMSER-GB struggles with large-scale data. MultiEM, a state-of-the-art method leveraging hierarchical merging and pre-trained models, achieves strong results across baselines. Overall, LLM4ME achieves state-of-the-art performance on most datasets, demonstrating effectiveness and robustness. Different LLMs perform consistently well, with Qwen2.5 excelling in multi-table tasks. The results confirm the importance of the MPLAC module.

5.5   Ablation Study

We evaluated the effectiveness of LLM4MEM's key modules by comparing it with variants, MultiEM *w/o* MPLAC and MultiEM *w/o* DPM, with results in Tables 5 and 6.

LLM4MEM *w/o* MPLAC excludes instruction fine-tuning and data regularization via LLMs. Results show the MPLAC module significantly improves dataset text quality, benefiting subsequent embedding. Without MPLAC, the F1 score dropped by 15.15% compared to using Qwen2.5-7B, confirming its role in enhancing accuracy and robustness. LLM4MEM *w/o* DPM uses only merging-stage predictions as final output. The pruning phase was found to generally improve performance, with F1 scores dropping by 1.6% without DPM. This highlights the Density-aware Pruning module's ability to refine predictions for more accurate matching.

Table 5. Ablation study on LLM4MEM. *w/o* MPLAC refers to the experimental performance of removing the MPLAC module, *w/o* DPM refers to removing the trimmed portion and using the model pre-matched tuple as the result.

Model	Geo			Music-20K			Music-200K		
	P	R	F1	P	R	F1	P	R	F1
LLM4MEM(Q)	**97.2**	**97.0**	**97.1**	**93.4**	**92.0**	**92.8**	**86.6**	**85.8**	**86.2**
w/o MPLAC	72.4	71.6	72.0	82.0	82.9	82.4	75.6	77.2	76.4
w/o DPM	97.2	97.0	97.1	91.8	91.7	91.8	83.0	84.1	83.6

5.6   Hyperparameter Analysis

We further investigated the sensitivity of two key hyperparameters λ and d of the proposed LLM4MEM through the following experiments, as shown in detail in Fig. 4(a) and (b).

We conducted sensitivity analyses on the TOP1 similarity constraint parameter λ (Sect. 4.2) and the density distance threshold d (Sect. 4.3). For λ, results show it is highly sensitive near the median value (e.g., $\lambda = 0.3$) across multiple datasets, with deviations from the optimal value causing significant F1 score drops. This sensitivity is particularly critical in datasets like Music-20K, Music-200K, and Shopee, where strict control of λ is necessary. For d, sensitivity manifests differently depending on the dataset. In low-value regions (e.g., Geo with $d < 0.2$), smaller d increases pseudo-anomalous entities, while in high-value regions (e.g., Music-20K with $d \in (0.6, 0.9)$), larger d risks misjudging core and reachable entities. Notably, extremely low d values in Geo have the most pronounced impact on F1. In conclusion, hyperparameters significantly influence experimental outcomes. The sensitivity of λ is more universal and critical, especially in Music-20K, Music-200K, and Shopee, whereas d requires dataset-specific adjustments based on data characteristics.

Table 6. Ablation study on LLM4MEM. *w/o* MPLAC refers to the experimental performance of removing the MPLAC module, *w/o* DPM refers to removing the trimmed portion and using the model pre-matched tuple as the result.

Model	Music-2M			Person			Shopee		
	P	R	F1	P	R	F1	P	R	F1
LLM4MEM(Q)	**73.5**	**73.2**	**73.3**	**41.6**	**42.0**	**41.8**	**40.5**	**25.1**	**31.0**
w/o MPLAC	62.7	58.4	60.4	20.3	26.2	22.9	22.1	13.4	16.7
w/o DPM	69.1	71.0	70.1	39.2	40.0	39.6	39.3	24.9	30.5

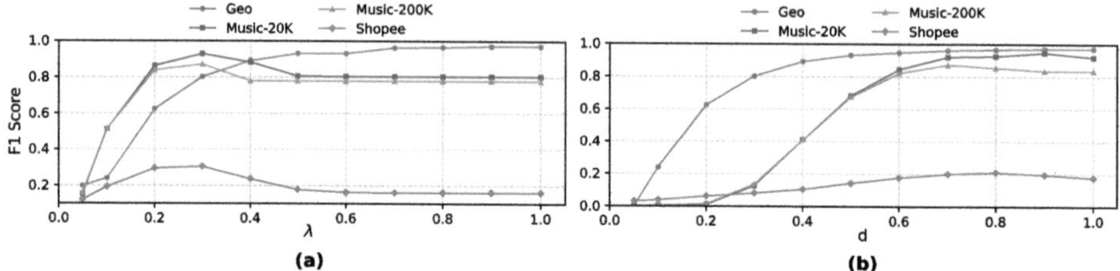

Fig. 4. The figure shows the sensitivity of key hyperparameters λ (a) and d (b) in the LLM4MEM method to experimental score F1.

6   Conclusion

In this paper, we explore Multi-Table Entity Matching (MEM) to identify equivalent entities between multiple tables. To unlock the power of Large Language Models (LLMs) for MEM, we propose a novel LLM-based framework for MEM, termed LLM4MEM. First, the multi-style prompt-enhanced attribute coordination module resolves semantic inconsistencies across schemas using LLMs, eliminating manual alignment. Second, the transitive consensus embedding matching mechanism tackles the combinatorial explosion via bidirectional top-1 filtering and graph-based propagation. Third, the density-aware pruning module improves matching quality by removing noise through spatial constraints. Experiments on 6 datasets show LLM4MEM achieves state-of-the-art performance, with a 5.1% F1 improvement over existing methods while maintaining linear complexity. Its unsupervised, schema-agnostic design ensures broad applicability. In future work, we will investigate domain adaptation and dynamic scenarios.

Acknowledgments. This work is supported by the National Natural Science Foundation of China (No. 62406319), and the Postdoctoral Fellowship Program of CPSF (No. GZC20232968).

References

1. Fan, M., et al.: Cost-effective in-context learning for entity resolution: a design space exploration. In: 2024 IEEE 40th International Conference on Data Engineering (ICDE) (2024)
2. Ge, C., Wang, P., Chen, L., Liu, X., Zheng, B., Gao, Y.: CollaborEM: a self-supervised entity matching framework using multi-features collaboration. IEEE Trans. Knowl. Data Eng. (2023)
3. Gokhale, C., et al.: Corleone: hands-off crowdsourcing for entity matching. In: International Conference on Management of Data, SIGMOD 2014, Snowbird, UT, USA, 22–27 June 2014. ACM (2014)
4. Grattafiori, A., Dubey, A., Jauhri, A., Pandey, A., Kadian, A., et al.: The Llama 3 herd of models (2024)
5. Howard, A., Liew, C., Wong, M., Dane, S.: Shopee - price match guarantee. Kaggle (2021)
6. Kwon, W., et al.: Efficient memory management for large language model serving with PagedAttention. In: Proceedings of the ACM SIGOPS 29th Symposium on Operating Systems Principles (2023)
7. Lerm, S., Saeedi, A., Rahm, E.: Extended affinity propagation clustering for multi-source entity resolution. In: BTW 2021 (2021)
8. Li, P., Cheng, X., Chu, X., He, Y., Chaudhuri, S.: Auto-FuzzyJoin: auto-program fuzzy similarity joins without labeled examples. In: International Conference on Management of Data, SIGMOD 2021. ACM (2021)
9. Li, Y., Li, J., Suhara, Y., Doan, A., Tan, W.: Deep entity matching with pre-trained language models. Proc. VLDB Endow. (2020)
10. Malkov, Y.A., Yashunin, D.A.: Efficient and robust approximate nearest neighbor search using hierarchical navigable small world graphs. IEEE Trans. Pattern Anal. Mach. Intell. (2020)
11. Mudgal, S., et al.: Deep learning for entity matching: a design space exploration. In: Proceedings of the 2018 International Conference on Management of Data, SIGMOD Conference 2018, Houston, TX, USA, 10–15 June 2018. ACM (2018)
12. Primpeli, A., Bizer, C.: Graph-boosted active learning for multi-source entity resolution. In: Hotho, A., et al. (eds.) ISWC 2021. LNCS, vol. 12922, pp. 182–199. Springer, Cham (2021). https://doi.org/10.1007/978-3-030-88361-4_11
13. Reimers, N., Gurevych, I.: Sentence-BERT: sentence embeddings using Siamese BERT-networks. In: Proceedings of EMNLP (2019)
14. Reimers, N., Gurevych, I.: Sentence-BERT: sentence embeddings using Siamese BERT-networks. In: Proceedings of the 2019 Conference on Empirical Methods in Natural Language Processing and the 9th International Joint Conference on Natural Language Processing, EMNLP-IJCNLP 2019. Association for Computational Linguistics (2019)
15. Saeedi, A., David, L., Rahm, E.: Matching entities from multiple sources with hierarchical agglomerative clustering. In: International Conference on Knowledge Engineering and Ontology Development (2021)
16. Saeedi, A., David, L., Rahm, E.: Matching entities from multiple sources with hierarchical agglomerative clustering. In: Proceedings of the 13th International Joint Conference on Knowledge Discovery, Knowledge Engineering and Knowledge Management, IC3K 2021, Volume 2: KEOD. SCITEPRESS (2021)
17. Saeedi, A., David, L., Rahm, E.: Matching entities from multiple sources with hierarchical agglomerative clustering. In: KEOD (2021)

18. Singh, R., et al.: Synthesizing entity matching rules by examples. Proc. VLDB Endow. (2017)
19. Qwen Team: Qwen2.5: a party of foundation models, September 2024
20. Falcon-LLM Team: The Falcon 3 family of open models, December 2024
21. Tu, J., et al.: Domain adaptation for deep entity resolution. In: International Conference on Management of Data, SIGMOD 2022, Philadelphia, PA, USA, 12–17 June 2022. ACM (2022)
22. Wang, P., Zeng, X., Chen, L., Ye, F., Mao, Y., et al.: PromptEM: prompt-tuning for low-resource generalized entity matching. Proc. VLDB Endow. (2022)
23. Wang, T., et al.: Match, compare, or select? An investigation of large language models for entity matching. In: Proceedings of the 31st International Conference on Computational Linguistics, COLING 2025, Abu Dhabi, UAE, 19–24 January 2025, pp. 96–109. Association for Computational Linguistics (2025)
24. Zeng, X., Wang, P., Mao, Y., Chen, L., Liu, X., Gao, Y.: MultiEM: efficient and effective unsupervised multi-table entity matching. In: 40th IEEE International Conference on Data Engineering, ICDE 2024. IEEE (2024)

Mongolian Speech Recognition Based on Semi-supervised Learning and Syllable Subword Modeling Units

Yuan Li[1,2,3], Yonghe Wang[1,2,3], ZhenJie Gao[1,2,3], and Feilong Bao[1,2,3(✉)]

[1] College of Computer Science, Inner Mongolia University, Hohhot, China
{liyuan,gzj}@mail.imu.edu.cn, {cswyh,csfeilong}@imu.edu.cn
[2] National & Local Joint Engineering Research Center of Intelligent Information Processing Technology for Mongolian, Hohhot, China
[3] Inner Mongolia Key Laboratory of Multilingual Artificial Intelligence Technology, Hohhot, China

Abstract. Mongolian is a low-resource language that lacks sufficient labeled data for end-to-end model training. Semi-supervised learning can significantly improve the performance of Mongolian speech recognition systems by utilizing low-cost unlabeled data. In this paper, we propose a pseudo-labeled semi-supervised speech recognition method for Mongolian based on syllable-level subword modeling units. Speech representations are extracted using a pre-trained model and discretized to generate pseudo-labels for automatic speech recognition (ASR) model pre-training. To enhance speech representation, we propose an end-to-end training method based on syllable subword modeling units. In our experiments, we utilized 1,560 h of unsupervised Mongolian speech data. The results indicate that the proposed method reduces the model's parameter count by 2.01%, while significantly enhancing model performance. Specifically, a relative reduction of 48.46% and 26.70% in WER is achieved with 10 and 100 h of supervised data, respectively, under non-autoregressive decoding. Additionally, under autoregressive decoding, WER shows a relative reduction of 52.21% and 13.38% for the same data conditions.

Keywords: Mongolian Speech Recognition · Low Resource Languages · Semi-Supervised Learning · Syllable Subword Modeling Units

1 Introduction

In recent years, automatic speech recognition (ASR) has made significant strides due to the successful application of supervised deep learning (DL) techniques [17,18]. However, one of the drawbacks of this approach is that it relies heavily on a large amount of supervised speech data, which may be difficult to obtain for resource-scarce languages.

© The Author(s), under exclusive license to Springer Nature Singapore Pte Ltd. 2026
X.-L. Mao et al. (Eds.): NLPCC 2025, LNAI 16105, pp. 221–233, 2026.
https://doi.org/10.1007/978-981-95-3352-7_18

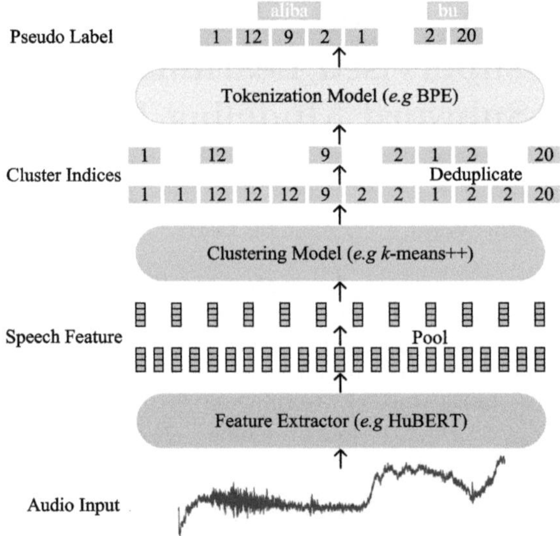

Fig. 1. An example of 0.6 s of Mongolian speech is given as input, and a relatively compact sequence of pseudo labels is output.

Additionally, in real application environments, ASR models need to adapt to a wide range of acoustic conditions such as environmental sounds, accents, and different speakers [5,15]. These practical needs have led to a surge of research in weakly supervised [12,16,24], unsupervised [1,9], and semi-supervised [26] acoustic feature learning for ASR tasks. For example, Singh et al. [16]. Combine video metadata and use remotely labeled weakly supervised methods. Baevski et al. [2] introduce wav2vec-U, which acquires speech representations through self-supervised learning and maps these representations to phonemes using adversarial training. Zhang et al. [26] use a diverse unlabeled dataset of audio for pre-training and self-training. However, related works have not been explored in detail for the Mongolian ASR task based on sequence-to-sequence models.

As we know, Mongolian is an agglutinative language like Japanese and Korean [7,12]. Words have complex morphological structures, usually, a word is composed of a root followed by several suffixes [3,10]. Due to this word-formation characteristic, millions of words can be generated. Therefore, building a speech recognition model for the Mongolian large vocabulary continuous speech recognition (LVCSR) system will suffer from data sparsity and out-of-vocabulary (OOV) problems [8,23]. Some studies propose to alleviate this problem by exploiting smaller meaning morpheme units. In [3], Bao et al. propose the use of a segmentation-based method to model the Mongolian LVCSR system and verify its effectiveness. More recently, in [19,22], the segmentation-based method is used to model the Neural Network (NN) based Mongolian ASR acoustic model and shows a remarkable promotion. In [22], Wang et al. use byte pair encoding (BPE) based subword modeling units to train an E2E-ASR model.

Table 1. Comparison of syllables and phonemes of different words followed with ending suffix -a'ca.

Ending suffix	Phonemes	Generated words	Words phonemes	Words syllable
-a'ca	al s	jam-a'ca	j a m al s	jam -a' ca
	g al s	nam_a-a'ca	n a m al g al s	na m_a -a' ca
	g wl s	cqmq-a'ca	q w m w g wl s	cq mq -a' ca
	wl s	tqqr-a'ca	t w r wl s	tqqr -a' ca

Semi-supervised methods can effectively leverage low-cost unlabeled data to improve the performance of ASR models on low-resource datasets. In this paper, we introduce a semi-supervised training method based on pseudo-labeling [21] for Mongolian. First, representational information is extracted from unlabeled speech data using a pre-training model and then discretized into pseudo-labels through a clustering algorithm. This discretization process reduces the complexity of modeling text units [4, 14]. Mongolian syllables are the logical units of pronunciation [11, 13]. A single syllable is a longer linguistic unit, and one to three Mongolian characters correspond to a syllable. Word can be segmented into a sequence of syllables. According to this characteristic, we propose a syllable-based subword modeling method. Experiments demonstrate that pre-training with pseudo labels significantly improves the performance of the E2E-ASR model on 10 and 100 h labeled Mongolian datasets. Moreover, the syllable subword system has a smaller model size and better recognition performance than the traditional letter subword system.

The contributions of this paper are twofold:

1. This paper presents the first investigation into the effectiveness of semi-supervised learning methods for Mongolian E2E-ASR. We demonstrate that leveraging unlabeled data can significantly reduces the Word Error Rate (WER) of low-resource Mongolian ASR systems.
2. We propose an end-to-end model training method for Mongolian based on syllable-level subword units, which has achieved remarkable performance. To the best of our knowledge, this is the first instance of using syllable-based acoustic subwords for modeling Mongolian E2E-ASR.

2 Mongolian Speech Recognition Based on Semi-Supervised Learning and Syllable Subword Modeling Units

To investigate the effectiveness of semi-supervised learning methods in Mongolian E2E-ASR, we generate pseudo-labels using unlabeled Mongolian speech data and develop a pre-trained encoder-decoder model, which is subsequently fine-tuned using supervised data. This section first describes the technique employed for generating pseudo-labels for Mongolian speech. Next, we provide a detailed account of the workflow for extracting syllable subword modeling units in Mongolian. Finally, we outline the complete process of implementing Mongolian E2E-ASR based on semi-supervised learning.

2.1   Mongolian Speech Pseudo Labels

In Fig. 1, the importance of pseudo labels in pre-training E2E-ASR systems is clearly illustrated, especially in scenarios where authentic textual annotations are not available. In E2E-ASR systems, the encoder processes an input audio sequence $X = (x_1, x_2, \ldots, x_m)$ to extract features, while the decoder generates the corresponding output text sequence $Y = (y_1, y_2, \ldots, y_n)$. Here, m and n denote the lengths of the input and output sequences, respectively, highlighting the temporal aspects of the speech recognition task.

The creation of pseudo labels begins by extracting features from the audio using a pre-trained model, such as HuBERT. These features, which capture detailed acoustic and phonetic information, are typically long in length, leading to potential computational inefficiencies. To tackle this, average pooling is utilized to shorten the sequence length while preserving key information. The pooled feature vectors are then discretized using k-means++ clustering, mapping each vector to a discrete cluster index, effectively transforming continuous features into pseudo-label indices. A subsequent deduplication step removes consecutive repetitions, which simplifies the representation. For example, a sequence like "a a l l l" is reduced to "a l", preserving the phonetic content in a more concise form.

To further compress the pseudo-label sequences and enhance their quality, subword tokenization techniques such as BPE are applied. BPE merges frequently co-occurring characters into larger subword units, striking a balance between fine-grained character-level information and more efficient word-level representations. As a result, the pseudo-character sequences are grouped into subword units, shortening the sequence length while maintaining the phonetic and semantic context. This process boosts the efficiency and effectiveness of pre-training, helping the model better capture the structural properties of the language. This method was originally designed for English, and we apply it to Mongolian speech recognition [21].

2.2   Syllable Subword Modeling Units

The syllable is defined based on human perception and speech production phenomenon typically assisted by stress patterns within a word. In Mongolian, we can categorize different types of syllables using their vowel (V) and consonant (C) content. For example, a syllable marked with CV consists of a sequence of consonant and vowel, such as ᠲ (Latin: ta, meaning: you); a syllable marked with CVC consists of a sequence of consonant, vowel and consonant, such as

Algorithm 1. Algorithms for Syllable Division in Mongolian

Require: token: A string $(c_1, c_2, \ldots, c_n)$ representing a Mongolian sequence.
Ensure: syllableList: A list of syllables obtained by segmenting the token.
1: Define vowel $= [\_, a, e, i, q, v, o, u, E]$
2: Initialize syllableList $= []$, indexList $= []$
3: Initialize tIndex $= 0$, index $= 0$
4: **for** $i = 0$ to length(token) $- 1$ **do**
5:     **if** token$[i] \in$ vowel and $i > 0$ and token$[i - 1] \neq _$ **then**
6:        Append i to indexList
7:     **end if**
8: **end for**
9: **if** length(indexList) ≤ 1 **then**
10:     Append token to syllableList
11:
12:     **return** syllableList
13: **end if**
14: Set endIndex $=$ indexList[last element]
15: **while** tIndex $<$ endIndex **do**
16:     **if** index $==$ last element of indexList **then**
17:        syllable $=$ token[tIndex : end]
18:        tIndex $=$ endIndex
19:        Append syllable to syllableList
20:     **else**
21:        **if** indexList[index $+ 1$] $-$ indexList[index] $== 1$ **then**
22:           **if** length(indexList) $>$ index $+ 2$ **then**
23:              syllable $=$ token[tIndex : indexList[index $+ 2$] $- 1$]
24:              tIndex $=$ indexList[index $+ 2$] $- 1$
25:           **else**
26:              syllable $=$ token[tIndex : end]
27:              tIndex $=$ endIndex
28:           **end if**
29:           index $\leftarrow$ index $+ 2$
30:        **else**
31:           syllable $=$ token[tIndex : indexList[index $+ 1$] $- 1$]
32:           tIndex $=$ indexList[index $+ 1$] $- 1$
33:           index $\leftarrow$ index $+ 1$
34:        **end if**
35:        Append syllable to syllableList
36:     **end if**
37: **end while**
38:
39: **return** syllableList

ᠲᠡᠭ (Latin: teg, meaning: zero). These two syllable forms cover close to three-quarters of Mongolian syllables, with other forms of syllables (such as V, VC, CCV, and so on) occurring with lower frequency.

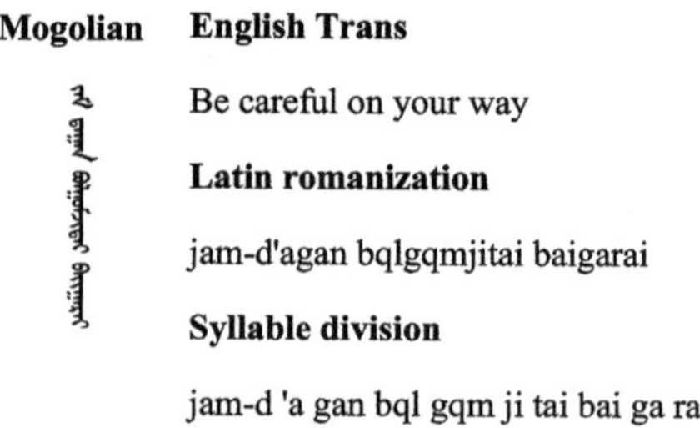

Mogolian   **English Trans**

Be careful on your way

Latin romanization

jam-d'agan bqlgqmjitai baigarai

Syllable division

jam-d 'a gan bql gqm ji tai bai ga rai

Fig. 2. Example of Mongolian syllable division.

The Mongolian syllable spans a longer period of time compared to the phonemic unit [7], and it is the logical unit of word pronunciation. Moreover, under the constraints of Mongolian vowel harmony rules, the pronunciation of the ending suffix is closely related to the preceding stem. For example, the ending suffix ↩ (Latin: -a'ca) has four different pronunciations depending on different stems. Therefore, we can use syllable segmentation to transform words containing multiple pronunciations into a fixed subword sequence (see Table 1), and modeling a syllable with a longer duration facilitates simultaneous learning of time and spectral variations information.

First, we perform syllable slicing, deduplication, and sorting of Mongolian words in the training set to create a subword dictionary for the model. Then, the annotated text of the speech is discretized according to the syllable subword dictionary during the training process. Subwords that are at the beginning of a word are labeled with '#', so that the output subwords can be recombined into words. We will now discuss how we implement syllable division. We define a set of vowel letters of the Mongolian Latin romanization alphabet: $\{\_, a, e, i, q, v, o, u, E\}$. Words are segmented according to the position of the vowel letters. Algorithm 1 details the process of syllable division for a sequence of words, and the *Syllable division* in Fig. 2 represents the syllable sequence corresponding to the Mongolian example sentence.

2.3   Model Structure and Training

The model comprises three modules: an encoder, a decoder, and a CTC module, as shown in Fig. 3. Both the encoder and decoder comprise a multi-head attention layer and a feedforward layer. At the base of the encoder, a depth-separable convolutional module is integrated to process the input speech feature sequences. This module encompasses dimensionality transformation, time-axis downsampling, and the addition of sinusoidal-cosinusoidal positional information. The multi-head attention layer enables the model to attend to information from different locations. The calculation method is as follows:

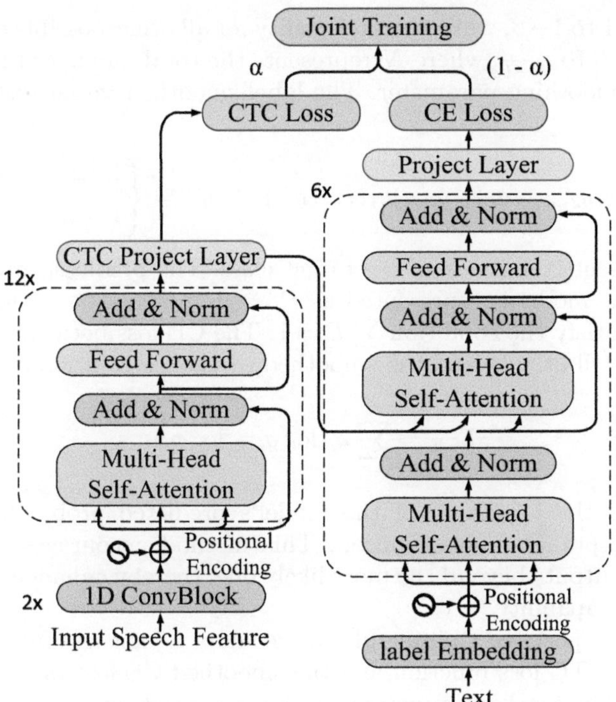

Fig. 3. During the pre-training phase, the weight α for the CTC loss function is set to zero to avoid instability caused by the absence of precise alignment labels, while in the supervised training phase, α is non-zero, enabling the joint optimization of the CTC and CE losses.

$$\text{SelfAttn}(Q, K, V) = \text{softmax}\left(\frac{QK^T}{\sqrt{d_k}}\right) V \tag{1}$$

$$\text{MultiHead}(Q, K, V) = \text{Concat}(h_1, h_2, \ldots, h_{n_h})W^O \tag{2}$$

$$h_i = \text{SelfAttn}(QW_i^Q, KW_i^K, VW_i^V) \tag{3}$$

among them, Q, K and V represent query, key, and value respectively, and d_k is the dimension of the key, n_h is the number of attention heads. The parameter matrices are as follows: $W^Q \in \mathbb{R}^{d_m \times d_q}, W^K \in \mathbb{R}^{d_m \times d_k}, W^V \in \mathbb{R}^{d_m \times d_v}, W^O \in \mathbb{R}^{d_m \times d_m}$, where d_m is the embedding dimension of the model. The feedforward network (FFN) consists of two fully connected layers with a Swish activation function in between. Moreover, residual connections and layer normalization are incorporated into the model.

During the pre-training phase, we use the smoothed CE loss function to train the E2E-ASR model. The probability of the true text classification output is adjusted from 1 to $1-\beta$, while the probability for all other possible classifications increases from 0 to $\frac{\beta}{N-1}$, where N represents the total number of classifications and β is the smoothing parameter. The label-smoothed target distribution q is expressed as:

$$q = (q_1, q_2, \ldots, q_{i-1}, q_i, q_{i+1}, \ldots, q_N), \quad q_i = \begin{cases} \frac{\beta}{N-1}, & \text{if } i \neq k \\ 1 - \beta, & \text{if } i = k \end{cases} \tag{4}$$

where k represents the index of the target class. The predicted probability distribution of the model is represented as $P = (p_1, p_2, \ldots, p_i, \ldots, p_N)$, where the probabilities satisfy the condition $\sum P = 1$. The CE loss between the predicted probability distribution p and the smoothed target distribution q is defined as:

$$L_{\mathrm{CE}} = \sum_{i=1}^{N} q_i (\log q_i - \log p_i) \tag{5}$$

where $\log p_i$ is the logarithm of the model's predicted probability for the i-th possible output text classification. This method encourages the model to explore other outputs beyond the most likely one, thereby enhancing the model's generalization capability.

During the supervised training phase, we adopt a joint loss function strategy, combining the CTC loss function and the smoothed CE loss function for model optimization. The total loss function can be expressed as:

$$\text{Loss} = \alpha L_{\mathrm{CTC}} + (1 - \alpha) L_{\mathrm{CE}} \tag{6}$$

where α is an adjustable parameter that balances the effects of the two loss functions. By combining the strengths of the CTC loss in alignment and the fine-grained probability adjustment capabilities of the CE loss, we enhance the model's effectiveness in speech recognition tasks.

3   Experiment

3.1   Dataset

We report the experiments on the MnASR database recorded by Inner Mongolia University [20]. The dataset contains recordings from 1,101 native speakers of Mongolian, including 383 males and 718 females, with approximately 1,560 h of training data, 8 h of validation data, and 12 h of test data. We use a training set of 1,560 h of unlabeled Mongolian speech data for semi-supervised learning. Subsequently, in the fine-tuning phase, we used supervised datasets of 1, 10, and 100 h to validate the effectiveness of the pre-training process.

To efficiently extract features from speech, we selected HuBERT as the feature extractor. HuBERT is a self-supervised audio model designed to learn acoustic features from unlabeled audio data. The model can be accessed at[1]. Additionally, Mel-frequency cepstral coefficients (MFCC) were used as a baseline for comparison in the experiment.

---

[1] https://github.com/facebookresearch/fairseq/tree/main/examples/hubert.

Table 2. Model parameters (M) and WER (%) for BPE and syllable systems with pseudo-labels generated by different feature extraction models for semi-supervised pre-training

Decoding	Feature Extraction	Hours of Data	Parameters (M)		Dev		Test	
			BPE	Syllable	BPE	Syllable	BPE	Syllable
CTC	None	1	44.6	43.7	97.82	92.71	97.85	92.88
	MFCC	1			97.52	92.63	97.77	92.69
	Hubert-base	1			97.18	92.43	97.58	92.54
	None	10			94.73	49.79	95.23	53.66
	MFCC	10			95.28	48.38	95.29	49.34
	Hubert-base	10			48.02	46.13	50.00	49.08
	None	100			24.61	19.01	26.40	20.73
	MFCC	100			22.53	17.88	24.03	19.65
	Hubert-base	100			18.16	**17.50**	20.18	**19.35**
Attention	None	1	44.6	43.7	98.32	95.78	98.44	96.52
	MFCC	1			98.13	95.66	98.21	96.31
	Hubert-base	1			97.85	95.28	97.89	95.87
	None	10			95.64	52.62	96.84	58.59
	MFCC	10			95.25	55.23	96.47	59.06
	Hubert-base	10			49.35	43.55	51.64	46.28
	None	100			15.83	14.07	17.11	15.78
	MFCC	100			15.18	13.84	16.12	15.52
	Hubert-base	100			14.08	**13.39**	15.28	**14.82**

3.2 Experimental Settings

For this experiment, we chose the baseline model Conformer under the Wenet framework [6,25]. During pre-training, the learning rate of the model is set to 0.002 and the batch size is set to 12. During supervised training, the learning rate is set to 0.004 and the batch size is set to 8.

To create a BPE [22] subword lexicon, the text from the training set is used to train the BPE model, which segments text into smaller units, balancing character and word representations to handle unknown words effectively. This process results in a lexicon comprising 5,000 subwords. To create a syllable subword lexicon, the text in the training set is used to perform syllable segmentation, deduplication, and sorting, thereby yielding a lexicon of 3,746 subwords. Due to the smaller number of modeling units, the model based on syllable subwords has the advantage of fewer parameters.

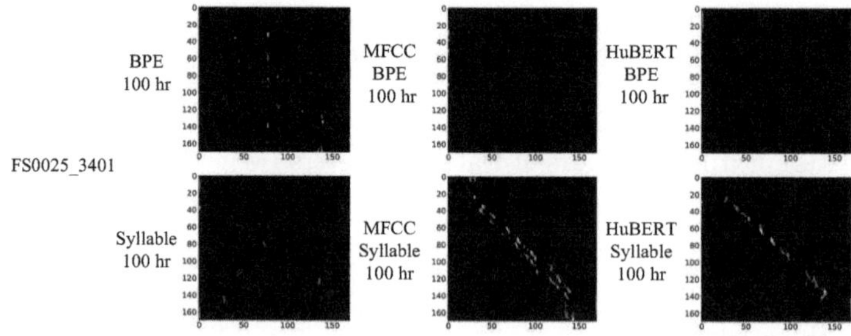

Fig. 4. Attention heatmaps for models using BPE and syllable modeling units with 100 h of labeled data under different pre-training conditions for test sample FS0025_3401.

In the experimental setup, two decoding methods were applied: Attention decoding, where the attention-based encoder-decoder (AED) component used autoregressive beam search, and CTC decoding, where the CTC part of the model employed greedy search, a non-autoregressive decoding method that is significantly faster but slightly lower in performance.

3.3   Experimental Result and Analysis

The Impact of Pre-training and Syllable-Based Tokenization on ASR Performance: Based on the results presented in Table 2, we can conclude that when the scale of pre-training data and supervised training data is moderately balanced, such as a ratio of 156:1, pre-training provides the most significant improvements to the model. However, as the amount of labeled training data increases and the ratio decreases to 15.6:1, the impact of pre-training diminishes significantly. Additionally, pre-training has a greater effect on BPE tokenization compared to syllable tokenization, as syllable tokenization inherently possesses stronger acoustic modeling capabilities. Syllable tokenization performs better in low-resource environments, consistently outperforming BPE tokenization regardless of whether pre-training is applied.

When combining these two methods, the experiments achieved the best results. With 1 h of supervised training data, HuBERT pre-training and syllable-based tokenization achieved relative improvements of 5.51% and 5.42% in the CTC decoding method. With 10 h of supervised training data, the combination achieved relative reductions of 51.30% and 48.46% in the CTC decoding method, and 56.45% and 52.21% in the attention decoding method. With 100 h of supervised training data, HuBERT pre-training and syllable-based tokenization achieved relative reductions of 28.89% and 26.70% in the CTC decoding method, and 15.41% and 13.38% in the attention decoding method. Clearly, the combination of these two approaches significantly enhances the performance of Mongolian ASR models in low-resource conditions.

Attention Heatmaps: The encoder attention heatmaps reveal in the Fig. 4 that syllable-based tokenization consistently demonstrates stronger alignment patterns compared to BPE-based tokenization, especially with HuBERT pre-training. The diagonal patterns in the "HuBERT Syllable 100 hr" heatmap highlight robust acoustic-phonetic modeling, which is less defined in the BPE counterparts. While HuBERT significantly improves attention alignment for both tokenization strategies, syllable-based models retain a clear advantage, showing better-focused attention and sharper alignments across all conditions.

BPE tokenization benefits notably from pre-training, particularly with HuBERT, as evident in the improvement of alignment patterns compared to MFCC or no pre-training. However, the improvement is insufficient to surpass the performance of syllable-based tokenization, which inherently captures acoustic features more effectively. These results demonstrate that syllable-based tokenization units, combined with pseudo-labels generated by HuBERT for pre-training, can achieve significant performance improvements in low-resource ASR tasks.

4 Conclusion

In this paper, we propose a semi-supervised speech recognition method based on syllable subword modeling units to cope with the low-resource problem in Mongolian speech recognition. We use Mongolian speech pseudo labels to pre-train the model. In the supervised training stage, we introduce an end-to-end training method based on syllable subword modeling units. The experiments demonstrate that, first, semi-supervised pre-training can utilize unlabeled speech data to improve the performance of models based on different subword modeling units. Second, the acoustic information modeling capability of the syllable subword modeling unit has a significant advantage over the traditional letter subwords. The above two approaches can work together to enhance the model's recognition performance. On 10 and 100 h of labeled data, the proposed method achieves a relative reduction in WER of 48.46% and 26.70%, respectively, under non-autoregressive decoding, and a relative reduction of 52.21% and 13.38%, respectively, under autoregressive decoding, while reducing the model parameters by 2.01%. In future research, we will explore other subword modeling units to further improve the performance of the Mongolian ASR system.

Acknowledgments. This work is supported by the National Natural Science Foundation of China (No. 62366037), Natural Science Foundation of Inner Mongolia (2025MS06001), Science and Technology Program of Inner Mongolia Autonomous Region (2025KYPT0041, 2025KYPT0064), Hohhot City Universities and Institutes Collaborative Innovation Project, Supporting the Reform and Development Funds for Local Universities, and Inner Mongolia Autonomous Region First-Class Discipline Scientific Research Special Project (No. YLXKZX-ND-036).

References

1. Baevski, A., Hsu, W.N., Conneau, A., Auli, M.: Unsupervised speech recognition. ANIPS **34**, 27826–27839 (2021)
2. Baevski, A., Zhou, Y., Mohamed, A., Auli, M.: wav2vec 2.0: a framework for self-supervised learning of speech representations. NeurIPS **33**, 12449–12460 (2020)
3. Bao, F., Gao, G., Yan, X., Wang, W.: Segmentation-based Mongolian LVCSR approach. In: ICASSP, pp. 8136–8139 (2013)
4. Chou, J.C., Chien, C.M., Hsu, W.N.: Toward joint language modeling for speech units and text. arXiv preprint arXiv:2310.08715 (2023)
5. Dua, M., Akanksha, Dua, S.: Noise robust automatic speech recognition: review and analysis. Int. J. Speech Technol. **26**(2), 475–519 (2023)
6. Gulati, A., Qin, J., Chiu, C.-C., et al.: Conformer: convolution-augmented transformer for speech recognition. arXiv preprint arXiv:2005.08100 (2020)
7. Janhunen, J.: The Mongolic Languages. Routledge (2006)
8. Liang, K., Liu, B., Hu, Y., et al.: MnTTS2: an open-source multi-speaker Mongolian text-to-speech synthesis dataset. In: National Conference on Man-Machine Speech Communication, pp. 318–329. Springer (2022)
9. Liu, A.H., Hsu, W.N., Auli, M., Baevski, A.: Towards end-to-end unsupervised speech recognition. In: SLT, pp. 221–228 (2023)
10. Liu, R., Bao, F., Gao, G., Zhang, H., Wang, Y.: A LSTM approach with subword embeddings for Mongolian phrase break prediction. In: ICCL, pp. 2448–2455 (2018)
11. Liu, R., Bao, F., Gao, G., Zhang, H., Wang, Y.: Phonologically aware BiLSTM model for Mongolian phrase break prediction with attention mechanism. In: PRICAI, pp. 217–231. Springer (2018)
12. Liu, R., Hu, Y., Zuo, H., Luo, Z., Wang, L., Gao, G.: Text-to-speech for low-resource agglutinative language with morphology-aware language model pretraining. IEEE/ACM TASLP **32**, 1075–1087 (2024)
13. Liu, R., Sisman, B., Bao, F., Yang, G., et al.: Exploiting morphological and phonological features to improve prosodic phrasing for Mongolian speech synthesis. TASLP **29**, 274–285 (2020)
14. Polyak, A., Adi, Y., Jade, C., et al.: Speech resynthesis from discrete disentangled self-supervised representations. arXiv preprint arXiv:2104.00355 (2021)
15. Radzikowski, K., Wang, L., Yoshie, O., Nowak, R.: Accent modification for speech recognition of non-native speakers using neural style transfer. EURASIP J. Audio Speech Music Process. **2021**(1), 1–10 (2021). https://doi.org/10.1186/s13636-021-00199-3
16. Singh, K., Manohar, V., Xiao, A., Edunov, S., et al.: Large scale weakly and semi-supervised learning for low-resource video ASR. arXiv preprint arXiv:2005.07850 (2020)
17. Sutskever, I., Vinyals, O., Le, Q.V.: Sequence to sequence learning with neural networks. NeurIPS **27** (2014)
18. Tian, Z., Yi, J., Tao, J., et al.: Spike-triggered non-autoregressive transformer for end-to-end speech recognition. arXiv preprint arXiv:2005.07903 (2020)
19. Wang, Y., Bao, F., Zhang, H., Gao, G.: Joint alignment learning-attention based model for grapheme-to-phoneme conversion. In: ICASSP, pp. 7788–7792 (2021)
20. Wang, Y., Wang, W.: Khalkha Mongolian dialect speech dataset (version 1), March 2023. Dataset

21. Wu, F., et al.: Wav2Seq: pre-training speech-to-text encoder-decoder models using pseudo languages. In: ICASSP, pp. 1–5 (2022)
22. Wu, Y., Wang, Y., Zhang, H., Bao, F., Gao, G.: MNASR: a free speech corpus for Mongolian speech recognition and accompanied baselines. In: O-COCOSDA, pp. 1–6 (2022)
23. Yonghe, W., Bao, F., Gao, G.: A comparative study on selecting acoustic modeling units for WFST-based Mongolian speech recognition. TALLIP **22**(10), 1–20 (2023)
24. Yusuyin, S., Ma, T., Huang, H., Zhao, W., Ou, Z.: Whistle: data-efficient multilingual and crosslingual speech recognition via weakly phonetic supervision. arXiv preprint arXiv:2406.02166 (2024)
25. Zhang, B., Wu, D., Peng, Z., et al.: WeNet 2.0: more productive end-to-end speech recognition toolkit. arXiv preprint arXiv:2203.15455 (2022)
26. Zhang, Y., Park, D.S., Han, W., et al.: BigSSL: exploring the frontier of large-scale semi-supervised learning for automatic speech recognition. JSTSP **16**(6), 1519–1532 (2022)

CEBFL: A Cost-Effectiveness-Based Approach to Defending Against Gradient Attack in Federated Learning

Zhi Hu[1], Zhuo Chang[1(✉)], Congpu Zhao[2], Yi Jin[3], and Dongping Gao[4(✉)]

[1] School of Cyber Security and Computer, Hebei University, Baoding 071000, China
changzhuo@hbu.edu.cn

[2] Chinese Academy of Medical Sciences, Peking Union Medical College Hospital, Beijing 100730, China
zhaocongpu@pumch.cn

[3] School of Computer and Information Technology, Beijing Jiaotong University, Beijing 100044, China
yjin@bjtu.edu.cn

[4] Institute of Medical Information, Chinese Academy of Medical Sciences, Peking Union Medical College, Beijing 100020, China
gaodp_gaodp@126.com

Abstract. Federated learning (FL) is a privacy-enhancing distributed machine learning framework, but attackers can reconstruct the client's private data from the exchanged model updates by launching a gradient inversion attack (GIA). Current defense methods struggle to strike an optimal balance between privacy protection and performance. In this paper, we propose a defense method driven by cost-effectiveness parameters, designed to safeguard privacy while maintaining the utility of the global model. This strategy increases the difficulty of data reconstruction by restricting the upload of parameters with high privacy leakage risks, while preserving knowledge-rich parameters to maintain model performance, achieving a better balance between privacy and utility. To validate the effectiveness of our method, we conduct experiments in both Computer Vision (CV) and natural language processing (NLP) tasks. The results show that our approach can effectively protect users' image and text privacy while preserving model performance as much as possible.

Keywords: Federated Learning · Gradient Inversion Attack · Privacy Preservation · Parameter Selection

1 Introduction

Federated learning (FL) [1] cite enables multiple clients to collaboratively train mod-els without uploading raw data. Under the coordination of cloud servers, each device uploads model parameters or updates instead of raw data, contributing to the global model while protecting the privacy of their local data. Due to its inherent privacy advantages, federated learning has been widely applied to natural language processing (NLP) tasks involving sensitive textual information, such as smart input methods and voice assistants on mobile devices [2],

© The Author(s), under exclusive license to Springer Nature Singapore Pte Ltd. 2026

X.-L. Mao et al. (Eds.): NLPCC 2025, LNAI 16105, pp. 234–246, 2026.
https://doi.org/10.1007/978-981-95-3352-7_19

electronic medical record analysis [3], dialogue systems [4], and data sharing scenarios constrained by privacy regulations such as GDPR [5].

Although federated learning avoids direct exposure of raw text data, recent studies have demonstrated that the model updates uploaded by clients may still leak private semantic information. Attackers can intercept or receive gradient updates and employ Gradient Inversion Attacks (GIA) [6–10] to reconstruct sensitive textual content from the original training samples, thereby compromising user privacy. In NLP models, structural components such as embedding layers and attention mechanisms cause gradients of certain parameters to contain rich linguistic information, making it easier for attackers to recover words or entire sentences. To mitigate GIAs, various defense strategies have been proposed. For example, differential privacy (DP) [11,12] adds random noise to gradients to obscure private data, but this approach often involves a trade-off between model performance and privacy. Gradient perturbation techniques, including quantization [13] and gradient compression (GC) [14], process gradients to restrict the information they convey. Additionally, cryptographic methods such as secure multiparty computation (SMC) [15,16] and homomorphic encryption (HE) [17,18] transmit encrypted gradient information across the network, safeguarding it from attackers. However, this will incur a lot of computational cost. Recent work has been focused on developing lightweight defenses that can strike a balance between model performance and privacy protection. GIAs primarily optimize virtual data by minimizing the distance between real gradients and virtual gradients. We observed that gradients that tend to produce significant differences are more advantageous for the reconstruction process, as they often carry a significant amount of training-related information. If we can avoid uploading updates for these parameters during the information upload phase, we can increase the difficulty of reconstruction and successfully defend against GIAs. In light of this finding, we designed a Cost-Effectiveness-Based (CEB) parameter selection method to resist GIAs. This method evaluates the sensitivity of each model parameter and limits the leakage of effective information by avoiding the upload of training updates for sensitive parameters. At the same time, it uses the Fisher Information Matrix (FIM) to measure the importance of model parameters, avoiding operations on parameters that carry a large amount of information, ensuring the accuracy of the processed model, and achieving a balance between performance and privacy.

Our contributions are summarized as follows.

1. We propose a lightweight parameter sensitivity calculation method, and show that removing some updates with high sensitivity can effectively defend against gradient reversal attacks.
2. We design a new parameter selection mechanism, which uses parameter sensitivity to assess the privacy disclosure risk of each parameter, uses FIM to measure the importance of the parameter, and comprehensively considers the two indicators to realize the trade-off between privacy and utility.

3. The experimental results indicate that this method can maintain good model performance and successfully defend against GIAs, effectively protecting the data privacy.

2   Related Work

FL is a privacy preserving distributed machine learning framework; however, the emergence of GIAs [6–10] poses a serious threat to data privacy, as attackers can reconstruct private training data from gradients shared by clients. To address this issue, researchers have conducted extensive studies and the main defense methods can be categorized into three types:

Cryptographic defense methods. HE [17,18] allows certain computations (such as addition) to be performed directly on encrypted gradients without decryption. Because the shared gradients are encrypted, attackers cannot intercept them, thus achieving defense without losing precision. SMC [15,16] defense methods are used to solve privacy protection issues in collaborative computations among a set of mutually distrustful participants, ensuring that input and output are not revealed to other participants during execution. Both methods prevent the leakage of gradient information to protect data privacy; however, they incur significant computational and communication costs.

Perturbation-based defense methods. DP [11,12] as a general privacy protection method, protects privacy by adding random noise to the original gradients. However, the addition of noise often leads to a loss in accuracy, requiring a trade-off between model performance and privacy protection. Yang et al. [19] combine FIM with DP to avoid the impact of noise on important parameters. Sun et al. [20] propose the Soteria scheme, which disrupts the intermediate features of the network to prevent attackers from reconstructing the actual input. Gao et al. [21] propose the ATS algorithm, which uses privacy-enhancing techniques to perturb input data and protect privacy.

Gradient pruning-based defense methods. The most common method is top-k [14] selection, which retains only the top-k gradient parameters with the largest absolute values. However, this method has been shown to provide insufficient privacy protection unless a high pruning ratio is used at the cost of accuracy. To avoid damaging accuracy with a high pruning ratio, Wang et al. [22] proposed Outpost, a privacy preserving method combining Top-k gradient pruning with adaptive noise addition. Zhang et al. [23] proposed a privacy protection scheme by pruning large gradients. By modifying only a few gradients, this approach makes the reconstructed images unrecognizable.

3   Methodology

3.1   Effect of Sensitive Gradients

First, let's review the process of GIAs, which optimizes the virtual data, narrows the distance between the virtual gradient and the real gradient, and makes the

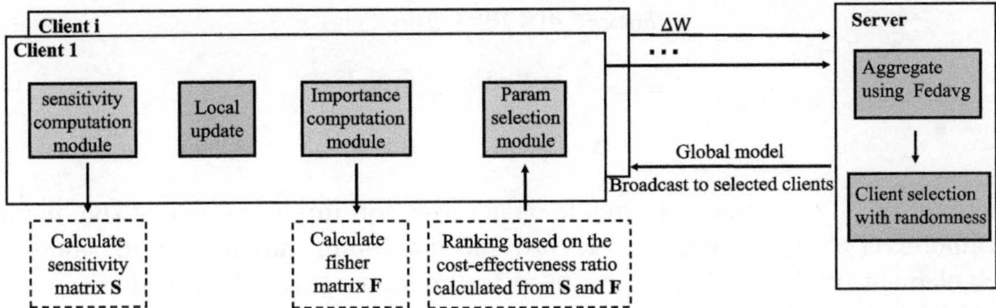

Fig. 1. Overview of CEBFL Defense architecture

virtual gradient fit to the real gradient, so as to achieve the purpose of reconstructing the training data. In this process, the Euclidean distance or cosine distance is often used as a loss function, and parameters that produce large differences between different inputs provide more information about the optimization process. If this part of the parameters can be effectively identified and hide the updates of these parameters, the reconstruction process will be greatly enhanced.

3.2   The Cost-Effectiveness-Based Parameter Selection Scheme

Based on this finding, we design a Cost-Effectiveness-Based (CEB) parameter selection scheme to resist GIAs. As shown in Fig. 1, the main process of the proposed parameter selection mechanism includes three parts: sensitivity calculation, importance evaluation, and parameter selection.

Sensitivity Calculation: Existing studies suggest that information leakage is the result of insufficient generalization performance or inadvertence memory [24, 25]. Understanding the memory of private information can be related to the generalization ability of the model: learning a model with good generalization ability can avoid recalling unnecessary information and make its parameters insensitive to small changes in input [26]. Based on this, if certain gradients are not sensitive to changes in the input data, it will be more challenging to reconstruct the input, which makes the success rate of the attack very low. The sensitivity is used to quantify the risk of information leakage. D_i represent the training data set owned by the client i. Before training the local model, we calculated the gradient of the model for each training data in D_i, and calculated its range to represent the variation range of the model parameter for D_i. The larger the variation range, the higher the sensitivity of the corresponding parameter to the input, the more beneficial information to the attacker, and the greater the risk of privacy leakage. The calculation process for sensitivity is as follows:

$$g_{\mathrm{max}} = \arg \max_{x_j \in D_i} g(\theta, x_j)$$

$$g_{\mathrm{min}} = \arg \min_{x_j \in D_i} g(\theta, x_j) \tag{1}$$

$$S = g_{\mathrm{max}} - g_{\mathrm{min}}$$

where $g(\theta, x_j)$ represents gradients generated for input x_j when the model parameter is θ. g_{max} and g_{min} record the maximum and minimum values of each element of the gradients produced for all $x_j(x_j \in D_i)$. S records the range at each element of the gradient and is used to measure the privacy risk of the corresponding model parameter.

Importance Evaluation: If only a single sensitivity index is used to guide parameter selection, the accuracy of the model will be damaged to some extent. In order to effectively guide parameter selection and avoid removing some parameters with large information, we choose to use FIM to quantify the information provided by model parameters. Parameters with more information can represent knowledge more effectively and play a crucial role in model prediction. Therefore, the model performance can be effectively maintained by avoiding the influence of information parameters. The FIM is closely related to the Hessian matrix, however, it is not feasible to use FIM or Hessian information directly in the context of deep learning because the possibilities are difficult to deal with. We use the empirical Fisher information matrix instead, which roughly approximates FIM and is often used to make calculations easier. We express the experience Fisher as:

$$F = \frac{1}{N} \sum_{i=1}^{N} \left(\nabla L(\theta_{t+1}^i, D_i) \cdot \nabla L(\theta_{t+1}^i, D_i)^T \right) \tag{2}$$

where F stands for the diagonal elements of the computed fisher information matrix, N stands for the number of samples, θ_{t+1}^i stands for the model parameter of client i at round t+1, D_i stands for the local data set owned by client i. $\nabla L(\theta_{t+1}^i, D_i)$ represents the gradient produced when the model parameters are θ_{t+1}^i and the input dataset is D_i.

Parameter Selection: After obtaining the two indicators, each client selects which gradients to discard during training based on them. First, a portion of gradients corresponding to parameters with high sensitivity is removed. These gradients are considered too sensitive, and retaining them may lead to privacy leakage. Then, for the remaining gradients, we consider both sensitivity and importance. Our goal is to retain parameters that are low-risk yet highly beneficial. Therefore, we compute the cost-effectiveness of each remaining parameter (with sensitivity as the cost and importance as the benefit). Gradients of parameters with lower cost-effectiveness are sequentially removed using a fixed step size until a predefined threshold is reached. This threshold is measured using the cosine distance between the perturbed gradient and the original gradient. By introducing this threshold, we ensure that the perturbed gradient deviates sufficiently from the original direction, making it harder for an attacker to recon-

---

Algorithm 1. FedAvg local training at client k with CEBFL.

1: **Input:** broadcast the global model with weights w_t of the current communication round t; local training dataset D_k; local training dataset D_k;

2: **Output:** Local model update Δw_k^t

3: Set local model weights same as the global model $w_k^t \leftarrow w^t$

4: Calculate parameter sensitivity $S \leftarrow (w_k^t, D_k)$ by Eq. 1

5: $w_k^t \leftarrow$ **local training** (w_k^t, D_k)

6: $\Delta w_k^t \leftarrow w_k^t - w^t$

7: compute experience fisher $F \leftarrow (w_k^t, D_k)$ by Eq. 2

8: Evaluate Cost-Effectiveness by $V \leftarrow F/S$

9: Perform pruning with threshold $\rho\%$ of w_k^t with the highest S and update perturbed w_k^t to $w_k^{t'}$

10: **while do**

11:     Perform pruning with threshold $s\%$ of $w_k^{t'}$ with the smallest V and update $w_k^{t'}$

12:     $d \leftarrow \dfrac{\Delta w_k^t \cdot \Delta w_k^{t'}}{\|\Delta w_k^t\| \|\Delta w_k^{t'}\|}$

13:     $s \leftarrow s + 1$

14:     **if** $d \geq$ thr **then**

15:         **break**

16:     **end if**

17: **end while**

18: $\Delta w_k^t \leftarrow \Delta \bar{w}$

19: Send the model update Δw_k^t to the server

---

struct the original data. At the same time, the threshold controls the degree of perturbation, avoiding excessive distortion that may harm the performance of the global model.

$$d = \cos \langle \mathbf{g}, \mathbf{g}^* \rangle \tag{3}$$

where d represents the cosine distance between the disturbed gradient and the original gradient, g represents the original gradient, and g^* represents the gradient after the disturbance. d is the hyperparameter in this experiment, and the intensity of privacy protection can be changed by adjusting the value of d.

The detailed implementation of CEBFL is shown in Algorithm 1.

4 Experiment

4.1 Experimental Setup

Data Sets: We evaluate the performance of the proposed scheme based on four datasets, MNIST, CIFAR10, CIFAR100, SST-2 and TREC.

Model: We use three models: one is the LeNet convolutional neural network, which has two convolutional layers and three fully connected layers; the second is the AlexNet model, which includes five convolutional layers and three fully connected layers; and the third is the BERT model, which is widely used for NLP tasks.

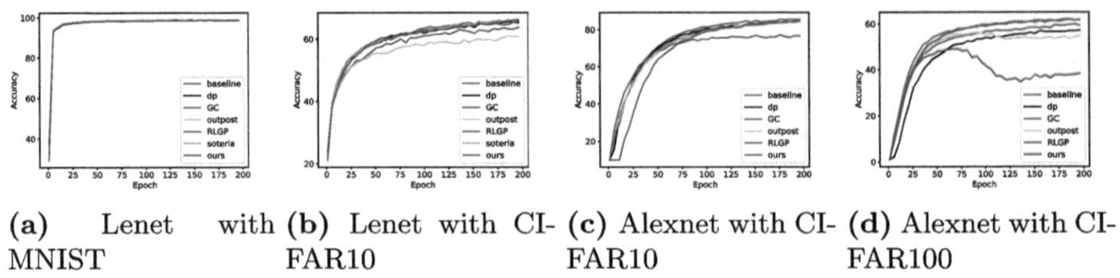

(a) Lenet with MNIST

(b) Lenet with CIFAR10

(c) Alexnet with CIFAR10

(d) Alexnet with CIFAR100

Fig. 2. Performance of various defense methods under IID setting.

Table 1. Performance Comparison of Defense Methods

	Lenet		Alexnet	
	MNIST	CIFAR10	CIFAR10	CIFAR100
Baseline	**98.92**	**66.09**	**85.56**	**61.87**
DP	<u>98.90</u>	65.83	84.60	57.91
GC	98.89	63.92	84.67	59.68
Soteria	**98.92**	<u>66.02</u>	–	–
Outpost	98.89	61.51	84.39	54.92
RLGP	98.89	65.36	76.11	38.29
Ours	98.86	65.94	<u>84.80</u>	<u>61.68</u>

Defense Baselines: We compare our proposed method with other defense mechanisms. The comparison includes DP, GC, Outpost, Soteria and RLGP. For GC, 80% of the smallest magnitude gradient values are pruned to zero. For DP, Gaussian noise with a standard deviation $\sigma = 0.01$ is added. For Soteria, the gradient pruning rate for fully connected layers is set to 50%. For Outpost 22 and RLGP 23, the hyperparameters are set according to those specified in the original paper. For our method, we set hyperparameters as $\rho = 10$, $s = 5$, $d = 0.9$.

Evaluation Metrics: To evaluate the effectiveness of defense mechanisms, we use mean squared error (MSE), structural similarity index measure (SSIM), learned perceptual image patch similarity (LPIPS) and peak signal-to-noise ratio (PSNR) as metrics to measure the distance between the reconstructed images and the original images.

Hyperparameter Configurations: We assume that the FL contains 100 clients. However, due to the large number of categories in the CIFAR-100 dataset, the number of clients is set to 20 when using the CIFAR-100 dataset. Local training uses the SGD optimizer with a learning rate $\eta = 0.01$. In each global round, 10 clients are selected to participate in the training. For the IID data distribution, each client has the same number and categories of data.

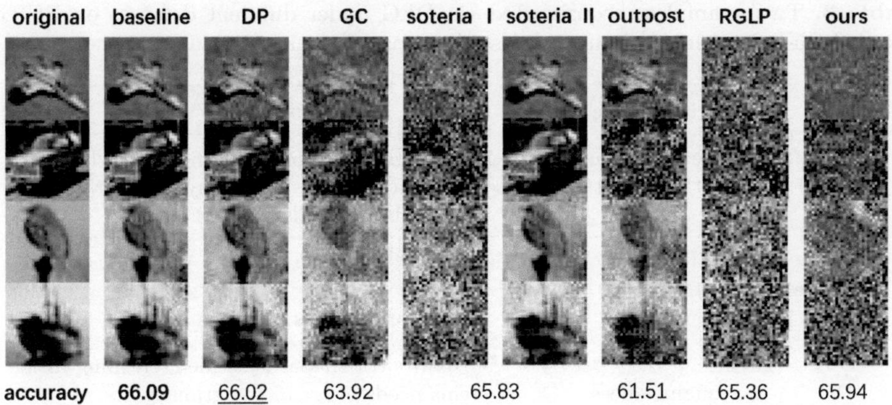

Fig. 3. Visualization of various defenses against IG attacks.

Table 2. Performance of various defense methods.

	Baseline	DP	GC	Soteria I	Soteria II	Outpost	RLGP	Ours
MSE (↑)	0.064	0.291	0.412	**0.417**	0.263	0.416	0.410	0.413
SSIM (↓)	0.837	0.569	0.285	0.073	0.841	0.091	0.053	**0.047**
LPTPS (↑)	0.001	0.007	0.063	0.208	0.02	0.195	0.203	**0.270**
PSNR (↓)	25.01	24.41	13.49	**9.67**	25.42	10.17	10.87	10.02

4.2 Accuracy Results

Figure 2 shows the training performance of both models on their respective test datasets. From the figure, it can be seen that for the LeNet model, on the MNIST dataset, all defense methods do not significantly affect accuracy of final model. This is also reflected in Table 1, where the accuracy difference between the best and worst cases is only 0.06%. On the CIFAR-10 dataset, the performance gap between different defense methods is more pronounced. The outpost method performs the worst, with an accuracy drop of 4.58%, while the Soteria method performs the best, with only a 0.07% decrease in accuracy. Our method is second, with a 0.15% drop in precision.

For the experimental results of the AlexNet, we do not provide the results for the Soteria method, as using Soteria on the AlexNet network incurs prohibitive computational costs. As shown in Table 2, among the remaining defense methods, our approach achieves the best performance, delivering accuracy comparable to baseline. The RLGP method achieves defense by eliminating partial large-value gradients. However, when dealing with datasets containing numerous categories, this approach impairs the model's ability to capture label information from the data, resulting in suboptimal performance on CIFAR-100 datasets.

Table 3. Two examples reconstructed via DLG under different defenses on BERT. Words high-lighted in red indicate those that appear in the original sentence.

	short sentence	long sentence
original	hide new secretions from the parental units	even horror fans will most likely not find what they are seeking with trouble every day; the movie lacks both thrills and humor.
Baseline	hide new secretions from the parental units	seeking they; thrill most not both day will are dung. troubleues humor horror the movie even and visitor progressess every fansrda
DP	gavin new hide from acquaint-ances parental theked	they fansplin most shepard justified; creeping inside are stems needs every movie grimsby horror not trouble even. boths the humorplanes day
GC	hide the secre-tions from units parental new	not unfolded dustin the lavish battled both demands thrill slotschel evacuate troubleplin; pounderapes movie horrors outer seeking vogel ding colloquiallyrda
RLGP	hideze secret the from cigar legal shiny	indie yielding sharpened unfolded the notalo easily bunker enacted are marc mosque trouble leash they horror voltage battled affects both jaw verdi choral turning dealings
outpost	hide theions new fraud devon calgaryions	say strait horror dessert guiana ad till smart every solve up even not location albeit chiefs chimney day dating save orbit will
ours	tires approached hide analogue abyss shiny pre-sided	indie horror unfolded yielding daggers equally easily dealings enacted measure patriots jaw trouble leash manifesto barlow voltage car-thage orphaned vhs eh r curses limbs famously

4.3   Defense Results

We compare our proposed method with other defense mechanisms, including DP, GC, Outpost, Soteria and RLGP. For Soteria method, we employed two different strategies during the attack process: one is a standard attack process (soteria **I**), and the other involves masking the gradients of the perturbed layers during the attack (soteria **II**).

Figure 3 shows the results of data reconstruction on the CIFAR-10 dataset. It can be observed that without any applied defenses, the training data can be reconstructed with minimal loss. The Soteria can effectively defend against the attack by pruning the gradient parameters of a single layer. However, the Soteria method becomes ineffective when the attacker masks the perturbed layers during image reconstruction. Our method removes the gradients of sensitive parameters, significantly increasing the difficulty of reconstruction. As a result, the reconstructed images are nearly indistinguishable to the human eye,

Table 4. Evaluation of Reconstruction Quality on SST-2

Metric	Baseline	DP	GC	RLGP	Outpost	Ours
Precision	1.000	0.510	0.791	0.468	0.475	**0.416**
Recall	1.000	0.530	0.808	0.498	0.497	**0.464**
F1	1.000	0.520	0.799	0.483	0.486	**0.419**
BLEU	1.000	0.046	0.095	0.039	0.041	**0.027**

resembling noise images. Table 2 shows the comparison of our defense method with other methods on different metrics. Our method achieves the best SSIM and LPIPS scores among all methods, and the other two metrics are also close to the best-performing Soteria method.

For NLP tasks, we evaluate the defense effectiveness using the DLG attack on the SST-2 dataset with the BERT model. We initialize the BERT model weights using a normal distribution, as opposed to using pretrained weights. This is because normal initialization tends to produce more non-zero gradients, which is more favorable for reconstructing the original text. Table 3 presents the defense performance of various methods on the BERT language model.

For NLP tasks, evaluation metrics commonly used in CV are not applicable. Instead, we use precision, recall, F1 score, and Bilingual Evaluation Understudy (BLEU) to assess defense performance. Precision measures the attacker's ability to correctly identify relevant words, while recall reflects the ability to recover all words from the ground-truth sentence. The F1 score is the average of precision and recall. BLEU is a widely used automatic evaluation metric in machine translation and text generation. It primarily measures the n-gram overlap between the candidate sentence and the reference sentence, focusing on surface-level word matching rather than semantic content. Table 4 reports the performance comparison of reconstructed texts across four evaluation metrics for each defense method. As shown in table, our defense method achieves the lowest values across four reconstruction metrics, demonstrating its effectiveness in preventing attackers from recovering original text data from gradients.

To further demonstrate the effectiveness of our method, we conducted defense performance experiments on the TREC dataset. The reconstruction results are shown in Tab. 5. Table 6 reports the performance of the reconstructed results on the TREC dataset across four evaluation metrics. On the TREC dataset, our method also demonstrates outstanding performance.

4.4   Time Consumption

We evaluated the time consumption of various defense methods on the LeNet network. When calculating the time consumption, we ran 600 global rounds for each method, recorded the total time taken, and used the average time per round as the final evaluation metric.

Table 5. Reconstruction Results on the TREC Dataset. Words high-lighted in red indicate those that appear in the original sentence.

Method	Reconstructed Text
original	How did perfdom develop in and then leave Russia?
Baseline	how did perfdom develop in and then leave russia?
DP	how did ser leavedom develop inf then how russia?
GC	how develop did leave ser organisations and then russiainsky?
RLGP	jewish begins bowling du lashes hatrew organisations leave russiainsky?
outpost	how develop thenfdomgre spilled ser sits leave russia?
ours	jewisheller bowling spilled hat gibraltar organisations leave russiainsky?

Table 6. Evaluation of Reconstruction Quality on TREC

Metric	Baseline	DP	GC	RLGP	Outpost	Ours
Precision	1.000	0.629	0.604	0.420	0.539	**0.388**
Recall	1.000	0.611	0.624	0.415	0.506	**0.401**
F1	1.000	0.620	0.614	0.417	0.522	**0.394**
BLEU	1.000	0.028	0.031	0.021	0.025	**0.021**

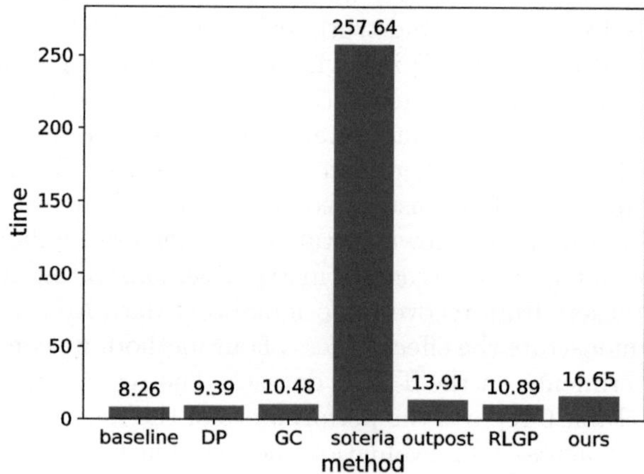

Fig. 4. Time consumption of various defense methods

Figure 4 shows the time consumption of various defense methods. For DP and GC, the time consumption is close to that of the baseline method, as they simply perform operations on the gradients without causing significant delays. Compared to the baseline approach, Soteria incurs a huge amount of time consumption because Soteria must learn the perturbed data representations in the FC layers of the model after each iteration. Our method provides a more accurate risk assessment compared to Outpost, but it inevitably incurs some additional time cost.

5   Conclusion

In this paper, we propose a defense method based on cost-effectiveness parameter selection to resist gradient reversal attacks. This defense method is light-weight and can achieve a better balance between privacy and performance. Specifically, we measure the risk of model parameter leakage by analyzing the differences between model parameters and various inputs, and assess the importance of model parameters using Fisher information. By considering these two metrics, we can precisely remove certain key gradients, thereby protecting data privacy while maintaining the model's accuracy. The experimental results demonstrate that the proposed method not only achieves strong protection efficacy in CV tasks, but also provides sufficient privacy guarantees for textual data in NLP applications.

Acknowledgments. This research was supported by the National Key Research and Development Program of China (2020AAA0104905), Major Project of the National Social Science Fund of China (19ZDA041), Hebei Provincial Natural Science Foundation (F2025201046).

Disclosure of Interests. The authors have no competing interests to declare that are relevant to the content of this article.

References

1. Kairouz, P., McMahan, H.B., Avent, B., et al.: Advances and open problems in federated learning. Found. Trends® Machine Learn. **14**(1–2), 1–210 (2021)
2. Hard, A., Rao, K., Mathews, R., et al.: Federated learning for mobile keyboard prediction. arXiv preprint arXiv:1811.03604 (2018)
3. Xu, J., Glicksberg, B.S., Su, C., et al.: Federated learning for healthcare informatics. J. Healthc. Inf. Res. **5**, 1–19 (2021)
4. Guo, T., Guo, S., Wang, J.: pFedPrompt: learning personalized prompt for vision-language models in federated learning. In: Proceedings of the ACM Web Conference 2023, pp. 1364-1374 (2023)
5. Regulation, P.: General data protection regulation. InTouch **25**, 1–5 (2018)
6. Zhu, L., Liu, Z., Han, S.: Deep leakage from gradients. Adv. Neural Inf. Process. Syst. **32** (2019)
7. Geiping, J., Bauermeister, H., et al.: Inverting gradients-how easy is it to break privacy in federated learning? Adv. Neural. Inf. Process. Syst. **33**, 16937–16947 (2020)
8. Zhu, J., Blaschko, M.B.: R-Gap: recursive gradient attack on privacy. In: Proceedings of the International Conference on Learning Representations (ICLR) (2021)

9. Yin, H., Mallya, A., Vahdat, A., et al.: See through gradients: image batch recovery via gradinversion. In: Proceedings of the IEEE/CVF Conference on Computer Vision and Pattern Recognition, pp. 16337–16346 (2021)
10. Li, Z., Zhang, J., Liu, L., et al.: Auditing privacy defenses in federated learning via generative gradient leakage. In: Proceedings of the IEEE/CVF Conference on Computer Vision and Pattern Recognition, pp. 10132–10142 (2022)
11. Abadi, M., Chu, A., Goodfellow, I., et al.: Deep learning with differential privacy. In: Proceedings of the ACM SIGSAC Conference on Computer and Communications Security, vol. 2016, pp. 308–318 (2016)
12. Wei, K., Li, J., Ding, M., et al.: Federated learning with differential privacy: Algorithms and performance analysis. IEEE Trans. Inf. Forensics Secur. **15**, 3454–3469 (2020)
13. Ovi, P.R., Dey, E., Roy, N., et al.: Mixed quantization enabled federated learning to tackle gradient inversion attacks. In: Proceedings of the IEEE/CVF Conference on Computer Vision and Pattern Recognition, pp. 5046–5054 (2023)
14. Lin, Y., Han, S., Mao, H., Wang, Y., Dally, W.J.: Deep gradient compression: reducing the communication bandwidth for distributed training. In: Proceedings of the International Conference on Learning Representations (ICLR) (2017)
15. Mohassel, P., Secureml, Z.Y.: A system for scalable privacy-preserving machine learning. In: 2017 IEEE Symposium on Security and Privacy (SP), pp. 19–38 (2017)
16. Chen, L., Xiao, D., Yu, Z., et al.: Secure and efficient federated learning via novel multi-party computation and compressed sensing. Inf. Sci. **667**, 120481 (2024)
17. Hijazi, N.M., Aloqaily, M., Guizani, M., et al.: Secure federated learning with fully homomorphic encryption for IoT communications. IEEE Internet Things J. **11**(3), 4289–4300 (2023)
18. Zhang C, Li S, Xia J, et al. BatchCrypt: efficient homomorphic encryption for Cross-Silo federated learning. In: 2020 USENIX Annual Technical Conference (USENIX ATC 20), pp. 493–506 (2020)
19. Yang, X., Huang, W., Ye, M.: Dynamic personalized federated learning with adaptive differential privacy. Adv. Neural. Inf. Process. Syst. **36**, 72181–72192 (2023)
20. Sun, J., Li, A., Wang, B., et al.: Soteria: provable defense against privacy leakage in federated learning from representation perspective. In: Proceedings of the IEEE/CVF Conference on Computer Vision and Pattern Recognition, pp. 9311–9319 (2021)
21. Gao, W., Guo, S., Zhang, T., et al.: Privacy-preserving collaborative learning with automatic transformation search. In: Proceedings of the IEEE/CVF Conference on Computer Vision and Pattern Recognition, pp. 114–123 (2021)
22. Wang, F., Hugh, E., Li, B.: More than enough is too much: adaptive defenses against gradient leakage in production federated learning. IEEE/ACM Trans. Netw. (2024)
23. Zhang, Z., Tianqing, Z., Ren, W., et al.: Preserving data privacy in federated learning through large gradient pruning. Comput. Secur. **125**, 103039 (2023)
24. Leino, K., Fredrikson, M.: Stolen memories: leveraging model memorization for calibrated White-Box membership inference. In: 29th USENIX security symposium (USENIX Security 20), pp. 1605–1622 (2020)
25. Carlini, N., Liu, C., Erlingsson, Ú., et al.: The secret sharer: evaluating and testing unintended memorization in neural networks. In: 28th USE-NIX Security Symposium (USENIX security 19), pp. 267–284 (2019)
26. Neyshabur, B., Bhojanapalli, S., McAllester, D., et al.: Exploring generalization in deep learning. Adv. Neural Inf. Process. Syst. **30** (2017)

IRSC: A Zero-Shot Evaluation Benchmark for Information Retrieval Based on Semantic Comprehension in Retrieval-Augmented Generation Scenarios

Hai Lin[1,2], Shaoxiong Zhan[1], Junyou Su[3], Hai-Tao Zheng[1,2(✉)], Hui Wang[2], Xin Su[4], and Ruitong Liu[1]

[1] Shenzhen International Graduate School, Tsinghua University, Shenzhen 518055, China
[2] Pengcheng Laboratory, Shenzhen 518055, China
`zheng.haitao@sz.tsinghua.edu.cn`
[3] Southern University of Science and Technology, Shenzhen 518055, China
[4] Tencent, Shenzhen 518055, China

Abstract. While conventional embedding benchmarks like MTEB provide generalized performance metrics, they fail to adequately evaluate the specialized requirements of embedding models in Retrieval-Augmented Generation (RAG) pipelines. Our IRSC benchmark addresses this gap through targeted assessment of five critical query types (Question, Title, Part-of-Paragraph, Keyword, Summary Retrieval) across multilingual scenarios. For instance, BGE-M3 achieves near-perfect Summary Retrieval (98.12) in IRSC despite moderate MTEB Retrieval scores (54.60), while S-Arctic-L demonstrates paradoxical failure in Title Retrieval (2.48) despite excelling in MTEB Reranking (63.67). These findings validate IRSC's capacity to expose task-specific competencies masked by conventional metrics. Our key innovation lies in the Similarity of Semantic Comprehension Index (SSCI), which quantifies cross-model semantic alignment through higher-order relationships rather than vector proximity. When applied to 21,000 bilingual queries in CorpusQTPKS, SSCI reveals fundamental differences in how models interpret queries. By bridging the gap between abstract metrics and real-world RAG requirements, IRSC establishes a task-aware evaluation framework that (1) identifies model specialization through multi-scenario testing, (2) enables cross-architecture comparability via SSCI, and (3) provides interpretable diagnostics for retrieval failures. All code, datasets, and a live demo are open-sourced to advance robust RAG system development (Project repository: https://github.com/Jasaxion/IRSC_Benchmark).

Keywords: Retrieval-Augmented Generation · Information Retrieval · Semantic Evaluation · Embedding Model Benchmark

H. Lin, S. Zhan and J. Su—Equal contribution.

© The Author(s), under exclusive license to Springer Nature Singapore Pte Ltd. 2026
X.-L. Mao et al. (Eds.): NLPCC 2025, LNAI 16105, pp. 247–259, 2026.
https://doi.org/10.1007/978-981-95-3352-7_20

# 1	Introduction

The rapid advancement of large language models (LLMs) has created growing demand for reliable Retrieval-Augmented Generation (RAG) systems, which mitigate key LLM limitations like factual hallucination and outdated knowledge [3]. As shown in Fig. 1, RAG enhances LLMs by integrating external knowledge, yet current evaluation methods remain inadequate. Existing benchmarks focus narrowly on tasks like semantic textual similarity while ignoring diverse retrieval scenarios and cross-model comparability [3,4].

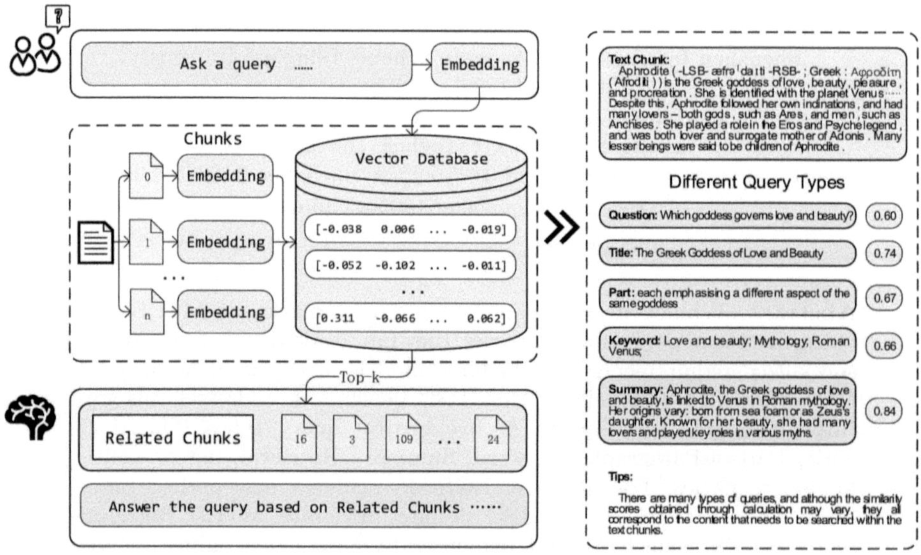

Fig. 1. In the question-answering process based on the RAG model, the first step is to divide the reference data into chunks and then extract vector features from these chunks using a embedding model. These vector embeddings are stored in a database. Next, when a user inputs a query, the system retrieves information from the database by searching for the top-k most similar chunks based on the query. These retrieved chunks are then used as reference materials to generate the answer.

Current metrics like cosine similarity [2] fail to address fundamental challenges in comparing embeddings across different models [1]. This limitation has led to incomplete evaluations where models appear comparable despite significant differences in semantic understanding. Moreover, most benchmarks lack multilingual support and task diversity needed for real-world RAG applications.

To address these gaps, we propose: (1) The IRSC Benchmark evaluating five retrieval tasks (Question, Title, Paragraph, Keyword, Summary retrieval) across English, Chinese and mixed-language datasets [4]; (2) The Similarity of Semantic Comprehension Index (SSCI) for cross-model semantic alignment measurement; and (3) CorpusQTPKS, a new 21,000-entry bilingual dataset with open-source code. Our evaluations of models like Snowflake-Arctic-Embed-S [16] and BGE-M3 [17] reveal previously overlooked task-specific performance variations.

The IRSC Benchmark and SSCI metric together provide a more comprehensive framework for developing robust RAG systems, while our open resources support community research into model interpretability and retrieval optimization.

2   Related Work

The field of Retrieval-Augmented Generation (RAG) has grown significantly to address limitations of Large Language Models (LLMs) in providing accurate, context-aware responses. We review key contributions and position our work within this landscape.

Benchmarking in RAG. Chen et al. proposed the Retrieval-Augmented Generation Benchmark (RGB), evaluating LLMs on noise robustness, negative rejection, information integration, and counterfactual robustness [3]. While RGB highlights LLM weaknesses in handling false information, it lacks coverage of diverse retrieval tasks critical for real-world RAG applications.

Multilingual Retrieval Datasets. Zhang et al. introduced MIRACL, a multilingual dataset with 700K annotated query-passage pairs across 18 languages [4]. Though valuable for linguistic diversity, MIRACL focuses solely on query-passage retrieval, omitting tasks like keyword or title retrieval.

RAG System Evaluations. Ogundepo et al. surveyed RAG evaluation methods, emphasizing metrics like nDCG and MRR [5]. Their work identifies challenges but lacks practical benchmarks integrating these metrics across retrieval tasks.

BEIR Benchmark. Thakur et al.'s BEIR benchmark unifies heterogeneous retrieval tasks [21]. However, it is limited to query-paragraph retrieval and excludes complex RAG scenarios.

Massive Text Embedding Benchmark (MTEB). Muennighoff et al. developed MTEB to evaluate embedding models across clustering, retrieval, and semantic similarity tasks [6]. While comprehensive, MTEB does not address retrieval-generation integration for RAG.

Multilingual QA. Longpre et al.'s MKQA dataset assesses multilingual QA systems via parallel questions [7]. Despite its utility, MKQA neglects broader retrieval tasks essential for RAG.

Our Contribution. We propose a novel benchmark evaluating five retrieval tasks (question, keyword, title, summary, and paragraph fragments) with multilingual support. Unlike prior work, our framework unifies cross-lingual retrieval and diverse tasks, bridging gaps in RAG evaluation.

3   The IRSC Benchmark

3.1   Desiderata

The IRSC benchmark is designed to evaluate the effectiveness of embedding models specifically within the context of RAG tasks. Unlike traditional benchmarks that focus broadly on sentence or paragraph length, IRSC hones in on the unique needs of RAG applications, which require supplementing knowledge to queries. This benchmark emphasizes five key data types to cover most RAG tasks:

Focus on RAG-Specific Retrieval Tasks: Unlike traditional benchmarks, IRSC focuses on expanding a query or brief information into a detailed response.

Emphasis on Cross-lingual Capabilities: IRSC evaluates models in multiple languages, particularly English and Chinese, to handle Mixed-Language queries and adapt to cross-lingual environments.

Comprehensive Evaluation Metrics: Standard retrieval metrics (nDCG-@10, MRR@10, MAP@10, precision@3, and recall@10) are used alongside new metrics like SSCI for deeper insights into semantic comprehension and retrieval capabilities.

Through these considerations, IRSC aims to set a new standard for evaluating embedding models in the context of RAG tasks, providing a more nuanced and applicable assessment framework.

3.2   Tasks and Evaluation

Existing benchmarks typically mix different queries together for testing, making it difficult to showcase the differences between various embedding models in RAG tasks at a more granular level. In response to this phenomenon, We have observed that the retrieval accuracy performance declines differently for different types of queries when facing varying database scale, as shown in Fig. 2.

We designed five different query types, and unified a more reasonable database scale. Figure 3 provides an overview of tasks and datasets available in IRSC. The benchmark consists of the following five task types:

Question → Paragraph: Evaluates retrieval of relevant paragraphs from a question, testing comprehension of inferential or causal semantics. Questions

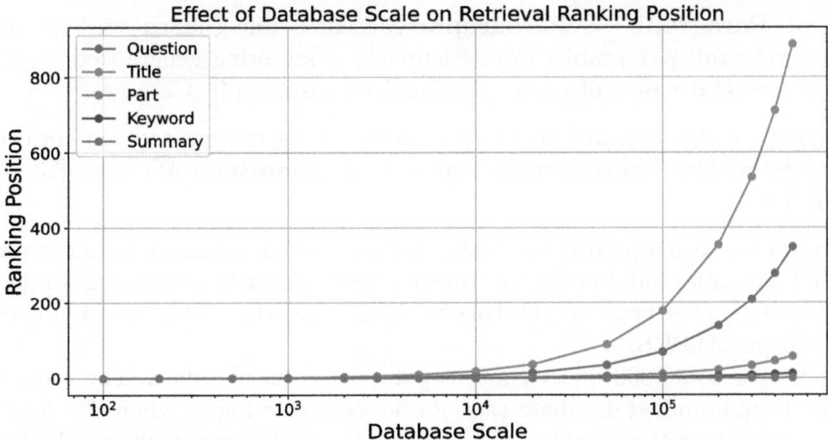

Fig. 2. This diagram illustrates how the ranking position of correct answers changes across different types of queries (question, title, part, keyword, summary) as the database scale increases. The X-axis represents increasing database scale, while the Y-axis shows the ranking position of correct answers, where lower values indicate better rankings.

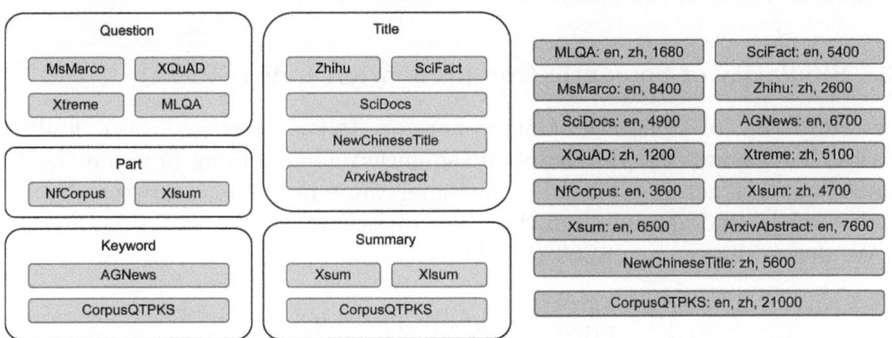

Fig. 3. The IRSC Benchmark is structured around five primary task types, each designed to evaluate different aspects of a model's retrieval capabilities. The red labels indicate the languages and quantities of each dataset.

may involve specific knowledge or reasoning, creating potential semantic shifts. **Datasets:** MsMARCO [8], XQuAD [9], Xtreme [10], MLQA [11].

Title → Paragraph: Tests matching concise titles to comprehensive paragraphs, assessing robustness under information sparsity. Titles condense key semantics, challenging the model's alignment ability. **Datasets:** zhihu[1], New-Title-Chinese[2], Arxiv-Abstract [12], SciDocs/SciFact [6].

---

[1] https://huggingface.co/datasets/suolyer/zhihu.
[2] https://huggingface.co/datasets/madao33/new-title-chinese.

Part of Paragraph → Paragraph: Measures fine-grained understanding by retrieving full paragraphs from fragments, countering generalized semantic embeddings. **Datasets:** nfcorpus [6] (English), xlsum [14] (Chinese).

Keyword → Paragraph: Assesses retrieval using fragmented semantic cues (keywords), unlike complete expressions in titles. **Datasets:** AG News [13], CorpusQTPKS.

Summary → Paragraph: Evaluates retrieval from summaries that preserve essential semantics, minimizing information loss. Focuses on matching condensed yet accurate representations. **Datasets:** XSum [15] (English), xlsum [14] (Chinese), CorpusQTPKS.

Each task uses 5000 query-content pairs as evaluation data. The remaining samples form a unified database (As can be seen from Fig. 2, when the database scale reaches more than 50,000, the performance of different tasks can be better distinguished. Considering the time cost of the evaluation, we selected 50,000 for Chinese and 50,000 for English, a total of 100,000) for retrieval across all tasks. During scoring, queries are used to search the unified database, and retrieval performance is evaluated based on the precision of retrieved indices against the ground truth. This standardized approach ensures robust and fair evaluation of the model's retrieval capabilities across various tasks.

3.3   Similarity of Semantic Comprehension Index (SSCI)

The Similarity of Semantic Comprehension Index, averaged over multiple queries. It measures the difference in semantic understanding between the two models' outputs across all queries. A higher value indicates a greater disparity in the models' understanding of the given questions.

We define the average SSCI ($\overline{\text{SSCI}}$) as:

$$\overline{\text{SSCI}} = \frac{1}{Q} \sum_{q=1}^{Q} \frac{|m1_q - m2_q|}{n}$$

Parameters:

- n: The length of each query result vector minus one, representing the maximum index of the retrieval results.
- $R1, R2$: These are matrices representing the results retrieved by the two different models over Q queries. Each matrix has dimensions $Q \times (n + 1)$. Each element is a binary value (0 or 1), where 1 indicates the position of the correct answer for each query.

For query q, the vectors $R1_q$ and $R2_q$ are defined as follows:

$$R1_q = [r_{11q}, r_{12q}, r_{13q}, \ldots, r_{1nq}, r_{1(n+1)q}]$$

$$R2_q = [r_{21q}, r_{22q}, r_{23q}, \ldots, r_{2nq}, r_{2(n+1)q}]$$

- $m1_q, m2_q$: These represent the positions of the correct answer in $R1_q$ and $R2_q$ respectively for query q. If there is no 1 in the vector, it is assigned a value of -1.

For query q:

$$m1_q = \begin{cases} n - \text{index}(R1_q, 1) & \text{if } 1 \in R1_q \\ -1 & \text{otherwise} \end{cases}$$

$$m2_q = \begin{cases} n - \text{index}(R2_q, 1) & \text{if } 1 \in R2_q \\ -1 & \text{otherwise} \end{cases}$$

where $\text{index}(R_q, 1)$ denotes the index position of the element equal to 1 in the vector R_q.

By using these metrics, IRSC aims to provide a comprehensive evaluation framework for assessing the performance of embedding models across diverse retrieval tasks.

4   Results

4.1   Experimental Setup

We evaluate models across three language settings using corresponding benchmark datasets:

English: Assessing retrieval performance on English-only tasks
Chinese: Testing capabilities in Chinese language contexts
All-Language: Evaluating cross-lingual performance on combined English-Chinese datasets

This comprehensive setup enables robust assessment of each model's retrieval capabilities across different linguistic contexts within the IRSC benchmark.

4.2   Main Results and Analysis

Benchmark Analysis. Based on Table 1, the experimental results reveal critical insights into model capabilities that conventional benchmarks fail to capture, demonstrating the unique value of our IRSC evaluation framework. While BGE-M3 dominates traditional MTEB metrics with strong performance in classification (60.35) and retrieval (54.60), our IRSC benchmark exposes its exceptional proficiency in RAG-specific tasks - achieving near-perfect summary retrieval (98.12) and superior keyword matching (86.68), capabilities obscured by MTEB's generic structure. Conversely, models like S-Arctic-L show paradoxical behavior: despite leading MTEB's reranking (63.67) and retrieval (58.36) tasks, they struggle fundamentally with IRSC's question retrieval (22.38) and title matching (2.48), highlighting how conventional benchmarks mask critical weaknesses

Table 1. IRSC Benchmark Results of S-Arctic Series, BGE Series, GTE Series, M3E Series, and MiniLM Series in All-Language for All Tasks. **IRSC:** Q = Question, T = Title, P = Part, K = Keywords, S = Summary **MTEB:** Cls = Classification, Clu = Clustering, MulL = Multilabel, Pair=Pair Classification, Retr=Retrieval

Model	IRSC					MTEB						
	Q	T	P	K	S	Cls	Clu	MulL	Pair	Rerank	Retr	STS
S-Arctic-S	30.67	35.66	45.88	63.02	53.34	46.33	37.39	14.84	71.53	40.03	39.84	58.08
S-Arctic-M	13.79	1.98	27.46	28.56	45.54	47.07	39.00	16.32	71.67	41.66	39.30	56.87
S-Arctic-L	22.38	2.48	31.26	38.04	43.94	57.39	**43.58**	18.94	76.71	**63.67**	**58.36**	70.11
BGE-M3	**69.72**	**86.40**	**79.64**	**86.68**	**98.12**	60.35	41.79	**20.10**	80.76	62.79	54.60	**74.12**
GTE-Small	50.99	73.60	69.16	78.76	82.84	47.28	40.90	16.27	71.44	45.77	35.99	62.77
GTE-Base	51.63	73.66	69.80	79.40	82.82	47.19	42.11	16.15	71.37	46.94	35.86	63.09
GTE-Large	52.05	73.72	69.84	79.36	81.80	47.61	42.14	17.91	71.74	48.87	38.23	63.47
M3E-Small	22.92	28.50	49.42	33.74	80.52	–	–	–	–	–	–	–
M3E-Base	59.12	78.40	75.62	83.68	96.44	–	–	–	–	–	–	–
M3E-Large	34.15	50.52	57.88	56.06	89.64	–	–	–	–	–	–	–
MiniLM-L6	45.89	61.68	60.66	70.42	54.84	46.49	38.90	15.05	71.31	41.45	33.30	61.52
MiniLM-L12	49.34	61.74	57.08	57.84	87.28	51.66	39.34	14.93	78.99	50.97	36.61	66.58

in contextual understanding. The GTE series exhibits another revealing pattern - while scaling from Small to Large brings minimal MTEB improvements (+0.42 in clustering), IRSC exposes meaningful gains in keyword (+0.64) and part-of-paragraph retrieval (+0.84), proving our benchmark's sensitivity to architectural refinements. Most strikingly, MiniLM-L12 achieves paradoxical supremacy in IRSC's summary retrieval (87.28) despite mediocre MTEB scores, suggesting specialized semantic comprehension that generic benchmarks cannot detect. These findings collectively validate IRSC's capacity to expose task-specific competencies and failure modes, providing practitioners with actionable insights for model selection beyond superficial metric comparisons. The absence of MTEB scores for the M3E series models (M3E-Small, M3E-Base, and M3E-Large) stems from their exclusion in the public MTEB benchmark leaderboard.

Radar Chart Analysis. Figur 4 presents radar charts visualizing model performance, where each axis represents the average of $r@10$, $m@10$, and $n@10$ scores across tasks. The charts reveal three key findings:

1. BGE-M3 dominates across all tasks (Question, Title, Part, Keyword, Summary), showing balanced, near-perfect coverage with particular strength in Summary tasks.
2. GTE and M3E series demonstrate competitive but uneven performance, with specific task-dependent strengths.

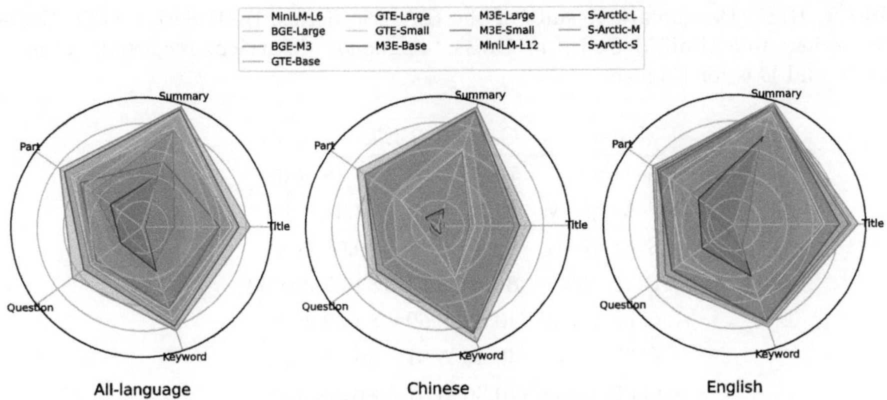

Fig. 4. Comparative Performance Radar Charts of S-Arctic Series, BGE Series, GTE Series, M3E Series, and MiniLM Series Models Across IRSC Benchmark's Question, Title, Part, Keyword and Summary Tasks in All-Language. **Metrics:** Average of Recall@10, MRR@10 and nDCG@10.

3. The S-Arctic series lags significantly behind, especially S-Arctic-M which shows the smallest coverage area, indicating limited effectiveness for these retrieval tasks.

These visualizations confirm BGE-M3 as the optimal choice for comprehensive retrieval performance.

Cross Language Analysis. Table 2 reveals critical insights about cross-lingual retrieval capabilities through systematic evaluation of 12 embedding models across four language scenarios. The results demonstrate a universal challenge in maintaining semantic alignment across languages, with most models showing significant performance degradation in cross-lingual tasks compared to their monolingual performance. BGE-M3 emerges as the most robust model, maintaining relatively stable performance across all scenarios (e.g., 86.30 C2C vs 62.60 C2E), suggesting its superior cross-lingual representation learning. However, other models reveal striking limitations - the GTE series collapses completely in E2C tasks (from 85 to <10), while M3E models show asymmetric performance (80.26 C2C vs 33.23 C2E), indicating fundamental gaps in their multilingual alignment capabilities. Interestingly, the performance patterns suggest that cross-lingual retrieval difficulty varies by direction, with English-to-Chinese proving particularly challenging for most models. These findings highlight that current embedding models, with the exception of BGE-M3, struggle to establish consistent cross-lingual semantic spaces, pointing to the need for more sophisticated multilingual training objectives that go beyond simple translation alignment.

Table 2. IRSC Benchmark Results of the S-Arctic Series, BGE Series, GTE Series, M3E Series, and MiniLM Series in Cross Languages. **Metrics:** recall@10. C is for Chinese and E is for English.

Model	C 2 C	C 2 E	E 2 E	E 2 C
S-Arctic-S	7.82	0.68	58.48	4.62
S-Arctic-M	12.72	0.14	14.41	2.08
S-Arctic-L	8.82	0.08	20.08	3.34
BGE-M3	**86.30**	**62.60**	84.27	**59.64**
GTE-Small	40.88	5.69	84.99	6.20
GTE-Base	40.48	5.81	86.13	8.66
GTE-Large	40.36	6.51	**86.93**	8.88
M3E-Small	74.86	6.60	13.27	1.90
M3E-Base	80.26	33.23	74.23	15.78
M3E-Large	76.48	24.20	36.59	6.88
MiniLM-L6	10.48	2.09	79.42	1.50
MiniLM-L12	55.86	38.41	58.72	45.58

4.3   SSCI Analysis

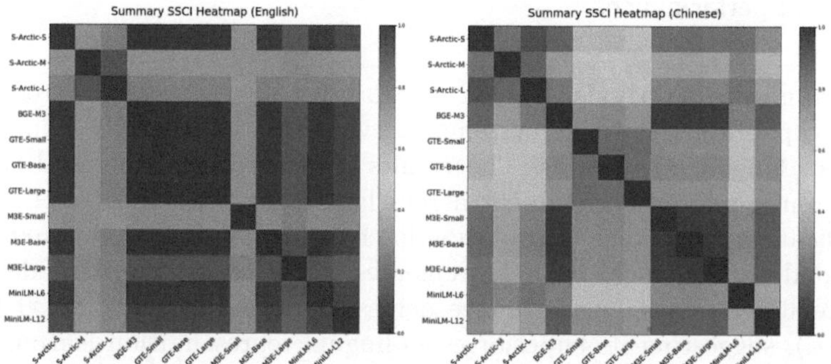

Fig. 5. Comparative SSCI Heatmaps of the S-Arctic Series, BGE Series, GTE Series, M3E Series, and MiniLM Series in the IRSC Benchmark's Summary Subtask Across Chinese and English. Smaller values indicate more consistent model performance.

In Fig. 5, we present detailed SSCI results for the Summary task across different languages and models. In English, most models display blue regions, indicating high consistency in semantic understanding. In contrast, the Chinese results exhibit more red regions, suggesting lower consistency and greater divergence among models. Examining the color distribution in Fig. 5 reveals that models within the same series generally exhibit higher semantic understanding consistency, whereas those from different series are more likely to diverge. These observations indicate significant differences in semantic understanding consistency across languages, with higher consistency in English compared to Chinese. Furthermore, models within the same series tend to have higher consistency, while those from different series are more prone to divergence.

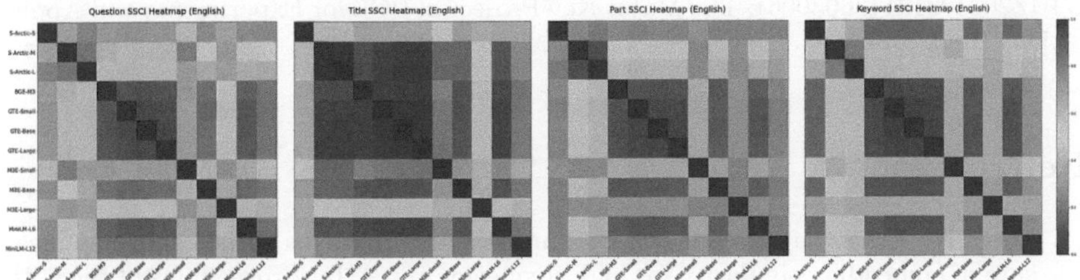

Fig. 6. Comparative SSCI Heatmaps of the S-Arctic Series, BGE Series, GTE Series, M3E Series, and MiniLM Series in the IRSC Benchmark's Question, Title, Part and Keyword Subtasks in English. Smaller values indicate more consistent model performance.

Figure 6 illustrates the SSCI heatmaps for models on four English tasks (excluding Summary), revealing varying degrees of divergence in model understanding across tasks. Unlike the Summary task, where most models show blue regions indicating high SSCI values, the other IRSC tasks reveal varying levels of red regions. This is particularly pronounced in the Title task, which shows extensive deep red regions, indicating significant divergence in semantic understanding among models. The Title task imposes higher demands on semantic understanding, highlighting differences in model performance across task types. While models show high consistency in the Summary task—possibly due to its clear objective and relatively smaller information processing requirements—the Title task requires complex context understanding and concise expression, leading to more pronounced divergences.

5   Conclusion

The IRSC Benchmark advances embedding model evaluation by systematically revealing task-specific capabilities that conventional single-metric assessments cannot detect. Unlike prior benchmarks focused on narrow tasks like semantic similarity, our framework exposes critical performance variations across five distinct retrieval scenarios (Question/Title/Paragraph/Keyword/Summary) and bilingual contexts through three key innovations: (1) The SSCI metric quantifies cross-model semantic alignment beyond cosine similarity's limitations, (2) Task-aware evaluation exposes surprising capability gaps (e.g., BGE-M3's consistent dominance vs S-Arctic's task-specific weaknesses), and (3) Cross-lingual analysis identifies language-agnostic patterns in semantic comprehension.

Acknowledgements. This research is supported by National Natural Science Foundation of China (Grant No.62276154); Research Center for Computer Network (Shenzhen) Ministry of Education, the Natural Science Foundation of Guangdong Province (Grant No.2023A1515012914 and 440300241033100801770); Basic Research Fund of Shenzhen City (Grant No. JCYJ20210324120012033, JCYJ20240813112009013 and GJHZ20240218113603006); The Major Key Project of PCL for Experiments and Applications (PCL2024A08).

References

1. Zhou, K., Ethayarajh, K., Card, D., Jurafsky, D.: Problems with cosine as a measure of embedding similarity for high frequency words. In: Proceedings of the 60th Annual Meeting of the Association for Computational Linguistics, vol. 2: Short Papers, pp. 401–423. Association for Computational Linguistics (2022)
2. Steck, H., Ekanadham, C., Kallus, N.: Is cosine-similarity of embeddings really about similarity? In: Companion Proceedings of the ACM on Web Conference 2024, pp. 887–890. ACM (2024)
3. Chen, J., Lin, H., Han, X., Sun, L.: Benchmarking large language models in retrieval-augmented generation. In: Proceedings of the AAAI Conference on Artificial Intelligence, vol. 38, no. 16, pp. 17754–17762. AAAI Press (2024)
4. Zhang, X., et al.: Making a MIRACL: multilingual information retrieval across a continuum of languages. arXiv preprint arXiv:2210.09984 (2023)
5. Yu, H., Gan, A., Zhang, K., Tong, S., Liu, Q., Liu, Z.: Evaluation of retrieval-augmented generation: a survey. arXiv e-prints, arXiv–2405 (2024)
6. Muennighoff, N., Tazi, N., Magne, L., Reimers, N.: MTEB: massive text embedding benchmark. In: Proceedings of the 17th Conference of the European Chapter of the Association for Computational Linguistics, pp. 2014–2037. Association for Computational Linguistics (2023)
7. Longpre, S., Lu, Y., Daiber, J.: MKQA: a linguistically diverse benchmark for multilingual open domain question answering. Trans. Assoc. Comput. Linguist. **9**, 1389–1406 (2021)
8. Bajaj, P., et al.: MS MARCO: a human generated MAchine reading COmprehension dataset. arXiv preprint arXiv:1611.09268 (2018)
9. Artetxe, M., Ruder, S., Yogatama, D.: On the cross-lingual transferability of monolingual representations. In: Proceedings of the 58th Annual Meeting of the Association for Computational Linguistics, pp. 421–431. Association for Computational Linguistics (2020). https://doi.org/10.18653/v1/2020.acl-main.421
10. Hu, J., Ruder, S., Siddhant, A., Neubig, G., Firat, O., Johnson, M.: Xtreme: a massively multilingual multi-task benchmark for evaluating cross-lingual generalisation. In: International Conference on Machine Learning, pp. 4411–4421. PMLR (2020)
11. Lewis, P., Oguz, B., Rinott, R., Riedel, S., Schwenk, H.: MLQA: evaluating cross-lingual extractive question answering. In: Proceedings of the 58th Annual Meeting of the Association for Computational Linguistics, pp. 7315–7330. Association for Computational Linguistics (2020)

12. Clement, C.B., Bierbaum, M., O'Keeffe, K., Alemi, A.A.: On the use of arXiv as a dataset (2019)
13. Zhang, X., Zhao, J., LeCun, Y.: Character-level convolutional networks for text classification. Adv. Neural Inf. Process. Syst. **28** (2015)
14. Joulin, A., Grave, E., Mikolov, P.B.T.: Bag of tricks for efficient text classification. In: EACL 2017, vol. 427 (2017)
15. Narayan, S., Cohen, S., Lapata, M.: Don't give me the details, just the summary! topic-aware convolutional neural networks for extreme summarization. In: 2018 Conference on Empirical Methods in Natural Language Processing, pp. 1797–1807. Association for Computational Linguistics (2018)
16. Merrick, L., Xu, D., Nuti, G., Campos, D.: Arctic-embed: scalable, efficient, and accurate text embedding models. arXiv preprint arXiv:2405.05374 (2024)
17. Chen, J., Xiao, S., Zhang, P., Luo, K., Lian, D., Liu, Z.: Bge m3-embedding: multi-lingual, multi-functionality, multi-granularity text embeddings through self-knowledge distillation. arXiv preprint arXiv:2402.03216 (2024)
18. Wang, Y., Sun, Q., He, S.: M3E: moka massive mixed embedding model (2023)
19. Li, Z., Zhang, X., Zhang, Y., Long, D., Xie, P., Zhang, M.: Towards general text embeddings with multi-stage contrastive learning. arXiv preprint arXiv:2308.03281 (2023)
20. Reimers, N., Gurevych, I.: Sentence-BERT: sentence embeddings using siamese BERT-networks. In: Proceedings of the 2019 Conference on Empirical Methods in Natural Language Processing, pp. 1–10. Association for Computational Linguistics (2019). http://arxiv.org/abs/1908.10084
21. Thakur, N., Reimers, N., Rücklé, A., Srivastava, A., Gurevych, I.: BEIR: a heterogeneous benchmark for zero-shot evaluation of information retrieval models. In: Thirty-fifth Conference on Neural Information Processing Systems Datasets and Benchmarks Track (Round 2), pp. 1–10. NeurIPS (2021). https://openreview.net/forum?id=wCu6T5xFjeJ

Evaluation Workshop

Overview of the NLPCC 2025 Shared Task 1: LLM-Generated Text Detection

Junchao Wu[1], Runzhe Zhan[1], Qianli Wang[1], Yulin Yuan[2], Lidia S. Chao[1], and Derek F. Wong[1(✉)]

[1] Natural Language Processing and Portuguese-Chinese Machine Translation Lab (NLP²CT), Department of Computer and Information Science, University of Macau, Macau, China
{lidiasc,derekfw}@um.edu.mo
[2] Department of Chinese Language and Literature, University of Macau, Macau, China
yulinyuan@um.edu.mo

Abstract. This paper introduces the achievements and findings of the shared task on Large Language Model (LLM) Generated Text Detection, organized as part of the 14th China National Conference on Natural Language Processing and Chinese Computing (NLPCC 2025). The primary objective of this shared task is to utilize machine learning techniques to develop detectors that can effectively distinguish between LLM-generated text and human-written text, thereby addressing the challenges posed by the rapid advancements of LLMs. The task garnered significant attention, attracting over 30 participating teams from both academia and industry, and 22 teams successfully submitted official results. In this paper, we provide a comprehensive overview of the task, including the dataset, task design, evaluation results, and an in-depth analysis of the submitted solutions. Furthermore, we introduce DetectRL-ZH, a newly released detection dataset, which aims to advance research in detecting LLM-generated Chinese texts (Shared Task Official Website: https://github.com/NLP2CT/NLPCC-2025-Task1).

Keywords: LLM-Generated Text Detection · AI Detection · Chinese

1 Introduction

With the rapid development of large language models (LLMs), the quality of their generated texts has increasingly approached that of human-written content and are widely adopted in various aspects of daily life [26]. However, these models also pose significant challenges, as they can generate misinformation, harmful content, or be misused in fields such as journalism, academia, and artistic creation [3,25]. As the capabilities of LLMs continue to improve, distinguishing between LLM-generated and human-written texts has become increasingly difficult, making effective differentiation an urgent and critical issue [26]. While

© The Author(s), under exclusive license to Springer Nature Singapore Pte Ltd. 2026

X.-L. Mao et al. (Eds.): NLPCC 2025, LNAI 16105, pp. 263–274, 2026.
https://doi.org/10.1007/978-981-95-3352-7_21

considerable progress has been made in detecting LLM-generated texts, existing research is mostly focused on English texts, with studies on Chinese texts remaining underexplored. To address this gap, we organized a shared task on detecting LLM-generated texts, aiming to develop more robust detection methods specifically for Chinese texts and advance research in this area.

In this shared task, participants were required to design and develop detection algorithms using the provided training dataset to distinguish between LLM-generated and human-written texts. We introduced DetectRL-ZH, a benchmark specifically designed for detecting LLM-generated Chinese texts. DetectRL-ZH covers four common writing scenarios: academic writing, news writing, creative writing, and social media, incorporating texts generated by widely used LLMs such as Qwen-turbo,[1] GLM-4-flash,[2] GPT-4o,[3] and Deepseek-V3.[4] The dataset was curated to simulate real-world scenarios, including a diverse range of paraphrased, adversarial, and data-mixed samples. During the evaluation phase, the submitted detectors underwent rigorous testing under conditions that closely aligned with real-world scenarios, enabling a comprehensive assessment of their practical effectiveness and robustness. To ensure fairness, participants were strictly prohibited from using external data or generating new data based on external knowledge. Furthermore, we conducted a detailed review of the training data and scripts submitted by leading participants to ensure the task's fairness.

The shared task attracted 30 participating teams from academia and industry, among which 22 teams successfully submitted official results.

In Sect. 2, we provide an overview of the task's background and related work. In Sect. 3, we detail the setup of the shared task, including our task description, dataset, baseline, and evaluation metrics. In Sect. 4, we summarize the systems developed by the participating teams and analyzes the evaluation results, offering valuable insights and discussions.

2   Related Work

2.1   Detection Methods

Current detection methods can generally be divided into two main categories: neural-based methods and statistical-based methods [26]. Neural-based methods typically employ supervised approaches, such as fine-tuning classifiers. While these methods can achieve relatively superior detection performance, they heavily rely on large amounts of training data and are prone to overfitting, which limits their ability to generalize effectively to out-of-distribution (OOD) data [12]. In contrast, statistical-based methods focus on identifying statistical features that can distinguish between two types of text and use distribution thresholds for classification, such as Log-Likelihood [17], Log-Rank [6], LRR [18], GECScore [27],

---

[1] https://qwenlm.github.io/zh/blog/qwen2.5-turbo/.
[2] https://bigmodel.cn/dev/activities/free/glm-4-flash.
[3] https://openai.com/index/hello-gpt-4o/.
[4] https://github.com/deepseek-ai/DeepSeek-V3.

Fast-DetectGPT [1], and Binoculars [9]. Although these methods may require impractical white-box access to the generator, their higher interpretability makes them more convincing and trustworthy to end-users.

2.2 Detection Benchmarks

Significant progress has been made in benchmarking for detecting LLM-generated texts, but most benchmarks primarily focus on English or multilingual datasets centered around English [26]. For example, benchmarks such as Turing-Bench [19], MGTBench [10], and MAGE [12] evaluate texts generated by LLMs across multiple domains and generators. While benchmarks such as M4 [23] and HC3 [8] incorporate multilingual data, including Chinese texts. However, these benchmarks are not specifically designed for Chinese detection tasks, and their diversity in terms of models and domains is limited. More importantly, these benchmarks still focus on idealized detection scenarios, lacking sufficient simulation and exploration of real-world application. In contrast, works like Stumbling Blocks [21], RAID [4], and DetectRL [28], have explored more challenging benchmarks aligned with real-world detection scenarios. However, these efforts remain predominantly focused on English, leaving the detection of LLM-generated Chinese texts with a notable lack of dedicated resources.

2.3 Detection Shared Tasks

To address the challenge of detecting LLM-generated text, several shared tasks have been organized. The 2023 ALTA Shared Task [15] focused on distinguishing between human-written and LLM-generated text, while the 2024 ALTA Shared Task [14] expanded this goal to include detecting LLM-generated sentences in human-machine hybrid articles. The CLIN33 Shared Task on the Detection of Text Generated by LLM [5] defined the problem as a binary classification task, using data from six domains in Dutch and English. Similarly, AuTexTification at IberLEF 2023 [16] divided the problem into two subtasks: binary classification and text attribution, covering English and Spanish across five domains. SemEval-2024 Task 8 [22] further broadened the scope to include English, Arabic, German, and Italian, and introduced three subtasks: binary classification, text attribution, and boundary detection in human-machine hybrid texts. Building on this, the COLING 2025 Workshop on Detecting AI-Generated Content [24] refined SemEval-2024 Task 8, with a stronger focus on detecting AI-generated content in academic writing and cross-domain detection.

3 Shared Task: LLM-Generated Text Detection

3.1 Overview

This shared task consists of two phases: the development phase (February 28 to April 10, 2025) and the testing phase (April 11 to April 20, 2025). During the development phase, participants can access the training and development

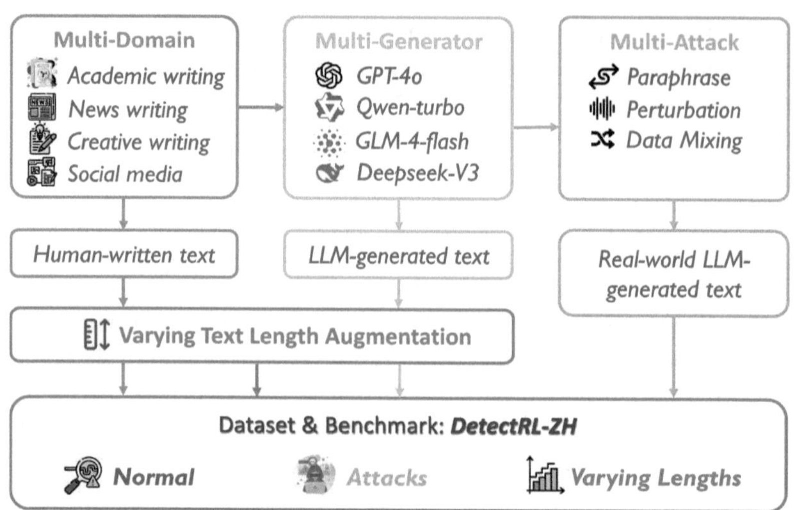

Fig. 1. The overview framework of DetectRL-ZH and shared task dataset.

sets, and use the development set to evaluate their detectors' robustness. To support the development of strong detection systems, participants are allowed to perform data augmentation based on the provided training data. However, data augmentation must be limited to processing or transforming the original data, such as creating new data samples through methods like cropping, splitting, word replacement, or format adjustment. It is crucial that any paraphrasing strictly preserves the original semantic meaning and does not introduce external knowledge or create entirely new content. This includes a prohibition on using generative LLMs for paraphrasing, as this could inadvertently introduce OOD knowledge and lead to unfair advantages, but allowing the use of traditional encoder-based models or Seq2seq models for paraphrasing. Additionally, the provided development set was strictly for model tuning and could not be used for training. Participants were also prohibited from optimizing their models specifically for the test set (e.g., by applying additional unsupervised methods on the test set).

After the testing phase began, participants were granted access to the test set texts and allowed multiple submissions, with only the final submission considered to prevent data leakage. After the testing phase concluded, test set labels were released for result verification and ablation studies.

3.2   Datasets

DetectRL-ZH. We introduce the DetectRL-ZH, a benchmark specifically designed for detecting LLM-generated text in Chinese as illustrated in Fig. 1. It is the Chinese extension of DetectRL [28], an English benchmark for detecting LLM-generated text in real-world scenarios. The human-written texts are sourced from CSL [13], CNewSum [20], ASAP [2], and STORAL [7], covering

Table 1. DetectRL-ZH Statistics.

Source	GPT4o	GLM	Qwen	DeepSeek	Normal		Attacks		Varying Length	
					Human	LLM	Human	LLM	Human	LLM
CSL	2,800	2,800	2,800	2,800	2,800	11,200	2,800	67,200	11,200	44,800
CNewSum	2,800	2,800	2,800	2,800	2,800	11,200	2,800	67,200	11,200	44,800
ASAP	2,800	2,800	2,800	2,800	2,800	11,200	2,800	67,200	11,200	44,800
STORAL	2,800	2,800	2,800	2,800	2,800	11,200	2,800	67,200	11,200	44,800
Total	11,200	11,200	11,200	11,200	11,200	44,800	11,200	268,800	44,800	179,200

four writing scenarios prone to misuse: academic writing, news writing, social media, and creative writing. The corresponding LLM-generated texts were produced using four widely used LLMs: Qwen-turbo, GLM-4-flash, GPT-4o, and Deepseek-V3. To ensure quality, we selected samples longer than 160 characters.

To better simulate real-world scenarios for detecting LLM-generated texts, we applied various attack methods to LLM-generated texts, including paraphrasing attacks, adversarial attacks, and data-mixing scenarios. Paraphrasing attacks aim to rewrite texts with semantic equivalence to alter their style or evade detection. Specifically, we employed two commonly used paraphrasing methods: (1) LLM-based text refinement and (2) back-translation via Google Translate. Adversarial attacks introduce character or word-level perturbations to confuse detectors [11]. We applied two types of noise in Chinese: (1) glyph replacement (substituting characters with visually similar ones) and (2) homophone replacement. The noise injection ratio was controlled between 0% and 5% of the total text, using a local dictionary of visually similar and homophonic characters. Data-Mixing scenario combines human-written and LLM-generated content. To construct such samples, we replaced approximately 25% of semantically complete content in LLM-generated texts with human-written content, ensuring that LLM-generated content remained above 50%. Content replacement was based on the sentence with the highest semantic similarity among human-written samples and categorized as (1) in-domain mixing or (2) out-domain mixing, depending on the source of the human-written samples.

To enhance the diversity of samples with varying lengths, we split texts at the sentence level, creating multiple versions of each sample approximating lengths of 64, 128, 256, and 512 characters. This approach evaluates the robustness of detectors across varying sample lengths.

As shown in Table 1, the dataset includes 11,200 human-written samples (2,800 per subdomain) and 44,800 LLM-generated samples, with each human-written sample paired with four LLM-generated versions. Additionally, 268,800 LLM-generated samples were created using six attack settings. For varying lengths, the dataset includes 44,800 human-written and 179,200 LLM-generated samples. Details of the prompts and parameters used are provided in Appendix A.1.

Table 2. Shared Task Dataset Split Details.

Split	Source	GPT4o	GLM	Qwen	DeepSeek	Human	LLM	Total
Train	ASAP	2,700	2,700	2,700	-	2,700	8,100	10,800
	CNewSum	2,700	2,700	2,700	-	2,700	8,100	10,800
	CSL	2,700	2,700	2,700	-	2,700	8,100	10,800
Dev	ASAP	100	100	100	-	100	300	400
	CNewSum	100	100	100	-	100	300	400
	CSL	100	100	100	-	100	300	400
	STORAL	-	-	-	800	800	800	1,600
Test	STORAL-Normal	-	-	-	2,000	2,000	2,000	4,000
	STORAL-Attacks	-	-	-	1,500	1,500	1,500	3,000
	STORAL-Attacks	-	-	-	2,000	2,000	2,000	4,000

Shared Task Data Setting. The dataset for the shared task is divided into three subsets: training, development, and test. All data were sampled from DetectRL-ZH. The detailed statistics are presented in Table 2.

The training set consists of human-written texts sampled from three domains: CSL, CNewSum, and ASAP. Corresponding LLM-generated texts were sampled from three distinct LLMs: GPT-4o, GLM-4-flash, and Qwen-turbo. As shown in Table 2, the training set includes a total of 32,400 samples, comprising 8,100 human-written texts and 24,300 LLM-generated texts.

The test set is divided into three settings: Normal, Attacks, and Varying Length, designed to evaluate the detector's performance across different aspects. In the Normal setting, human-written texts were sampled from a distribution entirely outside the training set, specifically from STORAL. This setting contains 2,000 human-written samples, with corresponding LLM-generated texts created by an OOD LLM, Deepseek-V3. In the Attacks setting, we applied various attack methods to 500 LLM-generated texts of Normal setting. These include paraphrasing attacks (back-translation via Google Translate), adversarial attacks (glyph replacement), and data-mixing scenarios (out-domain mixing). In the Varying Length setting, we sampled 500 LLM-generated texts in the normal setting and created corresponding samples with lengths of 64, 128, 256, and 512 characters. The statistics of test set are presented in Table 2, comprising 11,000 samples in total: 5,500 human-written and 5,500 LLM-generated.

The development set combines distributions from both the training and test sets. As shown in Table 2, it contains 2,800 samples in total: 1,100 human-written and 1,700 LLM-generated.

3.3 Baseline and Metrics

We fine-tuned the Chinese Roberta model[5] based on the training set to build a classifier as the baseline. We use the Hugging Face Trainer API for fine-tuning with 3 epochs, a learning rate of `1e-6`, and a batch size of `16`.

---

[5] https://huggingface.co/hfl/chinese-roberta-wwm-ext.

Table 3. Performance Comparison of Different Systems. Avg. F1 is the average score across the three settings. The dashed line represents the level of baseline.

System Name(ID)	Normal	Attacks	Varying Lengths	Avg. F1
LLM-Generated-System ⚇1	1.0000	0.9943	0.9770	**0.9904**
TeleAI ⚇2	0.9997	0.9823	0.8894	**0.9571**
POLYNLPCC ⚇3	0.9662	0.9100	0.9720	**0.9494**
AI Text Trackers	0.9730	0.9217	0.9389	**0.9445**
BlueSpace	0.9865	0.9533	0.8899	**0.9432**
MCI^2_LLMGTD	0.9900	0.8429	0.9110	**0.9146**
ZZU-NLP	0.9982	0.8389	0.8588	**0.8987**
DS	0.9484	0.7572	0.8727	**0.8594**
GenAuditor	0.9440	0.8673	0.7658	**0.8590**
Sprinting	0.8917	0.7930	0.8483	**0.8443**
ClassiFire	0.8922	0.8483	0.7858	**0.8421**
HC	0.9374	0.8219	0.7629	**0.8407**
YNU-HPCC	0.9940	0.8341	0.6517	**0.8266**
ZZUNLP	0.9997	0.9010	0.4464	**0.7824**
MSFLab	0.7357	0.7361	0.8706	**0.7808**
LLM-Generated Text Detection	0.9243	0.8149	0.5673	**0.7689**
SEIG-NLP	0.8782	0.7750	0.6480	**0.7671**
DUFL2025	0.9195	0.5146	0.7140	**0.7160**
ZZUNLP_Han	0.9597	0.5141	0.6170	**0.6969**
NPUNLP Research Group	0.7495	0.7217	0.3919	**0.6211**
PAK NLP	0.4892	0.4508	0.4902	**0.4767**
YouTuLab_Jarvis	0.3982	0.3974	0.4077	**0.4011**

3.4 Metrics

For evaluation metrics, we employ macro-averaged F1-Score, which effectively measures the performance of a classifier in binary classification task.

4 Participants' Submissions

4.1 Results and Ranks

A total of 22 submissions were received for the task, and the complete rankings are presented in Table 3. Based on the primary evaluation metric, 19 teams outperformed the baseline (62.59% macro F1-Score), with scores ranging from 99.04% to 69.69%. The competition among the top-performing teams was exceptionally intense, with significant performance differences observed. The first-place team achieved a macro F1 score of 99.04%, significantly outperforming the second and third-place teams: TeleAI (95.71%) and POLYNLPCC (94.94%). Close behind were AI Text Trackers (94.45%) and BlueSpace (94.32%), with only a marginal gap separating them from the third-place team.

4.2 Analysis and Discussion

High Performance of Current Detectors in Ideal Scenarios. Overall, compared to previous studies on detecting LLM-generated English text, the detection of LLM-generated Chinese text appears to be gradually evolving into a problem that can be effectively addressed. Under the Normal setting, most of the submitted systems have demonstrated high performance, with detection performance exceeding 95% and even approaching 100% in some cases outside specific domains and LLM distributions. This indicates that, within an ideal text length, current detectors can effectively distinguish between fully LLM-generated and human-written texts. Furthermore, cross-domain and cross-LLM robustness is no longer a significant challenge for existing systems.

Challenges in Complex and Real-World Scenarios. Experimental results on Attack and Varying Lengths reveal limitations in handling complex scenarios. When faced with diverse and complex LLM-generated texts in real-world scenarios or texts intentionally designed to evade detection, the performance of detectors significantly deteriorates. This highlights the current challenge in applying detectors beyond idealized datasets. Therefore, constructing more comprehensive benchmarks that better represent real-world scenarios is crucial for validating the effectiveness of detectors and advancing this field. Additionally, the robustness of existing detectors to texts of varying lengths remains problematic, underscoring the need for systems that can reliably handle text detection across different lengths.

Key Strategies and Insights for Advancing Detection. We identified several valuable approaches and insights from the systems of the participating teams, providing references for academic research and industrial applications. Overall, we found that Instruction Tuning demonstrated significant potential and robustness. Almost all teams adopting Instruction Tuning, including the first and second-place teams, achieved excellent results. Classifiers fine-tuned based on embedding showed moderate performance, with an average F1-Score of around 85%. However, results from AI Text Trackers team suggest that data augmentation and targeted optimizations, such as specialized classifiers for different text lengths, can improve performance. These classifiers, however, are prone to overfitting and require sufficiently diverse scenario coverage to ensure stability. Simple statistical-based methods were less effective. For example, English SOTA detectors such as Fast-DetectGPT and Binoculars, as well as methods relying on text style features, did not demonstrate strong competitiveness. However, integrating sufficient statistical features can enhance the practicality. The POLYNLPCC team achieved strong results using extensive statistical features, while the LLM-Generated-System improved robustness by combining statistical features with neural networks. Results based on statistical feature integration also offered better interpretability. Notably, results based on statistical feature integration also offered better interpretability. Furthermore, multi-feature integration, voting mechanisms, ensemble learning, and expert models proven to be effective strategies. Multi-feature integration combines diverse text features to achieve better performance than relying on single features, reducing overfitting and improving generalization in diverse scenarios. Voting mechanisms and ensemble learning enhance stability and performance by aggregating predictions from multiple top-n models. Expert models, tailored to specific distributions (e.g., text length or attack scenario), further boost detection by assigning the most suitable classifiers to specific tasks.

5   Conclusion

In this study, we introduce the dataset, baseline, participating systems, and a comprehensive analysis of various detection methods for NLPCC 2025 Shared Task 1: Detecting LLM-Generated Text. We focus on the Chinese language and present DetectRL-ZH, the first benchmark specifically designed to identify LLM-generated Chinese texts in real-world scenarios, covering diverse domains, text generators, and practical usage cases. While most submitted systems text under normal settings, their effectiveness drops significantly in attacks and varying lengths scenarios, highlighting the fragility of existing solutions. Notably, instruction fine-tuning exhibits surprising performance and significant potential for Chinese text detection. We hope that this shared task will encourage researchers to develop more robust and generalized detection methods. Furthermore, our findings offer valuable insights and directions for future work, advancing the research of LLM-generated text detection and promoting responsible artificial intelligence, especially in the Chinese context.

Acknowledgments. This work was supported in part by the Science and Technology Development Fund of Macau SAR (Grant Nos. FDCT/0007/2024/AKP, FDCT/0070/2022/AMJ, FDCT/060/2022/AFJ), the National Natural Science Foundation of China (Grant Nos. 62261160648, 62266013), the China Strategic Scientific and Technological Innovation Cooperation Project (Grant No. 2022YFE0204900), and the UM and UMDF (Grant Nos. MYRG-GRG2023-00006-FST-UMDF, MYRG-GRG2024-00165-FST-UMDF, EF2024-00185-FST, EF2023-00151-FST, EF2023-00090-FST).

A   Appendix

A.1   Data Generation Settings

All text generation tasks are conducted via API calls to the relevant LLM in a conversational format. For academic writing, the LLM is provided with the article title to generate a summary. For news articles, a summary is supplied to generate a complete article. For creative writing, the LLM is given the first sentence to write a full story. For social media content, it generates a complete comment based on the first sentence of a social commentary. We set the temperature as 1.0 to encourage diversity. The specific prompts are as follows:

> **Academic Writing**
>
> [{"role": "system", "content": "你是一个科研写作者。请根据论文的标题撰写摘要。"}, {"role": "user", "content": "论文标题：XXX\n 论文摘要："}]

> **News Writing**
>
> [{"role": "system", "content": "你是一个新闻写作者。请根据新闻摘要撰写新闻文章。"}, {"role": "user", "content": "新闻摘要：XXX\n 新闻文章："}]

> **Creative Writing**
>
> [{"role": "system", "content": "你是一个故事写作者。请根据故事的开头撰写完整的故事。"}, {"role": "user", "content": "故事开头：XXX\n 完整故事："}]

> **Social Media**
>
> [{"role": "system", "content": "你是一个评论写作者。请根据评论的开头撰写完整的评论。"}, {"role": "user", "content": "评论开头：XXX\n 完整评论："}]

References

1. Bao, G., Zhao, Y., Teng, Z., Yang, L., Zhang, Y.: Fast-detectgpt: efficient zero-shot detection of machine-generated text via conditional probability curvature. In: The Twelfth International Conference on Learning Representations, ICLR 2024, Vienna, Austria, 7–11 May 2024. OpenReview.net (2024)
2. Bu, J., et al.: ASAP: a Chinese review dataset towards aspect category sentiment analysis and rating prediction. In: Proceedings of the 2021 Conference of the North American Chapter of the Association for Computational Linguistics: Human Language Technologies, NAACL-HLT 2021, Online, 6–11 June 2021, pp. 2069–2079. Association for Computational Linguistics (2021)
3. Chen, C., Shu, K.: Combating misinformation in the age of LLMs: opportunities and challenges. AI Mag. **45**(3), 354–368 (2024)
4. Dugan, L., et al.: RAID: a shared benchmark for robust evaluation of machine-generated text detectors. In: Proceedings of the 62nd Annual Meeting of the Association for Computational Linguistics (Volume 1: Long Papers), ACL 2024, Bangkok, Thailand, 11–16 August 2024, pp. 12463–12492. Association for Computational Linguistics (2024)
5. Fivez, P., et al.: The CLIN33 shared task on the detection of text generated by large language models. Comput. Linguist. Neth. J. **13**, 233–259 (2024)
6. Gehrmann, S., Strobelt, H., Rush, A.M.: GLTR: statistical detection and visualization of generated text. In: Proceedings of the 57th Conference of the Association for Computational Linguistics, ACL 2019, Florence, Italy, 28 July–2 August 2019, Volume 3: System Demonstrations, pp. 111–116. Association for Computational Linguistics (2019)

7. Guan, J., Liu, Z., Huang, M.: A corpus for understanding and generating moral stories. In: Proceedings of the 2022 Conference of the North American Chapter of the Association for Computational Linguistics: Human Language Technologies, NAACL 2022, Seattle, WA, United States, 10–15 July 2022, pp. 5069–5087. Association for Computational Linguistics (2022)

8. Guo, B., et al.: How close is chatgpt to human experts? Comparison corpus, evaluation, and detection. CoRR abs/2301.07597 (2023). https://doi.org/10.48550/arXiv.2301.07597

9. Hans, A., et al.: Spotting LLMs with binoculars: zero-shot detection of machine-generated text. In: Forty-First International Conference on Machine Learning, ICML 2024, Vienna, Austria, 21–27 July 2024. OpenReview.net (2024)

10. He, X., Shen, X., Chen, Z., Backes, M., Zhang, Y.: Mgtbench: benchmarking machine-generated text detection. In: Proceedings of the 2024 on ACM SIGSAC Conference on Computer and Communications Security, CCS 2024, Salt Lake City, UT, USA, 14–18 October 2024, pp. 2251–2265. ACM (2024)

11. Krishna, K., Song, Y., Karpinska, M., Wieting, J., Iyyer, M.: Paraphrasing evades detectors of AI-generated text, but retrieval is an effective defense. In: Advances in Neural Information Processing Systems 36: Annual Conference on Neural Information Processing Systems 2023, NeurIPS 2023, New Orleans, LA, USA, 10–16 December 2023 (2023)

12. Li, Y., et al.: MAGE: machine-generated text detection in the wild. In: Proceedings of the 62nd Annual Meeting of the Association for Computational Linguistics (Volume 1: Long Papers), ACL 2024, Bangkok, Thailand, 11–16 August 2024, pp. 36–53. Association for Computational Linguistics (2024)

13. Li, Y., et al.: CSL: a large-scale Chinese scientific literature dataset. In: Proceedings of the 29th International Conference on Computational Linguistics, COLING 2022, Gyeongju, Republic of Korea, 12–17 October 2022, pp. 3917–3923. International Committee on Computational Linguistics (2022)

14. Mollá, D., Xu, Q., Zeng, Z., Li, Z.: Overview of the 2024 ALTA shared task: detect automatic AI-generated sentences for human-AI hybrid articles. CoRR abs/2412.17848 (2024). https://doi.org/10.48550/arXiv.2412.17848

15. Mollá, D., Zhan, H., He, X., Xu, Q.: Overview of the 2023 ALTA shared task: discriminate between human-written and machine-generated text. In: Proceedings of the 21st Annual Workshop of the Australasian Language Technology Association, ALTA 2023, Melbourne, Australia, 29 November–1 December 2023, pp. 148–152. Association for Computational Linguistics (2023)

16. Sarvazyan, A.M., González, J.Á., Franco-Salvador, M., Rangel, F., Chulvi, B., Rosso, P.: Overview of autextification at iberlef 2023: detection and attribution of machine-generated text in multiple domains. Proces. del Leng. Natural **71**, 275–288 (2023)

17. Solaiman, I., et al.: Release strategies and the social impacts of language models. CoRR abs/1908.09203 (2019). http://arxiv.org/abs/1908.09203

18. Su, J., Zhuo, T.Y., Wang, D., Nakov, P.: Detectllm: leveraging log rank information for zero-shot detection of machine-generated text. In: Findings of the Association for Computational Linguistics: EMNLP 2023, Singapore, 6–10 December 2023, pp. 12395–12412. Association for Computational Linguistics (2023)

19. Uchendu, A., Ma, Z., Le, T., Zhang, R., Lee, D.: TURINGBENCH: a benchmark environment for turing test in the age of neural text generation. In: Findings of the Association for Computational Linguistics: EMNLP 2021, Virtual Event/Punta Cana, Dominican Republic, 16–20 November 2021, pp. 2001–2016. Association for Computational Linguistics (2021)

20. Wang, D., Chen, J., Wu, X., Zhou, H., Li, L.: Cnewsum: a large-scale Chinese news summarization dataset with human-annotated adequacy and deducibility level. CoRR abs/2110.10874 (2021). https://arxiv.org/abs/2110.10874

21. Wang, Y., et al.: Stumbling blocks: stress testing the robustness of machine-generated text detectors under attacks. In: Proceedings of the 62nd Annual Meeting of the Association for Computational Linguistics (Volume 1: Long Papers), ACL 2024, Bangkok, Thailand, 11–16 August 2024, pp. 2894–2925. Association for Computational Linguistics (2024)

22. Wang, Y., et al.: Semeval-2024 task 8: multidomain, multimodel and multilingual machine-generated text detection. In: Proceedings of the 18th International Workshop on Semantic Evaluation, SemEval@NAACL 2024, Mexico City, Mexico, 20–21 June 2024, pp. 2057–2079. Association for Computational Linguistics (2024)

23. Wang, Y., et al.: M4: multi-generator, multi-domain, and multi-lingual black-box machine-generated text detection. In: Proceedings of the 18th Conference of the European Chapter of the Association for Computational Linguistics, EACL 2024 - Volume 1: Long Papers, St. Julian's, Malta, 17–22 March 2024, pp. 1369–1407. Association for Computational Linguistics (2024)

24. Wang, Y., et al.: Genai content detection task 1: English and multilingual machine-generated text detection: AI vs. human. CoRR abs/2501.11012 (2025). https://doi.org/10.48550/arXiv.2501.11012

25. Wu, J., Guo, J., Hooi, B.: Fake news in sheep's clothing: robust fake news detection against LLM-empowered style attacks. In: Proceedings of the 30th ACM SIGKDD Conference on Knowledge Discovery and Data Mining, KDD 2024, Barcelona, Spain, 25–29 August 2024, pp. 3367–3378. ACM (2024)

26. Wu, J., Yang, S., Zhan, R., Yuan, Y., Chao, L.S., Wong, D.F.: A survey on LLM-generated text detection: necessity, methods, and future directions. Comput. Linguistics **51**(1), 275–338 (2025)

27. Wu, J., et al.: Who wrote this? the key to zero-shot LLM-generated text detection is gecscore. In: Proceedings of the 31st International Conference on Computational Linguistics, COLING 2025, Abu Dhabi, UAE, 19–24 January 2025, pp. 10275–10292. Association for Computational Linguistics (2025)

28. Wu, J., et al.: Detectrl: benchmarking LLM-generated text detection in real-world scenarios. In: Advances in Neural Information Processing Systems 38: Annual Conference on Neural Information Processing Systems 2024, NeurIPS 2024, Vancouver, BC, Canada, 10–15 December 2024 (2024)

When Less is More: Minimal Prompts with LoRA for LLM Text Detection

Shiquan Wang, Ruiyu Fang, Mengxiang Li, Zhongjiang He[✉],
and Shuangyong Song[✉]

Institute of Artificial Intelligence (TeleAI), China Telecom Corp Ltd., Beijing, China
{wangsq23,fangry,hezj,songshy}@chinatelecom.cn

Abstract. This paper presents a method for detecting LLM-generated
Chinese text in the NLPCC 2025 Task 1. We utilize the Qwen2.5-72B-
Instruct model as the base, applying parameter-efficient fine-tuning using
Low-Rank Adaptation (LoRA) to optimize its performance on the detection task. Our approach integrates multiple models trained with different
configurations and combines their predictions using an ensemble learning strategy based on majority voting. Additionally, we evaluate GEC-
Score, a semantic-aware unsupervised baseline, for comparison. Through
comprehensive experiments, we show that our ensemble strategy significantly enhances the model's robustness and generalization ability across
different evaluation scenarios. In the final test, our method achieved an
average Macro-F1 score of 0.9665, securing second place in the competition. The results validate the effectiveness of the proposed method in
distinguishing between human-written and LLM-generated texts.

Keywords: LLM-generated Text Detection · Prompt Engineering

1 Introduction

In recent years, Large Language Models (LLMs) have undergone rapid and
unprecedented advancement. With their powerful natural language processing
capabilities, LLMs are able to generate text that not only exhibits fluent grammatical structure and coherent semantic logic but also closely mimics human
expression in terms of style and tone [1,7,13,24,32]. These capabilities have
enabled LLMs to be widely adopted across various domains such as education, media, and business, giving rise to innovative applications including intelligent writing assistants, personalized content recommendation systems, and automated customer service. These applications have significantly improved produc-
tivity and user experience.

However, the widespread deployment of LLMs has also introduced a range
of risks and challenges. In academic settings, the use of LLMs by students to
generate essays has raised concerns regarding academic integrity. In the media,

---

S. Wang and R. Fang—Equal contribution.

© The Author(s), under exclusive license to Springer Nature Singapore Pte Ltd. 2026

X.-L. Mao et al. (Eds.): NLPCC 2025, LNAI 16105, pp. 275–283, 2026.
https://doi.org/10.1007/978-981-95-3352-7_22

fake news articles can be mass-produced using LLMs, misleading public opinion. In cyberspace, scammers exploit LLM-generated text to craft persuasive narratives for fraud, posing serious threats to personal and financial security [6,22]. Against this backdrop, the ability to accurately and efficiently detect LLM-generated text has become a pressing issue for safeguarding information authenticity and maintaining social order. Addressing this challenge is now a critical research focus in the field of Natural Language Processing (NLP) [28].

To tackle this issue, the NLPCC 2025 Task 1 introduced a shared task on detecting LLM-generated Chinese text. The goal is to evaluate and advance techniques that distinguish human-written content from LLM-generated text across diverse domains. We participated in this competition and achieved second place. Our proposed method is based on the Qwen2.5-72B-Instruct model, enhanced with Low-Rank Adaptation (LoRA) fine-tuning, which significantly improves the model's task-specific adaptability and detection accuracy.

2   Related Work

With the widespread adoption of LLMs, the detection of LLM-generated text has become a critical research topic in the field of NLP. Existing detection methods can be broadly categorized into the following approaches:

2.1   Watermarking Techniques

Watermarking techniques embed imperceptible signals into the text generated by LLMs to facilitate later identification of the text's origin. These approaches include data-driven, model-driven, and post-processing watermarking methods. Data-driven methods introduce subtle perturbations into the training data, leading to outputs that exhibit identifiable statistical patterns [11]. Model-driven approaches modify model parameters to imprint unique generation signatures into the output [16,19]. Post-processing methods inject detectable patterns after the text is generated [33]. While watermarking offers a promising direction for tracing text provenance, it may degrade text quality and is vulnerable to adversarial attacks.

2.2   Statistical Methods

Statistical methods aim to identify LLM-generated text based on linguistic features or statistical characteristics of the generation process. Feature-based approaches analyze metrics like lexical richness and syntactic complexity to determine whether a text is LLM-generated [3,12]. White-box statistical methods leverage knowledge of the model's internal parameters and generation dynamics to detect anomalies [25,31]. In contrast, black-box methods evaluate statistical properties of the output without requiring access to the underlying model [34]. Although these methods are often efficient and interpretable, their generalizability across domains and languages remains limited.

2.3   Neural Network-Based Approaches

Neural network-based methods utilize deep learning models to build detectors for LLM-generated text. Feature-based classifiers extract various textual representations and feed them into traditional classifiers [2]. Pretrained classifiers, exemplified by encode text using pretrained language models and fine-tune them for detection tasks [9,21]. Other studies employ LLMs themselves as detectors leveraging the models' intrinsic language understanding capabilities for detection [4,17,23]. While these methods generally achieve high accuracy, they require substantial training resources and are heavily dependent on labeled data.

2.4   Human-Aided Approaches

Human-aided detection methods incorporate human expertise and reasoning to support the identification of LLM-generated text. For example, Human-in-the-Loop frameworks involve designing specific tasks or queries that allow human annotators to assess textual coherence, factual correctness, or domain-specific knowledge [15]. Other approaches leverage crowdsourcing platforms to collect multiple independent judgments, aggregating them to form a consensus [8,27]. While effective in handling complex and ambiguous cases, these methods are limited by subjectivity and scalability concerns.

3   Methodology

This section presents the methodology adopted in our solution for the NLPCC 2025 Task 1 competition. Our overall approach consists of three main components: prompt engineering, model fine-tuning with LoRA, and an ensemble strategy via majority voting.

3.1   Prompt Engineering

To enhance the ability of large language models to detect LLM-generated texts, we designed and compared a variety of prompt styles. Two representative examples are illustrated in Fig. 1. The prompt shown in Fig. 1(a) builds upon explicit role definition and task procedures, and further incorporates typical linguistic features commonly observed in LLM-generated texts—such as generic word usage, highly regular syntactic structures, and verbose content lacking in detail—with the aim of guiding the model through explicit cues. In contrast, the prompt in Fig. 1(b) adopts a more concise design that retains only the task definition and basic decision-making steps, without introducing additional heuristic descriptions or prior knowledge.

While the feature-enriched prompt demonstrated some heuristic value under specific input distributions, it also exhibited a higher risk of overfitting. In comparison, the concise and semantically clear prompt more effectively leveraged the model's intrinsic capabilities in language understanding and reasoning, resulting

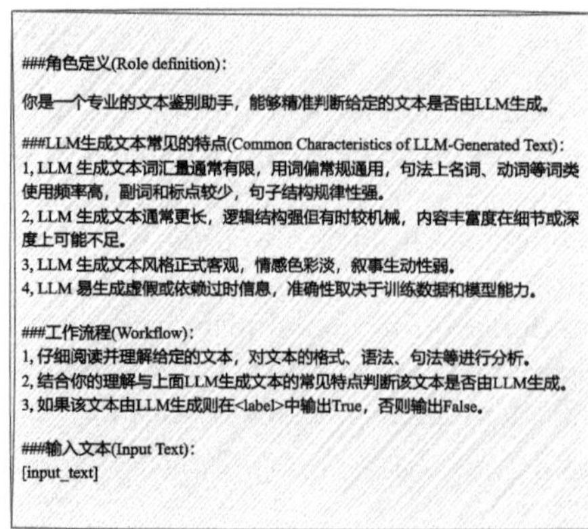

###角色定义(Role definition):

你是一个专业的文本鉴别助手，能够精准判断给定的文本是否由LLM生成。

###LLM生成文本常见的特点(Common Characteristics of LLM-Generated Text):
1,LLM 生成文本词汇量通常有限，用词偏常规通用，句法上名词、动词等词类使用频率高，副词和标点较少，句子结构规律性强。
2,LLM 生成文本通常更长，逻辑结构强但有时较机械，内容丰富度在细节或深度上可能不足。
3,LLM 生成文本风格正式客观，情感色彩淡，叙事生动性弱。
4,LLM 易生成虚假或依赖过时信息，准确性取决于训练数据和模型能力。

###工作流程(Workflow):
1,仔细阅读并理解给定的文本，对文本的格式、语法、句法等进行分析。
2,结合你的理解与上面LLM生成文本的常见特点判断该文本是否由LLM生成。
3,如果该文本由LLM生成则在<label>中输出True，否则输出False。

###输入文本(Input Text):
[input_text]

(a)

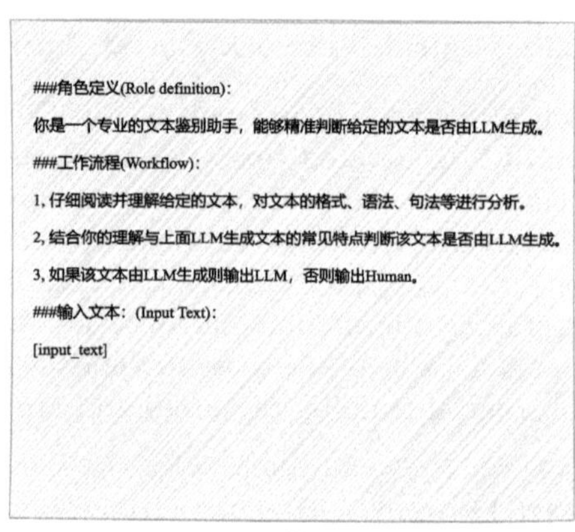

###角色定义(Role definition):

你是一个专业的文本鉴别助手，能够精准判断给定的文本是否由LLM生成。

###工作流程(Workflow):

1,仔细阅读并理解给定的文本，对文本的格式、语法、句法等进行分析。

2,结合你的理解与上面LLM生成文本的常见特点判断该文本是否由LLM生成。

3,如果该文本由LLM生成则输出LLM，否则输出Human。

###输入文本： (Input Text):

[input_text]

(b)

Fig. 1. Comparison of two prompt styles designed for detecting LLM-generated texts. (a): A feature-enriched prompt that incorporates explicit linguistic cues based on common characteristics of LLM-generated text. (b): A simplified prompt that provides only task instructions and basic decision steps, without additional heuristics.

in more stable and consistent performance on the validation set. Considering both accuracy and generalization, we ultimately adopted the simplified template shown in Fig. 1(b) as the core instruction design for the detection task.

3.2 Model Fine-Tuning with LoRA

To tailor the Qwen2.5-72B-Instruct model to the LLM-generated text detection task, we adopted a parameter-efficient fine-tuning strategy based on Low-Rank Adaptation (LoRA). Specifically, trainable LoRA modules were inserted into the attention subcomponents (q_proj, k_proj, v_proj, and o_proj), while the remaining parameters of the base model were kept frozen to preserve its general language capabilities. We set the LoRA rank to 8 and the scaling factor α to 16, using the AdamW optimizer with a learning rate of 1e-4 and applied cosine learning rate decay over 10 epochs. Training was conducted under the DeepSpeed ZeRO-3 framework with bf16 precision across 8*A100 GPUs. This approach effectively enhanced the model's performance on the detection task while maintaining architectural efficiency.

3.3 Ensemble Learning with Majority Voting

To improve robustness on the test set, we implemented a majority voting ensemble strategy. We selected the top three fine-tuned models based on their performance on the validation set. For each test instance, predictions were obtained from all three models, and the final label was determined by majority vote.

4 Experiments

4.1 Dataset Overview

To address the challenge of detecting text generated by LLMs, the NLPCC 2025 Task 1 introduced the DetectRL-ZH dataset. As a Chinese extension of the original English DetectRL dataset [29], DetectRL-ZH is designed to emulate real-world generation scenarios. It features diverse content types, including paraphrased texts, adversarial examples, and data mixture samples, offering a more comprehensive reflection of complex, practical applications.

The training set comprises data generated by three LLMs (GPT-4o, GLM-4-flash, and Qwen-turbo) across three domains (ASAP, CNewSum, and CSL) [5,10,14,18,26,32]. Within each domain, the ratio of LLM-generated to human-written texts is 3:1, yielding a total of 32,400 samples. The test set consists of 11,000 samples drawn from Storal, a creative writing domain generated using Deepseek-V3 [20]. This distribution is intentionally out-of-domain in terms of both topic and LLMs source, and is designed to rigorously evaluate the generalization ability of detection models.

4.2 Evaluation Metrics

The primary evaluation metric for the competition is the Macro F1 Score, which assesses the overall performance of models in distinguishing between LLM-generated and human-authored text. The test phase encompasses three distinct evaluation scenarios: (a) Normal, Standard generation detection; (b) Attacks, Robustness against adversarial examples (including hybrid, paraphrase, and perturbation attacks); (c) Varying Lengths, Detection performance across different text lengths. The final score is computed as the average F1 score across these three scenarios.

Table 1. Macro-F1 scores on the validation set for various base models and fine-tuning approaches

Model	Fine-tuning	Prompt	Dataset	Macro-F1
Qwen2.5-32B-Instruct	w/o	a	Dev	0.3259
Qwen2.5-32B-Instruct	w/o	b	Dev	0.4257
Qwen2.5-72B-Instruct	w/o	a	Dev	0.4262
Qwen2.5-72B-Instruct	w/o	b	Dev	0.4727
GECScore	w/o	/	Dev	0.8440
Qwen2.5-72B-Instruct + LoRA	w	a	Dev	0.9955
Qwen2.5-72B-Instruct + LoRA	w	b	Dev	**0.9993**

4.3   Base Model Experiments

Exploring with GECScore: To further explore the detection of syntactic and grammatical irregularities in LLM-generated text, we implemented GECScore [30] as an unsupervised baseline method for comparison. Originally designed for detecting LLM-generated content, GECScore evaluates the linguistic "abnormality" of a text by calculating probabilistic scores derived from a grammatical error correction model. Specifically, the method works by passing the input text through a GEC model, which generates corrections for potential grammatical errors. The difference between the original and corrected text is then used to assess the likelihood that the text was LLM-generated. In our implementation, we optimized the decision threshold using the validation set and applied the best threshold to the test set for performance evaluation. By using GECScore, we aimed to assess the effectiveness of leveraging syntactic inconsistencies as a feature for distinguishing between human and LLM-generated text.

Experiments Result: Table 1 presents the Macro-F1 scores of various models and approaches on the validation set. Among the untrained models, Qwen2.5-72B-Instruct achieved a baseline Macro-F1 score of 0.4727, outperforming its smaller counterparts—Qwen2.5-32B-Instruct—which underscores the importance of model capacity in detection tasks.

Remarkably, the unsupervised GECScore method yielded a strong score of 0.8440 without any model training, demonstrating its robustness and effectiveness as a zero-shot LLM-generated text detector.

Prompt design also significantly impacted performance. For both Qwen2.5-32B-Instruct and Qwen2.5-72B-Instruct models, prompt variant b consistently outperformed variant a, highlighting the importance of well-engineered prompts even in zero-shot settings. Specifically, Qwen2.5-32B-Instruct's score improved from 0.3259 to 0.4257, while Qwen2.5-72B-Instruct saw an increase from 0.4262 to 0.4727 when switching from prompt a to b.

The most significant performance gain was observed after applying LoRA-based fine-tuning on Qwen2.5-72B-Instruct, reaching a Macro-F1 score of 0.9993. This result validates the efficacy of parameter-efficient fine-tuning in enhancing detection performance and further motivates our use of this model as the foundation for ensemble inference.

Table 2. Test set performance (Macro-F1) across three evaluation scenarios

Method	Normal	Attacks	Varying Lengths	Avg. F1
GECScore	0.9198	0.3142	0.8153	0.6831
Majority Voting	**0.9997**	**0.9823**	**0.9175**	**0.9665**

4.4   Test Set Experiments

For final submission, we selected the top three performing models from the validation phase and applied a majority voting strategy to combine their predictions on the test set. This ensemble approach significantly improved stability and robustness across diverse test scenarios. As shown in Table 2, our submission achieved outstanding results in all evaluation categories, with an average Macro-F1 score of 0.9665, demonstrating strong generalization and resilience to distribution shifts and adversarial perturbations.

Furthermore, after the release of ground truth labels, we evaluated GECScore on the test set. By tuning its threshold on the validation set and applying it to the test predictions, we found that GECScore performed reasonably well in the Normal and Varying Lengths scenarios (0.9198 and 0.8153 respectively), but struggled in the Attacks scenario (0.3142). This indicates a limitation in its robustness against adversarial examples.

5   Conclusion

In this paper, we presented a method for detecting LLM-generated Chinese text in the NLPCC 2025 Task 1. By fine-tuning the Qwen2.5-72B-Instruct model with Low-Rank Adaptation, we achieved strong performance on the detection task. Our experiments compared various models and methods, revealing that GECScore, as a semantic-aware unsupervised baseline, performs well in zero-shot settings but lacks robustness in complex scenarios.

Through ensemble learning using majority voting on the top-performing models, we significantly improved robustness and generalization across different test scenarios. In the final evaluation, our method achieved an average Macro-F1 score of 0.9665, securing second place in the competition, validating the effectiveness of our approach. Future work will focus on refining detection mechanisms and exploring cross-lingual capabilities to improve adaptability to diverse types of generated text.

References

1. Achiam, J., et al.: GPT-4 technical report. arXiv preprint arXiv:2303.08774 (2023)
2. Aich, A., Bhattacharya, S., Parde, N.: Demystifying neural fake news via linguistic feature-based interpretation. In: Proceedings of the 29th International Conference on Computational Linguistics, pp. 6586–6599 (2022)
3. Arase, Y., Zhou, M.: Machine translation detection from monolingual web-text. In: Proceedings of the 51st Annual Meeting of the Association for Computational Linguistics (Volume 1: Long Papers), pp. 1597–1607 (2013)
4. Bhattacharjee, A., Liu, H.: Fighting fire with fire: can chatgpt detect AI-generated text? arXiv preprint arXiv:2308.01284 (2023)
5. Bu, J., et al.: Asap: a Chinese review dataset towards aspect category sentiment analysis and rating prediction. In: Proceedings of the 2021 Conference of the North American Chapter of the Association for Computational Linguistics: Human Language Technologies, pp. 2069–2079 (2021)

6. Chris, S.W.: AI bot chatgpt writes smart essays-should academics worry? Nature (2022)

7. DeepSeek-AI: Deepseek-r1: Incentivizing reasoning capability in LLMs via reinforcement learning (2025). https://arxiv.org/abs/2501.12948

8. Dugan, L., Ippolito, D., Kirubarajan, A., Shi, S., Callison-Burch, C.: Real or fake text?: investigating human ability to detect boundaries between human-written and machine-generated text. In: Proceedings of the AAAI Conference on Artificial Intelligence, vol. 37, pp. 12763–12771 (2023)

9. Fagni, T., Falchi, F., Gambini, M., Martella, A., Tesconi, M.: Tweepfake: about detecting deepfake tweets. PLoS ONE **16**(5), e0251415 (2021)

10. GLM, T., et al.: Chatglm: a family of large language models from GLM-130B TO GLM-4 all tools. arXiv preprint arXiv:2406.12793 (2024)

11. Gu, C., Huang, C., Zheng, X., Chang, K.W., Hsieh, C.J.: Watermarking pre-trained language models with backdooring. arXiv preprint arXiv:2210.07543 (2022)

12. Hamed, A.A., Wu, X.: Improving detection of chatgpt-generated fake science using real publication text: introducing xfakebibs a supervised-learning network algorithm (2023)

13. He, Z., et al.: Telechat technical report. arXiv preprint arXiv:2401.03804 (2024)

14. Hurst, A., et al.: GPT-4o system card. arXiv preprint arXiv:2410.21276 (2024)

15. Ippolito, D., Duckworth, D., Callison-Burch, C., Eck, D.: Automatic detection of generated text is easiest when humans are fooled. In: Proceedings of the 58th Annual Meeting of the Association for Computational Linguistics, pp. 1808–1822 (2020)

16. Kirchenbauer, J., Geiping, J., Wen, Y., Katz, J., Miers, I., Goldstein, T.: A watermark for large language models. In: International Conference on Machine Learning, pp. 17061–17084. PMLR (2023)

17. Li, X., et al.: Tele-FLM technical report. CoRR (2024)

18. Li, Y., et al.: CSL: a large-scale Chinese scientific literature dataset. In: Proceedings of the 29th International Conference on Computational Linguistics, pp. 3917–3923 (2022)

19. Liu, A., Pan, L., Hu, X., Meng, S., Wen, L.: A semantic invariant robust watermark for large language models (2024). arXiv:2310.06356

20. Liu, A., et al.: Deepseek-v3 technical report. arXiv preprint arXiv:2412.19437 (2024)

21. Lu, Y., et al.: Unified structure generation for universal information extraction. In: Proceedings of the 60th Annual Meeting of the Association for Computational Linguistics (Volume 1: Long Papers), pp. 5755–5772 (2022)

22. Pagnoni, A., Graciarena, M., Tsvetkov, Y.: Threat scenarios and best practices to detect neural fake news. In: Proceedings of the 29th International Conference on Computational Linguistics, pp. 1233–1249 (2022)

23. Rodriguez, J.D., Hay, T., Gros, D., Shamsi, Z., Srinivasan, R.: Cross-domain detection of GPT-2-generated technical text. In: Proceedings of the 2022 Conference of the North American Chapter of the Association for Computational Linguistics: Human Language Technologies, pp. 1213–1233 (2022)

24. Shao, J., Li, X.: AI flow at the network edge. IEEE Netw. (2025)

25. Su, J., Zhuo, T., Wang, D., Nakov, P.: Detectllm: leveraging log rank information for zero-shot detection of machine-generated text. In: Findings of the Association for Computational Linguistics: EMNLP 2023, pp. 12395–12412 (2023)

26. Wang, D., Chen, J., Wu, X., Zhou, H., Li, L.: Cnewsum: a large-scale Chinese news summarization dataset with human-annotated adequacy and deducibility level. arXiv preprint arXiv:2110.10874 (2021)

27. Weng, L., et al.: Towards an understanding and explanation for mixed-initiative artificial scientific text detection. arXiv preprint arXiv:2304.05011 (2023)
28. Wu, J., Yang, S., Zhan, R., Yuan, Y., Chao, L.S., Wong, D.F.: A survey on LLM-generated text detection: necessity, methods, and future directions. Comput. Linguist. 1–66 (2025)
29. Wu, J., et al.: Detectrl: benchmarking LLM-generated text detection in real-world scenarios. Adv. Neural. Inf. Process. Syst. **37**, 100369–100401 (2024)
30. Wu, J., et al.: Who wrote this? The key to zero-shot LLM-generated text detection is gecscore. In: Proceedings of the 31st International Conference on Computational Linguistics, pp. 10275–10292 (2025)
31. Wu, K., Pang, L., Shen, H., Cheng, X., Chua, T.S.: Llmdet: a third party large language models generated text detection tool. In: Findings of the Association for Computational Linguistics: EMNLP 2023, pp. 2113–2133 (2023)
32. Yang, A., et al.: Qwen2. 5 technical report. arXiv preprint arXiv:2412.15115 (2024)
33. Yoo, K., Ahn, W., Jang, J., Kwak, N.: Robust multi-bit natural language watermarking through invariant features. In: Proceedings of the 61st Annual Meeting of the Association for Computational Linguistics (Volume 1: Long Papers), pp. 2092–2115 (2023)
34. Yu, X., et al.: GPT paternity test: GPT generated text detection with GPT genetic inheritance. CoRR (2023)

EnsemJudge: Enhancing Reliability in Chinese LLM-Generated Text Detection Through Diverse Model Ensembles

Zhuoshang Wang[1,2], Yubing Ren[1,2(✉)], Guoyu Zhao[1,2], Xiaowei Zhu[1,2], Hao Li[1,2], and Yanan Cao[1,2]

[1] Institute of Information Engineering, Chinese Academy of Sciences, Beijing, China
{wangzhuoshang,renyubing}@iie.ac.cn
[2] School of Cyber Security, University of Chinese Academy of Sciences, Beijing, China

Abstract. Large Language Models (LLMs) are widely applied across various domains due to their powerful text generation capabilities. While LLM-generated texts often resemble human-written ones, their misuse can lead to significant societal risks. Detecting such texts is an essential technique for mitigating LLM misuse, and many detection methods have shown promising results across different datasets. However, real-world scenarios often involve out-of-domain inputs or adversarial samples, which can affect the performance of detection methods to varying degrees. Furthermore, most existing research has focused on English texts, with limited work addressing Chinese text detection. In this study, we propose EnsemJudge, a robust framework for detecting Chinese LLM-generated text by incorporating tailored strategies and ensemble voting mechanisms. We trained and evaluated our system on a carefully constructed Chinese dataset provided by NLPCC2025 Shared Task 1. Our approach outperformed all baseline methods and achieved first place in the task, demonstrating its effectiveness and reliability in Chinese LLM-generated text detection. Our code is available at https://github.com/johnsonwangzs/MGT-Mini.

Keywords: Large language models · Text detection · Ensemble learning

1 Introduction

Large Language Models (LLMs) have become increasingly integrated into daily life due to their impressive natural language generation capabilities. As LLMs continue to evolve and become more accessible, the cost of generating text has significantly decreased, leading to growing concerns over the misuse of LLM-generated content. For instance, students may use LLMs to write academic papers on their behalf, malicious actors might produce and disseminate harmful fake news, and hallucinated content from LLMs could spread misinformation, negatively impacting online communities. These issues pose serious challenges to the responsible development and deployment of LLMs.

© The Author(s), under exclusive license to Springer Nature Singapore Pte Ltd. 2026

X.-L. Mao et al. (Eds.): NLPCC 2025, LNAI 16105, pp. 284–295, 2026.
https://doi.org/10.1007/978-981-95-3352-7_23

As a result, detecting LLM-generated text has become an urgent and essential task. Early approaches were primarily rule-based, relying on the extraction of specific statistical features from the text for classification [1–3]. However, with the advancement of LLMs, LLM-generated text has become increasingly similar to human-written content, rendering such statistical methods progressively less effective. In recent years, training-based methods [4–9]—such as fine-tuning pretrained language models—and training-free approaches [10–14] based on generation probability have emerged. Nevertheless, these methods often suffer from notable limitations: rule-based approaches are labor-intensive and rely heavily on handcrafted rules; training-based methods tend to struggle with generalization to out-of-domain data; and training-free methods are sensitive to factors such as text length, making them less reliable for real-world deployment. Moreover, the majority of existing work has been conducted on English datasets, and the effectiveness of these methods on other languages, such as Chinese, remains underexplored.

In this paper, we propose an ensemble-based framework for LLM-generated text detection, aiming to optimize overall detection performance across diverse scenarios. Specifically, we treat each existing detection method as an independent base model and evaluate their performance differences when handling various types of text. We dynamically assign ensemble strategies to different inputs, each strategy applies differentiated voting weights to the individual models, thereby enabling the system to achieve optimal performance in aggregate. This framework effectively leverages the strengths of different models on different text types, ensuring robust and reliable performance across many real-world conditions.

Based on this framework, we develop a complete LLM-generated text detection system. We participate in the NLPCC2025 Shared Task 1, where we train and fine-tune our models using the official training set. Evaluation results show that our system achieves the highest macro F1 score compared to baseline models on the test set, which includes normal and adversarial texts. It is important to note that the test set differs significantly from the training set in terms of data distribution, and its construction methodology is entirely unknown to participants before the release of evaluation results. As a result, system optimization relies solely on anticipating potential adversarial strategies.

Our main contributions are as follows:

1. We evaluate the performance of several mainstream LLM-generated text detection methods on Chinese text data and assess their robustness against a variety of adversarial scenarios that may arise in real-world applications.
2. We propose an ensemble-based detection framework, EnsemJudge, which effectively integrates the strengths of multiple models by applying tailored strategies and ensemble voting rules to different types of text.
3. Based on this framework, we implement an extensible LLM-generated text detection system which achieves first place on the NLPCC2025 Shared Task 1, demonstrating its strong performance and reliability.

2   Related Work

Detecting LLM-generated texts has attracted increasing attention due to its critical role in enhancing transparency and preventing misuse. Existing detection methods primarily include training-based methods and training-free methods.

Training-based methods typically utilize supervised classifiers to differentiate human-written from LLM-generated texts, such as early RoBERTa classifiers [4]. Recent advancements like RADAR [5], DeTeCtive [6], DPIC [7], and Biscope [8] leverage adversarial training, contrastive learning, prompt reconstruction, and statistical features, respectively. However, these methods face significant limitations, particularly poor generalization to out-of-distribution (OOD) scenarios due to feature overfitting [15], prompting a shift toward training-free solutions.

Training-free methods exploit statistical and probabilistic text characteristics, bypassing model training. Techniques such as LogRank [1], Likelihood [2], and Entropy [3] analyze uncertainty metrics. DetectGPT [10] introduced contrastive perturbation paradigms, later enhanced by methods like Fast-DetectGPT [12] for improved efficiency, Binoculars [13] using cross-model perplexity, and Lastde++ [14] via Diversity Entropy. Despite advancements, computational efficiency and real-time detection remain key challenges.

3   Method

In this section, we present EnsemJudge, an ensemble-based framework for LLM-generated text detection. We begin by outlining the motivation for adopting an ensemble approach, followed by a detailed description of the framework.

3.1   Observation and Motivation

Although numerous LLM-generated text detection methods have been proposed in recent years [16], most of them are designed and evaluated on English datasets, with limited evidence of their effectiveness on Chinese text. Therefore, we first extract features or train models based on the training set and evaluate the performance of various detection methods on the development set.[1]

Data Augmentation. Based on existing data, we construct adversarial examples targeting potential evasion strategies, in order to simulate challenges that may arise in real-world LLM-generated text detection scenarios. We design two main types of adversarial methods. The first is back-translation, where an encoder-decoder model is used to translate the text generated by a LLM from the source language to a target language and then back to the source language.

---

[1] According to the guidelines of NLPCC2025 Shared Task 1, all data involved in the task are in Chinese, and participants are restricted to using only the officially provided training and development sets for system development; the use of external data is not permitted [17].

Prior studies have shown that detection accuracy drops significantly under paraphrasing attacks; thus, we use this method to simulate such attacks. The second method is text excerpting. We observe that many commercial detection tools reject inputs shorter than a minimum threshold, indicating that short-text detection remains a critical challenge.

Detection Method Evaluation. Given that our task targets LLM-generated text detection in practical application settings, we select a set of representative detection approaches for evaluation. Details of their implementation can be found in Sect. 4.1.

Rule-Based Methods. Rule-based methods are primarily used to detect common character patterns in text. In LLM-generated text, certain special tokens (e.g., \n\n) and frequently used phrases are more likely to appear. In contrast, human-written text tends to contain more clauses separated by commas and may exhibit more informal writing patterns, such as repeated punctuation marks. Although these approaches are mostly "ad-hoc", they can be highly effective when relevant patterns are present, often playing a decisive role in detection.

Training-Free Methods. We adopt three training-free detection methods, including two state-of-the-art approaches—Binoculars [13] and Fast-DetectGPT [12]—as well as a self-designed method named CommonToken. For Fast-DetectGPT, we experiment with different backbone models and both the normal and analytical modes. CommonToken operates by computing token frequency statistics from the positive and negative subsets of the training data. Given an input text, it simply compares the number of tokens originating from each subset and makes a prediction accordingly

Training-Based Methods. We employ three types of training-based methods. Following the work of Guo et al. [18], we fine-tune Chinese versions of RoBERTa and BERT [19] as classifiers. To evaluate the inherent capability of LLMs in detecting LLM-generated text, we also perform instruction tuning using LoRA on several Chinese LLMs. Additionally, building on the previously mentioned rule-based and training-free methods, we construct a hybrid feature model by concatenating the output representations from RoBERTa with the feature outputs of other detection methods. We then train a classification head on top of these combined features. We believe this integration helps leverage the strengths of both types of approaches.

Observation and Intuition. Based on the evaluation results, we make several key observations. It is worth noting that the test set released by the task organizers is more comprehensive than the evaluation set we construct from the training data in the early stage of the competition. Furthermore, we observe that the performance of various methods remains highly consistent across our self-constructed evaluation set and the final test set. Due to space limitations, we present only the key observations here; for detailed results and analysis, please refer to Sect. 4.2.

1. Several methods that perform well on English datasets exhibit noticeable performance degradation on Chinese datasets.
2. The effectiveness of each method varies across different types of text; individual methods tend to specialize in handling specific categories of content.
3. Detection methods show differing biases or tendencies when making binary decisions (i.e., classifying text as LLM-generated or human-written).
4. Methods of the same category tend to exhibit similar performance patterns; however, their actual effectiveness heavily depends on implementation details.
5. Certain adversarial strategies, such as back-translation or excerpting short text segments, can easily degrade the effectiveness of many detection methods.

Based on the above observations, we arrive at the following intuition: although an individual detection method may perform well on certain types of data, it is unlikely to maintain strong performance across all scenarios. Given the diversity of text encountered in real-world applications, the most effective way to ensure overall reliability of the detection system is to construct an ensemble model that integrates multiple methods through carefully designed decision strategies to leverage their respective strengths.

3.2 EnsemJudge: A Reliable Detection Framework

We begin by defining the notion of reliability in LLM-generated text detection, followed by a detailed introduction to the EnsemJudge framework.

Reliability in LLM-Generated Text Detection. Given a detection system S and a set of texts $\mathcal{D}$ generated by LLMs. The goal of S is to correctly predict whether a given text $t \in \mathcal{D}$ is human-written or LLM-generated. However, in real-world scenarios, the texts that S must detect are often not directly generated by the models but may have undergone adversarial modifications. We denote the set of all possible adversarial transformations as $\mathcal{F}$, and the detection target becomes the transformed set of texts $\mathcal{D}'$, where $\mathcal{D}' = \{f(t) \mid t \in \mathcal{D}, f \in \mathcal{F}\}$.

We define the reliability of a detection system S for a text set $\mathcal{D}$ and a set of adversarial transformations $\mathcal{F}$ as the expected performance of S over all adversarially modified texts. Formally, let $\mathrm{Acc}(S, t)$ be an indicator function that returns 1 if S correctly classifies t, and 0 otherwise. Then, the reliability $\mathrm{Rel}(S, \mathcal{D}, \mathcal{F})$ is defined as:

$$\mathrm{Rel}(S, \mathcal{D}, \mathcal{F}) = \mathbb{E}_{t \in \mathcal{D}, f \in \mathcal{F}}[\mathrm{Acc}(S, f(t))] \tag{1}$$

In practice, since enumerating all $f \in \mathcal{F}$ is infeasible, we approximate this expectation using a representative subset $\mathcal{F}' \subset \mathcal{F}$, such as selected text paraphrasing and excerpting attacks.

The EnsemJudge Framework. We propose EnsemJudge, a reliable ensemble framework for LLM-generated text detection tailored to real-world scenarios. By dynamically assigning integration strategies to different texts and assigning differentiated voting weights to each detection method under each strategy, the framework aims to optimize overall system performance. EnsemJudge effectively leverages the strengths of various detection methods across different text types, thereby ensuring reliability in diverse settings. The overall architecture is illustrated in Fig. 1.

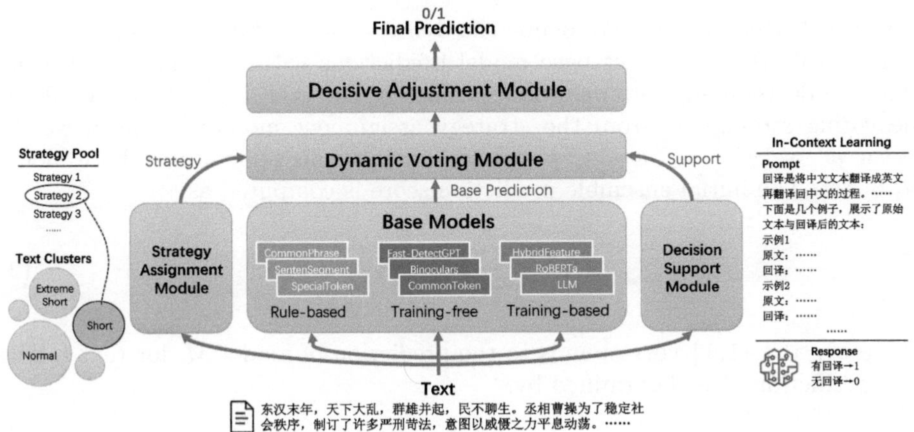

Fig. 1. The EnsemJudge Detection Framework.

Base Models. We begin by selecting a set of existing LLM-generated text detection methods $\mathcal{M}$. Each method $M_i \in \mathcal{M}$, regardless of its complexity, is treated as an independent base detection model, from which we obtain predictions across the entire dataset. The framework adopts a modular design, allowing the integration of any detection method in principle, as long as its prediction output $y_M = M(\cdot)$ is binary (i.e., 0 or 1).

Strategy Assignment Module. The strategy assignment module begins by analyzing the features of each input text $t \in \mathcal{D}$. Based on these features, it selects a subset of base models $\mathcal{M}^t = \{M_1^t, \cdots, M_n^t\}$ from the full set $\mathcal{M}$, and assigns predefined voting weights to the models within $\mathcal{M}^t$. Models not included in $\mathcal{M}^t$ do not contribute to the final decision.

The mapping from textual features to model subsets is determined in advance using a clustering-based approach. Specifically, we extract a set of lightweight features (e.g., text length, perplexity, etc.) for each text in the training set and perform clustering over these feature representations. For each resulting cluster, we evaluate the performance of all base models in $\mathcal{M}$, select an appropriate subset of models, and assign their voting weights to maximize detection performance— measured by metrics such as F1 score—on that cluster. The resulting voting configuration defines a strategy $r^t \in \mathcal{R}$, where $\mathcal{R}$ is the set of all learned strategies.

Decision Support Module. The decision support module is designed to handle samples that are difficult for the ensemble model to classify confidently. These samples typically yield voting scores near the decision threshold, resulting in higher uncertainty. This module relies on heuristic techniques to assist the ensemble decision-making process. For example, we incorporate large language models using in-context learning (ICL). Specifically, when the ensemble model exhibits uncertainty, we employ few-shot prompting to query the LLM and obtain a response d^t, which is then used to support or refine the prediction.

Dynamic Voting Module. We define the dynamic voting function as a weighted decision rule that combines base model predictions with optional adjustments from the decision support module. Specifically, for each input text $t \in \mathcal{D}$, let the voting strategy r^t from the strategy assignment module define a weight vector $\boldsymbol{w}^t = \{w^t_{M_1}, \ldots, w^t_{M_n}\}$, where each weight corresponds to a base model $M_i \in \mathcal{M}^t$. The initial ensemble prediction score is computed as:

$$s^t = \sum_{i=1}^{n} w^t_{M_i} \cdot v^t_{M_i} \tag{2}$$

where $v^t_{M_i} \in \{-1, 1\}$ corresponds to the prediction of model M_i for text t. The final prediction y^t is determined by:

$$y^t = \begin{cases} 1, & \text{if } s^t + \lambda \cdot d^t \geq \tau \\ 0, & \text{otherwise} \end{cases} \tag{3}$$

Here, $d^t \in [-1, 1]$ is the support signal from the decision support module, λ is a tunable parameter controlling the influence of the support module, and τ is the decision threshold.

Decisive Adjustment Module. The decisive module serves to make final adjustments to the voting results. In certain cases, LLM-generated or human-written texts exhibit highly distinctive features that can directly support classification. For example, double newline characters are typically only found in LLM-generated texts. However, this module also carries certain risks, as adversarial strategies can be designed to inject such representative features, potentially leading to misclassification. In our experiments, we observed that when the preceding ensemble voting component is sufficiently well-designed, this module can be safely omitted.

4   Experiments

In this section, we evaluate EnsemJudge for Chinese LLM-generated text detection based on the resources provided by NLPCC2025 Shared Task 1 [17]. We first present the details of the dataset, evaluation metrics, and system implementation, followed by a report of the evaluation results.

4.1   Experimental Settings

Datasets. The dataset used in this study is officially provided by the task organizers. It is divided into training, development, and test sets. Table 1 gives a summary of dataset statistics. The training set comes from a Chinese benchmark dataset named DetectRL-ZH [20], which is designed for detecting Chinese text produced by LLMs. The test set contains entirely out-of-domain data in terms of both content domain and LLM source. The evaluation covers three scenarios: normal, attack, and varying lengths. More details refer to the official documentation provided by the task organizers [17].

Table 1. Details of the dataset provided by NLPCC2025 Shared Task 1.

Split	Label Counts			Data Type		
	LLM	Human	Total	Normal	Attack	Varying Length
train	24300	8100	32400	✓	✕	✕
dev	1700	1100	2800	✓	✕	✕
test	5500	5500	11000	✓	✓	✓

System Implementation Details. We adopt the same base detection models as described in Sect. 3.1. Specifically, we employ four **rule-based methods**: SpecialToken, CommonPhrase, SentenceSegment, and ConsecutivePunctuation. For **training-free methods**, we used Binoculars [13], Fast-DetectGPT [12], and CommonToken. Binoculars is implemented with the Qwen2.5-7B [21] series as its backbone, while Fast-DetectGPT is tested with both the Qwen2.5-7B and GLM-4-9B [22] series. The tokenizer for CommonToken is based on GLM-4-9B. We also calculate classification thresholds for Binoculars and Fast-DetectGPT under different text lengths using the training set. For **training-based methods**, we fine-tune Chinese BERT and RoBERTa [19] models tailored to varying text lengths, as well as their corresponding hybrid-feature variants. In addition, we employe LoRA [23] fine-tuning via LlamaFactory [24], applying instruction tuning to Qwen2.5-7B-Instruct and GLM-4-9B-Chat, with Qwen2.5-7B-Instruct further adapted into several length-specific variants. The models trained on texts containing 110 to 150 words are referred to as the "short text" model, while the models trained on texts containing 55 to 75 words are referred to as the "extreme short text" model. For the **decision support module**, we employ Qwen2.5-72B-Instruct to identify back-translated samples via ICL. The few-shot demonstration examples are constructed by applying Chinese → English → Chinese back-translation to five samples from the training set, using the mbart-large-50-many-to-many-mmt model [25]. The hyperparameters used in our system can be found in Table 2. Due to space limitations, more details can be found in the code repository.

Metrics. According to the official setup of NLPCC2025 Shared Task 1 [17], we adopt macro F1-score as our primary evaluation metric. The reliability of each model is reflected by its macro F1 score on the entire test set, which includes a variety of adversarial samples to simulate real-world scenarios.

Table 2. The hyper-parameters used in our system. The order of the weights w corresponds to the order of the base models listed in Table 3.

text type	w_1	w_2	w_3	w_4	w_5	w_6	w_7	w_8	w_9	w_{10}	w_{11}	w_{12}	w_{13}	w_{14}	w_{15}	w_{16}	w_{17}	w_{18}	λ	τ
ext. short	0	10	0	10	10	60	60	55	60	0	0	0	0	0	95	400	10	0	250	0
short	0	10	0	10	40	40	40	35	40	0	0	0	0	40	95	400	40	0	150	0
medium	0	10	0	10	40	40	40	35	40	0	0	0	0	100	80	90	40	0	0	0
general	0	10	10	10	40	70	70	70	75	50	60	0	85	400	40	60	80	0	0	0

4.2 Evaluation Results

We evaluate the LLM-generated text detection system implemented based on the EnsemJudge framework on the official test set. Table 3 reports the macro F1 scores of the overall system as well as each base model across different test set partitions. Specifically, "Mixed", "Paraphrase" and "Perturbation" denote three types of adversarial attacks, while "64", "128", "256" and "512" indicate four different text lengths. Labels such as "5001-6000" represent the ID ranges of the corresponding subsets within the test set.

Table 3. Main results on test set.

Model Name	All	Normal	Attack			Varying Length (Short Text)			
			Mixed	Paraphrase	Perturbation	64	128	256	512
	1–11000	1–4000	4001–5000	5001–6000	6001–7000	7001–8000	8001–9000	9001–10000	10001–11000
SpecialToken	0.3334	0.3333	0.3338	0.3333	0.3333	0.3333	0.3333	0.3333	0.3333
ConsecutivePunctuation	0.3377	0.3367	0.3395	0.3400	0.3400	0.3333	0.3356	0.3400	0.3400
CommonPhrase	0.5299	0.5926	0.5122	0.6306	0.5325	0.3813	0.4020	0.4324	0.4681
SentenceSegment	0.5899	0.5919	0.6225	0.6361	0.6387	0.4864	0.5373	0.5627	0.6243
CommonToken(GLM-4-9B)	0.7327	0.7173	0.5958	0.8757	0.7584	0.6876	0.7065	0.7612	0.7744
Fast-DetectGPT(Qwen2.5-7B/Qwen2.5-7B-Instruct)	0.8298	0.9387	0.6400	0.7139	0.4355	0.8289	0.8419	0.8748	0.9230
Fast-DetectGPT-analytical(Qwen2.5-7B-Instruct)	0.8146	0.9775	0.4442	0.3808	0.3367	0.8036	0.8680	0.9160	0.9600
Fast-DetectGPT-analytical(GLM-4-9B-Chat)	0.8140	0.9414	0.6948	0.5924	0.5485	0.7212	0.8120	0.8455	0.9079
Binoculars(Qwen2.5-7B-Instruct/Qwen2.5-7B)	0.8317	0.9890	0.4828	0.3777	0.3444	0.8360	0.8880	0.9350	0.9800
ChineseBERT	0.7719	0.8592	0.5567	0.8561	0.8197	0.4624	0.5687	0.7636	0.8713
ChineseRoBERTa	0.7701	0.8426	0.5141	0.7041	0.8476	0.5566	0.6858	0.7773	0.9177
ChineseRoBERTa(Extreme Short Text)	0.8377	0.8694	0.5091	0.8583	0.8645	0.7751	0.8286	0.9057	0.9250
GLM-4-9B-Chat-LoRA	0.8907	0.9895	0.7984	0.9529	0.9920	0.3400	0.6127	0.9428	0.9970
Qwen2.5-7B-Instruct-LoRA	0.9409	**1.0000**	0.9970	0.9589	**0.9990**	0.4544	0.8444	0.9890	**1.0000**
Qwen2.5-7B-Instruct-LoRA(Extreme Short Text)	0.9057	0.9431	0.6562	0.7641	0.8827	0.9227	0.9479	0.9850	0.9910
Qwen2.5-7B-Instruct-LoRA(Short Text)	0.9572	0.9605	0.9064	0.9359	0.9610	0.9470	0.9700	0.9790	0.9870
HybridFeatureRoBERTa	0.8555	0.9214	0.5434	0.8545	0.9020	0.7232	0.8269	0.8901	0.9309
HybridFeatureRoBERTa(Extreme Short Text)	0.8204	0.8401	0.4673	0.7974	0.8274	0.8081	0.8510	0.9160	0.9148
EnsemJudge	**0.9922**	**1.0000**	**0.9970**	**0.9870**	**0.9990**	**0.9590**	**0.9780**	**0.9940**	**1.0000**

Overall Performance. Our system achieves the best performance on the overall test set as well as across all individual subsets. On non-adversarial samples, it reaches a perfect macro F1 score of 1.000, indicating completely correct predictions. Even on the full test set, the system achieves a macro F1 of 0.9922, with improvements up to 9.0% on certain individual subsets, demonstrating strong reliability. As illustrated in Fig. 2, different categories of detection methods exhibited substantial performance differences. Rule-based methods are largely ineffective, with macro F1 scores not exceeding 0.6. Training-free methods perform moderately better, with scores around 0.8. Training-based methods show the best results, reaching up to 0.95. Furthermore, for methods of the same type, we observe similar patterns when confronted with various adversarial

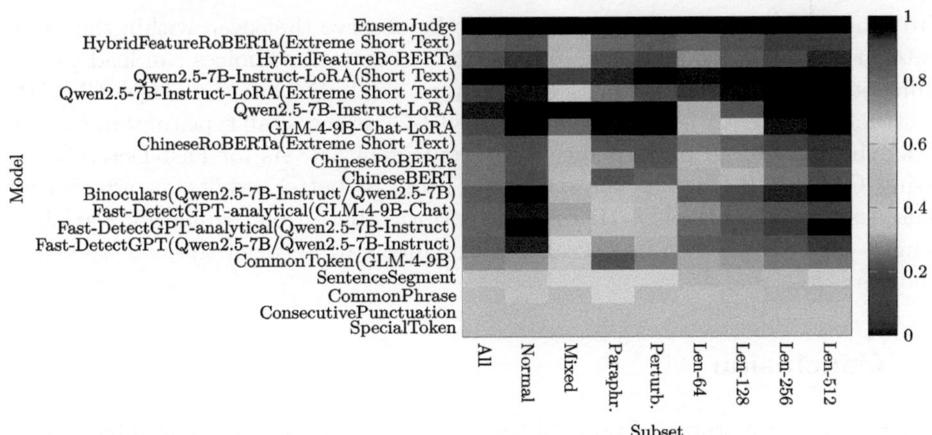

Fig. 2. Model performance (macro F1-score) for our system and different base models.

attacks. Their differences in performance primarily stem from specific implementation details.

Impact of Adversarial Attacks. We observe that different adversarial strategies have varying impacts on the models. Overall, the most effective adversarial method is mixing human-written and LLM-generated texts, while the most robust approach is fine-tuning LLMs. Notably, the fine-tuned Qwen2.5 model is barely affected by mixing or perturbation attacks with performance degradation under 1%, and shows less than a 5% drop under paraphrasing attacks. We speculate that this robustness may stem from Qwen2.5's superior pretraining mechanism, which grants it heightened sensitivity to global textual coherence and deep semantic structure, making it resistant to localized "camouflage." In contrast, these three types of attacks severely cripple training-free methods—e.g., Binoculars suffered over a 50% drop in performance. Interestingly, our proposed CommonToken outperforms all other non-training-based approaches under paraphrasing and perturbation attacks, achieving gains of 16% and 12% respectively, and ranking just behind fine-tuned LLMs.

Impact of Text Length. We find that text length has a significant impact on the performance of all detection methods. As the length increases, the F1 score generally improves. However, this performance gain became marginal when the length exceeds approximately 500 characters. For example, in the best-performing base model—the fine-tuned Qwen2.5—the performance improves by 39.0%, 14.5%, and 1.1% with increasing length. Our experiments show that building specialized models for short texts can effectively mitigate the negative effects of limited input length. For instance, setting length-aware decision thresholds for training-free methods or training models specifically on short-text data for training-based methods are both beneficial strategies. On extreme-short text subsets, the short-text variants of RoBERTa, Qwen2.5, and our hybrid feature model outperform their regular counterparts by 21.9%, 46.8%, and 8.5%, respectively.

Impact of Model Implementations. We observe that even within the same category of detection methods, different implementation choices can lead to significant performance differences. For instance, the LoRA fine-tuned Qwen2.5-7B-Instruct consistently outperforms GLM-4-9B-Chat across all types of input texts, achieving an overall performance improvement of 5%. As for Fast-DetectGPT, using GLM-4-9B-Chat as the backbone leads to better results on adversarial samples, whereas Qwen2.5-7B-Instruct performs better on regular and variable-length texts. However, the overall performance gap between the two backbone choices is less than 0.1%.

5   Conclusion

In this paper, we propose EnsemJudge, a reliable and extensible ensemble framework for LLM-generated text detection in real-world scenarios. By dynamically assigning voting strategies based on lightweight textual features and integrating a decision support module, EnsemJudge effectively leverages the strengths of diverse detection methods while mitigating their weaknesses. Our system is rigorously evaluated on the NLPCC2025 Shared Task 1 dataset, which includes both in-distribution and challenging out-of-distribution adversarial samples. The experimental results demonstrate that EnsemJudge achieves state-of-the-art performance, showing strong generalization and robustness across various text types and attack settings. This work highlights the importance of adaptive ensemble approaches for reliable LLM-generated text detection, especially in low-resource languages such as Chinese, and provides a practical foundation for future research and deployment in real-world applications.

Acknowledgments. This work is supported by the National Natural Science Foundation of China (No. U2336202).

References

1. Gehrmann, S., Strobelt, H., Rush, A.M.: Gltr: statistical detection and visualization of generated text. In: Proceedings of the 57th Annual Meeting of the Association for Computational Linguistics: System Demonstrations, pp. 111–116 (2019)
2. Hashimoto, T.B., Zhang, H., Liang, P.: Unifying human and statistical evaluation for natural language generation. In: Proceedings of the 2019 Conference of the North American Chapter of the Association for Computational Linguistics: Human Language Technologies, Volume 1 (Long and Short Papers), pp. 1689–1701 (2019)
3. Ippolito, D., Duckworth, D., Eck, D.: Automatic detection of generated text is easiest when humans are fooled. In: Proceedings of the 58th Annual Meeting of the Association for Computational Linguistics, pp. 1808–1822 (2020)
4. Solaiman, I., Brundage, M., Clark, J., et al.: Release strategies and the social impacts of language models. arXiv preprint arXiv:1908.09203 (2019)
5. Hu, X., Chen, P.Y., Ho, T.Y.: Radar: robust AI-text detection via adversarial learning. Adv. Neural. Inf. Process. Syst. **36**, 15077–15095 (2023)

6. Guo, X., He, Y., Zhang, S., et al.: Detective: detecting AI-generated text via multi-level contrastive learning. Adv. Neural. Inf. Process. Syst. **37**, 88320–88347 (2024)
7. Yu, X., Qi, Y., Chen, K., et al.: DPIC: decoupling prompt and intrinsic characteristics for LLM generated text detection. Adv. Neural. Inf. Process. Syst. **37**, 16194–16212 (2024)
8. Guo, H., Cheng, S., Jin, X., et al.: Biscope: AI-generated text detection by checking memorization of preceding tokens. Adv. Neural. Inf. Process. Syst. **37**, 104065–104090 (2024)
9. Song, Y., Yuan, Z., Zhang, S., et al.: Deep kernel relative test for machine-generated text detection. In: The Thirteenth International Conference on Learning Representations (2025)
10. Mitchell, E., Lee, Y., Khazatsky, A., et al.: Detectgpt: zero-shot machine-generated text detection using probability curvature. In: International Conference on Machine Learning, pp. 24950–24962. PMLR (2023)
11. Yang, X., Cheng, W., Wu, Y., et al.: DNA-GPT: divergent n-gram analysis for training-free detection of GPT-generated text. In: The Twelfth International Conference on Learning Representations (2024)
12. Bao, G., Zhao, Y., Teng, Z., et al.: Fast-detectGPT: efficient zero-shot detection of machine-generated text via conditional probability curvature. In: The Twelfth International Conference on Learning Representations (2024)
13. Hans, A., Schwarzschild, A., Cherepanova, V., et al.: Spotting LLMs with binoculars: zero-shot detection of machine-generated text. In: International Conference on Machine Learning, pp. 17519–17537. PMLR (2024)
14. Xu, Y., Wang, Y., Bi, Y., et al.: Training-free LLM-generated text detection by mining token probability sequences. arXiv preprint arXiv:2410.06072 (2024)
15. Chakraborty, S., Bedi, A.S., Zhu, S., et al.: On the possibilities of AI-generated text detection. arXiv preprint arXiv:2304.04736 (2023)
16. Wu, J., Yang, S., Zhan, R., et al.: A survey on LLM-generated text detection: necessity, methods, and future directions. Comput. Linguist. 1–66 (2025)
17. NLP2CT: NLPCC-2025 task 1 (2025). https://github.com/NLP2CT/NLPCC-2025-Task1. Accessed 08 May 2025
18. Guo, B., Zhang, X., Wang, Z., et al.: How close is chatgpt to human experts? Comparison corpus, evaluation, and detection. arXiv preprint arXiv:2301.07597 (2023)
19. Cui, Y., Che, W., Liu, T., et al.: Revisiting pre-trained models for Chinese natural language processing. In: Findings of the Association for Computational Linguistics: EMNLP 2020, pp. 657–668 (2020)
20. Wu, J., et al.: Detectrl: benchmarking LLM-generated text detection in real-world scenarios. Adv. Neural. Inf. Process. Syst. **37**, 100369–100401 (2024)
21. Qwen Team: Qwen2.5: A party of foundation models (2024). https://qwenlm.github.io/blog/qwen2.5/
22. Team GLM: Chatglm: a family of large language models from GLM-130B to GLM-4 all tools (2024)
23. Hu, E.J., Shen, Y., Wallis, P., et al.: Lora: low-rank adaptation of large language models. ICLR **1**(2), 3 (2022)
24. Zheng, Y., Zhang, R., Zhang, J., et al.: Llamafactory: unified efficient fine-tuning of 100+ language models. In: Proceedings of the 62nd Annual Meeting of the Association for Computational Linguistics, pp. 400–410 (2024)
25. Tang, Y., Tran, C., Li, X., et al.: Multilingual translation with extensible multilingual pretraining and finetuning. arXiv e-prints pp. arXiv–2008 (2020)

LOW-COST-AI-DETECTOR: An Efficient and Cost-Effective LLM-Generated Chinese Text Detection Model for NLPCC2025 Shared-Task 1

Yu Wang(✉) [ORCID], Zhirui Chen, Xinyan Yu, and Shaohui Yang

The Hong Kong Polytechnic University, Hong Kong 999077, China
janet-yu.wang@connect.polyu.hk

Abstract. Detecting texts generated by Large Language Models (LLMs) remains highly dependent on the availability of comprehensive training datasets. In response to NLPCC 2025 Shared Task 1, this paper introduces a low-cost yet effective detection system that combines traditional machine learning techniques with GECScore-based grammar correction. Our method demonstrates strong performance across both unseen domains and attacked data, all without the need for data augmentation, achieving an average F1 score of 94.94%. Key features used in our approach include entropy, perplexity, Chinese-English code-switching, special character usage, clause length, repetition, sentiment polarity, and grammar correction. Among the models evaluated, Random Forest emerged as the top performer. The proposed solution is both cost-efficient and resilient, offering reliable detection of LLM-generated content.

Keywords: AI detection · LLM-generated text · Machine learning

1 Introduction

In recent years, the rapid advancement of Large Language Models (LLMs) has significantly enhanced the quality and fluency of text generation [32]. Generative AI systems have found widespread applications across domains such as literary content creation [27], education [18], and news [19]. However, the misuse of AI-generated text has raised serious concerns, including the spread of misinformation [4], challenges to academic integrity [7], and disputes over copyright attribution [16]. According to recent research [13], there has been a significant surge in AI-generated news articles on mainstream websites, with a 55.4% increase between January 1, 2022, and May 1, 2023. Moreover, a staggering 45.7% rise in misinformation websites has been observed during the same period, highlighting a growing concern about the spread of false information. Against this backdrop, the development of AI-generated text detection technologies has emerged as a critical safeguard for the governance of digital content [32].

© The Author(s), under exclusive license to Springer Nature Singapore Pte Ltd. 2026
X.-L. Mao et al. (Eds.): NLPCC 2025, LNAI 16105, pp. 296–303, 2026.
https://doi.org/10.1007/978-981-95-3352-7_24

1.1   Challenges and Related Research

Detection of text generated by LLMs has become an increasingly critical challenge. Current studies have identified two key bottlenecks: limited cross-domain generalization [17] and insufficient robustness to adversarial attacks [32]. Many studies have proposed using probabilistic features—such as log-rank [24], entropy [34], and perplexity [30]—to capture statistical characteristics and differentiate between LLM-generated and human-written content [11,26]. However, their performance degrades significantly when applied to datasets with substantial domain discrepancies [8]. To address this, recent research has explored zero-shot detection methods based on LLMs [35], but these approaches often exhibit instability under adversarial editing. For instance, simple paraphrasing or synonym substitution can allow LLM-generated text to evade detection [25], making the task substantially more challenging. Meanwhile, the unique linguistic traits of Chinese—such as the absence of explicit word boundaries—further complicate the detection of character-level perturbations. Additionally, Chinese grammatical structures are frequently over-standardized by LLMs, yet current detection methods lack targeted solutions for these issues [31].

1.2   Task Description

The objective of this task is to develop robust automatic detectors capable of distinguishing between Chinese texts generated by LLMs and those written by humans. The task involves three datasets: training, validation, and test sets. A key limitation is that the validation data must not be used for model training, and no external data sources may be incorporated. The training data contains a total of 32,400 samples, consisting of three types of LLMs and three domains: online comments, news, and academic paper abstracts. The generators include GPT-4o [1], GLM-4-flash [12], and Qwen-turbo [28]. The validation dataset includes 2,800 samples and introduces a new domain: stories, while still covering the same three LLMs. The test data consists entirely of story texts that do not appear in the training set, and the LLMs used to generate them are unknown. This setup simulates a scenario where the detector encounters completely unseen data, presenting a significant challenge for accurate detection. Additionally, the test set includes attacked samples to assess the detector's robustness under complex conditions. These attacks fall into three categories:

- **Mixed Attacks**: Human-written content (less than 50%) is embedded within LLM-generated text at the paragraph or document level to confuse the detector.
- **Paraphrase Attacks**: Simulate non-native writing by translating LLM-generated text into English and back into Chinese using machine translation.
- **Perturbation Attacks**: Replace fewer than 5% of characters with visually similar ones to mimic human typos or introduce noise, aiming to evade detection.

Furthermore, to evaluate the detector's performance across various text lengths, a dataset comprising 2,000 non-adversarial LLM-human text pairs was constructed, with 500 pairs each at lengths of 64, 128, 256, and 512 characters.

1.3   Task Challenges

From the dataset, we identify two main challenges:

- **Generalization Across Domains:** Due to the restriction on using external data for model training and the fact that the test data contains entirely unseen content, it is essential to discover generalizable features that can effectively distinguish LLM-generated text from human-written text across different domains.
- **Robustness Against Attacks:** Given the presence of various attacks in the test set, it is necessary to develop a detector that performs reliably and robustly under such conditions. In this context, we argue that simple attack-based data augmentation is not sufficient. First, data augmentation often requires significant resources, including human effort, time, and computational power. Second, the diversity and unpredictability of attack types mean that when a new kind of attack emerges, existing augmentation strategies may no longer be effective. Therefore, a more generalizable and resilient detection approach is essential to handle a wide range of adversarial scenarios.

To address the challenges outlined above, we propose a detection method that combines machine learning models with GECScore [33]—a grammar correction scoring tool—to integrate both parameterized and non-parameterized knowledge. Our approach is designed to be robust across different domains and attack types without relying on data augmentation, making it both cost-effective and efficient.

2   Proposed Method

Based on previous research and our repeated experiments, we have identified the following valid features that can differentiate LLM-generated text from human text, as detailed in Table 1.

Among these 12 features, there are three categories. The first group, comprising features 1–5, consists of text-based features that capture stylistic differences between human-written and LLM-generated text. These features reflect observable patterns in writing behavior. For instance, humans often repeat words or phrases—such as "I, I mean, you know what I mean "—as they pause to think or self-correct during composition. In contrast, LLMs rarely produce such disfluencies. These features are relatively straightforward to extract using simple Python scripts.

The second group, features 6–11, includes statistical cues such as perplexity, log-likelihood, and entropy. Since LLMs generate text based on probabilistic models, their outputs tend to exhibit higher overall likelihoods compared to

Table 1. Features for differentiating LLM-generated and human Text.

Feature	Description
1. Chinese-English Mixed	Mixed-language content within a sentence or document
2. Special Functions Usage	Use of special characters, symbols, or formatting
3. Length of Clauses	Distribution of clause or sentence lengths
4. Repeated Texts	Repeated phrases or sentences
5. Sentiment Polarity	Emotional tone of the text
6. Perplexity	Language model perplexity score [30]
7. Log Likelihood	Log likelihood score [24]
8. Entropy	Entropy score [29]
9. Log-Rank	Log-rank score [24]
10. Log-Rank Ratio	Log-rank ratio score [26]
11. Norm Log-Rank Score	Normalized log-rank perturbation, robust extension [26]
12. GECScore	Grammar correctness score [33]

human-written text, which may include inconsistencies, hesitations, or errors. These statistical features are generally more robust, as they do not depend on specific content or domain. To compute them, we apply a sliding window approach and extract summary statistics such as the mean and standard deviation to represent the distribution of values across the text. The model we use to get statistics is BERT [9].

The third group consists of feature 12—GECScore (Grammar Error Correction Score)—which quantifies the grammatical correctness of a given text. As noted by Wu et al. [33], from the perspective of LLMs, human-written texts typically contain more grammatical errors than LLM-generated texts. This observation aligns with intuition and has been shown to generalize well across domains, demonstrating strong robustness against domain shifts. To compute this metric, we adopt a zero-shot approach using GPT-4o-mini [20], leveraging its grammar correction capabilities without requiring additional training or fine-tuning.

We integrate the numerical values of all 12 features into a single NumPy array as the input for model training. Each sample is represented by a 60-dimensional feature vector, capturing statistical summaries (e.g., mean, standard deviation) for features. Apart from extracting repeated text and computing the 12 features to construct a 60-dimensional feature vector, we do not perform any additional data preprocessing or data augmentation. Our approach relies solely on the original training data provided by the task organizers, ensuring a fair comparison under the shared task constraints.

To improve the generality of our detector, we use machine learning models and GECScore for detection. By effectively combining the parameterized knowledge of models with non-parameterized external knowledge bases, we enhance our detection capabilities. The structure is shown in Fig. 1. Within this combined framework, GECScore demonstrates strong adaptability across different domains, while the feature-based machine learning model exhibits high robustness against various types of attacks.

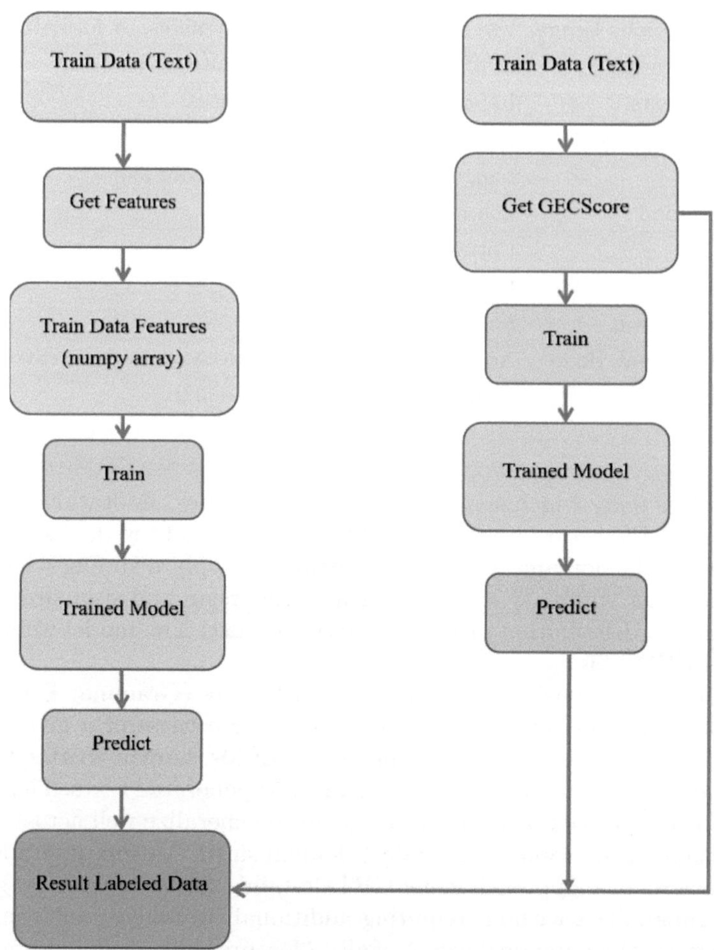

Fig. 1. Structure of the detector.

3   Experiment Results

Before conducting the main experiment, we performed a preliminary study to select the most suitable model. The training data consisted of CLS (academic writing) samples from the training dataset, while the development set served as the test data. We evaluated a range of models, including BERT [9], T5 [22], RoBERTa [15], Logistic Regression [14], Support Vector Classifier

(SVC) [6], Naive Bayes [23], K-Nearest Neighbors (kNN) [2], Decision Tree [21], Gradient Boosting [10], XGBoost [5], and Random Forest [3]. All models were trained using features extracted from the text data. Among these, Random Forest achieved the best performance and was therefore selected for making predictions on the test dataset. During validation, we observed that our system achieved an F1 score of up to 99.90% when processing text from similar domains. For test data, from Table 2, we can observe that our system demonstrates strong performance on this challenging task. Despite not employing data augmentation techniques, we ranked 3rd among 22 participating systems. Our model achieved consistently competitive results across normal data, adversarial attacks, and varying input lengths. Notably, all hyperparameter settings and configurations were kept at their default values.

Table 2. Performance comparison of different systems for test data.

System Name (ID)	Normal Data	Attacks Data	Varying Lens	Avg. F1 Score
LLM-Generated-System	1.0000	0.9943	0.9770	0.9904
TeleAI	0.9997	0.9823	0.8894	0.9571
Our System	**0.9662**	**0.9100**	**0.9720**	**0.9494**
AI Text Trackers	0.9730	0.9217	0.9389	0.9445
BlueSpace	0.9865	0.9533	0.8899	0.9432
MCI^2_LLMGTD	0.9900	0.8429	0.9110	0.9146
ZZU-NLP	0.9982	0.8389	0.8588	0.8987
DS	0.9484	0.7572	0.8727	0.8594
GenAuditor	0.9440	0.8673	0.7658	0.8590
Sprinting	0.8917	0.7930	0.8483	0.8443

3.1 Performance Analysis

One of the primary reasons our system did not achieve the top performance may be the absence of data augmentation. Given the diversity of domains and the variety of attack types—particularly perturbation attacks—our detector faced significant challenges. For instance, metrics like GECScore typically distinguish LLM-generated text from human-written text by identifying fewer grammatical errors in the former. However, when 5% of the characters in LLM-generated text are replaced with visually similar but incorrect characters, the resulting text may appear to have even more grammatical issues than human-written text, misleading the detector.

We believe that incorporating data augmentation strategies could substantially enhance the system's robustness and overall performance. However, to strike a balance between computational cost and performance, and to better simulate real-world deployment scenarios, we have opted to retain the current system.

4   Conclusion

For the LLM-generated text detection task, which involves the challenges of unseen domain texts and three types of adversarial attacks, we designed a detector that integrates machine learning models with GECScore to combine both parameterized and non-parameterized knowledge. Without relying on data augmentation, our system demonstrated strong performance across normal data, adversarial attacks, and varying input lengths, achieving an average F1 score of 94.94%.

This system offers a cost-effective and efficient solution for distinguishing LLM-generated Chinese text from human-written text, showing strong generalization ability when facing unseen texts and diverse data types. When tested on similar-domain data, the performance reached up to 99.90%, highlighting its strong potential for real-world applications. The system provides a practical foundation for regulating AI-generated content.

References

1. Achiam, J., et al.: Gpt-4 technical report. arXiv preprint arXiv:2303.08774 (2023)
2. Altman, N.S.: An introduction to kernel and nearest-neighbor nonparametric regression. Am. Stat. **46**(3), 175–185 (1992)
3. Breiman, L.: Random forests. Mach. Learn. **45**, 5–32 (2001)
4. Buchanan, B., Lohn, A., Musser, M., Sedova, K.: Truth, lies, and automation. Center Secur. Emerg. Technol. **1**(1), 2 (2021)
5. Chen, T., Guestrin, C.: Xgboost: a scalable tree boosting system. In: Proceedings of the 22nd ACM SIGKDD International Conference on Knowledge Discovery and Data Mining, pp. 785–794 (2016)
6. Cortes, C., Vapnik, V.: Support-vector networks. Mach. Learn. **20**(3), 273–297 (1995)
7. Cotton, D.R., Cotton, P.A., Shipway, J.R.: Chatting and cheating: ensuring academic integrity in the era of chatgpt. Innov. Educ. Teach. Int. **61**(2), 228–239 (2024)
8. Crothers, S., et al.: Machine-generated text detection in the wild: a real-world benchmark. arXiv preprint arXiv:2305.01848 (2023)
9. Devlin, J., Chang, M.W., Lee, K., Toutanova, K.: Bert: pre-training of deep bidirectional transformers for language understanding. In: Proceedings of the 2019 conference of the North American chapter of the association for computational linguistics: human language technologies, volume 1 (long and short papers), pp. 4171–4186 (2019)
10. Friedman, J.H.: Greedy function approximation: a gradient boosting machine. Ann. Stat. 1189–1232 (2001)
11. Gehrmann, S., Strobelt, H., Rush, A.M.: GLTR: Statistical detection and visualization of generated text. arXiv preprint arXiv:1906.04043 (2019)
12. GLM, T., et al.: Chatglm: A family of large language models from GLM-130b to GLM-4 all tools. arXiv preprint arXiv:2406.12793 (2024)
13. Hanley, H.W., Durumeric, Z.: Machine-made media: monitoring the mobilization of machine-generated articles on misinformation and mainstream news websites. In: Proceedings of the International AAAI Conference on Web and Social Media,d vol. 18, pp. 542–556 (2024)

14. Hosmer, D.W., Lemeshow, S., Sturdivant, R.X.: Applied Logistic Regression. John Wiley & Sons (2013)
15. Liu, Y., et al.: Roberta: A robustly optimized bert pretraining approach. arXiv preprint arXiv:1907.11692 (2019)
16. Lucchi, N.: Chatgpt: a case study on copyright challenges for generative artificial intelligence systems. Europ. J. Risk Regul. **15**(3), 602–624 (2024)
17. Mitchell, E., Lin, Y., Wu, A.B., Finn, C., Manning, C.D.: Detectgpt: zero-shot machine-generated text detection using probability curvature. In: International Conference on Learning Representations (ICLR) (2023)
18. Mittal, U., Sai, S., Chamola, V., et al.: A comprehensive review on generative AI for education. IEEE Access (2024)
19. Newman, N., Fletcher, R., Robertson, C.T., Ross Arguedas, A., Nielsen, R.K.: Reuters Institute digital news report 2024. Reuters Institute for the study of Journalism (2024)
20. OpenAI: Gpt-4o mini: advancing cost-efficient intelligence (July 2024). https://openai.com/index/gpt-4o-mini-advancing-cost-efficient-intelligence/. Accessed 21 May 2025
21. Quinlan, J.R.: Induction of decision trees. Mach. Learn. **1**(1), 81–106 (1986)
22. Raffel, C., et al.: Exploring the limits of transfer learning with a unified text-to-text transformer. J. Mach. Learn. Res. **21**(140), 1–67 (2020)
23. Rish, I.: An empirical study of the Naive Bayes classifier. In: IJCAI 2001 workshop on empirical methods in artificial intelligence, vol. 3, pp. 41–46 (2001)
24. Solaiman, I., et al.: Release strategies and the social impacts of language models. arXiv preprint arXiv:1908.09203 (2019)
25. Soni, A., Wade, T.: Detecting chatgpt-generated text with human-like errors. In: Proceedings of ACL 2023 (2023)
26. Su, J., Zhuo, T.Y., Wang, D., Nakov, P.: Detectllm: leveraging log rank information for zero-shot detection of machine-generated text. arXiv preprint arXiv:2306.05540 (2023)
27. Tang, X., Duan, X., Cai, Z.G.: Large language models for automated literature review: An evaluation of reference generation, abstract writing, and review composition (2025). https://arxiv.org/abs/2412.13612
28. Team, Q.: Qwen2 technical report. arXiv preprint arXiv:2412.15115 (2024)
29. Thomas Lavergne, T.U., Yvon, F.: Detecting fake content with relative entropy scoring **377** (2008)
30. Vasilatos, C., Alam, M., Rahwan, T., Zaki, Y., Maniatakos, M.: HowkGPT: investigating the Detection of ChatGPT-generated University Student Homework through Context-Aware Perplexity Analysis (Mar 2025). https://doi.org/10.48550/arXiv.2305.18226
31. Wang, R., et al.: Llm-detector: Improving AI-generated Chinese text detection with open-source LLM instruction tuning. arXiv preprint arXiv:2402.01158 (2024)
32. Wu, J., Yang, S., Zhan, R., Yuan, Y., Chao, L.S., Wong, D.F.: A survey on LLM-generated text detection: necessity, methods, and future directions. Comput. Linguist. 1–66 (2025)
33. Wu, J., et al.: Who wrote this? the key to zero-shot LLM-generated text detection is gecscore. arXiv preprint arXiv:2405.04286 (2024)
34. Wu, Z., Xiang, H.: MFD: multi-feature detection of LLM-generated text (2023)
35. Zhu, Y., et al.: Beat LLMs at their own game: Zero-shot LLM-generated text detection via querying chatgpt. In: Proceedings of EMNLP 2023 (2023)

Overview of the NLPCC 2025 Shared Task2: Evaluation of Essay On-Topic Graded Comments(EOTGC)

Haoxiang Dong[1], Xiayu Sun[1], Man Lan[1,2(✉)], Xiaopeng Bai[2,3], and Lixin Ye[3]

[1] School of Computer Science and Technology, East China Normal University, Shanghai, China
{hx_dong,10215102426}@stu.ecnu.edu.cn, mlan@cs.ecnu.edu.cn
[2] Shanghai Institute of AI for Education, East China Normal University, Shanghai, China
xpbai@zhwx.ecnu.edu.cn
[3] Department of Chinese Language and Literature, East China Normal University, Shanghai, China
lxye@cte.ecnu.edu.cn

Abstract. In recent years, the rapid rise of artificial intelligence technologies, particularly large language models(LLMs), has facilitated essay grading. However, current automated essay scoring tasks focus primarily on analyzing textual characteristics such as coherence, grammatical correctness, and clarity of expression to generate scores, while overlooking the critical relevance to essay writing requirements. In this paper, we present an overview of the Evaluation of Essay On-Topic Graded Comments(EOTGC) task in the NLPCC 2025 shared task, which focuses on assessing how well student writings align with writing requirements, maintain coherent central ideas, and use appropriate content. A total of 19 teams participated in this task, among which 9 teams submitted 127 submissions. This shared task sets up two tracks: (1)Relevance Scoring of Essays(RSE); (2)Generation of Relevance Comments(GRC). We detail the task definitions, dataset characteristics, evaluation metrics, and summarize the approaches adopted by participants. This work provides insights and assistance for future research in the field of essay on-topic graded comments.

Keywords: Relevance Scoring of Essays · Generation of Relevance Comments

1 Introduction

Essay writing is a cornerstone of Chinese education in middle and primary schools, serving as a critical indicator of students' language proficiency, logical reasoning, and analytical skills. Among the key dimensions of essay evaluation, *relevance to the topic*—whether the essay adheres to the prompt, conveys a

© The Author(s), under exclusive license to Springer Nature Singapore Pte Ltd. 2026
X.-L. Mao et al. (Eds.): NLPCC 2025, LNAI 16105, pp. 304–313, 2026.
https://doi.org/10.1007/978-981-95-3352-7_25

clear central idea, and uses appropriate content—plays a pivotal role in assessing students' comprehension and thought organization. Accurate relevance evaluation not only helps teachers provide targeted feedback but also supports the development of automated tools to streamline the assessment process [6], a task increasingly important with the integration of natural language processing in educational technology.

Despite advancements in NLP for essay analysis, existing research has primarily focused on global coherence, logical relations, or topic extraction [2,5,9]. Nevertheless, previous studies in this domain, although taking topic into account as an evaluation dimension, have overlooked the significance of topic relevance [4]. Relevance demands a nuanced understanding of how well an essay aligns with the prompt at both the sentence and paragraph levels, ensuring that the central idea is coherent and materials are contextually appropriate. For instance, a *"good"* essay might moderately meet topic requirements, while an *"unqualified"* one could severely deviate, highlighting the need for standardized, multi-level classification criteria. Additionally, generating constructive comments based on relevance analysis—another critical aspect of this task—requires models to synthesize evaluative insights into concise, educationally meaningful feedback, a challenge that bridges NLP and pedagogical expertise.

To address these gaps, the NLPCC 2025 provides the shared task 2 on Evaluation of Essay On-Topic Graded Comments, which is the 2nd task on Topic Graded Comments in NLPCC 2024 as well. The Track 1 Relevance Scoring of Essays (RSE) focuses on the multi-classification of essay relevance into five levels (*"Excellent"*, *"Good"*, *"Average"*, *"Qualified"*, *"Unqualified"*), using a combination of approximate *accuracy* and *Pearson*'s correlation to measure alignment with human judgments. And Track 2 Generation of Relevance Comments (GRC) entails generating grade-appropriate comments that critique the central idea and relevance, evaluated via linguistic quality (*PPLscore, Bertscore*) and human expert reviews.

A unique feature of this task is its dataset, comprising 185 essays from grades 3 to 9, each linked to grade-specific writing prompts. This diversity reflects real-world educational scenarios, challenging participants to handle age-dependent language complexity and topic requirements. By defining clear relevance standards and incorporating both scoring and comment generation, the task aims to foster research on automated essay evaluation that is both technically robust and pedagogically applicable.

A total of 19 teams participated in this task, among which 9 teams submitted 127 submissions. These submissions presented innovative approaches that leverage pre-trained language models, fine-tuning strategies, and generative techniques. Their solutions not only demonstrate state-of-the-art NLP methods but also highlight the challenges of aligning technical models with educational evaluation standards.

This overview paper is structured as follows. Section 2 details the competition tracks and task definitions, including scoring criteria and data formats. Section 3 describes the dataset, including grade distribution and annotation guidelines. Section 4 outlines the evaluation metrics for both scoring and generation tasks. Section 5 summarizes the approaches adopted by participating teams, while Sect. 6 presents the final results and analysis. Finally, Sect. 7 concludes the paper, discussing future directions for the evaluation of relevance-focused essays.

2   Competition Tracks and Task Definitions

The NLPCC 2025 shared task2 on Evaluation of Essay On-Topic Graded Comments is organized into two tracks, each targeting distinct yet complementary aspects of essay relevance assessment in primary and secondary education. The tracks are designed to comprehensively evaluate how well essays adhere to given topics and generate actionable feedback, reflecting the nuanced requirements of school-level writing curricula.

2.1   Relevance Scoring of Essays

Description and Definition. This track focuses on assessing the alignment between student essays and their respective topics, categorizing relevance into five hierarchical levels: *Excellent, Good, Average, Qualified,* and *Unqualified.* The task requires participants to develop models that evaluate how accurately an essay interprets the prompt, maintains a coherent central idea, and utilizes relevant content. Relevance scoring is framed as a multi - class classification problem, where each essay is assigned to one of the five levels based on criteria such as topic comprehension, content relevance, and central idea clarity. The Specific definitions for each relevance level are provided in Table 1.

2.2   Generation of Relevance Comments

Description and Definition. This track involves generating grade-appropriate comments that critique an essay's central idea and relevance to the given topic. The goal is to produce constructive feedback that highlights strengths and weaknesses in topic adherence, assisting teachers in instructional guidance and students in self-assessment. Comments must adhere to three core principles: (1) *Pedagogical Relevance*, aligning with the writing objectives of the corresponding grade (e.g., narrative coherence for lower grades, argument structure for higher grades); (2) *Sensitivity*, avoiding political, discriminatory, or illegal content; and (3) *Conciseness*, with a maximum length of 250 Chinese characters. Participants are required to synthesize insights from the essay's content and topic requirements into concise, actionable remarks that guide improvement while maintaining a supportive tone suitable for educational contexts.

3   Dataset Description

In this section, we discuss the characteristics and distribution of the dataset used in this study. The dataset comprises primary and secondary school essays completed by students in grades 3 to 9 within authentic writing contexts.

Table 1. Definition and Descriptive Specifications for Relevance Levels. Based on the requirements of the Curriculum Standards, the degree of topic adherence and compliance in essays was subdivided into five levels, with descriptive specifications defined for the criteria of each level.

Relevance Level	Description Standards
Excellent (优秀)	The essay perfectly meets the topic requirements, with an extremely appropriate focus and a distinct central idea. The content is meticulously selected to reinforce both the theme and its development.
Good (较好)	The essay fairly adheres to the topic, with a reasonably appropriate focus and a relatively clear central idea. The content is mostly relevant, contributing coherently to the theme.
Average (一般)	The essay generally aligns with the topic, featuring a moderately appropriate focus and a vaguely defined central idea. The content minimally satisfies thematic needs, with acceptable overall coherence.
Qualified (合格)	The essay does not fully deviate from the topic but shows weak focus and an unclear central idea. The content has low thematic relevance, requiring significant improvement in applicability.
Unqualified (不合格)	The essay severely deviates from the topic, with an inappropriate focus and a vague, unidentifiable central idea. The content is entirely irrelevant, demonstrating no connection to the theme.

3.1 Dataset Overview

In this study, 185 unit essays that comply with the requirements of the Chinese Curriculum Standards for Compulsory Education(Year 2022 version) were carefully selected by home-made product. These essays encompass diverse genres such as portrait writing, diary writing, imaginative writing, description of objects, landscape description, and narrative writing, as well as 14 different writing requirements. As shown in Table 2, the dataset consists of 185 essays spanning grades 3 to 9, with two writing requirements specified for each grade.

3.2 Annotation Process

To establish clear and operational evaluation criteria for essay topic adherence, providing teachers and students with an intuitive and quantifiable reference system, and enabling intelligent systems to automatically analyze writing topic adherence levels, this study developed a comprehensive essay topic adherence grading system under the guidance of authoritative experts in pedagogy and

Table 2. Distribution of the Dataset. Classified by grade, the dataset presents the number of topic requirements and essays, along with their distribution across each grade.

Grade(K)	3	4	5	6	7	8	9
Number of essay requirements	2	2	2	2	2	2	2
Number of essays		10	10	10	10	46	37	62

Chinese language literature, as shown in Table 2. The system aims to comprehensively improve the accuracy and effectiveness of essay evaluation.

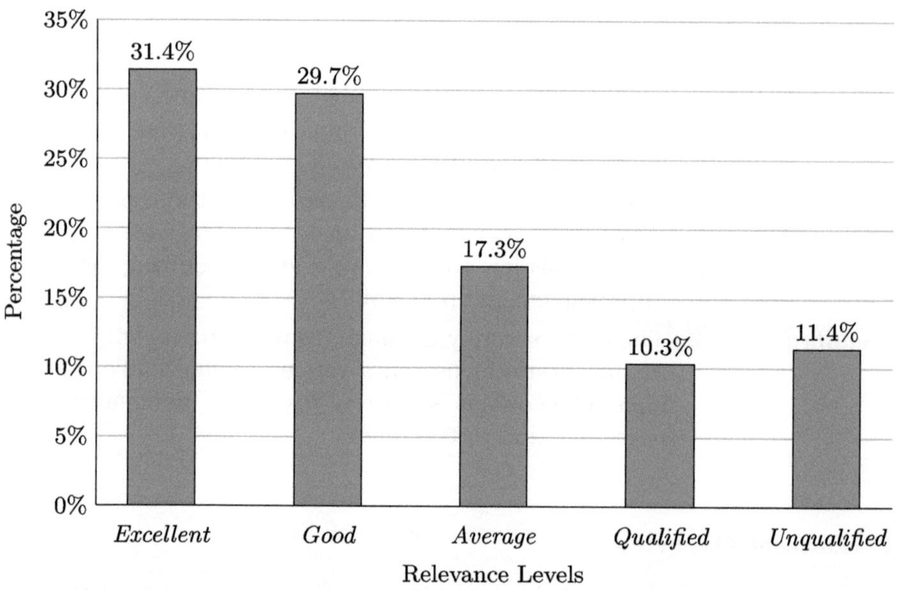

Fig. 1. The distribution of essays across five quality categories.

Manual annotation of the essays followed the content in Table 2, ensuring that the first sentence of each manually annotated comment clearly and accurately indicated the specific level of the essay's topic adherence. To enhance the quality and efficiency of data annotation, a set of comprehensive annotation guidelines was established under the guidance of educational experts and frontline Chinese teachers: (1)Annotators read the essay's "title" and "content" and provided grading comments on the essay's central theme and topic adherence, referring to the "writing requirements" of the "grade-specific" writing training. (2)Comments must not contain information related to politics, race, religious beliefs, ethnicity, violence, discrimination, or other content violating relevant laws and policies. (3)Comments should primarily use encouraging language, fully considering the characteristics of students at each grade level. They should avoid exaggerated praise, identifying both strengths and areas for improvement. (4)Comments should be 50–100 words in length, ideally around 100 words, and not exceed 150 words. (5)The first sentence of the annotation should briefly summarize the overall performance of the central theme and topic adherence, with levels assigned using a 5-point scale. (6)Comments should focus exclusively on the essay's central theme and topic adherence, excluding any other aspects (e.g., language expression, grammatical errors). Subsequently, an annotation team composed of postgraduate students in Chinese language and teacher education majors carefully revised the initially generated comments for each essay based on the established annotation guidelines and topic adherence grading criteria, resulting in a refined dataset containing 185 essays.

3.3   Dataset Distribution

As a case study, we present the distribution of topic relevance classifications in Track 1 data. Figure 1 depicts the percentage distribution of the 185 essays across each topic adherence level. This visualization not only highlights the diversity in topic adherence dimensions among the essays in the dataset but also reflects variations in writing abilities among primary and secondary school students, providing a critical perspective for in-depth analysis of writing instruction.

4   Evaluation Metrics

In this work, we employ distinct evaluation metrics for the two tracks of the EOTGC task, addressing the multi-class classification nature of Track 1 and the text generation requirements of Track 2.

For Track 1, we use three metrics to assess the alignment between essays and the topic. Approximate accuracy(ACC_A) measures the accuracy of the prediction while penalizing the magnitude of the error, which is defined as $ACC_A = \frac{1}{N} \sum_{i=1}^{N} S(d_i)$, where $S(d_i) = 1 - \frac{d_i}{4}$, $d_i = |y_i - \hat{y}_i|$. Here, N is the number of samples, y_i is the true label, $\hat{y}_i$ is the predicted label, and d_i represents the absolute difference between labels. The Pearson correlation coefficient(r) quantifies the linear relationship between the predicted and true labels. The final score normalizes and combines ACC_A and r with equal weight.

For Track 2, we employed Perplexity Score(PPLscore), Bertscore [1] to evaluate the generated topic-relevant comments. PPLscore is used to measure the quality and fluency of the generated text and Bertscore is used to assess semantic similarity between generated comments and reference annotations using BERT-based embeddings. For PPLscore, we employed the Baichuan2-7B-chat model [11] to compute it. In addition, we introduced human scoring. In this component, we recruited two Chinese teachers, established scoring guidelines, and evaluated the comments generated by sampling essays in a 1:10 ratio for each grade level in three dimensions: relevance of the core topic(70%), completeness of evaluation(20%), and expressive logic(10%). The final score is calculated by combining the normalized values of PPLscore, Bertscore, and human score, with weights of 0.1, 0.4, and 0.5, respectively.

5   Participated Systems

A total of 9 teams and 127 submissions have been submitted to this competition. Each team was allowed to submit results 5 times per day for each track, and all test results of the day were made public to facilitate adjustments and modifications to their schemes by the participating teams. Table 3 lists the detailed information of these participants and their final ranks.

Table 3. The detailed information of participated systems.

Rank	System Name	Organization	final score
1	**ZZUNLP_Han**	Zhengzhou University	71.50
2	**TW-NLP**	Beijing SmartDot Technology Co., Ltd	71.48
3	**liberty**	Soochow University	71.15
4	**Prompt**	Central China Normal University	70.25
5	**Fighting!**	Zhengzhou University	70.13
6	**DUFL2025**	Dalian University of Foreign Languages	69.04
7	**zzunlp**	Zhengzhou University	67.34
8	**炼丹师_zzunlp**	Zhengzhou University	66.36
9	**YNU-HPCC**	Yunnan University	62.08

5.1   Track 1. Relevance Scoring of Essays

In this track, multiple teams proposed innovative approaches. **ZZUNLP_Han** adopted a prompt enhancement approach based on chain-of-thought(CoT) [10] and in-context learning. They designed a unified prompt template that integrates step-by-step analytical CoT with few-shot samples to achieve a precise prediction of the five-level scoring criteria. **liberty** proposed a two-dimensional dynamic evaluation model, decomposing topic relevance into "degree of off-topic deviation" and "grade adaptability requirements". Two large language model agents were employed to process different features, with a third LLM agent fusing results for comprehensive scoring. **DUFL2025** developed a hybrid architecture combining an LLM multi-agent collaboration system with a BERT-assisted classification module, introducing a conflict arbitration agent to resolve discrepancies between LLMs and the BERT module [1] and ensure the reliability of classification results. **YNU-HPCC** leveraged synthetic data generation techniques, combining instruction fine-tuning and CoT training on the DeepSeek-R1-Distill-Qwen-7B model [3] to enable the model to generate structured reasoning processes and improve classification accuracy.

5.2   Track 2. Generation of Relevance Comments

For this track, **TW-NLP** adopted an iterative training approach combining Supervised Fine-Tuning(SFT) and Direct Preference Optimization(DPO) [7]. They utilized the provided topic-relevance comments as supervision data for SFT and optimized comment quality via DPO by comparing generated comments. **Prompt** framed the task as a standard conditional text generation problem, guiding the model to produce high-quality comments using few-shot examples. **YNU-HPCC** applied a two-stage strategy of Supervised Fine-Tuning and Gradient-Regularized Policy Optimization(GRPO) [8]. During the GRPO phase, they introduced custom reward signals, including length control and Track 1 results, to optimize comment quality and ensure alignment with relevance evaluation.

6   Results

Comprehensive analysis of the results presented in Table 4 and Table 5 reveals that several methods demonstrated exceptional performance in the competition.

In the Relevance Scoring of Essays, **TW-NLP** trained the QWQ-32B model [12] using the provided topic-relevant comments as thought processes, achieving promising performance. Meanwhile, the prompt enhancement approach based on chain-of-thought and in-context learning adopted by **ZZUNLP_Han**, as well as the two-dimensional dynamic evaluation model proposed by **liberty**, both achieved competitive results in this track, highlighting the effectiveness of chain-of-thought, in-context learning, and multi-evaluation perspectives.

Table 4. Results for Track 1: Relevance Scoring of Essays.

Rank	System Name	Organization	Track 1 Score
1	**TW-NLP**	Beijing SmartDot Technology Co., Ltd	**80.71**
2	**ZZUNLP_Han**	Zhengzhou University	78.22
3	**liberty**	Soochow University	78.13
4	**DUFL2025**	Dalian University of Foreign Languages	77.84
5	**Fighting!**	Zhengzhou University	75.23

When moving towards Generation of Relevance Comments(Track 2), **Prompt** delivered outstanding performance, indicating that guiding the model to generate high-quality comments through explicit prompts and few-shot examples was highly effective for this task. Both **YNU-HUCC** and **ZZUNLP_Han** achieved commendable results in this track, with the former outperforming the latter, demonstrating the feasibility and effectiveness of adopting a two-stage strategy of Supervised Fine-Tuning and GRPO in the Generation of Relevance Comments task.

Table 5. Results for Track 2: Generation of Relevance Comments.

Rank	System Name	Organization	Track 2 Score
1	**Prompt**	Central China Normal University	**68.38**
2	**YNU-HPCC**	Yunnan University	67.10
3	**ZZUNLP_Han**	Zhengzhou University	67.02
4	**Fighting!**	Zhengzhou University	66.73
5	**liberty**	Soochow University	66.50

Overall, the competition results demonstrate that the combination of fine-tuning methods and prompt enhancement approaches has shown significant effectiveness in these tasks. Additionally, innovative approaches such as training with comment content as thought processes, two-dimensional dynamic evaluation models, and two-stage strategies of supervised fine-tuning and GRPO have demonstrated their respective advantages.

7   Conclusions

This paper presents an overview of the Evaluation of Essay On-Topic Graded Comments (EOTGC) shared task at NLPCC 2025. We developed grading criteria for essay topic relevance, annotated a high-quality dataset for essay topic relevance, established an automated evaluation process and human scoring guidelines, and introduced the innovative approaches and results of participating teams. This work not only advances the frontiers of automated essay evaluation in NLP but also serves as a catalyst for integrating computational intelligence with educational assessment, envisioning a future where technology enhances equitable, insightful feedback for global writing instruction.

Acknowledgements. We appreciate the support from the Artificial Intelligence-Powered Research Paradigm Reform and Discipline Leap Plan (2024AI02004) from Shanghai Municipal Education Commission.

References

1. Devlin, J., Chang, M.W., Lee, K., Toutanova, K.: BERT: pre-training of deep bidirectional transformers for language understanding. In: Burstein, J., Doran, C., Solorio, T. (eds.) Proceedings of the 2019 Conference of the North American Chapter of the Association for Computational Linguistics: Human Language Technologies, Volume 1 (Long and Short Papers). pp. 4171–4186. Association for Computational Linguistics, Minneapolis, Minnesota (Jun 2019). https://doi.org/10.18653/v1/N19-1423, https://aclanthology.org/N19-1423/
2. Farag, Y., Yannakoudakis, H., Briscoe, T.: Neural automated essay scoring and coherence modeling for adversarially crafted input. arXiv preprint arXiv:1804.06898 (2018)

3. Guo, D., et al.: Deepseek-r1: Incentivizing reasoning capability in LLMs via reinforcement learning. arXiv preprint arXiv:2501.12948 (2025)

4. He, Y., Jiang, F., Chu, X., Li, P.: Automated Chinese essay scoring from multiple traits. In: Calzolari, N., et al., (eds.) Proceedings of the 29th International Conference on Computational Linguistics. pp. 3007–3016. International Committee on Computational Linguistics, Gyeongju, Republic of Korea (Oct 2022). https://aclanthology.org/2022.coling-1.266/

5. Jiang, Z., et al.: Improving domain generalization for prompt-aware essay scoring via disentangled representation learning. In: Rogers, A., Boyd-Graber, J., Okazaki, N. (eds.) Proceedings of the 61st Annual Meeting of the Association for Computational Linguistics (Volume 1: Long Papers). pp. 12456–12470. Association for Computational Linguistics, Toronto, Canada (Jul 2023). https://doi.org/10.18653/v1/2023.acl-long.696, https://aclanthology.org/2023.acl-long.696/

6. Liu, Y., Han, J., Sboev, A., Makarov, I.: Geef: a neural network model for automatic essay feedback generation by integrating writing skills assessment. Expert Syst. Appl. **245**, 123043 (2024)

7. Rafailov, R., Sharma, A., Mitchell, E., Manning, C.D., Ermon, S., Finn, C.: Direct preference optimization: Your language model is secretly a reward model. In: Thirty-seventh Conference on Neural Information Processing Systems (2023). https://openreview.net/forum?id=HPuSIXJaa9

8. Shao, Z., et al.: Deepseekmath: Pushing the limits of mathematical reasoning in open language models. arXiv preprint arXiv:2402.03300 (2024)

9. Song, W., Song, Z., Liu, L., Fu, R.: Hierarchical multi-task learning for organization evaluation of argumentative student essays. In: Bessiere, C. (ed.) Proceedings of the Twenty-Ninth International Joint Conference on Artificial Intelligence, IJCAI-20, pp. 3875–3881. International Joint Conferences on Artificial Intelligence Organization (7 2020).https://doi.org/10.24963/ijcai.2020/536, https://doi.org/10.24963/ijcai.2020/536, main track

10. Wei, J., et al.: Chain-of-thought prompting elicits reasoning in large language models. Adv. Neural. Inf. Process. Syst. **35**, 24824–24837 (2022)

11. Yang, A., et al.: Baichuan 2: Open large-scale language models. arXiv preprint arXiv:2309.10305 (2023)

12. Zheng, C., et al.: Processbench: Identifying process errors in mathematical reasoning. arXiv preprint arXiv:2412.06559 (2024)

Optimizing Automated Essay On-Topic Graded Comments via LLM-Based Prompt Augmentation

Zhongtian Hua[1], Mengyuan Wang[1], Meijia Yu[2], Yi Luo[1], Kunli Zhang[1], and Yingjie Han[1(✉)]

[1] Zhengzhou University, No.100 Science Avenue, Zhengzhou, China
{hzt1113,wangmengyuan}@gs.zzu.edu.cn, nancetide@stu.zzu.edu.cn,
{ieklzhang,ieyjhan}@zzu.edu.cn
[2] Henan University of Science and Technology, No.263 Kaiyuan Avenue,
Luoyang, China
240320261531@stu.haust.edu.cn

Abstract. Essay writing is a crucial component of middle school Chinese education. The NLPCC 2025 Evaluation of Essay On-Topic Graded Comments (EOTGC) task centers on evaluating primary and secondary school essays. It includes two subtasks: Relevance scoring of essays (Track1) and Generate relevance comments (Track2). This paper proposes a Progressive Augmented-Prompt Fusion framework (PAPF) based on Large Language Models (LLMs), which integrates multiple prompt enhancement techniques including role-playing, task decomposition, Chain-of-Thought, and In-Context Learning into structured prompt templates. The framework progressively guides the model to conduct more accurate essay writing evaluation through a hierarchical, step-by-step approach. Based on this framework, we carefully designed detailed prompt words for Track1 and Track2 respectively according to the actual evaluation requirements, and significantly improved the model's performance without fine-tuning with training data. Our approach achieves the highest overall score across all leaderboards. Extensive comparative and ablation experiments have confirmed the effectiveness and universality of our method.

Keywords: Essay On-Topic Graded Comments · Large Language Model · Prompt Augmentation

1 Introduction

Essay writing constitutes a critical component of junior high school Chinese language education, serving not only as a manifestation of students' linguistic expression capabilities but also as a significant indicator of their logical thinking and comprehension abilities. Topic relevance stands as one of the pivotal dimensions in writing assessment and a crucial reference point for teachers' writing instruction. With the widespread application of Natural Language Processing

© The Author(s), under exclusive license to Springer Nature Singapore Pte Ltd. 2026
X.-L. Mao et al. (Eds.): NLPCC 2025, LNAI 16105, pp. 314–324, 2026.
https://doi.org/10.1007/978-981-95-3352-7_26

(NLP) technologies in educational domains, an increasing number of automated essay analysis tools have been employed to support writing pedagogy and evaluation. Early-stage research primarily focused on identifying central ideas from complete essays, while subsequent studies attempted to analyze textual paragraph structures and logical coherence. [1,2]

The NLPCC2025 Evaluation of Essay On-Topic Graded Comments (EOTGC) task targets primary and secondary school students' compositions through two subtasks: relevance assessment (Track1) and relevance-based comment generation (Track2). [12]Specifically, Track1 employs multi-dimensional scoring criteria including accuracy of topic comprehension, content relevance, and completeness, ultimately selecting the most appropriate rating from five tiers ("Excellent", "Good", "Average", "Qualified", and "Unqualified") as the final evaluation. Track2 requires machines to conduct comprehensive relevance analysis between essays and topics, automatically generating tailored comments to assist teachers in assessment and instructional guidance. This initiative aims to establish unified relevance evaluation standards while providing technical support for automated essay scoring and pedagogical applications.

The rapid advancement of Large Language Models (LLMs) has demonstrated exceptional capabilities in semantic understanding and generation, achieving widespread implementation and superior performance across NLP domains. [3]LLMs based systems enable rapid, objective quantitative scoring against predefined criteria (e.g., grammatical accuracy, lexical diversity, logical coherence) while providing immediate feedback. [6]Therefore, we utilized LLMs as the base models for this evaluation task and constructed a Progressive Augmented-Prompt Fusion framework (PAPF) to guide the models in conducting more accurate essay writing assessments. This framework integrates multiple prompt enhancement methods, including role-playing, task decomposition, Chain-of-Thought, and In-Context Learning. Based on the framework and the specific characteristics of Track1 and Track2, we meticulously designed detailed prompt words for each. Specifically, for Track1, since it is essentially a classification task, we incorporated a few examples into the framework to prompt the model to accurately predict the five-level scores. For Track2, we designed a prompt template for automatic comment generation based on the framework, which emphasizes thematic consistency and employs task decomposition techniques to break down the generation process into several consecutive steps, ensuring compliance with the writing requirements of different score levels and generating standardized and targeted language output. Our method performed outstandingly in the evaluation task, achieving the highest overall score among all participants. The contributions of this work can be summarized as follows:

I. We propose a framework named PAPF that integrates multiple prompt-enhancement techniques to guide LLMs to think step by step, and carefully design prompt templates for each sub-task based on their distinct characteristic quantities.

II. By optimizing prompt templates without fine-tuning, we conserve computational resources while maintaining superior evaluation performance, ranking first among all teams in terms of overall score.

III. Comparative experiments and ablation studies across multiple models validate the effectiveness and universality of our approach.

2   Methodology

An overview of our approach is illustrated in Fig. 1. We designed a unified prompt template PAPF for Track1 and Track2, and carefully crafted prompt words based on the distinct characteristics of Track1 and Track2. In Track1, we additionally incorporated few-shot examples to assist the model in achieving more precise classification. Then, we fed the prompt and the essay to be detected into the LLM together, obtaining two sets of selectable answers. Finally, we extracted the corresponding scores and comments from the two sets of answers and concatenated them to obtain the final answer.

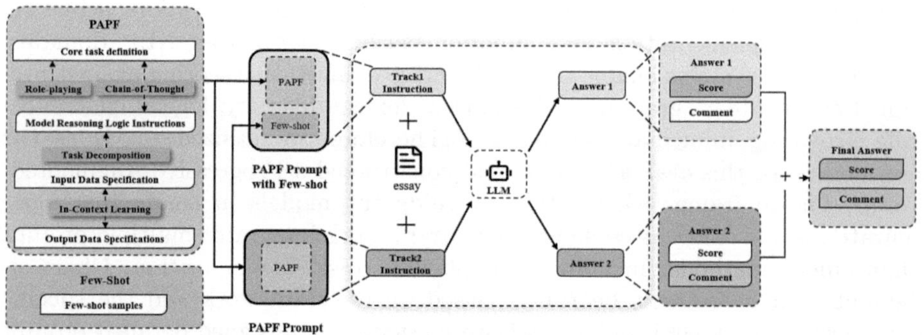

Fig. 1. The overview of our approach. We've designed a framework called PAPF, which integrates multiple prompt - enhancement methods. It's used for Track2's essay comments generation task. For Track1's essay scoring task, we add Few - shot to PAPF. Finally, we extract the required content from the two generated Answers by the LLM and piece it together to get the final Answer.

2.1   LLM

Large Language Models (LLMs) are a type of deep learning - based natural language processing model with a massive number of parameters (typically billions or even hundreds of billions) [7]. They are trained on large - scale text data, enabling them to capture intricate language patterns and semantic information. This endows them with robust language understanding and generation capabilities. LLMs excel in handling a variety of natural language tasks, such as text generation, question answering, machine translation, and summarization, playing a pivotal role in driving the advancement of natural language processing technologies.

In this evaluation task, to examine the impact of model modes (including inference and generative modes), model parameters, and model types on task performance, as well as to validate the effectiveness and universality of our proposed method, we selected Qwen2.5-72B [4], Qwen2.5-Max [4], DeepSeek-R1-671B [5], and QwQ-Max [11] as our foundational models.

2.2   Prompt Engineering

Prompt Engineering is a technique for designing inputs to large language models. By carefully crafting input prompts, it guides the model to respond as desired [8]. It significantly impacts the quality and relevance of model outputs. The design encompasses various aspects, including the format of the prompt (such as in the form of a question or instruction), the provision of contextual information (like background and examples), and the integration of task - specific requirements. Effective prompt engineering can greatly enhance the performance of large language models in specific tasks, better aligning them with real - world application scenarios. We have selected prompt enhancement methods including role-playing, Chain-of-Thought(CoT), task decomposition, and In-Context Learning, and integrated them into our PAPF framework to help LLMS think and complete tasks from the simple to the complex. Through role-playing, LLMS can quickly understand the background of the task. Afterwards, through CoT the and task decomposition, we guide the LLM to think more deeply. Finally, through In-Context Learning, we help the LLM further understand the core of the task and control its output style.

2.3   Progressive Augmented-Prompt Fusion Framework

The PAPF framework architecture (Chinese-English bilingual version) is shown in Fig. 2. We mainly construct it from three dimensions: core task definition, model reasoning logic instructions, and input-output examples.

Core Task Definition: We explicitly delineate the task's input-output specifications and employ role-playing strategies to guide the model in emulating the cognitive patterns and expressive styles of domain-specific evaluators, thereby generating contextually aligned responses. Within this section, we rigorously define the boundaries of Track1's five-tier scoring criteria (e.g., distinguishing nuanced differences between adjacent score brackets) and simultaneously establish Track2's operational constraints, including permissible modification scopes and prohibited evaluation biases. This dual specification mechanism ensures both tasks maintain alignment with pedagogical evaluation principles while preventing scoring criterion drift or recommendation overreach.

Model Reasoning Logic Instructions: Implement phased analysis using chain-of-thought [9] for both subtasks. For Track1, we adopt a hierarchical rating approach that guides the model to progressively assess essay scores based on their thematic relevance. For Track2, the model is instructed to perform comprehensive summarization based on initial predictions, generate targeted evaluations with revision suggestions, and conduct in-depth analytical synthesis.

Input-Output specifications: We provide the model with a limited number of contextual samples as in-context demonstrations [10], serving as reference patterns to ensure output consistency. These exemplars maintain structural alignment between input prompts and desired output formats while preserving task-specific characteristics.

The complete version of the prompt template utilized in this study will be provided in the appendix. For Task 2, we have carefully designed detailed prompt words based on the specific requirements and characteristics of the task within this framework. For Track1, we have additionally introduced several sample essays in the prompt as reference materials. Given that Track1 contains five different essay scoring levels, we have accordingly integrated representative sample data for each scoring level in the prompt. By using a small number of examples, large language models can distinguish the differences between compositions at different scoring levels through comparative analysis, enhancing the model's ability to determine the best scoring level.

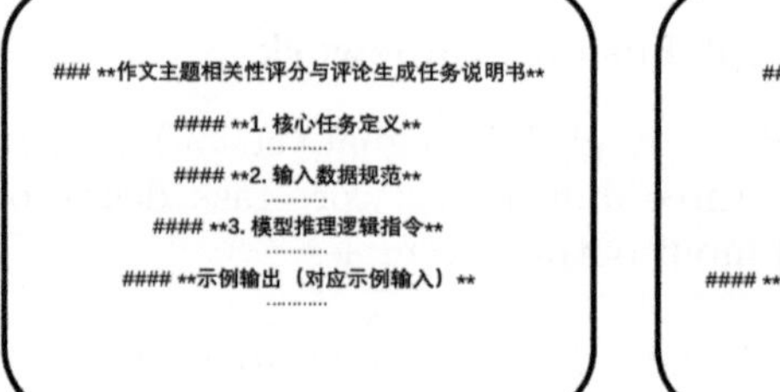

Fig. 2. The architecture of PAPF. PAPF consists of four parts: core task definition, input data specification, model logical reasoning instructions, and example output. Different prompt - enhancement methods are incorporated in each part to ensure more accurate responses from the LLM.

3   Experiments

3.1   Experimental Setup

We compared the four aforementioned large language models using three methods: baseline prompt (only informing the LLM of the task objective withou prompt augmentation),PAPF prompt with less few-shot, and PAPF prompt with more few-shot.

3.2   Dataset and Metrics

In this competition, the dataset and sample set are provided by the organizer. It should be noted that the organizer only provides a test set, without offering a training set or validation set. This means that participants need to employ specific data augmentation methods to construct their own training sets, or compete directly without a training set. This represents a major challenge of the competition. The two sub - tasks of this competition share the same dataset. The description of each data field in the sample set is shown in the table below.

Table 1. Description of Each Field in the Sample set.

Field Name	Description
grade	Grade of student who write the essay.
requirement	Essay topic.
title	Essay title.
content	Essay content.
classification	Rating classification for essay-topic relevance (not present in the test set)
comment	Generated commentary on essay-topic relevance (not present in the test set)

The evaluation corpus comprises 185 student essays spanning grades 3 through 9. Each grade level includes two distinct writing prompts (denoted as "requirement" in data fields). For instance, the annotation "5/5" for third-grade essays indicates 5 essays corresponding to the first writing prompt and 5 to the second, with analogous distributions maintained across other grades, as shown in the table below.

Table 2. Test Set Data Distribution

Grade	3	4	5	6	7	8	9
Number of essay questions	2	2	2	2	2	2	2
Number of essays	5/5	5/5	5/5	5/5	20/26	25/12	32/30

For Track 1, the competition utilizes a composite evaluation metric that integrates both Approximate Accuracy and the Pearson Correlation Coefficient to calculate the final score of model predictions.

Approximate Accuracy. This metric measures the prediction accuracy of the model by considering the magnitude of the error between the predicted results and the true labels. Here, N is the number of samples, $S(d_i) = (1 - d_i/4)$, $d_i = |y_i - \hat{y}_i|$, y_i is the true label, and $\hat{y}_i$ is the predicted result.

$$ACC_A = \frac{1}{n} \sum_{i=1}^{N} S(d_i) \tag{1}$$

Pearson Correlation Coefficient. This metric measures the linear relationship between the predicted results and the true labels. Here, y_i is the true label, $\overline{y}$ is the mean of the true labels, $\hat{y}_i$ is the predicted result, and $\bar{\hat{y}}$ is the mean of the predicted results.

$$r = \frac{\sum (y_i - \overline{y})(\hat{y}_i - \bar{\hat{y}})}{\sqrt{\sum (y_i - \overline{y})^2}\sqrt{\sum (\hat{y}_i - \bar{\hat{y}})^2}} \tag{2}$$

Final Score. The final score for Track 1 is calculated by normalizing the approximate accuracy and Pearson correlation coefficient, weighting each by 0.5, and summing them.

$$Track1\_Score = 0.5 * ACC_A + 0.5 * (\frac{1+r}{2}) \tag{3}$$

For Track 2, the competition employs a composite evaluation framework that integrates PPLscore, BERTScore, and human evaluation to compute the final score for model-generated writing assessments.

PPLscore. PPLscore is used to measure the model's predictive ability for a given text sequence. In the formula, N represents the number of words in the test text, w_i is the i-th word in the sequence, and $P(w_i|w_1, w_2, ...w_{i-1})$ represents the model's predicted probability for the i-th word. For PPLscore, we use the baichuan-7b-chat model for calculation.

$$PPL_{score} = exp(-\frac{1}{N} \sum_{i=1}^{N} logP(w_i|w_1, w_2, ...w_{i-1})) \tag{4}$$

Bertscore. BERTScore is an automated evaluation metric for text generation that leverages contextual embeddings from BERT-based pre-trained models to compute token-level similarity between candidate sentences and reference sentences.

Human. In this evaluation process, experts in primary and secondary school essay writing to manually score a fixed selection of essays from each grade at a 1:10 ratio, with the average score serving as the human score.

Final Score. The final score is calculated by normalizing the PPLscore and weighting it by 0.1, adding the Bertscore weighted by 0.4, and adding the normalized human score weighted by 0.5.

$$Track2\_Score = 0.10 * \frac{\frac{1}{PPL_{score}} - 0.02}{0.18} + 0.40 * Bertscore + 0.5 * \frac{human}{100} \quad (5)$$

3.3 Results and Analysis

The experimental (contrastive and ablation) results are in Table 3.

Table 3. Experimental Results.

Model	base-prompt	PAPF-prompt	more few-shot	Track1_score	Track2_score
Qwen2.5-72B	✓			0.6983	0.6379
		✓		0.7378	**0.6878**
		✓	✓	**0.7822**	0.6593
Qwen2.5-Max	✓			0.6701	0.6184
		✓		0.7294	0.6381
		✓	✓	0.7413	0.6243
QwQ-Max	✓			0.6693	0.5542
		✓		0.7077	0.5940
		✓	✓	0.7325	0.5863
DeepSeek-R1	✓			0.6972	0.5714
		✓		0.7376	0.5916
		✓	✓	0.7732	0.5758

Overall, Qwen2.5-72B got the highest scores in Track1 and Track2. DeepSeek-R1 was the second. The poor performance of the QwQ-Max and Qwen-Max models, which contrasts sharply with the top two, is surprising. Because models with larger parameter sizes are generally expected to perform better due to their more knowledge. From the experimental results. Specifically, we can draw the following conclusions from the experimental results:

Superiority of PAPF. Regardless of the model type, the model using the prompt constructed based on the PAPF framework outperforms the model using the baseline prompt, both in Track1 and Track2. This demonstrates the effectiveness and universality of PAPF, which can be applied to most large language models.

Generative Models' Advantage. By comparing the performance of Qwen2.5-72B with DeepSeek-R1, as well as the performance of Qwen-Max and QwQ-Max, we can find that the performance of the generative model is superior to that of the reasoning models at the same level. This situation is particularly evident in Track2. This indicates that in the field of essay scoring, the evaluation criteria of generative models are closer to those of humans, and the generated essay comments are also closer to the real evaluation style of teachers.

Parameter Scale's Limited Impact. Comparing Qwen2.5-72B and Qwen2.5-Max, parameter scale doesn't affect performance in this domain. This is the case in both Track1 and Track2. Smaller models even outperform larger ones. But this conclusion applies only to models with parameters over 32B, as we didn't test smaller ones because of the lack of time.

Few-shot Samples' Different Effects. Few-shot samples in prompts boost track1 scores by offering more grading references, enabling accurate ratings. However, in track2, they restrict model performance by making outputs resemble the sample style.

To sum up, we finally used PAPF with less few-shot to deal with Track2 and PAPF with more few-shot to deal with Track1. Eventually, we achieved a comprehensive score of 0.7150 and ranked first among all the participants

4   Conclusion

This study adopts LLM as the basic model and proposes a framework PAPF that integrates several prompt enhancement methods to address the challenges in NLPCC2025 EOTGC. By integrating prompt enhancement strategies such as Chain-of-Thought, In-Context Learning, and role-playing into the prompt, we significantly improved the performance of the model in automatic writing evaluation without fine-tuning the model. The results of the ablation experiment show that our PAPF can effectively support essay scoring and comment generation, achieving strong performance with minimal resource consumption. The comparative experiments further show that PAPF can play a role in improving the model performance on different LLMS, verifying its effectiveness and universality. Ultimately, we chose the Qwen2.5-72B model to participate in the competition and won the first place (Fig. 3, Fig. 4, Fig. 5, Fig. 6, Fig. 7 and Tables 1, 2).

A   Appendix

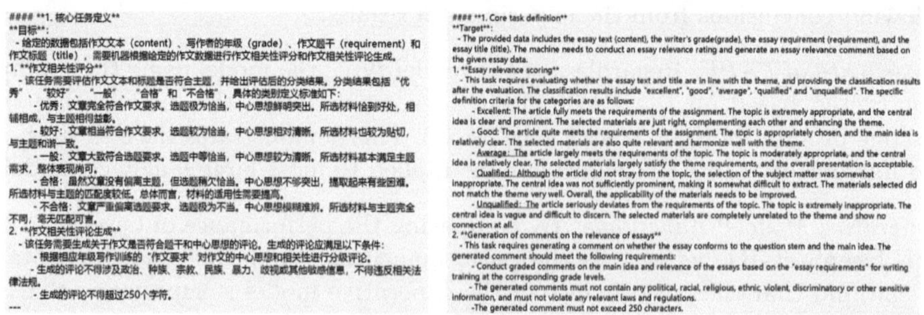

1. 核心任务定义
目标:
 - 给定的数据包括作文文本（content）、写作者的年级（grade）、作文题干（requirement）和作文标题（title），需要机器根据给定的作文数据进行作文相关性评分和作文相关性评论生成。
1. **作文相关性评分**
 - 该任务需要评估作文文本和标题是否符合主题，并给出评估后的分类结果。分类结果包括"优秀"、"较好"、"一般"、"合格"和"不合格"，具体的类别定义标准如下：
  - 优秀：文章完全符合作文要求。选题极为恰当，中心思想鲜明突出。所选材料恰到好处，相辅相成，与主题相得益彰。
  - 较好：文章相当符合作文要求。选题较为恰当，中心思想相对清晰。所选材料也较为贴切，与主题和谐一致。
  - 一般：文章大致符合选题要求。选题中等恰当，中心思想较为清晰。所选材料基本满足主题需求，整体表现尚可。
  - 合格：虽然文章没有偏离主题，但选题稍欠恰当。中心思想不够突出，提取起来有些困难。所选材料与主题的匹配度较低。总体而言，材料的适用性需要提高。
  - 不合格：文章严重偏离选题要求。选题极为不当。中心思想模糊难辨。所选材料与主题完全不同，毫无匹配可言。
2. **作文相关性评论生成**
 - 该任务需要生成关于作文是否符合题干和中心思想的评论。生成的评论应满足以下条件：
  - 根据相应年级写作训练的"作文要求"对作文的中心思想和相关性进行分级评论。
  - 生成的评论不得涉及政治、种族、宗教、民族、暴力、歧视或其他敏感信息，不得违反相关法律法规。
  - 生成的评论不得超过250个字符。
---

1. Core task definition
Target:
 - The provided data includes the essay text (content), the writer's grade(grade), the essay requirement (requirement), and the essay title (title). The machine needs to conduct an essay relevance rating and generate an essay relevance comment based on the given essay data.
1. **Essay relevance scoring**
 - This task requires evaluating whether the essay text and title are in line with the theme, and providing the classification results after the evaluation. The classification results include "excellent", "good", "average", "qualified" and "unqualified". The specific definition criteria for the categories are as follows:
  - Excellent: The article fully meets the requirements of the assignment. The topic is extremely appropriate, and the central idea is clear and prominent. The selected materials are just right, complementing each other and enhancing the theme.
  - Good: The article quite meets the requirements of the assignment. The topic is appropriately chosen, and the main idea is relatively clear. The selected materials are also quite relevant and harmonize well with the theme.
  - Average: The article largely meets the requirements of the topic. The topic is moderately appropriate, and the central idea is relatively clear. The selected materials largely satisfy the theme requirements, and the overall presentation is acceptable.
  - Qualified: Although the article did not stray from the topic, the selection of the subject matter was somewhat inappropriate. The central idea was not sufficiently prominent, making it somewhat difficult to extract. The materials selected did not match the theme very well. Overall, the applicability of the materials needs to be improved.
  - Unqualified: The article seriously deviates from the requirements of the topic. The topic is extremely inappropriate. The central idea is vague and difficult to discern. The selected materials are completely unrelated to the theme and show no connection at all.
2. **Generation of comments on the relevance of essays**
 - This task requires generating a comment on whether the essay conforms to the question stem and the main idea. The generated comment should meet the following requirements:
  - Conduct graded comments on the main idea and relevance of the essays based on the "essay requirements" for writing training at the corresponding grade levels.
  - The generated comments must not contain any political, racial, religious, ethnic, violent, discriminatory or other sensitive information, and must not violate any relevant laws and regulations.
  -The generated comment must not exceed 250 characters.

Fig. 3. This figure shows the "core task definition" part of the prompt template we used.

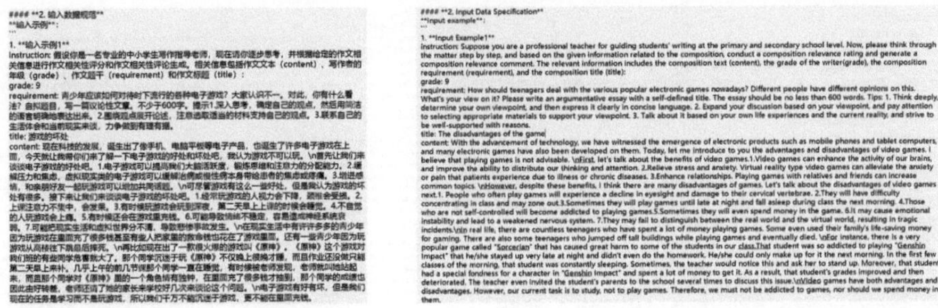

Fig. 4. This figure presents the input section of the "context example" in our prompt template.

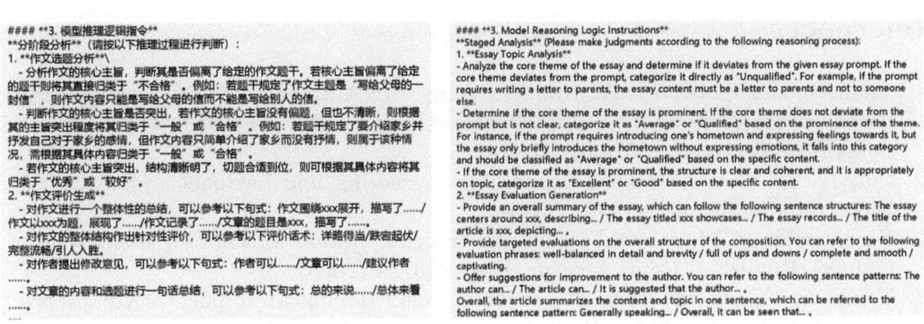

Fig. 5. This figure displays the "model logical reasoning instruction" part of our prompt template.

4. 最终输出格式要求
1. **输出作文相关性评分时只需输出最后的分类结果，不要输出别的东西。
2. **输出作文相关性评论时只需输出最后的评论，不要输出别的东西，并且保证输出的内容满足**核心任务定义**中的评论生成条件。

示例输出（与示例输入一一对应）

1. **输出示例1**
classification:一般
comment:文章以《游戏的坏处》为题，却先写游戏的好处，然后再列举了游戏的坏处，并运用举例论证的方法加深读者印象，突出了游戏的危害。结尾处作者总结了全文，但不够精当，语言也较为随意。建议作者注意文体特征，紧紧围绕中心论点展开写作，选取适当的论据，运用恰当的语言，避免写出四不像的文章。总的来说，本文没有跑题。
2. **输出示例2**
classification:较好
comment:作文围绕作者春日登山的经历展开写作，先介绍了老家山的特点，接着通过移步换景的写作手法描述了作者从山脚到半山腰再到山顶一路的风景见闻，多次运用比喻的修辞手法，感官体验充分。建议作者增加一些自己的感受描写，使文章更富有真情实感。总体来看，作文主题鲜明，切题恰当。

4. Final output format requirements
1. When outputting the relevance score of the composition, only the final classification result should be provided; no other information should be included.
2. When outputting the relevance comment of the composition, only the final comment should be provided; no other information should be included, and it must meet the comment generation conditions specified in the "Core Task Definition".

Output Examples(corresponding one-to-one with input examples)

1. **Output Example1**
classification:Average
comment:The article is titled "The Disadvantages of Games", but it begins by presenting the benefits of games, and then lists the disadvantages. It uses the method of giving examples to deepen the readers' impression and highlights the harm of games. At the end, the author summarizes the entire article, but the summary is not precise and the language is rather casual. It is suggested that the author pay attention to the characteristics of the writing style, focus on the central argument when writing, select appropriate evidence, use appropriate language, and avoid writing something that doesn't make sense. Overall, this article has not strayed from the topic.
2. **Output Example2**
classification:Good
comment:The essay is centered around the author's experience of climbing the mountain in spring. It first introduces the characteristics of the mountain in the hometown. Then, through the writing technique of changing scenes, it describes the author's scenery and experiences from the foot of the mountain to the halfway point and finally to the top. The essay frequently employs the rhetorical device of metaphor, and the sensory experience is fully realized. It is suggested that the author add some descriptions of his own feelings to make the article more full of genuine emotions. Overall, the theme of the essay is clear and appropriate to the topic.

Fig. 6. This figure illustrates the output section of the "context example" in our prompt template.

3. **输出示例3**
classification:合格
comment:作文围绕作者家乡南京展开写作，详细介绍了南京历史背景、人文景观，后半段介绍了作者最喜欢的地方夫子庙老门东，表达了对期间美食的喜爱之情。但是作文体裁是抒情，要求表达出对家乡怀有的情感，文章前面大半篇幅没有一句表达了作者的感情，只是单纯的介绍，后半段也只提到喜爱之情，较为片面，建议作者仔细审题。总体来说，作文偏离题目要求。
4. **输出示例4**
classification:优秀
comment:作文以"作业机问世记"为题，想象了作者发明了可以帮助学生完成各科作业的机器，但是这个机器的发行对全国教育体系造成了不良影响，最后作者决定回收机器并销毁的故事。作文故事情节跌宕起伏，引人入胜，对于作业机功能和科学技术的描述十分详细。总体来看，作文中心明确，科幻感十足，符合作文要求。
5. **输出示例5**
classification:不合格
comment:这篇作文切题和中心不合格。题目的要求是限定给父母写一封书信，但是本文的收信对象却是刘思岩，是作者的好朋友而非父母，因此不符合题目要求，属于跑题。建议作者在行文前仔细审题，确定正确的受话人之后再展开写作，避免跑题。
```

3. **Output Example3**
classification:Qualified
comment:The essay is centered around the author's hometown, Nanjing. It provides a detailed account of Nanjing's historical background and cultural attractions. The latter part introduces the author's favorite place, the Confucius Temple Old Men's District, expressing his love for the local cuisine. However, the essay is of the lyrical genre, and it is required to convey the emotions towards the hometown. The majority of the first part of the essay does not express the author's feelings at all; it is merely a simple description. The latter part only mentions the love, which is rather one-sided. It is suggested that the author carefully review the topic. Overall, the essay deviates from the requirements of the topic.
4. **Output Example4**
classification:Excellent
comment:The composition is titled "The Advent of the Exercise Machine", imagining the story that the author invented a machine that could help students complete their homework in various subjects. However, the release of this machine had a negative impact on the national education system. Eventually, the author decided to recycle and destroy the machine. The plot of the composition is full of ups and downs and fascinating. The description of the functions of the operation machine and science and technology is very detailed. Overall, the composition has a clear central theme and a strong sense of science fiction, meeting the requirements of an essay.
5. **Output Example5**
classification:Unqualified
comment:This essay focuses on the author's hometown Nanjing. However, the essay fails to meet the requirements of the topic and the main idea. The task stated in the question is to write a letter to one's parents, but the recipient in this essay is Liu Siyan, an author's good friend rather than the parents. Therefore, it does not meet the requirements of the question and is considered as straying from the topic. It is suggested that the author carefully review the question before writing and determine the correct recipient before starting the composition to avoid straying from the topic.
```

Fig. 7. This figure shows the "few - shot examples" part of the prompt template specifically designed for Track 1.

References

1. Yuan, S., He, T., Huang, H., Hou, R., Wang, M.: Automated Chinese essay scoring based on deep learning. Comput. Mater. Contin. 65(1), 817–833 (2020). https://doi.org/10.32604/cmc.2020.010471

2. Lin, L., Li, C.: Automated Chinese essay scoring and feedback system (2008). http://hdl.handle.net/11536/43549

3. Xiaohuashi: an LLM-based intelligent tutoring system for Chinese essay writing. Chinese/English J. Educ. Measur. Eval. 4(3), 4 (2023)

4. Yang, A., Yang, B., Hui, B., et al.: Qwen2 Technical Report arXiv preprint arXiv:2407.10671 (2024). https://arxiv.org/abs/2407.10671

5. DeepSeek-AI, D.G., Yang, D., et al.: DeepSeek-R1: incentivizing reasoning capability in LLMs via Reinforcement Learning arXiv preprint arXiv:2501.12948, (2025). https://arxiv.org/abs/2501.12948

6. Zhang, J., et al.: System Report for CCL24-Eval Task 7: multi-Error Modeling and fluency-targeted pre-training for Chinese essay evaluation. arXiv preprint arXiv:2407.08206 (2024). https://arxiv.org/abs/2407.08206

7. Kalyan, K.S.: A Survey of GPT-3 family large language models including ChatGPT and GPT-4. arXiv preprint arXiv:2310.12321 (2023). https://arxiv.org/abs/2310.12321

8. Wang, J., et al.: Review of Large Vision Models and Visual Prompt Engineering. arXiv preprint arXiv:2307.00855 (2023). https://arxiv.org/abs/2307.00855

9. Masikisiki, B., Marivate, V., Hlope, Y.: Investigating the efficacy of large language models in reflective assessment methods through chain of thoughts prompting arXiv preprint arXiv:2310.00272 (2023). https://arxiv.org/abs/2310.00272

10. Chen, Y., Zhang, Y., Yu, J., Yang, L., Xia, R.: In-Context learning for knowledge base question answering for unmanned systems based on large language models. arXiv preprint arXiv:2311.02956 (2023). https://arxiv.org/abs/2311.02956

11. QwQ-32B: Embracing the Power of Reinforcement Learning. Qwen Team, (2025). https://qwenlm.github.io/blog/qwq-32b/ Accessed 6 Mar 2025

12. NLPCC 2025 shared task 2: evaluation of essay on-topic graded comments. CUBENLP (2025). https://github.com/cubenlp/EOTGC-2025NLPCC Accessed 30 Apr 2025

Decomposing Topic Relevance: A Multi-agent LLM Approach for Automated Essay Scoring and Feedback

Xinyue Kang and Fang Kong[(✉)]

Natural Language Processing Lab, Soochow University, Suzhou, China
`20244227013@stu.suda.edu.com`, `kongfang@suda.edu.cn`

Abstract. In Chinese language education, compositions reflect students' language and reasoning skills. Topic relevance assesses cue comprehension and content focus, thereby guiding instructional strategies. Current state-of-the-art Large Language Models (LLMs), including architectures such as GPT-4, tend to perform poorly in assessing topic relevance, often producing erroneous judgements and generating feedback that lacks practical applicability. This study proposes an innovative zero sample Automatic Essay Scoring(AES) framework that innovatively deconstructs the core assessment dimension of 'Topic Relevance' and divides it into 'Degree of Topic Deviation' and 'grade adaptation requirements' as two key subcharacteristics. At the same time, this study proposes a three-step strategy that utilises the capabilities of LLMs to progressively achieve composition content comprehension, multivariate evaluation and feedback generation, thereby compensating for the shortcomings of traditional Automatic Essay Comment Generation(AECG) systems. Ultimately, depending on the score, different levels of comments and suggestions are given. By systematically eliciting the assessment capabilities of the LLM, our approach performs well across multiple automated assessment metrics and manual assessments, demonstrating its great potential for real-world applications.

Keywords: Automated Essay Evaluation · Topic Relevance · Large Language Models · Automatic Essay Comment Generation · Developmental Writing Assessment

1 Introduction

Essay writing is a foundational component of Chinese education, serving as a critical measure of students' language proficiency, logical thinking, and comprehension skills. Among the key evaluation criteria, relevance to the topic is particularly important, as it reflects students' ability to analyze prompts, organize ideas coherently, and maintain focus throughout their writing. For educators, relevance serves as a valuable indicator for designing targeted instructional strategies to enhance students' writing skills. A relevant essay not only adheres strictly to the topic's requirements but also explores its implicit topics, demonstrating depth of understanding and clarity of expression.

© The Author(s), under exclusive license to Springer Nature Singapore Pte Ltd. 2026

X.-L. Mao et al. (Eds.): NLPCC 2025, LNAI 16105, pp. 325–336, 2026.
https://doi.org/10.1007/978-981-95-3352-7_27

In recent years, the integration of natural language processing (NLP) technologies into educational tools has opened new avenues for automated essay analysis. researchers have begun learning models for scoring content-based traits. such as convolutional neural networks (CNNs) [9], long- and short-term memory networks (LSTMs) [8,12]. At the same time, there is a growing interest in specific aspects such as coherence, grammatical accuracy, and clarity of expression. For instance, Hussein et al., [4] modified the overall scoring model by replacing its output layer with multiple specialized layers, each dedicated to evaluating a single trait. However, existing AES systems for Chinese essays often overlook topic relevance and fail to provide detailed feedback.

Meanwhile, AECG faces significant challenges due to the complexity and difficulty of generating detailed, meaningful feedback that addresses relevance, coherence, and depth—particularly in the nuanced context of Chinese writing [14]. research on automatic essay comment generation (AECG) remains limited— some studies employ T5 models or synthesize strengths and weaknesses to generate critiques, yet these methods offer only superficial assistance and do little to enhance the thematic relevance of essays [6,13]. As the development of LLMs has progressed, the results of several empirical studies have shown that LLMs can provide an operational function for the AECG, although the results show a regression effect [10].

Although LLMs have demonstrated excellent performance in several natural language processing tasks, their potential for application in the field of AES and AECG has not been fully explored.

In this paper, we propose an innovative zero-sample scoring framework that significantly improves the performance of LLMs in essay topic relevance evaluation by systematically stimulating their assessment capabilities.The proposed system participated in the NLPCC-2025 Shared Task 2.This shared task consists of two tracks, Our method achieved an Score of 0.7813 in track1, 0.6650 in track2, it ranked third in all track.

The rest of this paper is organized as follows. The related work is introduced in Sect. 2 A detailed description of the Automatic Essay Scoring (AES) and Automatic Essay Comment Generation (AECG) and model is provided in Sect. 3 The experiment and results are discussed in Sect. 4 Finally, Sect. 5 presents the conclusion.

2 Related Work

2.1 Automatic Essay Scoring

Initially, AES aims at evaluating and scoring essays with machine learning (Dikli, 2006) [3]. Early AES systems Focus on feature engineering. Use off-the-shelf machine learning algorithms to train classifiers or regressors for scoring. For example, Lowlevel features include length-based features [11], High-level features include readability features [12], With the advent of the neural NLP era, researchers have begun learning models for scoring content-based traits. such as convolutional neural networks (CNNs), long short-term memory networks

(LSTMs) [8,12], AES has typically predicted the overall or trait ranking or numerical score of an article by analysing a range of textual features such as coherence, grammatical correctness and clarity of expression.[2]These models obtained superior performance compared with traditional methods. LLMs has a great deal of common sense knowledge that can be utilised to perform a variety of tasks. In recent years, an increasing number of essay scoring tasks have been built on LLM. Lee present a zero-shot prompting framework to elicit essay scoring capabilities in LLMs [5],A series of experimental sets conducted on public and private datasets by xu et al. highlights the significant advantages of LLM-based AES systems [5]. These studies explore the potential for utilising the capabilities of modern LLMs in AES tasks.

AES is a promising alternative to teacher assessment that can greatly address inconsistencies in scoring criteria across assessors, but provides little feedback to students to improve their papers. In this study, our goal was not only to predict scores, but also to generate constructive feedback on topic relevance.

2.2 Automatic Essay Comment Generation

AECG targets at generating effective feedback for different students to purposefully revise their essays, thereby improving writing skills. Despite the large number of existing studies on AES, there are few studies focusing on AECGs. Early studies mostly relied on predefined rules and rubric templates to generate feedback by matching grammatical errors or keywords. These methods provide mostly superficial help, but fall short in enhancing the thematic relevance of the article [6,13]. For AEGC to perform well on topics it has not seen before, it needs to draw on external knowledge, and LLMs can help the model acquire this knowledge by providing examples.

However, directly using LLMs to comment on essays, the feedback provided by these models is often too general to help students target and improve their essays [10]. The importance of breaking down the task of generating feedback in the AECG domain into steps and presenting intermediate results has been studied [7]. This study bridges the gap in feedback generation by utilising the capabilities of the LLMs for step-by-step synthetic content comprehension, multifaceted assessment and feedback generation.

3 Methodology

3.1 Task Definition

NLPCC2025 Evaluation of Essay On-Topic Graded Comments Competition primary and secondary school students' essays, with an emphasis on relevance evaluation and the generation of comments based on relevance analysis. The model utilizes the provided metadata (including grade, requirement, title, and content) to generate relevance evaluation and the generation of comments based on relevance analysis. The goal is to create a model that can generate comments that meet this requirement. In the final stage, relevance evaluation and comments based on relevance analysis are generated based on the test dataset, and the text generated by the model is submitted for evaluation.

3.2 Motivation

Specifically, Topic Relevance has long been used as a core indicator in composition assessment, but its underlying structure is ambiguous. Conventional studies usually treat it as a single dimension and fail to distinguish between: Topic Drift: Whether the author sticks to the topic or not. Developmental Appropriateness: differences in the depth of subject matter required in different school years. This generalised assessment led to two types of misjudgements: false negatives: primary schools students' associative writing was misjudged as "off-topic"; and false positives: high school students' over-embellishment masking thematic ambiguity was not detected.

In recent years, large models have excelled in text generation and comprehension tasks, offering new possibilities for automated feedback generation. Based on this, this study first proposed a two-dimensional dynamic assessment model using LLMs, which innovatively deconstructed the core assessment dimension of topic relevance, and divided it into two key subcharacteristics: (1) the degree of topic departure: to quantify the extent to which the content of the essay deviates from the given topic, and to assess whether the writer consistently focuses on the core topic;(2) Grade-level adaptability requirements: Dynamically adjust the scale of topicrelevance to the writing standards of different grades (e.g., primary schools, middle school, and high school), reflecting the concept of developmental evaluation. Rubrics should differentiate expectations. For lower-grade students, assessment should focus on evaluating their observational skills and emotional expressiveness in writing. For upper-grade students, evaluation should prioritize their logical coherence and critical thinking proficiency. In the end, the LLMs generates a comprehensive final score by integrating the scores from multiple dialogue sessions. Next, we propose a three-step strategy that utilizes the capabilities of LLMs to progressively achieve content comprehension, multifaceted evaluation, and feedback generation for essays, thereby compensating for the shortcomings of traditional scoring systems in terms of suggestions for essay improvement.

3.3 Track 1: Generate Relevance Scores

This paper presents an innovative zero-sample scoring framework that significantly improves the performance of LLMs in essay topic relevance assessment by systematically eliciting their assessment abilities. The Overall architectural framework is shown in Fig. 1.

In terms of method implementation, LLMs may be overloaded in a single response. Therefore, each trait prompt is handled exclusively by a separate LLM agent, forming an LLM-based trait inference generation system.

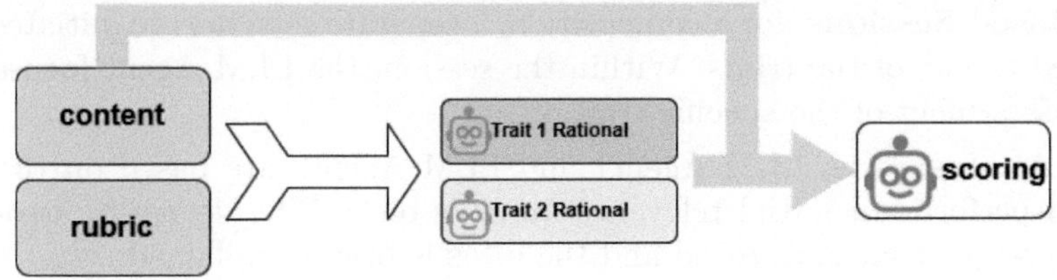

Fig. 1. The overall architecture of our model.

Prompt design plays a crucial role in unlocking the reasoning ability of LLMs. Their reasoning ability benefits from subproblem decomposition of complex problems. LLMs provide a more rational evaluation of compositions when specifically targeting a particular aspect of topic relevance on a level-by-level basis, inspiring us to design the following steps for prompting, as shown in the Fig. 2:

Fig. 2. The diagram of Methodological Steps.

Trait-Based Sessions: for a composition, 2 separate sessions are initiated, each dedicated to one of the traits. Within the session, the LLM Agent focuses only on the assessment of the specific trait.

Initial Analysis: the LLM Agent1 and LLM Agent2 are based on the input text and perform an initial relevance analysis on it. The degree of association with the target trait is assessed and the basis is briefly explained.

Scoring: LLM Agent3 synthesises the evaluations and bases provided by LLM Agent1 and LLM Agent2, and combines them with the preset scoring criteria to quantitatively assess them in two dimensions. The ratio of 40% and 60% is the best result obtained through multiple experiments

The system gives full play to the advantages of LLMs in textual assessment: the trait agent not only generates qualitative assessment results based on the quantitative scale, but also outputs detailed textual justifications simultaneously. This approach ensures a high degree of consistency between the assessment results and the scoring criteria, while providing an interpretable basis for assessment. As shown in Fig. 2, this trait dialogue mechanism not only transforms the AES task into a manageable set of sub-problems, but also effectively prevents inter-trait assessments from interfering with each other.

3.4 Track 2: Generate Comments Based on Relevance Analysis

In recent years, LLMs have excelled in text generation and comprehension tasks, providing new possibilities for automated feedback generation. This study proposes a three-step strategy that utilises the capabilities of LLMs to progressively achieve composition content comprehension, multifaceted evaluation and feedback generation, thereby compensating for the shortcomings of traditional scoring systemsThe Overall architectural framework is shown in Fig. 3.

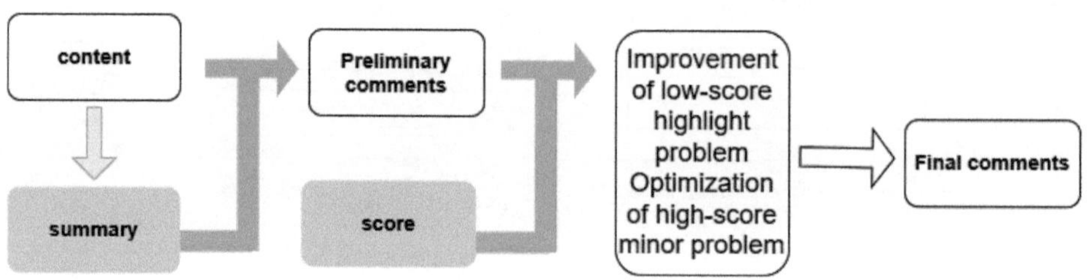

Fig. 3. Overall architectural framework of Track 2.

Summary Generation: The large model first performs a deep reading of the essay to generate a concise summary. The summary serves as an intermediate representation of the text that filters out noise, preserves core semantics, and mitigates the overfitting of redundant information by the scoring model. The model's ability to understand the text is enhanced by pre-generating the summary, a step designed to ensure that the model accurately captures the core content and logical structure of the essay. Summary generation not only helps the model understand the text, but also provides a basis for subsequent evaluation.

> **Prompt1 :Summary generation**
> Please generate a concise and accurate Chinese abstract for the following article, which requires: 1. extract the core ideas and key information of the article 2. maintain objectivity and neutrality, without adding personal opinions 3. keep the number of words between [100-200]. 4. use clear and concise language

Preliminary Assessment: Based on the summary and the original text, the model evaluates the essay against predefined scoring criteria. This step simulates a human teacher's review process and generates an initial qualitative analysis rather than a single score.

> **Prompt2 :preliminary assessment**
> Your task is to critically and in detail judge whether the paper meets the requirements of the topic. Evaluation criteria: Excellent: the item fully meets the requirements of the composition. ... GOOD: The article fits the composition fairly well. .... Moderate: the essay generally meets the requirements of the chosen topic. T..... Pass: While the essay does not stray from the topic, ... Fail: The essay deviates significantly from the chosen topic...... The final needs to be critically summarized,limited to 180 words

Generate Comments: Based on the multifaceted evaluations generated in Step 2 (e.g., 'weak logic of argumentation', 'insufficient expression of emotion'), the model adjusts the weighting based on the classification of the scores obtained from Track 1: if the total score is low, it highlights the suggestions for improvement in the low-scoring dimensions; if the total score is high, it filters out the minor problems. If the total score is low, the improvement suggestions of low-scoring dimensions will be highlighted; if the total score is high, the secondary issues will be filtered to provide advanced suggestions.

> **Prompt3 :Generate comments**
> You are a professional language teacher who is responsible for the overall evaluation of a student's essay based on other teachers' comments and the final score of the essay. Analyze and critique the given essay in a very, very concise manner, keeping the word count strictly within 180 words. Output Requirements: Language is concise, professional and instructive. The evaluation should be objective and fair, recognizing both strengths and weaknesses. Clear structure, in the order of "Overview - Analysis - Recommendations - Summary". Sample output (for reference): The article is titled "xxxxx" and centers on xxxxx, showing xxxxx (theme/emotion)

> through xxxxx (technique/content). The text is x x x (strengths) but x x x (weaknesses). Suggestions x x x (suggestions for improvement). Overall, this paper x x x x (overall assessment).

4   Experiments

4.1   Dataset

This task 2 uses a zero-shot text generation task. The evaluation dataset contains 185 essays covering grades 3 to 9. Each grade contains answers to two different writing prompts. Each data contains grade, requirement, title, and content.

4.2   Experimental Setup

Large language models, like the qwen [1] series from Tongyi Qianwen and OpenAI's GPT [2], excel in text generation and under standing, producing coherent and high-quality text. In order to generate high-quality Chinese reviews, we selected the LLMs of the Qwen family: Qwen-max. The temperature of all LLMs was set to 0.3. Other sampling hyperparameters were set by default.

4.3   Evaluation Metrics

Track 1: The evaluation framework combines adjusted accuracy with statistical correlation metrics:

Adjusted Accuracy (ACC$_\mathbf{A}$):

$$ACC_A = \frac{1}{N} \sum_{i=1}^{N} \left(1 - \frac{|y_i - \hat{y}_i|}{4} \right) \tag{1}$$

where N denotes the total number of samples, y_i represents the ground truth label, and $\hat{y}_i$ is the predicted value. This metric incorporates a linear penalty term scaled to the [0,4] error range, following established practices for continuous scoring.

Pearson Correlation Coefficient:

$$r = \frac{\sum(y_i - \bar{y})(\hat{y}_i - \bar{\hat{y}})}{\sqrt{\sum(y_i - \bar{y})^2 \sum(\hat{y}_i - \bar{\hat{y}})^2}} \tag{2}$$

This statistic measures the linear dependence between predictions and ground truth, with values ranging from -1 to 1.

Composite Score:

$$\text{Score} = 0.5 \times ACC_A + 0.5 \times \left(\frac{1+r}{2} \right) \tag{3}$$

The balanced combination of accuracy and normalized correlation addresses both prediction precision and trend consistency, aligning with regression evaluation best practices.

Track 2: A tripartite evaluation framework integrates automated metrics with human assessment:

Perplexity Score:

$$\text{PPL} = \exp\left(-\frac{1}{N}\sum_{i=1}^{N}\log P(w_i|w_{1:i-1})\right) \tag{4}$$

Computed using the baichuan-7b-chat language model, this metric quantifies text fluency through language model probability distributions. Raw PPL values are normalized to [0,1] using min-max scaling.

Semantic Similarity: We employ BERTScore, which calculates cosine similarity between contextual embeddings of generated and reference texts. This approach captures semantic coherence better than traditional n-gram matching.

Expert Evaluation: A panel of three certified language arts educators with ≥ 5 years teaching experience assessed samples using criteria derived from national curriculum standards. Following stratified sampling (1:10 ratio per grade)

Composite Scoring:

$$\text{Score} = 0.1 \times \text{PPL}_{\text{norm}} + 0.4 \times \text{BERTScore} + 0.5 \times \left(\frac{\text{Human}}{100}\right) \tag{5}$$

where PPL_{norm} is linearly normalized using training set statistics ($\mu = 0.02$, $\sigma = 0.18$). This weighting scheme follows contemporary NLG evaluation frameworks.

4.4   Experimental Results and Analysis

The results are summarized in Table 1, which presents the performance of the models across tracks

The proposed multi-agent collaborative framework demonstrates superior performance in essay topic evaluation tasks, achieving a score of 0.7813 . Ablation

Table 1. Official Results.

Rank	System Name	Track1	Track2	Total
1	ZZUNLP_Han	0.7822	0.6702	0.7150
2	TW-NLP	0.8071	0.6532	0.7148
3	**liberty**	**0.7813**	**0.6650**	**0.7115**
4	Prompt	0.7307	0.6838	0.7025
5	Fighting!	0.7523	0.6673	0.7013
6	DUFL2025	0.7784	0.6317	0.6904
7	zzunlp	0.6999	0.6558	0.6734
8	_zzunlp	0.6725	0.6577	0.6636
9	YNU-HPCC	0.5455	0.6710	0.6208

Table 2. The results of Track1 on the test set.

Methods	score
OurMethod	0.7813
w/o agent1	0.7302
w/o agent2	0.6925

studies reveal statistically significant performance degradation when removing core components (Table 2):

without agent1: Removing agent1 results in a 6.5% performance degradation, as it is responsible for analyzing the consistency of topic and content. For example, the model can recognize the match between the topic of "Growing Up" and the arguments of "Physical Growth" and "Mental Maturity" in the text of "That Moment I Grew Up", which is in line with the design requirement of "Complementing the Selected Material with the topic". The design requirement of "the choice of material and the topic complement each other" is met.

without agent2: Removing agent2 reduces the performance by 11.4%, which indicates that its ability to recognize the clarity and uniqueness of topics is crucial. For example, the grade module in the framework guides agent2 to locate the thematic depth requirements of different class segments through hierarchical labeling (e.g., "3", "5") to avoid evaluation bias.

Table 3. The results of Track2 on the test set.

Methods	score
OurMethod	0.6650
w/o summary	0.6475
w/o score	0.6256

As shown in Table 3, the OurMethod proposed in this paper achieves the optimal performance on the Track2 test set (Score=0.6650), which is significantly better than the ablation experimental model:

without summary: the performance decreases by 2.7%, indicating that the summary module significantly improves the focusing of Preliminary comments by generating content summaries.

without score: performance decreases by 5.9%, demonstrating the critical role of the scoring module in the differentiation of high and low scores, which allows LLMs to generate more focused comments based on the level of scores.

5   Conclusion

This paper describes an approach that with LLMs to improve the efficiency and quality of relevance assessment and relevance analysis based comment generation. The interpretability of the process is improved by decomposing the task into multiple subtasks and assigning specific responsibilities to each agent to improve process interpretability. This approach demonstrates the potential of LLMs to assist instructors in essay assessment and teaching guidance.

The main contribution of this paper is the proposal of an innovative zero-sample scoring framework that significantly improves the performance of LLMs in essay topic relevance assessment by systematically eliciting their assessment abilities.

Although the method has many advantages, it also has some limitations. First, LLM-generated relevance evaluations may remain inaccurate. Future research directions include incorporating Retrieval Augmented Generation (RAG) techniques to construct a repository of expert exemplars in essays, which may entail the collection of high- and low-scoring exemplars with detailed rubrics describing strengths and weaknesses. These improvements are expected to further enhance the quality of automated dissertation analyses and provide stronger support for assisting faculty with dissertation assessment and teaching guidance.

Acknowledgement. This work was supported by the Project 62276178 under the National Natural Science Foundation of China, the Key Project 23KJA520012 under the Natural Science Foundation of Jiangsu Higher Education Institutions, the project 22YJCZH091 of Humanities and Social Science Fund of Ministry of Education and the Priority Academic Program Development of Jiangsu Higher Education Institutions.

References

1. Bai, J., et al.: Qwen technical report. arXiv preprint arXiv:2309.16609 (2023). https://arxiv.org/abs/2309.16609
2. Brown, T.: Language models are few-shot learners. In: Advances in Neural Information Processing Systems. NeurIPS 2020, vol. 33, pp. 1877–1901. Springer, Heidelberg (2020)
3. Dikli, S.: An overview of automated scoring of essays. J. Technol. Learn. Assess. **5**(1) (2006)
4. Hussein, M.A., Hassan, H.A., Nassef, M.: A trait-based deep learning automated essay scoring system with adaptive feedback. Int. J. Adv. Comput. Sci. Appl. **11**(5) (2020)
5. Lee, S., Cai, Y., Meng, D., et al.: Unleashing large language models' proficiency in zero-shot essay scoring. In: Proceedings of the 2024 Conference on Empirical Methods in Natural Language Processing, EMNLP 2024, pp. 181–198. Association for Computational Linguistics, Miami, Florida, USA (2024). https://doi.org/10.18653/v1/2024.findings-emnlp.10
6. Lu, X., Mahesh, A., Shen, Z., et al.: Exploring the limits of transfer learning with a unified text-to-text transformer. J. Mach. Learn. Res. **21**(1) (2020)

7. Lu, X., Mahesh, A., Shen, Z., Dudley, M., Sano, L., Wang, X.: Exploring LLM-generated feedback for economics essays: how teaching assistants evaluate and envision its use (2025). http://arxiv.org/abs/2505.15596
8. Riordan, B., Horbach, A., Cahill, A., Zesch, T., Lee, C.: Investigating neural architectures for short answer scoring. In: Proceedings of the 12th Workshop on Innovative Use of NLP for Building Educational Applications, pp. 159–168 (2017)
9. Taghipour, K., Ng, H.T.: A neural approach to automated essay scoring. In: Proceedings of the 2016 Conference on Empirical Methods in Natural Language Processing, pp. 1882–1891. Association for Computational Linguistics, Austin, Texas (2016)
10. Xia, W., Mao, S., Zheng, C.: Empirical study of large language models as automated essay scoring tools in English composition: Taking TOEFL independent writing task for example (2024). https://arxiv.org/abs/2401.03401
11. Yannakoudakis, H., Briscoe, T.: Modeling coherence in ESOL learner texts. In: Proceedings of the Seventh Workshop on Building Educational Applications Using NLP, pp. 33–43. Association for Computational Linguistics, Montréal, Canada (2012)
12. Zesch, T., Wojatzki, M., Scholten-Akoun, D.: Task-independent features for automated essay grading. In: Proceedings of the Tenth Workshop on Innovative Use of NLP for Building Educational Applications, pp. 224–232. Association for Computational Linguistics, Denver, Colorado (2015)
13. Zhang, Z., Guan, J., Xu, G., et al.: Automatic comment generation for Chinese student narrative essays. In: Proceedings of the 2022 Conference on Empirical Methods in Natural Language Processing: System Demonstrations, pp. 214–223. Association for Computational Linguistics, Abu Dhabi, UAE (2022)
14. Zhuang, X., Wu, H., Shen, X., et al.: TOREE: evaluating topic relevance of student essays for Chinese primary and middle school education. In: Findings of the Association for Computational Linguistics: ACL 2024, pp. 5749–5765. Association for Computational Linguistics, Bangkok, Thailand (2024). https://aclanthology.org/2024.findings-acl.342/

Overview of the NLPCC 2025 Shared Task 3: Comprehensive Argument Analysis for Chinese Argumentative Essay

Zheqin Yin[1], Yupei Ren[1,2], Man Lan[1,2(✉)], Yuanbin Wu[1], Aimin Zhou[1,2],
and Xiaopeng Bai[3]

[1] School of Computer Science and Technology, East China Normal University,
Shanghai, China
{zqyin,ypren}@stu.ecnu.edu.cn, {mlan,ybwu,amzhou}@cs.ecnu.edu.cn
[2] Shanghai Institute of AI for Education, East China Normal University,
Shanghai, China
[3] Department of Chinese Language and Literature, East China Normal University,
Shanghai, China
xpbai@zhwx.ecnu.edu.cn

Abstract. This paper provides a comprehensive overview of NLPCC 2025 shared task 3: **C**omprehensive **A**rgument Analysis for **C**hinese **A**rgumentative **E**ssay (CACAE). Based on the foundation of the annotation of argument component in the first edition of AMCAE, this year's competition introduces the addition of argument relations between components, facilitating nuanced analysis and robust evaluation of computational models. There are 14 teams registered for this task and we received 23 submissions in total from 5 teams. This paper also summarizes some of the techniques used by teams that achieved top performance. More information can be accessed at https://github.com/cubenlp/NLPCC-2025-Shared-Task3.

Keywords: Argument Mining · Argument Component Detection · Argument Relation Identification

1 Introduction

Argument Mining (AM), as a critical task in natural language processing (NLP), aims to identify and structure argument components, such as claims and premises, and their interrelations within texts [3]. This capability holds profound significance in educational contexts, particularly for analyzing argumentative essays composed by students, as it can help cultivating critical thinking, thereby benefiting both learners and educators. For students, AM-driven feedback transcends holistic scores by offering trait-specific evaluations. For teachers, AM systems automate the labor-intensive evaluation of argumentative structures, enabling scalable and consistent assessment aligned with rubric criteria [1,2,14].

© The Author(s), under exclusive license to Springer Nature Singapore Pte Ltd. 2026

X.-L. Mao et al. (Eds.): NLPCC 2025, LNAI 16105, pp. 337–346, 2026.
https://doi.org/10.1007/978-981-95-3352-7_28

However, several limitations persist in current research: **1) Insufficient focus on Chinese argumentative essays**. Existing studies demonstrate a marked underrepresentation of Chinese argumentative writing, especially in comparison to the extensive body of work on English argumentative texts [6,7,9,10]. **2) Shallow relational modeling limits theoretical insights**. Many existing datasets only capture binary relations—primarily support and attack—between argument components, restricting the depth of interaction modeling. This limitation hampers the development of more nuanced and theoretically informed computational models for Chinese argumentation [4,6,8,11,12].

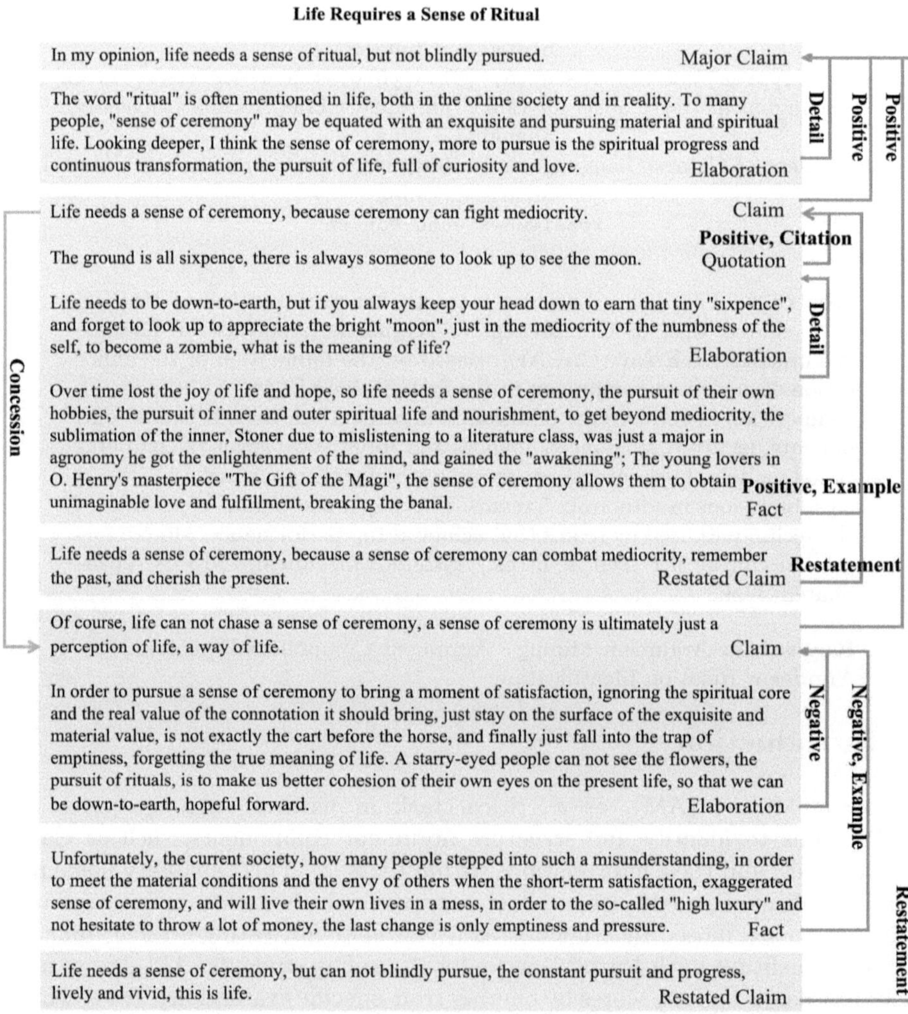

Fig. 1. Visual representation of CACAE.

In light of these limitations, we organize the **C**omprehensive **A**rgument Analysis for **C**hinese **A**rgumentative **E**ssay (CACAE) competition, which focuses on fine-grained and comprehensive argument mining for Chinese argumentative essays. Building upon the AMCAE dataset from NLPCC 2024 Shared Task 5—which provides detailed annotations of argument components based on essays written by Chinese high school students—our updated dataset further includes precise annotations of argument relations, enabling more granular and structured analysis. This initiative aims to establish a solid foundation for advancing automated evaluation models and deepening the understanding of argumentation characteristics in Chinese discourse. Additionally, it provides a practical platform that bridges theoretical research and real-world applications, allowing researchers to systematically assess their approaches [13]. A visual overview of the task is shown in Fig. 1.

This overview paper is organized as follows: Sect. 2 presents a detailed description of the task settings, including background information, label definitions, and task formats. Section 3 outlines the construction of the dataset, detailing the annotation process and inter-annotator agreement (IAA) results. Section 4 introduces the evaluation metrics used for both tracks, along with the final scoring methodology employed to rank participating systems. Section 5 provides an overview of the submitted systems and their corresponding results. Finally, Sect. 6 concludes the paper.

2   Task Definition

Understanding argumentative texts should not be limited to identifying argument components alone; it is equally important to capture the underlying argument relations among them. Therefore, this shared task includes two tracks: **1) Track 1: Argument Component Detection (ACD)**: This track aims to build the fundamental argumentative structure by identifying the argument components. Given an essay as input, the output is expected to be the argument component categories of each sentence, which indicates the role it serves within the text. **2) Track 2: Argument Relation Identification (ARI)**: The objective of this task is to extract and classify the possible argument relations between various argument components, thereby forming an comprehensive understanding of the author's argumentative logic.

2.1   Argument Component Detection (ACD)

Task Description. Argument components detection for argumentative essays is important for the assessment of argumentative essays. This task takes the whole argumentative essay as input and categorizes each sentence in it into 4 categories of assertion, evidence, elaboration, and others at a coarse-level. According to the content and location of the assertion sentence, this task further divides assertion into main claim, claim and restate claim. This task divides evidence into fact, anecdote, quotation, proverb and axiom according to the type and source of evidence as well.

Task Definition. In this track, an essay will be inputted and the model needs to predict the fine-grained category of argument components to which each sentence belongs. More formally, for a document D, we provide the division of sentences, i.e., $D = [s^1, ..., s^n]$, and a prediction of the fine-grained type to which each sentence belongs, i.e., $\hat{y}^1, ..., \hat{y}^n, \hat{y}^i \in \{$ *Major Claim, Claim, Restate Claim, Fact, Anecdote, Quotation, Proverb, Axiom, Elaboration, Others*$\}$ is required. Detailed definition of each category is shown in Table 1.

Table 1. The division of argument components and their definitions.

Coarse	Fine	Definition
Assertion	Major Claim	The main idea or proposition of the entire document.
	Claim	Secondary ideas around the major claim.
	Restate Claim	Restatement of the major claims or claims
Evidence	Fact	Specific facts, historical facts or phenomena in society
	Anecdote	Examples that happened to the author
	Quotation	Citing of the writings of famous people
	Proverb	Idioms or phrases passed down among the masses
	Axiom	Recognized common sense or scientific laws
Elaboration	-	Explanatory notes or analytical discussions of the assertion
Others	-	Sentences that do not fall into the above categories

2.2 Argument Relation Identification (ARI)

Task Description. Argument relation identification aims to reveal the internal argumentative connection between the components. By identifying the supportive, refuting, causal and other relationships between argument components, it is possible to understand the argumentative structure of the text in a more comprehensive way, and thus to grasp more accurately the author's point of view and the intent of the argument. As depicted in Fig. 1, an essay is segmented into multiple chunks, with argumentative relationships annotated between pairs of chunks where such relationships exist.

Task Definition. Given an input essay D_c that has m sentence chunks ($D_c = [c^1, ..., c^m]$), this track aims to predict the possible argument relation between chunks $\mathcal{AR} = \{(i_{from}, i_{to}, r)\}, i_{from}, i_{to} \in [1, m]$. A chunk of sentences is adjacent sentences (with the same argument component type) that plays similar role in the text. In this track, 10 types of argument relationships are defined at a finer level of granularity, focusing on the relationships between different types of argument components. Table 2 provides detailed definition for each category. In addition, to make it easier, we consider each sentence in chunk c_i has the same relation r to each sentence in chunk c_j if $r = [r_1, r_2, \cdots]$ exists from c_i to c_j, where $r_k \in \{$ *Positive, Negative, Comparative, Example, Citation, Metaphorical, Hypothetical, Restatement, Detail, Background* $\}$, as defined in Table 2.

Table 2. The division of argument relation types and their definitions

Aspect	Label	Definition
Stance-based	Positive	A method that directly validates the correctness of a viewpoint by using elaboration or evidence consistent with the viewpoint to support it, emphasizing direct affirmation of the viewpoint.
	Negative	A method that indirectly proves the correctness of a viewpoint through elaboration or evidence that are contrary to the viewpoint. It emphasizes the negation of opposing viewpoints, thereby achieving the purpose of the argumentation.
	Comparative	A shorthand for positive and negative argumentation, is an argumentative approach that involves contrasting and comparing two items to highlight their differences, thereby making the conclusion more evident and persuasive.
Evidence-based	Example	An argumentation method that proves a thesis through concrete, or typical examples.
	Citation	An argumentation method that proves a thesis by using quotations or axioms.
Discourse-based	Metaphorical	By employing metaphorical rhetoric, familiar things are used as metaphors to argue the correctness of a viewpoint. In drawing parallels between two items with similar characteristics, the artful use of metaphors often serves to better elucidate concepts, making the argument more vivid and interesting.
	Hypothetical	Analyzing evidence from the opposite side based on hypothesis to infer its authenticity and reliability, thus robustly supporting a thesis.
	Restatement	For argument of the type *restated claim*, its relation with the target argument (*major claim* or *claim*) is defined as restatement relation.
	Detail	When an argument (*elaboration* type) primarily aims to further explain or analyze other content, it establishes a detail relation with the corresponding argument (*assertion* or *evidence* type).
	Background	When an argument (*elaboration* type) primarily serves the function of introducing background, it constructs a background relation with the corresponding argument (*assertion* or *evidence* type).

3   Dataset Description

The dataset in this work derives from the argumentative essay corpus CEAMC [5], comprising essays authored by Chinese high school students. Building upon the original annotation framework where fine-grained argument components were systematically categorized at the sentence level, we implemented an additional annotation layer to capture inter-component argument relations. This section elaborates on two aspects: (1) the annotation process, and (2) the annotation results.

3.1   Annotation Process

The annotation team comprised three undergraduate linguistics students, three graduate researchers specializing in discourse analysis, and two senior Chinese language education specialists. All annotators completed structured training modules before the official annotation commences. The annotation protocol incorporated a preliminary calibration phase wherein annotators were assigned to systematically label a representative subset sampled from the dataset. The primary objectives of this phase were to standardize annotator interpretation of the schema guidelines and facilitate task acclimatization. Subsequent to the initial labeling phase conducted by the annotators, experts performed systematic validation of the assigned labels and formulated constructive feedback for quality optimization. This iterative refinement mechanism, implemented across a three-month development cycle, enabled the creation of a meticulously annotated corpus.

3.2 Annotation Result

Inner-**A**nnotator **A**greement (IAA) analysis was conducted after the annotation. We employed *Cohen's Kappa*, which ranges from 0 to 1, to measure annotation consistency. The results are as follows:

- Sentence chunk agreement: 0.95 for sentence unit boundaries.
- Relation agreement: 0.68 for argumentative linkage identification.

Both the metrics exceed 0.60 and constitutes acceptable research-grade reliability. The observed divergence between component and relation agreement aligns with theoretical expectations given the increased cognitive complexity of relational annotation tasks.

4 Evaluation Metrics

The evaluation process employs automated metrics to assess the performance of submitted systems. For Track 1, the composite score is derived from two distinct components: the $MicroF1$ score and the $MacroF1$ score of fine-grained category predictions. The formal scoring function is defined as:

$$Score_{Track1} = 0.5 \times MicroF1_{Track1} + 0.5 \times MacroF1_{Track1} \tag{1}$$

In contrast, Track 2 adopts a simplified evaluation protocol where system performance is quantified solely through the $MicroF1$ metric:

$$Score_{Track2} = MicroF1_{Track2} \tag{2}$$

To account for the inherent discrepancy in task complexity between the two tracks, differential weighting coefficients are applied in the final ranking computation. This weighting scheme aims to incentivize participants to focus on addressing more complex challenges while maintaining balanced system performance. Therefore, we formulated Eq. 1 and Eq. 2 as Eq. 3:

$$Score = 0.4 \times Score_{Track1} + 0.6 \times Score_{Track2} \tag{3}$$

5 Participated Systems

This section provides an outline of the teams and organizations involved in this task, as well as an analysis of the submissions. In addition, this section provides an overview of some representative techniques used in participated systems.

5.1 Participation Overview

This research task garnered attention from both academic and commercial sectors, as evidenced by the substantial number of participants. A total of 14 teams enrolled in the task. These participants included academic institutions such as universities, as well as commercial entities. Table 3 provides detailed information regarding the registered systems and their respective affiliations, offering an overview of the diverse backgrounds and expertise of the participating teams.

Table 3. Teams and their organizations that registered this task.

System Name	Organization
ZZU-NLP	Zhengzhou University
西西恩优NLP	Central China Normal University
Moon	Zhengzhou University
YouTuLab_Jarvis	Tencent YouTu Lab, Jarvis Research Center
TW-NLP	Beijing SmartDot Technology Co., Ltd.
YNU-HPCC	Yunnan University
CCNU NLP	Central China Normal University
xlarge	Dalian University of Technology
HITSZ-HLT	Harbin Institute of Technology, Shenzhen
BLCU LCC Lab	Beijing Language and Culture University
Phd wu	Zhengzhou University
Bits	XUTELI School, Beijing Institute of Technology (BIT)
炼丹师_zzunlp(LDS_zzunlp)	Zhengzhou University
Prompt	Central China Normal University
Total Number	14

5.2 Submission Analysis

In the phrase of testing, participants have no restrictions for submission count. We received 23 times of submission in total, and among 14 teams registered for the task, 5 teams submitted their predictions. Their results are shown in Table 4. We observed a variety of methods used by these participants. Additionally, different scale of models of LLMs were utilized. Below are some representative examples.

LDS_zzunlp employed additional open source data to fine-tune Qwen2-7b via LoRA for Track 1, aiming to enhance its ability to follow instructions and adapt

Table 4. The final leader board of this task. This table presents the scores for both tracks along with detailed metric values for all participated systems. Note all scores in this table are presented as percentages (%).

Rank	Team	Track1		$Score_{Track1}$	Track2 $Score_{Track2}$	Score
		Micro F1	Macro F1			
1	炼丹师_zzunlp	75.24	55.71	65.48	10.26	32.35
2	TW-NLP	72.34	35.29	53.82	8.84	26.83
3	Moon	64.02	36.88	50.45	10.86	26.69
4	Prompt	73.79	43.65	58.72	3.58	25.64
5	xlarge	36.75	27.84	36.75	0.00	12.92

to the task requirements. They experimented with two methods: (1) directly classifying sentences into ten fine-grained categories, and (2) first performing coarse-grained classification followed by fine-grained classification based on the coarse category. After preliminary testing, they found that the second approach yielded better results and thus adopted it for model fine-tuning. During test data generation,we employed a voting mechanism, generating multiple answers for each input through different sampling strategies and selecting the most frequently occurring answer as the final output. For Track 2, given the uncertainty of which two sentences in an article have a relationship, they conducted pairwise discrimination among all sentences. Considering the computational complexity, we leveraged the API of Qwen-72B to directly generate answers. Similar voting mechanism was applied, where multiple answers were generated for each input using various sampling strategies, and the most frequent answer was chosen as the final result.

TW-NLP primarily utilized the Qwen2.5-32B model for both Track 1 and Track 2. In Track 1, they conducted a comparative analysis between the QWQ-32B and Qwen2.5-32B models. The latter, when fine-tuned using LoRA, achieved a $Score_{Track1}$ of 53.82, indicating its superior performance in this setting. For Track 2, the team explored various prompt designs for the Qwen2.5-32B model. They observed that ensembling the outputs from two distinct prompts led to an improvement in overall recall, mitigating the low recall observed when using individual prompts. This strategy resulted in a F1 score of 8.84, demonstrating the effectiveness of prompt ensembling in enhancing task performance.

For Track 1, *Moon* employed the Qwen2.5-34B-Instruct model, applying LoRA for fine-tuning on an A800 GPU. A carefully crafted prompt was designed to explicitly define the task of classifying sentences from argumentative essays into ten distinct categories. This prompt was then used to perform instruction-tuning. For Track 2, the team primarily adopted prompt-based strategies. Specifically, they leveraged the Qwen2.5-72B-Instruct model in a zero-shot setting via API calls, without further parameter updates. The resulting performance, as reflected in their $Score_{Track2}$, demonstrates the model's strong capability in addressing the task without the need for additional fine-tuning.

6   Conclusions

This paper presents an overview of NLPCC Shared Task 3: Comprehensive Argument Analysis for Chinese Argumentative Essays. The task introduces a more fine-grained analysis to argument analysis by not only focusing on the identification of argument components but also incorporating the recognition of argument relations. This addition enables a deeper understanding of the discourse structure and reasoning flow within argumentative essays. To support this task, we constructed a high-quality annotated corpus, with labels verified by domain experts to ensure reliability and annotation consistency. A total of 14 teamsregistered for the task, and 5 teams submitted valid system outputs, which were scored using standard evaluation metrics. This paper also gives an overview of the submitted systems, highlights several approaches, and presents the final leaderboard results. Notably, LLMs—especially o1-like models such as QwQ—demonstrated strong performance in both tracks, showcasing their ability to handle complex argumentation structures .

Acknowledgements. We appreciate the support from the Shanghai Municipal Education Commission through the Artificial Intelligence-Powered Research Paradigm Reform and Discipline Leap Plan (2024AI02004).

References

1. Afrin, T., Wang, E.L., Litman, D.J., Matsumura, L.C., Correnti, R.: Annotation and classification of evidence and reasoning revisions in argumentative writing. In: Workshop on Innovative Use of NLP for Building Educational Applications (2020). https://api.semanticscholar.org/CorpusID:220059860
2. Janda, H.K., Pawar, A., Du, S., Mago, V.: Syntactic, semantic and sentiment analysis: the joint effect on automated essay evaluation. IEEE Access **7**, 108486–108503 (2019). https://doi.org/10.1109/ACCESS.2019.2933354
3. Lawrence, J., Reed, C.: Argument mining: a survey. Comput. Linguist. **45**(4), 765–818 (2019). https://aclanthology.org/J19-4006
4. Park, J., Cardie, C.: A corpus of eRulemaking user comments for measuring evaluability of arguments. In: International Conference on Language Resources and Evaluation (2018). https://api.semanticscholar.org/CorpusID:21689265
5. Ren, Y., et al.: CEAMC: Corpus and Empirical Study of Argument Analysis in Education via LLMs. In: Conference on Empirical Methods in Natural Language Processing (2024). https://api.semanticscholar.org/CorpusID:274060298
6. Rocha, V.H.N., Silveira, I.C., Pirozelli, P., Mauá, D.D., Cozman, F.G.: Assessing good, bad and ugly arguments generated by ChatGPT: a new dataset, its methodology and associated tasks. In: Portuguese Conference on Artificial Intelligence (2024). https://api.semanticscholar.org/CorpusID:266757593
7. Song, W., Song, Z., Liu, L., Fu, R.: Hierarchical multi-task learning for organization evaluation of argumentative student essays. In: International Joint Conference on Artificial Intelligence (2020). https://api.semanticscholar.org/CorpusID:220484146

8. Srivastava, P., Bhatnagar, P., Goel, A.: Argument mining using BERT and self-attention based embeddings. In: 2022 4th International Conference on Advances in Computing, Communication Control and Networking (ICAC3N), pp. 1536–1540 (2022). https://api.semanticscholar.org/CorpusID:257219765
9. Stab, C., Gurevych, I.: Parsing argumentation structures in persuasive essays. Comput. Linguist. **43**(3), 619–659 (2017)
10. Wang, H., Huang, Z., Dou, Y., Hong, Y.: Argumentation mining on essays at multi scales. In: International Conference on Computational Linguistics (2020). https://api.semanticscholar.org/CorpusID:227230893
11. Wang, H., Huang, Z., Dou, Y., Hong, Y.: Argumentation mining on essays at multi scales. In: Scott, D., Bel, N., Zong, C. (eds.) Proceedings of the 28th International Conference on Computational Linguistics, pp. 5480–5493. International Committee on Computational Linguistics, Barcelona, Spain (Online) (2020). https://doi.org/10.18653/v1/2020.coling-main.478, https://aclanthology.org/2020.coling-main.478
12. Wang, X., Lee, Y., Park, J.: Automated evaluation for student argumentative writing: A survey. ArXiv **abs/2205.04083** (2022). https://api.semanticscholar.org/CorpusID:248571754
13. Yang, H., He, Y., Bu, X., Xu, H., Guo, W.: Automatic essay evaluation technologies in chinese writing—a systematic literature review. Appl. Sci. **13**(19) (2023). https://doi.org/10.3390/app131910737, https://www.mdpi.com/2076-3417/13/19/10737
14. Zupanc, K., Bosnić, Z.: Advances in the field of automated essay evaluation. Informatica (Slovenia) **39** (2016). https://api.semanticscholar.org/CorpusID:34396

Knowledge-Enhanced and Event-Rule Guided Framework for Fine-Grained Argument Mining in Chinese Essays

Tao Liu[1], Yunlong Li[1], Yifan Li[1], Bohan Yu[1], Aoze Zheng[1], Kunli Zhang[1], Hongying Zan[1(✉)], and Ming Peng[2]

[1] School of Computer and Artificial Intelligence, Zhengzhou University, Zhengzhou, China
{taoliu01,lylyun}@gs.zzu.edu.cn, iehyzan@zzu.edu.cn
[2] School of Computer Science, Wuhan University, Wuhan, China
pengm@whu.edu.cn

Abstract. Argument Mining is crucial for uncovering the logical structure and reasoning process within texts, particularly in educational scenarios such as argumentative essay analysis. The NLPCC 2025 Shared Task on Argument Mining in Chinese argumentative essays introduces two subtasks: Argument Component Detection (ACD) and Argument Relation Identification (ARI). In this paper, we propose two corresponding methods—Track1 and Track2—to address these challenges. For Track1, we design a fine-grained data augmentation strategy by refining category labels with domain-specific and contextual information, enabling Large Language Models (LLMs) to generate diverse, high-quality samples. These are then used to fine-tune models through LoRA to improve category understanding. For Track2, we introduce a knowledge-enhanced relation identification method that combines prompt-based LLM generation with rule-based scoring and filtering to improve relation precision. In both tracks, we apply a majority voting strategy across multiple strong LLMs to enhance robustness. Experimental results demonstrate that our approach achieves state-of-the-art performance, validating the effectiveness of the proposed framework for fine-grained argument mining in Chinese essays.

Keywords: Argument Mining · Data Augmentation · LoRA · Knowledge Enhancement

1 Introduction

Argument Mining plays an essential role in understanding how ideas are logically connected within a text. Through detailed analysis of argument structures, one can better follow the author's reasoning and identify how claims and evidence support each other. This not only improves comprehension but also helps reveal the deeper logic behind a writer's argument.

© The Author(s), under exclusive license to Springer Nature Singapore Pte Ltd. 2026
X.-L. Mao et al. (Eds.): NLPCC 2025, LNAI 16105, pp. 347–357, 2026.
https://doi.org/10.1007/978-981-95-3352-7_29

In this context, the NLPCC 2025 Shared Task on Argument Mining in Chinese argumentative essays focuses on building models that can identify and link argumentative elements. The dataset includes essays written by Chinese high school students, with expert annotations that highlight various argument components and their relationships. The task encourages deeper analysis of essay structure, supporting applications in education such as writing feedback and reasoning training.

This shared task consists of two tracks. Track 1 focuses on Argument Component Detection (ACD) [5], where the goal is to label each sentence with its argumentative role, such as claim, evidence, or elaboration. Track 2, Argument Relation Identification (ARI) [6], targets the identification of logical links between these components, helping to form a complete argumentative structure.

In this paper, we propose two methods corresponding to Track1 and Track2. For Track1, due to the lack of sufficient data to support the model in learning sentence categories in argumentative prose, we introduce a data augmentation approach. This method refines fine-grained categories by incorporating relevant domains and scenarios, enabling LLMs to generate more diverse and detailed training samples. After obtaining adequate annotated data, we apply LoRA-based fine-tuning to inject task-specific knowledge into the model, thereby improving its task comprehension. We further adopt a majority voting strategy to determine the final output by combining predictions from three models: Qwen2.5-7B-Instruct [9], InternLM3-8B, and Deepseek-R1-Distill-Qwen-7B [2]. For Track2, we leverage the strong reasoning capabilities of LLMs and external knowledge-based rules to identify relationships between sentences. Based on the sentences and corresponding relation types generated in Track1, we design a classification schema and prompt templates for argumentative prose generation to extract inter-sentence relations. After obtaining the initial relation predictions, we apply a rule-based scoring system, constructed from relation-type descriptions, to evaluate and filter the results. Finally, we perform majority voting over the outputs of three models: DeepSeek-V3 [3], Qwen2.5-72B-Instruct [9], and DeepSeek-R1 [2] to determine the final predictions.

In summary, our contributions are as follows:

- We propose a fine-grained data augmentation method for the Track1 classification task. By expanding the relation schema with contextual domains and scenarios, we generate more diverse samples. We then apply LoRA-based fine-tuning to inject task-specific knowledge, effectively improving the model's understanding of sentence categories in argumentative texts.
- We introduce a knowledge-enhanced relation filtering method. Based on initial predictions generated by LLMs, we use external rule-based relation descriptions to evaluate and filter the results, significantly improving the accuracy and reliability of relation identification.
- Extensive experimental results demonstrate that our approach achieves state-of-the-art performance, validating the effectiveness of the proposed methods.

2   Related Work

As computer technology advances, its applications in language education have expanded, offering new avenues for text analysis. Researchers have used computer-assisted technologies to extract key arguments and their premises, providing insights into complex textual structures [7,11]. Classification techniques that differentiate argumentative claims from conclusions have also proven valuable for automated text scoring and guiding student writing [10]. Additionally, some studies categorize texts by function, aiding in content organization [8]. These studies primarily use feature-based and neural network-based methods. The former relies on intricately designed features for structured data [12], while the latter leverages deep learning to automatically extract complex semantic features [4,13]. Research also shows that incorporating contextual information can improve the accuracy of argument component classification, highlighting deep learning's potential in managing text coherence [1]. Despite significant progress, gaps remain in current research, particularly in the fine-grained classification of argument types—a capability that is critical for uncovering an essay's logical structure, optimizing pedagogical approaches, and strengthening students' argumentative skills. Existing methods facilitate the identification and coarse categorization of arguments, but they do not systematically delineate detailed argument subtypes, limiting their practical utility in educational settings. A deeper investigation into argument type taxonomy would not only advance theoretical understanding but also substantially enhance instructional effectiveness.

3   Method

3.1   Task Definition

Track1. Given an argumentative essay $D = \{s_1, s_2, \ldots, s_n\}$, our task is to predict the label $\hat{y}$ for each sentence s_i. This involves first classifying each sentence into one of four coarse-grained categories, and then further subdividing it into one of ten fine-grained categories.

Track2. For an argumentative essay $D = \{s_1, s_2, \ldots, s_n\}$, there are relationships defined vertically between the sentences. This part aims to identify the relationships between different sentences. The goal is to predict the potential argumentative relationships that may exist between sentence blocks. A sentence block refers to adjacent sentences in the text that serve similar roles (having the same type of argumentative components).

3.2   Data Synthesis

The evaluation data consists of 3 articles, totaling approximately 30 sentences. Due to the scarcity of this data, it is difficult to conduct generalization experiments. Therefore, we chose to use data synthesis techniques. As shown in Fig. 2, we divide the process into two stages: The first stage (Category Subdivision and

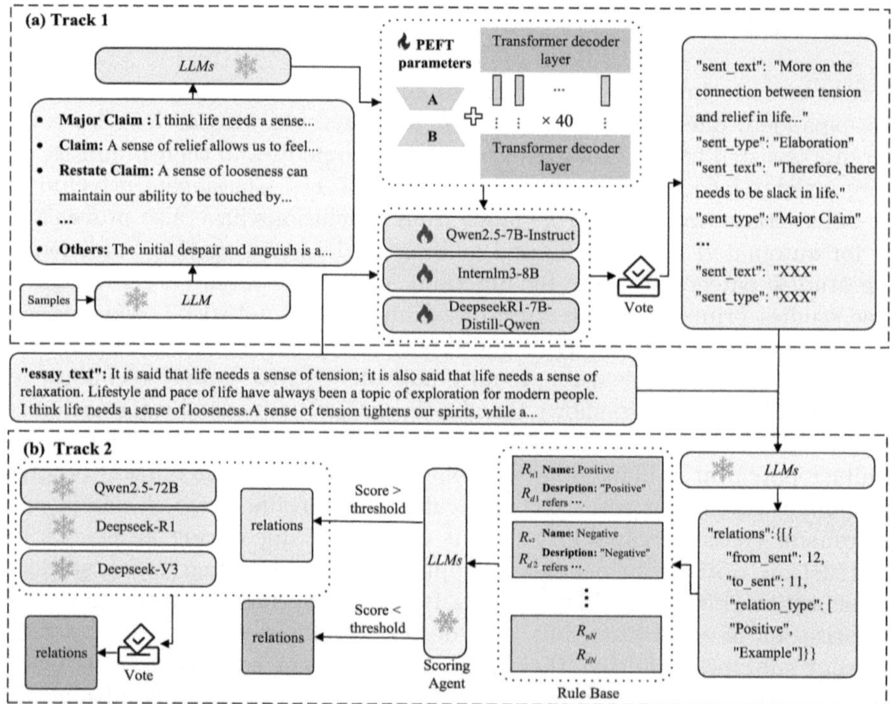

Fig. 1. The architecture diagram is divided into two main parts: *Top* represents the workflow of Track1, *Bottom* illustrates the process of Track2.

Expansion) starts from fine-grained categories, analyzing them and, in combination with specific domains and scenarios, forms a more explicit and diverse detailed category library. In the second stage (Precise Data Generation), we focus on the diversity of sentences by increasing variation in three aspects: lexical, syntactic, and stylistic. From the perspective of sentence quality, we ensure the quality of the generated sentences through constraints on grammatical rules, semantic consistency, and noise control. Finally, we generate sentences related to the categories using the detailed category library created in the first stage. After obtaining relevant categories and corresponding sentences, we perform a quality review to determine whether a sentence belongs to the specified category. After the quality review and screening, we obtain the final set of sentences.

3.3   Knowledge Filtering and Event Consistency

Track1. As mentioned in the previous section, we have constructed a large amount of synthetic data. The purpose of data augmentation is to obtain a high-quality candidate set for subsequent processes. We utilized several open-source large language models and conducted multiple zero-shot tests on the augmented development set. Ultimately, we selected Qwen2.5-7B-Instruct, InternLM3-8B,

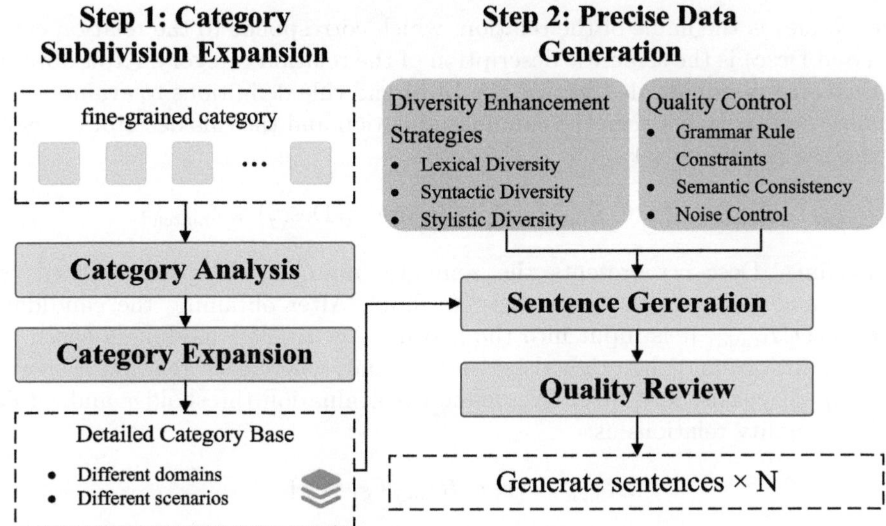

Fig. 2. Data Augmentation Workflow. The process begins with category refinement to create more fine-grained labels. Based on these refined categories, diverse generation strategies combined with quality control measures are used to produce candidate sentences. Finally, an LLM is employed to filter and select high-quality sentence-label pairs, resulting in a reliable and diverse augmented dataset.

and Deepseek-R1-Distill-Qwen-7B as the baseline models for instruction fine-tuning, and employed LoRA for parameter-efficient fine-tuning. Due to the differences in task understanding and text generation capabilities among the models, the output of a single model is often limited. To fully leverage the strengths of each model, we further performed voting fusion on the outputs of different models, effectively reducing single-model bias and enhancing the stability and robustness of the predictions. Based on this, we achieved excellent results and conducted experiments using Track2 on the final outcomes as shown in Fig. 1 a.

Track2. To further improve the accuracy and robustness of the relationship extraction results, we designed the Track 2 architecture as shown in Fig. 1 b. This method primarily consists of three key modules: the rule matching module, the scoring discrimination module, and the multi-model voting fusion module. First, from Track 1, we obtain the initial set of relationship candidates R_{init}, and then based on the acquired R_{init} and relationship categories R, we inject it into the prompt template and use the LLM to generate the initial results. Next, for each result, we match the relationships r_i with the pre-built rule set $B = \{R_1, R_2, \ldots, R_m\}$. We obtain the relationship rule corresponding to each matched relationship. The relationship rule R_j is defined as a pair:

$$R_j = (Name_j, Desc_j)$$

Here, Name_j is the name of the relation, which corresponds to the relation category, and Desc_j is the semantic description of the relation category. After obtaining the corresponding rules, we use the LLM and rule definitions to evaluate the semantic similarity between the candidate relation and the rule description, generating the candidate set:

$$R_{\text{cand}} = \{r_i \in R_{\text{init}} \mid \exists R_j \in B, \text{sim}(r_i, \text{Desc}_j) > \delta_{\text{match}}\}$$

Here, $\text{sim}(r_i, \text{Desc}_j)$ represents the semantic matching function realized by M_{match}, and δ_{match} is the matching threshold. After obtaining the candidate relation set R_{cand}, it is input into the Scoring Agent. This module is based on rule descriptions and the original textual content, where each relation is scored with a quality score $s_i \in [0, 1]$. We define the evaluation threshold τ and retain the high-quality relations as:

$$R_{\text{high}} = \{r_i \in R_{\text{cand}} \mid s_i > \tau\}$$

After the scoring process through the Scoring Agent, I will perform voting on the high-quality relation set R_{high} from multiple large language models (such as Deepseek-V3, Qwen2.5-72B-Instruct, Deepseek-R1). We use majority voting to combine the model results, forming the final output.

4 Experiments

4.1 Dataset

Dataset Introduction. The dataset used in this paper is from "Task 3: Argument Mining in Chinese Argumentative Essays." In this task, each sentence of the argumentative essay is treated as an input unit and is carefully classified into one of the following categories: Major Claim, Claim, Restate Claim, Fact, Anecdote, Quotation, Proverb, Axiom, Elaboration, and Others. In Track 2, we define 14 types of argumentative relationships with a finer granularity from both vertical (focusing on relationships between different types of argumentative elements) and horizontal (focusing on relationships between the same types of argumentative elements) perspectives, as shown in Fig. 3. 1). The relationship between **Elaboration** and **Claim** includes: Positive Argumentation, Negative Argumentation, Refinement Relationship, Background Relationship, Metaphorical Argumentation, Hypothetical Argumentation, and Contrastive Argumentation. 2). The relationship between **Elaboration** and **Premise** includes: Refinement Relationship, Background Relationship. 3). The relationship between **Premise** and **Elaboration** includes: Positive Argumentation, Negative Argumentation, Exemplification Argumentation, Quotation Argumentation, and Contrastive Argumentation. 4). The relationship between **Premise** and **Claim** includes: Positive Argumentation, Negative Argumentation, Exemplification Argumentation, Quotation Argumentation, Metaphorical Argumentation, and Contrastive Argumentation. 5). The relationship between **Subclaim** and **Main Claim** includes: Positive Argumentation, Negative Argumentation. 6). The relationship between **Restating Claim** and **Subclaim** includes: Restatement Relationship. 7). The relationship between **Restating Claim** and **Main Claim** includes: Restatement Relationship.

Data Synthesis. We perform data synthesis using LLM, expanding the three articles from Track 1 into approximately 50 additional argumentative essays. These essays are sourced from a composition website. We used web scraping techniques to gather about 80 articles and selected approximately 50 high-quality ones. At the same time, we utilized a large model for synthesis, generating about 1057 textual sentences and labeled their fine-grained categories using LLM. The categories and the number of synthesized data are shown in Table 1.

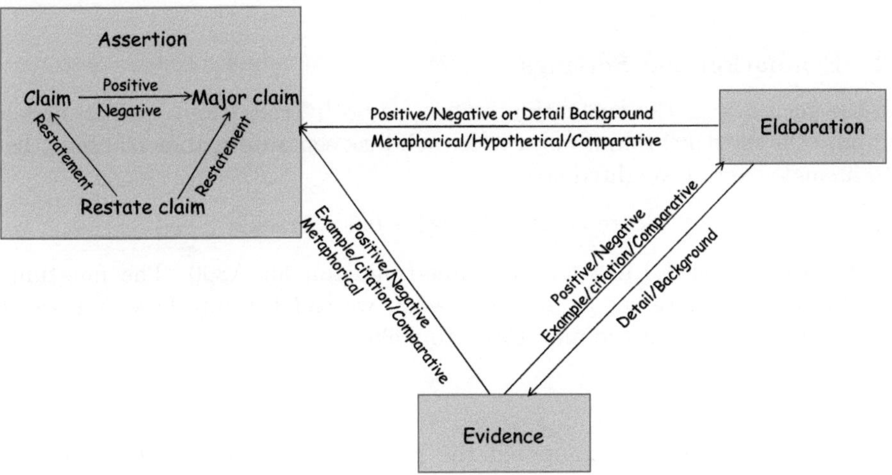

Fig. 3. Example of a relational link types for track 2.

Table 1. Synthesis Data Categories and Their Counts. MC for Major Claim; C for Claim; RC for Restate Claim; F for Fact; A for Anecdote; Q for Quotation; P for Proverb; A for Axiom; E for Elaboration; and O for Others.

Dataset	MC	C	RC	F	A	Q	P	A	E	O	Overall
Origin	3	7	3	11	x	1	x	1	42	x	69
Synthesis	50	123	45	179	4	44	4	5	590	40	1057

Table 2. Pretrained Models Parameters and LoRA Parameters

setting	parameter
Epochs	5
Learning_rate	5e-5
Batch_Size	4
Max_token	4096
Optimizer	AdamW
Gradient_accumulation_steps	8
LoRA_Rank	128
LoRA_Alpha	512
LoRA_Target	all

4.2 Evaluation and Settings

We use accuracy as the evaluation metric for both Track1 and Track2: first we compute the identification accuracy for each task separately, then combine them into a single overall weighted score.

$$Score = 0.4 \times Track1 + 0.6 \times Track2$$

For Track1, we used LLM for Lora fine-tuning,on an A800. The fine-tuning hyperparameters were set as 2. For Track2, we call the interface and set the temperature to 0.7 and the max token to 4096.

4.3 Results

As shown in Table 3, we compared the performance of different methods on the Track1 and Track2 tasks. The results show that individual models such as Qwen2.5-7B-Instruct and InternLM3-8B-Instruct perform similarly without data augmentation, with higher scores on Track1 but weaker performance on Track2. With data augmentation, Qwen2.5-7B-Instruct shows slight improvement on Track1, but Track2 remains at a lower level. Decspeck-R1-7B-distill performs well without augmentation, particularly on Track1, but still lags behind on Track2 compared to other models. The model ensemble strategy (VOTE) shows significant improvement in overall performance, especially after applying data augmentation, achieving the highest overall score on both Track1 and Track2. The experimental results demonstrate that data augmentation and multi-model voting strategies can significantly enhance task performance, validating the effectiveness of our framework for fine-grained argument mining tasks. And we submit last result with ovrall score 26.69, but our best results can achieve 29.9.

5 Ablation Study

This experiment compared the performance of various models before and after applying synthetic data augmentation to validate its impact. As shown in

Table 3. Performance of different methods on the Track1 and Track2 tasks.

Method	Data Synthesis	Track1	Track2	Overall
Qwen2.5-7B-Instruct	x	48.32	6.72	23.36
InternLM3-8B-Instruct	x	47.37	8.02	23.76
Deepseek-R1-Distill-Qwen-7B	x	52.30	7.68	25.53
Qwen2.5-7B-Instruct	✓	50.45	**10.86**	26.69
VOTE (Qwen2.5, InternLM3, Deepseek-R1)	x	55.10	9.92	27.93
VOTE(Qwen2.5, InternLM3, Deepseek-R1)	✓	**58.48**	10.11	29.9

Table 4, data synthesis consistently improves the performance of all models, especially in Track1 and Track2 tasks, with the highest improvements seen in Deepspeck-R1-7B-Qwen and InternLM3-8B. The combination of data synthesis and enhanced model architectures demonstrates the effectiveness of improving model performance across both tasks. Notably, DeepseekR1-7B-Distill-Qwen demonstrated more accurate identification and linking across categories after augmentation, suggesting that synthetic data helps models learn more robust feature representations.

Table 4. Performance of different models on the Track1 and Track2 tasks in Data Synthesis.

Track1 Models	Data Synthesis	Track1 Models	Track1	Track2	Overall
Qwen2.5-7B-Instruct	x	Qwen2.5-72B-Instruct	48.32	6.72	23.36
InternLM3-8B-Instruct	x	Deepseek-V3	47.37	8.02	23.76
Deepseek-R1-Distill-Qwen-7B	x	Deepseek-R1	52.3	7.68	25.53
Qwen2.5-7B-Instruct	✓	Qwen2.5-72B-Instruct	57.1	9.92	27.99
InternLM3-8B	✓	Deepseek-V3	56.32	8.28	32.35
Deepseek-R1-Distill-Qwen-7B	✓	Deepseek-R1	55.58	9.37	32.35

6   Conclusion

In summary, this paper presents two effective methods for the NLPCC 2025 Shared Task on Argument Mining in Chinese argumentative essays, targeting the sub-tasks of argument component detection and relation identification. For component detection, we propose a fine-grained data augmentation strategy combined with LoRA-based fine-tuning, which significantly improves the model's ability to understand sentence categories. For relation identification, we introduce a knowledge-based filtering method that enhances the accuracy of inter-sentence relation recognition. A voting-based strategy is used to further improve the overall system performance. Extensive experimental results show that our approach achieves leading performance on both Track1 and the overall evaluation metric, demonstrating the effectiveness of our proposed methods.

7 Limitation

Despite the promising results, several limitations remain. First, the model still struggles with understanding complex rhetorical devices such as metaphor and irony, as well as handling ambiguous semantic expressions. Second, its performance becomes less stable when processing long essays with cross-paragraph, long-range dependencies. Additionally, the current rule-based knowledge construction process relies heavily on manual design and lacks the ability to generalize automatically. Future work will focus on automated knowledge extraction, hierarchical semantic modeling, and improving the model's adaptability to complex textual structures, aiming to further enhance the effectiveness and applicability of argument mining in Chinese argumentative essays.

References

1. Cabessa, J., Hernault, H., Mushtaq, U.: In-context learning and fine-tuning GPT for argument mining (2024)
2. DeepSeek-AI, et al.: DeepSeek-R1: Incentivizing reasoning capability in LLMs via reinforcement learning (2025)
3. DeepSeek-AI, Liu, A., et al.: DeepSeek-v3 technical report (2025)
4. Eger, S., Daxenberger, J., Gurevych, I.: Neural end-to-end learning for computational argumentation mining. In: Barzilay, R., Kan, M.Y. (eds.) Proceedings of the 55th Annual Meeting of the Association for Computational Linguistics (Volume 1: Long Papers), pp. 11–22. Association for Computational Linguistics, Vancouver, Canada (2017)
5. Gao, Y., Wang, H., Zhang, C., Wang, W.: Reinforcement learning based argument component detection (2017)
6. Gemechu, D., Ruiz-Dolz, R., Reed, C.: ARIES: A general benchmark for argument relation identification. In: Ajjour, Y., Bar-Haim, R., El Baff, R., Liu, Z., Skitalinskaya, G. (eds.) Proceedings of the 11th Workshop on Argument Mining (ArgMining 2024), pp. 1–14. Association for Computational Linguistics, Bangkok, Thailand (2024)
7. Nguyen, H., Litman, D.: Extracting argument and domain words for identifying argument components in texts. In: Cardie, C. (ed.) Proceedings of the 2nd Workshop on Argumentation Mining, pp. 22–28. Association for Computational Linguistics, Denver, CO (2015)
8. Peldszus, A., Stede, M.: From argument diagrams to argumentation mining in texts: a survey. Int. J. Cogn. Informatics Nat. Intell. 7, 1–31 (2013)
9. Yang, A., et al.: Qwen2.5 technical report (2025)
10. Sazid, M.T., Mercer, R.E.: A unified representation and a decoupled deep learning architecture for argumentation mining of students' persuasive essays. In: Lapesa, G., Schneider, J., Jo, Y., Saha, S. (eds.) Proceedings of the 9th Workshop on Argument Mining, pp. 74–83. International Conference on Computational Linguistics, Online and in Gyeongju, Republic of Korea (2022)

11. Stab, C., Gurevych, I.: Identifying argumentative discourse structures in persuasive essays. In: Moschitti, A., Pang, B., Daelemans, W. (eds.) Proceedings of the 2014 Conference on Empirical Methods in Natural Language Processing (EMNLP), pp. 46–56. Association for Computational Linguistics, Doha, Qatar (2014)
12. Wachsmuth, H., Al-Khatib, K., Stein, B.: Using argument mining to assess the argumentation quality of essays. In: Matsumoto, Y., Prasad, R. (eds.) Proceedings of COLING 2016, the 26th International Conference on Computational Linguistics: Technical Papers, pp. 1680–1691. Osaka, Japan (2016)
13. Wang, H., Huang, Z., Dou, Y., Hong, Y.: Argumentation mining on essays at multi scales. In: Scott, D., Bel, N., Zong, C. (eds.) Proceedings of the 28th International Conference on Computational Linguistics, pp. 5480–5493. International Committee on Computational Linguistics, Barcelona, Spain (Online) (2020)

Comprehensive Argument Mining
for Chinese Argumentative Essays Using
Large Language Models

Yu Song, Bohan Yu, Aoze Zheng, Pengcheng Wu, Tao Liu, Xia Liu,
Hongying Zan, and Kunli Zhang[✉]

School of Computer and Artificial Intelligence, Zhengzhou University,
Zhengzhou, China
alexyu010120@gs.zzu.edu.cn

Abstract. Argument mining in Chinese essays is a challenging task due
to the diversity of argumentative structures. In NLPCC 2025 Shared
Task 5, we explored the use of large language models for comprehensive
argument analysis. For argumentative component detection, we decouple
the task into two stages. We first perform coarse-grained classification,
then refine the results with fine-grained classification, both accomplished
through fine-tuning large language models. For argument relation identification, we apply automated prompt engineering, beginning with a manually designed seed prompt and iteratively expanding and testing candidate prompts on simple data to select and optimize the best template.
Our approach enhances contextual understanding and achieves strong
performance in both argumentative component detection and argument
relation identification, with our method achieving first place in the evaluation.

Keywords: Argument Mining · Large Language Models · Natural
Language Processing

1 Introduction

Argument mining aims to automatically identify argumentative components
and their structural relationships within essays, and has become an important
research direction in natural language processing [8]. Early approaches typically
relied on syntactic trees or graph-based models, utilizing handcrafted rules or
shallow features to capture local dependencies between argument elements [15]
[12]. However, these methods often struggled to incorporate the global structure
of the text, resulting in limited performance on complex argumentative discourse.

With the development of deep learning, pre-trained language models such as
BERT [5] and RoBERTa [9] have emerged as the dominant techniques, leveraging self-attention mechanisms to capture long-range semantic dependencies
and achieving substantial improvements across various argument mining tasks

© The Author(s), under exclusive license to Springer Nature Singapore Pte Ltd. 2026
X.-L. Mao et al. (Eds.): NLPCC 2025, LNAI 16105, pp. 358–366, 2026.
https://doi.org/10.1007/978-981-95-3352-7_30

[19] [2]. Nevertheless, most of these models focus on local semantic understanding, and their ability to model document-level argumentative structure remains limited [4].

Recently, the advent of large language models (LLMs) has opened new possibilities for argument mining, enabling more effective modeling of both sentence-level semantics and document-level structure [1] [16]. In the NLPCC 2025 Shared Task 5, we explored the use of large language models for comprehensive argument analysis in Chinese argumentative essays. For argument component detection, we designed a two-stage framework: first, we applied LLMs to perform coarse-grained and fine-grained classification for each sentence, while incorporating paragraph-level contextual information to enhance structural understanding. For argument relation identification, we adopted automated prompt engineering, generating and optimizing prompts to guide LLMs in identifying relations between sentences without further parameter tuning. Our method achieved first place in argument component detection and second place in argument relation identification, ranking first overall in the competition.

2   Task Description

2.1   Track 1. Argumentative Component Detection (ACD)

This task aims to identify the argumentative component of each sentence in Chinese high school students' essays. Each sentence is first classified into four coarse-grained categories: assertion, evidence, elaboration, or others. Assertion sentences are further divided into major claim, claim, and restate claim, while evidence is refined into fact, anecdote, quotation, proverb, and axiom, according to the content and source. In total, ten fine-grained categories are defined, enabling detailed structural analysis of argumentative essays.

2.2   Track 2. Argument Relation Identification (ARI)

This task focuses on identifying the logical and argumentative relations between components within an essay. Based on the component types recognized in ACD, the system determines whether a relation exists between pairs of sentences, and further classifies the relation into a set of predefined categories, which are constrained by the types of the sentence pair involved. For example, a claim may support another claim or be supported by a reason, while a lead may be related to a background or detail. These relation types vary depending on the combination of sentence roles, rather than forming a single fixed label set. This task aims to uncover the internal logical structure and argumentative coherence of the essay, providing deeper insight into its reasoning process.

3   Related Work

Argument mining has emerged as a prominent research topic in NLP, targeting the automatic identification of argumentative components and their relations in various genres of text [3,8]. Early work in this area primarily relied on rule-based methods, syntactic parsing, and graph structures to model argument components and relations [12,15]. For instance, Peldszus and Stede applied joint prediction models for discourse parsing in argument mining, while Stab and Gurevych proposed feature-rich approaches for analyzing persuasive essays.

The introduction of deep learning significantly advanced the field. Neural network models such as RNNs and CNNs were first applied to argument mining tasks [6,11]. With the success of pre-trained language models like BERT [5] and RoBERTa [9], researchers achieved substantial improvements in both argument component detection and relation classification by leveraging contextualized word embeddings and self-attention mechanisms [19]. However, these models tend to focus more on local semantic understanding and often struggle to capture global argumentative structure in long documents.

Recently, LLMs such as GPT-3 [10] and GPT-4 [16] have demonstrated strong capabilities in zero-shot and few-shot learning, enabling prompt-based approaches for argument mining. Prompt engineering has attracted increasing attention, allowing users to elicit desired behaviors from LLMs by designing and optimizing input prompts instead of fine-tuning model parameters [13,17]. In argument mining, methods based on prompt selection, prompt generation, and iterative prompt optimization have been shown to improve relation extraction and classification tasks with minimal annotation cost [16].

Despite these advances, most previous work has focused on English, while research on argument mining for Chinese texts, particularly student essays, remains relatively limited [14]. Our approach addresses this gap by integrating two-stage fine-tuning and automated prompt engineering with LLMs for comprehensive argument analysis in Chinese argumentative essays.

4   Methods

4.1   Track 1 (ACD)

In this subtask, we use a two-stage fine-tuning framework to identify argumentative components in Chinese argumentative essays, consisting of coarse-grained classification and fine-grained classification, as shown in Fig. 1.

First, for coarse-grained classification, we split the original essay into individual sentences and input each sentence along with its context from the entire essay into a large language model. Let the input essay be $E = \{s_1, s_2, \ldots, s_n\}$, where s_i denotes the i-th sentence. We use the fine-tuned LLM to classify each sentence, obtaining the coarse-grained label $C_i^{\text{coarse}} \in \{\text{Assert}, \text{Evid}, \text{Elab}, \text{Other}\}$ for each sentence. Specifically, the coarse-grained classification process can be represented as:

$$C_i^{\text{coarse}} = \text{LLM}_{\text{coarse}}(s_i, E) \tag{1}$$

Here, $\text{LLM}_{\text{coarse}}$ refers to the LLM fine-tuned for coarse-grained classification.

After performing coarse-grained classification, we proceed to fine-grained classification. For sentences labeled as 'Assertion', we further categorize them

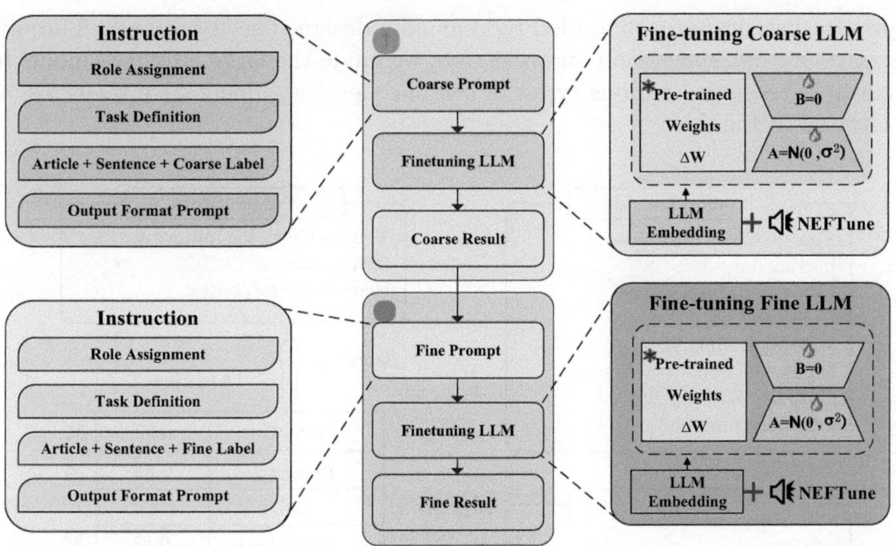

Fig. 1. Two-stage fine-tuning framework for argumentative component classification with document-level context.

into more specific types, such as 'Major Claim' or 'Claim'. For sentences labeled as 'Evidence', we further distinguish between 'Fact', 'Anecdote', 'Quotation', etc. The fine-grained classification process utilizes the coarse-grained label C_i^{coarse} for each sentence and fine-tunes the LLM again to obtain the fine-grained classification label C_i^{fine}. This process can be represented as:

$$C_i^{\text{fine}} = \text{LLM}_{\text{fine}}(s_i, C_i^{\text{coarse}}, E) \tag{2}$$

Here, LLM_{fine} refers to the LLM fine-tuned for fine-grained classification.

The input format for both stages includes the sentence content and the context of the entire essay to ensure that the LLM can fully understand the relationship between the sentence and the overall essay structure. The input format is as follows:

$$\text{Input} = \langle \text{Sentence} : s_i, \text{Context} : E \rangle \tag{3}$$

Through this two-stage fine-tuning process, we successfully combine contextual information and accurately identify the argumentative components in Chinese argumentative essays.

4.2   Track 2 (ARI)

In Track 2, our goal is to identify argumentative relations between sentence pairs in Chinese argumentative essays, such as support, rebuttal, comparison, example, and citation. Inspired by Automated Prompt Engineering [20], we adopt a prompt-based approach guided by manually designed seed prompts. Through iterative prompt generation and selection, we guide the large language model to accurately recognize various types of sentence-level argumentative relations, as illustrated in Fig. 2.

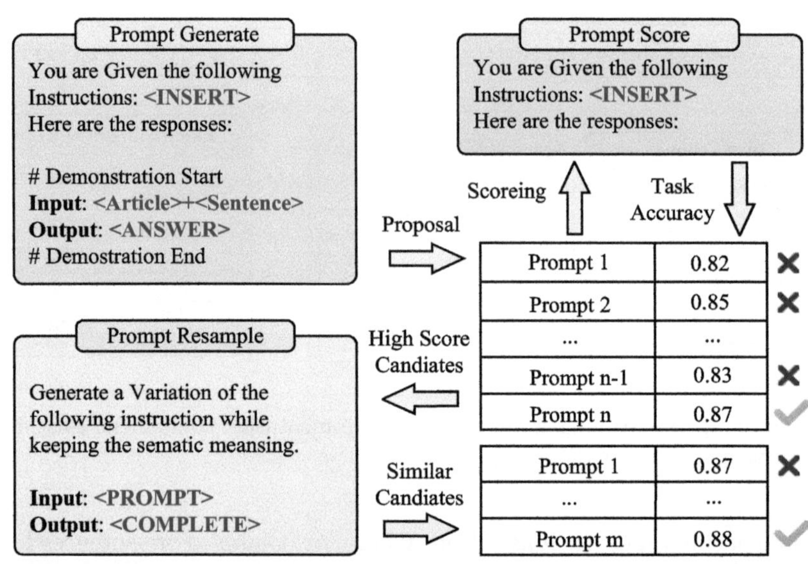

Fig. 2. The process of using automated prompt engineering to generate and select the optimal prompt.

We start by manually designing a seed prompt P_0 that poses a basic question or task, such as 'Does sentence 1 support sentence 2?'. The LLM is then used to generate multiple extended prompts $P_1, P_2, \ldots, P_m$ based on the seed, each covering different relation types or task details. These candidate prompts are evaluated on a small validation set, and the best-performing template P_{best} is selected according to an evaluation metric $\mathcal{L}(P_i)$:

$$P_{\text{best}} = \arg \max_{P_i \in \{P_1, P_2, \ldots, P_m\}} \mathcal{L}(P_i) \tag{4}$$

Once the optimal prompt P_{best} is selected, we iteratively expand and test new prompts, always retaining and building upon the best-performing template in each round, until convergence.

Finally, the selected optimal prompt P_{best} is used to instruct the LLM to predict the relation type R_{ij} for any sentence pair (s_i, s_j):

$$R_{ij} = \text{LLM}(s_i, s_j, P_{\text{best}}) \tag{5}$$

This automated prompt engineering framework allows us to efficiently identify argumentative relations without further fine-tuning, making the overall approach highly flexible and data-efficient.

5   Experiments

5.1   Dataset and Model

For Track 1, the training data is sourced from the training set of NLPCC 2024 Shared Task 5 on Argument Mining for Chinese Argumentative Essays. After data cleaning to avoid overlap with the test set, we retained 12 essays as our dataset. Each essay was segmented into individual sentences, resulting in a total of 480 sentences. These sentences were randomly divided into a training set and a validation set according to an 8:2 split, yielding 384 sentences for training and 96 for validation. For Track 2, the training data is constructed from the data samples provided in the official task documentation. The test set for both tracks is the official test set from NLPCC 2025 Shared Task 3.

In Track 1, we selected Qwen2.5-7B-Instruct [18] as the primary model and applied LoRA [7] for instruction-based fine-tuning. For Track 2, we utilized Qwen2.5-72B-Instruct [18] as the model for generating and optimizing prompts.

5.2   Hyperparameter Settings

All experiments were performed on a single NVIDIA A800 GPU to ensure consistent computational resources and reproducibility. The main hyperparameters used for model training and fine-tuning, including optimizer, learning rate, batch size, and LoRA rank, are detailed in Table 1.

Table 1. Hyperparameter Settings

Hyperparameters	Settings
Batchsize	4
Gradient accumulation steps	1
Initial learning rate	1e−5
Optimizer	AdamW
Lr scheduler	Cosine
Max grad norm	1.0
Max input length	4096
LoRA rank	64
LoRA alpha	256
Neftune noise	3.0 (ACD)

We applied LoRA to all linear layers of the model, while keeping the other parameters fixed during fine-tuning. The weights achieving the best performance on the validation set were chosen as the final checkpoint.

5.3　Evaluation Metrics

ACD. The final score for component detection is calculated as the average of the micro-average F1 and macro-average F1:

$$\text{Score}_{\text{track 1}} = 0.5 \times \text{Micro-F1} + 0.5 \times \text{Macro-F1} \tag{6}$$

ARI. For relation identification, the evaluation metric is the micro-average F1 score computed over all relation categories. The final score is reported as:

$$\text{Score}_{\text{track 2}} = \text{Micro-F1}_{\text{relation}} \tag{7}$$

The overall score is computed as a weighted sum of the scores from both tracks, with Track 1 accounting for 40% and Track 2 for 60%:

$$\text{Overall Score} = 0.4 \times \text{Score}_{\text{track 1}} + 0.6 \times \text{Score}_{\text{track 2}} \tag{8}$$

5.4　Results and Analysis

ACD. Our experimental results are shown in Table 2. Starting with Qwen2.5-7B-Instruct as the baseline, we achieve a Micro-F1 score of 31.73% on the ACD task. Introducing document-level context results in a substantial improvement, with Micro-F1 increasing to 51.84%. This highlights the importance of incorporating global contextual information, which enables the model to better understand the structural role of each sentence within the essay. When both document-level context and the coarse-to-fine classification strategy are applied, the Micro-F1 further improves to 65.48%. This demonstrates that, in addition to global context, task decoupling plays a crucial role. The coarse-to-fine framework effectively reduces label confusion and learning difficulty, resulting in a much stronger ability to accurately identify argumentative components in Chinese essays.

Table 2. Performance of our method on the ACD task.

Method	Micro-F1 (%)
Qwen2.5-7B-Instruct (baseline)	31.73
+ Document-level Context	51.84
+ Coarse-to-fine Classification + Document-level Context	65.48

ARI. Our results for the ARI task are presented in Table 3. The baseline Qwen2.5-72B-Instruct model achieves a Micro-F1 of 7.13%. With automated prompt engineering, performance improves to 8.54% after just one iteration. Notably, increasing the number of prompt engineering iterations to five further boosts the Micro-F1 to 10.26%. These results clearly indicate that the iterative process of automated prompt engineering plays a crucial role in improving relation identification, with additional iterations leading to significant gains in model performance.

Table 3. Performance comparison on the ARI task with different numbers of prompt engineering iterations.

Method	Micro-F1 (%)
Qwen2.5-72B-Instruct (baseline)	7.13
+ Automated Prompt Engineering (iteration = 1)	8.54
+ Automated Prompt Engineering (iteration = 5)	10.26

6 Conclusion

In this paper, we presented our methods for NLPCC 2025 Shared Task 5 Comprehensive Argument Analysis for Chinese Argumentative Essay. For argumentative component detection, we adopted a two-stage fine-tuning framework combining coarse-to-fine classification with document-level context to enhance the model's ability to recognize sentence roles. For relation identification, we leveraged automated prompt engineering based on Qwen2.5-72B-Instruct, and demonstrated that iterative prompt optimization effectively improved relation prediction. Our approach integrates task decoupling and global contextual modeling to address the challenges of complex argumentative structures. On the final test set, our method achieved strong performance, ranking first in argument component detection, second in relation identification, and first overall in the competition.

References

1. Achiam, J., et al.: GPT-4 technical report. arXiv preprint arXiv:2303.08774 (2023)
2. Cabessa, J., Hernault, H., Mushtaq, U.: Argument mining with fine-tuned large language models. In: Proceedings of the 31st International Conference on Computational Linguistics, pp. 6624–6635 (2025)
3. Five years of argument mining: Cabrio, E., Villata, S. A data-driven analysis. In: IJCAI. **18**, 5427–5433 (2018)
4. Chen, Z., Chen, W., Xu, J., Liu, Z., Zhang, W.: Beyond semantics: learning a behavior augmented relevance model with self-supervised learning. In: Proceedings of the 32nd ACM International Conference on Information and Knowledge Management, pp. 4516–4522 (2023)

5. Devlin, J., Chang, M.W., Lee, K., Toutanova, K.: Bert: Pre-training of deep bidirectional transformers for language understanding. In: Proceedings of the 2019 conference of the North American chapter of the association for computational linguistics: human language technologies, volume 1 (long and short papers), pp. 4171–4186 (2019)

6. Eger, S., Daxenberger, J., Gurevych, I.: Neural end-to-end learning for computational argumentation mining. arXiv preprint arXiv:1704.06104 (2017)

7. Hu, E.J., et al.: Lora: low-rank adaptation of large language models. ICLR $\mathbf{1}(2)$, 3 (2022)

8. Lippi, M., Torroni, P.: Argumentation mining: state of the art and emerging trends. ACM Trans. Internet Technol. (TOIT) $\mathbf{16}(2)$, 1–25 (2016)

9. Liu, Y., et al.: Roberta: a robustly optimized BERT pretraining approach. arXiv preprint arXiv:1907.11692 (2019)

10. Mann, B., et al.: Language models are few-shot learners. arXiv preprint arXiv:2005.14165 $\mathbf{1}(3)$ (2020)

11. Nguyen, H., Litman, D.: Argument mining for improving the automated scoring of persuasive essays. In: Proceedings of the AAAI Conference on Artificial Intelligence. vol. 32 (2018)

12. Peldszus, A., Stede, M.: Joint prediction in MST-style discourse parsing for argumentation mining. In: Proceedings of the 2015 Conference on Empirical Methods in Natural Language Processing, pp. 938–948 (2015)

13. Pryzant, R., Iter, D., Li, J., Lee, Y.T., Zhu, C., Zeng, M.: Automatic prompt optimization with "gradient descent" and beam search. arXiv preprint arXiv:2305.03495 (2023)

14. Ren, Y., et al.: Ceamc: corpus and empirical study of argument analysis in education via LLMs. In: Findings of the Association for Computational Linguistics: EMNLP 2024, pp. 6949–6966 (2024)

15. Stab, C., Gurevych, I.: Identifying argumentative discourse structures in persuasive essays. In: Proceedings of the 2014 Conference On Empirical Methods In Natural Language Processing (EMNLP), pp. 46–56 (2014)

16. Wadhwa, S., Amir, S., Wallace, B.C.: Revisiting relation extraction in the era of large language models. In: Proceedings of the conference. Association for Computational Linguistics. Meeting. vol. 2023, p. 15566 (2023)

17. Wei, J., et al.: Chain-of-thought prompting elicits reasoning in large language models. Adv. Neural. Inf. Process. Syst. $\mathbf{35}$, 24824–24837 (2022)

18. Yang, Q.A., et al.: Qwen2.5 technical report. ArXiv $\mathbf{abs/2412.15115}$ (2024). https://api.semanticscholar.org/CorpusID:274859421

19. Zhang, G., Lillis, D., Nulty, P.: Can domain pre-training help interdisciplinary researchers from data annotation poverty? a case study of legal argument mining with BERT-based transformers. In: Proceedings of the Workshop on Natural Language Processing for Digital Humanities, pp. 121–130 (2021)

20. Zhou, Y., et al.: Large language models are human-level prompt engineers. In: The Eleventh International Conference on Learning Representations (2022)

Overview of the NLPCC 2025 Shared Task 4: Multi-modal, Multilingual, and Multi-hop Medical Instructional Video Question Answering Challenge

Bin Li[1], Shenxi Liu[2], Yixuan Weng[3], Yue Du[1], Yuhang Tian[2], and Shoujun Zhou[1(✉)]

[1] Shenzhen Institute of Advanced Technology, Chinese Academy of Sciences, Shenzhen, China
{b.li2,yue.du2,sj.zhou}@siat.ac.cn
[2] School of Computer Science and Technology, Beijing Institute of Technology, Beijing, China
{liushenxi,tianyuhang}@bit.edu.cn
[3] School of Engineering, Westlake University, Hangzhou, China
https://cmivqa.github.io/

Abstract. Following the successful hosts of the 1-st (NLPCC 2023 Foshan) CMIVQA and the 2-rd (NLPCC 2024 Hangzhou) MMIVQA challenges, this year, a new task has been introduced to further advance research in multi-modal, multilingual, and multi-hop medical instructional question answering (M4IVQA) systems, with a specific focus on medical instructional videos. The M4IVQA challenge focuses on evaluating models that integrate information from medical instructional videos, understand multiple languages, and answer multi-hop questions requiring reasoning over various modalities. This task consists of three tracks: multi-modal, multilingual, and multi-hop Temporal Answer Grounding in Single Video (M4TAGSV), multi-modal, multilingual, and multi-hop Video Corpus Retrieval (M4VCR) and multi-modal, multilingual, and multi-hop Temporal Answer Grounding in Video Corpus (M4TAGVC). Participants in M4IVQA are expected to develop algorithms capable of processing both video and text data, understanding multilingual queries, and providing relevant answers to multi-hop medical questions. We believe the newly introduced M4IVQA challenge will drive innovations in multimodal reasoning systems for healthcare scenarios, ultimately contributing to smarter emergency response systems and more effective medical education platforms in multilingual communities[1]Official Website: https://cmivqa.github.io/

Keywords: Multilingual medical instructional video · Multi-hop question answering · Video retrieval · Temporal answer grounding

---

B. Li and S. Liu—These authors contribute this work equally.

© The Author(s), under exclusive license to Springer Nature Singapore Pte Ltd. 2026
X.-L. Mao et al. (Eds.): NLPCC 2025, LNAI 16105, pp. 367–379, 2026.
https://doi.org/10.1007/978-981-95-3352-7_31

1   Introduction

Recent advancements in AI-assisted healthcare have demonstrated potential across various clinical scenarios [1–3], particularly in imaging diagnosis [4,5] and personalized treatment consultation [6,7]. The development of Video Question Answering (VideoQA) technology in the medical domain has achieved significant breakthroughs in extracting information from video content and answering related queries [8,9]. However, significant gaps persist in the development of reasoning systems capable of handling multimodal domain knowledge [10,11]. Existing medical VideoQA systems still face three fundamental challenges: (1) temporal grounding of cross-modal evidence, (2) multilingual semantic alignment, and (3) multi-hop reasoning across the video corpus.

To advance research and application in this field, NLPCC 2025 has introduced the Multi-modal, Multilingual, and Multi-hop Medical Instructional Question Answering (M4IVQA) challenge, specifically focusing on instructional medical videos. This task includes three tracks:: multi-modal, multilingual, and multi-hop Temporal Answer Grounding in Single Video (M4TAGSV), multi-modal, multilingual, and multi-hop Video Corpus Retrieval (M4VCR) and multi-modal, multilingual, and multi-hop Temporal Answer Grounding in Video Corpus (M4TAGVC). The main goals of the M4IVQA challenge include:

1. **Multi-hop reasoning**: The task requires systems to perform multi-step inference across heterogeneous information sources within or across videos. This reflects the complexity of real medical questions, which often require combining multiple pieces of evidence rather than relying on a single visual cue [12].
2. **Multimodal fusion**: Effective performance depends on the model's ability to jointly understand and integrate diverse modalities [13], including instructional narration [14], visual demonstrations [15], and on-screen text [16] (e.g., captions or annotations), which are all essential components in medical video content.
3. **Cross-video temporal grounding**: This involves not only retrieving the most semantically relevant videos, but also accurately pinpointing the temporal boundaries of answer-containing segments. Such a capability is critical in medical education and practice, where relevant knowledge may be dispersed across different procedural videos or case demonstrations.

The design of the M4IVQA task is closely aligned with the practical demands of medical education and emergency information access. In surgical scenarios, the ability to rapidly locate key operational procedures within videos can be life-saving. In educational contexts, intelligent question-answering systems empower learners to better comprehend complex medical techniques by referencing precise visual evidence [17,18]. Moreover, multilingual support ensures that high-quality medical instructional content can transcend language barriers, thereby reaching and benefiting a broader global audience.

This paper provides a comprehensive overview of the M4IVQA task, including its design motivations, dataset composition, evaluation framework, and potential application scenarios. Through this challenge, we aim to advance research in medical AI, multimodal reasoning, and cross-lingual understanding, ultimately contributing to improved global medical training and more accessible dissemination of emergency knowledge.

2   Task Introduction

2.1   Definition of Each Track

The M4IVQA challenge aims to promote the development of medical instructional video question-answering technology, especially in reasoning ability. This task requires participants to develop algorithms capable of processing both video and text data, understanding user's queries [19], and providing relevant answers to multi-hop medical questions. The M4IVQA task is divided into three challenging subtasks, which is described as follows.

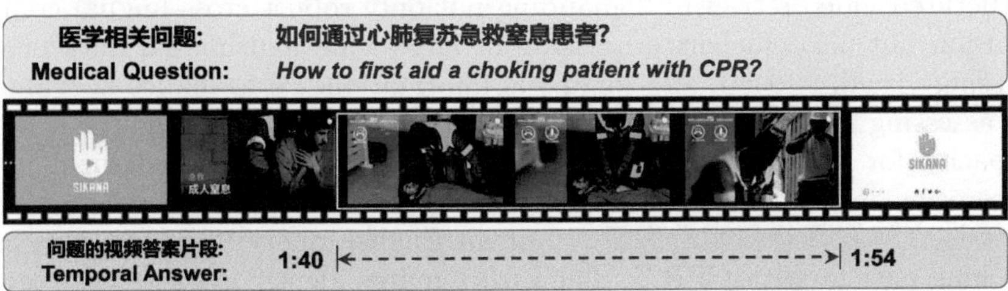

Fig. 1. Introduction of the multi-modal, multilingual, and multi-hop Temporal Answer Grounding in Singe Video (M4TAGSV) track.

1. M4TAGSV: This track targets temporal answer grounding in a single video. Given a natural-language question in both Chinese or English language, AI systems must precisely identify the contiguous temporal span that contains the requisite visual evidence. Accordingly, the track benchmarks fine-grained video comprehension and high-resolution temporal localization, thereby laying the groundwork for the more complex corpus-level tasks. As illustrated in Fig. 1, for the Chinese query "如何通过心肺复苏急救窒息患者？" or its English counterpart "How to first aid a choking patient with CPR?", the correct prediction is the segment 01:40-01:54. We also prepared knowledge graphs in different languages, which are derived from Wikipedia or common knowledge bases [20]. As shown in Fig. 2, the "CPR" in the knowledge graph helps the model understand professional medical terms and perform more complex multi-hop reasoning.

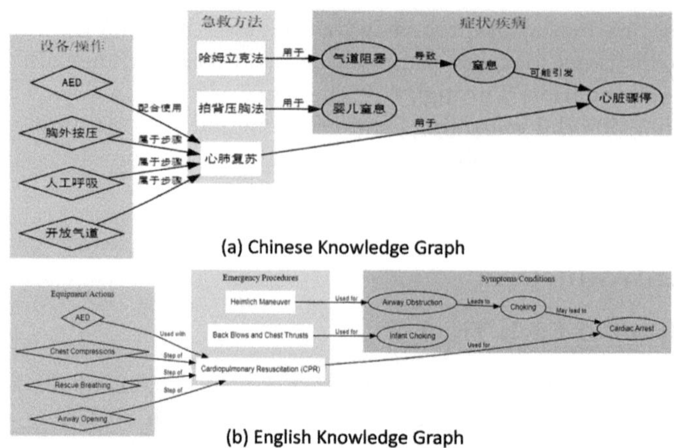

Fig. 2. Illustration of the knowledge graph derived from the given medical video.

2. M4VCR: This track integrates a domain-specific knowledge graph to facilitate structured video retrieval, demanding not only robust cross-lingual comprehension but also efficient processing of large-scale multimodal data encompassing visual, textual, and linguistic information. Performance is evaluated by assessing the relevance ranking of returned videos, measuring the system's capacity for information retrieval and semantic relevance judgment across heterogeneous sources. As illustrated in Fig. 3, consider a Chinese query: "如何通过心肺复苏急救窒息患者？" or an English query: "How to first aid a choking patient with CPR?". The task requires identifying the most semantically aligned video within the corpus.

3. M4TAGVC: This task combines the key challenges of the first two tracks, requiring systems to retrieve relevant videos from large-scale corpora and precisely localize answer-containing temporal segments (e.g., "visual answers"). This task assesses holistic capabilities in video comprehension, cross-corpus information retrieval, cross-lingual semantic alignment, and temporal grounding–integrating multi-hop reasoning across visual, textual, and linguistic data. As shown in Fig. 4, given a query like the Chinese "如何通过心肺复苏急救窒息患者？" or the English "How to first aid a choking patient with CPR?", the system shall first identify semantically matched videos and then pinpoint the exact time span (e.g., 1:40â"1:54 s) where the answer is demonstrated. This requires a model for corpus-level retrieval and fine-grained temporal localization.

2.2 Evaluation Metrics

The M4IVQA challenge utilizes a holistic framework of evaluation metrics that assess participating systems through multiple dimensions. These metrics not

Fig. 3. Introduction of the multi-modal, multilingual, and multi-hop Video Corpus Retrieval (M4VCR) track.

Fig. 4. Introduction of the multi-modal, multilingual, and multi-hop Temporal Answer Grounding in Video Corpus (M4TAGVC) track.

only examine the correctness of system outputs but also quantify their precision levels and ranking capabilities, ensuring a thorough and equitable assessment process.

1. M4TAGSV: Our primary evaluation metric is the Intersection over Union (IoU), which measures the overlap extent between predicted and ground-truth regions of interest [14]. To achieve a holistic performance assessment across all test scenarios, we compute the mean IoU (mIoU). Drawing from prior research, we integrate supplementary evaluation metrics. A key addition is the "R@n, IoU $= \mu$" metric, which evaluates instances where the overlap between predicted temporal spans and ground-truth moments surpasses a threshold μ among the top-n retrieved segments. In our specific evaluation

framework, we fix n at 1 and examine μ values of 0.3, 0.5, and 0.7. These metrics are formalized by the following equations.

$$IOU = \frac{A \cap B}{A \cup B}$$

$$mIOU = \left(\sum_{i=1}^{N} IOU_i \right) / N \tag{1}$$

where A and B represent different spans, and $\sum_{i=1}^{N} IOU_i$ represent IoU $= 0.3/0.5/0.7$ respectively, $N=3$.

2. M4VCR: We utilized the standard evaluation metrics in video retrieval [21,22], specifically the "R@n" metric with n set to 1, 10, and 50. This metric quantifies the system's recall performance at varying retrieval depths. To assess the effectiveness of multilingual medical instructional video retrieval, we incorporated the Mean Reciprocal Rank (MRR) score. As a holistic measure, MRR evaluates both the correctness of retrieved results and the positional ranking of accurate entries, defined by the following calculation:

$$MRR = \frac{1}{|V|} \sum_{i=1}^{|V|} \frac{1}{Rank_i} \tag{2}$$

Here, $|V|$ represents the number of videos in the corpus. For each testing sample V_i, $Rank_i$ denotes the position of the ground-truth target video in the predicted list.

In this track, the primary ranking metric is the "verall" score, which combines the R@1, R@10, R@50, and MRR scores:

$$Overall = \frac{1}{|M|} \sum_{i=1}^{|M|} Value_i \tag{3}$$

Here, $|M|$ is the number of evaluation metrics (4 in this case, corresponding to R@1, R@10, R@50, and MRR), and $Value_i$ denotes the i-th metric score.

3. M4TAGVC: We retained the Intersection over Union (IoU) metric in the first task to evaluate the precision of temporal localization. Additionally, the second task incorporates retrieval-oriented metrics, including the "R@n" (with n set to 1, 10, and 50) and mean reciprocal rank (MRR) scores. To integrate these, we introduce the "R@1—mIoU, R@10—mIoU, and R@50—mIoU" metrics, which compute the average IoU values at different retrieval depths, offering a comprehensive assessment of model performance. Participating models' final rankings in this task are primarily determined by a composite score termed "Average," derived from the mean of three indicators (denoted as $Value_i'$ for the i-th indicator): R@1—mIoU, R@10—mIoU, and R@50—mIoU. The specific calculation formula is as follows:

$$Average = \frac{1}{|M'|} \sum_{i=1}^{|M'|} Value_i' \tag{4}$$

where the $|M'| = 3$.

2.3   Dateset

```json
[
  {
    "id":60,
    "video_id":"L8wKeHJANR0",
    "Chinese_question":"如何使用弓箭步来缓解膝关节疼痛？",
    "English_question":"How to use Lunges to relieve knee pain?",
    "start_second":840,
    "end_second":906,
    "video_captions":[
      {
        "Ch_caption":"很开心今天又跟大家见面",
        "Eng_caption":"I'm very happy to meet you all again today",
        "start":6.0,
        "end":9.0,
        "duration":3.0
      }...
    ]
  }...
]
```

Fig. 5. Dataset examples of the M4IVQA shared task.

The M4IVQA challenge builds upon the dataset of MMIVQA [2] and incorporates new knowledge graphs, utilizing a specially constructed multilingual medical instructional video dataset with unique and comprehensive characteristics, as illustrated in Fig. 5. Sourced from medical educational channels on YouTube via the Pytube tool[1], the dataset covers diverse topics such as first aid, medical emergency management, and medical education, ensuring professional and varied content. A core feature is its multilingual design: each video includes both Chinese and English subtitles directly extracted from YouTube, alongside corresponding questions and answers in both languages. Chinese questions (Chinese_question) are manually crafted by Chinese medical experts, while English questions (English_question) are translated and reviewed by native English-speaking physicians to guarantee linguistic accuracy and professional rigor. The dataset's foundation in MMIVQA, combined with the integration of new knowledge graphs, enriches its structure for comprehensive multimodal and multilingual evaluation.

---

[1] https://github.com/pytube/.

To ensure data quality, annotations are meticulously conducted by professionals with medical backgrounds. Each video may contain multiple question-answer pairs, where semantically equivalent questions map to a single unique answer. Every question is annotated with precise answers and timestamps (start and end seconds) to anchor responses to specific video segments. Additionally, the dataset includes automatically generated Chinese and English subtitles via Whisper[2], providing participants with supplementary textual context beyond the video content. A distinctive feature of the dataset is its detailed sample annotations for the M4TAGV task, including "id" (for video retrieval indexing) and YouTube's unique "video_id". The "id" identifiers remain non-public during the competition to maintain evaluation fairness. For comprehensive dataset details and download links, participants can access the GitHub repository at https://github.com/cmivqa/NLPCC2025_M4IVQA, which offers extensive resource support for model development and testing.

Table 1. Details of the datasets in NLPCC shared task 4.

Dataset	Videos	QA pairs	KG Nums.	Ch_Q.AvgLen.	Eng_Q.AvgLen.	Video Avg. Len.
Train	1228	5840	28490	17.16	6.97	263.3
Dev	200	983	4637	17.81	7.26	242.4
Test	200	1022	5011	17.48	7.44	310.9

All the Train, Dev and Test files in the M4IVQA dataset include videos, audio, and corresponding subtitles. To maintain consistency, all the Chinese questions and subtitles have been converted to Simplified Chinese. As shown in Table 1, the dataset is divided into three subsets: Train, Dev, and Test sets. The Train set contains 1228 videos with 5840 QA pairs, the Dev set includes 200 videos with 983 QA pairs, and the Test set consists of 200 videos with 1022 QA pairs. The Knowledge Graph (KG) number (Triple) for train set is 28490, 4637 for the Dev set, and 5011 for the Test set. The average length of Chinese questions (AvgLen. Ch_Q) is 17.16 characters for the Train set, 17.81 for the Dev set, and 17.48 for the Test set. For English questions (Eng_Q AvgLen.), the average lengths are 6.97, 7.26, and 7.44 words for Train, Dev, and Test sets respectively. The average video length (Video Avg. Len.) varies across the sets, with 263.3 s for Train set, 242.4 s for Dev set, and 310.9 s for Test set.

3   Evaluation Results

There are a total of 21 teams registered for the NLPCC 2025 Shared Task 4. During the testing phase, 10 teams submitted their results. Here is a brief introduction to the representative systems designed by **Baichuan** for track 1, **DIMA** for track 2, and **MedEcho** for track 3 (Tables 2, 3 and 4).

---

[2] https://github.com/openai/whisper.

Table 2. Final Results of the track 1.

Rank	Team ID	R@1,IoU=0.3	R@1,IoU=0.5	R@1,IoU=0.7	mIoU(R@1)
1	Baichuan	0.5133	0.3612	0.2103	0.3717
2	Ouc_AI [23]	0.5088	0.3542	0.2054	0.3637
3	SEU	0.4719	0.3314	0.1973	0.3411
4	SETAG [24]	0.4775	0.3209	0.1898	0.3389
5	BIGG	0.4099	0.2863	0.1544	0.2977
6	PIPINSTALL [2]	0.4055	0.2911	0.1454	0.2898
7	Random Pick Method [1]	0.0571	0.0465	0.0358	0.0397

Table 3. Final Results of the track 2.

Rank	Team ID	R@1	R@10	R@50	MRR	Overall
1	DIMA	0.3264	0.4211	0.5177	0.3407	1.6059
2	NYU	0.3213	0.4137	0.5104	0.3354	1.5808
3	sun [25]	0.3121	0.4078	0.4966	0.3245	1.5410
4	DSG-1 [26]	0.2644	0.3545	0.4414	0.2887	1.3491
5	Wjh	0.2744	0.3312	0.4117	0.2551	1.2724
6	GEN [2]	0.1311	0.1074	0.0978	0.1142	0.4505
7	Random Pick Method [1]	0.03438	0.03668	0.05238	0.04428	0.1674

For Track 1, the Baichuan team developed a RAG - enhanced multi - modal fusion framework. They take medical videos, queries, subtitles, and knowledge graphs as inputs, where RAG enriches the query and subtitle text by retrieving relevant information from the knowledge graph. The CLIP aligns video frames and queries to get a rough time interval. Then, we adopt the feature extractor to separately extract visual and textual features [29]. Pseudo - label generators guide the training of visual and textual predictors. A mutual knowledge transfer module is used between modalities to improve the prediction accuracy of start and end times. The whole framework is optimized through a supervised learning loop to achieve accurate localization of answers in medical videos.

Table 4. Final Results of the track 3.

Rank	Team ID	R@1|mIoU	R@10|mIoU	R@50|mIoU	Average
1	MedEcho	0.1284	0.2417	0.3243	0.2314
2	NYU	0.1202	0.2366	0.3133	0.2233
3	IIEleven [27]	0.1141	0.2343	0.3098	0.2200
4	Nsddd [28]	0.1078	0.2145	0.2997	0.2112
5	Random Pick Method [1]	0.0247	0.0397	0.0509	0.0384

For the track 2, the DIMA team proposed a three-stage retrieval-rerank framework. In the 1-st stage, subtitle chunks are enriched with knowledge-graph facts, encoded by LaBSE [30], and organized into a hierarchical index. In the 2-nd stage, a similarity-based traversal prunes low-score branches of this index and returns a compact pool of top candidate segments. In 3-rd stage, a lightweight multilingual LLM reranks these segments, and max-pool aggregation yields the final video ranking, augmenting the fine-grained multilingual relevance.

For Track-3, the MedEcho team proposed a multi-hop knowledge-enhanced cross-modal retrieval framework designed for multilingual medical instructional video question answering. The approach begins by extracting visual and textual features using CLIP-ViT and a BERT-based encoder [31], respectively. Each video is decomposed into aligned frame-subtitle pairs, and a transformer-based cross-modal alignment module is applied to fuse these features and capture fine-grained semantic relationships [32]. To address modality imbalance and enable efficient retrieval, a subtitle-level embedding library is constructed through temporal modeling. Moreover, the method retrieves relevant knowledge triples from an external medical knowledge graph and performs multi-hop reasoning via a RAG module to generate an enhanced query representation that better reflects the underlying medical intent. During training, contrastive learning is conducted between the enhanced query and both positive and negative subtitle segments to improve retrieval robustness. At inference time, they compute cosine similarity between the enhanced query vector and subtitle embeddings, with the final answer span determined by the position and value of the highest-scoring match in the similarity matrix.

4   Conclusion

This paper comprehensively overviews the NLPCC 2025 Shared Task 4: Multi-modal, Multilingual, and Multi-hop Medical Instructional Video Question Answering (M4IVQA). We introduced this innovative task, which comprises three challenging tracks: Multi-modal, Multilingual, Multi-hop Temporal Answer Gr-ounding in Single Video (M4TAGSV), Multi-modal, Multilingual, Multi-hop Video Corpus Retrieval (M4VCR), and Multi-modal, Multilingual, Multi-hop Temporal Answer Grounding in Video Corpus (M4TAGVC). These tracks were designed to push the boundaries of multi-modal fusion, multi-hop reasoning, and cross-lingual semantic alignment in the medical domain. We detailed the specially curated dataset used for this competition, highlighting its unique features such as bilingual (Chinese and English) content, professional medical annotations, cross-modal alignment, and diverse medical scenarios with multi-modal instructional elements. While the results of this competition demonstrate significant progress in multi-modal and cross-lingual medical video question answering, there remains substantial room for improvement before such systems can be deployed in real-world applications. The challenge of accurately integrating multi-modal evidence, performing multi-hop reasoning across video corpora, and achieving accurate visual answer localization, proves to be a complex task that requires further research and development. In conclusion, we believe that the M4IVQA task has opened up new avenues for research at the intersection of medical AI, multi-modal learning, cross-lingual understanding, and multi-hop reasoning, fostering advancements in global medical training and emergency knowledge dissemination.

Acknowledgement. This work was supported by the Natural Science Foundation of Guangdong Province (No. 2023A1515010673), in part by the Shenzhen Science and Technology Innovation Bureau key project (No. JSGG20220831110400001, No. CJGJZD 20230724093303007,KJZD20240903101259001), in part by Shenzhen Medical Research Fund (No. D2404001), in part by Shenzhen Engineering Laboratory for Diagnosis and Treatment Key Technologies of Interventional Surgical Robots (XM HT20220104009), and the Key Laboratory of Biomedical Imaging Science and System, CAS, for the Research platform support.

References

1. Li, B., et al.: Overview of the NLPCC 2023 shared task: chinese medical instructional video question answering. In: CCF International Conference on Natural Language Processing and Chinese Computing, pp. 233–242. Springer (2023)
2. Li, B., Weng, Y., Song, Q., Liang, L., Min, X., Zhou, S.: Overview of the NLPCC 2024 shared task 7: Multi-lingual medical instructional video question answering. In: CCF International Conference on Natural Language Processing and Chinese Computing, pp. 429–439. Springer (2024)
3. Wang, Y., Zhong, J., Kumar, R.: A systematic review of machine learning applications in infectious disease prediction, diagnosis, and outbreak forecasting (2025)
4. Lu, S., Liu, Y., Kong, A.W.: TF-icon: diffusion-based training-free cross-domain image composition. In: Proceedings of the IEEE/CVF International Conference on Computer Vision, pp. 2294–2305 (2023)
5. Xinlei, Yu., et al.: Ich-prnet: a cross-modal intracerebral haemorrhage prognostic prediction method using joint-attention interaction mechanism. Neural Netw. **184**, 107096 (2025)
6. Yu, X., et al.: Ich-SCNET: Intracerebral hemorrhage segmentation and prognosis classification network using clip-guided sam mechanism. In: 2024 IEEE International Conference on Bioinformatics and Biomedicine (BIBM), pp. 2795–2800. IEEE (2024)
7. Bačić, B., Vasile, C., Feng, C., Ciucă, M.G.: Towards nation-wide analytical healthcare infrastructures: a privacy-preserving augmented knee rehabilitation case study. arXiv preprint arXiv:2412.20733 (2024)
8. Wen, Z., Li, B.: Learning to unify audio, visual and text for audio-enhanced multilingual visual answer localization. arXiv preprint arXiv:2411.02851 (2024)
9. Bi, J., et al.: and Yunpu Ma. Self-pruning intrinsic selection method for training-free multimodal data selection, Prism (2025)
10. Lu, S., Zhou, Z., Lu, J., Zhu, Y., Kong, A.W.: Robust watermarking using generative priors against image editing: from benchmarking to advances. arXiv preprint arXiv:2410.18775 (2024)
11. Li, L., Lu, S., Ren, Y., Kong, A.W.: Set you straight: auto-steering denoising trajectories to sidestep unwanted concepts. arXiv preprint arXiv:2504.12782 (2025)

12. Xia, F., et al.: Lingyi: medical conversational question answering system based on multi-modal knowledge graphs. arXiv preprint arXiv:2204.09220 (2022)
13. Bi, J., et al.: Llava steering: cisual instruction tuning with 500x fewer parameters through modality linear representation-steering (2025)
14. Weng, Y., Li, B.: Visual answer localization with cross-modal mutual knowledge transfer. In: ICASSP 2023-2023 IEEE International Conference on Acoustics, Speech and Signal Processing (ICASSP), pp. 1–5. IEEE (2023)
15. Zhong, J., Wang, Y.: Enhancing thyroid disease prediction using machine learning: a comparative study of ensemble models and class balancing techniques (2025)
16. Qiu, S., et al.: A generative adversarial network-based investor sentiment indicator: superior predictability for the stock market. Mathematics **13**(9), 1476 (2025)
17. Jing, P., Cui, K., Zhang, J., Li, Y., Yuting, S.: Multimodal high-order relationship inference network for fashion compatibility modeling in internet of multimedia things. IEEE Internet Things J. **11**(1), 353–365 (2024)
18. Ke, Z., Zhou, S., Zhou, Y., Chang, C., Zhang, R.: Detection of AI deepfake and fraud in online payments using GAN-based models. arXiv preprint arXiv:2501.07033 (2025)
19. He, Y., et al.: Enhancing intent understanding for ambiguous prompts through human-machine co-adaptation. arXiv preprint arXiv:2501.15167 (2025)
20. Lu, S., Wang, Z., Li, L., Liu, Y., Kong, A.M.: Mace: mass concept erasure in diffusion models. In: Proceedings of the IEEE/CVF Conference on Computer Vision and Pattern Recognition, pp. 6430–6440 (2024)
21. Yi, Q., et al.: Score: story coherence and retrieval enhancement for AI narratives. arXiv preprint arXiv:2503.23512 (2025)
22. Li, B., Weng, Y., Sun, B., Li, S.: Learning to locate visual answer in video corpus using question. In: ICASSP 2023 - 2023 IEEE International Conference on Acoustics, Speech and Signal Processing (ICASSP), pp.1–5 (2023)
23. Zhang, H., Zheng, C., He, Y., Zhao, Y., Lai, Y.: Improving multilingual temporal answering grounding in single video via LLM-based translation and OCR enhancement. In: CCF International Conference on Natural Language Processing and Chinese Computing, pp. 145–156. Springer (2024)
24. Zhou, Z., Liu, J., Cheng, S., Luo, H., Gu, Y., Ye, J.: Improving cross-modal visual answer localization in chinese medical instructional video using language prompts. In: CCF International Conference on Natural Language Processing and Chinese Computing, pp. 221–232. Springer (2023)
25. Yu, G., et al.: Mqua: multi-level query-video augmentation for multilingual video corpus retrieval. In: CCF International Conference on Natural Language Processing and Chinese Computing, pp. 353–364. Springer (2024)
26. Lei, N., et al.: A two-stage chinese medical video retrieval framework with LLM. In: CCF International Conference on Natural Language Processing and Chinese Computing, pp. 211–220. Springer (2023)
27. Ma, T., Hu, Y., Jiang, S., Yin, Z., Zang, T.: Multilingual temporal answer grounding in video corpus with enhanced visual-textual integration. In: CCF International Conference on Natural Language Processing and Chinese Computing, pp. 471–483. Springer (2024)
28. Cheng, S., Zhou, Z., Liu, J., Ye, J., Luo, H., Gu, Y.: A unified framework for optimizing video corpus retrieval and temporal answer grounding: fine-grained modality alignment and local-global optimization. In: CCF International Conference on Natural Language Processing and Chinese Computing, pp. 199–210. Springer (2023)

29. Cui, K., et al.: Correlation-aware cross-modal attention network for fashion compatibility modeling in UGC systems. ACM Transactions on Multimedia Computing, Communications and Applications (2024)
30. Feng, F., Yang, Y., Cer, D., Arivazhagan, N., Wang, W.: Language-agnostic BERT sentence embedding. arXiv preprint arXiv:2007.01852 (2020)
31. Li, B., Weng, Y., Xia, F., Sun, B., Li, S.: Vpai_lab at medvidqa 2022: a two-stage cross-modal fusion method for medical instructional video classification. In: Proceedings of the 21st Workshop on Biomedical Language Processing, pp. 212–219 (2022)
32. Jing, P., Cui, K., Guan, W., Nie, L., Yuting, S.: Category-aware multimodal attention network for fashion compatibility modeling. IEEE Trans. Multimedia **25**, 9120–9131 (2023)

Multi-hop Knowledge-Enhanced Query Reasoning for Multi-modal Medical Video QA

Yangchengyu Zhou[1]([✉]), Jiayuan Wu[2], and Yunze Li[1]

[1] School of Computer Science, Wuhan University, Wuhan, China
{zhouyangchengyu,smallphan}@whu.edu.cn
[2] School of Electronics Engineering and Computer Science, Peking University, Beijing, China
2200012869@stu.pku.edu.cn

Abstract. Multi-modal medical instructional video question answering (MMI-VQA) requires precise alignment of visual and textual information, along with complex multi-hop reasoning over external knowledge sources. Existing approaches often struggle to effectively integrate multi-modal signals and external knowledge for accurate retrieval and temporal localization. In this paper, we propose a multi-hop knowledge-enhanced cross-modal retrieval framework for NLPCC-2025 Task 4. Our method first encodes subtitles and their temporally aligned video frames through dedicated encoders, and performs cross-modal interaction and temporal modeling to construct a fine-grained retrieval library. Given an input query, relevant knowledge triples are retrieved from an external medical knowledge graph and enhanced through multi-hop reasoning in a Retrieval-Augmented Generation (RAG) module, producing an enriched query representation. The enhanced query vector is then used to compute similarity scores with subtitle segment embeddings in the retrieval library, enabling retrieval of top-k relevant segments and prediction of their temporal spans. Our framework effectively combines external medical knowledge with multi-modal understanding, offering a scalable solution for complex medical instructional video QA scenarios.

Keywords: Multi-modal Retrieval · Knowledge Graph · Multi-hop Reasoning · Question Answering

1 Introduction

With the rapid growth of online educational platforms, instructional videos have become a dominant modality for delivering domain-specific knowledge, particularly in fields such as medicine and emergency care [1–3]. Compared with traditional text-based materials, these videos offer rich multimodal information–visual demonstrations, spoken language, and textual cues–making them highly effective for conveying complex procedures [4]. However, the sheer volume and

© The Author(s), under exclusive license to Springer Nature Singapore Pte Ltd. 2026

X.-L. Mao et al. (Eds.): NLPCC 2025, LNAI 16105, pp. 380–392, 2026.
https://doi.org/10.1007/978-981-95-3352-7_32

length of such videos pose a major challenge: users often struggle to locate precise information related to their queries, especially when it is buried deep within multilingual, multimodal content across a large video corpus [5].

To tackle this issue, prior research has explored temporal answer grounding (TAG), which aims to retrieve the most relevant video segments in response to natural language questions. Recent approaches leverage both subtitles and visual frames via cross-modal fusion, and some have considered multilingual settings [6]. However, most existing methods still rely on shallow semantic matching and assume that the answer lies within a single video [7]. These assumptions limit their generalization to real-world scenarios where understanding a query often requires deeper reasoning and external domain knowledge. Notably, current models lack the ability to perform multi-hop inference based on structured knowledge, such as medical knowledge graphs, which is essential for answering complex medical questions that go beyond the observable content in the video [8].

To overcome these challenges, we tackle this limitation through the use of structured external knowledge to enhance the retrieval of relevant video segments. In medical instructional videos, many queries require connecting multiple domain-specific concepts that are not explicitly co-located or sequentially presented within a single video [9]. To bridge this semantic gap, we utilize external medical knowledge graphs composed of entityrelationentity triples and apply multi-hop reasoning to generate the enriched version of the original query. This enhanced query captures deeper semantic intent, facilitating more accurate retrieval across a large-scale, multilingual, and multimodal video corpus (Fig. 1).

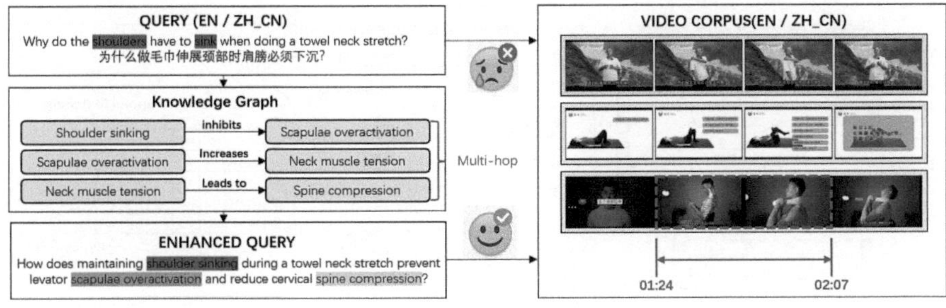

Fig. 1. By leveraging a medical knowledge graph and multi-hop reasoning, the original query is enriched with critical concepts such as "scapulae overactivation" and "spine compression", bridging the semantic gap and enabling accurate retrieval of relevant video segments.

To this end, we propose a novel Multi-hop Knowledge-enhanced Cross-modal Retrieval Framework tailored for the NLPCC 2025 Task 4: Multi-modal, Multilingual, and Multi-hop Medical Instructional Video QA. We first encode all subtitle segments and their aligned video frames using a text encoder and a visual encoder, respectively. These are fused through a cross-modal module [10] to construct session-level embeddings for each video. All session representations are indexed to form a searchable corpus [11]. Given a user query, we extract relevant triples from an external medical knowledge graph [12] and apply a Retrieval-Augmented Generation (RAG) module [13] to perform multi-hop reasoning, producing an enhanced query. This enhanced query is then encoded and compared with the session representations using cosine similarity to retrieve the top-K most relevant video segments.

Our main contributions are summarized as follows:

1. We design a cross-modal session encoder that effectively integrates textual subtitles and corresponding video frames for fine-grained segment representation (Sect. 2.2).
2. We introduce a multi-hop knowledge-enhanced reasoning module that utilizes structured medical triples to enrich query semantics (Sect. 2.4).
3. We demonstrate that our method significantly outperforms existing baselines on the NLPCC 2025 Task 4 benchmark (Sect. 3.4).

2   Methods

We propose a multi-modal retrieval framework with multi-hop knowledge-enhanced reasoning for medical instructional video QA, as illustrated in Fig. 2.

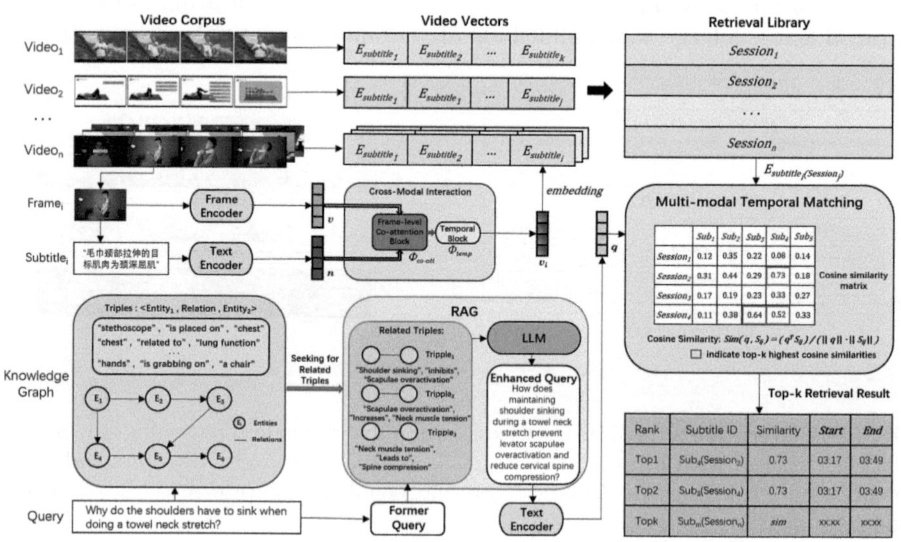

Fig. 2. Architecture of our multi-hop knowledge-enhanced cross-modal retrieval framework for NLPCC-2025 Task 4. Video subtitles and aligned frames are fused to build a retrieval library. Given a query, relevant knowledge triples guide multi-hop reasoning to enhance the query representation, which is used to retrieve relevant segments with temporal spans.

2.1 Video Preprocessing and Encoding

For a given video corpus consisting of n videos, each video V_i is represented by a sequence of frames $\{F_{i1}, F_{i2}, \ldots, F_{im}\}$, where m denotes the number of frames in video V_i. Each video also contains a sequence of subtitles $\{S_{i1}, S_{i2}, \ldots, S_{in}\}$, where each subtitle S_{ij} corresponds to a specific frame F_{ij} in the video, where j denotes the index of both the frame and subtitle.

Each frame F_{ij} is passed through a frame encoder [14] to extract its feature vector $\mathbf{v}_{ij} \in \mathbb{R}^d$, where d is the dimensionality of the frame embedding. This process is expressed as:

$$\mathbf{v}_{ij} = \text{FrameEncoder}(F_{ij}) \tag{1}$$

Similarly, each subtitle S_{ij} is encoded using a text encoder, such as BERT [15] or RoBERTa [16], to obtain a dense vector $\mathbf{n}_{ij} \in \mathbb{R}^d$, which captures the semantic meaning of the subtitle text. The subtitle encoding process is formulated as:

$$\mathbf{n}_{ij} = \text{TextEncoder}(S_{ij}) \tag{2}$$

After finishing this step, we have a set of encoded vectors $\{\mathbf{v}_{i1}, \mathbf{v}_{i2}, \ldots, \mathbf{v}_{im}\}$ for the video frames and $\{\mathbf{n}_{i1}, \mathbf{n}_{i2}, \ldots, \mathbf{n}_{in}\}$ for the subtitles, where each subtitle S_{ij} corresponds to the frame F_{ij} of the same index. These vectors will be used in the subsequent Cross-Modal Interaction module for further fusion and integration.

2.2 Cross-Modal Interaction

For each subtitle segment S_{ij} in video V_i, we first extract its text feature vector $\mathbf{n}_{ij}$ using the text encoder, and obtain the corresponding frame feature vector $\mathbf{v}_{ij}$ using the frame encoder. Each pair of $\mathbf{n}_{ij}$ and $\mathbf{v}_{ij}$ is then processed by a frame-level co-attention block [17] to facilitate cross-modal interaction and enrich mutual information between modalities. This operation is formulated as:

$$\mathbf{c}_{ij} = \Phi_{co\text{-}att}(\mathbf{v}_{ij}, \mathbf{n}_{ij}) \tag{3}$$

where $\Phi_{co\text{-}att}$ denotes the co-attention function, which enables joint reasoning over the visual and textual features at the frame-subtitle level.

Through the cross-modal co-attention between video frames and their corresponding subtitles, our model captures fine-grained semantic relationships between visual content and its aligned textual description. This interaction enriches the fused features by leveraging contextual information from individual frame-subtitle pairs [18].

The resulting sequence of fused features for video V_i is denoted as $\mathbf{C}_i = \{\mathbf{c}_{i1}, \mathbf{c}_{i2}, \ldots, \mathbf{c}_{in}\}$, where n is the number of subtitles in V_i. To capture the temporal dependencies across these fused features, we apply a temporal block [19], defined as:

$$\mathbf{V}_i = \Phi_{temp}(\mathbf{C}_i) \tag{4}$$

where Φ_{temp} represents the temporal encoding function that models sequential relationships within the fused cross-modal feature sequence.

The output $\mathbf{V}_i = \{\mathbf{v}_{i1}, \mathbf{v}_{i2}, \ldots, \mathbf{v}_{in}\}$ comprises temporally enhanced, cross-modal feature vectors corresponding to each subtitle-frame pair in video V_i. These vectors will be further projected into the retrieval embedding space in the next stage.

2.3   Retrieval Library Construction

Given the temporally enhanced cross-modal feature sequence $\mathbf{V}_i = \{\mathbf{v}_{i1}, \ldots, \mathbf{v}_{in}\}$ obtained from the Cross-Modal Interaction module for video V_i, we project each feature vector $\mathbf{v}_{ij}$ into a shared retrieval embedding space. This embedding operation transforms the modality-fused features into vector representations suitable for efficient similarity computation during retrieval [20]. Formally, the embedding process is defined as:

$$\mathbf{E}_{subtitle_{ij}} = \Phi_{emb}(\mathbf{v}_{ij}) \tag{5}$$

where Φ_{emb} denotes the embedding function, typically implemented as a linear projection or multi-layer perceptron (MLP), which maps the fused feature vector $\mathbf{v}_{ij}$ to the retrieval space embedding $\mathbf{E}_{subtitle_{ij}}$. For each video V_i, we aggregate the embeddings of all its subtitle-frame pairs to construct a session representation:

$$\mathbf{S}_i = \{\mathbf{E}_{subtitle_{i1}}, \mathbf{E}_{subtitle_{i2}}, \ldots, \mathbf{E}_{subtitle_{in}}\} \tag{6}$$

where $\mathbf{S}_i$ represents the session for video V_i, comprising the embeddings of all subtitle segments in the video.

Finally, we construct the retrieval library $\mathcal{R}$ by collecting the session representations of all videos in the video corpus:

$$\mathcal{R} = \{\mathbf{S}_1, \mathbf{S}_2, \ldots, \mathbf{S}_N\} \tag{7}$$

where N is the total number of videos in the corpus. The retrieval library $\mathcal{R}$ serves as the search space for downstream query retrieval, enabling efficient matching between the query representation and the embedded video subtitle segments [21].

This retrieval library structure ensures that each video is decomposed into fine-grained subtitle-level embeddings while maintaining session-level organization, supporting precise and efficient multi-modal retrieval in the subsequent stages.

2.4   Query Processing and RAG Enhancement

Given an input query Q, we first leverage an external medical knowledge graph $\mathcal{G}$ to retrieve relevant knowledge triples. The knowledge graph $\mathcal{G}$ [22] is composed of entities and relations, structured as triples in the form of $\langle e_h, r, e_t \rangle$, where e_h

and e_t represent the head and tail entities, and r denotes the relation between them.

To extract the relevant triples $\mathcal{T}_Q$ associated with the input query, we perform entity linking and relation matching between the query text and the knowledge graph $\mathcal{G}$:

$$\mathcal{T}_Q = \Phi_{\mathrm{KG}}(Q, \mathcal{G}) \tag{8}$$

where Φ_{KG} denotes the knowledge retrieval function that identifies all triples in $\mathcal{G}$ closely related to the query Q (Fig. 3).

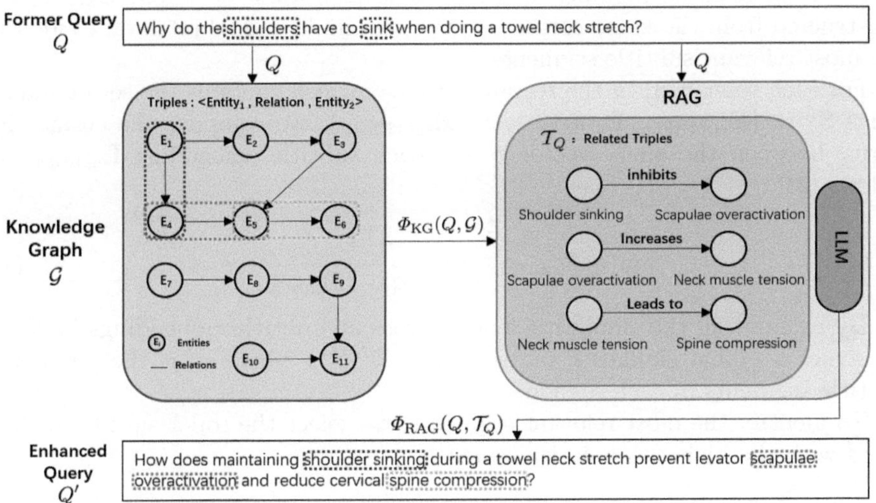

Fig. 3. Multi-hop reasoning over knowledge graph triples $\mathcal{T}_Q$ enables the RAG module to transform the input query Q into an enhanced query Q', bridging the semantic gap for accurate retrieval.

The retrieved set of triples $\mathcal{T}_Q$ is then passed to the Retrieval-Augmented Generation (RAG) module. The RAG module performs multi-hop reasoning over the set of knowledge triples, leveraging a large language model (LLM) to generate an enhanced query Q', which integrates explicit reasoning paths derived from $\mathcal{T}_Q$. The enhancement process is formulated as:

$$Q' = \Phi_{\mathrm{RAG}}(Q, \mathcal{T}_Q) \tag{9}$$

where Φ_{RAG} represents the multi-hop reasoning and generation process conducted by the RAG module.

Finally, the enhanced query Q' is encoded using the same text encoder applied in the video preprocessing stage to obtain the query embedding vector $\mathbf{q}$:

$$\mathbf{q} = \Phi_{\text{text\_enc}}(Q') \tag{10}$$

where $\Phi_{\text{text\_enc}}$ denotes the text encoder that transforms the enhanced query into its corresponding vector representation. The resulting query vector $\mathbf{q}$ is then used to retrieve relevant candidates from the retrieval library $\mathcal{R}$ in the subsequent stage.

2.5 Multi-Modal Retrieval and Answer Extraction

Given the enhanced query vector $\mathbf{q}$ obtained from the Query Processing & Query Enhancement module, and the retrieval library $\mathcal{R} = \{\mathbf{S}_1, \mathbf{S}_2, \ldots, \mathbf{S}_N\}$ constructed from the video corpus, we perform multi-modal retrieval to identify the most relevant subtitle segments.

For each session $\mathbf{S}_j$ in the retrieval library, which contains the set of embeddings $\mathbf{S}_j = \{\mathbf{E}_{\text{subtitle}_{j1}}, \mathbf{E}_{\text{subtitle}_{j2}}, \ldots, \mathbf{E}_{\text{subtitle}_{jn}}\}$, we compute the cosine similarity between the query vector $\mathbf{q}$ and each subtitle embedding $\mathbf{E}_{\text{subtitle}_{ji}}$ as follows [23] :

$$\text{Sim}(\mathbf{q}, \mathbf{E}_{\text{subtitle}_{ji}}) = \frac{\mathbf{q}^{\top} \mathbf{E}_{\text{subtitle}_{ji}}}{\|\mathbf{q}\| \cdot \|\mathbf{E}_{\text{subtitle}_{ji}}\|} \tag{11}$$

By calculating the similarity scores across all subtitle embeddings in $\mathcal{R}$, we construct a global similarity matrix $\mathbf{M} \in \mathbb{R}^{N \times m}$, where m is the number of subtitle segments in each session.

To identify the most relevant segments, we select the top-k subtitle embeddings with the highest similarity scores:

$$\mathcal{T}_{\text{top-}k} = \text{Top-}k(\mathbf{M}) \tag{12}$$

where $\mathcal{T}_{\text{top-}k}$ denotes the set of top-k subtitle segments ranked by their similarity to the query $\mathbf{q}$.

For each retrieved subtitle segment, we return its corresponding session identifier, subtitle index, similarity score, and temporal information, including the start and end timestamps $(t_{\text{start}}, t_{\text{end}})$ derived from the subtitle metadata:

$$\text{Result} = \left\{(\text{Session}_j, \text{Subtitle}_i, \text{Sim}, t_{\text{start}}, t_{\text{end}})\right\} \in \mathcal{T}_{\text{top-}k} \tag{13}$$

This retrieval process enables accurate alignment between the user query and the most semantically relevant segments in the video corpus, providing precise temporal localization of the answer.

3   Experiments

3.1 Dataset

The dataset used in this study is officially provided for NLPCC 2025 Task 4 (M4IVQA Challenge), and it consists of three subsets: training, validation, and

Table 1. Statistics of the NLPCC 2025 M4IVQA dataset.

Dataset	Videos	QA pairs	Ch_Q Avg. Len.	Video Avg. Len.
Train Set	1,228	5,840	17.16	263.3
Dev Set	200	983	17.81	242.4
Test Set	200	1,022	18.22	310.9

test sets. Each subset contains a multilingual medical instructional video corpus, along with annotations for questions and corresponding answer locations.

Detailed information about the dataset is shown in Table 1. The video corpus comprises 1,628 videos collected from YouTube medical instructional channels, with subtitles automatically generated using the Whisper model and converted to simplified Chinese. Each video is segmented into spans based on the start and end timestamps of the subtitles. Each annotated sample mainly consists of three components: the question (in both Chinese and English), the video ID where the answer is located, and the temporal boundaries of the answer span. For questions with the same semantics, there is a unique answer across the entire corpus, although a single video may contain answers to multiple different questions. To ensure fairness, the answer locations in the test set are not provided to participants.

3.2 Metrics

Based on the official evaluation protocol of NLPCC 2025 Task 4, we adopt Intersection over Union (IoU) and mean Intersection over Union (mIoU) as our primary evaluation metrics. Specifically, we treat the task as localizing the answer span in the video, and use "R@n, IoU $= \mu$" to denote whether the predicted span overlaps with the ground truth span by more than μ in the top-n retrieved segments.

The definitions of IoU and mIoU are as follows:

$$\mathrm{IoU} = \frac{A \cap B}{A \cup B} \tag{14}$$

$$\mathrm{mIoU} = \frac{1}{n} \sum_{i=1}^{n} \mathrm{IoU}_i \tag{15}$$

where A and B represent different temporal spans. The IoU measures the overlap between the predicted answer span and the ground-truth span, while mIoU is the average IoU over all evaluation samples. In our experiments, we adopt $n = 1$ and $\mu \in \{0.3, 0.5, 0.7\}$ to evaluate the answer localization performance. The official ranking of this track is primarily based on the mIoU score, while other metrics are reported for comprehensive analysis.

During model inference, for each test question Q^{test} and the video corpus $Corpus_v$, we construct candidate pairs as:

$$Samples^{test} = \{Q^{test}, Video_i\}, \quad Video_i \in Corpus_v \tag{16}$$

The model computes a relevance score for each candidate pair based on the similarity between the question and the predicted answer span in the video. Specifically, the model generates a localization matrix M^i_{span} for each video $Video_i$, and selects the maximum value as the retrieval score. The corresponding row and column in the matrix indicate the predicted start and end timestamps of the answer span:

$$Score_i = \max\left(M^i_{span}\right) = M^i_{span}(start_i, end_i) \tag{17}$$

We rank all candidate spans by their retrieval scores, select the top-n candidates, and compare their predicted $(start_i, end_i)$ with the ground-truth span $(st\hat{a}rt, e\hat{n}d)$. If any candidate span achieves an IoU greater than μ, the retrieval is considered successful. In our experiments, we report R@1, IoU=0.3/0.5/0.7 and the overall mIoU score to evaluate the performance of our method.

3.3   Experiment Environment and Hyperparameters

Our model is implemented using the PyTorch framework. The data preprocessing stage was performed on a local machine equipped with an NVIDIA GeForce RTX 3070 Ti GPU, while model training and evaluation were conducted on an NVIDIA A100 GPU server to ensure efficient computation.

For the visual modality, we extracted 3 frames per second from each video to balance between computational efficiency and visual coverage [24]. Each frame was processed using the CLIP-ViT model to obtain visual embeddings [25]. For the textual modality, we utilized the subtitles provided in the dataset, which were tokenized and encoded using a BERT-base model [26]. These features were further fused through a transformer encoder to capture cross-modal interactions.

During training, we set the maximum input token length to 512, a batch size of 8, and adopted a hidden size of 768 for the transformer layers. We used the AdamW optimizer with a learning rate of 5×10^{-5} and trained the model for 20 epochs. Model selection was based on the highest mIoU score achieved on the validation set, and early stopping was applied to prevent overfitting. To ensure reproducibility, we conducted experiments with three different random seeds and reported the average performance across these runs. The preprocessing pipeline processes the video content approximately 6 min per second on average.

3.4   Main Results

We evaluate our proposed method **MedEcho** on the official test set of the NLPCC 2025 M4IVQA dataset and compare it with several representative baselines, including RANDOMPICK [27] [28], Nsddd [29], IIEleven [30], and the NYU

Table 2. Performance comparison on the NLPCC 2025 M4IVQA dataset. The best results are highlighted in bold.

Method	R@1—mIoU	R@10—mIoU	R@50—mIoU	Average
RANDOMPICK	0.0247	0.0397	0.0509	0.0384
Nsddd [29]	0.1078	0.2145	0.2997	0.2112
IIEleven [30]	0.1141	0.2343	0.3098	0.2200
NYU	0.1202	0.2366	0.3133	0.2233
MedEcho (Ours)	**0.1284**	**0.2417**	**0.3243**	**0.2314**

2025 submission. The evaluation results are presented in Table 2. All methods are assessed using Recall at different thresholds of mean Intersection-over-Union (mIoU), including R@1, R@10, and R@50, with an average performance metric.

Our method outperforms all competing approaches across all evaluation metrics. Notably, MedEcho achieves the best performance in R@1, R@10, and R@50, resulting in the highest average score of 0.2314. Compared to the strongest baseline IIEleven, MedEcho yields a relative improvement of 5.2% in the overall average. These gains are attributed to our cross-modal fusion mechanism, integration of structured knowledge, and a more precise temporal grounding pipeline. The results confirm the effectiveness of our approach in addressing the challenges posed by multilingual and multimodal instructional video QA tasks.

3.5   Ablation Study

To investigate the effectiveness of each major component in our proposed method, we conduct a comprehensive ablation study. Specifically, we analyze the contributions of three key modules: the visual encoder, the cross-modal alignment mechanism, and the KG-RAG enhancement module. Table 3 summarizes the performance after removing each component individually. All experiments are conducted under the same settings as the main evaluation.

Table 3. Ablation study results of MedEcho. The best results for each metric are highlighted in bold.

Method	R@1—mIoU	R@10—mIoU	R@50—mIoU	Average
MedEcho (Ours)	**0.1284**	**0.2417**	**0.3243**	**0.2314**
w/o Vision	0.1103	0.2271	0.2917	0.2097
w/o Cross-Modal Alignment	0.1042	0.2015	0.2874	0.1977
w/o KG-RAG Enhancement	0.0984	0.1943	0.2811	0.1913

As shown in Table 3, removing any individual module results in a clear drop in performance, confirming that each component plays a significant role. In particular, removing KG-RAG enhancement leads to the largest degradation (from

0.2314 to 0.1913), suggesting that structured knowledge is crucial for complex medical question understanding. Similarly, the cross-modal alignment module contributes significantly to temporal localization, with its removal causing a noticeable decline in R@10 and R@50. The absence of visual features also lowers overall accuracy, demonstrating that visual information provides important complementary cues to subtitles. These results validate the design of our model and highlight the synergy between vision, language, and knowledge.

4   Conclusion

In this paper, we propose a multi-hop knowledge-enhanced cross-modal retrieval framework for the Multi-modal, Multilingual, and Multi-hop Medical Instructional Video Question Answering Challenge (NLPCC-2025 Task 4). This task aims to retrieve the most relevant subtitle segments and predict their temporal spans for medical queries in a large-scale multi-modal video corpus. Our method encodes subtitles and corresponding frames through dedicated encoders, applies cross-modal interaction and temporal modeling to construct a retrieval library, and enhances the input query via multi-hop reasoning over external knowledge triples using a RAG module. The enriched query representation is then used to retrieve top-k relevant subtitle segments along with their temporal spans.

However, our method still has limitations: it is constrained by external knowledge coverage and simplified visual-textual interaction strategies. In the future, we will target enhancing multimodal integration through dynamic KG optimization. We hope this study contributes to the development of medical instructional video QA systems and inspires more future research in multi-modal video retrieval and reasoning.

References

1. Li, S., Li, B., Sun, B., Weng, Y.: Towards visual-prompt temporal answer grounding in instructional video. IEEE Transactions on Pattern Analysis and Machine Intelligence (2024)
2. Bačić, B., Vasile, C., Feng, C., Ciucă, M.G.: Towards nation-wide analytical healthcare infrastructures: a privacy-preserving augmented knee rehabilitation case study. arXiv preprint arXiv:2412.20733 (2024)
3. Li, B., Liu, S., Weng, Y., Du, Y., Tian, Y., Zhou, S.: Overview of the NLPCC 2025 shared task 4: multi-modal, multilingual, and multi-hop medical instructional video question answering challenge. arXiv preprint arXiv:2505.06814 (2025)
4. Li, B., Weng, Y., Song, Q., Liang, L., Min, X., Zhou, S.: Overview of the NLPCC 2024 shared task 7: multi-lingual medical instructional video question answering. In: Derek F., Wong, Wei, Z., Yang, M (eds) Natural Language Processing and Chinese Computing, pp. 429–439, Singapore, 2025. Springer Nature Singapore
5. Lei, J., Yu, L., Berg, T., Bansal, M.: TVQA: Localized. Compositional Video Question Answering, In EMNLP (2018)
6. Mun, J., Cho, M., Han, B.: Local-global video-text interactions for temporal grounding. In: CVPR (2020)

7. Chen, S., Zhao, Y., Jin, Q., Wu, Q.: Fine-grained video-text retrieval with hierarchical graph reasoning. In: Proceedings of the IEEE/CVF Conference on Computer Vision and Pattern Recognition (CVPR), pp. 10638–10647 (2020)

8. Yasunaga, M., Ren, H., Bosselut, A., Liang, P.: QA-GNN: reasoning with Language Models and Knowledge Graphs for Question Answering. In: NAACL (2021)

9. He, Y., T al.: Enhancing intent understanding for ambiguous prompts through human-machine co-adaptation. arXiv preprint arXiv:2501.15167 2025

10. Jiasen, L., Batra, D., Parikh, D.: and Stefan Lee. Pretraining Task-Agnostic Visiolinguistic Representations for Vision-and-Language Tasks. In NeurIPS, VilBERT (2019)

11. Yi, Q., et al.: Score: story coherence and retrieval enhancement for AI narratives. arXiv preprint arXiv:2503.23512 (2025)

12. Di, Y., Shi, H., Ma, R., Gao, H., Liu, Y., Wang, W.: Fedrl: a reinforcement learning federated recommender system for efficient communication using reinforcement selector and hypernet generator. ACM Transactions on Recommender Systems (2024)

13. Lewis, P., et al.: Retrieval-Augmented Generation for Knowledge-Intensive NLP Tasks. In: NeurIPS (2020)

14. Radford, A., et al.: Learning Transferable Visual Models from Natural Language Supervision. In: ICML (2021)

15. Devlin, J., Chang, M., Lee, K., Toutanova, K.: BERT: pre-training of Deep Bidirectional Transformers for Language Understanding. arXiv preprint arXiv:1810.04805 (2019)

16. Li, B., et al.: Distinct but correct: generating diversified and entity-revised medical response. Sci. China Inf. Sci. **67**(3), 132106 (2024)

17. Hur, C., et al.: Narrating the video: boosting text-video retrieval via comprehensive utilization of frame-level captions. In: Proceedings of the IEEE/CVF Conference on Computer Vision and Pattern Recognition (CVPR) (2025)

18. He, Y., et al.: Enhancing low-cost video editing with lightweight adaptors and temporal-aware inversion. arXiv preprint arXiv:2501.04606 (2025)

19. Bertasius, G., Wang, H., Torresani, L.: Is Space-Time Attention All You Need for Video Understanding? In: ICML (2021)

20. Gao, Y., Gao, Y., Wei, Y., Yang, Y.: Multi-modal graph neural network for joint reasoning on vision and scene text. In: Proceedings of the IEEE/CVF Conference on Computer Vision and Pattern Recognition (CVPR), pp. 12577–12586 (2020)

21. Miech, A., Alayrac, J.B., Smaira, L., Laptev, I., Sivic, J., Zisserman, A.: End-to-End Learning of Visual Representations from Uncurated Instructional Videos. In: CVPR (2020)

22. Vrandečić, D., Krötzsch, M.: Wikidata: A Free Collaborative Knowledgebase. Commun. ACM **57**(10), 78–85 (2014)

23. Dong, J., Li, X., Xu, C.: Dual Encoding for Zero-Example Video Retrieval. In: CVPR (2019)

24. Yu, X., et al.: Ich-scnet: intracerebral hemorrhage segmentation and prognosis classification network using clip-guided SAM mechanism. arXiv preprint arXiv:2411.04656 (2024)

25. Xinlei, Yu., et al.: Ich-prnet: a cross-modal intracerebral haemorrhage prognostic prediction method using joint-attention interaction mechanism. Neural Netw. **184**, 107096 (2025)

26. Di, Y., Shi, H., Wang, X., Ma, R., Liu, Y.: Federated recommender system based on diffusion augmentation and guided denoising. ACM Trans. Inf. Syst. **43**(2), 1–36 (2025)

27. Weng, Y., Li, B.: Visual answer localization with cross-modal mutual knowledge transfer. In: ICASSP 2023 - 2023 IEEE International Conference on Acoustics, Speech and Signal Processing (ICASSP), pp. 1–5 (2023)
28. Li, B., Weng, Y., Sun, B., Li, S.: Learning to locate visual answer in video corpus using question. In: ICASSP 2023 - 2023 IEEE International Conference on Acoustics, Speech and Signal Processing (ICASSP), pp. 1–5 (2023)
29. Li, B., et al.: Overview of the NLPCC 2023 shared task: Chinese medical instructional video question answering. In: Natural Language Processing and Chinese Computing, volume 14267 of Lecture Notes in Computer Science, pp. 233–242. Springer (2023)
30. Ma, T., Hu, Y., Jiang, S., Yin, Z., Zang, T.: Multilingual temporal answer grounding in video corpus with enhanced visual-textual integration. In: Proceedings of the NLPCC Shared Task on Multilingual Medical Instructional Video QA (MMIVQA) (2024)

Hierarchical Indexing with Knowledge Enrichment for Multilingual Video Corpus Retrieval

Yu Wang[1(✉)], Tianhao Tan[2], and Yifei Wang[3]

[1] School of Computing and Information, University of Pittsburgh, Pittsburgh, PA, USA
yuw235@pitt.edu
[2] Wuhan University of Technology, Wuhan, China
tantianhao@whut.edu.cn
[3] Hunan University, Changsha, China
wangyifei0411@hnu.edu.cn

Abstract. Retrieving relevant instructional videos from multilingual medical archives is crucial for answering complex, multi-hop questions across language boundaries. However, existing systems either compress hour-long videos into coarse embeddings or incur prohibitive costs for fine-grained matching. We tackle the Multilingual Video Corpus Retrieval (mVCR) task in the NLPCC-2025 M4IVQA challenge with a multi-stage framework that integrates multilingual semantics, domain terminology, and efficient long-form processing. Video subtitles are divided into semantically coherent chunks, enriched with concise knowledge-graph (KG) facts, and organized into a hierarchical tree whose node embeddings are generated by a language-agnostic multilingual encoder. At query time, the same encoder embeds the input question; a coarse-to-fine tree search prunes irrelevant branches, and only the top-ranked chunks are re-scored by a lightweight large language model (LLM). This design avoids exhaustive cross-encoder scoring while preserving chunk-level precision. Experiments on the mVCR test set demonstrate state-of-the-art performance, and ablation studies confirm the complementary contributions of KG enrichment, hierarchical indexing, and targeted LLM re-ranking. The proposed method offers an accurate and scalable solution for multilingual retrieval in specialized medical video collections.

Keywords: Multilingual Video Corpus Retrieval · Knowledge Graph · Tree-Based Search · Large Language Model

1 Introduction

Online video has become a primary medium for disseminating information, and medical instructional content is increasingly recognized for conveying complex

© The Author(s), under exclusive license to Springer Nature Singapore Pte Ltd. 2026
X.-L. Mao et al. (Eds.): NLPCC 2025, LNAI 16105, pp. 393–404, 2026.
https://doi.org/10.1007/978-981-95-3352-7_33

health topics [1–3]. However, their sheer volume and unstructured nature make it challenging to locate specific information. This work addresses the Multilingual Video Corpus Retrieval (mVCR) task in the NLPCC-2025 M4IVQA challenge [4,5]. The objective is to retrieve the most relevant untrimmed video from a large, multilingual collection, even when the query language differs from the video's subtitles. Effective retrieval faces three key challenges: achieving robust multilingual semantics, efficiently processing lengthy videos rich in medical terminology, and bridging the gap between concise queries and comprehensive video content [6–8].

Existing retrieval strategies, however, fail to meet the specific demands of the mVCR task. Dual-encoder models [9–11] enable fast lookup through shared queryvideo embeddings but cannot capture the extensive temporal structure of long videos [12]. Multilingual alignment techniques, whether via machine translation [13] or unified embedding spaces [14], often provide insufficient coverage of the domain-specific terminology crucial to medical content. Sophisticated temporal models [15–17] are typically designed for monolingual data and, therefore, miss essential cross-language semantics. Neural re-rankers based on cross-encoders [6,18] or LLMs [19] deliver precise relevance scores but incur prohibitive computational costs when applied as first-stage filters for large corpora, limiting practical scalability. Consequently, no single approach simultaneously achieves efficient multilingual retrieval, fidelity to medical terminology [20], and tractable processing of long videos.

To overcome these limitations, we introduce a multi-stage framework that delivers efficient and accurate mVCR. Subtitles are segmented into semantic chunks, enriched with KG facts, and then organized using LaBSE [21] embeddings into a hierarchical index for coarse-to-fine retrieval. An embedded query initiates a tree search that prunes irrelevant branches early to reduce search costs. Finally, only the top candidate chunks are re-ranked by a lightweight multilingual LLM, yielding nuanced relevance scores without processing the entire corpus.

The main contributions of this work are:

(1) A modular architecture that combines semantic chunking, domain-specific KG enrichment, and multilingual embeddings to enable scalable search in long medical videos.
(2) A dynamic tree-pruning strategy that balances efficiency and precision by narrowing the search space before LLM re-ranking.
(3) State-of-the-art results on the mVCR test set, supported by ablation studies that isolate the impact of KG enrichment, hierarchical indexing, and LLM re-ranking.

2 Related Work

Early video retrieval struggled with semantic gaps due to its reliance on low-level features and metadata. Deep dual encoders [9–11] improved scalability via independent indexing of joint query-video embeddings. However, they often neglected fine-grained cross-modal interactions and struggled to represent long temporal sequences [12]. Transformers have further enhanced temporal reasoning, with models like CLIP4Clip [22] demonstrating the efficacy of frame aggregation. Subsequent refinements in temporal alignment using sliding windows or segment attention [15,16] also showed promise. Nevertheless, these methods are predominantly monolingual and general-domain, making them unsuitable for domain-specific terminology and multilingual queries in mVCR.

Multilingual retrieval initially relied on machine translation, but poor translation quality limited performance, spurring direct alignment techniques that embed sentences into unified semantic spaces. Models like LaBSE [21] and other language-agnostic embeddings proved effective for multilingual sentence retrieval and on benchmarks like VATEX [14], which contains bilingual captions for short videos. Nonetheless, VATEX's short videos differ significantly from the long, procedural, terminology-dense medical videos in mVCR. Adapting these techniques to specialized, lengthy, code-mixed content remains challenging.

Knowledge Graphs (KGs) offer structured relational information to mitigate vocabulary discrepancies between queries and video content. Early strategies involved query expansion and path-based reasoning for enhanced recall [23]. VideoGraph [24] integrates KG entities with shot-level video features for open-domain search, while BioSyn [25] uses UMLS to link clinical terms by synthesizing synonyms, improving retrieval in noisy settings. Despite these advances, most KG-augmented approaches focus on text or short video clips. Effectively incorporating KG information into long, multilingual instructional videos while preserving temporal coherence remains unaddressed.

Large Language Models (LLMs) significantly advanced re-ranking by capturing nuanced query-document semantics [26,27]. BERT-based cross-encoders [6,18] substantially outperform traditional passage re-ranking methods. Prompting large generative models for zero-shot relevance scoring also shows consistent multilingual improvements [19]. Their computational expense remains a primary drawback, as cross-encoders scale quadratically with input length, making them unsuitable as first-stage filters for large collections of long videos. This computational bottleneck significantly challenges the application of advanced semantic matching to long-form, multilingual video retrieval.

3   Methods

Our multi-stage framework addresses the mVCR challenge of retrieving relevant videos when the query and subtitle languages differ. At its core, our pipeline enriches subtitles with KG facts and builds a hierarchical index for each video, enabling efficient coarse-to-fine retrieval. The system consists of two main phases: Hierarchical Index Construction (Sect. 3.2) and Retrieval & Ranking (Sects. 3.3-3.4). This design effectively scales to long videos while bridging language gaps between queries and video content.

3.1   Task Formulation

Let $\mathcal{V} = \{v_1, \ldots, v_N\}$ denote a collection of N medical instructional videos. Each video v_i is associated with a set of subtitles $\mathcal{S}_i$ (in its original language L_i) and a collection of relevant KG triples $\mathcal{K}_i$. Let $\mathcal{Q}$ be the space of user queries, where a query $Q \in \mathcal{Q}$ may be expressed in any supported language L_Q. The objective is to learn a retrieval function $f : \mathcal{Q} \times \mathcal{V} \rightarrow$ Ranking that generates a ranked list of videos from $\mathcal{V}$ based on their relevance to a given query Q (Fig. 1).

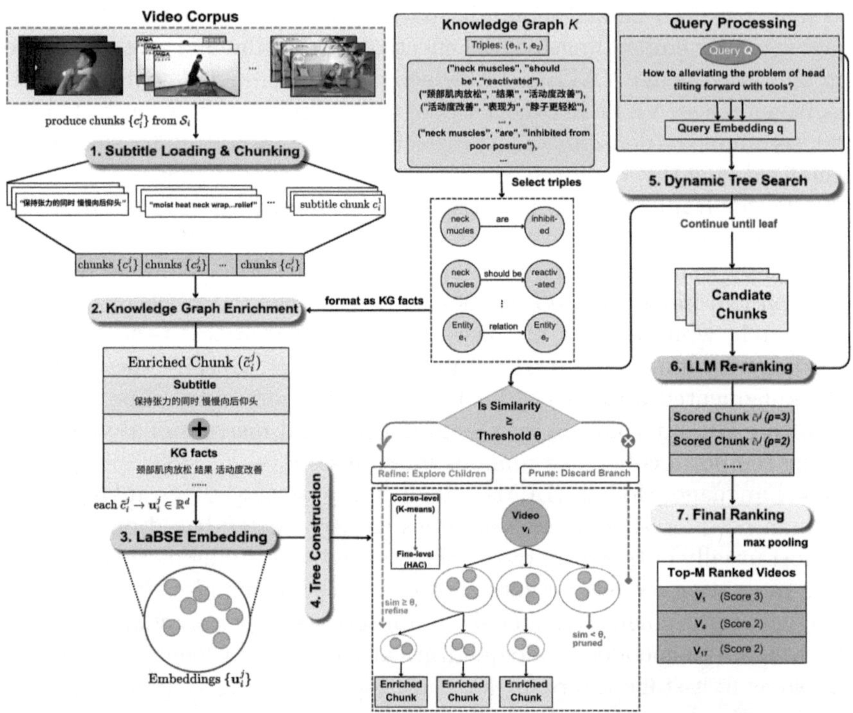

Fig. 1. Overview of proposed multilingual video retrieval pipeline.

3.2   Hierarchical Index Construction

For each video $v_i \in \mathcal{V}$, we construct an enriched hierarchical index $\mathcal{T}_i$ through three key steps: segmenting subtitles into semantic chunks, enhancing these chunks with relevant KG context, and organizing them into a hierarchical tree structure.

Subtitle Loading and Semantic Chunking. Segmenting lengthy instructional videos requires preserving semantic coherence. We begin by loading subtitle data $\mathcal{S}_i = \{\ell_1, \ldots, \ell_{m_i}\}$ for each video and performing basic text cleaning.

To avoid disrupting the instructional flow of arbitrary divisions, our approach employs semantic chunking based on the similarity between adjacent subtitle lines. The LaBSE model, with its strong multilingual representation capabilities, provides embeddings for these subtitle lines:

$$\mathbf{e}(\ell_k) = \text{LaBSE}(\ell_k) \in \mathbb{R}^d \tag{1}$$

where $\mathbf{e}(\ell_k)$ represents the d-dimensional embedding for subtitle line ℓ_k. Chunk boundaries are detected by identifying points where the cosine similarity between adjacent embeddings falls below an empirically tuned threshold τ:

$$\cos(\mathbf{e}(\ell_k), \mathbf{e}(\ell_{k+1})) < \tau \tag{2}$$

This boundary detection yields a sequence of chunks $c_i^1, \ldots, c_i^{M_i}$ for video v_i, each containing semantically coherent subtitle lines in the original language L_i.

KG Enrichment via Text Concatenation. To enhance semantic representation with domain knowledge, each chunk c_i^j is enriched using the set of KG triples $\mathcal{K}_i$ relevant to its corresponding video v_i. We identify medical entities in c_i^j using a multilingual Named Entity Recognizer, specifically an XLM-RoBERTa model fine-tuned for multilingual NER [28]. These entities directly guide the selection of relevant knowledge. Specifically, for each identified entity, we retrieve all triples from the video's pre-filtered set $\mathcal{K}_i$ where it appears as either the subject or the object. This enrichment occurs via straightforward text concatenation: key information from the retrieved triples, such as entity relationships and types, is converted into concise, factual statements and appended to the chunk's original text. The resulting enriched chunk, $\tilde{c}_i^j$, thus integrates relevant domain knowledge while preserving the original content structure.

Tree Construction. The hierarchical organization of enriched chunks forms the foundation of our efficient retrieval approach. We encode each enriched chunk into a vector representation using LaBSE:

$$\mathbf{u}_i^j = \text{LaBSE}(\tilde{c}_i^j) \tag{3}$$

where $\mathbf{u}_i^j$ represents the enriched chunk in the shared multilingual semantic space. We implement a two-level clustering strategy to create a structure that captures both broad topics and specific details. First, K-means partitions the set of embeddings $\{\mathbf{u}_i^j\}$ for video v_i into K coarse clusters that serve as first-level nodes representing major topics. Then, for each coarse cluster, we apply HAC to develop deeper tree levels that reveal finer-grained subtopics. Each node n in the resulting tree $\mathcal{T}_i$ stores a representative embedding $\mathbf{e}_n$, calculated as the centroid of $\mathcal{C}_n$, the set of embeddings corresponding to all chunks descended from node n:

$$\mathbf{e}_n = \frac{1}{|\mathcal{C}_n|} \sum_{\mathbf{u} \in \mathcal{C}_n} \mathbf{u} \tag{4}$$

This centroid $\mathbf{e}_n$ effectively summarizes the semantic content of node n. The completed hierarchical structure $\mathcal{T}_i$, whose leaf nodes are the individual enriched chunks $\tilde{c}_i^j$, enables the efficient coarse-to-fine search.

3.3   Query Processing and Initial Retrieval

After constructing hierarchical indices for all videos, our system processes incoming user queries and performs efficient retrieval across these structured representations to identify relevant candidate chunks.

Query Processing. Given a user query Q in language L_Q, we encode it using the same LaBSE model employed during the indexing phase:

$$\mathbf{q} = \text{LaBSE}(Q) \tag{5}$$

This consistent encoding projects the query vector $\mathbf{q}$ and the chunk embeddings $\mathbf{u}_i^j$ into a shared multilingual semantic space, enabling comparisons based on conceptual similarity rather than exact lexical matching. Consequently, the system gains inherent robustness against linguistic variations, such as those introduced by translation.

Dynamic Tree Search. Rather than exhaustively comparing the query against all chunks, we implement a coarse-to-fine search strategy that leverages the hierarchical index $\mathcal{T}_i$ of each video. The search commences by computing the cosine similarity between the query embedding $\mathbf{q}$ and the embeddings $\mathbf{e}_n$ of the first-level (K-means) cluster nodes. Using a predefined relevance threshold θ, only top-level clusters whose similarity exceeds this threshold are retained, effectively pruning irrelevant branches early in the search. For each qualifying cluster, the search recursively descends its subtree (generated by HAC), applying the same pruning logic at each level to traverse only promising branches. This traversal continues until reaching leaf nodes (the enriched chunks $\tilde{c}_i^j$) via unpruned paths. The resulting candidate set comprises all leaf nodes reached through this process. Each candidate is recorded as a tuple $(\text{video\_id}, \text{chunk\_id}, \cos(\mathbf{q}, \mathbf{u}_i^j), \tilde{c}_i^j)$, with its cosine similarity serving as an initial relevance score. These candidates are then ranked to form a top-M list, $\mathcal{C}_{\text{top}}$, for subsequent re-ranking. This hierarchical search offers significant computational improvements over a brute-force scan. By dynamically pruning the search space, it ensures the expensive LLM re-ranker processes only a few top candidates, which is critical for balancing high precision with the scalability and low latency required for large video corpora.

3.4   LLM Re-ranking and Video Aggregation

While embedding similarity provides efficient initial retrieval, achieving optimal ranking requires a deeper semantic understanding. In this final phase, we refine the ranking of candidate chunks using a multilingual LLM and then aggregate these scores to produce video-level results.

Multilingual LLM Re-ranking. Embedding-based similarity captures broad semantic relationships but often misses nuanced relevance factors crucial for medical queries. To address this limitation, we implement LLM-based re-ranking that leverages multilingual understanding capabilities. For each candidate chunk $\tilde{c}_i^j \in \mathcal{C}_{\text{top}}$, we prompt the LLM with the original query Q (in language L_Q) and the chunk's enriched text $\tilde{c}_i^j$ (in its original language L_i). The model then produces a scalar relevance rating $\rho(\tilde{c}_i^j)$ on a 1–3 scale (where 3 indicates highest relevance), providing a fine-grained assessment that surpasses simple vector similarity. While the LLM's nuanced semantic understanding leads to highly effective scoring, this performance comes with a trade-off: the model's internal reasoning is largely opaque, limiting its interpretability.

Video-level Aggregation and Ranking. The mVCR task requires video-level rankings rather than chunk-level results. We aggregate the chunk scores for each video v_i using max pooling, which assigns each video the highest relevance score achieved by any of its evaluated chunks:

$$\text{Score}(v_i) = \max_{\tilde{c}_i^j \in \mathcal{C}_{\text{top}}^i} \rho(\tilde{c}_i^j) \tag{6}$$

where $\mathcal{C}_{\text{top}}^i$ represents the set of top chunks belonging to video v_i. This approach prioritizes videos containing highly relevant content chunks, even if other portions are less pertinent. The final output ranks all videos $\{v_1, \ldots, v_N\}$ in descending order of $\text{Score}(v_i)$.

4   Experiments

4.1   Dataset and Evaluation

The dataset features medical instructional videos crawled from YouTube, with textual content that includes original subtitles and generated captions in both Chinese and English. The corresponding question-answer pairs consist of Chinese questions manually authored by medical experts and English questions that are translated and refined by native-speaking medical doctors. Each question corresponds to a specific temporal segment of a video, and multiple related questions may point to the same answer segment. The dataset is divided into training, validation, and test sets (Table 1).

Following the challenge protocol [29], retrieval performance is measured using Recall@n (R@n) with $n \in \{1, 10, 50\}$, which indicates the percentage of queries where the correct video appears among the top-n results. The Mean Reciprocal Rank (MRR) [30] is calculated as:

$$\text{MRR} = \frac{1}{|V|} \sum_{i=1}^{|V|} \frac{1}{\text{Rank}_i} \tag{7}$$

Table 1. Statistics of the Medical Instructional Video Dataset, including the number of videos, QA pairs, vocabulary size, and average lengths for the Train/Dev/Test splits.

Dataset	Videos	QA pairs	Vocab Size	Avg. Ch. Q. Len.	Avg. Eng. Q. Len.	Avg. Video Len.
Train	1,228	5,840	6,582	17.16	6.97	263.3
Dev	200	983	1,743	17.81	7.26	242.4
Test	200	1,022	2,234	18.22	7.44	310.9

where $|V|$ represents the number of test queries, and Rank_i is the position of the ground-truth video in the predicted list for the i-th query. The Overall score, serving as the main ranking criterion, is calculated by summing the four metrics:

$$\text{Overall} = \sum_{i=1}^{|M|} \text{Value}_i \tag{8}$$

where $|M| = 4$ is the number of evaluation metrics, and Value_i represents the value of the i-th metric.

4.2 Main Results

Table 2. Retrieval performance comparison of our proposed framework against other methods on the mVCR test set.

Method	R@1	R@10	R@50	MRR	Overall
RANDOMPICK [29,31]	0.0343	0.0523	0.0442	0.0442	0.1674
GEN [32]	0.1311	0.1074	0.0978	0.1142	0.4505
Wjh	0.2744	0.3312	0.4117	0.2551	1.2724
DSG-1 [33,34]	0.2644	0.3545	0.4414	0.2887	1.3491
sun [35]	0.3121	0.4078	0.4966	0.3245	1.5410
NYU	0.3213	0.4137	0.5104	0.3354	1.5808
DIMA (Ours)	**0.3264**	**0.4211**	**0.5177**	**0.3407**	**1.6059**

We evaluate our proposed method against several strong baselines from previous mVCR challenges using five standard metrics: R@1, R@10, R@50, MRR, and the Overall score. Key competitors include GEN [32], which implemented a retrieval framework based on approaches surveyed in recent literature. DSG-1 [33,34] developed a two-stage retrieval-reranking pipeline that employed GPT-3.5[1] for video summary generation and RoBERTa [36] for initial retrieval, followed by a CCGS-VCR analyzer for re-ranking. The MQuA approach [35], from

---

[1] https://poe.com/GPT-3.5-Turbo.

the 2024 challenge, leveraged the DeBERTa-v2-710M-Chinese [37] model combined with Multi-Level Video Moment Refinement (MVMR) and enhanced it with Multilingual Query Paraphrase Generation (MQPG) using Few-shot ChatGPT [38].

As shown in Table 2, our proposed method achieves state-of-the-art performance across all evaluation metrics on the mVCR test set, achieving the highest scores in R@1 (0.3264), R@10 (0.4211), R@50 (0.5177), MRR (0.3407), and Overall (1.6059).

Compared to GEN [32], our method demonstrates substantial improvements with absolute increases of 0.1953↑ in R@1, 0.3137↑ in R@10, 0.4199↑ in R@50, 0.2265↑ in MRR, and 1.1554↑ in Overall score. Against the stronger DSG-1 approach [33,34], we achieve notable improvements: 0.0620↑ for R@1, 0.0666↑ for R@10, 0.0763↑ for R@50, 0.0520↑ for MRR, and 0.2568↑ for Overall score. Furthermore, our method outperforms the sun team's MQuA approach [35] with consistent gains of 0.0143↑ in R@1, 0.0133↑ in R@10, 0.0211↑ in R@50, 0.0162↑ in MRR, and 0.0649↑ in Overall score.

These consistent improvements validate the effectiveness of our multi-stage retrieval framework. The performance gains are particularly significant for R@1 and MRR metrics, highlighting the superior precision of our approach in retrieving the most relevant video as the top result for multilingual medical video retrieval tasks.

4.3   Ablation Study

We conduct ablation experiments to evaluate the impact of each core component by systematically removing modules from our framework. Generally, all reported percentage changes represent relative decreases from the full system's performance. Removing domain-specific KG enrichment decreases the Overall score by 6.6% and R@1 by 7.6%. These results confirm KG enrichment's crucial role in enhancing semantic representations, particularly in bridging specialized medical terminology between queries and video content.

When our hierarchical index is replaced with flat retrieval, performance degrades further, with the Overall score dropping by an additional 2.7%. Notable declines appear in MRR (12.4%) and R@50 (8.4%), showing that flat indexing struggles with long-form videos even under relaxed retrieval criteria. The magnitude of this performance gap underscores the effectiveness of the hierarchical organization for efficient pruning and improved precision (Table 3).

LLM re-ranking is the most critical component, as evidenced by the substantial 12.9% decrease in Overall score when removed from the pipeline. Performance metrics show the most significant deterioration here, with R@10 and MRR falling by 14.2% and 14.6% respectively. Such pronounced degradation relative to other ablations demonstrates that the LLM's nuanced understanding of query-video semantic relationships is critical for achieving state-of-the-art performance in multilingual medical video retrieval.

Table 3. Impact of removing key components from the proposed framework on retrieval performance.

Method	R@1	R@10	R@50	MRR	Overall
DIMA	**0.3264**	**0.4211**	**0.5177**	**0.3407**	**1.6059**
w/o KG Enrichment	0.3017	0.3943	0.4878	0.3154	1.4992
w/o Hierarchical Index	0.2968	0.3887	0.4741	0.2985	1.4581
w/o LLM Re-ranking	0.2855	0.3614	0.4612	0.2911	1.3992

5   Conclusion

We have presented a solution to the mVCR challenge that addresses key limitations in retrieving multilingual medical videos. By integrating language-agnostic embeddings with domain knowledge and efficient hierarchical search, our framework achieves both computational scalability and multilingual precision. Experiments demonstrate state-of-the-art performance across all metrics, and ablation studies confirm that each component makes complementary contributions to the effectiveness of multilingual video retrieval.

To build upon this work, future directions include exploring structured KG reasoning with methods like graph neural networks to overcome the limitations of text concatenation. We will also investigate knowledge distillation to create a more compact and efficient LLM re-ranker. Finally, incorporating visual features for true multi-modal retrieval remains a key priority to further boost precision and scalability.

References

1. Li, S., Li, B., Sun, B., Weng, Y.: Towards visual-prompt temporal answer grounding in instructional video. IEEE Trans. Pattern Anal. Mach. Intell. **01**, 1–18 (2024)
2. Zhong, J., Wang, Y.: Enhancing thyroid disease prediction using machine learning: a comparative study of ensemble models and class balancing techniques. 2025
3. Wang, Y., Zhong, J., Kumar, R.: A systematic review of machine learning applications in infectious disease prediction, diagnosis, and outbreak forecasting. 2025
4. Li, B., Weng,Y., Song, Q., Liang, L., Min, X., Zhou, S.: Overview of the NLPCC 2024 shared task 7: multi-lingual medical instructional video question answering. In: Wong, D.F., Wei, Z., Yang, M., (eds) Natural Language Processing and Chinese Computing, pp. 429–439, Singapore, 2025. Springer Nature Singapore
5. Li, B., Liu, S., Weng, Y., Du, Y., Tian, Y., Zhou, S.: Overview of the NLPCC 2025 shared task 4: multi-modal, multilingual, and multi-hop medical instructional video question answering challenge. arXiv preprintarXiv:2505.06814 (2025)
6. Kong, Z., et al.: Spvit: enabling faster vision transformers via latency-aware soft token pruning. In: European conference on computer vision, pp. 620–640. Springer (2022)
7. Ke, Z., Zhou, S., Zhou, Y., Chang, C.H., Zhang, R.: Detection of AI deepfake and fraud in online payments using GAN-based models. arXiv preprint arXiv:2501.07033 (2025)

8. Kong, Z., et al.: Peeling the onion: hierarchical reduction of data redundancy for efficient vision transformer training. Proc. AAAI Conf. Artifi. Intell. **37**, 8360–8368 (2023)

9. Mithun, N.C., Li, J., Metze, F., Roy-Chowdhury, A. K.: Learning joint embedding with multimodal cues for cross-modal video-text retrieval. In: Proceedings of the 2018 ACM on International Conference on Multimedia Retrieval, ICMR '18, pp. 19–27, New York, NY, USA, 2018. Association for Computing Machinery

10. Dong, J., Li, X., Chaoxi, X., Shouling Ji., Yang, G., Wang, X.: Dual encoding for zero-example video retrieval, Yuan He (2019)

11. Yu, Y., Kim, J., Kim, G.: A joint sequence fusion model for video question answering and retrieval (2018)

12. Yu, P., et al.: Q-tempfusion: quantization-aware temporal multi-sensor fusion on bird's-eye view representation. In: Proceedings of the Winter Conference on Applications of Computer Vision (WACV), pp. 5489–5499 (2025)

13. Braslavski, P., Verberne, S., Talipov, R.: Show me how to tie a tie: evaluation of cross-lingual video retrieval. In: Fuhr, N., et al (eds) Experimental IR Meets Multilinguality, Multimodality, and Interaction, pp. 3–15, Cham, 2016. Springer International Publishing

14. Wang, X., Jiawei, W., Chen, J., Li, L., Wang, Y.-F., Wang, W.Y.: A large-scale, high-quality multilingual dataset for video-and-language research, Vatex (2020)

15. Ma, Y., Guohai, X., Sun, X., Yan, M., Zhang, J., Ji, R.: End-to-end multi-grained contrastive learning for video-text retrieval, X-clip (2022)

16. Zhao, S., Zhu, S., Wang, X., Yang, Y.: Centerclip: token clustering for efficient text-video retrieval. In: Proceedings of the 45th International ACM SIGIR Conference on Research and Development in Information Retrieval, SIGIR '22, pp. 970–981. ACM (2022)

17. Zhao, P., Fan, R., Wang, S., Shen, L., Zhang, Q., Ke, Z., Zheng, T.: Contextual bandits for unbounded context distributions (2025)

18. Nogueira, R., Cho, K.: Passage re-ranking with BERT (2020)

19. Adeyemi, M., Oladipo, A., Pradeep, R., Lin, R.: Zero-shot cross-lingual reranking with large language models for low-resource languages (2023)

20. Li, B., et al.: Distinct but correct: generating diversified and entity-revised medical response. Sci. China Inf. Sci. **67**(3), 132106 (2024)

21. Feng, F., Yang, Y., Cer, D., Arivazhagan, N., Wang., W.: Language-agnostic BERT sentence embedding (2022)

22. Luo, H.: Clip4clip: an empirical study of clip for end to end video clip retrieval (2021)

23. Xiong, C., Power, R., Callan, J.: Explicit semantic ranking for academic search via knowledge graph embedding. In: Proceedings of the 26th International Conference on World Wide Web, WWW '17, pp. 1271–1279, Republic and Canton of Geneva, CHE, 2017. International World Wide Web Conferences Steering Committee

24. Rossetto, L., et al.: Videograph - towards using knowledge graphs for interactive video retrieval. In: MultiMedia Modeling: 27th International Conference, MMM 2021, Prague, Czech Republic, June 22–24, 2021, Proceedings, Part II, pp. 417–422, Berlin, Heidelberg, 2021. Springer-Verlag

25. Sung, M., Jeon, H., Lee, J., Kang, J.: Biomedical entity representations with synonym marginalization. In: Jurafsky, D., Chai, J., Schluter, N., Tetreault, J., (eds) Proceedings of the 58th Annual Meeting of the Association for Computational Linguistics, pp. 3641–3650, Online, July 2020. Association for Computational Linguistics

26. Shen, Y., et al.: Altgen: Ai-driven alt text generation for enhancing EPUB accessibility. arXiv preprint arXiv:2501.00113 (2024)

27. Zhang, H., et al.: Comparative analysis of large language models for context-aware code completion using safim framework. arXiv preprint arXiv:2502.15243 (2025)

28. Mehta, R., Varma, V.: LLM-RM at semeval-2023 task 2: multilingual complex NER using XLM-roberta. In: Proceedings of the 17th International Workshop on Semantic Evaluation (SemEval-2023) (2023)

29. Li, B., Weng, Y., Sun, B., Li, S.: Learning to locate visual answer in video corpus using question. In: ICASSP 2023 - 2023 IEEE International Conference on Acoustics, Speech and Signal Processing (ICASSP), pp.1–5. IEEE (2023)

30. Chapelle, O., Metlzer, D., Zhang, Y., Grinspan, P.: Expected reciprocal rank for graded relevance. In: Proceedings of the 18th ACM Conference on Information and Knowledge Management, CIKM '09, pp. 621–630, New York, NY, USA, 2009. Association for Computing Machinery

31. Weng, Y., Li, B.: Visual answer localization with cross-modal mutual knowledge transfer. In: ICASSP 2023-2023 IEEE International Conference on Acoustics, Speech and Signal Processing (ICASSP), pp. 1–5. IEEE (2023)

32. Li, B., Weng, Y., Song, Q., Liang, L., Min, X., Zhou, S.: Overview of the nlpcc 2024 shared task 7: multi-lingual medical instructional video question answering. In: Wong, D.F., Wei, Z., Yang, M., (eds) Natural Language Processing and Chinese Computing, pp. 429–439, Singapore, 2025. Springer Nature Singapore

33. Lei, N., et al.: A two-stage chinese medical video retrieval framework with LLM. In: Liu, F., Duan, N., Xu, Q., Hong, Y., (eds) Natural Language Processing and Chinese Computing, pp. 211–220, Cham, 2023. Springer Nature Switzerland

34. Li, B., et al.: Overview of the NLPCC 2023 shared task: Chinese medical instructional video question answering. In: Liu, F., Duan, N., Xu, N., Hong, Y., (eds) Natural Language Processing and Chinese Computing, pp. 233–242, Cham, 2023. Springer Nature Switzerland

35. Yu, G., et al.: Mqua: multi-level query-video augmentation for multilingual video corpus retrieval. In: Wong, D. F., Wei, Z., Yang, Z., (eds) Natural Language Processing and Chinese Computing, pp. 353–364, Singapore, 2025. Springer Nature Singapore

36. Liu, Y., et al.: and Veselin Stoyanov. A robustly optimized bert pretraining approach, Roberta (2019)

37. He, P., Liu, X., Gao, J., Chen, W.: Decoding-enhanced BERT with disentangled attention, Deberta (2021)

38. OpenAI. Introducing chatgpt: optimizing language models for dialogue (2022). https://openai.com/index/chatgpt/, Accessed 04 May 2025

Hierarchical RAG-Driven Multi-hop Reasoning for Medical Video Question Answering

Ruohan Gao, Qijun Zhao, and YangQianQian Chen[✉]

Sichuan University, Chengdu, China
{2022141510122,2021141460269}@stu.scu.edu.cn, qjzhao@scu.edu.cn

Abstract. In medical video understanding, the m^3TAGSV task faces challenges in bridging cross-lingual knowledge gaps, modeling cross-modal interactions, and enabling multi-hop reasoning across video segments. To address these, we propose a hierarchical Retrieval-Augmented Generation (RAG)-enhanced tri-modal framework comprising two parallel pathways: (a) a visual predictor using 3D CNNs with temporal shift modules for spatiotemporal feature extraction and (b) a textual predictor processing questions, subtitles, and RAG-augmented knowledge from multilingual medical graphs. The RAG component enriches textual representations via structured triple retrieval, while joint optimization under ground-truth (GT) supervision employs contrastive learning and temporal localization losses to align multimodal features and localize answer segments. A hierarchical attention mechanism aggregates cross-modal and cross-segment evidence for multi-hop reasoning, with cross-modal alignment ensuring precise grounding. Our contributions include a novel tri-modal fusion architecture, an RAG-based multilingual knowledge retrieval mechanism, a hierarchical attention framework for multi-hop reasoning, and a GT-supervised training scheme for accurate temporal answer grounding.

Keywords: m^3TAGSV task · Tri-modal fusion · Retrieval-Augmented Generation (RAG) · Multi-hop reasoning

1 Introduction

Medical video question localization (VQL) is of critical importance in clinical decision-making and medical education [1–4]. With recent advancements in multimodal fusion infrastructures [5–8], the capability to process complex videos and educational content has been significantly enhanced [9]. However, the task remains challenging stemming from the inherent complexity of medical videos and the substantial semantic gap between visual and textual information [10,11]. To address these issues, our proposed framework harnesses Retrieval-Augmented Generation (RAG) to incorporate external medical knowledge into the textual input of the textual predictor. Coupled with Ground-Truth (GT)-supervised

© The Author(s), under exclusive license to Springer Nature Singapore Pte Ltd. 2026
X.-L. Mao et al. (Eds.): NLPCC 2025, LNAI 16105, pp. 405–416, 2026.
https://doi.org/10.1007/978-981-95-3352-7_34

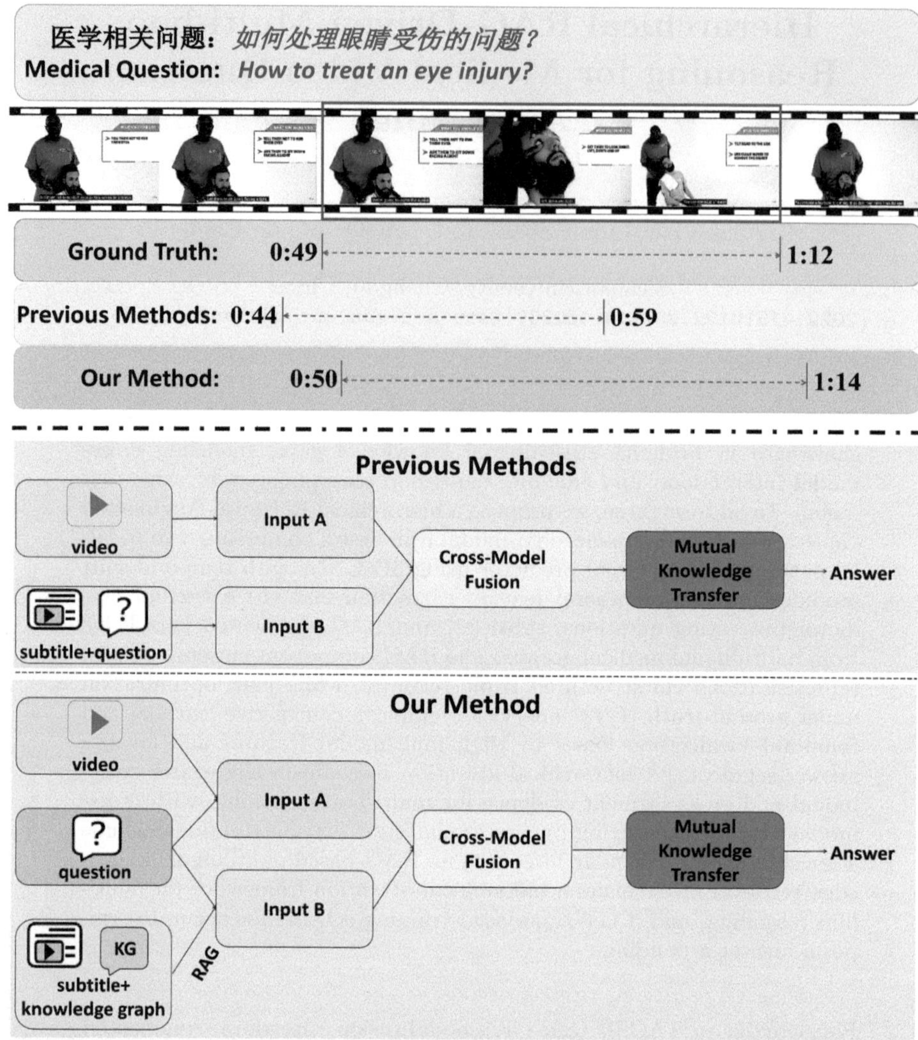

Fig. 1. Task description of the visual answer localization, where the following is the paradigm of the previous methods and our method.

learning for both visual and textual predictors, this approach facilitates more accurate feature representation learning. The framework's architecture, featuring cross-modal alignment and mutual knowledge transfer, further leverages these components to achieve superior performance in VQL (Fig. 1).

Our research focuses on Track 1 of the NLPCC2025 challenge, the multi-modal, Multilingual, and Multi-Hop Temporal Answer Grounding in Single Video (m³TAGSV) task. Given a medical/health question and an untrimmed Chinese medical instructional video, the goal is to accurately localize the corresponding temporal segment (start and end time points) in the video. This requires the model to understand the question and integrate multi-modal video information accurately.

Previous approaches [12,13] to medical video question localization typically took video and a combined input of a concatenated subtitle and question input. As depicted in Fig. 2, when addressing the medical question "How to treat an eye injury?", a prior method identified a segment from $0 : 44$ to $0 : 59$, showing a significant deviation from the Ground Truth $(0 : 49 - 1 : 12)$. Building on the foundation of such prior work, we conducted a comprehensive comparative analysis and identified limitations in multi-modal input processing and knowledge integration.

To overcome these challenges, we introduce an enhanced methodology. Our approach treats the question as an independent input modality and integrates a knowledge graph (KG) with Retrieval-Augmented Generation (RAG) for subtitle processing. Specifically, we utilize video, an independent question, and subtitle + KG (processed by RAG) as inputs. As shown in Fig. 2, our method localizes the segment from $0 : 50$ to $1 : 14$, which is much closer to the Ground Truth.

Drawing from experimental results and comparative evaluations, we summarize the following key observations:

1. By isolating the question input, our method can more effectively utilize the question's semantic guidance for visual feature extraction, as illustrated in the input section of our method in the figure.
2. The RAG module efficiently integrates knowledge from the KG, enriching the textual input and enabling more precise understanding, as reflected in the subtitle + KG processing part.
3. The improved input structure and knowledge integration mechanism endow our method with enhanced robustness in handling multi-modal information, significantly reducing the deviation from the Ground Truth, as evident from the comparison of localization results.

2   Related Work

Multi-modal Video Question Localization: Extensive research has investigated multi-modal video question localization by integrating visual and textual information. VideoBERT [14], an early attempt, leverages masked language modeling and frame prediction in a BERT-like architecture, although it primarily depends on simple concatenation and lacks fine-grained alignment mechanisms. HERO [15] and UniVL [16] adopt dual-encoder or fusion-based architectures to learn joint representations, but often fail to model long-range dependencies effectively. MMBT [17] applies early fusion via a transformer, though its attention mechanism becomes computationally intensive for long-duration medical videos. Notably, most existing approaches assume clean, well-structured input and are ill-suited to the noisy and heterogeneous nature of real-world medical video data.

Multilingual Processing in the Medical Domain: Multilingual modeling in medical applications has predominantly utilized general-purpose pre-trained models such as mBERT [18] and XLM-R [19]. These models are trained on broad corpora and exhibit limited command of medical terminology, resulting in inadequate performance in domain-specific applications. While domain-specific models like BioBERT [20] and PubMedBERT [21] have substantially improved English medical understanding, non-English medical resources—particularly in Chinese—remain severely under-represented [22]. Furthermore, these models are typically restricted to text-based tasks and lack the capability to incorporate visual or auditory cues for comprehensive question answering.

Multi-hop Question Answering: Multi-hop question answering (QA), which requires reasoning over multiple information units, has been extensively explored through datasets such as HotPotQA [23] and MuSiQue [24]. HotPotQA, for instance, builds graphs over supporting facts and employs graph neural networks to model reasoning paths [25]. However, these techniques are largely designed for purely textual contexts [26], limiting their applicability in multimedia settings. In medical instructional videos, information is fragmented across visual frames, subtitles, and sometimes audio, posing challenges for applying conventional textual reasoning techniques. Recent methods like E-Graph [27] demonstrate potential in graph-based multi-modal fusion, yet remain insufficiently robust for precise temporal grounding. Overall, although notable advancements have been made in multi-modal learning, multilingual modeling, and multi-hop reasoning, few methods effectively integrate all these elements for complex medical video QA. Our proposed Baichuan framework fills this gap by combining RAG-enhanced textual reasoning, CLIP-based visual-textual alignment, and pseudo-label supervision within a unified training paradigm.

3   Proposed Method

The model processes medical videos, user queries, subtitles, and knowledge graphs as inputs. Medical videos are decomposed into frame sequences, while queries and subtitles are tokenized into word embeddings. A pre-trained CLIP model aligns video frames with textual queries to generate coarse-grained temporal intervals via semantic similarity. For visual feature extraction, a 3D convolutional network (e.g., 3D-ResNet) captures spatio-temporal features from frames. For text, a Transformer-based encoder (e.g., BERT) encodes the semantic content of the query and subtitles. Visual and textual features are fed into lightweight pseudo-label generators, which compute similarity to labeled data and produce pseudo-labels for supervised training of unimodal predictors.

3.1   Inputs for Predictors

Input for Visual Predictor: The input to the visual predictor comprises a medical video and a natural language query (e.g., "How to treat an eye injury?"). The video is uniformly sampled into frames, each aligned with a timestamp. A visual feature extractor encodes spatio-temporal features, denoted as A^V, which

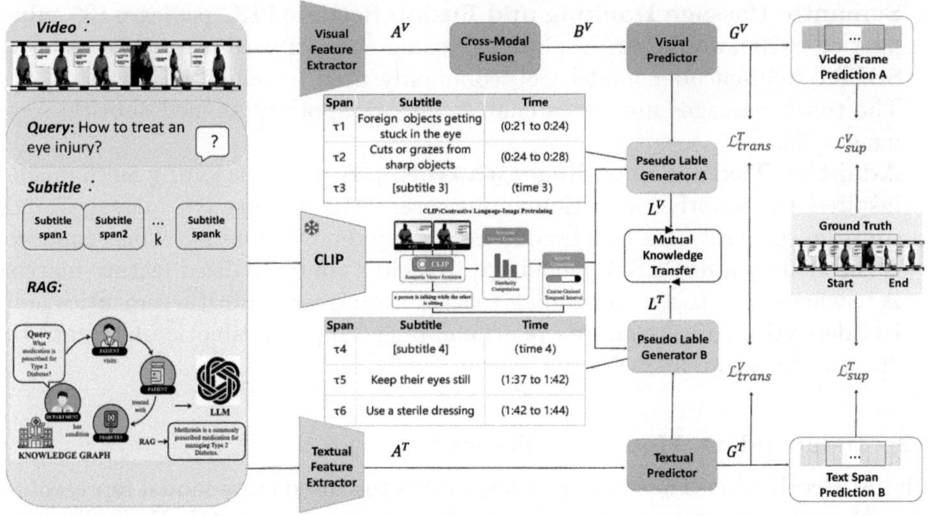

Fig. 2. Overview of the proposed multimodal video question localization framework.

capture essential visual context related to the query. This ensures the visual modality retains critical information for identifying relevant segments.

Input for Textual Predictor: The textual predictor receives the query, associated subtitles, and augmented text from a Retrieval-Augmented Generation (RAG) module [28–30]. Subtitles are segmented into temporal spans aligned with the video timeline. Below, we elaborate on the RAG technique, a key component for enhancing textual semantics.

Retrieval–Augmented Generation (RAG) Technique. RAG serves as a knowledge integration module, dynamically linking raw text inputs with structured medical knowledge from a knowledge graph (KG) [31]. For a user query (e.g., "How to treat an eye injury?"), the RAG pipeline operates in four stages, following established knowledge-augmented NLP practices [32]:

1. **Linguistic Structure Parsing** The query is processed using a lightweight medical NER model (e.g., `spaCy` [33]) to identify key semantic elements such as `ANATOMY` (eye), `CONDITION` (injury), and `PROCEDURE` (treatment). Dependency parsing extracts relational information (e.g., "treat" as the action), in accordance with medical language processing workflows [34].
2. **Knowledge Graph Subgraph Extraction** A two-hop breadth-first search (BFS) is executed on a medical KG based on the UMLS ontology [35], which encodes entities (e.g., `MEDICATION`, `PROCEDURE`) and relations (e.g., "has_treatment"). Nodes are augmented with clinical guidelines (e.g., "Ocular Trauma Management Protocol") and linked to evidence-based resources [36]. This strategy captures both direct treatment protocols and contextual information such as contraindications [37].

3. **Semantic Passage Ranking and Fusion** Retrieved KG passages (35 snippets of 50200 words) are ranked by cosine similarity to the query using a SBERT dual-encoder model [38], commonly used in semantic retrieval [39]. The top-k passages are concatenated with temporally aligned subtitle segments [40].

4. **Adaptive Textual Encoding with Gating** A trainable gating mechanism, inspired by adaptive attention frameworks [41], weights KG passages and subtitles, generating a fused sequence (maximum 512 tokens). This sequence is encoded by a RoBERTa model [42] to yield a contextualized feature matrix $\mathbf{A}^T$, where each token embedding reflects both query/subtitle semantics and KG-derived medical concepts (e.g., mapping "apply antibiotic ointment" to "topical fluoroquinolone").

3.2 Independent Modal Predictors

Visual Predictor: The visual predictor takes the fused cross-modal representation B^V and outputs continuous start/end timestamps $G^V = (V_s, V_t)$, indicating the temporal boundaries of the relevant video segment. To capture both coarse and fine-grained cues, it employs a span-based regression framework that first predicts frame-level probability distributions, followed by boundary refinement. Specifically, B^V is input into a temporal modeling module—either stacked convolutions or a transformer encoder—to aggregate long-range context, producing contextualized frame embeddings. These are passed to a multi-layer perceptron (MLP) that outputs normalized offsets, optimized via the following loss:

$$\mathcal{L}_{\text{sup}}^V = \tfrac{1}{2}\big[(V_s - G_s^T)^2 + (V_t - G_t^T)^2\big]. \tag{1}$$

A visual temporal attention mechanism is typically applied to emphasize semantically salient frames before regression, sharpening focus on key medical actions (e.g., incision, dressing).

Textual Predictor: The textual predictor processes the feature sequence A^T comprising the query, time-aligned subtitles, and RAG-augmented text—and predicts discrete start/end indices (S_s, S_t) corresponding to the subtitle span. Token embeddings are encoded using a bidirectional transformer or Bi-LSTM to capture both local syntax and global discourse. A classification or regression head then estimates span boundaries: classification-based variants minimize cross-entropy, while regression-based ones use mean squared error. To handle varying span lengths and linguistic complexity, positional encodings are combined with multi-scale temporal convolutions. Although later stages may apply cross-attention between modalities, the textual predictor relies solely on self-attention, enabling high-precision localization. Its supervised loss mirrors that of the visual branch:

$$\mathcal{L}_{\text{sup}}^T = \tfrac{1}{2}\big[(S_s - G_s^T)^2 + (S_t - G_t^T)^2\big]. \tag{2}$$

3.3   CLIP-Guided Semantic Alignment and Pseudo Labeling

A frozen CLIP model bridges visual and textual modalities via three steps:

Semantic Embedding: Sampled video frames and the query are encoded by CLIP's visual and text encoders, respectively.

Similarity Computation: Cosine similarities between video frame embeddings and the query embedding produce a semantic similarity score sequence.

Temporal Constraint Generation: A threshold is applied to these scores to select a coarse-grained interval, mapping to soft constraints for pseudo-label generation.

Two pseudo-label generators utilize these constraints: Generator A produces visual pseudo-labels L^V, while Generator B generates textual pseudo-labels L^T from RAG-enhanced semantic input.

Mutual Knowledge Transfer: To bridge modality gaps, a bidirectional knowledge transfer module is introduced. Visual predictions (L^V) inform textual span selection, while textual predictions (L^T) highlight temporal video regions. Transfer consistency losses are defined as:

$$\mathcal{L}^V_{\text{trans}} = \text{Dist}(L^V, \hat{L}^V), \quad \mathcal{L}^T_{\text{trans}} = \text{Dist}(L^T, \hat{L}^T). \tag{3}$$

where $\hat{L}^V$ and $\hat{L}^T$ are cross-modal pseudo-labels, and $\text{Dist}(\cdot)$ (e.g., mean squared error) measures their consistency.

3.4   Training Objective

The total training loss integrates supervised and pseudo-supervised objectives:

$$\mathcal{L}_{\text{total}} = \mathcal{L}^V_{\text{sup}} + \mathcal{L}^T_{\text{sup}} + \lambda_1 \mathcal{L}^V_{\text{trans}} + \lambda_2 \mathcal{L}^T_{\text{trans}}. \tag{4}$$

Here, λ_1 and λ_2 balance the supervised and cross-modal consistency losses. This end-to-end framework enables accurate localization of query-relevant segments by integrating unimodal learning, CLIP-based semantic alignment, and knowledge transfer.

3.5   Supervised Learning Loop

The framework is structured around a supervised learning loop. Both the visual predictor (taking video and query as input) and the textual predictor are trained using ground truth. Cross-modal transfer is co-optimized with the supervision stage, forming a closed-loop from unimodal analysis to multimodal fusion, ensuring each component contributes to accurate localization.

4   Experiments

4.1   Data Analysis and Experimental Settings

The dataset for NLPCC 2025 Shared Task 4 focuses on the multilingual temporal answer grounding task in Chinese medical instructional videos. Each data sample includes an untrimmed medical video, a natural language question, and annotated temporal intervals indicating the answer span. Videos were obtained from a Chinese medical YouTube channel using the Pytube tool, and subtitles were generated using the Whisper model. To standardize the input format, both subtitles and questions were converted to Simplified Chinese. The task also provides a knowledge base derived from Wikidata, which is used as external domain knowledge to enhance semantic understanding via our RAG module.

The dataset is divided into three subsets: a training set, a development set, and a test set. The training set consists of 1228 videos and 5840 question-answer (QA) pairs. The development set, used for model validation and ablation studies, contains 200 videos and 983 QA pairs. Test A, designated for final evaluation, comprises 200 videos and 1022 QA pairs. The average question length and video durations are summarized in Table 1.

Table 1. Dataset Statistics.

Split	Videos	QA Pairs	Tokens	Ch_Q Avg. Len	Eng_Q Avg. Len	Avg. Video Len
Train	1228	5840	6582	17.16	6.97	263.3
Dev	200	983	1743	17.81	7.26	242.4
Test A	200	1022	2234	18.22	7.44	310.9

Since no official validation set is provided, we randomly split the training data using a 4:1 ratio to create a held-out validation set [43]. This validation set is used for hyperparameter tuning and ablation analysis. All models are implemented using PyTorch and trained on NVIDIA V100 GPUs. The Adam optimizer is used with a learning rate of 1×10^{-4} [44]. The regularization parameters for mutual knowledge transfer, λ_1 and λ_2, are empirically set to 0.5 to balance supervised learning and cross-modal consistency losses. Videos are uniformly sampled to extract frames, and subtitle segments are aligned with temporal spans using timestamp metadata.

4.2 Main Results

To evaluate the effectiveness of our method, we compare the full Baichuan model with multiple strong baselines and top-performing systems from previous NLPCC tracks. The evaluation metrics include Recall@1 at three IoU thresholds (0.3, 0.5, and 0.7), as well as mean IoU. As shown in Table 2, Baichuan achieves the highest performance across all metrics.

Our method significantly outperforms earlier approaches, including VideoBERT-based models and multilingual fine-tuned baselines. These improvements are primarily attributed to the integration of domain-specific knowledge via RAG, improved video-text alignment through CLIP, and the use of mutual pseudo-label supervision. These components enable the model to better interpret complex medical procedures and reduce localization errors.

Table 2. Main results on the NLPCC 2025 Test set.

Method	R@1 IoU = 0.3	R@1 IoU = 0.5	R@1 IoU = 0.7	mIoU (R@1)
Random Pick [1,2]	0.0571	0.0465	0.0358	0.0397
PIPINSTALL [2]	0.4055	0.2911	0.1454	0.2898
BIGG [2]	0.4099	0.2863	0.1544	0.2977
SETAG [45]	0.4775	0.3209	0.1898	0.3389
Ouc_AI [46]	0.5088	0.3542	0.2054	0.3637
SEU [4]	0.4719	0.3314	0.1973	0.3411
Baichuan (Ours)	**0.5133**	**0.3612**	**0.2103**	**0.3717**

4.3   Ablation Study

To further examine the contribution of each component, we conduct ablation studies by removing one module at a time: RAG, CLIP alignment, and pseudo-labeling. The corresponding results are presented in Table 3.

Table 3. Ablation study results on the validation set.

Variant	R@1 IoU = 0.3	R@1 IoU = 0.5	R@1 IoU = 0.7	mIoU (R@1)
Full Model (Ours)	**0.5133**	**0.3612**	**0.2103**	**0.3717**
w/o RAG Module	0.5043	0.3511	0.2021	0.3598
w/o CLIP Alignment	0.4818	0.3489	0.1973	0.3445
w/o Pseudo Labels	0.4769	0.3297	0.1884	0.3297

Each component contributes significantly to overall performance. Removing the RAG module deprives the model of domain-specific knowledge, limiting its capacity to interpret complex medical semantics. Omitting CLIP alignment reduces cross-modal matching accuracy, resulting in noisier span predictions. Eliminating pseudo-labels removes soft supervision, which is especially beneficial in low-resource settings. These findings validate the effectiveness of our architectural choices.

5   Conclusion

This work proposes a RAG-enhanced multi-modal fusion framework for the task of multilingual temporal answer grounding in medical instructional videos. The architecture integrates Wikidata-derived medical knowledge via retrieval-augmented generation (RAG) to enrich textual queries and subtitles, employs CLIP-based visual-text alignment to align relevant video frames with question embeddings, and uses pseudo-label learning to enhance supervision. This approach achieved state-of-the-art results on the NLPCC 2025 Shared Task 4, ranking first in Track 1. Extensive ablation studies confirm that each component - external knowledge integration, fine-grained cross-modal alignment, and pseudo-label supervision makes a significant contribution, thereby enabling more precise temporal localization of answers and enhanced semantic clarity in complex medical contexts By bridging semantic gaps in medical video question answering through structured knowledge, the framework substantially improves answer fidelity and interpretability. Future work will extend this framework to additional languages and more diverse and comprehensive knowledge sources, and will evaluate its applicability in real-world clinical training scenarios, thereby strengthening its generalizability and practical impact.

References

1. Li, B., et al.: Overview of the NLPCC 2023 shared task: Chinese medical instructional video question answering. In: CCF International Conference on Natural Language Processing and Chinese Computing, pp. 233–242. Springer, Cham (2023). https://doi.org/10.1007/978-3-031-44699-3_21
2. Li, B., Weng, Y., Song, Q., Liang, L., Min, X., Zhou, S.: Overview of the NLPCC 2024 shared task 7: multi-lingual medical instructional video question answering. In: Wong, D.F., Wei, Z., Yang, M. (eds.) Natural Language Processing and Chinese Computing, pp. 429–439. Springer Nature Singapore, Singapore (2025). https://doi.org/10.1007/978-981-97-9443-0_38
3. Li, S., Li, B., Sun, B., Weng, Y.: Towards visual-prompt temporal answer grounding in instructional video. IEEE Trans. Pattern Anal. Mach. Intell. **46**(12), 8836–8853 (2024)
4. Li, B., Liu, S., Weng, Y., Du, Y., Tian, Y., Zhou, S.: Overview of the NLPCC 2025 shared task 4: multi-modal, multilingual, and multi-hop medical instructional video question answering challenge. arXiv preprint arXiv:2505.06814 (2025)
5. Lu, S., Liu, Y., Kong, A.W.K.: TF-ICON: diffusion-based training-free cross-domain image composition. In: Proceedings of the IEEE/CVF International Conference on Computer Vision, pp. 2294–2305 (2023)
6. Xin, Y., Junlong, D., Wang, Q., Lin, Z., Yan, K.: VMT-adapter: parameter-efficient transfer learning for multi-task dense scene understanding. In: Proceedings of the AAAI Conference on Artificial Intelligence, vol. 38, pp. 16085–16093 (2024)
7. Xin, Y., Junlong, D., Wang, Q., Yan, K., Ding, S.: MmAP: multi-modal alignment prompt for cross-domain multi-task learning. In: Proceedings of the AAAI Conference on Artificial Intelligence, vol. 38, pp. 16076–16084 (2024)
8. Bi, J., et al.: LLaVa steering: visual instruction tuning with $500\times$ fewer parameters through modality linear representation-steering (2025)
9. Xin, Y., et al.: V-petl bench: a unified visual parameter-efficient transfer learning benchmark. In: Advances in Neural Information Processing Systems, vol. 37, pp. 80522–80535 (2024)
10. Li, B., Weng, Y., Sun, B., Li, S.: Learning to locate visual answer in video corpus using question. In: ICASSP 2023-2023 IEEE International Conference on Acoustics, Speech and Signal Processing (ICASSP), pp. 1–5. IEEE (2023)

11. Zong, C., Li, B., Zhou, S., Wan, J., Zhang, L.: Ask2loc: learning to locate instructional visual answers by asking questions. arXiv preprint arXiv:2504.15918 (2025)
12. Weng, Y., Li, B.: Visual answer localization with cross-modal mutual knowledge transfer. In: ICASSP 2023-2023 IEEE International Conference on Acoustics, Speech and Signal Processing (ICASSP), pp. 1–5. IEEE (2023)
13. Tian, Y., Guo, X., Wang, J., Li, B., Zhou, S.: Video temporal grounding with multi-model collaborative learning. Appl. Sci. **15**(6), 3072 (2025)
14. Sun, C., Myers, A., Vondrick, C., Murphy, K., Schmid, C.: VideoBERT: a joint model for video and language representation learning. In: Proceedings of the IEEE International Conference on Computer Vision (ICCV) (2019)
15. Li, D., Yatskar, M., Yin, D., Hsieh, C.J., Chang, K.W.: Hero: hierarchical encoder for video+ language omni-representation pre-training. In: Conference on Empirical Methods in Natural Language Processing (EMNLP) (2020)
16. Luo, Y., et al.: Univl: a unified video and language pre-training model for multi-modal understanding and generation. arXiv preprint arXiv:2002.06353 (2020)
17. Kiela, D., et al.: Supervised multimodal bitransformers for classifying images and text. In: Advances in Neural Information Processing Systems (NeurIPS) (2019)
18. Devlin, J., Chang, M.W., Lee, K., Toutanova, K.: BERT: pre-training of deep bidirectional transformers for language understanding. In: North American Chapter of the Association for Computational Linguistics (NAACL) (2019)
19. Conneau, A., et al.: Unsupervised cross-lingual representation learning at scale. In: Annual Meeting of the Association for Computational Linguistics (ACL) (2020)
20. Lee, J., et al.: BioBERT: a pre-trained biomedical language representation model for biomedical text mining. Bioinformatics (2020)
21. Gu, Y., et al.: Domain-specific language model pretraining for biomedical natural language processing. ACM Trans. Comput. Healthcare (2021)
22. Wang, M., et al.: Lost in multilinguality: dissecting cross-lingual factual inconsistency in transformer language models. arXiv preprint arXiv:2504.04264 (2025)
¡error l=”308” c=”Invalid
command: paragraph not started.” /¿
23. Yang, Z., Qi, P., Zhang, S., et al.: Hotpotqa: a dataset for diverse, explainable multi-hop question answering. In: Conference on Empirical Methods in Natural Language Processing (EMNLP) (2018)
24. Trivedi, H., et al.: Musique: a multihop question answering dataset with realistic paragraphs. In: Conference on Empirical Methods in Natural Language Processing (EMNLP) (2022)
25. Wang, M., Stoll, A., Lange, L., Adel, H., Schütze, H., Strötgen, J.: Bring your own knowledge: a survey of methods for LLM knowledge expansion. arXiv preprint arXiv:2502.12598 (2025)
26. Feng, H., Gao, Y.: Ad placement optimization algorithm combined with machine learning in internet e-commerce (2025)
27. Fang, H., et al.: Hierarchical contextualized contrastive learning for multimodal retrieval. In: Annual Meeting of the Association for Computational Linguistics (ACL) (2022)
28. Feng, H., Dai, Y., Gao, Y.: Personalized risks and regulatory strategies of large language models in digital advertising. arXiv preprint arXiv:2505.04665 (2025)
29. Wu, S., Huang, X., Lu, D.: Psychological health knowledge-enhanced LLM-based social network crisis intervention text transfer recognition method. arXiv preprint arXiv:2504.07983 (2025)
30. Bi, J., et al.: Cot-kinetics: a theoretical modeling assessing LRM reasoning process (2025)

31. Lewis, P., et al.: Retrieval-augmented generation for knowledge-intensive NLP tasks. In: Advances in Neural Information Processing Systems (NeurIPS) (2020)
32. Wang, Y., et al.: Semantic-aware knowledge integration for multimodal NLP. In: Annual Meeting of the Association for Computational Linguistics (ACL) (2022)
33. Hoffmann, M., et al.: Training data compression for deep neural networks in NLP. arXiv preprint arXiv:2002.08217 (2020)
34. Zhou, X., et al.: Medical language processing with deep learning. ACM Trans. Intell. Syst. Technol. (2019)
35. Bodenreider, O.: The unified medical language system (UMLs): integrating biomedical terminology. Nucleic Acids Res. **32**(D1), D267–D270 (2004)
36. Shah, N.H., et al.: Translational bioinformatics: the science of turning biomedical data into knowledge for human health. Ann. Rev. Biomed. Data Sci. **1**, 1–24 (2018)
37. Sun, Y., et al.: Openke: an open toolkit for knowledge embedding. In: AAAI Conference on Artificial Intelligence (AAAI) (2021)
38. Reimers, N., Gurevych, I.: Sentence-BERT: sentence embeddings using siamese BERT-networks. In: Conference on Empirical Methods in Natural Language Processing (EMNLP) (2019)
39. Gao, T., Yao, X., Chen, D.: Simcse: simple contrastive learning of sentence embeddings. In: Annual Meeting of the Association for Computational Linguistics (ACL) (2021)
40. Guan, Y., et al.: Multimodal knowledge graph construction and application: a survey. arXiv preprint arXiv:2301.09896 (2023)
41. Jaderberg, M., et al.: Reading wikipedia to answer open-domain questions. In: Annual Meeting of the Association for Computational Linguistics (ACL) (2016)
42. Liu, Y., et al.: RoBERTa: a robustly optimized BERT pretraining approach. arXiv preprint arXiv:1907.11692 (2019)
43. Li, B., Weng, Y., Xia, F., Sun, B., Li, S.: VPAI_lab at MedVidQA 2022: a two-stage cross-modal fusion method for medical instructional video classification. In: Proceedings of the 21st Workshop on Biomedical Language Processing, pp. 212–219 (2022)
44. Wang, M., Adel, H., Lange, L., Strötgen, J., Schütze, H.: Rehearsal-free modular and compositional continual learning for language models. In: Proceedings of the 2024 Conference of the North American Chapter of the Association for Computational Linguistics: Human Language Technologies (Volume 2: Short Papers), pp. 469–480 (2024)
45. Zhou, Z., Liu, J., Cheng, S., Luo, H., Gu, Y., Ye, J.: Improving cross-modal visual answer localization in Chinese medical instructional video using language prompts. In: CCF International Conference on Natural Language Processing and Chinese Computing, pp. 221–232. Springer (2023). https://doi.org/10.1007/978-3-031-44699-3_20
46. Zhang, H., Zheng, C., He, Y., Zhao, Y., Lai, Y.: Improving multilingual temporal answering grounding in single video via LLM-based translation and OCR enhancement. In: CCF International Conference on Natural Language Processing and Chinese Computing, pp. 145–156. Springer (2024). https://doi.org/10.1007/978-981-97-9443-0_12

Overview of NLPCC 2025 Shared Task 5: Chinese Government Text Correction with Knowledge Bases

Yang Song, Yuxiang Jia, Yuchen Yan, Jiajia Cui, Lingling Mu, and Hongfei Xu

Zhengzhou University, Henan 450001, China
{ieyxjia,iellmu}@zzu.edu.cn, {yanyuchen,jjcui}@gs.zzu.edu.cn,
hfxunlp@foxmail.com

Abstract. In recent years, the field of Chinese text error correction has advanced rapidly, with machine learning-based correction algorithms significantly improving performance. However, existing research often overlooks the integration of Knowledge Bases (KBs) to guide error correction, despite their potential value in rectifying critical factual errors or dynamically adjusting correction results based on KB updates. In this paper, we develop specialized KBs and datasets for the automatic text error correction of Chinese government documents. The datasets are built upon authentic news corpora, real-world user inputs and their needs. Furthermore, we present KB-oriented metrics to evaluate text correction performance on knowledge-related terms. We test the baseline performances of several Large Language Models (LLMs), including Deepseek, Qwen, GLM, and Baichuan, for their exceptional language understanding and reasoning capabilities, and then report the performances and methods of five systems participating in the shared task.

Keywords: Chinese Text Error Correction · Knowledge Base · Large Language Model

1 Introduction

The core objective of the Chinese text error correction task is to identify and rectify errors in Chinese texts. In recent years, with the rapid advancement of Natural Language Processing (NLP), Chinese text error correction has made significant progress [2,8–13]. It is a helpful proofreading application and is also beneficial for the other applications [1,5,6,15].

However, it should be noted that while existing efforts on error correction have achieved remarkable success in detecting and correcting spelling and grammatical errors empowered by Pre-trained Language Models (PLMs) [3,4,14,16–19], they still exhibit notable deficiencies when handling factual errors involving domain-specific knowledge. Correcting such errors typically requires precise mastery and flexible application of specialized knowledge, however, current correction methods generally lack knowledge integration mechanisms. Incorporating

© The Author(s), under exclusive license to Springer Nature Singapore Pte Ltd. 2026
X.-L. Mao et al. (Eds.): NLPCC 2025, LNAI 16105, pp. 417–428, 2026.
https://doi.org/10.1007/978-981-95-3352-7_35

knowledge resources can help error correction systems correct text that contradicts objective facts. Particularly noteworthy is the dynamic update capability of Knowledge Bases (KBs), enabling continuous tracking of the latest facts and knowledge to ensure error correction results remain updated.

In this work, we construct specialized knowledge bases and datasets for Chinese government text error correction, based on authentic news corpora and real-world user inputs. The KBs developed in this study encompasses a rich variety of categories, including official information, policy/spirit names, standard expressions, fixed phrases, idioms and so on, as detailed in Fig. 2. We use match based methods to locate related KB terms in sentences, and construct training set, validation set and test set by extracting sentences with KB matches in news corpora and real user inputs with human corrections. To evaluate the performance of error correction systems regarding KB terms, we introduce four evaluation metrics for the correction with KBs: KB Accuracy (KB-Acc), KB precision (KB-P), KB Recall (KB-R), and KB F0.5 score (KB-F0.5). These metrics aim at precisely assessing the error correction capability of systems in handling KB related errors.

Given the exceptional capabilities of Large Language Models (LLMs) in semantic understanding and knowledge utilization, we select Deepseek, Qwen, GLM and Baichuan as baseline systems, and test their performances with an instruction template which integrates KB terms into the correction of the input sentences. We have organized NLPCC 2025 shared task 5 based on the resources. The shared task has attracted 10 teams from both the universities and industries, with five teams ultimately submitted system results. The results provided in Tables 4 and 6 show the challenge of the task.

2   Task Description

The Chinese Government Text Correction (CGTC) shared task aims to detect and correct spelling and grammatical errors in Chinese government texts with the help of knowledge bases. It is highly related to Chinese Spelling Error Correction (SEC) and Chinese Grammatical Error Correction (GEC) but has special characteristics with respect to the domain and the user needs. For example, in government text correction, misspelling of policy names or containing factual errors are usually considered more serious than grammatical errors.

For the input sentence to correct, we employ matching based methods (described in Sect. 3.1) to extract KB terms from the corresponding KBs. The correction model is expected to generate correct outputs based on both the input sentence and the extracted corresponding KB terms. Two main challenges of the task are that: 1) the KB terms extracted based on matching are not always helpful, and sometimes may be misleading, as shown in Fig. 1, and 2) the model has to decide whether to use the KB terms and how to leverage the KB terms for correction, while a large part of KB terms may be of low-frequency in the pre-training data and it is normally hard for models to take care of long-tail cases.

原始句子：我院以"筑牢中华民族共同体意识"工作为契机。
Original sentence: Our institute takes the work of building the consciousness of the Chinese nation community as an opportunity.
知识库条目(KB term)：铸牢中华民族共同体意识(forging the consciousness of the Chinese nation community)
纠错结果：我院以"铸牢中华民族共同体意识"工作为契机。✔
Corrected: Our institute takes the work of forging the consciousness of the Chinese nation community as an opportunity.
参考答案：我院以"铸牢中华民族共同体意识"工作为契机。
Reference: Our institute takes the work of forging the consciousness of the Chinese nation community as an opportunity.

原始句子：严格党的组织生活，抓好党员学习教育，不断提高党员素质。
Original sentence: Strictly enforce the Party's organizational life, focus on the study and education of Party members, and continuously improve the quality of Party members.
知识库条目(KB term)：党史学习教育(the study and education of Party history)
纠错结果：严格党的组织生活，抓好党史学习教育，不断提高党员素质。✘
Corrected: Strictly enforce the Party's organizational life, focus on the study and education of Party history, and continuously improve the quality of Party members.
参考答案：严格党的组织生活，抓好党员学习教育，不断提高党员素质。
Reference: Strictly enforce the Party's organizational life, focus on the study and education of Party members, and continuously improve the quality of Party members.

Fig. 1. Positive and negative examples for KB corrections.

3   Data Construction

To support the research on the task, 1) we construct knowledge bases of 10 governmental document relevant categories, 2) we build a synthetic dataset by extracting sentences which have at least one KB term matching from Chinese news corpora, and 3) we collect real user inputs, extract the sentences resulting in KB matches, and manually annotate correction results to build the development and test sets.

3.1   Knowledge Bases and Matching Methods

The constructed KBs encompass 10 categories: Event Information, Organization Information, Official Information, Geographic Information, Laws and Regulations, Policy/Spirit Names, Idioms, Fixed Phrases, Standard Expressions and Document Reference. The examples of each KB type are shown in Fig. 2, and the numbers of KB terms in each KB type are shown in Table 1.

We implement 4 matching based algorithms to extract KB terms for input sentences.

Event Information Matching Algorithm. The algorithm first finds all event names in the event information KB in the input sentence, and returns the found events and their corresponding times in the event information KB.

事件信息(Event Information)
(中国共产党第二十次全国代表大会, 会议时间, 2022年10月16日-2022年10月22日)
(The 20th National Congress of the Communist Party of China, Meeting
Time, 2022. 10. 16-2022. 10. 22)

机构信息(Organization Information)
(中华人民共和国发展和改革委员会, 发改委)
(National Development and Reform Commission of the People's Republic of China,
National Development and Reform Commission)

领导人信息(Official Information)
(马朝旭, 中华人民共和国外交部副部长、外交部党委委员)
(Ma Zhaoxu, Vice Minister of Foreign Affairs of the People's Republic of China、
Member of the Party Committee of the Ministry of Foreign Affairs)

地域信息(Geographic Information)
(石家庄市, 河北省)
(Shijiazhuang City, Hebei Province)

法律法规(Laws and Regulations)
中华人民共和国立法法
The Legislation Law of the People's Republic of China

政策精神名称(Policy/Spirit Names)
"两弹一星" 精神
The Spirit of "Two Bombs, One Satellite"

成语(Idioms)
全力以赴
Spare no effort

固定用语(Fixed Phrases)
不忘初心、牢记使命
Stay true to our original aspiration and
keep our mission firmly in mind.

规范表述(Standard Expressions)
党代会胜利召开
The Party Congress was
successfully convened

文件引用(Document Reference)
(最高人民检察院是最高检察机关，领导地方各级人民检察院和专门人民检察院的工作，
对全国人民代表大会和全国人民代表大会常务委员会负责并报告工作。)
(The Supreme People's Procuratorate is the highest procuratorial organ,
leading the work of the people's procuratorates at all local levels and the
specialized people's procuratorates. It is responsible to and reports work to
the National People's Congress and its Standing Committee.)

Fig. 2. Knowledge base examples.

Official Information Matching Algorithm. The algorithm finds all position titles
in the official information KB in the input sentence, and returns all found position titles and corresponding names in the official information KB.

Geographical Information Matching Algorithm. The algorithm finds the cities or
counties in the geographical KB in the input sentence. For found counties, the
algorithm tries to find the existence of any city or province name in the input
sentence, and returns the city-county or province-county pairs in the geographical KB of the counties if a city/province name was found in the input sentence.
For found cities, the algorithm searches all province names in the input sen-

Table 1. Statistics of knowledge bases.

KB types	Amount
Event Information	137
Organization Information	100
Official Information	4,054
Geographic Information	3,595
Laws and Regulations	1,178
Policy/Spirit Names	54
Idioms	9,341
Fixed Phrases	124
Standard Expressions	80
Document Reference	54,593

tence, and returns the province-city pairs in the geographical KB of the cities if a province name was found in the input sentence.

Matching based on Sequences' Similarity. For the KB elements inside the other KBs, we compute the sequences' similarity ratio using the python's difflib for the KB matching. We find the sub-span of the input sentence which leads to highest sequence similarity to the KB term, and returns the KB term if the similarity ratio is larger than a threshold.

Table 2. Amount of extracted sentences for training data synthesis for each KB type. A sentence may fall in more than one KB types at the same time.

KB type	Amount (number of sentences)
Event Information	15,279
Organization Information	3,005,692
Official Information	29,432
Geographic Information	835,391
Laws and Regulations	33,220
Policy Spirit Names	235,515
Idioms	2,536,394
Fixed Phrases	626,967
Standard Expressions	17,325
Document Reference	50,253

3.2   Training Set Synthesis

It is difficult to collect large-scale real text error correction datasets, especially when we require the input sentences for correction containing KB-related errors. However, the scale of the training set may be crucial for obtaining good performance with some machine learning approaches. So we provide a dataset for large-scale training set synthesis.

We first collect sentences from available online news. Specifically, we leverage the Chinese part of the newscrawl corpus [7], and crawl $522M$ deduplicated sentences from the government websites. We normalize the sentences with NFKC and convert traditional Chinese into simplified Chinese through OpenCC. Next, we use the KB matching algorithms (described in Sect. 3.1) to iterate the collected sentences. We keep the sentences with at least one KB match and augment the sentences with corresponding matched KB terms. As a result, we obtain around $644M$ sentences together with KB terms for data synthesis. The statistics over 10 KB types are as shown in the Table 2.

The extracted sentences can be categorized into two types: exact match or partial match. For exact match, the KB term directly appears in the sentence, and the data synthesis can be facilitated by introducing errors into the sentence through modifying the matched KB element, and train the model to correct the modified error sentence into the original sentence with the help of the extracted KB term. For partial match, we may assume the extracted sentences are normally correct, and train the model to re-generate the extracted sentence with both the sentence and matched KB terms as input. In this way, the model is trained to ignore surface matched but unrelated KB terms.

3.3   Validation and Test Data

To test the performance in real-world cases, we collect real user inputs for the construction of the validation and test sets. We only keep the sentences with matched KB terms, and manually annotate the correction results. The annotation team comprises native Chinese-speaking graduate students and Chinese linguistic experts working on Chinese government text correction. Each sentence is randomly assigned to 2 native Chinese-speaking graduate students and the linguistic experts decide the final correction result if the annotation results for a same sentence are different. The annotation agreement is 95.16%.

After sentence selection and annotation, we obtained 806 sentences, their corresponding matched KB terms and manually annotated correction results. The statistics w.r.t. KB types are as shown in Table 3. We randomly sampled 306 of them as the validation set and used the remained 500 instances for testing.

3.4   Evaluation Metrics

We evaluate with the traditional Precision (P), Recall (R) and F0.5 scores implemented by the ChERRANT toolkit. In addition, we also compute the Accuracy (Acc) and P/R/F0.5 scores only for the correction operations on KB terms to directly measure the correction performances regarding KBs.

Table 3. Statistics of annotated instances for validation and testing.

KB types	Amount
Event Information	11
Organization Information	198
Official Information	15
Geographic Information	43
Laws and Regulations	9
Policy/Spirit Names	72
Idioms	370
Fixed Phrases	115
Standard Expressions	104
Document Reference	56

知识库条目(KB term)：感激不尽(was endlessly grateful)

原始句子：赵某某对巡察组干部感激不已。
Original sentence: Zhao Jun was immensely grateful to the inspection team cadres.

大模型输入(模板)：
已知成语信息：感激不尽
请对句子中可能的错误进行纠正，只输出结果，不要输出其它内容：
赵军对巡察组干部感激不已。
LLM input(template):
Known idiom: was endlessly grateful
Please correct any possible errors in the sentence and only output the result without any additional content:
Zhao Jun was immensely grateful to the inspection team cadres.

大模型输出(纠错结果)：赵军对巡察组干部感激不尽。
LLM output(correction result): Zhao Jun was endlessly grateful to the inspection team cadres.

Fig. 3. An example for the LLM template.

4   LLM Baselines

We selected several representative LLMs as baselines for their exceptional language generation and comprehension capabilities, including DeepSeek, Qwen, GLM and Baichuan. We instruct the LLMs for text correction using the template in Fig. 3. Despite that we have prompted the LLMs to only generate the correction result, sometimes the model may still generate the other outputs, we extract the most similar sentence from the LLM outputs as the correction result.

We first tested the performance of LLMs of around 7B parameters, with and without KB terms in the prompt. Results in Table 4 show that: 1) the task is challenging for the tested LLMs, Qwen 3 8B with thinking enabled only achieves a highest KB F0.5 score of 12.38, and 2) providing KB terms generally leads to better performance than without KB terms.

Table 4. Results of LLMs without (w.o) or with (w) KB terms. The "-t" suffix indicates enabling thinking for Deepseek and Qwen.

LLM			ChERRANT				KB		
			P	R	F0.5	Acc	P	R	F0.5
w.o KB	Deepseek-R1	Qwen-7B-t	0.43	8.43	0.53	30.18	0.59	11.11	0.73
		Qwen-7B	0.55	9.64	0.67	31.49	0.64	11.11	0.79
	Qwen	2.5-7B	1.89	22.89	2.32	39.72	3.02	38.89	3.70
		3-8B-t	1.01	10.84	1.23	57.90	3.05	16.67	3.64
		3-8B	100.00	1.20	**5.75**	89.22	0.00	0.00	0.00
	GLM	4-9B	1.47	14.46	1.79	44.61	2.22	22.22	2.71
		4-9B-Z1	0.73	19.28	0.91	24.05	0.85	22.22	1.05
	Baichuan		2.23	14.46	2.68	66.24	7.09	27.78	**8.33**
w KB	Deepseek-R1	Qwen-7B-t	1.34	21.69	1.65	32.37	1.76	27.78	2.16
		Qwen-7B	1.53	24.10	1.88	33.02	2.69	41.67	3.31
	Qwen	2.5-7B	4.35	39.76	5.29	38.01	6.07	69.44	7.42
		3-8B-t	4.39	30.12	5.30	60.62	10.36	55.56	**12.38**
		3-8B	100.00	1.20	**5.75**	89.22	0.00	0.00	0.00
	GLM	4-9B	3.59	28.92	4.35	44.12	5.70	55.56	6.94
		4-9B-Z1	1.77	30.12	2.18	25.40	2.30	44.44	2.84
	Baichuan		3.68	16.87	4.37	59.91	6.82	33.33	8.11

We also tested the effects of LLM model sizes on performance with Deepseek and Qwen 2.5. Results in Table 5 show that larger models generally bring about higher F0.5 scores.

5 System Submissions

10 teams registered for the shared task, and 5 teams ultimately submitted the results.

CGT-Corrector. They adopt a computationally efficient approach by fine-tuning the Qwen2.5-14B-Instruct model on $20k$ representative samples carefully selected through multi-dimensional evaluation considering textual features, knowledge relevance and category distribution. By systematically introducing controlled noise patterns, they constructed an optimized training set.

KARTC. They propose a knowledge-aware error correction framework consisting of three modules. The Error Detection Module analyzes input texts to separately identify semantic errors and knowledge errors. The Candidate Sentence Generation Module, guided by error detection, generates multi-source candidate sentences in separate channels. The Over-Correction Mitigation Rewriting

Table 5. Results of LLMs with varying sizes.

LLM		ChERRANT			KB			
		P	R	F0.5	Acc	P	R	F0.5
Deepseek-R1	Qwen-1.5B-t	0.40	6.02	0.49	35.40	0.40	5.56	0.49
	Qwen-1.5B	0.61	9.64	0.75	35.57	0.78	11.11	0.96
	Qwen-7B-t	1.34	21.69	1.65	32.37	1.76	27.78	2.16
	Qwen-7B	1.53	24.10	1.88	33.02	2.69	41.67	3.31
Qwen	2.5-0.5B	1.34	15.66	1.64	46.15	2.71	25.00	3.30
	2.5-1.5B	3.36	30.12	4.09	41.78	5.79	61.11	7.07
	2.5-7B	4.35	39.76	**5.29**	38.01	6.07	69.44	**7.42**

Table 6. Results of submitted systems.

System		ChERRANT			KB			
		P	R	F0.5	Acc	P	R	F0.5
CGT-Corrector		47.76	22.38	**38.93**	84.20	46.94	41.82	**45.82**
KARTC		38.26	30.77	36.48	79.64	34.57	50.91	36.94
QEFDA	result1	13.08	11.89	12.82	77.72	17.02	14.55	16.46
	result2	17.19	15.38	16.79	74.14	15.28	20.00	16.03
	result3	8.29	12.59	8.90	65.93	6.90	14.55	7.71
CoT-LoRA		4.77	38.46	5.78	33.02	4.08	47.27	4.99
Sky		0.33	3.50	0.40	59.68	2.55	7.27	2.93

Module employs a knowledge-aware fusion rewriting mechanism based on the candidate set and original sentence, aiming at enhancing correction robustness and semantic retention while mitigating over-correction.

QEFDA. They employ Parameter-Efficient Fine-tuning (PEFT) with QLoRA to fine-tune Qwen-2.5-7B-Instruct on Lang8, HSK and the task-specific dataset which is formatted into error-correction pairs (incorrect-correct sentence pairs). To further improve generalization, they augment the task dataset through techniques including synonym replacement and random deletion.

CoT-LoRA. They extract data from the training set and reformat them into prompt-completion pairs for the LoRA fine-tuning of Qwen2.5-7B-Instruct and Yi1.5-7B-Instruct. To enhance the performance, they implement a voting mechanism to ensemble predictions from multiple fine-tuned models and select the optimal output through majority voting.

Results in Table 6 show that: 1) despite fine-tuning a larger model (Qwen2.5 14B Instruct), the data selection mechanism considering textual features, knowledge relevance and category distribution employed by CGT-Corrector seems very effective, and they obtains the highest F0.5 scores and largest improvements over our baselines, 2) the collaborative framework proposed by KARTC also leads to large performance gains over our baselines, their method also obtains the highest recall, probably due to the use of an separate error detection module, and 3) QEFDA also achieves higher performance than our baselines, showing that fine-tuning simply on error-correction pairs and employing simple data augmentation strategies are beneficial for the task compared to instruct LLMs without fine-tuning.

6   Conclusion

In NLPCC 2025 shared task 5, we investigate the use of knowledge bases for Chinese government text correction. Specifically, we construct a number of KBs and corresponding methods to match potential KB terms in sentences. We extract a large dataset for training set synthesis, with each instance inside the dataset has resulted in at least one KB match. We also collect and annotate the development and test sets for the task based on real user inputs. For evaluation, we develop KB oriented metrics to evaluate the performance of text correction regarding KB terms. We report the performance of instructing several mainstream LLMs, with thinking enabled or disabled, and with various model sizes. The shared task has attracted registrations from 10 teams, with 5 teams ultimately submitted the final results. We report their methods and the performances of submitted systems. Data selection strategy and collaborative modeling have been proven effective in the shared task.

Acknowledgments. We appreciate our reviewer for the insightful comments and suggestions. This work is partially supported by the National Natural Science Foundation of China (Grant No. 62306284), China Postdoctoral Science Foundation (Grant No. 2023M743189), and the Natural Science Foundation of Henan Province (Grant No. 232300421386).

References

1. Afli, H., Qiu, Z., Way, A., Sheridan, P.: Using SMT for OCR error correction of historical texts. In: Calzolari, N., et al. (eds.) Proceedings of the Tenth International Conference on Language Resources and Evaluation (LREC 2016), pp. 962–966. European Language Resources Association (ELRA), Portorož, Slovenia (2016). https://aclanthology.org/L16-1153/
2. Cao, H., Yuan, L., Zhang, Y., Ng, H.T.: Unsupervised grammatical error correction rivaling supervised methods. In: Bouamor, H., Pino, J., Bali, K. (eds.) Proceedings of the 2023 Conference on Empirical Methods in Natural Language Processing, pp. 3072–3088. Association for Computational Linguistics, Singapore (2023). https://doi.org/10.18653/v1/2023.emnlp-main.185
3. Chang, H., et al.: Overview of CCL23-eval task: Chinese learner text correction. In: Sun, M., Qin, B., Qiu, X., Jiang, J., Han, X. (eds.) Proceedings of the 22nd Chinese National Conference on Computational Linguistics (Volume 3: Evaluations), pp. 239–249. Chinese Information Processing Society of China, Harbin, China (2023). https://aclanthology.org/2023.ccl-3.27/

4. Gan, Z., Xu, H., Zan, H.: Self-supervised curriculum learning for spelling error correction. In: Moens, M.F., Huang, X., Specia, L., Yih, S.W.T. (eds.) Proceedings of the 2021 Conference on Empirical Methods in Natural Language Processing, pp. 3487–3494. Association for Computational Linguistics, Online and Punta Cana, Dominican Republic (2021). https://doi.org/10.18653/v1/2021.emnlp-main.281

5. Gao, J., Li, X., Micol, D., Quirk, C., Sun, X.: A large scale ranker-based system for search query spelling correction. In: Huang, C.R., Jurafsky, D. (eds.) Proceedings of the 23rd International Conference on Computational Linguistics (Coling 2010), pp. 358–366. Coling 2010 Organizing Committee, Beijing, China (2010). https://aclanthology.org/C10-1041/

6. Gupta, H., Del Corro, L., Broscheit, S., Hoffart, J., Brenner, E.: Unsupervised multi-view post-OCR error correction with language models. In: Moens, M.F., Huang, X., Specia, L., Yih, S.W.T. (eds.) Proceedings of the 2021 Conference on Empirical Methods in Natural Language Processing, pp. 8647–8652. Association for Computational Linguistics, Online and Punta Cana, Dominican Republic (2021). https://doi.org/10.18653/v1/2021.emnlp-main.680

7. Kocmi, T., et al.: Findings of the WMT24 general machine translation shared task: the LLM era is here but MT is not solved yet. In: Haddow, B., Kocmi, T., Koehn, P., Monz, C. (eds.) Proceedings of the Ninth Conference on Machine Translation, pp. 1–46. Association for Computational Linguistics, Miami, Florida, USA (2024). https://doi.org/10.18653/v1/2024.wmt-1.1

8. Li, W., Luo, W., Peng, G., Wang, H.: Explanation based in-context demonstrations retrieval for multilingual grammatical error correction. In: Chiruzzo, L., Ritter, A., Wang, L. (eds.) Proceedings of the 2025 Conference of the Nations of the Americas Chapter of the Association for Computational Linguistics: Human Language Technologies (Volume 1: Long Papers), pp. 4881–4897. Association for Computational Linguistics, Albuquerque, New Mexico (2025). https://aclanthology.org/2025.naacl-long.251/

9. Li, W., Wang, H.: Detection-correction structure via general language model for grammatical error correction. In: Ku, L.W., Martins, A., Srikumar, V. (eds.) Proceedings of the 62nd Annual Meeting of the Association for Computational Linguistics (Volume 1: Long Papers), pp. 1748–1763. Association for Computational Linguistics, Bangkok, Thailand (2024). https://doi.org/10.18653/v1/2024.acl-long.96

10. Liu, Y., Li, Z., Jiang, H., Zhang, B., Li, C., Zhang, J.: Towards better utilization of multi-reference training data for Chinese grammatical error correction. In: Ku, L.W., Martins, A., Srikumar, V. (eds.) Findings of the Association for Computational Linguistics: ACL 2024, pp. 3044–3052. Association for Computational Linguistics, Bangkok, Thailand (2024). https://doi.org/10.18653/v1/2024.findings-acl.180

11. Sun, C., She, L., Lu, X.: Two issues with Chinese spelling correction and a refinement solution. In: Ku, L.W., Martins, A., Srikumar, V. (eds.) Proceedings of the 62nd Annual Meeting of the Association for Computational Linguistics (Volume 2: Short Papers), pp. 196–204. Association for Computational Linguistics, Bangkok, Thailand (2024). https://doi.org/10.18653/v1/2024.acl-short.19

12. Wang, X., et al.: VisCGEC: Benchmarking the visual Chinese grammatical error correction. In: Chiruzzo, L., Ritter, A., Wang, L. (eds.) Proceedings of the 2025 Conference of the Nations of the Americas Chapter of the Association for Computational Linguistics: Human Language Technologies (Volume 1: Long Papers), pp. 5054–5068. Association for Computational Linguistics, Albuquerque, New Mexico (2025). https://aclanthology.org/2025.naacl-long.261/

13. Wang, X., Mu, L., Zhang, J., Xu, H.: Multi-pass decoding for grammatical error correction. In: Al-Onaizan, Y., Bansal, M., Chen, Y.N. (eds.) Proceedings of the 2024 Conference on Empirical Methods in Natural Language Processing, pp. 9904–9916. Association for Computational Linguistics, Miami, Florida, USA (2024). https://doi.org/10.18653/v1/2024.emnlp-main.553
14. Xu, L., Wu, J., Peng, J., Fu, J., Cai, M.: FCGEC: fine-grained corpus for Chinese grammatical error correction. In: Goldberg, Y., Kozareva, Z., Zhang, Y. (eds.) Findings of the Association for Computational Linguistics: EMNLP 2022, pp. 1900–1918. Association for Computational Linguistics, Abu Dhabi, United Arab Emirates (2022). https://doi.org/10.18653/v1/2022.findings-emnlp.137
15. Yang, Y., Wu, H., Zhao, H.: Attack named entity recognition by entity boundary interference. In: Calzolari, N., Kan, M.Y., Hoste, V., Lenci, A., Sakti, S., Xue, N. (eds.) Proceedings of the 2024 Joint International Conference on Computational Linguistics, Language Resources and Evaluation (LREC-COLING 2024), pp. 1734–1744. ELRA and ICCL, Torino, Italia (2024). https://aclanthology.org/2024.lrec-main.153/
16. Yin, X., Wan, X., Zhang, D., Yu, L., Yu, L.: Overview of the NLPCC 2023 shared task: Chinese spelling check. In: Natural Language Processing and Chinese Computing (2023). https://doi.org/10.1007/978-3-031-44699-3_30
17. Zhang, Y., et al.: MuCGEC: a multi-reference multi-source evaluation dataset for Chinese grammatical error correction. In: Carpuat, M., de Marneffe, M.C., Meza Ruiz, I.V. (eds.) Proceedings of the 2022 Conference of the North American Chapter of the Association for Computational Linguistics: Human Language Technologies, pp. 3118–3130. Association for Computational Linguistics, Seattle, United States (2022). https://doi.org/10.18653/v1/2022.naacl-main.227
18. Zhang, Y., et al.: Nasgec: a multi-domain Chinese grammatical error correction dataset from native speaker texts. arXiv:2305.16023 (2023)
19. Zhao, Y., Jiang, N., Sun, W., Wan, X.: Overview of the NLPCC 2018 shared task: grammatical error correction. In: Zhang, M., Ng, V., Zhao, D., Li, S., Zan, H. (eds.) NLPCC 2018. LNCS (LNAI), vol. 11109, pp. 439–445. Springer, Cham (2018). https://doi.org/10.1007/978-3-319-99501-4_41

CGT-Corrector: Chinese Government Text Correction with Knowledge Bases

Sheng Chen, Fangkun Zhao, Zimeng Bai, Lujie Niu, Caixia Yuan,
and Xiaojie Wang$^{(\boxtimes)}$

Center of Intelligence Science and Technology, Beijing University of Posts and
Telecommunications, Beijing, China
`{chen0626,1529343535,zimengbai,lujien,yuancx,xjwang}@bupt.edu.cn`

Abstract. Chinese text correction plays a crucial role in the field of
natural language processing. However, its development is hampered by
several challenges, including the complexity of error types, the high cost
of data collection, and the difficulty of accurately correcting key factual
errors in domain-specific texts. This paper focuses on the research of Chinese government text correction based on knowledge bases (KB). Given
that general large language models (LLMs) have achieved good semantic understanding capabilities after pre-training, we propose the CGT-
Corrector: Chinese Government Text Correction with Knowledge Bases.
CGT-Corrector encompasses three key stages. Firstly, a data processing
framework that integrates M&T labeling and diversity sampling is constructed. This framework effectively addresses the issue of imbalanced
data distribution and significantly reduces the training cost. Secondly, a
diverse noise generation and instruction optimization strategy based on
large language models is designed, which greatly enhances the model's
generalization ability to handle complex errors. Finally, we have successfully achieved efficient training for Chinese government text correction
based on knowledge bases. Our approach has achieved 1st place at the
NLPCC-2025 Shared Task 5.

Keywords: Chinese Government Text Correction · Large Language
Models · M&T Labeling · Diversity Sampling

1 Introduction

Chinese, as a major natural language, is a key information dissemination medium
vital to daily life and professional scenarios. However, due to its linguistic complexity, diverse input methods, and user errors, practical text often contains
mistakes—undermining communication accuracy and even causing misunderstandings or serious issues. Amid exponential information growth, manual proofreading has become increasingly inefficient, highlighting the urgent need for automated text correction technologies.

© The Author(s), under exclusive license to Springer Nature Singapore Pte Ltd. 2026
X.-L. Mao et al. (Eds.): NLPCC 2025, LNAI 16105, pp. 429–441, 2026.
https://doi.org/10.1007/978-981-95-3352-7_36

Fig. 1. The examples of Chinese government text correction.

In recent years, machine learning-based methods [3, 5, 9, 11, 15] have advanced Chinese text correction, but new challenges arise with evolving text diversity and model technology. Firstly, Chinese text errors are highly diverse. Early approaches requires over 100K labeled instances [6, 10, 14], facing issues like labor-intensive data collection, high computational costs, and imbalanced distributions. Moreover, current methods focus on general-domain spelling and grammatical correction but overlook key factual errors in specialized texts. Domain-specific linguistic patterns (e.g., medical literature's dense terminology like "冠状动脉粥样硬化性心脏病" and "炉甘石") hinder model transfer, as their precision and specificity make context-only correction ineffective.

This paper focuses on text correction in domain of Chinese government texts. Figure 1 shows the examples of Chinese government text correction. As illustrated in Fig. 1(a), without a referable domain knowledge base, models are unable to detect errors in texts due to a lack of understanding of critical knowledge. Figure 1(b) demonstrates that for general-purpose models, after incorporating a referable domain knowledge base, they are capable of correcting relatively simple key factual errors. However, complex errors may not necessarily be resolved effectively.

To address the aforementioned issues, we propose the **CGT-Corrector**: Chinese **G**overnment **T**ext Correction with Knowledge Bases, which leverages general large language models (LLMs) and fully exploits their powerful language comprehension and knowledge reasoning capabilities acquired through pre-training. Our goal is to achieve efficient Chinese government text correction with lower computational resource consumption. In the face of challenges posed by imbalanced data distribution and the complexity of real-world scenarios, we innovatively propose a data balancing strategy. To prevent learning bias, we perform M&T labeling on the matching degrees between retrieved knowledge types and texts, as well as apply balanced sampling within each label group. Additionally, we introduce a diversity sampling mechanism based on text similarity quantification, which enhances the diversity of training data and ensures the model's ability to capture various error patterns. In terms of data generation, we utilize LLMs to simulate diverse noise, expanding the boundaries of text error types. We adopt an optimized instruction generation strategy that integrates manual and LLM-generated prompts, preserving task adaptability while aligning with LLM pre-training language style to enhance data controllability and correction performance. Our main contributions are summarized as follows:

1. We propose a data sampling framework that integrates M&T labeling and diversity sampling, effectively resolving the issue of imbalanced data distribution and reducing model training costs.
2. We design a data augmentation that contains diverse noise generation and instruction optimization strategy based on LLMs, significantly enhancing the model's generalization ability for complex error types.
3. We validate the effectiveness of our method in the domain of Chinese government texts and provide a novel solution for knowledge-sensitive text correction in specific domains.

2 Method

The overall framework of our proposed method is illustrated in Fig. 2. To obtain balanced and diverse training data, we design our approach from four dimensions including **Explicit M&T labeling** in Sect. 2.2, **Implicit Semantic Sampling** in Sect. 2.2, **Diverse Noise Simulation** in Sect. 2.3, **Diverse Instruction Construction** in Sect. 2.3. After acquiring these data, we perform supervised fine-tuning on LLMs to enhance performance.

2.1 Task Definition

Chinese government text correction based on knowledge bases aims to leverage the retrieved knowledge to improve the ability to correct key factual errors in Chinese texts. For each given text $text_{input}$ to be corrected, a referable key entity knowledge set $K = \{Type_1 : [Entity_1^1, ...], Type_2 : [Entity_2^1, Entity_2^2, ...], ...\}$ containing multiple types of knowledge will be provided. Before generating the corrected text $text_{output}$, it is necessary to determine whether to refer to the provided entity knowledge set to modify the entities that may contain errors in the text.

2.2 Data Sampling

The diversity of training data optimizes text error-correction model training by enhancing efficiency and final performance. It acts as a natural regularizer,

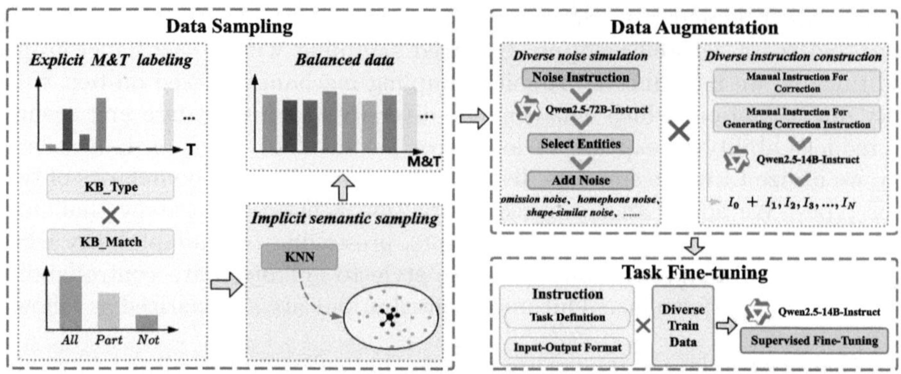

Fig. 2. The overall framework of our method. To ensure the diversity of training data, we first perform M&T labeling based on retrieved knowledge type and whether the knowledge matches the text. Then, within each label group, we adopt semantic-based diversity sampling. Next, we use large-scale LLMs to naturally simulate the diversity of text errors. Meanwhile, we prompt the LLMs performing the error-correction task to generate suitable instructions for executing the task by themselves. Finally, we obtain a dataset suitable for training to fine-tune smaller LLMs.

reducing overfitting and enabling faster convergence by exposing the model to varied errors, domains, and linguistic styles. For each instance x_i in dataset D, it contains original correct text $text_i$ and knowledge set k_i, we respectively perform **Explicit M&T labeling** and **Implicit Semantic Sampling** to obtain a balanced and diverse dataset D'.

Explicit M&T Labeling. Considering the text error correction task based on knowledge bases, we have designed two different dimensions for the provided knowledge: match($\mathcal{M}$) and type($\mathcal{T}$).

Definition 1. *Based on whether the provided knowledge matches the text to be corrected, match(x_i) has three possible values, including all match, partial match, and not match at all, which is shown in Eq. 1.*

$$match(x_i) = m_p, m_p \in \mathcal{M} = \{m_1, m_2, m_3\}$$
$$m_1 = all, m_2 = partial, m_3 = not \tag{1}$$

Definition 2. *For the type of provided knowledge, the label type(x_i) can be a single knowledge type {"成语信息"} or a combination of multiple knowledge types {"机构信息", "固定搭配"}, as shown in Eq. 2.*

$$type(x_i) = t_q \in \mathcal{T} = \{t_1, ..., t_{|\mathcal{T}|}\}$$
$$t_1 = \{Type_1\}, t_2 = \{Type_2\}, ..., t_{|\mathcal{T}|} = \{Type_1, Type_2, ..., Type_{|Type|}\} \tag{2}$$

By orthogonally crossing these two dimensions, we have obtained training data with $|\mathcal{M}| \times |\mathcal{T}|$ real-world retrieval scenarios. The data $\mathcal{D}_{m_p,t_q}$ in retrieval scenario m_p and t_q ($p \in [1, |\mathcal{M}|], q \in [1, |\mathcal{T}|]$) is shown as follows:

$$\mathcal{D}_{m_p,t_q} = \{x_i \mid match(x_i) = m_p \quad \& \quad type(x_i) = t_q\} \tag{3}$$

Implicit Semantic Sampling. To balance the sample distribution and enhance the diversity of the training data, we sample fixed number of instances from each $\mathcal{D}_{m_p,t_q}$. We have improved the conventional random sampling method by quantifying the diversity of samples to select training samples $\mathcal{D}'_{m_p,t_q}$ with stronger semantic diversity, thereby obtaining a dataset D' with balanced KB types and diverse text semantics.

Diversity Quantification. Traditional random sampling assigns the same diversity weight to each sample. To properly quantify diversity weights, we follow the idea of "MAYBE ONLY 0.5% DATA IS NEEDED" [1] and experimented with the K-means approach. Specifically:

(1) Obtain embeddings for all texts to be corrected.
(2) Cluster all the embeddings, where the number of clusters corresponds to the number of instances to be sampled.
(3) Quantify the diversity of instance x_i as d_i based on the number of instances within its respective cluster. Specifically, we define diversity inversely proportional to the concentration of instances in a given area since the larger the number of instances in a cluster, the lower the diversity. This relationship is the following transformation:

$$d_i = 1 - \frac{d_i - \min(d)}{\max(d) - \min(d)} \tag{4}$$

However, this method may encounter situations where the similarity between some instance pairs from different clusters exceeds that of pairs within the same cluster, which contradicts our diversity objectives. To address this issue, we propose an alternative approach using K-Nearest Neighbors (KNN) [4] to quantify diversity d' more properly. As shown in Eq. 5, we calculate the average similarity of a sample to its top-N nearest neighbors and use this as the similarity weight s_i.

$$s_i = \frac{1}{N} \sum_{j \in \mathcal{N}} Similarity(text_i, text_j) \tag{5}$$

$$d'_i = 1 - \frac{s_i - \min(s)}{\max(s) - \min(s)} \tag{6}$$

Diversity-Based Sampling. For diversity-based sampling, we partition the interval $[0, 1)$ into 100 equally-spaced sub-intervals, $[0, 0.01)$, $[0.01, 0.02)$, ..., $[0.99, 1)$, where $sample_{0-0.01}$ denote the number of sampled instances in the interval $[0, 0.01)$. To ensure that samples with higher diversity are more likely to be selected, we enforce the following conditions:

$$sample_{0.99-1} > sample_{0.98-0.99} > \cdots > sample_{0-0.01}$$
$$sample_{0.99-1} + sample_{0.98-0.99} + \cdots + sample_{0-0.01} = |\mathcal{D}'_{m_p,t_q}| \tag{7}$$

where the sampling rate changes linearly across intervals.

2.3   Data Augmentation

To obtain diverse error types and natural task instructions, we first use relatively large LLMs to simulate the error types that may occur in text error correction tasks with knowledge base. Then, we generate appropriate instructions for executing the task based on smaller LLMs that will be used for testing in the future. Finally, these instructions are orthogonally combined with the diverse original data in Sect. 2.2 for final training. The relevant prompts used in this section can be found in the Appendix A.

Diverse Noise Simulation. To reduce usage costs, we use large-scale LLMs to simulate noise, and efficiently transfer their language understanding and error-correction capabilities to small models through knowledge distillation. This enables small models to acquire powerful error-correction logic with limited parameters and achieve lightweight deployment. When simulating noise, we adopt a preset-error-type-free instruction (I_{noise}) and high inference temperature. This allows us to leverage large models to mine real and diverse error text $text'_i$ based correct text $text_i$ and retrieved knowledge k_i for each instance x_i in D', avoiding the limitations of manual annotation.

$$text'_i = LLM(I_{noise}, text_i, k_i) \tag{8}$$

Diverse Instruction Construction. A single manually designed instruction is difficult to exhaust all possible expressive forms of problem descriptions, while models can expand the diversity of instructions through their own generative capabilities. At the same time, when generating instructions, models will automatically integrate the semantic associations learned during pre-training. The process of "externalizing internal knowledge" with I_{ins} makes the instructions generated by the model closer to its own semantic understanding boundaries and expression habits. We also consider that explicit guidance of human intentions is crucial in this task, so we balance controllability and diversity by mixing manually designed instructions I_{manual} with model-generated instructions $I_{generated}$.

$$\mathcal{I}_{generated} = \{LLM(I_{ins}, task)\} \tag{9}$$

2.4 Training Loss

We conduct supervised training loss on LLMs.

$$\mathcal{L} = -\frac{1}{|D'|} \sum_{i=1}^{|D'|} \sum_{l=1}^{L-1} \log P(text_{i,l+1} \mid I_i; text'_i; k_i; text_{i,1:l}) \tag{10}$$

The instruction I_i is sampled from the sets $\mathcal{I}_{\mathrm{manual}} \cup \mathcal{I}_{\mathrm{generated}}$ for each x_i. We denote the corresponding original corrected text as $text_i$. By sampling and augmenting by Sect. 2.2 and 2.3, we set the text as $text'_i$ and the retrieved knowledge as k_i. $|D'|$ represents the number of all sampled data and L represents the sequence length (Table 2).

3 Experiment Setup

3.1 Dataset and Metric

Table 1. The statistical information for each dataset.

Dataset	Wrong	Right	KB	all_match	partial_match	not_match
Train	-	6448361	6448361	5734601	154091	559669
Dev	306	306	306	113	14	179
Test	500	-	500	188	15	297

Table 2. The original distribution of knowledge types in three datasets.

Dataset	规范表述	机构信息	政策精神名称	成语信息	领导信息	地域信息	法律法规	事件信息	固定用语	引用
Train	70	115	54	9316	1623	11300	854	95	122	17600
Dev	30	26	12	123	1	16	2	1	19	7
Test	32	26	14	171	0	30	5	1	29	10

Dataset. We conduct experiments using the dataset provided by NLPCC2025 Shared Task 5: Chinese Government Text Correction with Knowledge Bases, which is divided into train, dev, and test sets. The statistical details are shown in Table 1.

Metric. In this task, we employ two evaluation methods to assess the model. On one hand, we continue using the Cherrant method proposed for grammatical error correction in the MUCGEC work [13], which involves evaluating the Precision (Prec), Recall (Rec), and $F_{0.5}$ between the output sentence and gold edits. On the other hand, we adopt the evaluation method provided by NLPCC2025 Shared Task 5, including the correction accuracy and miscorrection probability with respect to the KB elements.

3.2   Baselines

We select different LLM backbones and prompt methods as our baselines. The chosen models include closed-source LLMs GPT-4o [7], GPT-4.1[1], open-source LLMs DeepSeek-v3 [8], and open-source smaller LLMs Qwen2.5-14B-Instruct [12]. There are three prompt methods: (1) zero-shot: directly prompting the LLMs to generate the final answer; (2) naive few-shot: randomly selecting examples from the training set for few-shot prompting; (3) dynamic few-shot: selecting similar examples from the training set as prompts based on sentence similarity.

3.3   Implementation Details

We use BGE-M3 [2] as the retriever for calculating similarity between texts and select LLMs backbones of different scales to verify the effectiveness of our method, including Qwen2.5-14B-Instruct, Qwen2.5-7B-Instruct, Qwen2.5-3B-Instruct, and smaller Qwen2.5-1.5B-Instruct. We sample instances by KNN diversity sampling. When fine-tuning LLMs, we set the learning rate to 1e-6 and the batch size to 64. The training is conducted on four A800 GPUs with DeepSpeed within 3 h.

4   Result and Analysis

4.1   Overall Performance

Table 3 shows our evaluation results on different models. In the baseline models, both precision and recall show an upward trend with increasing model scale. However, precision is generally lower than recall. For example, Deepseek-V3 has a precision of 21.21 and a recall of 87.50 on KB-Related metrics. This indicates that existing LLMs cannot properly decide whether to use the retrieved knowledge, leading to excessive reliance on such knowledge for correction. Our fine-tuned LLMs significantly improve precision while slightly reducing recall. As a result, on the dev set, the KB-Related $F_{0.5}$ score of our 7B model reaches 31.86, exceeding that of large-scale LLMs such as Deepseek-V3, which is 25.00. On the test set, the KB-Related $F_{0.5}$ score of our 14B model reaches 45.82, achieving leading performance in NLPCC-2025 Shared Task 5.

---

[1] https://openai.com/index/gpt-4-1/.

Table 3. The main result of our experiments. Due to the poor instruction-following capabilities of the 1.5B and 3B models, their results are not included.

Methods		Cherrant			KB-Related			
		Prec(%)	Rec(%)	$F_{0.5}$(%)	Acc(%)	Prec(%)	Rec(%)	$F_{0.5}$(%)
Dev								
Baselines	7B	17.22	37.14	19.29	63.04	16.82	75.00	19.91
	14B	16.51	51.43	19.11	50.00	13.82	87.50	16.61
	14B + naive few-shot	16.85	44.29	19.23	51.12	14.57	91.67	17.52
	14B + dynamic few-shot	17.49	45.71	19.95	55.97	15.83	79.17	18.85
	GPT-4o-2025-05-13	19.21	41.43	21.51	61.54	17.43	79.17	20.65
	GPT-4.1-2025-04-14	22.93	51.43	25.79	54.92	17.42	95.83	20.83
	Deepseek-V3	25.22	41.43	27.36	64.94	21.21	87.50	25.00
Ours	1.5B-SFT	37.84	20.00	32.11	81.90	23.33	29.17	24.31
	3B-SFT	37.50	30.00	35.71	78.54	21.74	41.67	24.04
	7B-SFT	45.28	34.29	**42.55**	81.30	28.89	54.17	**31.86**
	14B-SFT	45.10	32.86	41.97	82.02	27.03	41.67	29.07
Test								
Ours	3B-SFT	40.33	18.88	32.85	82.61	41.18	38.18	40.54
	7B-SFT	38.03	18.88	31.62	81.74	38.00	34.55	37.55
	14B-SFT	47.76	22.38	**38.95**	84.20	46.94	41.82	**45.82**

4.2   Ablation Study

To validate the effectiveness of our approach, we conduct ablation studies on sampling strategy, noise simulation and instruction diversity components.

Table 4. The ablation results of sampling strategy in our methods. Experiments are conducted on dev dataset with Qwen2.5-14B-Instruct. For each sampling method, we sample a total of 20k instances for training.

Methods	Cherrant			KB-Related			
	Prec(%)	Rec(%)	$F_{0.5}$(%)	Acc(%)	Prec(%)	Rec(%)	$F_{0.5}$(%)
− Explicit type + Random Sample	20.00	31.43	21.57	74.51	19.40	54.17	22.26
+ Explicit type + Random Sample	44.44	28.57	40.00	78.72	21.74	41.67	24.04
+ Explicit type + Kmeans Sample	42.78	31.27	39.85	80.30	24.60	39.86	26.37
+ Explicit type + KNN Sample	45.10	32.86	41.97	82.02	27.03	41.67	29.07

Sampling Strategy. The result is presented in Table 4. Owing to the highly imbalanced distribution of samples, direct sampling from the entire dataset yields 22.26 KB-Related $F_{0.5}$. After performing simple label crossing, random sampling of data from each crossed label achieves an improvement of 1.78 compared to overall sampling, which intuitively demonstrates the significance of enhancing data diversity for final performance. Given that semantic information is orthogonal to KB types, methods based on semantic clustering and semantic similarity have brought improvements of 2.33 and 5.03, respectively. This also indicates that our KNN method outperforms K-means in measuring diversity, leading to a 2.7 improvement.

Table 5. The ablation results of noise simulation in our methods. Experiments are conducted on dev and test dataset with Qwen2.5-14B-Instruct.

Methods	Cherrant				KB-Related		
	Prec(%)	Rec(%)	$F_{0.5}$(%)	Acc(%)	Prec(%)	Rec(%)	$F_{0.5}$(%)
Dev							
Original	45.10	32.86	41.97	82.02	27.03	41.67	29.07
Balanced (0.5:0.5:1)	57.89	31.43	49.55	83.86	31.25	41.67	32.89
Diverse (1:1:1)	55.56	35.71	50.00	81.94	25.71	37.50	27.44
Test							
Original	47.76	22.38	38.95	84.20	46.94	41.82	45.82
Balanced (0.5:0.5:1)	50.00	19.58	38.15	84.81	50.00	36.36	46.51
Diverse (1:1:1)	55.93	23.08	43.54	85.36	52.38	40.00	49.33

Table 6. The ablation results of instruction diversity in our methods. Experiments are conducted on dev dataset with Qwen2.5-14B-Instruct.

Methods	Cherrant			KB-Related			
	Prec(%)	Rec(%)	$F_{0.5}$(%)	Acc(%)	Prec(%)	Rec(%)	$F_{0.5}$(%)
Manual	53.85	40.00	50.36	78.75	23.53	50.00	26.32
Generated	44.90	31.43	41.35	76.76	18.00	37.50	20.09
Manual+Generated	45.10	32.86	41.97	82.02	27.03	41.67	29.07

Noise Simulation. We compare some methods of noise ratios under controls m_1, m_2, and m_3. Original noise (our submission) refers to the result based on Data Sampling, where noise is added to all samples belonging to m_1 and m_2, while no noise is added to samples of m_3. Balance noise means that the total number of noisy samples is controlled to be in a 1:1 ratio with the number of noiseless samples, and these noise allocations are evenly distributed between m_1

and m_2. Diverse noise indicates that we consider the diversity on M to balance the samples of m_1, m_2, and m_3, while still not adding noise to m_3. Therefore, the ratio of noisy samples to noiseless samples is 2:1. The result is shown in Table 5. In the test of KB-Related $F_{0.5}$, the balanced noise scheme only improves the score by 0.69 (from 45.82 to 46.51) compared with the original scheme. However, using the diverse noise ratio further improves the score by 2.82, which matches the diverse idea throughout our paper.

Instruction Diversity. We compare the impacts of different instruction sources. The result is shown in Table 6. When using instruction sets $I_{generate}$ generated solely by LLMs, although the language style is consistent with the base model, the insufficient understanding of the task leads to an indicator of 20.09 on KB-Related $F_{0.5}$. In contrast, instructions incorporating human prior knowledge I_{manual} bring a 6.23 improvement on KB-Related $F_{0.5}$. Finally, the hybrid approach of combining I_{manual} and $I_{generate}$ achieves the optimal result of 29.07, which demonstrates the importance of instruction diversity.

5   Conclusion

We propose the CGT-Corrector: Chinese Government Text Correction with Knowledge Bases. By **Explicit M&T labeling** and **Implicit Semantic Sampling**, we make the original data distribution more balanced and diverse. Furthermore, LLM-driven **Noise Simulation** and **Instruction Construction** optimization strategy addresses complex error types and fully leverage the pretrained knowledge of LLMs, respectively. Finally, we achieve leading performance in NLPCC-2025 Shared Task 5 with a 14B model's $F_{0.5}$ score of 45.82 and validate the effectiveness of its innovative components through ablation studies.

6   Limitations

Although we have made many improvements to data samples and noise, there is still significant room for improvement in terms of instructions and training methods: (1) The current approach mainly generates instructions by leveraging the task understanding of LLMs during pre-training. In the future, we will design a scheme to automatically find the optimal instructions. (2) The current scheme does not explicitly model whether to use the retrieved knowledge. We hope to explicitly model the participation proportion of knowledge. (3) In text error correction tasks, the proportion of correct text often far exceeds that of erroneous text. Therefore, simple supervised fine-tuning is likely to be biased. In the future, we hope to balance texts of different difficulty levels.

A   Appendix

All prompts used in the experiment are shown in Fig. 3.

Instruction for Simulating Noise

<kb>是在<text>中出现的一些字符串，请你随机选择<kb>中的一个或多个，并根据你选择的<kb>在<text>的对应位置加入一些文本错误的噪声。注意：
1. <text>加入的噪声是和你选择的<kb>对应的且有关联的，噪声应确保出现在你选择的<kb>上。
2. <text>加入的噪声是符合真实中文文本可能出现的噪声的。
3. 直接返回加入噪声后的文本，输出格式为<output>加入噪声的文本</output>。

Manual Instruction for Correction

你是一位中文政府文本纠错助手，在中文政府文本中一些文本错误需要依靠外部知识库来判断是否需要进行修改。
我将提供给你一个可能含有文本错误的中文政府文本<text>和这个文本对应的一个字典形式的参考知识库<kb>。首先，你需要判断文本<text>中和<kb>相关联的位置是否存在文本错误；然后，当你认为含有错误时你需要参考<kb>对<text>相关联的位置进行恰当的修改，当你认为不含有错误时则直接返回<text>。注意：
1. 你只需要关注和知识库相似的文本片段中是否含有错误。
2. 不要对原始文本中的标点符号或没有错误的位置进行修改。
3. 对于'领导信息'类的知识，当出现领导名称和参考知识库<kb>不一致时，应尊重<text>原文。
4. 输出格式为'<output>text</output>'。

Manual Instruction for Generating Correction Instruction

任务定义：近年来，中文文本纠错取得了快速发展，基于机器学习的纠错算法显著提升了性能。然而，当前的研究通常缺乏对利用知识库指导纠错的考量，而知识库有助于纠正关键事实性错误或根据知识库的变化调整纠错结果。我们基于真实用户输入，专门为政府公文自动文本纠错开发了一个数据集和知识库。
为解决以上任务，将采用指令微调的方式对模型进行训练。指令微调是一种通过向模型提供明确的指令来引导模型生成所需输出的方法。现在，请你根据任务定义和你的内部知识，为模型生成N个指令，该指令应明确地指示模型如何基于知识库进行中文政府文本纠错。
你生成的多样化指令将会被随机选择并拼接在<text>待纠正文本</text>和<kb>参考知识库</kb>之前作为一条完整的训练数据，以指导模型进行文本纠错。请确保生成的指令能够覆盖各种可能的文本纠错场景，并能够有效地利用知识库进行纠错。

Some Cases of Generating Correction Instructions

1. 全面审查整个文档，寻找可以进一步优化和完善的地方，包括但不限于语言流畅度、逻辑连贯性等方面，并根据知识库提供的最佳实践进行改进。
2. 请根据提供的知识库，修正<text>待纠正文本</text>中的所有语法错误和事实性错误，特别是涉及特定政策名称或术语的地方。

Fig. 3. Prompts for CGT-Corrector.

References

1. Chen, H., Zhang, Y., Zhang, Q., et al.: Maybe only 0.5% data is needed: a preliminary exploration of low training data instruction tuning. arXiv preprint arXiv:2305.09246 (2023)
2. Chen, J., Xiao, S., Zhang, P., et al.: Bge m3-embedding: Multi-lingual, multi-functionality, multi-granularity text embeddings through self-knowledge distillation. arXiv preprint arXiv:2402.03216 (2024)
3. Cheng, X., Xu, W., Chen, K., et al.: SpellGCN: incorporating phonological and visual similarities into language models for Chinese spelling check. In: Proceedings of the 58th Annual Meeting of the Association for Computational Linguistics, pp. 871–881. Association for Computational Linguistics (2020)
4. Douze, M., Guzhva, A., Deng, C., et al.: The faiss library. arXiv preprint arXiv:2401.08281 (2024)
5. Hong, Y., Yu, X., He, N., et al.: FASPell: a fast, adaptable, simple, powerful Chinese spell checker based on DAE-decoder paradigm. In: Proceedings of the 5th Workshop on Noisy User-generated Text (W-NUT 2019), pp. 160–169. Association for Computational Linguistics (2019)
6. Hu, Y., Meng, F., Zhou, J.: CSCD-NS: a Chinese spelling check dataset for native speakers. In: Proceedings of the 62nd Annual Meeting of the Association for Computational Linguistics (Volume 1: Long Papers), pp. 146–159. Association for Computational Linguistics (2024)
7. Hurst, A., Lerer, A., Goucher, A.P., et al.: Gpt-4o system card. arXiv preprint arXiv:2410.21276 (2024)
8. Liu, A., Feng, B., Xue, B., et al.: Deepseek-v3 technical report. arXiv preprint arXiv:2412.19437 (2024)

9. Omelianchuk, K., Atrasevych, V., Chernodub, A., et al.: GECToR – grammatical error correction: tag, not rewrite. In: Proceedings of the Fifteenth Workshop on Innovative Use of NLP for Building Educational Applications, pp. 163–170. Association for Computational Linguistics (2020)
10. Wang, D., Song, Y., Li, J., Han, J., Zhang, H.: A hybrid approach to automatic corpus generation for chinese spelling check. In: Proceedings of the 2018 conference on empirical methods in natural language processing, pp. 2517–2527. Association for Computational Linguistics (2018)
11. Xu, L., Wu, J., Peng, J., et al.: FCGEC: Fine-grained corpus for Chinese grammatical error correction. In: Findings of the Association for Computational Linguistics: EMNLP 2022, pp. 1900–1918. Association for Computational Linguistics (2022)
12. Yang, A., Yang, B., Zhang, B., et al.: Qwen2. 5 technical report. arXiv preprint arXiv:2412.15115 (2024)
13. Zhang, Y., Li, Z., Bao, Z., et al.: MuCGEC: a multi-reference multi-source evaluation dataset for Chinese grammatical error correction. In: Proceedings of the 2022 Conference of the North American Chapter of the Association for Computational Linguistics: Human Language Technologies, pp. 3118–3130. Association for Computational Linguistics (2022)
14. Zhao, Y., Jiang, N., Sun, W., Wan, X.: Overview of the NLPCC 2018 shared task: grammatical error correction. In: Zhang, M., Ng, V., Zhao, D., Li, S., Zan, H. (eds.) NLPCC 2018. LNCS (LNAI), vol. 11109, pp. 439–445. Springer, Cham (2018). https://doi.org/10.1007/978-3-319-99501-4_41
15. Zhou, Y., Porwal, U., Konow, R.: Spelling correction as a foreign language. arXiv preprint arXiv:1705.07371 (2017)

KARTC: Knowledge-Aware Rewriting with Large Language Models for Chinese Government Text Correction

Lei Hu, Wenting Zhang, Lihua Tan, Zhiwen Xie,
and Guangyou Zhou[✉]

Central China Normal University, Wuhan, China
`gyzhou@mail.ccnu.edu.cn`

Abstract. This paper aims to address the challenge of correcting semantic, syntactic, and knowledge-related errors in Chinese government texts. The existing methods often overlook content-level inaccuracies and knowledge inconsistencies. To address the above issue, we propose a knowledge-aware rewriting method with large language models (LLMs) for Chinese government text correction (in short KARTC). The proposed KARTC comprehensively integrates structured knowledge bases (KBs) with LLMs with a three-stage hierarchical task-chain framework. To demonstrate the effectiveness of the proposed KARTC, we conduct the experiments on NLPCC 2025 shared task 5. The results show that KARTC achieves the 79.64% in term of accuracy, and ranks the 2nd place on NLPCC 2025 shared task 5.

Keywords: Large Language Model · Chinese Government Text Correction · Text Rewriting

1 Introduction

In official documents within the government and judicial sectors, the accuracy, consistency, and standardization of textual content are of utmost importance. These documents play a central role in policy dissemination, legal proceedings, and public communication. Any inaccuracies can lead to serious misunderstandings and legal consequences. Therefore, ensuring the quality of official documents is crucial for maintaining the enforcement of policies and the impartiality of the law. However, current research on Chinese text correction [1] predominantly focuses on superficial errors such as spelling and grammar, with insufficient attention to content-level errors involving external knowledge, entity logic, and expression standards [2].

Existing methods for Chinese text correction are mostly based on Seq2Seq [3] and Seq2Edit [4] models. These methods perform well in correcting superficial errors but still face challenges when dealing with complex word order changes in Chinese [5,6]. With the rise of LLMs, researchers have started to explore their application in Chinese grammatical error correction (CGEC). However, due to

© The Author(s), under exclusive license to Springer Nature Singapore Pte Ltd. 2026
X.-L. Mao et al. (Eds.): NLPCC 2025, LNAI 16105, pp. 442–452, 2026.
https://doi.org/10.1007/978-981-95-3352-7_37

the flexibility and context-dependence of Chinese grammatical structures, LLMs still face significant challenges in Chinese error correction. Although existing knowledge-augmented text correction methods can correct factual errors, they still need improvement in multi-source knowledge fusion and real-time consistency validation. These issues are particularly prominent in the field of government document correction, where revisions must strictly conform to formal policy frameworks while maintaining syntactic fluency and semantic fidelity. Moreover, existing methods often lead to overcorrection and loss of original intent when dealing with semantic and knowledge errors in complex contexts, which further highlights the need for a more nuanced and controlled approach. To address these challenges, NLPCC 2025 shared task 5 introduced a Chinese government text correction task with KB, aiming to promote more effective identification and repair of semantic and knowledge errors by systems in real-world application scenarios.

To tackle the aforementioned issues, we propose the KARTC framework. This framework addresses the shortcomings of existing methods through the coordinated processing of three core modules: error detection, candidate generation, and controlled rewriting. First, the Error Detection Module provides precise error localization and type judgment by combining semantic, syntactic, and knowledge error detection, laying the foundation for the subsequent correction process. Second, the Candidate Generation Module generates a diverse set of correction candidates through semantics-enhanced and knowledge-enhanced rewriting strategies, reducing dependence on a single correction pattern. Finally, the Controlled Rewriting Module follows the "minimum intervention" principle to ensure that errors are corrected while preserving the original sentence style and intent. To further enhance the system's performance, we integrate pre-trained language models with knowledge base information, effectively addressing the insufficiencies of existing methods in complex contexts. Our main contributions include:

- We propose KARTC, a hierarchical framework that integrates structured knowledge bases with LLMs, significantly enhancing error correction accuracy for Chinese government texts through three-stage collaborative processing.
- We implement a controlled rewriting module with dual-objective optimization to balance KB consistency and minimal text intervention, ensuring corrections preserve original document intent and formal style.
- Our system achieves the 2nd place on NLPCC 2025 shared task 5. Specifically, it obtains an $F_{0.5}$ score of 36.48% in traditional error correction and a knowledge alignment accuracy of 79.64%.

2   Related Work

Compared to the well-established research on English Grammatical Error Correction, CGEC remains in its nascent stage of development. Early CGEC studies primarily focused on non-native learner texts in Chinese as a Foreign Language scenarios, which exhibit high explicit error rates due to learners' linguistic limitations [7].

In the field of CGEC, traditional methods are largely inherited from general Grammatical Error Correction (GEC) approaches, primarily focusing on Seq2Seq and Seq2Edit models. Seq2Seq models, which treat CGEC as a translation-like task, rely heavily on large-scale labeled sentence pairs to achieve performance, leading to extremely high data annotation costs [8]. Seq2Edit models, such as GECToR [9], aim to generate corrections by predicting edit tags for tokens, but they struggle with errors involving complex word order changes, a common issue in Chinese.

With the rise of LLMs [10], researchers have explored their application in CGEC [11,12], but LLMs face significant challenges. LLMs' free-generation paradigm often violates the "minimum change principle" central to CGEC, leading to corrections that deviate excessively from the original text and perform poorly on traditional metrics like Precision (P) and Recall (R) [13]. This is partly due to Chinese grammatical structures being more flexible and context-dependent than Indo-European languages, making it harder for LLMs trained on English-centric data to generalize to CGEC. Additionally, the scarcity of high-quality, large-scale CGEC datasets exacerbates LLMs' difficulties in learning subtle error patterns specific to Chinese [14].

3   Method

In this task, we propose KARTC, a method designed to improve error correction accuracy for government-related texts by combining structured KB information with the generative power of LLMs.

KARTC adopts a three-stage chained task framework: Error Detection, Candidate Generation, and Controlled Rewriting. This layered approach mitigates the problem of overcorrection often seen in knowledge-injected LLMs.

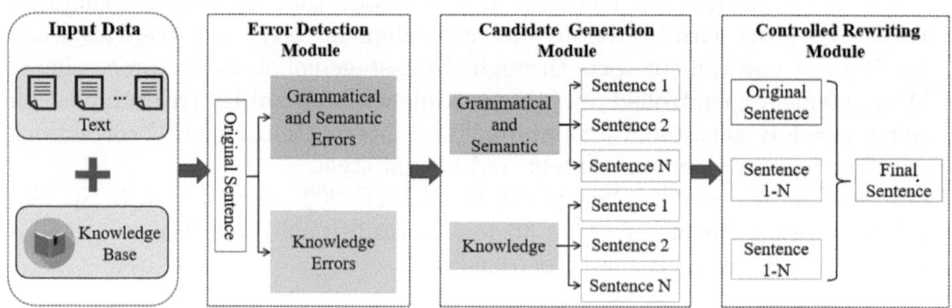

Fig. 1. The framework of KARTC.

As illustrated in Fig. 1, KARTC first employs the Error Detection Module to detect potential errors, including grammatical, semantic, and knowledge-based inconsistencies. Based on these results, the Candidate Generation Module produces correction candidates that align with both the sentence meaning and external knowledge. In the final stage, the Controlled Rewriting Module applies corrections with a focus on minimal intervention, ensuring errors are corrected while preserving the original sentence style and intent. By progressively refining corrections through this chained design, KARTC balances semantic accuracy, knowledge consistency, and stylistic fidelity, offering a precise solution for error correction in government text scenarios.

3.1   Error Detection Module

The primary objective of the Error Detection Module is to automatically detect semantic error types within an input sentence and further determine the presence of knowledge-related errors based on an external KB. This process not only supplies essential error information for subsequent candidate generation and controlled rewriting but also serves as a precise diagnostic foundation for the overall correction pipeline.

Given the input sentence set $S = \{S_1, S_2, ..., S_n\}$, this module aims to learn a mapping function $f_{judge} : S \rightarrow E \times \{0, 1\}$, where $C = \{e_1, e_2, ..., e_m\}$ denotes the set of semantic error categories (e.g., grammatical errors, ambiguity, semantic conflicts), and $\{0, 1\}$ indicates the binary label for knowledge-related errors (1 for present, 0 otherwise).

To achieve this, we first encode the sentence using a pretrained language model to obtain its semantic representation vector:

$$h = Encoder(S) \in R^d, \tag{1}$$

where d is the dimensionality of the hidden vector.

Subsequently, two separate classifiers are employed to predict the semantic error types and knowledge error existence:

$$\hat{y}_{semantic} = softmax(W_s h + b_s), \hat{y}_{knowledge} = \sigma(w_k^T h + b_k), \tag{2}$$

where W_s, b_s are the weights and bias of the semantic error classifier, and w_k, b_k are the parameters for the binary knowledge error classifier. $\sigma(\cdot)$ denotes the sigmoid activation function.

During training, the module minimizes the combined cross-entropy loss:

$$L = L_{semantic} + \alpha L_{knowledge}, \tag{3}$$

where $L_{semantic} = -\sum_{i=1}^{m} y_i log \hat{y}_i$ is the semantic classification loss, and $L_{knowledge}$ represents the binary classification loss. The hyperparameter α balances the influence of the two tasks.

Importantly, knowledge error detection relies on alignment with the external KB. Specifically, entities within the sentence are matched against factual triples in the KB. If discrepancies are identified, the sentence is labeled as containing a knowledge error.

The output of this module provides both the distribution of semantic error categories and a binary knowledge error indicator, which directly influences the candidate generation strategies and the rewriting granularity in downstream modules. This ensures a coherent chain of tasks across the entire correction framework.

3.2 Candidate Generation Module

Upon completing the error detection phase, KARTC proceeds to the candidate generation stage. This module aims to produce a set of semantically coherent and knowledge-consistent candidate corrections for each text fragment S_i that has been identified as potentially erroneous, based on its associated knowledge subset K_i. These candidate sentences serve as crucial inputs for the subsequent controlled rewriting process.

Formally, the candidate generation is defined through a conditional generation function:

$$C_i = G(S_i, K_i), \tag{4}$$

where $G(\cdot)$ denotes a context-aware text generation model that takes both the fragment S_i and the knowledge subset K_i as input, and outputs a candidate set $C_i = \{C_{i_1}, C_{i_2}, ..., C_{i_k}\}$. Each candidate aims to maintain the semantic fidelity of the original fragment while ensuring factual consistency with the provided knowledge.

To enhance the quality and relevance of generated candidates, KARTC incorporates a "minimal revision priority" constraint within the prompt design. This constraint enforces the model to perform only a single, necessary modification per generation, thereby reducing the risk of excessive rewriting and semantic drift. Such a strategy promotes fine-grained corrections and maintains the overall stylistic and contextual integrity of the input sentence.

Importantly, KARTC distinguishes between semantic errors and knowledge-related errors by generating two separate candidate sets:

$$C_i^{semantic} = G_{semantic}(S_i, K_i), C_i^{knowledge} = G_{knowledge}(S_i, K_i), \tag{5}$$

where $G_{semantic}$ focuses on correcting grammatical and semantic issues, while $G_{knowledge}$ targets factual inaccuracies by aligning the output with domain knowledge. This dual-generation strategy ensures targeted and domain-aware correction suggestions.

To further enhance semantic precision, KARTC employs a local attention mechanism that explicitly models the semantic discrepancy between the input fragment S_i and its corresponding knowledge subset K_i. The local attention weight is defined as:

$$\alpha_{i,j} = \frac{exp(h_{S_i} \cdot h_{K_j})}{\sum_l exp(h_{S_i} \cdot h_{K_l})}, \tag{6}$$

where h_{S_i} and h_{K_j} denote the contextual embeddings of S_i and K_j, respectively. The dot product measures their semantic relevance, allowing the model to prioritize knowledge elements most pertinent to the fragment while suppressing irrelevant noise.

Finally, the aggregated candidate set for all erroneous fragments is constructed as:

$$C = \bigcup_{i=1}^{n}(C_i^{semantic} \bigcup C_i^{knowledge}). \tag{7}$$

Equation (7) will be utilized in the controlled rewriting phase for contextually accurate and knowledge-grounded text revision.

3.3   Controlled Rewriting Module

The Controlled Rewriting Module serves as the pivotal component of the KARTC framework, tasked with generating high-quality sentence corrections while adhering to the principles of precision and controllability. Unlike conventional end-to-end generative correction methods, KARTC emphasizes a "necessity-first, minimal intervention" design philosophy. This ensures that revisions are applied only when warranted, avoiding unnecessary structural alterations and preserving the original sentence's semantic intent and stylistic nuances.

Formally, given an original sentence S_i and its associated candidate set $C_i = \{c_{i1}, c_{i2}, ..., c_{ik}\}$, the controlled rewriting process employs a strategy function $R(\cdot)$ to select the most appropriate correction, resulting in the final revised output S_i':

$$S_i' = R(S_i, C_i, K_i), \tag{8}$$

where K_i denotes the relevant knowledge subset corresponding to S_i, ensuring knowledge consistency throughout the revision process. The strategy function $R(\cdot)$ optimizes for two primary objectives: (1) the alignment between each candidate sentence and the KB, and (2) the preservation of semantic proximity to the original sentence. This trade-off is captured by the following optimization formulation:

$$R(S_i, C_i, K_i) = arg \max_{c \in C_i}(\lambda_1 \cdot Align(c, K_i) - \lambda_2 \cdot Dist(S_i, c)), \tag{9}$$

where:

- $Align(c, K_i)$ quantifies the semantic and factual alignment between candidate c and knowledge subset K_i, leveraging the same semantic-knowledge alignment function as in the error detection stage;
- $Dist(S_i, c)$ measures the edit distance between S_i and c implemented via token-level Levenshtein distance, acting as a regularization term to discourage unnecessary modifications;
- λ_1 and λ_2 are tunable coefficients balancing alignment fidelity and conservative rewriting.

Through this dual-objective optimization, KARTC ensures that the rewriting process corrects actual errors while minimizing stylistic or structural distortions, effectively achieving fine-grained sentence optimization.

4   Experiments

4.1   Data Analysis and Experimental Settings

The task provides a training set and a validation set. The training set comprises 6,448,361 instances, with an average length of 62.26. Notably, the training set provided by the competition organizer lacks error annotation and correction forms. The organizer directly split the text and supplemented knowledge-base information via retrieval. The validation set totals 306 instances, among which 50 contain errors. Due to the limited data availability, a random sampling of 6,000 sentences was first conducted from the training set, followed by a semantic fluency assessment. Based on the assessment results, 2,000 sentences with higher fluency scores were selected for subsequent processing. Then, by integrating the error categories from the validation set, we generated 200 error sentences for subsequent method evaluation. The experiments employ the model Qwen2.5-32B-Instruct-GPTQ-Int8. The experiments were conducted on hardware equipped with 4 V100 GPUs, leveraging the vLLM framework to ensure efficient model inference.

4.2   Metrics

In the evaluation framework, the distinction between the metrics in Table 1 (traditional text correction) and Table 2 (knowledge-base correction) lies in the operational definitions of TP, FP, and FN, rather than the calculation of P (precision) and R (recall). For traditional text correction (Table 1), let $TP_{Cherrant}$ denote the number of correctly identified and corrected linguistic errors, $FP_{Cherrant}$ represent the number of non-errors mistakenly flagged as errors, and $FN_{Cherrant}$ signify the number of undetected actual linguistic errors. The precision P and recall R are calculated as:

$$P = \frac{TP}{TP + FP} \tag{10}$$

$$R = \frac{TP}{TP + FN} \tag{11}$$

For knowledge-base correction (Table 2), let TP_{kb} be the number of corrections that accurately align with knowledge bases (e.g., resolving factual mismatches), FP_{kb} denote unwarranted modifications to knowledge-consistent content, and FN_{kb} represent unaddressed knowledge errors. Let TN be the number of knowledge-base entries absent in both reference and generated texts. The relevant metrics are given by:

$$F_{0.5} = \frac{(1 + 0.5^2) \times P \times R}{0.5^2 \times P + R} \tag{12}$$

$$ACC = \frac{TP_{kb} + TN}{TP_{kb} + TN + FP_{kb} + FN_{kb}} \tag{13}$$

Although the mathematical forms of P and R are identical for both tables, their semantic meanings differ fundamentally due to the distinct definitions of TP, FP, and FN. Table 1 evaluates linguistic correctness, while Table 2 assesses knowledge-driven accuracy, reflecting the dual-focus design of the evaluation framework.

4.3   Main Results

The evaluation results of our team in the NLPCC 2025 shared task 5 have been released. Our team achieved the 2nd place ranking, demonstrating competitive performance in this task. The specific evaluation results are shown in Table 1 and Table 2.

Table 1. Experimental results on NLPCC 2025 shared task 5 regarding the traditional Cherrant evaluation.

Rank	TP	FP	FN	P (%)	R (%)	F0.5 (%)
top1	32	35	111	47.76	22.38	38.93
top2 (ours)	44	71	99	38.26	30.77	36.48
top3	17	113	126	13.08	11.89	12.82

Table 2. Experimental results on NLPCC 2025 shared task 5 regarding the knowledge-based error correction evaluation.

Rank	ACC (%)	P (%)	R (%)	F0.5 (%)
top1	84.20	46.94	41.82	45.82
top2 (ours)	79.64	34.57	50.91	36.94
top3	77.72	17.02	14.55	16.46

4.4   Ablation Study

To validate the effectiveness of our framework's components, we conducted ablation studies on two key parameters: error detection rounds (EDR: 0, 1, 3) and candidate set limits (CSL: 1, 3, 7). EDR determines whether error detection precedes candidate generation: EDR $= 0$ skips detection and directly assumes errors exist, while EDR$\geq$1 performs iterative error detection to filter invalid tokens. CSL controls the maximum number of candidates per category: CSL $=$ 1 retains only the original sentence; CSL $=$ 3 adds one grammatical & semantic candidate and one knowledge-base candidate; CSL $=$ 7 allows three candidates from each category.

Experimental results (Table 3 and Table 4) revealed distinct performance patterns. Without error detection (EDR = 0), increasing CSL from 1 to 7 improved ACC from 45.95% to 51.69%, but P remained low (12.64%–8.94%) due to high false positives (FP = 159–163), indicating that unrestricted candidate generation introduces noise. With error detection (EDR$\geq$1), FP dropped sharply to 63–66, boosting ACC to 72.73%–73.48% and P to 20.73%–21.43%. This highlights EDR's critical role in filtering low-confidence candidates. The optimal configuration (EDR = 3, CSL = 7) achieved the highest $F_{0.5}$ score (25.00%) by balancing R = 75.00% and P = 21.43%, demonstrating that iterative error detection combined with diversified candidates maximizes performance. These results underscore the necessity of coupling controlled candidate diversity with error detection to mitigate precision-recall trade-offs in error correction systems.

Table 3. Confusion matrix metrics of ablation experiments under different EDR and CSL.

Parameters		Confusion Matrix Items			
EDR	CSL	TP	FP	FN	TN
0	1	23	159	1	113
0	3	13	178	11	170
0	7	16	163	8	167
1	3	17	63	7	177
1	7	17	63	7	175
3	3	17	65	7	176
3	7	18	66	6	174

Table 4. Evaluation metrics of ablation experiments under different EDR and CSL.

Parameters		Evaluation Metrics			
EDR	CSL	ACC (%)	P (%)	R (%)	$F_{0.5}$(%)
0	1	45.9	12.6	95.8	15.3
0	3	49.2	68.1	54.2	82.5
0	7	51.7	89.4	66.7	10.8
1	3	73.5	21.2	70.8	24.7
1	7	73.3	21.2	70.8	24.7
3	3	72.8	20.7	70.8	24.2
3	7	72.7	21.4	75.0	25.0

5   Conclusion

In this paper, we propose KARTC, which adopts a multi-stage chained pipeline to enhance error correction accuracy in complex scenarios. Ranked second in NLPCC 2025 shared task 5, the framework demonstrates innovation through integrated dual-path error detection that synergistically identifies linguistic anomalies and knowledge conflicts while preserving semantic coherence. By combining semantic-knowledge dual rewriting strategies to generate diversified candidates, it overcomes limitations of conventional single-pattern correction. The knowledge-aware consistency modeling further mitigates over-correction risks.

While the current cascaded training may underutilize cross-module feature interactions, future work will develop end-to-end joint training paradigms and investigate prompt-learning based knowledge fusion to optimize the precision-recall equilibrium in domain-specific correction tasks.

Acknowledgments. This work was supported by the National Natural Science Foundation of China under Grant 62377021, the China Postdoctoral Science Foundation under Grant Number 2024M751062, financially supported by self-determined research funds of CCNU from the colleges basic research and operation of MOE (No. CCNU24XJ010, CCNU22QN015 and CCNU24ai011), and the Natural Science Foundation of Hubei Province for Distinguished Young Scholars (No. 2023AFA096).

References

1. Wang, Y., Wang, Y., Liu, J., Liu, Z.: A comprehensive survey of grammar error correction (2020)
2. Tang, C., Wu, X., Wu, Y.: Are pre-trained language models useful for model ensemble in Chinese grammatical error correction? In: Rogers, A., Boyd-Graber, J., Okazaki, N. (eds.) Proceedings of the 61st Annual Meeting of the Association for Computational Linguistics (Volume 2: Short Papers), pp. 893–901, Toronto, Canada, July 2023. Association for Computational Linguistics
3. Kaneko, M., Mita, M., Kiyono, S., Suzuki, J., Inui, K.: Encoder-decoder models can benefit from pre-trained masked language models in grammatical error correction (2020)
4. Li, S., Zhao, J., Shi, G., Tan, Y., Huifang, X., Chen, G., Lan, H., Lin, Z.: Chinese grammatical error correction based on convolutional sequence to sequence model. IEEE Access **7**, 72905–72913 (2019)
5. Cao, H., Yuan, L., Zhang, Y., Ng, H.T.: Unsupervised grammatical error correction rivaling supervised methods. In: Bouamor, H., Pino, J., Bali, K. (eds.) Proceedings of the 2023 Conference on Empirical Methods in Natural Language Processing, pp. 3072–3088, Singapore, December 2023. Association for Computational Linguistics
6. Rothe, S., Mallinson, J., Malmi, E., Krause, S., Severyn, A.: A simple recipe for multilingual grammatical error correction. In: Zong, C., Xia, F., Li, W., Navigli, R. (eds.). Proceedings of the 59th Annual Meeting of the Association for Computational Linguistics and the 11th International Joint Conference on Natural Language Processing (Volume 2: Short Papers), pp. 702–707, Online, August 2021. Association for Computational Linguistics

7. Zhao, Y., Jiang, N., Sun, W., Wan, X.: Overview of the NLPCC 2018 shared task: grammatical error correction. In: Zhang, M., Ng, V., Zhao, D., Li, S., Zan, H. (eds.) NLPCC 2018. LNCS (LNAI), vol. 11109, pp. 439–445. Springer, Cham (2018). https://doi.org/10.1007/978-3-319-99501-4_41
8. Shao, Y., et al.: Cpt: a pre-trained unbalanced transformer for both Chinese language understanding and generation. arXiv preprint arXiv:2109.05729 (2021)
9. Omelianchuk, K., Atrasevych, V., Chernodub, A., Skurzhanskyi, O.: GECToR – grammatical error correction: Tag, not rewrite. In: Burstein, J., et al. (eds.) Proceedings of the Fifteenth Workshop on Innovative Use of NLP for Building Educational Applications, pp. 163–170, Seattle, WA, USA → Online, July 2020. Association for Computational Linguistics
10. Zhao, W.X., et al.: A survey of large language models, Peiyu Liu (2025)
11. Wang, Y., Wang, B., Liu, Y., Wu, D., Che, W.: LM-combiner: A contextual rewriting model for Chinese grammatical error correction. In: Calzolari, N., Kan, M.-Y., Hoste, V., Lenci, A., Sakti, S., Xue, N. (eds.) Proceedings of the 2024 Joint International Conference on Computational Linguistics, Language Resources and Evaluation (LREC-COLING 2024), pp. 10675–10685, Torino, Italia, May 2024. ELRA and ICCL
12. Liu, X., Xu, B., Yang, M., Cao, H., Zhu, C., Zhao, T., Lu, W.: A chain-of-task framework for instruction tuning of llms based on Chinese grammatical error correction. In: Proceedings of the 31st International Conference on Computational Linguistics, pp. 8623–8639 (2025)
13. Fang, T., et al.: Is chatgpt a highly fluent grammatical error correction system? a comprehensive evaluation (2023)
14. Jin, W., Jiang, F., Wang, X., Ma, N., Zhang, Y.: Research and analysis of grammatical error correction technology for Chinese documents. J. Comput. Commun. **12**(8), 202–223 (2024)

Overview of the NLPCC 2025 Shared Task: Gender Bias Mitigation Challenge

Yizhi Li[1,2], Ge Zhang[1], Hanhua Hong[2], Yiwen Wang[1,2], and Chenghua Lin[2(✉)]

[1] Multimodal Art Projection Research Community, Manchester, USA
yizhi.li@hotmail.com
[2] University of Manchester, Manchester, USA
chenghua.lin@manchester.ac.uk

Abstract. As natural language processing for gender bias becomes a significant interdisciplinary topic, the prevalent data-driven techniques, such as pre-trained language models, suffer from biased corpus. This case becomes more obvious regarding those languages with less fairness-related computational linguistic resources, such as Chinese. To this end, we propose a Chinese cOrpus foR Gender bIas Probing and Mitigation (**CORGI-PM**), which contains **32.9k** sentences with high-quality labels derived by following an annotation scheme specifically developed for gender bias in the Chinese context. It is worth noting that CORGI-PM contains 5.2k gender-biased sentences along with the corresponding bias-eliminated versions rewritten by human annotators. We pose three challenges as a shared task to automate the mitigation of textual gender bias, which requires the models to detect, classify, and mitigate textual gender bias. In the literature, we present the results and analysis for the teams participating this shared task in NLPCC 2025.

Keywords: Bias Mitigation · Bias Detection · Fairness for Chinese Corpus

1 Introduction

There is a growing consensus that the identification and prevention of toxic gender attitudes and stereotypes are of vital importance for society [3]. Given that gender-biased information can be presented and disseminated extensively in textual form, it is of paramount significance to develop automatic approaches for detecting and alleviating textual gender bias. As the blooming of open-source models and training corpus [2, 12, 33, 41, 43], Natural language processing (NLP) community has found extensive applications in text-related scenarios and has exerted a considerable influence on gender bias issues [7]. On one hand, pre-trained language models (LMs), which serve as a crucial technique in modern NLP, have been demonstrated to absorb the subjective gender bias present in the internet-wise training corpus and even have the potential to amplify it [10, 17, 34, 45]. On the other hand, the application of cutting-edge NLP techniques for exploring and mitigating gender bias holds increasing promise. This status in quo necessitates the construction of high-quality corpora to facilitate the research for gender bias mitigation.

Y. Wang—Independent Researcher.

© The Author(s), under exclusive license to Springer Nature Singapore Pte Ltd. 2026
X.-L. Mao et al. (Eds.): NLPCC 2025, LNAI 16105, pp. 453–464, 2026.
https://doi.org/10.1007/978-981-95-3352-7_38

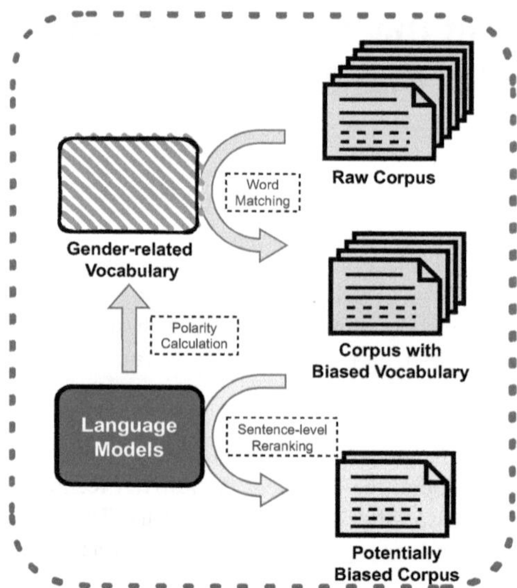

Fig. 1. Pipeline of Retrieving and Filtering Potentially Biased Sentences Candidate Pool from Raw Corpus for Human Annotation.

Building a high-quality text corpus has been one of the key tangents in improving NLP applications for debiasing gender stereotypes in texts [31]. Some researchers introduce *automatic* annotation techniques, such as gender-swapped based methods, to create corpora for gender bias mitigation [20,27,47]. While it is attractive to build a large-scale corpus without heavy labor, automatic gender-swapped based methods highly depend on the quality of base language models and are prone to creating nonsensical sentences [31]. To address this issue, some works devote effort to developing *human-annotated* corpora for gender bias mitigation. However, these corpora either mainly focus on word- or grammar-level bias [28,37,49,50], without considering the nuanced biases appearing in specific contexts. Or some of the corpora concentrate only on sexism-related topics [5,6,13,23]. Moreover, existing works on gender bias exclusively focus on English [7], where few datasets exist for other influential languages such as Chinese. We aim to tackle the aforementioned issues by providing a high-quality Chinese corpus for contextual-level gender bias probing and mitigation with a hybrid pipeline including automatic corpus filtering and human annotation.

To this end, we propose the Chinese cOrpus foR Gender bIas Probing and Mitigation (**CORGI-PM**) dataset, which consists of **32.9k** human-annotated sentences, including both gender-biased and non-biased samples. To construct the initial candidate pool for further processing, we propose an automatic method to build a potentially gender-biased sentence set from existing large-scale Chinese corpora, as illustrated in Fig. 1. Inspired by the metric leveraging language models for gender bias score calculation proposed in [4], the samples containing words of high gender bias scores are first recalled at this stage. Following the retrieval, the samples are then reranked and filtered according to their sentence-level gender-biased probability [14]. After the candidate pool construction, we select human annotators with qualified educational backgrounds and design an annotation scheme to label the acquired sentences.

During the annotation, the candidates are classified into biased and non-biased classes, and the biased samples are further categorized into three fine-grained categories considering their contexts. To facilitate research in bias mitigation research, we also require the annotators to paraphrase the biased sentences into gender-neutral ones while maintaining invariant semantics to build a parallel subset corpus. Based on the labeled corpus, we further pose three challenges in CORGI-PM, *i.e.*, gender bias **detection**, **classification**, and **mitigation**, which come with clear definitions and evaluation protocols for NLP tasks in gender bias probing and mitigation. In order to provide referential baselines and benchmarks for our proposed challenges, we conduct random data splitting with balanced labels and implement experiments on pre-trained language models in zero-shot, in-context learning, and fine-tuning paradigms. We discuss the experimental settings and provide result analysis in Sect. 5.

In summary, we provide a well-annotated Chinese corpus for gender bias probing and mitigation, along with clearly defined corresponding challenges. With a properly designed annotation scheme, CORGI-PM provides a corpus of high quality that assists models in detecting gender bias in texts. More importantly, other than the 22.5k human-annotated non-biased samples, all the 5.2k biased sentences in our corpus are further labeled with gender bias subclasses and companies with parallel bias-free versions provided by the annotators[1].

2   Related Work

Gender Bias Corpus. High-quality gender bias corpus, especially contextual-level gender bias corpus, is significant for mitigating gender bias contained in language models, but hard to collect. Previous research work widely uses gender-swapping to build a corpus for evaluation or mitigate gender bias in LMs [16,46]. Metrics and corpus are introduced to measure gender bias in abusive languages as well [9,13,24]. Word-level Chinese gender bias corpora have been proposed about adjectives [50], and careers [30]. [46] also shares an automatically constructed Chinese sentence-level gender-unbiased data set. In sharp contrast, CORGI-PM is the first human-annotated Chinese gender bias detection dataset, one of the rare gender bias classification datasets [24], and the first human-annotated gender-bias correction dataset.

Bias Detection and Correction. Different Gender Bias Evaluation Testsets (GBETs) have been designed to automatically evaluate models trained for specific tasks for gender bias [16,32,38]. Word-swapping is the most widely used technique for gender bias correction and widely used to mitigate the gender bias in hate-speech [25], regional bias mitigation [18], knowledge graph [21], sentiment analysis [16], and the general language model [45]. As a comparison, CORGI-PM serves as a manual standard dataset for testing LMs' ability to measure and mitigate gender bias.

---

[1] To eliminate the data contamination, we additionally provide 100 samples for each task in addition to the original splits [42].

Table 1. Overall Statistics of the CORGI-PM Dataset. The notations, **AC**, **DI**, and **ANB** represent specific bias labels described in Sect. 3.2.

Sample Category	Quantity		
	Train	Valid	Test
Biased AC	1.90k	235	237
DI	2.70k	334	337
ANB	2.47k	306	309
Non-biased	21.4k	516	526
Overall	30.1k	1391	1409

3   Data Collection

3.1   Sample Filtering

We propose an automatic processing method to recall, rerank, and filter annotation candidates from raw corpora using a two-stage filtering from word-level to sentence-level, as illustrated in Fig. 1. The Chinese sentence samples are mainly screened out from the SlguSet [48] and the CCL corpus [39]. To recall gender-biased words or retrieve candidate sentences with gender bias scores, we compare the target word/sentence representations with the *seed direction*, which can be calculated by the subtraction between the word embeddings of she and he [4, 14]. We leverage different Chinese LMs including ERNIE [44], CBert [8], and Chinese word vectors [26] to acquire the word-level and sentence-level representations. For word-level filtering, we use the mentioned metric to build a vocabulary of high bias scores and recall sentences containing such words from the raw corpora with exact matches. We compute gender bias scores of the crawled sentences and group them by the gender bias keywords acquired in the previous stage for sentence-level filtering. The final sentences for annotation are then selected according to a specific global threshold score and an in-group threshold rank.

Table 2. Linguistic Characteristics of the Corpus. *Word, Dictionary, and Character* separately denote the total Chinese word number, total unique Chinese word number, and total character number of the specific categories. The sentence lengths are defined as the number of containing characters.

Linguistic Info.	Non-biased			Biased			Corrected Biased		
	Train	Valid	Test	Train	Valid	Test	Train	Valid	Test
Word	724k	18.9k	17.7k	228k	24.8k	28.3k	265k	27.1k	30.0k
Dictionary	574k	14.4k	14.1k	167k	18.4k	20.4k	191k	19.9k	21.5k
Character	1,156k	30.1k	28.1k	358k	39.2k	44.4k	417k	42.8k	46.9k
Sent. Length	53.952	58.397	53.473	85.837	76.087	85.214	99.839	82.853	89.939

3.2   Annotation Scheme

The annotation scheme is designed for gender bias probing and mitigation. For gender bias probing, the annotators are required to provide the following information given a sentence: whether gender bias exists; if so, how the bias is established. For gender bias mitigation, the corrected non-biased version of the biased sentences is also required. We further describe the annotation scheme details in the following paragraphs.

Existence and Categorization.   The annotators are required to annotate whether the sentence is gender-biased (**B**) or non-biased (**N**) in contextual-level or word-level, and further clarify how the bias is established. Given that our raw data is collected using gender-related keywords or from gender-related corpus, the samples annotated without gender bias are useful human-annotated negative samples for detecting gender bias. To additionally provide information about gender bias categorization, we classify gender bias types into three subtypes: (1) Gender Stereotyped activity and career choices (**AC**); (2) Gender Stereotyped descriptions and inductions (**DI**); and (3) Expressed gender-stereotyped attitudes, norms and beliefs (**ANB**). The classification standard is inspired by [15] and further summed up into the mentioned subtypes.

Bias Mitigation.   Annotators are further required to mitigate the gender bias of selected sentences while keeping the original semantics. We also ask our annotators to diversify the expressions if applicable. The major revision patterns can be summarized as follows: (1). *Replace* the gender-specific pronouns with neutral pronouns. (2). *Replace* the gender-specific adjectives with neutral descriptions with similar semantics definitions. (3). *Add* additional comments to neutralize the sentences that cannot be directly mitigated.

As shown in Fig. 2, the three mitigation revision patterns could cover various cases in the selected sentences. These three major mitigation annotation patterns are not used exclusively in the annotation but can be used in combination. Except for the three mentioned patterns, we require the annotators to apply several other linguistic skills to cover corner cases, including deleting gender-specific pronouns and replacing vehicles in gender-related metaphors.

4   CORGI-PM Corpus Analysis

In this section, we report the linguistic statistics of CORGI-PM as Table 1. We conduct a balanced splitting to create the valid and test set considering the negative-positive ratio and bias subclass proportion in the global distribution. As revealed in Table 2[2], we observe two major differences between the biased sentences and the corresponding human debiased ones: the debiased are usually longer and have more diverse expressions, revealed by the sentence length and the vocabulary size metrics. Except for the samples debiased with additional neutralization comments, we hypothesize that it is due to human annotators' intention to keep the semantic information unchanged and the sentence coherent while mitigating gender bias. In this case, they may use more conjunctions and longer descriptions compared to some gender-biased inherent expressions.

---

[2] We use the Jieba (https://github.com/fxsjy/jieba to parse.

Quality Monitoring and Control. We used a standardized operating method and educated our annotators to achieve high-quality annotations as follows:

(1). **Annotators**   We have 6 annotators, which were all native speakers of Chinese. Annotators were only qualified to do the annotation if they went through

	Original Sentence	Edit Sentence
Change the Pronoun	清洁阿姨一边扫地一边赞扬。	清洁工一边扫地一边赞扬。
	(The cleaning woman praised while sweeping the floor.)	(The cleaners praised while sweeping the floor.)
	我，有时文静，有时却调皮得像一个男孩。	我，有时文静，有时调皮。
	(I, sometimes quiet, but sometimes naughty like a boy.)	(I, sometimes quiet, sometimes naughty.)
Change the Gender-specific Adjectives	在小王眼里，李某高大帅气、温柔体贴，而且风趣幽默，是一个十分优质的青年男性。	在小王眼里，李某身材高大、外表好看、温柔体贴，而且风趣幽默，是一个十分优质的青年。
	(In the eyes of Wang, Li is tall and handsome, gentle and considerate, and funny, a very high-quality young male.)	(In the eyes of Wang, Li is tall, good-looking, caring and gentle, and funny, a very high-quality young people.)
	沙峰起伏，金光灿灿，宛如一座金山，像绸缎一样柔软，少女一样娴静。	沙峰起伏，金光灿灿，宛如一座金山，像绸缎一样柔软，宁静。
	(The sandy peaks are undulating and golden, like a golden mountain, as soft as silk and as serene as a maiden.)	(The sandy peaks are undulating and golden, like a golden mountain, as soft and serene as silk.)
Add Comments	我想要世界，而世界当时属于男人们。	我想要世界，而世界当时属于男人们。评：世界应当属于人们，与男女无关。
	(I want the world, and the world then belonged to the men.)	(I wanted the world, and the world then belonged to the men. Comment: The world should belong to people, not to men and women.)
	哎哟，果然每个追梦男人的背后，都有个不世俗的后方！	哎哟，果然每个追梦男人的背后，都有个不世俗的后方！评：这种感慨是错误的，将男女的家庭分工固定化，剥除女性就业的权利，应予以鄙弃。
	(Oops, indeed, behind every dream-chasing man, there is an unsophisticated back!)	(Oops, indeed, behind every dream-chasing man, there is an unsophisticated back! Comment: This is a wrong feeling that fixes the domestic division of labor between men and women and strips women of their employment rights, which should be despised.)

Fig. 2. Case Study of Mitigation Annotation Patterns.

several societal [15,40] and computer science research works [31,47] about gender bias before the annotation procedure. All annotators held a bachelor's degree. [36] points out that expert annotators are more cautious and can improve the corpus quality with a large margin, which proves the necessity of our training procedure. We also kept the number of male and female annotators equal.

(2). **Gender Equality of Raw Corpus**   In the raw data collection procedure, we keep the number of man-related keywords and woman-related keywords equal and make the number of samples recalled according to different keywords balanced. As a result, the raw data and the final data should hold gender equality.

(3). **Annotation Procedure**   Our annotation procedure is separated into two stages. In the first stage, annotators are encouraged to not enter any samples that they are not certain about. In the second stage, we have annotators cross-checking annotations. We did not enter any contradictory samples.

(4). **Inter-annotator Agreement**   Given the domain and purpose of the dataset, we want to build the dataset as high quality as possible. After an initial annotation round with 6 annotators, we also report inter-annotator agreement in Table 3 to verify annotation reliability, where the IAA among three annotators on bias classification, detection, and mitigation is 0.802, 0.935, and 0.987, respectively.

Table 3. Inter-Annotator Agreement (IAA)

	Classification	Detection	Mitigation
IAA	0.802	0.935	0.987

Word Cloud Analysis. We provide word cloud analysis of Ernie and Chinese-Electra in the section about adjectives and career words. More available word cloud analysis will be available in our public repository. The words are ranked according to the absolute value of their gender bias score calculated along the method used by [4,14]. There is a noticeable word-level gender stereotype according to the word cloud. For example, a man is robust and a woman is motherly, a man is suitable for a fitness instructor and a woman is suitable for a choreographer. We also conduct word cloud analysis for language models pre-trained by different corpora.

5   Derived Gender Bias Mitigation Challenges

To provide a clear definition for automatic textual gender bias probing and mitigation tasks, we propose corresponding challenges and standardize the evaluation protocols. We address two tasks, bias detection and classification, for gender bias probing to evaluate how well the language models can distinguish the biased contexts. Furthermore, we formalize the gender mitigation challenge as a sentence correction task to benchmark the bias mitigation ability of the language models.

5.1 Challenges of Detection and Classification

Definition. We regard both the gender bias detection and classification challenges as *supervised classification* tasks and evaluate them with metrics of consensus. The gender bias detection challenge can be regarded as a binary classification task, where the model is required to predict the probability that a given sentence contains gender bias. As described in § 3.2, biased samples are further categorized into one or more kinds. Therefore, we can address the gender classification challenge as a multi-label classification task. The precision, recall, and F1-score are selected as the main metrics in these two challenges. Class-wise metrics and macro average summarized evaluation are required through both valid and test sets to show the performance of language models.

Experiment Settings. Then we use the test sets to perform a classification query on the saved file. The processing time for the classification of gender bias is approximately 1 h. We calculated the precision, recall, and F1 score to analyze model performance. We test the performance on both "yes" and "no" detection.

5.2 Challenge of Mitigation

Definition. The gender bias mitigation challenge can be regarded as a sentence correction task, where the model is required to generate a non-biased version of a biased sentence. As a natural language generation task, the model outputs could be evaluated by N-gram based metrics.

Experiment Settings. Regarding the decision on *evaluation metrics,* we conduct extensive human evaluations on the debiased sentences considering both gender bias and coherence aspects. In human evaluation, we shuffle the debiased written by humans and different models, and asked annotators to grade the results using the answer range from 1-*not at all* to 7-*extremely gender biased/extremely fluent* without providing the information of the source. Additionally, we use automated reference-based metrics to evaluate the bias mitigated sentences [29], including BLEU [22], ROUGE-L [19], and METEOR [1].

6 Leaderboard

Table 4 presents the leaderboards for all the tasks, listing only the top-performing teams and

Table 4. The leaderboards for all tasks. Our baseline model is underscored.

Task	Team	Performance
Detection	ZZU-NLP	.850
	ZZU-NLP_DS	.741
	Cloud Lab	.720
	YNU-HPCC	.714
	Prompt	.712
	MAP-Neo	.653
Classification	ZZU-NLP	.646
	Team0071	.548
	Hu	.531
	MAP-Neo	.526
	YNU-HPCC	.509
	Prompt	.505
Mitigation	ZZU-NLP	.294
	Team0071	.293
	YNU-HPCC	.293
	Prompt	.288
	IR901	.271
	MAP-Neo	.091
Overall	ZZU-NLP	.597
	YNU-HPCC	.505
	Prompt	.502
	Cloud Lab	.479
	ZZU-NLP_DS	.472
	MAP-Neo	.423

our baseline model MAP-Neo. For each task, a representative evaluation metric is selected to compare model performance across teams. Specifically, for the detection and classification tasks—both formulated as binary classification problems—the F1 score is used as the primary performance metric. For the mitigation task, model performance is assessed using the average of BLEU, METEOR, and ROUGE-L F1 scores. An overall ranking is then derived by averaging each team's scores across the three tasks. The results demonstrate that Team ZZU-NLP achieved the highest performance in all three tasks, thereby securing the top overall position in the shared task.

Notably, while many teams achieved strong results in the detection task, performance declined considerably in the classification task, with some models even falling below the baseline. Furthermore, the performance remain consistently low across all submissions for the mitigation task. This performance discrepancy supports the validity of our stepwise three-task framework, which introduces increasing complexity in a reasonable and structured difficulty progression. Furthermore, the outcomes underscore the persistent challenges in accurately identifying and effectively mitigating gender bias in Chinese-language texts. They highlight the need for models to possess both a deep understanding of gender bias and advanced linguistic capabilities to identify and appropriately revise gender-biased content.

7   Conclusion

We introduce CORGI-PM, the first Chinese human-annotated corpus designed specifically for probing and mitigating gender bias in text. This corpus also serves as the basis for defining and evaluating metrics across three challenges, aimed at testing the performance of state-of-the-art language models in detecting, classifying, and mitigating textual gender bias. Our proposed challenges are intended to establish benchmarks for assessing the capabilities of language models in this domain. Our experiments and the submissions demonstrate that the fine-grained subclass labels in our sentences enhance the models' ability to probe for gender bias, while our parallel, human-written debiased data provides robust supervision for training generative language models. We also analyze the performance of submissions from participating teams. The results highlight the persistent challenges in identifying and mitigating gender bias in Chinese corpora, underscoring the value of our work. In conclusion, we suggest that future research utilizing CORGI-PM could significantly advance the field of NLP by improving methods for both probing and mitigating gender bias in textual data.

Limitations

There are several major limitations in this research work. Due to the high requirement of annotators for annotating gender-biased sentences and correcting such sentences, we only choose annotators with higher education, which may lead to potential cognitive bias. In addition, CORGI-PM mainly focuses on gender bias but has not explored the bias phenomenon across different domains or disciplines, which could be potentially derived from the comprehensive benchmark for LLMs [11,35].

References

1. Agarwal, A., Lavie, A.: Meteor: an automatic metric for mt evaluation with high levels of correlation with human judgments. In: Proceedings of WMT-08 (2007)
2. Bai, J., et al.: Qwen technical report. arXiv preprint arXiv:2309.16609 (2023)
3. Blodgett, S.L., Barocas, S., Daumé III, H., Wallach, H.: Language (technology) is power: a critical survey of "bias" in nlp. In: ACL, June 2020. https://www.microsoft.com/en-us/research/publication/language-technology-is-power-a-critical-survey-of-bias-in-nlp/
4. Bolukbasi, T., Chang, K.W., Zou, J.Y., Saligrama, V., Kalai, A.T.: Man is to computer programmer as woman is to homemaker? debiasing word embeddings. In: NIPS (2016)
5. Chiril, P., Benamara, F., Moriceau, V.: "be nice to your wife! the restaurants are closed": Can gender stereotype detection improve sexism classification? In: Findings of the Association for Computational Linguistics: EMNLP 2021, pp. 2833–2844 (2021)
6. Chiril, P., Moriceau, V., Benamara, F., Mari, A., Origgi, G., Coulomb-Gully, M.: An annotated corpus for sexism detection in French tweets. In: Proceedings of the 12th Language Resources and Evaluation Conference, pp. 1397–1403 (2020)
7. Costa-jussà, M.R.: An analysis of gender bias studies in natural language processing. Nature Mach. Intell. **1**(11), 495–496 (2019)
8. Cui, Y., Che, W., Liu, T., Qin, B., Wang, S., Hu, G.: Revisiting pre-trained models for chinese natural language processing. arXiv preprint arXiv:2004.13922 (2020)
9. Dixon, L., Li, J., Sorensen, J., Thain, N., Vasserman, L.: Measuring and mitigating unintended bias in text classification. In: Proceedings of the 2018 AAAI/ACM Conference on AI, Ethics, and Society, AIES '18, pp. 67–73. Association for Computing Machinery, New York (2018). https://doi.org/10.1145/3278721.3278729
10. Dong, X., Wang, Y., Yu, P.S., Caverlee, J.: Disclosure and mitigation of gender bias in llms. arXiv preprint arXiv:2402.11190 (2024)
11. Du, X., et al.: Supergpqa: scaling llm evaluation across 285 graduate disciplines. arXiv preprint arXiv:2502.14739 (2025)
12. Gao, L., et al.: The pile: an 800gb dataset of diverse text for language modeling. arXiv preprint arXiv:2101.00027 (2020)
13. Jiang, A., Yang, X., Liu, Y., Zubiaga, A.: Swsr: a Chinese dataset and lexicon for online sexism detection. Online Soc. Networks Media **27**, 100182 (2022)
14. Jiao, M., Luo, Z.: Gender bias hidden behind Chinese word embeddings: the case of Chinese adjectives. In: Proceedings of the 3rd Workshop on Gender Bias in Natural Language Processing, pp. 8–15 (2021)
15. King, T.L., Scovelle, A.J., Meehl, A., Milner, A.J., Priest, N.: Gender stereotypes and biases in early childhood: a systematic review. Australas. J. Early Childhood **46**(2), 112–125 (2021)
16. Kiritchenko, S., Mohammad, S.: Examining gender and race bias in two hundred sentiment analysis systems. In: Proceedings of the Seventh Joint Conference on Lexical and Computational Semantics, pp. 43–53. Association for Computational Linguistics, New Orleans, Louisiana, June 2018. https://doi.org/10.18653/v1/S18-2005, https://aclanthology.org/S18-2005
17. Kotek, H., Dockum, R., Sun, D.: Gender bias and stereotypes in large language models. In: Proceedings of the ACM Collective Intelligence Conference, pp. 12–24 (2023)
18. Li, Y., Zhang, G., Yang, B., Lin, C., Ragni, A., Wang, S., Fu, J.: HERB: Measuring hierarchical regional bias in pre-trained language models. In: He, Y., Ji, H., Li, S., Liu, Y., Chang, C.H. (eds.) Findings of the Association for Computational Linguistics: AACL-IJCNLP 2022, pp. 334–346. Association for Computational Linguistics, Online only, November 2022. https://doi.org/10.18653/v1/2022.findings-aacl.32, https://aclanthology.org/2022.findings-aacl.32/

19. Lin, C.Y.: Rouge: A package for automatic evaluation of summaries. In: Text summarization branches out, pp. 74–81 (2004)
20. Lu, K., Mardziel, P., Wu, F., Amancharla, P., Datta, A.: Gender bias in neural natural language processing. In: Logic, Language, and Security, pp. 189–202. Springer (2020)
21. Madaan, N., Mehta, S., Agrawaal, T., Malhotra, V., Aggarwal, A., Gupta, Y., Saxena, M.: Analyze, detect and remove gender stereotyping from bollywood movies. In: Friedler, S.A., Wilson, C. (eds.) Proceedings of the 1st Conference on Fairness, Accountability and Transparency. Proceedings of Machine Learning Research, vol. 81, pp. 92–105. PMLR (23–24 Feb 2018), https://proceedings.mlr.press/v81/madaan18a.html
22. Papineni, K., Roukos, S., Ward, T., Zhu, W.J.: Bleu: a method for automatic evaluation of machine translation. In: Proceedings of the 40th annual meeting of the Association for Computational Linguistics, pp. 311–318 (2002)
23. Parikh, P., et al.: Multi-label categorization of accounts of sexism using a neural framework. arXiv preprint arXiv:1910.04602 (2019)
24. Parikh, P., et al.: Multi-label categorization of accounts of sexism using a neural framework. In: Proceedings of the 2019 Conference on Empirical Methods in Natural Language Processing and the 9th International Joint Conference on Natural Language Processing (EMNLP-IJCNLP), pp. 1642–1652. Association for Computational Linguistics, Hong Kong, China, November 2019. https://doi.org/10.18653/v1/D19-1174, https://aclanthology.org/D19-1174
25. Park, J.H., Shin, J., Fung, P.: Reducing gender bias in abusive language detection. In: Proceedings of the 2018 Conference on Empirical Methods in Natural Language Processing. pp. 2799–2804. Association for Computational Linguistics, Brussels, Belgium (Oct-Nov 2018). https://doi.org/10.18653/v1/D18-1302, https://aclanthology.org/D18-1302
26. Qiu, Y., Li, H., Li, S., Jiang, Y., Hu, R., Yang, L.: Revisiting correlations between intrinsic and extrinsic evaluations of word embeddings. In: Chinese Computational Linguistics and Natural Language Processing Based on Naturally Annotated Big Data, pp. 209–221. Springer (2018)
27. Rudinger, R., Naradowsky, J., Leonard, B., Van Durme, B.: Gender bias in coreference resolution. arXiv preprint arXiv:1804.09301 (2018)
28. Sahai, S., Sharma, D.: Predicting and explaining french grammatical gender. In: Proceedings of the Third Workshop on Computational Typology and Multilingual NLP, pp. 90–96 (2021)
29. Sharma, S., El Asri, L., Schulz, H., Zumer, J.: Relevance of unsupervised metrics in task-oriented dialogue for evaluating natural language generation. CoRR abs/1706.09799 (2017). http://arxiv.org/abs/1706.09799
30. Srivastava, A., et al.: Beyond the imitation game: quantifying and extrapolating the capabilities of language models. arXiv preprint arXiv:2206.04615 (2022)
31. Sun, T., et al.: Mitigating gender bias in natural language processing: Literature review. arXiv preprint arXiv:1906.08976 (2019)
32. Sun, T., et al.: Mitigating gender bias in natural language processing: Literature review. In: Proceedings of the 57th Annual Meeting of the Association for Computational Linguistics, pp. 1630–1640. Association for Computational Linguistics, Florence, Italy, July 2019. https://doi.org/10.18653/v1/P19-1159, https://aclanthology.org/P19-1159
33. Wake, A., et al.: Yi-lightning technical report. arXiv preprint arXiv:2412.01253 (2024)
34. Wan, Y., Pu, G., Sun, J., Garimella, A., Chang, K.W., Peng, N.: "Kelly is a warm person, joseph is a role model": gender biases in llm-generated reference letters. arXiv preprint arXiv:2310.09219 (2023)
35. Wang, Y., et al.: Mmlu-pro: A more robust and challenging multi-task language understanding benchmark. In: The Thirty-eight Conference on Neural Information Processing Systems Datasets and Benchmarks Track (2024)

36. Waseem, Z.: Are you a racist or am I seeing things? annotator influence on hate speech detection on Twitter. In: Proceedings of the First Workshop on NLP and Computational Social Science, pp. 138–142. Association for Computational Linguistics, Austin, Texas, November 2016. https://doi.org/10.18653/v1/W16-5618, https://aclanthology.org/W16-5618
37. Webster, K., Recasens, M., Axelrod, V., Baldridge, J.: Mind the gap: a balanced corpus of gendered ambiguous pronouns. Trans. Assoc. Comput. Linguist. **6**, 605–617 (2018)
38. Webster, K., Recasens, M., Axelrod, V., Baldridge, J.: Mind the GAP: A balanced corpus of gendered ambiguous pronouns. Trans. Assoc. Comput. Linguist. **6**, 605–617 (2018). https://doi.org/10.1162/tacl_a_00240, https://aclanthology.org/Q18-1042
39. Weidong, Z., Rui, G., Baobao, C., Yirong, C., Chen, L.: Development of Peking University CCL Corpus. In: Chinese Corpus Linguistic Journal (Jan 2019)
40. Xu, H., Zhang, Z., Wu, L., Wang, C.J.: The cinderella complex: word embeddings reveal gender stereotypes in movies and books. PLoS ONE **14**(11), e0225385 (2019)
41. Young, A., et al.: Yi: open foundation models by 01. ai. arXiv preprint arXiv:2403.04652 (2024)
42. Zhang, G., Li, Y., Wu, Y., Zhang, L., Lin, C., Geng, J., Wang, S., Fu, J.: Corgi-pm: A Chinese corpus for gender bias probing and mitigation (2023). https://arxiv.org/abs/2301.00395
43. Zhang, G., et al.: Map-neo: Highly capable and transparent bilingual large language model series. arXiv preprint arXiv:2405.19327 (2024)
44. Zhang, Z., Han, X., Liu, Z., Jiang, X., Sun, M., Liu, Q.: Ernie: enhanced language representation with informative entities. arXiv preprint arXiv:1905.07129 (2019)
45. Zhao, J., Wang, T., Yatskar, M., Ordonez, V., Chang, K.W.: Men also like shopping: reducing gender bias amplification using corpus-level constraints. In: Proceedings of the 2017 Conference on Empirical Methods in Natural Language Processing, pp. 2979–2989. Association for Computational Linguistics, Copenhagen, Denmark, September 2017. https://doi.org/10.18653/v1/D17-1323, https://aclanthology.org/D17-1323
46. Zhao, J., Wang, T., Yatskar, M., Ordonez, V., Chang, K.W.: Gender bias in coreference resolution: Evaluation and debiasing methods. In: Proceedings of the 2018 Conference of the North American Chapter of the Association for Computational Linguistics: Human Language Technologies, Volume 2 (Short Papers), pp. 15–20. Association for Computational Linguistics, New Orleans, Louisiana, June 2018. https://doi.org/10.18653/v1/N18-2003, https://aclanthology.org/N18-2003
47. Zhao, J., Zhou, Y., Li, Z., Wang, W., Chang, K.W.: Learning gender-neutral word embeddings. arXiv preprint arXiv:1809.01496 (2018)
48. Zhao, J., Du, B., Zhu, S., Liu, P.: Construction of Chinese sentence-level gender-unbiased data set and evaluation of gender bias in pre-training language. In: Proceedings of the 20th Chinese National Conference on Computational Linguistics, pp. 564–575 (2021)
49. Zhou, P., et al.: Examining gender bias in languages with grammatical gender. arXiv preprint arXiv:1909.02224 (2019)
50. Zhu, S., Liu, P.: Great males and stubborn females: a diachronic study of corpus-based gendered skewness in Chinese adjectives. In: Proceedings of the 19th Chinese National Conference on Computational Linguistics, pp. 31–42. Chinese Information Processing Society of China, Haikou, China, October 2020. https://aclanthology.org/2020.ccl-1.4

From Detection to Mitigation: Addressing Gender Bias in Chinese Texts via Efficient Tuning and Voting-Based Rebalancing

Chengyan Wu[1,2], Yiqiang Cai[1,2], Yufei Cheng[3], and Yun Xue[1,2(✉)]

[1] Guangdong Provincial Key Laboratory of Quantum Engineering and Quantum Materials, School of Electronic Science and Engineering (School of Microelectronics), South China Normal University, Guangdong, China
`{chengyan.wu,yiqiangcai}@m.scnu.edu.cn`
[2] Guangdong Provincial Key Laboratory of Intelligent Information Processing, Guangdong, China
`xueyun@m.scnu.edu.cn`
[3] School of Business, Yangzhou University, Yangzhou, China

Abstract. This paper presents our team's solution to Shared Task 7 of NLPCC-2025, which focuses on sentence-level gender bias detection and mitigation in Chinese. The task aims to promote fairness and controllability in natural language generation by automatically detecting, classifying, and mitigating gender bias. To address this challenge, we adopt a fine-tuning approach based on large language models (LLMs), efficiently adapt to the bias detection task via Low-Rank Adaptation (LoRA). In terms of data processing, we construct a more balanced training set to alleviate class imbalance and introduce heterogeneous samples from multiple sources to enhance model generalization. For the detection and classification sub-tasks, we employ a majority voting strategy that integrates outputs from multiple expert models to boost performance. Additionally, to improve bias generation detection and mitigation, we design a multi-temperature sampling mechanism to capture potential variations in bias expression styles. Experimental results demonstrate the effectiveness of our approach in bias detection, classification, and mitigation. Our method ultimately achieves an average score of 47.90%, ranking fourth in the shared task.

Keywords: Text Classification · Text Rewriting · Class-imbalance · Majority Voting

1 Introduction

With the widespread application of artificial intelligence technologies in real-world scenarios such as recruitment, question answering, translation, and recommendation, the issue of potential gender bias in models has increasingly attracted

---

C. Wu and Y. Cai—Equal contribution.

© The Author(s), under exclusive license to Springer Nature Singapore Pte Ltd. 2026
X.-L. Mao et al. (Eds.): NLPCC 2025, LNAI 16105, pp. 465–476, 2026.
https://doi.org/10.1007/978-981-95-3352-7_39

attention. Some researchers argue that identifying and preventing harmful gender bias is of significant societal importance [3]. Gender bias refers to a preference for or prejudice against one gender over another [21]. It manifests in various components of natural language processing (NLP) systems, including training data, pre-trained models, and algorithms [4,11,40]. Bias present in any of these components can lead to gender-biased predictions in NLP systems, sometimes even amplifying existing biases [39]. The propagation of gender bias through NLP algorithms poses the risk of reinforcing harmful stereotypes, thereby affecting downstream applications. This phenomenon can have serious real-world consequences; for example, there is concern that automated resume screening systems may exhibit a preference for male applicants when gender is the only distinguishing factor.

Since most gender bias in real life is expressed and disseminated through text, developing models capable of detecting and mitigating gender bias in textual content is particularly critical [36]. Researchers have proposed training models using gender-swapped corpora [18], though such methods heavily rely on the quality of the underlying models. To address this issue, some studies have adopted supervised training on manually annotated biased corpora, but these approaches tend to focus primarily on lexical-level bias [31]. Moreover, most existing methods have been developed for English and lack adaptation to Chinese [9]. With the recent rapid development of large language models (LLMs), such as GPT, Claude, and Deepseek, it has become feasible to employ LLMs for gender bias-related tasks. Trained on massive corpora, LLMs possess a deep understanding of complex linguistic phenomena and are capable of identifying subtle and implicit gender-discriminatory expressions.

In this work, we propose an LLM-based framework for detecting and mitigating gender bias in Chinese text. Our approach leverages the CORGI-PM dataset [36] and employs Low-Rank Adaptation (LoRA) to efficiently fine-tune the model for bias detection tasks. For the classification subtask, we address label imbalance through data recombination and improve performance via ensemble prediction using majority voting from multiple expert models. Furthermore, to enhance the diversity of generated de-biased texts, we design a multi-temperature sampling strategy that captures stylistic variations in biased expressions.

The contributions of this work are as follows:

- We propose a unified framework for Chinese gender bias probe and mitigation, utilizing parameter-efficient fine-tuning (LoRA) to adapt large language models across all subtasks with minimal computational overhead.
- To address label imbalance and ambiguity in the classification subtask, we design a data recombination approach combined with majority voting from multiple expert models, significantly enhancing classification robustness.
- For the mitigation subtask, we introduce a multi-temperature sampling strategy to increase the diversity and stylistic variation of bias-corrected outputs, improving both linguistic richness and bias coverage.

2   Related Work

2.1   Text Style Transfer

Previous approaches to Text Style Transfer (TST) can be categorized based on the type of training data used, namely parallel and non-parallel data methods. Parallel data-based methods typically adopt a sequence-to-sequence framework [28], which can be implemented using architectures such as Transformer [29] and LSTM [19]. However, due to the scarcity of parallel data in real-world scenarios, these methods are often impractical. Consequently, the majority of TST research focuses on non-parallel data. Non-parallel data methods primarily fall into three categories: prototype editing [13], disentanglement-based approaches [38], and pseudo-parallel corpus construction [12].

Recently, LLMs have transformed the landscape of TST in natural language processing. In exploring how to leverage LLMs for TST effectively, Reif et al. [26] enhanced LLM performance through few-shot prompting, while Liu et al. [16] proposed a dynamic prompt generation method to guide the model in producing text with the desired style. Although prompt engineering has proven useful, the performance of LLMs is highly sensitive to prompt variations [42], which may lead to instability in output quality. In contrast, using fine-tuned LLMs for TST has been shown to yield more consistent results. Motivated by these insights, this work adopts a hybrid approach, combining prompt-based guidance with further fine-tuning of the model to perform bias-mitigated style transfer for gender discrimination. This method integrates the strengths of both strategies, enabling the model to produce high-quality outputs while maintaining greater stability.

2.2   Text Classification

Text classification refers to the task of assigning predefined categories to text sequences. In recent years, with the rapid development of social networks, blogs, and forums, as well as the continuous expansion of online academic resource repositories, research on text classification has become increasingly important. Early approaches to text classification mostly relied on manually constructed features [20,24], and used machine learning algorithms for classification. For example, Chen et al. [6] employed simple logistic regression methods for classifying textual information, while Hinrich et al. [27], considering computational efficiency in machine learning, adopted a Naive Bayes classifier for document classification.

With the rise of deep learning models, text classification has entered a new stage of development. CNNs and RNNs are representative architectures in deep learning. Chen et al. [7] applied CNNs to sentence-level text classification tasks, extracting local features using multiple convolutional kernels. Given that CNNs are less effective in capturing long-range dependencies in text, Zhou et al. [41] proposed a hybrid CNN-RNN model for long-text classification tasks. With the advancement of LLMs, researchers have also begun using these models for text classification tasks. Devlin et al. [10] introduced the BERT model, which unified many NLP downstream tasks and has been widely applied to text classification. Raffel et al. [25] proposed the T5 framework, which reformulates text classification as a text generation task. Inspired by these developments, this study adopts an instruction-tuned large language model to determine whether a given sentence contains gender-biased content.

2.3 LoRA Framework

LLMs have achieved remarkable success in natural language processing tasks [8], demonstrating powerful emergent abilities [32]. However, directly training LLMs requires substantial computational resources. To address this, various fine-tuning methods have been proposed to reduce resource demands, with an increasing number of researchers adopting lightweight fine-tuning techniques to adapt LLMs to different downstream tasks.

For the task of gender bias detection and mitigation, this work employs LoRA for fine-tuning. LoRA works by keeping the original model weights frozen and introducing trainable low-rank decomposition matrices as adapter modules at each layer of the model. Compared to the base LLM, these adapter modules contain significantly fewer trainable parameters, enabling efficient adaptation to new tasks with limited data. Compared to earlier tuning methods such as Prefix-Tuning [14] and P-Tuning v2 [17], LoRA offers advantages including fewer modified layers and easier training, making it a more efficient and scalable fine-tuning approach.

3 Methods

In this section, we first define the task, followed by a detailed description of our proposed method. The architecture of our model is illustrated in Fig. 1. Overall, we propose a fine-tuning strategy for LLMs that integrates efficient adaptation with class-balancing techniques. We also describe the majority voting strategy employed in our approach.

3.1 Problem Statement

The task focuses on detecting, classifying, and mitigating gender bias in Chinese texts, and is structured into three subtasks:

Bias Detection. Given a sentence, the model is required to determine whether it contains gender bias. Each input sentence is labeled as either biased (B) or non-biased (N). The output is a boolean value: **true** if the sentence contains gender bias, and **false** otherwise.

Bias Classification. For sentences identified as biased, the model must further classify the bias into one or more predefined categories: (1) AC: Gender-stereotyped activities and career choices. (2) DI: Gender-stereotyped descriptions

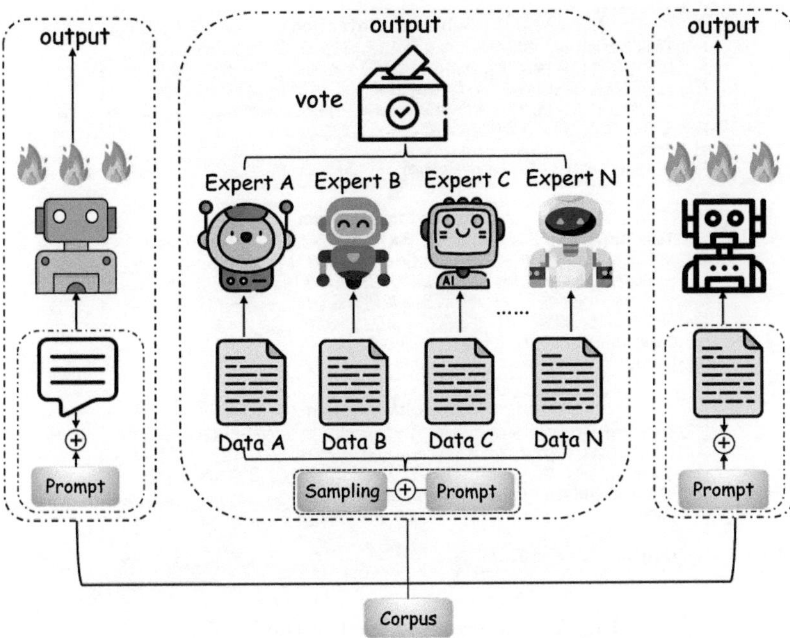

Fig. 1. The overall framework of the proposed method. From left to right, it illustrates the specific implementations of subtasks 1, 2, and 3.

and inductions. (3) ANB: Expressed gender-stereotyped attitudes, norms, and beliefs. The output is a multi-hot vector indicating the presence of each bias type (e.g.,[1, 0, 0] indicates the presence of the AC bias type.).

Bias Mitigation. Given a biased sentence, the goal is to generate a revised version that mitigates or removes the gender bias while preserving the original semantics. This may involve rewriting, substituting biased expressions, or adding neutralizing commentary.

3.2   Prompt Setting

Figure 2 illustrates the prompt design used in our framework. For all three subtasks, we adopt a unified prompt structure that consists of role-playing, task description, and test examples. Specifically, for subtasks 2 and 3, we convert the original multi-hot vectors into textual descriptions of bias types, enabling the model to interpret and process them in natural language form. In particular, the bias categories in subtask 3 are obtained based on the predictions from subtask 2 and subsequently incorporated into the model input.

3.3   Class Balance and Lora Fine-Tuning

For subtask 1, we perform efficient LoRA fine-tuning [30] on the model using 4,172 biased data instances. For subtask 2, the training set consisting of 21,418

Fig. 2. The prompts used in the LLMs.

unbiased instances is randomly split into five subsets. Each subset is then randomly combined with the biased data at approximately a 1:1 ratio to construct diverse training sets. In addition to preserving the completeness of the data, we also create a combined dataset that includes all biased and unbiased instances without any splitting. For subtask 3, we generate texts with different styles by varying the temperature settings.

3.4 Majority Voting

In text classification tasks within the field of natural language processing, voting mechanisms are commonly employed as ensemble strategies to aggregate predictions from multiple models and improve overall performance. For instance, Onan and Wu et al. [22,33,34] proposed a weighted voting scheme for sentiment analysis, where model outputs are combined with different weights to enhance classification accuracy. Similarly, Yin et al. [35] leveraged prompt engineering techniques with large language models (LLMs) and adopted a majority voting strategy for multi-label classification of social media texts, achieving notable improvements in model performance.

The core advantage of such methods lies in their ability to allow each individual expert to focus on different subspaces or characteristics of the training data. This fosters diversity among models while enhancing the robustness of the overall system. Inspired by ensemble learning [1,5], our work incorporates a six-expert voting system, where each expert is fine-tuned on a differently restructured version of the training dataset. This diversification results in experts having distinct predictive preferences and biases. However, due to class imbalance or the presence of rare categories, some experts may struggle with specific classes, making single-expert predictions unreliable.

To address this issue, we design a majority voting mechanism: when more than three out of six experts agree on a prediction, we take this majority decision as the final output. In cases where no majority is formed, the system retains the original confidence scores for downstream processing. This strategy effectively mitigates overfitting to specific training features by individual experts, and enhances the generalization capability and stability of the model, particularly in challenging bias-type classification tasks.

4   Experiments

4.1   Datasets

The CORGI-PM dataset [37] consists of Chinese sentences collected from diverse sources such as social media and news commentaries, with a focus on gender bias in the Chinese socio-cultural context. The dataset contains approximately 329,000 sentences, each annotated with high-quality labels by annotators with backgrounds in linguistics and gender studies, using an annotation scheme specifically designed for gender bias. The annotations include the type of bias, the target of the bias, and fine-grained subcategory labels, enabling deeper understanding and analysis of gender bias in text. The entire dataset is divided into training, validation, and test sets to ensure robust and fair evaluation. Table 1 presents more detailed statistics of the dataset.

Table 1. Size of sentences for the official datasets.

	# biased	# non-biased	Total
Train	4172	21418	25590
Dev	516	516	1032
	subtask1	**subtask2&3**	**Total**
Test	200	200	400

4.2   Training Details

We use the `Qwen2.5-7B-Instruct`[1] model, with a learning rate of 3×10^{-4}, batch size of 8, and 4 training epochs. The inference temperature is set to 0.1 for subtasks 1 and 2, while for subtask 3, the temperature values range over {0.01, 0.1, 0.3} (As shown in Table 4). Our experiments are conducted using the `PyTorch` deep learning framework, and we adopt a mainstream LoRA fine-tuning strategy. Notably, we employ the `llama-factory`[2] tool to facilitate model training.

---

[1] https://huggingface.co/Qwen/Qwen2.5-7B-Instruct.
[2] https://github.com/hiyouga/LLaMA-Factory.

Table 2. Top-4 official overall result of NLPCC2025 Task7.

Rank	System Name	Task1 Score	Task2 Score	Task3 Score	Average Score
1	ZZU-nlp	0.850	0.646	0.294	0.597
2	YNU-HPCC	0.714	0.509	0.293	0.505
3	Prompt	0.712	0.505	0.288	0.502
4	Cloud Lab	0.720	0.453	0.265	0.479

Table 3. Precision, Recall and F1 score of experiments for subtask 1.

Rank	System Name	Precision	Recall	F1
1	ZZU-nlp	0.798	0.910	0.850
2	Cloud Lab	0.566	0.990	0.720
3	YNU-HPCC	0.645	0.800	0.714
4	Prompt	0.552	1.000	0.712

4.3   Evaluation Metrics

Tasks related to gender bias are typically evaluated using different metrics depending on the subtask: detection and classification tasks are assessed using the F1 score, while mitigation tasks are evaluated based on the average of BLEU, METEOR, and ROUGE-L F1 scores.

BLEU [23] is an automatic evaluation metric based on n-gram precision matching. In this metric, BP refers to the brevity penalty, which is used to penalize excessively short outputs, and p_n represents the n-gram precision score.

$$BLEU = BP \cdot \exp\left(\sum_{n=1}^{N} w_n \cdot \log p_n \right) \tag{1}$$

METEOR [2] is an evaluation metric designed to assess the quality of generated text, primarily developed to address the limitations of early metrics such as BLEU. The core formula is shown below, where F denotes the weighted harmonic mean, and Penalty represents the penalty term.

$$METEOR = F_{\mathrm{mean}} \cdot (1 - \text{Penalty}) \tag{2}$$

Table 4. Performance of each subtask at different temperatures.

Temperature	Task1 Score	Task2 Score	Task3 Score
0.01	0.720	0.453	0.394
0.1	0.720	0.453	0.393
0.3	0.720	0.453	0.392

ROUGE-L [15] is a variant of the ROUGE evaluation metric. The corresponding formula is shown below, where F1 denotes the harmonic mean of precision and recall, and LCS(X, Y) represents the length of the longest common subsequence between sequences X and Y.

$$R_{\text{LCS}} = \frac{\text{LCS}(X, Y)}{m} \tag{3}$$

$$P_{\text{LCS}} = \frac{\text{LCS}(X, Y)}{n} \tag{4}$$

$$F_{\text{LCS}} = \frac{(1 + \beta^2) \cdot R_{\text{LCS}} \cdot P_{\text{LCS}}}{R_{\text{LCS}} + \beta^2 \cdot P_{\text{LCS}}} \tag{5}$$

4.4   Results and Analysis

Tables 2, 3, 5, and 6 present the average overall scores and subtask-specific scores of the top four teams in terms of overall performance.

In subtask 1, our method ranks second in the final leaderboard, demonstrating the effectiveness of our fine-tuning strategy. We perform efficient fine-tuning based on the Qwen model, focusing on how different hyperparameter configurations affect performance in bias detection. In particular, our optimization in LoRA design and learning rate scheduling confirms the practical value of our efficient parameter search strategy.

In subtask 2, there exists a performance gap between our approach and the top-performing team. We adopt a data compression and reorganization strategy, restructuring the original dataset according to different bias categories and training multiple sub-models to perform classification. The final prediction is produced via a multi-expert voting mechanism. While this method improves the model's ability to identify common bias types, we reuse the same hyperparameters from subtask 1 without task-specific tuning, which limits the model's upper-bound performance. Furthermore, our approach to class imbalance considers only the ratio between biased and non-biased data, while overlooking the imbalance within the biased categories. We plan to address this by incorporating loss re-weighting, oversampling, and data augmentation strategies to enhance the model's recognition of long-tail categories.

In subtask 3, we also fine-tune the model and focus on the impact of generation strategies on the quality of bias mitigation. We fix most parameters and vary the temperature during generation to produce more diverse and expressive rewrites. Due to resource and submission constraints, we explore only three temperature values, which may not cover the optimal search space. Additionally, we retain the same training configuration used in subtask 1 without further tuning for text generation quality. In future work, we plan to introduce evaluation metrics such as BLEU, BERTScore, and MAUVE, and implement automatic temperature selection or multi-pass generation with reranking to improve the diversity and controllability of the outputs. Notably, the competition limits us to three final submissions, and we do not submit our best-performing configuration, indicating that our model still has room for further improvement.

Table 5. Precision, Recall and F1 score of experiments for subtask 2.

Rank	System Name	Precision	Recall	F1
1	ZZU-nlp	0.543	0.576	0.646
2	YNU-HPCC	0.463	0.565	0.509
3	Prompt	0.496	0.513	0.505
4	Cloud Lab	0.510	0.409	0.453

Table 6. BLEU, METEOR and ROUGE-L score of experiments for subtask 3.

Rank	System Name	BLEU	METEOR	ROUGE-L			Average
				Precision	Recall	F1	
1	ZZU-nlp	0.013	0.417	0.464	0.452	0.452	0.294
2	YNU-HPCC	0.013	0.414	0.472	0.448	0.453	0.293
3	Prompt	0.011	0.418	0.430	0.462	0.434	0.288
4	Cloud Lab	0.009	0.391	0.367	0.461	0.394	0.265

5 Conclusion

In this paper, we propose a unified framework for gender bias detection and mitigation, with a primary focus on the challenge of class imbalance. To address this, we design a simple yet effective prompt-based fine-tuning approach. Specifically, we recombine biased and unbiased samples to construct multiple resampled subsets, each of which is used to train an expert model based on a pretrained backbone. The final prediction is obtained via majority voting across these experts, which enhances the model's ability to recognize minority-class biases. In addition, we further improve performance through efficient hyperparameter tuning, including LoRA fine-tuning and temperature adjustments. Our team ranks fourth in the NLPCC-2025 Task 7 competition, demonstrating the effectiveness of the proposed approach in real-world scenarios.

References

1. Agbesi, V.K., Chen, W., Yussif, S.B., Ukwuoma, C.C., Gu, Y.H., Al-Antari, M.A.: Mutcelm: an optimal multi-textCNN-based ensemble learning for text classification. Heliyon **10**(19) (2024)
2. Banerjee, S., Lavie, A.: Meteor: an automatic metric for MT evaluation with improved correlation with human judgments. In: Proceedings of the ACL Workshop on Intrinsic and Extrinsic Evaluation Measures for Machine Translation and/or Summarization, pp. 65–72 (2005)
3. Blodgett, S.L., Barocas, S., Daumé III, H., Wallach, H.: Language (technology) is power: a critical survey of "bias" in NLP. arXiv preprint arXiv:2005.14050 (2020)
4. Bolukbasi, T., Chang, K.W., Zou, J.Y., Saligrama, V., Kalai, A.T.: Man is to computer programmer as woman is to homemaker? debiasing word embeddings. In: Advances in Neural Information Processing Systems **29** (2016)

5. Cang, Y., Yang, W., Sun, D., Ye, Z., Zheng, Z.: Albert-driven ensemble learning for medical text classification. J. Comput. Technol. Software **3**(6) (2024)

6. Chen, W., et al.: A comparative study of logistic model tree, random forest, and classification and regression tree models for spatial prediction of landslide suscep-tibility. CATENA **151**, 147–160 (2017)

7. Chen, Y.: Convolutional neural network for sentence classification. Master's thesis, University of Waterloo (2015)

8. Chu, Y., et al.: Qwen2-audio technical report. arXiv preprint arXiv:2407.10759 (2024)

9. Costa-Jussà, M.R.: An analysis of gender bias studies in natural language process-ing. Nat. Mach. Intell. **1**(11), 495–496 (2019)

10. Devlin, J., Chang, M.W., Lee, K., Toutanova, K.: Bert: pre-training of deep bidi-rectional transformers for language understanding. In: Proceedings of the 2019 conference of the North American Chapter of the Association for Computational Linguistics: Human Language Technologies, volume 1 (Long and Short Papers), pp. 4171–4186 (2019)

11. Garg, N., Schiebinger, L., Jurafsky, D., Zou, J.: Word embeddings quantify 100 years of gender and ethnic stereotypes. Proc. Natl. Acad. Sci. **115**(16), E3635–E3644 (2018)

12. Jin, Z., Jin, D., Mueller, J., Matthews, N., Santus, E.: IMAT: unsupervised text attribute transfer via iterative matching and translation. arXiv preprint arXiv:1901.11333 (2019)

13. Li, J., Jia, R., He, H., Liang, P.: Delete, retrieve, generate: a simple approach to sentiment and style transfer. arXiv preprint arXiv:1804.06437 (2018)

14. Li, X.L., Liang, P.: Prefix-tuning: Optimizing continuous prompts for generation. arXiv preprint arXiv:2101.00190 (2021)

15. Lin, C.Y.: Rouge: A package for automatic evaluation of summaries. In: Text Sum-marization Branches Out, pp. 74–81 (2004)

16. Liu, Q., Qin, J., Ye, W., Mou, H., He, Y., Wang, K.: Adaptive prompt routing for arbitrary text style transfer with pre-trained language models. In: Proceedings of the AAAI Conference on Artificial Intelligence. vol. 38, pp. 18689–18697 (2024)

17. Liu, X., et al.: P-tuning v2: prompt tuning can be comparable to fine-tuning uni-versally across scales and tasks. arXiv preprint arXiv:2110.07602 (2021)

18. Lu, K., Mardziel, P., Wu, F., Amancharla, P., Datta, A.: Gender bias in neural natural language processing. In: Logic, Language, and Security: Essays Dedicated to Andre Scedrov on the Occasion of His 65th Birthday, pp. 189–202 (2020)

19. Memory, L.S.T.: Sepp hochreiter and jürgen schmidhuber. Neural Comput. **9**(8), 1735 (1997)

20. Mikolov, T., Chen, K., Corrado, G., Dean, J.: Efficient estimation of word repre-sentations in vector space. arXiv preprint arXiv:1301.3781 (2013)

21. Moss-Racusin, C.A., Dovidio, J.F., Brescoll, V.L., Graham, M.J., Handelsman, J.: Science faculty's subtle gender biases favor male students. Proc. Natl. Acad. Sci. **109**(41), 16474–16479 (2012)

22. Onan, A., Korukoğlu, S., Bulut, H.: A multiobjective weighted voting ensemble classifier based on differential evolution algorithm for text sentiment classification. Expert Syst. Appl. **62**, 1–16 (2016)

23. Papineni, K., Roukos, S., Ward, T., Zhu, W.J.: Bleu: a method for automatic evaluation of machine translation. In: Proceedings of the 40th annual meeting of the Association for Computational Linguistics, pp. 311–318 (2002)

24. Pennington, J., Socher, R., Manning, C.D.: Glove: global vectors for word representation. In: Proceedings of the 2014 Conference on Empirical Methods in Natural Language Processing (EMNLP), pp. 1532–1543 (2014)
25. Raffel, C., et al.: Exploring the limits of transfer learning with a unified text-to-text transformer. J. Mach. Learn. Res. **21**(140), 1–67 (2020)
26. Reif, E., Ippolito, D., Yuan, A., Coenen, A., Callison-Burch, C., Wei, J.: A recipe for arbitrary text style transfer with large language models. arXiv preprint arXiv:2109.03910 (2021)
27. Schütze, H., Manning, C.D., Raghavan, P.: Introduction to Information Retrieval, vol. 39. Cambridge University Press, Cambridge (2008)
28. Sutskever, I., Vinyals, O., Le, Q.V.: Sequence to sequence learning with neural networks. In: Advances in Neural Information Processing Systems, vol. 27 (2014)
29. Vaswani, A., et al.: Attention is all you need. In: Advances in Neural Information Processing Systems, **30** (2017)
30. Wang, X., Aitchison, L., Rudolph, M.: Lora ensembles for large language model fine-tuning. arXiv preprint arXiv:2310.00035 (2023)
31. Webster, K., Recasens, M., Axelrod, V., Baldridge, J.: Mind the gap: a balanced corpus of gendered ambiguous pronouns. Trans. Assoc. Comput. Linguist. **6**, 605–617 (2018)
32. Wei, J., et al.: Chain-of-thought prompting elicits reasoning in large language models. Adv. Neural. Inf. Process. Syst. **35**, 24824–24837 (2022)
33. Wu, C., Fang, W., Dai, F., Yin, H.: A model ensemble approach with LLM for Chinese text classification. In: Xu, H., et al. (eds.) CHIP 2023. CCIS, vol. 2080, pp. 214–230. Springer, Singapore (2023). https://doi.org/10.1007/978-981-97-1717-0_20
34. Wu, C., Lin, Z., Fang, W., Huang, Y.: A medical diagnostic assistant based on LLM. In: China Health Information Processing Conference, pp. 135–147. Springer (2023)
35. Yin, K., Liu, C., Mostafavi, A., Hu, X.: Crisissense-LLM: instruction fine-tuned large language model for multi-label social media text classification in disaster informatics. arXiv preprint arXiv:2406.15477 (2024)
36. Zhang, G., et al.: Corgi-pm: a Chinese corpus for gender bias probing and mitigation. arXiv preprint arXiv:2301.00395 (2023)
37. Zhang, G., et al.: Corgi-PM: a Chinese corpus for gender bias probing and mitigation (2023). https://arxiv.org/abs/2301.00395
38. Zhang, Z., et al.: Style transfer as unsupervised machine translation. arXiv preprint arXiv:1808.07894 (2018)
39. Zhao, J., Wang, T., Yatskar, M., Ordonez, V., Chang, K.W.: Men also like shopping: Reducing gender bias amplification using corpus-level constraints. arXiv preprint arXiv:1707.09457 (2017)
40. Zhao, J., Wang, T., Yatskar, M., Ordonez, V., Chang, K.W.: Gender bias in coreference resolution: Evaluation and debiasing methods. arXiv preprint arXiv:1804.06876 (2018)
41. Zhou, C., Sun, C., Liu, Z., Lau, F.: A C-LSTM neural network for text classification. arXiv preprint arXiv:1511.08630 (2015)
42. Zhu, K., et al.: Promptrobust: towards evaluating the robustness of large language models on adversarial prompts. In: Proceedings of the 1st ACM Workshop on Large AI Systems and Models with Privacy and Safety Analysis, pp. 57–68 (2023)

A Progressive Framework for Addressing Gender Bias in Chinese NLP: Detection, Classification, and Mitigation

Chenyang Li[1], Junshuai Zhang[2], Long Zhang[2(✉)], and Qiusheng Zheng[2]

[1] Faculty of Artificial Intelligence in Education, Central China Normal University,
Wuhan, China
`cyl@mails.ccnu.edu.cn`
[2] School of Cyberspace Security, Zhongyuan University of Technology,
Zhengzhou, China
`{2023116731,zhanglong,zqs}@zut.edu.cn`

Abstract. This paper aims to address the challenges of gender bias in the field of Chinese Natural Language Processing by proposing a methodology comprising three progressive tasks: gender bias detection, fine-grained bias classification, and bias mitigation. For the bias detection and classification tasks, this study employs the BERT language model as a foundation and introduces a Fast Gradient Method (FGM) adversarial training strategy to enhance model robustness. Through a five-model ensemble strategy based on predetermined model ranking and hierarchical decision-making principles, precise identification of gender bias in text and in-depth analysis of bias types are achieved. For the bias mitigation task, this study leverages Large Language Models (LLMs), guiding them with carefully designed few-shot prompts to rewrite biased text into neutral and fluent expressions. This research aims to provide a systematic solution for gender bias governance in the Chinese NLP domain, promoting the development of fairer and more inclusive language technologies. This progressive framework, moving from detection to detailed classification and then to active mitigation, allows for a more comprehensive approach to tackling gender bias compared to addressing each stage in isolation, reflecting the comprehensiveness and depth of the methodology.

Keywords: Gender Bias Detection · Bias Classification · Large Language Models · Adversarial Training

1 Introduction

Gender bias is prejudice based on gender, often expressed through explicit or implicit gendered language (such as pronoun usage implying that a specific gender possesses inherent traits like leadership) [1], erroneously attributing certain traits to a specific gender, thereby reinforcing social stereotypes and exacerbating systemic inequality [2]. Gender bias issues are prevalent in Chinese

© The Author(s), under exclusive license to Springer Nature Singapore Pte Ltd. 2026
X.-L. Mao et al. (Eds.): NLPCC 2025, LNAI 16105, pp. 477–487, 2026.
https://doi.org/10.1007/978-981-95-3352-7_40

Natural Language Processing [3] and are complicated by the scarcity of high-quality annotated datasets [4] and the tendency of pre-trained models to amplify existing biases [5]. Furthermore, unique Chinese linguistic phenomena such as homophonous third-person pronouns in spoken language (tā for he/she/it), and gender stereotypes embedded in certain characters, words, and titles [6], intertwined with deep-seated socio-cultural factors, pose unique challenges for bias governance, requiring careful consideration [7].

This study aims to systematically address the issue of gender bias in Chinese text, focusing on robust gender bias detection and fine-grained classification of bias types. It proposes the RobustBERT-Fusion method. This method, built upon the BERT pre-trained language model [8], introduces an FGM adversarial training strategy [9], compelling the model to learn more fundamental and robust bias patterns. Concurrently, it proposes a five-model ensemble strategy based on predetermined model ranking and hierarchical decision-making principles to further optimize overall performance [10]. To mitigate gender bias in text, it proposes a rewriting approach, the FairFewshot-Gen method. This method, based on multiple large language models [11], is guided by few-shot prompts [12]. It constructs prompts containing clear task instructions and 15 high-quality examples. Through an iterative optimization strategy, it guides the rewriting process to generate new sentences from the original ones with gender bias eliminated.

2   Task Definition

2.1   Sub-task 1: Gender Bias Detection

The core objective of this sub-task is to train a model that can automatically identify whether a given Chinese sentence contains gender bias. The model needs to analyze the input sentence and ultimately output a binary classification result: whether the sentence is Biased (B) or Non-biased (N). Data samples are shown in Fig. 1.

Input: This thought began to burn her like a flame; she could no longer control herself—pride, self-esteem, vanity, restraint... all melted away.
Output: Biased

Fig. 1. Gender Bias Detection.

2.2   Sub-task 2: Gender Bias Classification

Building upon Sub-task 1 (bias detection), Sub-task 2 aims to conduct a deeper and more detailed analysis of those sentences already identified as containing gender bias. Its core objective is to further classify these biased sentences into three predefined specific bias categories, including AC, DI, and ANB. Data samples are shown in Fig. 2.

> **Input:** This thought began to burn her like a flame; she could no longer control herself—pride, self-esteem, vanity, restraint... all melted away.
> **Output:** DI (Gender stereotypes in descriptions/inductions)

Fig. 2. Gender Bias Classification.

2.3   Sub-task 3: Gender Bias Mitigation

The core objective of this sub-task is to develop a model capable of mitigating or eliminating gender bias in a given Chinese sentence. The model needs to process the input gender-biased sentence, using methods such as word replacement, sentence rewriting, rephrasing, or (in a broader sense) providing a more neutral and objective "commentary-style" alternative version, to generate a new version of the sentence that is free of gender bias or has significantly reduced gender bias. The final output should strive to eliminate bias while preserving the core semantic information of the original sentence as much as possible, and ensuring the fluency and naturalness of the generated text. Data samples are shown in Fig. 3.

> **ori_sentence:** This thought began to burn her like a flame; she could no longer control herself—pride, self-esteem, vanity, restraint... all melted away.
> **edit_sentence:** This thought began to burn like a flame; the protagonist could no longer control themselves—pride, self-esteem, vanity, restraint... all melted away.

Fig. 3. Gender Bias Mitigation.

3   Model Architecture

3.1   RobustBERT-Fusion

To optimize the performance of bias detection and bias type analysis, enhance generalization ability, and improve system stability, we propose RobustBERT-Fusion. This framework adopts a five-model ensemble strategy [13] based on predetermined model ranking and hierarchical decision-making principles [14], leveraging 'collective intelligence' to enhance judgment. This strategy selects five Chinese BERT models (ERNIE [15], BERT-wwm [16], RoBERTa-wwm-ext [17], MacBERT [18], and NEZHA [19]). For each model, Fast Gradient Method (FGM) adversarial training is introduced—aiming to enhance its resistance to subtle textual perturbations and learn more fundamental bias patterns.

Afterward, they are pre-ranked based on their performance on a validation set. When predicting new samples, the system makes hierarchical decisions based on the degree of consensus among the five models' votes: if there is a unanimous vote (5-0) or an absolute majority (4-1), the majority opinion is adopted. When the vote results in a simple majority (3-2), the judgment of the highest-ranked model in the predetermined ranking serves as the final decision. This ensemble strategy forms a dual-guarantee system. It combines the robustness of individual models enhanced by FGM with the intelligent decision-making capabilities of hierarchical integration (especially the decisive power of high-ranking models in critical disagreements). This aims to comprehensively improve detection accuracy and ensure more reliable judgments when faced with complex and ambiguous expressions of bias. The model framework is shown in Fig. 4.

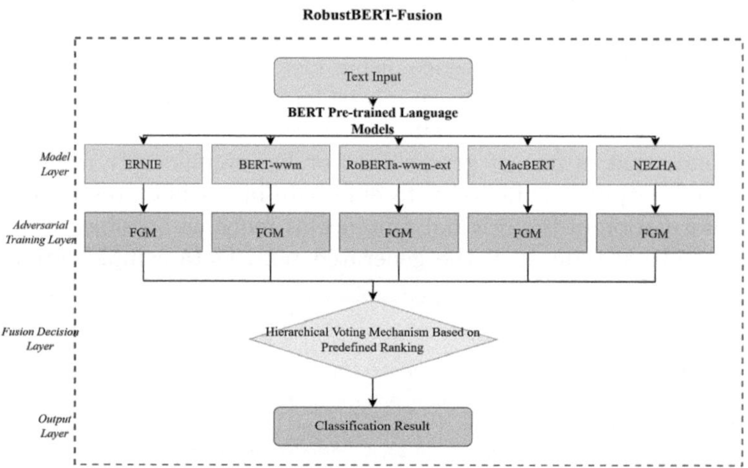

Fig. 4. RobustBERT-Fusion Model Framework.

3.2   FairFewshot-Gen

To effectively guide Large Language Models (LLMs) in performing bias mitigation tasks, we propose FairFewshot-Gen, a framework that employs a Few-Shot Prompting strategy. This strategy provides the LLM with in-context learning [20] by including clear task instructions and 15 high-quality 'biased sentence-mitigated sentence' pairs as 'live examples' in the input prompt. This specifically demonstrates the desired output characteristics (neutral, fluent, and accurately debiased) to the LLM without requiring updates to the model parameters. The key to achieving high-quality bias mitigation lies in an iterative optimization closed loop of 'prompt-generate-evaluate-adjust': this process involves not only the continuous optimization of task instruction wording and example selection but also the meticulous adjustment of LLM decoding parameters. For instance, a lower temperature value is typically chosen to ensure output determinism and fidelity, complemented by an appropriate top-p parameter to balance the diversity and coherence of the generated text. This ensures that the LLM achieves the desired effect on this complex and somewhat subjective task. The model framework is shown in Fig. 5.

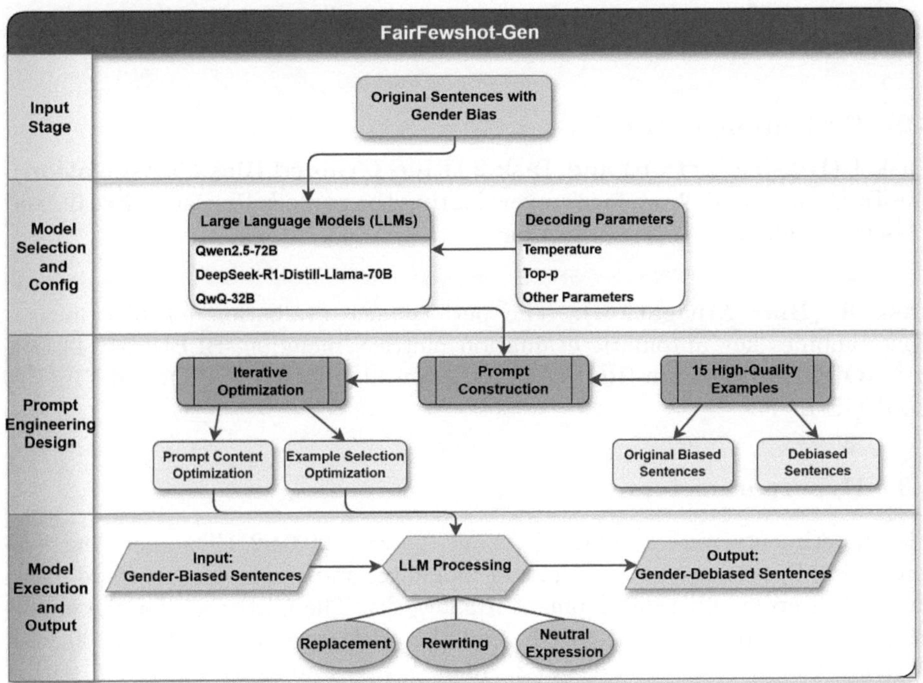

Fig. 5. FairFewshot-Gen Model Framework.

4 Experimental Setup

4.1 Dataset

Task 1 and Task 2: This study uses the officially provided dataset for model training and validation. For Task 1 (gender bias binary classification detection), the training set contains 21,418 non-biased texts and 4,172 biased texts. The validation set consists of 516 non-biased and 516 biased texts to achieve a balanced evaluation. Building on this, Task 2 (fine-grained bias classification) uses all biased samples from Task 1's training and validation sets (4,172 and 516 samples, respectively) as its initial training and validation data. These samples are further annotated into three predefined subcategories: gender stereotypes in activities/career choices (AC), descriptions/inductions (DI), or attitudes/norms/beliefs (ANB). To further enhance the training data for Task 2, we additionally performed fine-grained AC/DI/ANB annotation on 200 biased samples from Task 1's original test set, which were not used in Task 1's training or validation phases. These were then added to Task 2's training data, expanding the total training sample size for Task 2 to 4,372.

Task 3: For Task 3 (bias mitigation), this study's data application focuses on constructing efficient Few-Shot Prompts. Specifically, we meticulously selected 15 high-quality examples from the 4,688 data records provided by the officials.

4.2 Evaluation Metrics

Task 1 (Bias Detection) and Task 2 (Fine-Grained Bias Classification): For Task 1 and Task 2, we focus on evaluating the model's Precision, Recall, and F1-score in identifying bias categories.

Task 3 (Bias Mitigation): The performance evaluation for bias mitigation combines key automatic evaluation metrics, including BLEU, METEOR, and ROUGE-L Precision (ROUGE-L_P), Recall (ROUGE-L_R), and F1-score (ROUGE-L_F1).

4.3 Hyperparameters

The experiments were conducted on an Ubuntu 20.04.2 LTS operating system, using Python as the development language, and employing the Paddle and PyTorch deep learning development frameworks. The CPU used for the experiments was an Intel Core i7-9700F, and the GPU was an NVIDIA V100 with 32 GB of VRAM. For Tasks 1 and 2, AdamW was used as the optimizer, with a batch size set to 4, a learning rate of 3×10^{-5}, maxlen set to 512, and 15 epochs. For Task 3, the batch size was set to 32, the learning rate was set to 2×10^{-5}, and maxlen set to 512.

5 Results and Analysis

5.1 Results for Task 1 (Gender Bias Detection)

Table 1. Results for Task 1 (Gender Bias Detection).

Model	Precision	Recall	F1
RobustBERT	0.538	1.000	0.699
RobustBERT-Fusion	0.552	1.000	0.712

The RobustBERT-Fusion model proposed in this study exhibits unique performance characteristics in the gender bias detection task. Experimental results show that the model achieved a Recall of 1.000 in identifying biased categories, with a Precision of 0.552, and a comprehensive F1-score of 0.712. This result clearly reveals the model's core strengths and areas for improvement: it can comprehensively capture all actual gender bias samples, ensuring high sensitivity to potentially harmful content. However, the relatively low precision also suggests a certain level of false positives in its judgments, meaning some non-biased content is mistakenly identified as biased. Nevertheless, the F1-score of 0.712 still indicates that the model achieves a good level of overall performance. Based on the performance of the current model's perfect recall but moderate accuracy, in the future, the accuracy can be optimized by requiring 4/5 model consistency and setting a 0.8 confidence threshold for 3-2 divergence situations to reduce misjudgment. The evaluation results are shown in Table 1.

The trade-off between the model's perfect recall and moderate precision is a common challenge in the field of bias detection, potentially influenced by a combination of specific design strategies adopted in this study. Firstly, the adopted five-model (ERNIE, BERT-wwm, RoBERTa-wwm-ext, MacBERT, and NEZHA) hierarchical decision fusion strategy, especially giving the highest pre-ranked model decisive power when votes are close (e.g., 3-2), might lead to a tendency to classify borderline or ambiguous cases as biased to maximize risk aversion. Secondly, the uniform application of Fast Gradient Method (FGM) adversarial training to all base models, while significantly enhancing their resistance to subtle textual perturbations and prompting them to learn more fundamental bias features, might also have unintentionally lowered the model's sensitivity threshold for potential bias signals, leading to over-generalization on some neutral or borderline expressions, thereby causing misjudgments.

5.2   Results for Task 2 (Fine-Grained Bias Classification)

Table 2. Results for Task 2 (Fine-grained Bias Classification).

Model	Precision	Recall	F1
RobustBERT	0.494	0.487	0.491
RobustBERT-Fusion	0.496	0.513	0.505

On the fine-grained gender bias classification task (Task 2), the RobustBERT-Fusion framework achieved a Precision of 0.496, a Recall of 0.513, and an F1-score of 0.505. These figures indicate that the model achieved a moderate level of overall performance in distinguishing among the three predefined bias subcategories (AC, DI, ANB). The similar values for Precision and Recall reflect that the model does not show a particular tendency between misclassifying one bias subcategory as another (affecting precision) and failing to identify all instances of a specific subcategory (affecting recall), indicating a relatively balanced overall judgment. The evaluation results are shown in Table 2.

Although the RobustBERT-Fusion framework demonstrated a certain capability in fine-grained bias identification, the F1-score of 0.505 also reveals that this three-way classification task is significantly more complex than the binary bias detection in Task 1. The current performance level may be influenced by several factors: firstly, subtle semantic differences and overlaps might exist among the three bias categories (AC, DI, ANB), increasing the difficulty for the model to accurately distinguish them; secondly, although data augmentation increased the training samples to 4,372, the data volume (especially for certain specific subcategories) might still be insufficient for training five large-scale BERT models to achieve high precision on such a detailed three-way classification task; furthermore, while FGM adversarial training and the hierarchical fusion strategy aim to enhance robustness and accuracy, their optimal configuration for this multi-classification task and their specific contributions to performance still have room for further optimization and in-depth analysis.

Based on Fig. 6 analysis, the most commonly confused stereotypes (ACs) are misclassified as discriminatory language (DI), with 48 samples of such errors occurring, indicating that the model has difficulties in distinguishing these two types of biases with similar semantics. Overall, the model has the strongest ability to identify bias hypothesis (ANB), while the most difficult to identify stereotypes (AC). This may be because there are overlapping features in language expression between stereotypes and discriminatory language, making it difficult for the model to accurately distinguish the nuances of the two, and it is necessary to improve classification performance by improving feature extraction or enhancing training data for AC categories.

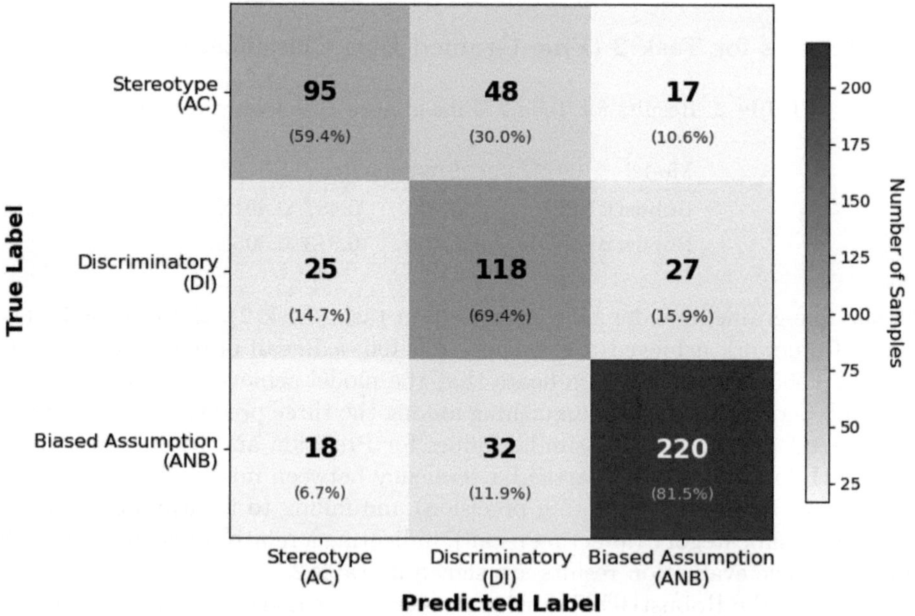

Fig. 6. Confusion Matrix Gender Bias Classification.

5.3   Results for Task 3 (Gender Bias Mitigation)

In the automatic evaluation for Task 3, the FairFewshot-Gen framework achieved a ROUGE-L_F1 score of 0.434, a BLEU score of 0.011, and a METEOR score of 0.418. The ROUGE-L_F1 and METEOR scores (0.434 and 0.418, respectively) indicate to some extent that there is lexical sequence overlap and a certain degree of semantic similarity between the model-generated mitigated text and the reference text. The METEOR score, in particular, which considers synonyms and stem matching, suggests that the model may have, to some extent, captured the desired semantic rewriting direction. However, the significantly low BLEU score (0.011) typically indicates a low degree of exact n-gram matching (especially for shorter, consecutive phrases) between the generated text and the reference text. This might reflect considerable differences in specific wording choices in the generated text, or that the mitigation strategy involved deep rewriting that significantly differs from the surface form of the reference text. The evaluation results are shown in Table 3.

Table 3. Results for Task 3 (Gender Bias Mitigation).

Model	ROUGE-L_F1	BLEU	METEOR
baseline(no fewshot)	0.370	0.008	0.389
FairFewshot-Gen	0.434	0.011	0.418

6   Conclusion

The main contribution of this study lies in proposing and validating two innovative multi-model collaborative frameworks to address the issue of gender bias in Chinese text. Firstly, for bias detection (Task 1) and fine-grained classification (Task 2), we designed the RobustBERT-Fusion framework: this framework innovatively integrates five diverse Chinese BERT models (ERNIE, BERT-wwm, RoBERTa-wwm-ext, MacBERT, and NEZHA) that have undergone FGM adversarial training. It fuses them through a set of decision rules based on predetermined model ranking and hierarchical voting, forming a dual guarantee that considers both individual model robustness and integrated intelligent decision-making. This framework achieved perfect recall in the bias detection task and promising performance in the fine-grained classification task. Secondly, for the bias mitigation task (Task 3), we constructed the FairFewshot-Gen framework. This framework systematically applies Large Language Models (LLMs) by combining Few-Shot Prompting, which includes 15 'in-context examples,' with an iterative 'prompt-generate-evaluate-adjust' optimization loop (covering prompt instructions, example selection, and decoding parameter tuning). This has preliminarily validated its potential in the task of rewriting biased Chinese text. In summary, these two frameworks provide a comprehensive solution—from detection and classification to mitigation—and a preliminary empirical basis for the identification, deep understanding, and effective handling of gender bias in the field of Chinese Natural Language Processing.

References

1. Doughman, J., Khreich, W., El Gharib, M., et al.: Gender bias in text: origin, taxonomy, and implications. In: Proceedings of the 3rd Workshop on Gender Bias in Natural Language Processing, pp. 34–44 (2021)
2. Sun, T., Gaut, A., Tang, S., et al.: Mitigating gender bias in natural language processing: literature review. arXiv preprint arXiv:1906.08976 (2019)
3. Chen, Y., Mahoney, C., Grasso, I., et al.: Gender bias and under-representation in natural language processing across human languages. In: Proceedings of the 2021 AAAI/ACM Conference on AI, Ethics, and Society, pp. 24–34 (2021)
4. Park, J.H., Shin, J., Fung, P.: Reducing gender bias in abusive language detection. arXiv preprint arXiv:1808.07231 (2018)
5. Chen, T., Hirota, Y., Otani, M., et al.: Would Deep generative models amplify bias in future models? In: Proceedings of the IEEE/CVF Conference on Computer Vision and Pattern Recognition, pp. 10833–10843 (2024)
6. Ye, S.: From maximality to bias: biased a-not-a questions in Mandarin Chinese. In: Semantics and Linguistic Theory, pp. 355–375 (2020)
7. Lu, K., Mardziel, P., Wu, F., et al.: Gender bias in neural natural language processing. In: Logic, Language, and Security: Essays Dedicated to Andre Scedrov on the Occasion of His 65th Birthday, pp. 189–202 (2020)
8. Devlin, J., Chang, M.W., Lee, K., et al.: Bert: pre-training of deep bidirectional transformers for language understanding. In: Proceedings of the 2019 Conference of the North American Chapter of the Association for Computational Linguistics: Human Language Technologies, Volume 1 (Long and Short Papers), pp. 4171–4186 (2019)
9. Miyato, T., Maeda, S., Koyama, M., et al.: Virtual adversarial training: a regularization method for supervised and semi-supervised learning. IEEE Trans. Pattern Anal. Mach. Intell. **41**(8), 1979–1993 (2018)
10. Yang, Y., Lv, H., Chen, N.: A survey on ensemble learning under the era of deep learning. Artif. Intell. Rev. **56**(6), 5545–5589 (2023)
11. Thakur, H., Jain, A., Vaddamanu, P., et al.: Language models get a gender makeover: mitigating gender bias with few-shot data interventions. arXiv preprint arXiv:2306.04597 (2023)
12. Liu, P., Yuan, W., Fu, J., et al.: Pre-train, prompt, and predict: a systematic survey of prompting methods in natural language processing. ACM Comput. Surv. **55**(9), 1–35 (2023)
13. Clark, C., Yatskar, M., Zettlemoyer, L.: Don't take the easy way out: ensemble based methods for avoiding known dataset biases. arXiv preprint arXiv:1909.03683 (2019)
14. Mahabadi, R.K., Belinkov, Y., Henderson, J.: End-to-end bias mitigation by modelling biases in corpora. arXiv preprint arXiv:1909.06321 (2019)
15. Zhang, Z., Han, X., Liu, Z., et al.: ERNIE: enhanced language representation with informative entities. arXiv preprint arXiv:1905.07129 (2019)

16. Zhang, Y., Liao, X., Chen, L., et al.: Multi-BERT-wwm model based on probabilistic graph strategy for relation extraction. In: Health Information Science: 10th International Conference, HIS 2021, Melbourne, VIC, Australia, October 25–28, 2021, Proceedings 10, pp. 95–103. Springer International Publishing (2021). https://doi.org/10.1007/978-3-030-90885-0_9
17. Liu, Y., Ott, M., Goyal, N., et al.: RoBERTa: a robustly optimized BERT pre-training approach. arXiv preprint arXiv:1907.11692 (2019)
18. Cui, Y., Che, W., Liu, T., et al.: Revisiting pre-trained models for Chinese natural language processing. arXiv preprint arXiv:2004.13922 (2020)
19. Wei, J., Ren, X., Li, X., et al.: Nezha: neural contextualized representation for Chinese language understanding. arXiv preprint arXiv:1909.00204 (2019)
20. Li, T., Zhang, G., Do, Q.D., et al.: Long-context LLMs struggle with long in-context learning. arXiv preprint arXiv:2404.02060 (2024)

Qwen-Gender: A Chain-of-Thought Based Multi-task Gender Bias Mitigation System

Ning Li, You Zhang[✉], Jin Wang, Dan Xu, and Xuejie Zhang

School of Information Science and Engineering, Yunnan University, Kunming, China
lining@stu.ynu.edu.cn, yzhang0202@ynu.edu.cn

Abstract. Gender bias mitigation is an integral aspect of ensuring fair and equitable technological outcomes from artificial intelligence (AI) and natural language processing (NLP) systems. While large language models (LLMs) have demonstrated exceptional performance across diverse domains, their reliance on few-shot and zero-shot inference paradigms often fails to address inherent biases, posing risks of perpetuating discriminatory outputs. To address this issue, we propose a multi-task framework called Qwen-Gender, designed for parameter-efficient fine-tuning of the Qwen2.5-7B-Instruct LLM to automate gender bias detection, classification, and mitigation. First, a multi-task chain-of-thought (CoT) prompting strategy that generates CoT-based analyses to guide model fine-tuning while preserving the model's foundational analytical capabilities. Next, a low-rank adaptation (LoRA) and a 4-bit quantization strategy are utilized to optimize multi-task collaboration without overburdening computational resources. Experimental results on the enhanced CORGI-PM dataset show that Qwen-Gender achieved second place in NLPCC 2025 Shared Task 7, demonstrating strong scalability and interpretability in Chinese gender bias mitigation tasks, and providing an effective pathway toward building fairer language model systems.

Keywords: Gender Bias Mitigation System · Chain-of-Thought Reasoning · Parameter-Efficient Fine-Tuning

1 Introduction

With the increasing integration of natural language processing (NLP) technologies into everyday applications, gender bias embedded in textual data and algorithmic models [1,3] poses a significant threat to the development of fairness, inclusion and the development of ethical artificial intelligence (AI) systems [15]. Addressing this issue requires robust, scalable systems that are capable of not only detecting biased language, but also categorizing and mitigating it in a semantically faithful manner [2].

To address this challenge in the context of the Chinese language, the CORGI-PM project constructed the first sentence-level Chinese corpus dedicated to the detection and mitigation of gender bias [18]. On this basis, NLPCC 2025 proposes

© The Author(s), under exclusive license to Springer Nature Singapore Pte Ltd. 2026
X.-L. Mao et al. (Eds.): NLPCC 2025, LNAI 16105, pp. 488–499, 2026.
https://doi.org/10.1007/978-981-95-3352-7_41

Table 1. An example in NLPCC Shared Task 7

Subtask	Input Example	Output Example
1	`{"text"`: "她讲起话来，总是尖声尖气，扭扭捏捏。"`}`	Label: B
	`{"text"`: "盲人中医师通过自学取得文凭。"`}`	Label: N
2	`{"ori_sentence"`: "剽悍的黑甲羽林卫仗剑立。"`}`	$[0,1,0] \Rightarrow$ DI
3	`{"ori_sentence"`: "剽悍的黑甲羽林卫仗剑立。"`}`	"高大的黑甲羽林卫仗剑立。"

Note: AC=gender stereotyped activity and career choices, DI=gender stereotyped descriptions and inductions, and ANB=expressed gender stereotyped attitudes, norms and beliefs

a comprehensive shared task that consists of three interrelated subtasks (as shown in Table 1): **Gender Bias Detection**, **Gender Bias Classification**, and **Gender Bias Mitigation**.

Although large language models (LLMs) perform well in many tasks, they usually rely on zero-shot or few-shot reasoning and are not specifically trained for bias detection tasks, making them difficult to cope with bias-related challenges [12]. In addition, comprehensive fine-tuning suffers from the "catastrophic forgetting" problem, which may weaken the model's original context learning and chain-of-thought (CoT) reasoning capabilities [21], and has high computational overhead.

To overcome the aforementioned limitations, this paper proposes Qwen-Gender, a multi-task framework based on the Qwen2.5-7B-Instruct model that leverages CoT prompting techniques [20] to achieve unified modeling of bias detection, classification, and mitigation [11]. The framework designs a hierarchical multi-task CoT prompt that sequences the three subtasks according to their difficulty and dependency, enabling the large language model to systematically uncover implicit biases in natural language texts and generate interpretable reasoning chains. Importantly, these CoT-based reasoning chains serve as guidance during model fine-tuning, helping to preserve the model's intrinsic reasoning capabilities while aligning it with bias analysis objectives. Furthermore, the framework incorporates parameter-efficient fine-tuning (PEFT) techniques, such as low-rank adaptation (LoRA) [6] and 4-bit quantization [17], to enhance training efficiency without sacrificing performance. Experimental results demonstrate that Qwen-Gender achieves strong performance across all three subtasks: detection F1 of 0.714, classification macro-F1 of 0.509, and mitigation average score of 0.293. Although lexical overlap is low (BLEU=0.013), high METEOR (0.414) and ROUGE-L (0.453) scores indicate effective preservation of semantic information during text rewriting.

Our main contributions include the following four aspects:

- We investigate the relatedness among three subtasks and propose a multi-task framework that mainly contains a multi-task CoT prompt for generating CoT-based analysis and instructing unified downstream task fine-tuning.
- To better leverage the instinctive reasoning capabilities of LLM, we augmented the original samples among three subtasks with CoT-based analysis, which guides the model for fine-tuning.
- The framework introduces LoRA and 4-bit-quantization strategies to optimize the LLM, reducing memory consumption and training costs without compromising the model's performance.
- Experimental results on the enhanced CORGI-PM dataset demonstrate the effect of our framework, which achieved second place in NLPCC 2025 Shared Task 7, highlighting its potential to advance fairness in AI systems.

2   Related Work

2.1   Recent Advances in Bias Detection and Mitigation

With growing attention to algorithmic fairness, the NLP community has increasingly prioritized the identification and mitigation of social biases embedded in both datasets and language models. Early research predominantly centered on English corpora, revealing gender, racial, and occupational stereotypes in word embeddings (e.g., Word2Vec, GloVe) and pre-trained models (e.g., BERT) [1,3]. These foundational studies introduced key bias evaluation metrics (e.g., WEAT, SEAT) and inspired diverse mitigation techniques, including data augmentation, embedding debiasing, and counterfactual training [7,10,13].

More recently, research efforts have expanded to address bias in multilingual and low-resource language contexts. In the Chinese domain, the CORGI-PM dataset marks a significant advancement, offering fine-grained annotations and comprehensive benchmarks across detection, classification, and mitigation tasks. Contemporary approaches increasingly emphasize explainability and controllability, leveraging human-in-the-loop reasoning and guided generation techniques to enhance both fairness and semantic fidelity [14,20].

2.2   CoT Reasoning for Bias Tasks

CoT prompting [20] is a recent technique that encourages large language models to break down complex reasoning tasks into intermediate steps. Initially developed for mathematical and logical reasoning, CoT has proven effective in interpretability-centric NLP tasks, such as bias detection and classification [19,22]. By explicitly prompting models to "think aloud," CoT improves both prediction accuracy and transparency, providing human-readable explanations that enhance trust in bias-sensitive applications.

Within bias mitigation, CoT enables a multi-step understanding process—first identifying the presence of bias, then diagnosing its category, and finally rewriting the biased content with contextual awareness. These explicit reasoning traces support both generalization and interpretability, benefiting developers and evaluators alike. Recent work, including ours, extends CoT by incorporating supervised fine-tuning on CoT-annotated corpora.

2.3 Parameter-Efficient Fine-Tuning and Quantization

PEFT methods, such as LoRA [6], provide a lightweight alternative to full model tuning, allowing the efficient adaptation of large language models under constrained computational budgets. LoRA operates by introducing trainable low-rank matrices into select layers (typically attention projections), thereby achieving substantial memory savings with minimal performance degradation.

To further improve memory efficiency, LoRA is often combined with quantization techniques such as 4-bit NormalFloat (NF4) quantization [17,24]. This hybrid strategy enables practical fine-tuning on consumer-grade hardware, while still supporting long-context reasoning and multi-task learning. Our framework adopts this approach to fine-tune Qwen2.5-7B-Instruct for integrated bias detection, classification, and rewriting.

Together, CoT reasoning and PEFT form the technical backbone of our approach, enabling scalable, interpretable, and high-performance gender bias mitigation in Chinese.

3 Methodology

3.1 Task Description

NLPCC-2025 Shared Task 7 addresses gender bias mitigation in Chinese texts through three interrelated subtasks:

- **Subtask 1. Gender Bias Detection**: A binary classification task requiring models to determine whether a given Chinese sentence contains gender-biased expressions.
- **Subtask 2. Gender Bias Classification**: For sentences annotated as containing gender bias, this multi-label classification task requires assigning one or more category labels from three fine-grained dimensions: gender stereotyped activity and career choices (AC), gender stereotyped descriptions and inductions (DI), and expressed gender stereotyped attitudes, norms and beliefs (ANB)
- **Subtask 3. Gender Bias Mitigation**: A text-to-text generation task demanding the system rewrite biased sentences into neutral equivalents while preserving original semantics.

For pursuing these tasks, we formulate them as follows, where the notation X, $D \in \{B/1, N/0\}$, $C = [C_{AC}, C_{DI}, C_{ANB}] \in \{0, 1\}$, and M represent input text, gender bias detection label, gender bias classification label, and gender-bias mitigated text of one sample in training dataset. For gender bias detection and classification tasks, the final prediction (i.e., 0 or 1) is obtained through X. For gender bias mitigation, the response M is generated with LLMs given M.

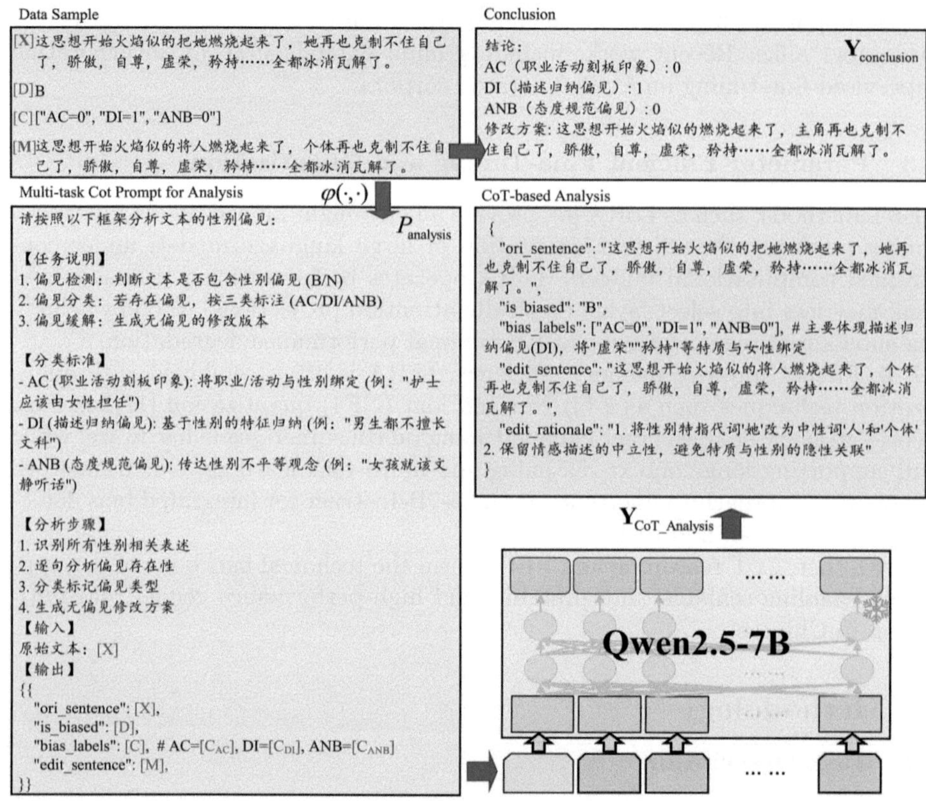

Fig. 1. Multi-task CoT-based Prompt for Analysis.

3.2 Qwen-Gender Model

In this section, we will introduce our method in the NLPCC 2025 Task 7, including two main procedures: CoT-based Analysis (Fig. 1) and Multi-task Fine Tune (Fig. 2). In the phase of CoT-based Analysis, the proposed framework utilizes data sample to generated CoT-based analysis. In the subsequent phase, we construct training samples by integrating each original input with its corresponding CoT-based analysis, thereby forming reasoning-aware data for model fine-tuning.

CoT-Based Analysis. Although subtasks 1-3 have distinct objectives, all three subtasks share the same input data and exhibit interrelated logical and difficulty-based dependencies. Specifically, subtask 1 to 2 represents a transition from coarse-grained to fine-grained bias identification, while Task 3 further refines the identified biases by performing bias mitigation based on the results obtained from the preceding tasks. To leverage the relationships among these tasks, this paper introduces a multi-task CoT prompt to guide the large language model in generating coherent and interpretable reasoning across subtasks, as shown in

CoT-based Data Sample

[X] 这思想开始火焰似的把她燃烧起来了，她再也克制不住自己了，骄傲，自尊，虚荣，矜持……全都冰消瓦解了。

[Y] {
    "ori_sentence": "这思想开始火焰似的把她燃烧起来了，她再也克制不住自己了，骄傲，自尊，虚荣，矜持……全都冰消瓦解了。",
    "is_biased": "B",
    "bias_labels": ["AC=0", "DI=1", "ANB=0"], # 主要体现描述归纳偏见(DI)，将"虚荣""矜持"等特质与女性绑定
    "edit_sentence": "这思想开始火焰似的将人燃烧起来了，个体再也克制不住自己了，骄傲，自尊，虚荣，矜持……全都冰消瓦解了。",
    "edit_rationale": "1.将性别特指代词'她'改为中性词'人'和'个体' 2.保留情感描述的中立性，避免特质与性别的隐性关联"
}

结论：
AC（职业活动刻板印象）：0
DI（描述归纳偏见）：1
ANB（态度规范偏见）：0
修改方案：这思想开始火焰似的燃烧起来了，主角再也克制不住自己了，骄傲，自尊，虚荣，矜持……全都冰消瓦解了。

Multi-task Cot Prompt for Fine Tune

$P_{finetune}$

请按照以下框架分析文本的性别偏见：

【任务说明】
1. 偏见检测：判断文本是否包含性别偏见 (B/N)
2. 偏见分类：若存在偏见，按三类标注 (AC/DI/ANB)
3. 偏见缓解：生成无偏见的修改版本

【分类标准】
- AC (职业活动刻板印象): 将职业/活动与性别绑定 (例："护士应该由女性担任")
- DI (描述归纳偏见): 基于性别的特征归纳 (例："男生都不擅长文科")
- ANB (态度规范偏见): 传达性别不平等观念 (例："女孩就该文静听话")

【分析步骤】
1. 识别所有性别相关表述
2. 逐句分析偏见存在性
3. 分类标记偏见类型
4. 生成无偏见修改方案
【输入】
原始文本：[X]
【输出】

[Y] $[\mathbf{Y}_{\text{CoT\_Analysis}} ; \mathbf{Y}_{\text{clusion}}]$

Qwen2.5-7B

LoRA

Hidden States $\mathbf{h'}$

W + B A

Hidden States $\mathbf{h}$

Fig. 2. Fine-tuning Qwen-Gender with LoRA-Enhanced Qwen2.5-7B.

Fig. 1. This prompt ensures that the model not only performs individual tasks effectively but also maintains a coherent and interpretable analysis across the entire pipeline [23].

As shown in Fig. 1, the multi-task CoT prompt is denoted as P_{analysis} for CoT reasoning. To guarantee input and output quality, we enforce a JSON-structured format for each sample d, which contains four field including "ori_sentence" for $\mathbf{X}$, "is_biased" for D, "bias_labels" for C, and "edit_sentence" for $\mathbf{M}$. To generate CoT-based analysis $\mathbf{Y}_{\text{CoT\_Analysis}}$, we first integrate P_{analysis} and d and then feed it into frozen Qwen2.5-7B-Instruct, formally:

$$\mathbf{Y}_{\text{CoT\_Analysis}} = \text{Qwen2.5} - 7\text{B} - \text{Instruct}(\varphi(P_{\text{analysis}}, \mathbf{X}, \text{D}, \text{C}, \mathbf{M})) \quad (1)$$

where $\varphi(\cdot, \cdot)$ represents the integration operations between prompts and samples. To ensure that the fine-tuning of downstream tasks can clearly obtain structured outputs, we introduce an additional summary of the output results, denoted as $P_{\text{conclusion}}$.

Multi-task Fine Tune. First, we construct CoT-based samples by aggregating the multi-task CoT prompt P_{finetune} and the input text $\mathbf{X}$ [19]. The output of each sample is formed by concatenating the corresponding conclusion output $\mathbf{Y}_{\text{conclusion}}$ and the CoT-based output $\mathbf{Y}_{\text{CoT\_Analysis}}$.

Inspired by PEFT methods that introduce a lightweight module to enable PLMs to be adapted to downstream tasks, we utilize the LoRA modules to implement our Qwen-gender frame-work. In detail, let $W \in R^{d_{in} \times d_{out}}$ be the pre-trained matrix weights in LLM, where d_{in} and d_{out} are the dimensionalities; $\mathbf{h}$ and $\mathbf{h}'$ be the hidden states as the inputs and outputs of W; $\Delta W = A \cdot B$ be the low-rank parameters of LoRA [6], where $A \in R^{d_{in} \times r}$, $B \in R^{r \times d_{out}}$, and $r \ll \min(d_{in}, d_{out})$. Therefore, corresponding adaptation can be formulated as:

$$\mathbf{h}' = W\mathbf{h} + \Delta W\mathbf{h} = (W + \Delta W)\mathbf{h} \tag{2}$$

During the training phase, only ΔW is updated while W is fixed. The final optimization loss function can be defined as:

$$\text{Loss}(\text{Qwen2.5} - 7\text{B} - \text{Instruct}(\varphi(P_{\text{finetune}}, \mathbf{X})), [\mathbf{Y}_{\text{CoT\_Analysis}}; \mathbf{Y}_{\text{conclusion}}]) \tag{3}$$

4   Experiment

4.1   Dataset and Evaluation Metrics

Dataset. The groundbreaking CORGI-PM dataset [16] establishes the first sentence-level Chinese corpus for gender bias detection and mitigation [25]. This enhanced version comprises the following components (Table 2):

Table 2. Dataset Composition

Dataset		Biased Samples	Non-biased Samples	Total
Training Set		4,172	21,418	25,590
Validation Set		516	516	1,032
Test Set	Detection Task	N/A	N/A	200
	Classification Task	200	0	200
	Mitigation Task	200	0	200

The training set consists of 25,590 texts, including 4,172 biased samples and 21,418 non-biased samples. The biased samples are annotated with triplets: original sentence (ori_sentence), multi-label bias types (bias_labels), and manually revised sentence (edit_sentence), whereas the non-biased samples are provided as plain text. These data cover a wide range of stereotypical gender expressions commonly found in Chinese contexts.

The validation set contains 1,032 class-balanced samples (516 biased and 516 non-biased), which are used for model selection and hyperparameter tuning. This balanced composition helps ensure stable evaluation across categories.

The test set is divided into two evaluation modules. The detection task includes 200 mixed-format samples requiring binary classification (biased and non-biased). The classification-mitigation task involves 200 biased samples in ori_sentence format, where models must predict multi-class bias labels and generate debiased versions of the input. Human-edited revisions serve as references for generative evaluation, such as replacing gendered pronouns like "她" with neutral terms like "主角".

To enhance robustness and simulate real-world deployment, external data integration is permitted during model development.

Evaluation Metrics. To comprehensively assess model performance on gender bias tasks, a phased multi-dimensional evaluation [8] framework is implemented:

- Bias Detection (Binary Classification). It evaluates Precision (proportion of true biased samples among identified cases) [5], Recall (ratio of correctly detected biased samples), and F1-score (harmonic mean) to quantify the system's accuracy and completeness in identifying gender-biased text [9].
- Bias Classification (Ternary Categorization). It computes macro-averaged Precision, Recall, and F1-score across three subcategories: AC, DI and ANB. This approach prevents evaluation bias caused by class imbalance.
- Bias Mitigation (Text Generation). It uses BLEU that measures surface-level similarity via n-gram overlap between generated and reference texts [13, 26], METEOR that enhances semantic evaluation through synonym matching and morphological variants, and ROUGE-L that assesses completeness of bias removal using longest common subsequence analysis.

The arithmetic mean of these three metrics ensures compliance with formal and semantic fidelity requirements, and serves as the basis for official rankings, which are determined by task-specific metrics: F1-scores for detection/classification tasks, and the average of BLEU, METEOR, and ROUGE-L F1 scores for mitigation evaluation.

4.2   Implementation Details

Subtask 1 and 2 Experimental Procedure. For Subtask 1 (Bias Detection) and Subtask 2 (Bias Classification), we use the prompt template introduced in the method section to guide the model in identifying three types of gender bias. The model generates a response containing a three-digit binary label representing the presence of each bias type.

We extract the prediction result by locating the three-digit label in square brackets following "Final Answer:". If no such label is found, a fallback regular expression is applied to capture the first valid three-digit 0/1 sequence. The result is parsed into a 3-dimensional bias label. For Subtask 1, a sample is considered biased if any of the three dimensions equals 1. The results are saved in JSON format.

During inference, we log the input, model response, and parsed result for each sample to facilitate debugging. Final outputs are stored in the specified directory[1]

Subtask 3 Experimental Procedure. For Subtask 3 (Bias Mitigation), we adopt the multi-step instruction prompt introduced in the method section to guide the model in identifying and revising gender-biased text while preserving the original meaning.

We use generation parameters of temperature of 0.7, top_p of 0.9, and a max length of 300 tokens. After generation, we extract the revised sentence using regular expressions. The original input, the model's revision, and the full output are saved for further evaluation. All results are stored in structured JSON files.

4.3   Results

Table 3. Detection, Classification and Mitigation final task results

Detection			Classification			Mitigation				
Precision	Recall	F1	Precision	Recall	F1	BLEU	METEOR	ROUGE-L		
								Precision	Recall	F1
0.645	0.8	0.714	0.463	0.565	0.509	0.013	0.414	0.472	0.448	0.453

The experimental results demonstrate differentiated performance across three subtasks. In the bias detection task, the model achieved its highest F1-score of 0.714, with recall reaching 0.8 while precision stood at 0.645 [4]. This pattern suggests strong coverage of potential biases alongside a noticeable tendency for false positives. For bias classification, the macro-average F1-score reached 0.509. The observed disparity between precision (0.463) and recall (0.565) reflects inherent class imbalance among the AC, DI, and ANB categories. Regarding bias mitigation, the metrics showed substantial divergence. The low BLEU-4 score of 0.013 indicates limited lexical overlap, whereas the METEOR score of 0.414 and ROUGE-L F1 score of 0.453 [13] collectively confirm the model's capability to preserve semantic content during text modification (Table 3).

---

[1] The code of this paper is available at: https://github.com/jiyuaner/YNU-HPCC-at-NLPCC2025.

Table 4 presents the comparative performance of our approach (YNU-HPCC) against other participating teams in the competition, Our method secured second place overall.

Table 4. Teams Ranking with Task Scores

Ranking	Name	Task1	Task2	Task3	Average
1	ZZU-nlp	0.850	0.646	0.294	0.597
2	**YNU-HPCC**	**0.714**	**0.509**	**0.293**	**0.505**
3	Prompt	0.712	0.505	0.288	0.502
4	Cloud Lab	0.720	0.453	0.265	0.479

Notably, while our team achieved the second-highest average score, the performance gap among the top three teams was relatively small (within 0.095 points). Our approach demonstrated balanced performance across all three tasks compared to other methods.

5 Conclusion

This study presents Qwen-Gender, a novel framework for gender bias mitigation in Chinese NLP systems through multi-task chain-of-thought reasoning and parameter-efficient fine-tuning of the Qwen2.5-7B-Instruct model. Our approach successfully addresses three critical challenges in bias mitigation: detection (achieving 0.714 F1-score), classification (0.509 macro-F1), and text rewriting (0.293 average generation score). The system's strong performance earned second place in NLPCC 2025 Shared Task 7, demonstrating particular strength in semantic preservation during bias mitigation (0.414 METEOR, 0.453 ROUGE-L) despite lower lexical overlap (0.013 BLEU). Future directions encompass cross-linguistic data expansion, hierarchical model architecture design, and refined evaluation metrics for generative mitigation tasks.

Acknowledgments. This work was supported by the National Natural Science Foundation of China (NSFC) under Grant Nos. 61966038 and 62266051. We would like to thank the anonymous reviewers for their constructive comments.

References

1. Bolukbasi, T., Chang, K.-W., Zou, J.Y., Saligrama, V., Kalai, A.T.: Man is to computer programmer as woman is to homemaker? arXiv preprint arXiv:1607.06520 (2016)
2. Sun, T.,et al.: Mitigating gender bias in natural language processing. In: Proceedings of ACL, pp. 417–430 (2019)

3. Sheng, E., Chang, J., Gupta, N., Baldridge, J.: Woman is to homemaker as man is to office worker: debiasing word embeddings. In: Proceedings of NAACL, pp. 2347–2360 (2021)

4. Zhao, J., Wang, T., Yatskar, M., Ordonez, V., Chang, K.-W.: Gender bias in multilingual NLP models. In: Proceedings of COLING, pp. 1123–1135 (2020)

5. Dev, S., Sheng, E., Li, N., Prabhakaran, V.: Measuring personal bias in language models. In: Proceedings of AIES, pp. 88–94 (2020)

6. Hu, E.J., Shen, Y., Wallis, P., Allen-Zhu, Z., Li, Y., Wang, L.: LoRA: low-rank adaptation of large language models. In: Proceedings of ICLR (2022)

7. Vig, J., Gehrmann, S., Belinkov, Y.: Causal mediation analysis for analyzing language models. In: Proceedings of EMNLP, pp. 5008–5021 (2020)

8. Nadeem, M., Bethke, A., Reddy, S.: StereoSet: measuring stereotypical bias in pretrained language models. In: Proceedings of ACL, pp. 629–645 (2021)

9. Webster, K., Recasens, M., Axelrod, V., Baldridge, J.: Measuring gendered correlations in pre-trained language models. In: Findings of EMNLP, pp. 787–803 (2020)

10. Blodgett, S.L., Barocas, S., Daumé III, H., Wallach, H.: Language (technology) is power: a critical survey of "Bias" in NLP. In: Proceedings of FAccT, pp. 352–365 (2021)

11. Zhang, Q., Zhou, J., Zhang, Y., Chen, H., et al.: Qwen Technical Report. Technical Report, Alibaba Group (2023)

12. Zmigrod, R., Mielke, S.J., Wallach, H., Cotterell, R.: Counterfactual data augmentation for mitigating gender bias in languages with rich morphology. In: Proceedings of ACL, pp. 1651–1661 (2019)

13. Gehman, S., Gururangan, S., Sap, M., Choi, Y., Smith, N.A.: RealToxicityPrompts: evaluating neural toxic degeneration in language models. In: Proceedings of NeurIPS (2020)

14. Lin, Y., Jiang, Y., Huang, L.: Cross-lingual transfer learning for multilingual bias mitigation. In: Proceedings of ACL, pp. 6873–6886 (2022)

15. Bender, E.M., Gebru, T., McMillan-Major, A., Shmitchell, S.: On the dangers of stochastic parrots: can language models be too big? In: Proceedings of FAccT, pp. 610–623 (2021)

16. Caliskan, A., Bryson, J.J., Narayanan, A.: Semantics derived automatically from language corpora contain human-like biases. Science **355**(6324), 183–186 (2017)

17. Dettmers, T., Lewis, M., Shleifer, S., Zettlemoyer, L.: 8-bit optimizers via blockwise quantization. In: Proceedings of NeurIPS (2022)

18. Zhang, G., et al.: CORGI-PM: a Chinese corpus for gender bias probing and mitigation. arXiv preprint arXiv:2301.00395 (2023)

19. Liu, P., Yuan, W., Fu, J., Jiang, Z., Hayashi, H., Neubig, G.: Pre-train, prompt, and predict: a systematic survey of prompting methods in natural language processing. In: Proceedings of ACL, pp. 1–68 (2023)

20. Sheng, E., Choi, E., Chen, S., He, P., Chen, W., Chang, K.-W.: Societal biases in language generation: progress and challenges. In: Proceedings of EMNLP, pp. 190–206 (2021)

21. Navigli, R., Conia, S., Ross, B.: Biases in large language models: origins, inventory, and discussion. J. Data Inform. Qual. **15**(2), 1–21 (2023)

22. Wei, J., et al.: Chain-of-thought prompting elicits reasoning in large language models. In: NeurIPS (2022)

23. Zhang, X., Liu, H., Wang, D., Zhou, J.: Bias detection with chain-of-thought prompting. In: Proceedings of EMNLP, pp. 4560–4572 (2023)

24. Frantar, E., Alistarh, D.: GPTQ: accurate post-training quantization for generative transformers. arXiv preprint arXiv:2210.17323 (2022)
25. Fu, Y., Li, Q., Tang, D., Duan, N., Zhou, M.: Chinese gender bias evaluation dataset for pretrained language models. In: Proceedings of COLING, pp. 1075–1085 (2022)
26. Hartvigsen, T., Hwang, J.D., Sakaguchi, K., Daumé III, H., Boyd-Graber, J.: Toxi-Chat: a framework for evaluating human-chatbot conversations about unconscious bias. In: Proceedings of ACL, pp. 3200–3215 (2022)

Detection, Classification, and Mitigation of Gender Bias in Large Language Models

Xiaoqing Cheng[1], Hongying Zan[1(✉)], Lulu Kong[1], Jinwang Song[1], and Min Peng[2]

[1] Zhengzhou University, Zhengzhou, China
{xqcheng,kll,jwsong}@gs.zzu.edu.cn, iehyzan@zzu.edu.cn
[2] Wuhan University, Wuhan, China
pengm@whu.edu.cn

Abstract. With the rapid development of large language models (LLMs), they have significantly improved efficiency across a wide range of domains. However, recent studies have revealed that LLMs often exhibit gender bias, leading to serious social implications. Detecting, classifying, and mitigating gender bias in LLMs has therefore become a critical research focus. In the NLPCC 2025 Shared Task 7: Chinese Corpus for Gender Bias Detection, Classification and Mitigation Challenge, we investigate how to enhance the capabilities of LLMs in gender bias detection, classification, and mitigation. We adopt reinforcement learning, chain-of-thoughts (CoT) reasoning, and supervised fine-tuning to handle different Subtasks. Specifically, for Subtasks 1 and 2, we leverage the internal reasoning capabilities of LLMs to guide multi-step thinking in a staged manner, which simplifies complex biased queries and improves response accuracy. For Subtask 3, we employ a reinforcement learning-based approach, annotating a preference dataset using GPT-4. We then apply Direct Preference Optimization (DPO) to mitigate gender bias by introducing a loss function that explicitly favors less biased completions over biased ones. Our approach ranked first across all three subtasks of the NLPCC 2025 Shared Task 7.

Keywords: Gender Bias · Large Language Models · Reinforcement Learning · Chain-of-Thought Reasoning

1 Introduction

Large language models, characterized by their extensive parameterization and large-scale training corpora, have been widely applied across various domains, bringing substantial convenience and efficiency [24]. However, recent studies have shown that these models often exhibit gender bias due to imbalances in their training data [18]. Such biases risk perpetuating gender inequality, reinforcing stereotypical social norms, and undermining fairness, thereby leading to serious societal consequences. As a result, detecting, classifying, and mitigating gender

© The Author(s), under exclusive license to Springer Nature Singapore Pte Ltd. 2026
X.-L. Mao et al. (Eds.): NLPCC 2025, LNAI 16105, pp. 500–511, 2026.
https://doi.org/10.1007/978-981-95-3352-7_42

bias in large language models has become increasingly important. In response to these challenges, the NLPCC 2025 Task 7 was introduced, focusing on the identification and mitigation of gender bias in Chinese-language data.

Existing bias evaluation methods can be categorized into data-level [29], model-level [12], output-level [4], and human-involved, each targeting distinct sources and manifestations of bias. These approaches are often constrained by high computational and data annotation costs, and may face challenges in scalability and consistency. Existing methods for gender bias mitigation can be broadly categorized into two types: prompt-based [14,25] approaches and fine-tuning-based [10] approaches. However, these approaches often suffer from limited control over fine-grained bias mitigation and require substantial computational resources, which restrict their scalability and practicality.

Based on the above considerations, we propose different methods to address the three subtasks. For Subtask 1 and Subtask 2, which focus on bias detection and classification [15,17], we employ supervised fine-tuning in combination with chain-of-thought (CoT) reasoning [20,31]. Specifically, we first inject gender bias-related knowledge into the large language model through supervised fine-tuning. Then, leveraging the model's reasoning capabilities, we design task-specific prompts that guide the model to decompose complex problems into simpler ones. This staged reasoning process enables the model to think step by step with logical structure, thereby improving the accuracy of its predictions. For Subtask 3, which involves rewriting sentences to eliminate gender bias [7,11,23] while preserving the original meaning, we adopt a reinforcement learning [21,26] approach. We begin by using GPT-4 [28] to construct a set of preference data pairs from the original training set. Based on this, we train a DPO [27,30] (Direct Preference Optimization) model by designing a loss function [6,8] that encourages the model to generate less biased rewritings. To enhance the coverage and diversity of our training data, we further supplement it with samples collected from the CORGI-PM [34] dataset.

Experimental results demonstrate the effectiveness of our approach across all three tasks: gender bias detection, classification, and mitigation. Our system achieved No.1 in Subtask 1, Subtask 2, and Subtask 3, as well as the highest overall ranking in NLPCC 2025 Task 7.

Our main contributions are summarized as follows:

- We contribute a fine-grained dataset for gender bias detection and classification, as well as a preference dataset constructed via AI feedback. Specifically, in building the preference dataset, we leverage GPT-4 to generate counterexamples. These counterexamples are paired with corresponding unbiased sentences from the training data to form high-quality preference pairs suitable for preference-based optimization.
- We introduce a chain-of-thought (CoT) strategy for gender bias detection and classification. By designing task-specific prompts, we guide LLMs to reason step by step, improving both accuracy and interpretability.

- We propose a novel DPO-based debiasing framework that mitigates gender bias in generated text while preserving semantic intent, enabling LLMs to prefer less biased completions.

2 Related Work

2.1 Bias Evaluation

Existing methods for evaluating and classifying gender bias in large language models (LLMs) can be broadly categorized into four categorizes. (1) Data-level approaches primarily focus on identifying and quantifying biases inherent in the training corpora of LLMs. Common strategies include data distribution analysis, data sources analysis, sentiment analysis, and annotation bias analysis. (2) Model-level methods aim to detect biases that arise during the training or inference processes of LLMs, often employing fairness metrics and counterfactual-based evaluations. (3) Output-level evaluations assess how LLMs respond to different demographic groups and whether their outputs maintain fairness and neutrality, typically through techniques such as counterfactual testing, stereotype detection, sentiment and toxicity analysis. (4) Human-involved evaluations incorporate human judgment to capture complex, context-dependent biases in LLM outputs.

2.2 Bias Mitigation

Existing gender bias mitigation methods can generally be divided into three major categorizes. (1) prompt-based approaches attempt to reduce bias by crafting prompts that incorporate fairness-related cues, thereby steering the model toward generating more neutral outputs. (2) Fine-tuning-based techniques [33,34] focus on retraining models with balanced datasets and utilize a variety of advanced strategies, such as causal debiasing, manipulation of feature subspaces, contrastive learning for self-debiasing, and interventions at the module level. (3) Inference-time debiasing methods concentrate on altering the decoding process during inference, either by constraining token selection at each step or by generating multiple candidate outputs and selecting the least biased among them.

3 Methods

Figure 1 illustrates an overview of our proposed framework for addressing the three subtasks. Supervised fine-tuning serves as the foundation for all three tasks. Building upon this, we design task-specific strategies tailored to the unique characteristics of each subtask. Our approach primarily integrates two distinct techniques: chain-of-thought reasoning, which is applied to Subtask 1 and Subtask 2, and a reinforcement learning-based method, which is mainly employed for Subtask 3. In the following sections, we provide detailed descriptions of each method respectively.

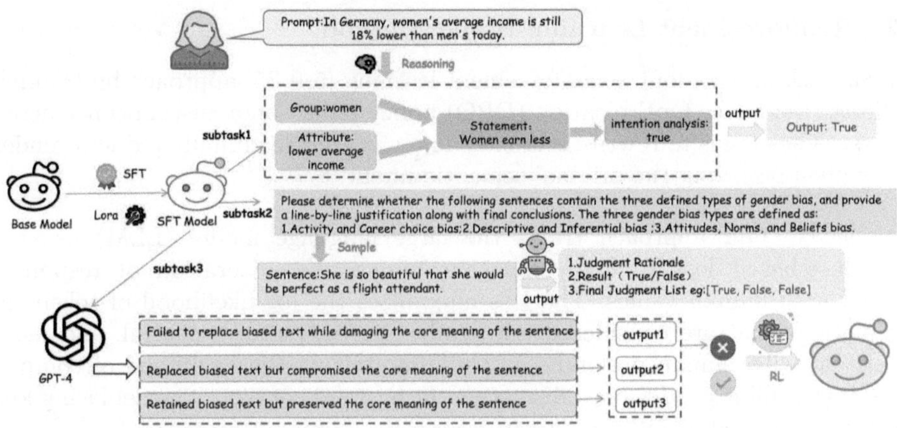

Fig. 1. The overall framework for bias detection, classification, and mitigation.

3.1   Chain-of-Thought Reasoning

Task1: Bias Detection. For Subtask 1, we randomly sample a portion of the CORGI-PM dataset [34] and combine it with the official training data provided by the organizers to construct the raw dataset for fine-tuning the large language model. Following [16], during training and inference, we instruct the model to respond in a structured format comprising three steps:

Groups and Attribute Identification: The model is first required to identify the social group mentioned in the sentence (e.g., "women" in the example) and the associated attribute assigned to the group (e.g., "lower average income").

Bias Judgment: Next, the model is asked to determine whether describing the identified group with the given attribute (e.g., "women earn less") constitutes a biased statement (e.g., answer: "true").

Agreement Analysis and Label Assignment: Finally, the model must assess whether the sentence expresses agreement with the biased statement identified in step 2. If the sentence aligns with the biased implication, the output label is set to "True"; otherwise, if the sentence opposes or questions the implication, the label is set to "False".

Task2: Bias Classification. For Subtask 2, which involves a multi-label classification task, it is challenging for the model to simultaneously make accurate predictions across multiple categories, especially when it may not fully understand the semantic distinctions among the labels. To address this, our prompt is carefully designed to enhance label comprehension and step-by-step reasoning.

Specifically, we first define the meaning of the three labels involved in the task. Then, we ask the model to independently assess whether the given sentence belongs to each label. For each assessment, the model is required to provide a justification before producing a binary decision (i.e., whether the label applies). In the final step, the model is instructed to synthesize the outcomes of the three individual judgments and generate a combined overall answer.

3.2 Reinforcement Learning-Based Method

For Subtask 3, we adopt a reinforcement learning [5,9,35] approach by training a Direct Preference Optimization (DPO) policy model on a custom-constructed dataset. The goal is to rewrite sentences in a way that maximally reduces gender bias while preserving the original semantic intent.

Framework. Our approach trains the large language model (LLM) using a preference-based loss function that encourages the generation of responses aligned with human values. The loss maximizes the log-likelihood of tokens in completions that are considered less gender-biased, more respectful, and more consistent with human preferences, while minimizing the likelihood of completions that exhibit gender bias, disrespect, or harmful content. The debiasing loss function is defined as follows:

$$\mathcal{L}_{\mathrm{DPO}}(\pi; \pi_{\mathrm{ref}}) = -\mathbb{E}_{(x,y_w,y_l)\sim D}\left[\log \sigma\left(\beta \log \frac{\pi(y_w \mid x)}{\pi_{\mathrm{ref}}(y_w \mid x)} - \beta \log \frac{\pi(y_l \mid x)}{\pi_{\mathrm{ref}}(y_l \mid x)}\right)\right] \tag{1}$$

where π represents the target policy, and π_{ref} denotes the reference policy. Each training instance (x, y_w, y_l) is sampled from the Fairness Preference Dataset D, where x is the prompt, y_w and y_l are the preferred and less preferred responses, respectively. β controls the degree of divergence of π from the reference policy π_{ref}. To prevent the model from diverging excessively from the original data distribution, a reference model is incorporated through a KullbackâĂŞLeibler (KL) divergence term. This training objective penalizes the model when it produces biased outputs and rewards it for generating less biased alternatives, thereby encouraging the production of respectful and non-harmful language.

Dataset. To better guide the DPO model in learning human-aligned preferences, we carefully constructed a dedicated dataset for DPO training. Specifically, for each prompt in the training set, we leverage GPT-4 to generate sentences following predefined rules. The generated sentence was treated as the dispreferred response, while the human-edited version from the training data served as the preferred response. These preference pairs were then used to train the DPO model.

The dataset construction process is illustrated in Fig. 1. We adopted GPT-4 to generate counterfactual examples by replacing parts of the original sentence, aiming to produce contrastive pairs that align with the goals of our task. In particular, we consider three types of counterfactuals: (i) biased content is not replaced and the core meaning of the sentence is distorted; (ii) biased content is replaced, but the core meaning is still distorted; and (iii) biased content is retained, but the core meaning is preserved. To ensure coverage of these cases, we designed different prompting strategies to guide GPT-4 in generating high-quality counterfactual responses. This design allows the DPO model to better distinguish between factual and counterfactual examples, thereby improving its ability to rewrite biased sentences in a way that reduces gender bias while maintaining semantic fidelity.

4 Experiments

4.1 Datasets and Metrics

Datasets. We conduct our experiments using the dataset provided in Shared Task 7 of NLPCC 2025. In addition, we randomly sample a subset of data from CORGI-PM to supplement our training set. The statistics of the three tasks are summarized in Table 1. For each task, the data is divided into training, validation, and test sets.

Table 1. Dataset statistics for each subtask.

Task	Train	Valid	Test	Total
SubTask1	12224	1032	200	12924
SubTask2	4872	516	200	5472
SubTask3	3672	516	200	4372

Evaluation Metrics. Task 1: Bias Detection. This task is formulated as a binary classification problem. Given a sentence, the goal is to determine whether it contains gender bias.

We adopt a commonly used evaluation metric: F1-score, which are defined as follows:

$$\text{F1-score} = \frac{2 \cdot \text{Precision} \cdot \text{Recall}}{\text{Precision} + \text{Recall}} \tag{2}$$

where Precision denotes the fraction of correctly predicted positive instances among all predicted positives, and Recall denotes the fraction of correctly predicted positive instances among all actual positives.

Task 2: Gender Bias Classification. This task focuses on categorizing identified gender biases into three types: Activity and Career Choices (AC), Gender Stereotyped Descriptions and Inductions (DI), Expressed Gender-stereotyped Attitudes, Norms and Beliefs (ANB)

We adopt both class-wise and macro-averaged evaluation metrics: F1-score. Class-wise metrics for class i are defined as:

$$\text{F1}_i = \frac{2 \cdot \text{Precision}_i \cdot \text{Recall}_i}{\text{Precision}_i + \text{Recall}_i} \tag{3}$$

where $i \in \{1, 2, 3\}$ indexes the three predefined gender bias types.

The macro-averaged scores are computed as the unweighted mean over all K classes:

$$\text{Macro-F1} = \frac{1}{K} \sum_{i=1}^{K} \text{F1}_i \tag{4}$$

In this task, $K = 3$, corresponding to the three gender bias categories.

Task 3: Gender Bias Mitigation. This task focuses on rewriting biased sentences to mitigate gender bias while preserving the core meaning of the original text. The goal is to generate unbiased variants of the input sentences.

We adopt a commonly used evaluation metric: BLEU.

BLEU evaluates the overlap of n-grams between the generated sentence and one or more reference sentences. It emphasizes precision and includes a brevity penalty to penalize overly short outputs.

4.2   Baselines

(1) LLM Zero-shot. We evaluate several large language models in a zero-shot setting on all three tasks to serve as baselines. The models include Chinese Tiny LLM (2B) [13], Qwen2.5-Instruct (7B) [19], Yi-1.5 (6B) [3], and GPT-4o.

(2) SFT Training. We fine-tune the base models on the training datasets provided for the three tasks. The performance is compared with our proposed chain-of-thought prompting method and reinforcement learning-based method.

(3) Reward-guided Generation. We adopt the reward-guided decoding framework. Specifically, the loss for reward model training is defined as:

$$\mathcal{L}_{\mathrm{RM}}(x, y_w, y_l; \theta) = \log \sigma \left(r([x, y_w]) - r([x, y_l]) \right) \tag{5}$$

where θ is the parameter set of the reward model, $\sigma(\cdot)$ is the sigmoid function, and $r([x, y])$ denotes the scalar reward for a given input-response pair.

Given the context $x_{<t}$ and timestep t, the reward-guided token scoring function is defined as:

$$s(v, x_{<t}) = \mathrm{LM}(v \mid x_{<t}) + w \cdot r([x_{<t}, v]) \tag{6}$$

where $\mathrm{LM}(v \mid x_{<t})$ is the model's likelihood for token v, and w is a scalar weight for the reward.

(4) BiasDPO. We follow the setup proposed in BiasDPO [1], where an additional debiasing dataset is constructed and used to train a DPO model. The resulting DPO model is then used on all three tasks.

(5) Without Data Expansion. To assess the effect of external data, we fine-tune the base model using only the official NLPCC 2025 task dataset, without incorporating any supplementary samples from the CORGI-PM dataset.

4.3   Experimental Settings.

All experiments are conducted using Qwen2.5-7B-Instruct as the base model. We used the LLaMA Factory [22] framework for training. The training configurations for SFT and DPO are shown in Table 2.

For SFT Training and Reward-guided Generation baselines, we also adopt Qwen2.5-7B-Instruct as the base model. In Reward-guided Generation, where a reward model is required, we use Meta-LLaMA3-8B-Instruct [2] as the backbone to train the reward model. The training configuration for the reward model is shown in Table 2.

Table 2. Hyperparameter settings: left for SFT training, right for DPO training and RM training.

Hyper-parameter	Value		Hyper-parameter	Value
Lora Alpha	16		Lora Alpha	32
Lora Rank	8		Lora Rank	16
Optimizer	AdamW		Optimizer	AdamW
Train Batch Size	1		Train Batch Size	1
Train Epochs	2		Train Epochs	2
Learning Rate	1×10^{-5}		Learning Rate	8×10^{-6}
Max Gradient Norm	0.3		Max Gradient Norm	0.3
Warmup Ratio	0.03		Warmup Ratio	0.03
Max Sequence Length	1024		Max Sequence Length	1024

4.4   Experimental Results and Analysis

In this section, we present a comprehensive comparison between our proposed method and various baselines, which constitutes the core results of our main experiments. In addition, we conduct a series of ablation studies to validate the effectiveness of each component in our framework. Finally, we perform an error analysis by examining typical failure cases, aiming to gain deeper insights into the challenges of the task and to inform future improvements.

Main Experimental Results. We compare all baseline methods with our proposed approach on the validation sets, and report the results in Table 3. Compared with several strong baselines, our method achieves the best performance across all three tasks, demonstrating its effectiveness. Interestingly, we observe that the ARGs-based method also performs competitively, suggesting that reinforcement learning-based strategies are generally effective for bias mitigation, and that the benefit is not limited to DPO-style optimization. However, we also find that BiasDPO, despite being trained with a reinforcement learning objective, does not perform as well. Upon closer examination, we attribute this to the dataset used in BiasDPO, which may not be well aligned with the specific settings of our tasks. This finding indirectly supports the effectiveness of our approach to constructing contrastive pairs via GPT-4 sampling, which ensures task relevance and better supervision.

Table 3. Main results on the validation sets of the three subtasks.

Methods	Models	Subtask1	Subtask2	Subtask3
LLM Zero-shot	Chinese Tiny LLM (2B)	0.24	0.32	0.154
	Qwen2.5-Instruct (7B)	0.69	0.58	0.218
	Yi-1.5 (9B)	0.68	0.58	0.215
	GPT-4o	0.82	0.67	0.259
SFT Training	Qwen2.5-Instruct (7B)	0.72	0.59	0.248
ARGS	Qwen2.5-Instruct (7B)	0.83	0.61	0.269
BiasDPO	Qwen2.5-Instruct (7B)	0.75	0.63	0.223
Ours	Qwen2.5-Instruct (7B)	**0.87**	**0.68**	**0.286**
w/o Dataset Expansion	Qwen2.5-Instruct (7B)	0.85	0.65	0.265
w/o CoT	Qwen2.5-Instruct (7B)	0.72	0.59	-
w/o RL	Qwen2.5-Instruct (7B)	-	-	0.248

Ablation Study. To investigate the contribution of different components in our method, we conduct ablation studies by individually removing the following modules: (1) the data expansion component, (2) the chain-of-thought (CoT) reasoning mechanism, and (3) the reinforcement learning (RL) optimization. The results are presented in the lower part of Table 3. We observe that removing the data expansion module leads to an average performance drop across all three tasks. Furthermore, when the CoT module and the reinforcement learning method are removed, the performance on the corresponding tasks also decreases. These results highlight the effectiveness of both the CoT reasoning and reinforcement learning components in our proposed framework.

More Results. We further compared the performance of our proposed method combined with different base models, including Qwen2.5-3B and Baichuan2-13B [32]. The experimental results are presented in Table 4.

Table 4. More results of different models on three subtasks.

Methods	Models	Subtask1	Subtask2	Subtask3
LLM Zero-shot	Baichuan2-13B	0.58	0.54	0.198
	Qwen2.5-3B	0.61	0.52	0.193
Ours	Baichuan2-13B	0.69	0.66	0.232
	Qwen2.5-3B	0.65	0.65	0.227

Error Analysis. Table 5 presents the error distribution on Subtask 2. We randomly sampled 50 error cases and manually analyzed each one to identify its error type. Our analysis revealed that, Among the three categories, the error rate for gender-stereotypical activities and career choices (AC) is 26%, for gender-stereotypical descriptions and inferences (DI) is 38%, and for gender-stereotypical attitudes, norms, and beliefs (ANB) is 36%. These results suggest that instances involving descriptive and inferential gender stereotypes (DI) pose greater challenges for computational models, potentially due to their implicit and context-dependent nature.

Table 5. Error Analysis.

Error Type	Ratio
Activity and Career Choices (AC)	26%
Gender Stereotyped Descriptions and Inductions (DI)	38%
Expressed Gender-stereotyped Attitudes, Norms and Beliefs (ANB)	36%

5   Conclusion

In this paper, we present a framework to address gender bias in large language models (LLMs), targeting bias detection, classification, and mitigation tasks in NLPCC 2025 Shared Task 7. By integrating chain-of-thought (CoT) reasoning, supervised fine-tuning, and reinforcement learning via Direct Preference Optimization (DPO), our method effectively enhances the reasoning and debiasing capabilities of LLMs. Notably, we construct a high-quality preference dataset and utilize GPT-4 to guide bias-aware learning. Experimental results demonstrate that our method achieves state-of-the-art performance across all three subtasks, ranking first in the competition. These findings highlight the potential of combining structured reasoning and preference-based optimization to mitigate social biases in LLMs, paving the way for more fair and responsible language generation systems.

References

1. Allam, A.: Biasdpo: Mitigating bias in language models through direct preference optimization. arXiv preprint arXiv:2407.13928 (2024)
2. Alsariera, Y.A., Adeyemo, V.E., Balogun, A.O., Alazzawi, A.K.: Ai meta-learners and extra-trees algorithm for the detection of phishing websites. IEEE Access **8**, 142532–142542 (2020)
3. Arias, D.C., De Buyzere, M.L., Chirinos, J.A., Rietzschel, E.R., Segers, P.: Yi 1.5 ten years of ageing in the middle-aged does not increase input impedance or wave reflection—insights from the asklepios study. Artery Res. **26**(Suppl 1), S5–S6 (2020)

4. Banerjee, P., et al.: All should be equal in the eyes of lms: counterfactually aware fair text generation. In: Proceedings of the AAAI Conference on Artificial Intelligence, vol. 38, pp. 17673–17681 (2024)
5. Chen, R., et al.: Diffpo: diffusion-styled preference optimization for efficient inference-time alignment of large language models. arXiv preprint arXiv:2503.04240 (2025)
6. Chen, R., Hu, T., Feng, Y., Liu, Z.: Learnable privacy neurons localization in language models. arXiv preprint arXiv:2405.10989 (2024)
7. Chen, Ret al.: Identifying and mitigating social bias knowledge in language models. In: Findings of the Association for Computational Linguistics: NAACL 2025, pp. 651–672 (2025)
8. Chen, R., et al.: Fast model debias with machine unlearning. Adv. Neural. Inf. Process. Syst. **36**, 14516–14539 (2023)
9. Chen, R., Zhang, X., Luo, M., Chai, W., Liu, Z.: Pad: Personalized alignment of llms at decoding-time. arXiv preprint arXiv:2410.04070 (2024)
10. Cheng, R., Ma, H., Cao, S., Shi, T.: Rlrf: reinforcement learning from reflection through debates as feedback for bias mitigation in llms. arXiv preprint arXiv:2404.10160 (2024)
11. Cheng, X., Chen, R., Zan, H., Jia, Y., Peng, M.: Biasfilter: An inference-time debiasing framework for large language models. arXiv preprint arXiv:2505.23829 (2025)
12. Doan, T.V., Wang, Z., Hoang, N.N.M., Zhang, W.: Fairness in large language models in three hours. In: Proceedings of the 33rd ACM International Conference on Information and Knowledge Management, pp. 5514–5517 (2024)
13. Du, X., et al.: Chinese tiny llm: pretraining a chinese-centric large language model. arXiv preprint arXiv:2404.04167 (2024)
14. Echterhoff, J., Liu, Y., Alessa, A., McAuley, J., He, Z.: Cognitive bias in decision-making with llms. arXiv preprint arXiv:2403.00811 (2024)
15. Fan, Z., Chen, R., Hu, T., Liu, Z.: Fairmt-bench: benchmarking fairness for multi-turn dialogue in conversational llms. arXiv preprint arXiv:2410.19317 (2024)
16. Fan, Z., Chen, R., Liu, Z.: Biasguard: a reasoning-enhanced bias detection tool for large language models. arXiv preprint arXiv:2504.21299 (2025)
17. Fan, Z., Chen, R., Xu, R., Liu, Z.: Biasalert: a plug-and-play tool for social bias detection in llms. arXiv preprint arXiv:2407.10241 (2024)
18. Gallegos, I.O., et al.: Bias and fairness in large language models: a survey. Comput. Linguist. **50**(3), 1097–1179 (2024)
19. Hui, B., et al.: Qwen2. 5-coder technical report. arXiv preprint arXiv:2409.12186 (2024)
20. Kojima, T., Gu, S.S., Reid, M., Matsuo, Y., Iwasawa, Y.: Large language models are zero-shot reasoners. Adv. Neural. Inf. Process. Syst. **35**, 22199–22213 (2022)
21. Lee, H., et al.: Rlaif vs. rlhf: scaling reinforcement learning from human feedback with ai feedback. arXiv preprint arXiv:2309.00267 (2023)
22. Li, Y., Wang, Z., Fu, T., Cui, G., Yang, S., Cheng, Y.: From drafts to answers: unlocking llm potential via aggregation fine-tuning. arXiv preprint arXiv:2501.11877 (2025)
23. Li, Y., et al.: Fairsteer: inference time debiasing for llms with dynamic activation steering. arXiv preprint arXiv:2504.14492 (2025)
24. Liu, Y., Iter, D., Xu, Y., Wang, S., Xu, R., Zhu, C.: G-eval: Nlg evaluation using gpt-4 with better human alignment. arXiv preprint arXiv:2303.16634 (2023)
25. Liu, Z., Chen, Z., Zhang, M., Ren, Z., Chen, Z., Ren, P.: Zero-shot position debiasing for large language models. CoRR (2024)

26. Ouyang, L., et al.: Training language models to follow instructions with human feedback. Adv. Neural. Inf. Process. Syst. **35**, 27730–27744 (2022)
27. Rafailov, R., Hejna, J., Park, R., Finn, C.: From r to q*: Your language model is secretly a q-function. arXiv preprint arXiv:2404.12358 (2024)
28. Rafailov, R., Sharma, A., Mitchell, E., Manning, C.D., Ermon, S., Finn, C.: Direct preference optimization: Your language model is secretly a reward model. Adv. Neural. Inf. Process. Syst. **36**, 53728–53741 (2023)
29. Wang, A., Morgenstern, J., Dickerson, J.P.: Large language models cannot replace human participants because they cannot portray identity groups. arXiv e-prints pp. arXiv–2402 (2024)
30. Wang, B., et al.: Exploring the limits of domain-adaptive training for detoxifying large-scale language models. Adv. Neural. Inf. Process. Syst. **35**, 35811–35824 (2022)
31. Wei, J., et al.: Chain-of-thought prompting elicits reasoning in large language models. Adv. Neural. Inf. Process. Syst. **35**, 24824–24837 (2022)
32. Yang, A., et al.: Baichuan 2: Open large-scale language models. arXiv preprint arXiv:2309.10305 (2023)
33. Zhang, C., Zhang, L., Wu, J., He, Y., Zhou, D.: Causal prompting: debiasing large language model prompting based on front-door adjustment. In: Proceedings of the AAAI Conference on Artificial Intelligence, vol. 39, pp. 25842–25850 (2025)
34. Zhang, G., et al.: Corgi-pm: a chinese corpus for gender bias probing and mitigation (2023). https://arxiv.org/abs/2301.00395
35. Zhang, X., Chen, R., Feng, Y., Liu, Z.: Persona-judge: personalized alignment of large language models via token-level self-judgment. arXiv preprint arXiv:2504.12663 (2025)

Overview of the NLPCC 2025 Shared Task 8: Personalized Emotional Support Conversation

Zhengda Jin, Bingbing Wang, Geng Tu, and Ruifeng Xu[✉]

Harbin Institute of Technology, Shenzhen, China
{220110515,bingbing.wang,22b951011}@stu.hit.edu.cn, xuruifeng@hit.edu.cn

Abstract. This paper provides a detailed overview of the NLPCC 2025 Shared Task 8, which focused on personalized emotional support conversation. Addressing the dual challenges of acquiring high-quality, nuanced datasets for emotional support and the limitations of generic Large Language Model (LLM) responses, this task aims to encourage the development of systems capable of delivering empathetic and contextually relevant support by taking individual user characteristics into account. The central objective is to train models on a newly created dataset, Uni-Conv, to generate supportive dialogue that acknowledges and responds to users' unique profiles and situations. This paper outlines the motivation behind the task, the creation and specific details of the UniConv dataset, the evaluation framework employed, the approaches taken by the participating teams, and a summary of the achieved results. Looking ahead, we anticipate that continued exploration and refinement of personalized modeling approaches will pave the way for the development of next-generation emotional support systems that are more attuned to user needs and more human-centered. A total of 3 teams participated in the task, submitting 12 system results.

Keywords: Emotional Support Conversation · Individual Characteristics · Large Language Models

1 Introduction

Emotional support conversation (ESC) systems are dedicated to alleviating users' emotional distress and assisting them in navigating various challenges [12,14]. These systems play a crucial role in a multitude of domains, including social interaction, mental health care, and customer service [13].

Previously, the datasets for ESC systems have primarily originated from psychotherapy recordings, online databases, and questionnaires [10,17]. While these sources can provide high-quality data, acquiring them often entails significant costs and time investment. In recent years, Large Language Models (LLMs) have demonstrated potential in generating empathetic responses; however, these responses often tend to be formulaic and redundant. To enhance the effectiveness of ESC systems, it is increasingly important to create high-quality ESC datasets and leverage them to fine-tune LLMs, enabling the generation of more empathetic and contextually relevant replies [20,22].

© The Author(s), under exclusive license to Springer Nature Singapore Pte Ltd. 2026
X.-L. Mao et al. (Eds.): NLPCC 2025, LNAI 16105, pp. 512–520, 2026.
https://doi.org/10.1007/978-981-95-3352-7_43

However, these datasets have often failed to capture the nuances of users' individual characteristics, including their traits and specific circumstances. For instance, consider an individual with the following profile: Female, John Doe, 35 years old, holds a Master's degree, works as a technology professional, enjoys hiking, possesses project management skills, and is currently facing work-related stress. Her consultation is: "I've been feeling very down lately, and the work pressure is immense. I've tried to relax, but it doesn't seem to help. I feel hopeless and see no light at the end of the tunnel." A generic response might be: "Just keep trying, things will eventually get better." In contrast, a response that considers the user's individual characteristics could be: "Given that you work in the high-pressure tech industry, let's talk about your communication at work. You have project management skills, perhaps organizing a team discussion could be beneficial for you." Compared to the former, the latter response acknowledges the user's profession in the demanding tech sector and inquires about her workplace communication, making the dialogue more relevant. Furthermore, instead of offering a vague, encouraging remark like the former, it leverages the user's project management skills by suggesting a team discussion, reinforcing her professional value. This personalized approach can make users feel understood and empowered, indicating that incorporating individual characteristics can significantly enhance the effectiveness of emotional support.

In this paper, we present a dataset called UniConv for emotional support conversations that incorporates diverse individual characteristics. UniConv is rich in content, encompassing a variety of real-world personal scenarios, and can be utilized for the customization of emotional support.

Ultimately, ten teams submitted registration information, and three teams submitted final results. We will discuss the detailed task information in Sect. 3, the content of the dataset in Sect. 4, and the evaluation results in Sect. 5.

2   Related Work

Emotional support is a crucial aspect of human-computer interaction [5], and the development of effective emotional support chatbots heavily relies on the availability of comprehensive, real-world datasets [16]. While early efforts [10] involved manual curation, the scalability of such approaches is limited. Recent advancements in large language models (LLMs) have spurred research into their potential as emotional support agents, with a growing emphasis on dataset augmentation techniques [6,22] and leveraging LLMs to enhance existing datasets [15,21]. For instance, the ESCoT dataset [20] aims to improve dialogue explainability, and Synth-Empathy [8] focuses on generating synthetic empathetic data.

The development of emotional support conversation (ESC) models has evolved from rule-based systems [23] to data-driven approaches [2] incorporating techniques like hierarchical graph networks [12] and smaller Transformer models [18]. More recently, the focus has shifted towards utilizing pre-trained language models [3] and LLMs [19] to create more advanced and adaptable ESC solutions. However, a key challenge that remains is addressing individual user differences to provide truly personalized emotional support.

3   Task Overview

The objective of this task is for participants to train models on the provided dataset, enabling emotional support dialogue models to consider users' individual characteristics. The goal is to generate responses that are more relevant and directly address the core concerns of users, rather than providing broad and unhelpful replies.

Through this task, we aim to identify which models and methods can more accurately capture users' individual characteristics and, based on an understanding of these traits, provide effective emotional support. Participants are required to input both the user's personal characteristics and utterances into the model for training. These personal characteristics encompass a variety of scenarios. During testing, we will comprehensively evaluate the model's performance on both seen and unseen scenarios.

4   Dataset Description

The UniConv dataset was constructed using a multi-agent role-playing framework called UniESC. This framework simulates real-world emotional support dialogue scenarios to generate high-quality, personalized emotional support conversation data. The framework defines three key roles in this process: the *Seeker* who needs emotional support, the *School Supporter* who provides support strategies based on different psychological orientations, and the *Supervisor* who evaluates various support strategies and selects the most appropriate response. Specifically, a diverse group of Seekers with rich individual characteristics was created by randomly sampling and leveraging the generation capabilities of GPT-4o. Each Supporter proposed initial responses based on the Seeker's personality and situation, guided by their respective psychological approaches. Subsequently, through multi-turn discussions utilizing a Theory of Mind (ToM) mechanism, the Supporters could simulate human thinking patterns, comprehensively considering the psychological states of the Seeker and each other, and iteratively refining their responses. Finally, the Supervisor selected the most suitable response from these options to form the final dialogue data. This process not only ensured the personalization and diversity of the conversations but also employed strict filtering criteria to retain only high-quality dialogues that could improve the Seeker's emotional state and align with their preferences. Ultimately, this resulted in the UniConv dataset, comprising 1500 dialogues and 30,000 utterances, providing a valuable data resource for research on emotional support dialogue systems.

We have split the dataset into training, validation, and test sets with a ratio of 8:1:1. Each sample includes the user's individual characteristics and twenty turns of dialogue. An example of a sample is illustrated in Table 1. We encourage participants to design models that take the user's individual characteristics into account.

Table 1. Dataset Example

Character

Name: Lucas Thompson	**Nickname**: Luke	**Age**: 28	**Sex**: Male

Appearance: Tall, athletic build, short brown hair

Education Background: High School Diploma

Occupation: Warehouse Associate

Emotion Type: Anxious and Sad

Problem Type: Ongoing Depression and Job Insecurity

Hobby: Playing video games

Situation: Not having enough friends nearby. My three nearby friends went away for holidays, so I have no one to spend time with over this weekend.

Dialog

Seeker: I'm feeling really lonely and anxious this weekend since my friends are away, and the job uncertainty is making everything seem even worse.

Supporter: It sounds like the absence of your friends is really weighing on you, especially with all the stress from work. That's such a tough situation to be in, and it's completely understandable to feel anxious about it.

Seeker: I appreciate your understanding; it really helps to talk about it. I'm trying to find some ways to distract myself this weekend, maybe by diving into some video games.

Supporter: Diving into some video games sounds like a fun way to pass the time! Just remember, it's also okay to feel what you're feeling; you're not alone in this.

... (partial dialog omitted) ...

Seeker: I'll definitely make it a point to keep these discussions going; they feel so uplifting. It's nice to be reminded that I'm not navigating this alone and that I can gain strength from these connections.

Supporter: It's wonderful to hear that these discussions uplift you! Knowing you're not alone can truly help you tap into the strength of your connections. Keep engaging in those conversations; they're so valuable for your emotional well-being!

5   Results

5.1   Evaluation Metrics

To comprehensively evaluate the quality of the generated responses, we adopted a multi-faceted approach that considered both their fidelity to the reference responses and their intrinsic linguistic properties. Participants were tasked with providing the model's response for each turn in every dialogue within the test set, which were then rigorously compared against the reference responses to establish a benchmark for evaluation.

The consistency between these generated and reference responses was quantified using standard metrics such as METEOR (ME) [1], which accounts for synonyms and stemming, BLEU-4 (B-4) [11], which assesses n-gram precision,

ROUGE-L (R-L) [9], focusing on the longest common subsequence, and VectorExtrema (Ext) [4], which evaluates semantic similarity at the sentence level. Beyond mere accuracy, we also recognized the importance of generating diverse and engaging conversational turns. To this end, we employed Distinct-2 (D-2) and Distinct-3 (D-3) [7] to measure the richness of the generated vocabulary in terms of bigrams and trigrams, respectively. Recognizing the limitations of purely statistical metrics in capturing the overall quality of a dialogue response, we further incorporated a human-like evaluation by utilizing ChatGPT-4. This allowed us to assess more abstract qualities such as the relevance of the response within the conversational context, its grammatical correctness and natural flow (fluency), the degree to which it provides meaningful information (informativeness), and the logical connection between the response and the preceding turns (logical coherence), yielding a global quality score (G-Score). The prompt we used in ChatGPT-4 is shown in Table 2.

Table 2. Prompt for ChatGPT-4

Evaluate the generated response (1-5 scale) considering:

1. Relevance to input

2. Match with reference

3. Fluency and coherence

Input: {input}

Reference: {reference}

Generated: {generated}

Score (1-5 only):

The final overall evaluation score was then calculated by assigning weights to each of these diverse metrics and summing them, as illustrated below:

$$\text{Score} = 0.2 \times \text{ME} + 0.2 \times \text{B-4} + 0.2 \times \text{R-L} + 0.1 \times \text{Ext}$$
$$+ 0.1 \times \text{D-2} + 0.1 \times \text{D-3} + 0.1 \times \text{G-Score}$$

5.2 Participants

A total of 3 teams submitted 12 results throughout the evaluation period. In addition to the final submission deadline, we established four intermediate submission deadlines, each separated by a one-day interval leading up to the final date. For each of these intermediate deadlines, the last submission received on that day was designated as the official result for that particular day. Across the multiple submissions made over the entire period, the submission yielding the best overall score was selected as the team's top-performing result. Following each submission deadline, on the subsequent day, we publicly announced each team's cumulative overall score, their ranking relative to the other teams, and the individual scores for each evaluation metric. This public announcement was based on each team's best submission to date, as well as their last submission from the preceding day. By implementing these multiple spaced submission opportunities and the regular public dissemination of metric scores, our aim was to facilitate a process that would actively assist participating teams in iteratively improving the expressive capabilities of their models.

5.3   Main Results

As clearly indicated in Table 3, the team ZZUNLP_Adventure achieved the highest overall score of 42.69, demonstrating a consistent lead across nearly all sub-metrics. In particular, they outperformed other teams significantly in ME, BLEU-4, ROUGE-L, and G-Score, which are key metrics for evaluating both emotional alignment and linguistic quality. This suggests that their model not only generated emotionally appropriate responses but also maintained strong fluency and relevance.

Interestingly, this top-ranked team used a relatively compact model—a fine-tuned 7B parameter Qwen2 model—and still surpassed competitors that used significantly larger models (72B and 32B Qwen2.5, respectively). This highlights the importance of effective fine-tuning strategies and task-specific adaptation, rather than simply scaling up model size. It also implies their training data selection or prompt engineering could have been particularly well-aligned with the task requirements.

In contrast, the second and third place teams, despite utilizing larger models, scored only marginally different from each other (39.62% vs. 38.99%), and both fell behind most notably in ME and R-L, which may indicate limitations in emotional expression or response richness. Notably, the third-place team outperformed others in D-3, suggesting their model produced more diverse responses, but perhaps at the expense of emotional consistency or coherence.

Table 3. Rank of the Task (%)

Rank	Team	Score	ME	B-4	R-L	Ext	D-2	D-3	G-Score
1	ZZUNLP_Adventure	42.69	32.83	8.90	34.70	96.48	30.57	55.35	91.60
2	TeleAI	39.62	27.21	6.25	29.89	96.22	30.99	55.12	87.20
3	NewFolder	38.99	25.85	5.04	27.84	96.22	31.58	57.77	86.84

6   Conclusion

In this paper, we provide a comprehensive overview of the NLPCC 2025 Shared Task 8. Emotionally supportive dialogue systems play a crucial role in various domains; however, the acquisition of high-quality datasets for this task is relatively expensive, and existing datasets often fall short in capturing individual user characteristics effectively. To address this limitation, we propose a novel approach by constructing an emotionally supportive dialogue dataset enriched with individual traits. This was achieved through a multi-agent role-playing framework integrated with the ToM mechanism. Building upon this unique dataset, we collected emotionally supportive dialogue models developed by three participating teams specifically for this shared task. We conducted a thorough evaluation of these models' emotional support capabilities using our newly created dataset. The results demonstrate that employing targeted strategies can significantly enhance a mode's ability to capture individual characteristics, thereby enabling them to provide more effective emotional support to the dialogue partner. We eagerly anticipate future work that can further explore the potential of our proposed dataset and the submitted models.

Acknowledgement. This work was partially supported by the National Natural Science Foundation of China 62576120, Natural Science Foundation of Guang Dong 2023A1515012922, the Shenzhen Foundational Research Funding JCYJ20220818102415032, Guangdong Provincial Key Laboratory of Novel Security Intelligence Technologies 2022B1212010005 and CIPSC-SMP-ZHIPU Large Model Cross-Disciplinary Fund ZPCG20241119405.

References

1. Banerjee, S., Lavie, A.: METEOR: An automatic metric for MT evaluation with improved correlation with human judgments. In: Goldstein, J., Lavie, A., Lin, C.Y., Voss, C. (eds.) Proceedings of the ACL Workshop on Intrinsic and Extrinsic Evaluation Measures for Machine Translation and/or Summarization, pp. 65–72. Association for Computational Linguistics, Ann Arbor, Michigan (Jun 2005). https://aclanthology.org/W05-0909/
2. Cheng, Y., et al.: Improving multi-turn emotional support dialogue generation with lookahead strategy planning (2022). https://arxiv.org/abs/2210.04242
3. Deng, Y., Zhang, W., Yuan, Y., Lam, W.: Knowledge-enhanced mixed-initiative dialogue system for emotional support conversations. In: Rogers, A., Boyd-Graber, J., Okazaki, N. (eds.) Proceedings of the 61st Annual Meeting of the Association for Computational Linguistics (Volume 1: Long Papers), pp. 4079–4095. Association for Computational Linguistics, Toronto, Canada (Jul 2023). https://doi.org/10.18653/v1/2023.acl-long.225, https://aclanthology.org/2023.acl-long.225/
4. Forgues, G., Pineau, J., Larchevêque, J.M., Tremblay, R.: Bootstrapping dialog systems with word embeddings. In: Nips, Modern Machine Learning and Natural Language Processing Workshop, vol. 2 (2014)
5. Huang, M., Zhu, X., Gao, J.: Challenges in building intelligent open-domain dialog systems (2020). https://arxiv.org/abs/1905.05709
6. Kang, D., et al.: Can large language models be good emotional supporter? mitigating preference bias on emotional support conversation (2024). https://arxiv.org/abs/2402.13211

7. Li, J., Galley, M., Brockett, C., Gao, J., Dolan, B.: A diversity-promoting objective function for neural conversation models. In: Knight, K., Nenkova, A., Rambow, O. (eds.) Proceedings of the 2016 Conference of the North American Chapter of the Association for Computational Linguistics: Human Language Technologies, pp. 110–119. Association for Computational Linguistics, San Diego, California (Jun 2016). https://doi.org/10.18653/v1/N16-1014, https://aclanthology.org/N16-1014/

8. Liang, H., et al.: Synth-empathy: Towards high-quality synthetic empathy data (2024). https://arxiv.org/abs/2407.21669

9. Lin, C.Y.: ROUGE: A package for automatic evaluation of summaries. In: Text Summarization Branches Out, pp. 74–81. Association for Computational Linguistics, Barcelona, Spain (Jul 2004). https://aclanthology.org/W04-1013/

10. Liu, S., et al.: Towards emotional support dialog systems. In: Zong, C., Xia, F., Li, W., Navigli, R. (eds.) Proceedings of the 59th Annual Meeting of the Association for Computational Linguistics and the 11th International Joint Conference on Natural Language Processing (Volume 1: Long Papers), pp. pp. 3469–3483. Association for Computational Linguistics, Online (Aug 2021). https://doi.org/10.18653/v1/2021.acl-long.269, https://aclanthology.org/2021.acl-long.269/

11. Papineni, K., Roukos, S., Ward, T., Zhu, W.J.: Bleu: a method for automatic evaluation of machine translation. In: Isabelle, P., Charniak, E., Lin, D. (eds.) Proceedings of the 40th Annual Meeting of the Association for Computational Linguistics, pp. 311–318. Association for Computational Linguistics, Philadelphia, Pennsylvania, USA (Jul 2002). https://doi.org/10.3115/1073083.1073135, https://aclanthology.org/P02-1040/

12. Peng, W., Hu, Y., Xing, L., Xie, Y., Sun, Y., Li, Y.: Control globally, understand locally: a global-to-local hierarchical graph network for emotional support conversation (2022). https://arxiv.org/abs/2204.12749

13. Yang, A., et al.: Qwen2.5 technical report (2025). https://arxiv.org/abs/2412.15115

14. Rains, S.A., Pavlich, C.A., Lutovsky, B., Tsetsi, E., Ashtaputre, A.: Support seeker expectations, support message quality, and supportive interaction processes and outcomes: the case of the comforting computer program revisited. J. Soc. Personal Relationships **37**(2), 647–666 (2020). https://doi.org/10.1177/0265407519876359

15. Rashkin, H., Smith, E.M., Li, M., Boureau, Y.L.: Towards empathetic open-domain conversation models: a new benchmark and dataset. In: Korhonen, A., Traum, D., Màrquez, L. (eds.) Proceedings of the 57th Annual Meeting of the Association for Computational Linguistics, pp. 5370–5381. Association for Computational Linguistics, Florence, Italy (Jul 2019). https://doi.org/10.18653/v1/P19-1534, https://aclanthology.org/P19-1534/

16. Sharma, A., Miner, A., Atkins, D., Althoff, T.: A computational approach to understanding empathy expressed in text-based mental health support. In: Webber, B., Cohn, T., He, Y., Liu, Y. (eds.) Proceedings of the 2020 Conference on Empirical Methods in Natural Language Processing (EMNLP), pp. 5263–5276. Association for Computational Linguistics, Online (Nov 2020). https://doi.org/10.18653/v1/2020.emnlp-main.425, https://aclanthology.org/2020.emnlp-main.425/

17. Shen, S., Welch, C., Mihalcea, R., Pérez-Rosas, V.: Counseling-style reflection generation using generative pretrained transformers with augmented context. In: Pietquin, O., et al. (eds.) Proceedings of the 21th Annual Meeting of the Special Interest Group on Discourse and Dialogue, pp. 10–20. Association for Compu-

tational Linguistics, 1st virtual meeting (Jul 2020). https://doi.org/10.18653/v1/2020.sigdial-1.2, https://aclanthology.org/2020.sigdial-1.2/

18. Tu, Q., Li, Y., Cui, J., Wang, B., Wen, J.R., Yan, R.: MISC: A mixed strategy-aware model integrating COMET for emotional support conversation. In: Muresan, S., Nakov, P., Villavicencio, A. (eds.) Proceedings of the 60th Annual Meeting of the Association for Computational Linguistics (Volume 1: Long Papers), pp. 308–319. Association for Computational Linguistics, Dublin, Ireland (May 2022). https://doi.org/10.18653/v1/2022.acl-long.25, https://aclanthology.org/2022.acl-long.25/

19. Zhang, Q., Naradowsky, J., Miyao, Y.: Ask an expert: leveraging language models to improve strategic reasoning in goal-oriented dialogue models. In: Rogers, A., Boyd-Graber, J., Okazaki, N. (eds.) Findings of the Association for Computational Linguistics: ACL 2023. pp. 6665–6694. Association for Computational Linguistics, Toronto, Canada (Jul 2023). https://doi.org/10.18653/v1/2023.findings-acl.417, https://aclanthology.org/2023.findings-acl.417/

20. Zhang, T., Zhang, X., Zhao, J., Zhou, L., Jin, Q.: ESCoT: towards interpretable emotional support dialogue systems. In: Ku, L.W., Martins, A., Srikumar, V. (eds.) Proceedings of the 62nd Annual Meeting of the Association for Computational Linguistics (Volume 1: Long Papers), pp. 13395–13412. Association for Computational Linguistics, Bangkok, Thailand (Aug 2024). https://doi.org/10.18653/v1/2024.acl-long.723, https://aclanthology.org/2024.acl-long.723/

21. Zheng, C., Sabour, S., Wen, J., Zhang, Z., Huang, M.: AugESC: dialogue augmentation with large language models for emotional support conversation. In: Rogers, A., Boyd-Graber, J., Okazaki, N. (eds.) Findings of the Association for Computational Linguistics: ACL 2023, pp. 1552–1568. Association for Computational Linguistics, Toronto, Canada (Jul 2023). https://doi.org/10.18653/v1/2023.findings-acl.99, https://aclanthology.org/2023.findings-acl.99/

22. Zheng, Z., Liao, L., Deng, Y., Qin, L., Nie, L.: Self-chats from large language models make small emotional support chatbot better. In: Ku, L.W., Martins, A., Srikumar, V. (eds.) Proceedings of the 62nd Annual Meeting of the Association for Computational Linguistics (Volume 1: Long Papers), pp. 11325–11345. Association for Computational Linguistics, Bangkok, Thailand (Aug 2024). https://doi.org/10.18653/v1/2024.acl-long.611, https://aclanthology.org/2024.acl-long.611/

23. van der Zwaan, J.M., Dignum, V., Jonker, C.M.: A conversation model enabling intelligent agents to give emotional support. In: Ding, W., Jiang, H., Ali, M., Li, M. (eds.) Modern Advances in Intelligent Systems and Tools. Springer, Berlin (2012). https://doi.org/10.1007/978-3-642-30732-4_6

Optimizing LLMs for Personalized Emotional Support with Future Cues and Response Diversity

Jinwang Song[1], Hongying Zan[1(✉)], Haixin Liu[1], Yifan Li[1], Lulu Kong[1], Xiaoqing Cheng[1], Kunli Zhang[1], and Min Peng[2]

[1] Zhengzhou University, Zhengzhou, China
{jwsong,lhxin,lyfan,kll,xqcheng}@gs.zzu.edu.cn,
{iehyzan,ieklzhang}@zzu.edu.cn
[2] Wuhan University, Wuhan, China
pengm@whu.edu.cn

Abstract. Personalized Emotional Support Conversation (PESC) systems are crucial for providing effective emotional solace tailored to users' unique needs. This paper details our first-place system in the NLPCC 2025 Shared Task 8 on PESC. To address the challenge of enhancing Large Language Models' (LLMs') ability to generate personalized and highly supportive responses in this task, we proposed and integrated a series of innovative optimization strategies. Key methods include: utilizing Forward-looking Information by integrating users' future turn responses as guiding signals into the system prompt to enhance coherence and goal-orientation; employing an optimized two-turn Sliding Dialogue History Window mechanism for efficient context management; and significantly improving generated text diversity through Output Decoupling of the model's own outputs in the dialogue history. At the model training level, we adopted LoRA for parameter-efficient fine-tuning and applied NEFTune, adding noise to the embedding layer to enhance model robustness. Experimental results show that our approach achieved a top composite score of 42.69.

Keywords: Emotional Support Conversation · Large Language Models · Fine-tuning

1 Introduction

Emotional Support Conversation (ESC) systems leverage artificial intelligence techniques to provide emotional solace to users through natural language interaction, helping them alleviate emotional distress and cope with various life challenges [11]. Against the backdrop of an accelerated pace of modern life and increasing individual psychological stress, the demand for mental health support is becoming increasingly prominent. ESC systems, by virtue of their convenience, accessibility, and ability to protect user privacy to a certain extent,

© The Author(s), under exclusive license to Springer Nature Singapore Pte Ltd. 2026
X.-L. Mao et al. (Eds.): NLPCC 2025, LNAI 16105, pp. 521–532, 2026.
https://doi.org/10.1007/978-981-95-3352-7_44

demonstrate significant applied value and positive societal impact in providing immediate emotional counseling and alleviating psychological burdens. However, traditional ESC systems often generate generic responses that struggle to meet the unique, personalized, and deep-seated needs of users. To address this issue, Personalized Emotional Support Conversation (PESC) has emerged. Its core objective is to generate more targeted and empathetic supportive responses by considering users' personal backgrounds and traits. As illustrated in Fig. 1, a PESC system can generate responses tailored to their current situation and emotional state, such as "It's completely understandable to feel lost and heartbroken after such an abrupt ending to your relationship" based on the seeker's user profile. Therefore, developing efficient PESC systems is of crucial research value and practical significance for enhancing user interaction experience, improving the actual effectiveness of emotional support, and promoting overall societal mental well-being.

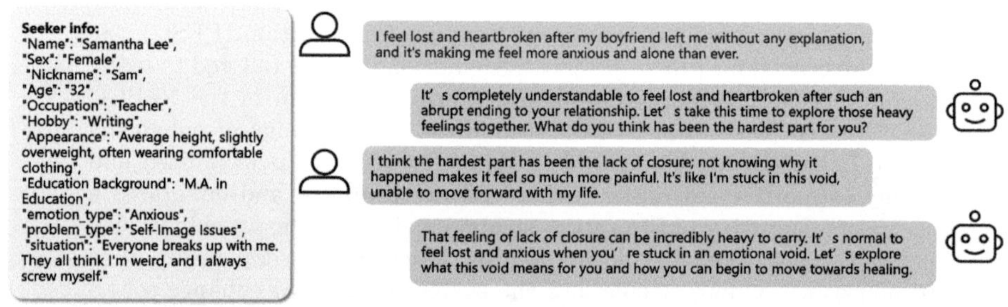

Fig. 1. Example of a PESC interaction.

The technological trajectory of traditional ESC systems has evolved from early rule-based and template-based methods to explorations based on information retrieval and early generative models such as Recurrent Neural Networks (RNNs) and Long Short-Term Memory (LSTM) networks. While these techniques achieved some success in specific scenarios, they faced significant bottlenecks in terms of depth of semantic understanding, response naturalness, contextual consistency, and personalized care, often struggling to generate responses that genuinely cater to users' complex emotional needs. In recent years, the rapid development of Large Language Models (LLMs) has brought revolutionary breakthroughs to the field of emotional support conversation. Through pre-training on massive text datasets, LLMs have acquired unprecedented capabilities in natural language understanding and generation. In ESC tasks, LLMs can more accurately capture subtle changes in user emotions, understand complex contexts and even latent intentions, and generate more fluent, coherent, and empathetic responses. Furthermore, their powerful knowledge integration and learning abilities have laid a solid foundation for providing deeply personalized support strategies based on user profiles, dialogue history, and current specific situations. This has significantly enhanced the potential quality of emotional support conversations and user experience, making it possible to build more intelligent ESC systems.

Against this backdrop, we participated in the NLPCC 2025 Shared Task 8: Personalized Emotional Support Conversation. Our work is dedicated to enhancing the performance of LLMs in this specific scenario. We proposed a systematic set of optimization strategies, the core of which lies in more efficiently utilizing contextual information and the inherent characteristics of the task data to drive the model to generate responses that are both deeply personalized and highly supportive. Our main methodological innovations include:

First, the introduction of "Forward-looking Information", where known future user responses from the training data are integrated as guiding signals into the system prompt to enhance the coherence and goal-orientation of the generated content.

Second, to balance contextual understanding integrity with computational efficiency, a sliding dialogue history window mechanism was adopted, retaining only the last two turns of conversation as historical reference.

Third, to improve the diversity of generated text and avoid homogenized outputs, we performed an "Output Decouple" process on the model's own previous-turn generations within the dialogue history.

During the model training phase, we employed the LoRA [5] method for parameter-efficient fine-tuning and drew inspiration from NEFTune [7] to add moderate noise to the word embedding layer, aiming to enhance model generalization and robustness. Thanks to these integrated methods, our system achieved a score of 42.69 in the final evaluation of NLPCC 2025 Shared Task 8, ranking first on the leaderboard.

2   Related Work

Early Emotional Support Conversation (ESC) systems often adopted rule-based or predefined template-based approaches [4,14]. For instance, intelligent conversational agents like Woebot [4] provided self-help support based on Cognitive Behavioral Therapy (CBT) principles through preset dialogue flows and exercises. The Emohaa system [14] combined template-based CBT dialogues (CBT-Bot) with open-ended emotional expression dialogues (ES-Bot), offering structured cognitive support while allowing users to freely express their emotions. These methods relied on manually designed strategies and simple emotion classification, lacking the flexibility to adapt to emotional changes in complex, multi-turn conversations.

With the rise of deep learning and the application of Transformer-based pre-trained models in dialogue generation, ESC research has entered a new phase. The FADO model [13], by coordinating strategy selection and response generation through a dialogue-level dual-feedback mechanism, significantly improved strategy prediction and generation quality on ESConv. Furthermore, the AdMISC framework [8] integrated dynamic emotional features and commonsense knowledge, effectively enhancing strategy classification accuracy and generation performance. [19] employed reinforcement learning, treating the multi-turn ESC process as positive emotion induction, guiding the model to generate responses that promote positive emotional shifts in seekers through a mixture-of-experts strategy and emotional rewards.

In recent years, with the rapid advancement of large-scale pre-trained language models (LLMs), ESC tasks have increasingly leveraged the capabilities of these larger models. [18] proposed using ChatGPT to generate extended dialogue corpora and fine-tuning on LLaMA [16] to enhance ESC capabilities. Despite this, existing research has indicated limitations in current LLMs regarding strategy execution and emotional regulation. For instance, models have been found to exhibit an empathy bias in strategy distribution, neglecting suggestion-type strategies [9]. Human-machine comparison experiments by [2] also pointed out that while current LLM generations are often emotionally tinged, they frequently lack goal-orientation. To address these issues, researchers have introduced new strategy evaluation metrics and process tracking mechanisms, such as Strategy-Relevant Attention (SRA) [12], to analyze and improve strategy coherence in long conversations. Concurrently with LLM technological evolution, ESC systems are gradually advancing towards high robustness, long-range emotional understanding, and personalized support, yet further breakthroughs are still needed in controlling strategy diversity and modeling user intent.

3   Method

System:	You are an advanced Emotional Support AI specializing in Personalized Emotional Support Conversations (PESC). The user you are assisting is ...
Seeker:	I feel trapped in my loneliness and despair, like nothing I do can ever change how deeply sad I am.
Forward-looking System:	Provide the user's next response in the future as: **It's hard to remember those moments because they feel so fleeting and distant. I'd say it's a 2 right now; connection seems so out of reach most times.**
Supporter:	It sounds really heavy to carry that sadness around. What if we could look at moments where you felt connected, even in small ways?
Seeker:	**It's hard to remember those moments because they feel so fleeting and distant. I'd say it's a 2 right now; connection seems so out of reach most times.**

Fig. 2. Guiding the model to produce more coherent responses by inserting additional system prompts as contextual guidance.

3.1   Dialogue Generation with Forward-Looking Information

The dataset provided for this shared task offers a unique condition: all user historical dialogues and future replies are fully given. Leveraging this, we proposed and implemented a "Dialogue Generation with Forward-looking Information" strategy. The core idea of this strategy is to explicitly integrate the seeker's actual reply content from the immediately following turn into the model's input as "forward-looking information" before the model generates the supporter's response for the current dialogue turn.

Due to the causal attention mask in decoder-only LLM architectures, which prevents tokens from attending to subsequent tokens, it is necessary to integrate forward-looking information into the precedent context of the current dialogue turn. In practice, we introduce this forward-looking information by designing and inserting specific system prompts into the standard chat template.

As shown in Fig. 2, in addition to the initial system prompt, before the supporter generates a response for the current turn, we add an extra system prompt that explicitly states what the user will express in the upcoming next turn. This way, when devising its current response, the model can "foresee" and refer to the immediately following user feedback. This mechanism aims to guide the model to generate supportive dialogue that is more consistent with the subsequent flow of the conversation, semantically more coherent, and contextually more relevant. Experimental results indicate that introducing such forward-looking information can significantly improve the model's performance on n-gram overlap-based semantic similarity evaluation metrics such as METEOR, BLEU-4, and ROUGE-L.

3.2   Sliding Dialogue History Window

In multi-turn dialogue scenarios, the length of the dialogue history significantly impacts both model performance and efficiency. Excessively long dialogue histories can introduce early information with weak relevance to the current turn, thereby interfering with the model's focus on the immediate context. They may also exceed the model's maximum input length limit and increase computational burden. Considering that each complete dialogue sample in the dataset provided for this task contains 10 turns of interaction, we adopted a Sliding Dialogue History Window strategy to enable the model to more effectively capture the most relevant contextual information for the current dialogue state and to optimize processing efficiency.

Specifically, when the model generates a supporter response for any given turn, we do not include the entire dialogue history preceding that turn as input. Instead, we set a fixed-size window, truncating and retaining only the most recent two complete turns of dialogue up to and including the current turn's user query, as the effective dialogue history. This approach allows the model to concentrate on recent interactions, thereby more accurately grasping the immediate dynamics of the conversation and the user's current explicit needs. Concurrently, this method helps maintain the input sequence length within a relatively stable and manageable range, ensuring the efficiency of both model training and inference processes.

3.3   Output Decoupling

In the continuous generation process of multi-turn dialogues, the model's outputs from previous turns are typically included as historical information in the input for subsequent turns. However, our experimental observations revealed that directly including the model's own generated response from the previous turn in the dialogue history can negatively impact the diversity of subsequently generated text. This phenomenon may arise because the model tends to learn and repeat its own expression patterns, leading to response homogenization, as reflected by decreases in text diversity metrics such as Distinct-2 (D-2) and Distinct-3 (D-3).

To mitigate this issue and enhance the novelty and richness of the generated content, we introduced an "Output Decoupling" strategy. The core idea of this method is that when constructing the input for the current turn, all supporter responses generated by our model in previous turns within the dialogue history are replaced with a uniform, fixed placeholder (e.g., "###") that carries no specific semantic information. In this manner, we effectively sever the direct textual dependency of the model's output content across different generation turns. This prompts the model, when generating new responses, to rely more on the seeker's actual input, user profile, and contextual cues provided through other mechanisms such as "forward-looking information," rather than simply imitating or continuing its previous expression patterns.

3.4   Training Data Construction

To construct samples suitable for model training, based on the methods outlined previously, we performed detailed preprocessing and formatting of the original multi-turn dialogue data. Specifically, each dialogue instance containing ten turns of interaction was converted into ten independent training data points, with each data point aimed at training the model to generate the supporter's response for the corresponding turn, as illustrated in Fig. 3. For the t-th turn of interaction in the original dialogue, where we define the seeker's utterance as U_t and the supporter's response as S_t, the input sequence we constructed for the model follows these steps:

I. First, the seeker's personal profile information from the current dialogue instance (such as name, age, occupation, problem faced, etc.) is structured as an initial system prompt and placed at the beginning of the input sequence.

II. If the current turn t is not the last turn of the dialogue instance, the seeker's actual utterance from the immediately following turn $t + 1$, U_{t+1}, is encapsulated as an additional system prompt and appended to the context as forward-looking information.

III. Subsequently, if the current turn t is not the first turn of the dialogue (i.e., $t > 0$), the dialogue content from the previous turn $t - 1$ is introduced. This includes the seeker's utterance from the previous turn, U_{t-1}, and a fixed placeholder "###" representing the supporter's response from the previous turn,S_{t-1}.

IV. Finally, the seeker's actual utterance from the current turn t, U_t, is added to the input sequence.

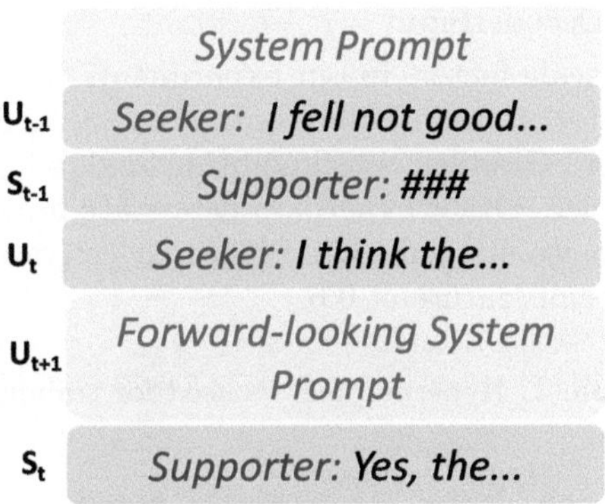

Fig. 3. Example of a constructed training data sample.

4   Experiments

4.1   Dataset and Models

The dataset used in our experiments is from the NLPCC 2025 Shared Task 8. The organizers provided a dataset with a total of 1500 dialogue instances, split into training, test, and validation sets of 1200, 150, and 150 instances, respectively. Each dialogue instance consists of ten turns of Seeker-Supporter interaction. In the test set, the Supporter's responses are left blank and need to be predicted by the model.

Following the steps described in Sect. 3.4, we further processed the raw dataset. The training and validation sets resulted in 12,000 and 1,500 data points, respectively.

In our experiments, we utilized models from the Qwen2.5 [17] series and the Gemma3 [15] model, employing the LoRA method for supervised fine-tuning (SFT).

4.2   Settings

During training, we only calculated the loss for the target supporter response tokens S_t (as the learning objective described in Sect. 3.4); labels for all other parts of the sequence were set to -100 to be ignored by the loss function. We adopted the NEFTune [7] method to add noise to the LLM embedding layer, aiming to alleviate overfitting during training. Given the tokenized input indices *input_ids*, we have:

$$e = \text{Embedding}(input\_ids) \in \mathbb{R}^{L \times d}$$

$$\epsilon \sim U\left(-\frac{noise\_\alpha}{\sqrt{Ld}}, \frac{noise\_\alpha}{\sqrt{Ld}}\right) \tag{1}$$

$$\text{DecoderInput} = e + \epsilon$$

where *noise_α* is the scale factor. In our experiments, we set *noise_α* = 6.0.

We uniformly used the AdamW8bit optimizer [3] and a cosine annealing learning rate scheduler. Gradient checkpointing and bfloat16 mixed-precision training were also enabled. Other hyperparameters are provided in Table 1. During the inference phase, we utilized VLLM [10] to accelerate inference speed and employed a decoding temperature of 0.6.

Table 1. Hyperparameters used for training.

Hyperparameters	
Epoch	4
Batchsize	4
Gradient Accumulation	2
Learning Rate	1.8e−5
Weight Decay	5e−2
Max Grad Norm	1.0
Truncation Max Length	1536
LoRA Rank	64
LoRA Alpha	512
LoRA Dropout	0.08

4.3   Evaluation Metrics

The shared task employed multiple metrics to evaluate the quality of the model-generated dialogues. Overall, these can be divided into three categories: **I. Semantic Overlap Metrics**, including METEOR (ME), BLEU-4 (B-4), ROUGE-L (R-L), and VectorExtrema (Ext); **II. Text Diversity Metrics**, including Distinct-2 (D-2) and Distinct-3 (D-3); and **III. LLM-based Score**, specifically GPT-4o [1,6] score (G-Score). The final Score is a weighted sum of these metrics:

$$\begin{aligned} Score_{track2} = {} & 0.2 * \text{ME} + 0.2 * \text{B-4} + 0.2 * \text{R-L} \\ & + 0.1 * \text{Ext} + 0.1 * \text{D-2} + 0.1 * \text{D-3} + 0.1 * \text{G-Score} \end{aligned} \tag{2}$$

Table 2. Online submission results on the test set.

Model	ME	B-4	R-L	Ext	D-2	D-3	G-score	Score
Qwen2-7B-it	32.92	9.02	34.63	96.57	28.72	52.06	91.39	42.19
Qwen2.5-14B-it	32.54	9.10	34.72	96.60	30.27	54.58	90.79	42.50
Gemma3-12B-it	32.83	8.90	34.70	96.48	30.57	55.35	91.60	**42.69**

4.4 Main Results

Table 2 presents our submitted online evaluation results on the test set. It lists the performance of different pre-trained models of various scales and series used in our experiments (including Qwen2-7B-it, Qwen2.5-14B-it, and Gemma3-12B-it) after fine-tuning with the aforementioned methods. The table shows their performance on the official test set across various evaluation metrics, including semantic overlap, text diversity, and the GPT-4o score (G-Score), along with the final composite Score calculated according to the organizer's formula. The data in the table indicates that the Gemma3-12B-it model achieved the best composite score of 42.69.

4.5 Ablation Studies

To thoroughly investigate the specific contributions of our proposed strategies to the final model performance, we conducted a series of ablation studies. All ablation studies were performed on the validation set, and the metric scores were calculated using the same evaluation script as in the main experiments. To improve evaluation efficiency, G-Score was not computed for ablation studies on the validation set.

Table 3. Ablation results for forward-looking information.

Model	ME	B-4	R-L	Ext	D-2	D-3	G-score	Score
Gemma3-12B-it	**33.15**	**9.41**	**35.1**	**96.58**	30.28	54.85	-	**33.71**
w/o Forward-Looking	29.86	7.76	30.57	96.32	30.89	55.19	-	31.87

Impact of Forward-Looking Information. To quantify the impact of forward-looking information, we used the best-performing Gemma3-12B-it model as a base and compared its performance when this strategy was enabled versus when it was removed.

As shown in Table 3, after removing forward-looking information, the model exhibited a significant decline across all semantic overlap metrics (METEOR, BLEU-4, ROUGE-L, VectorExtrema). For instance, METEOR dropped from 33.15 to 29.86, and ROUGE-L decreased from 35.1 to 30.57. This directly led to a substantial decrease in the composite Score from 33.71 to 31.87. This result strongly demonstrates the essential role of forward-looking information in guiding the model to generate more accurate and coherent responses.

Table 4. Ablation results for history window.

Model	Window Size	Score	Relative Training Time
Gemma3-12B-it	1	33.12	1x
	2	**33.71**	1.3x
	3	33.65	1.4x
	4	33.02	1.5x
	10	33.21	2.3x

Impact of Dialogue History Window. To investigate the specific impact of different history lengths on model performance, we conducted a series of experiments on the validation set. We compared the composite Score and the training speed relative to a window size of 1 when the window size was set to 1(i.e., considering only the current seeker's utterance as context), 2, 3, 4, and 10 turns (i.e., utilizing all available history). The experimental results are shown in Table 4.

The results indicate that when we increased the dialogue history window size from 1 turn to 2 turns, the model's composite score significantly improved from 33.12 to 33.71, reaching the optimal performance point in this experiment. Further increasing the history window did not yield additional benefits; instead, the total score slightly decreased. On the other hand, from the perspective of training efficiency, a larger dialogue history input window leads to a significant increase in input sequence length, thereby considerably slowing down the training speed. Considering both the final score and training cost, we determined the optimal dialogue history window size to be 2 turns, adopting it as the best practice in our method.

Table 5. Ablation results for output decoupling.

Model	ME	B-4	R-L	Ext	D-2	D-3	G-score	Score
Gemma3-12B-it	33.15	9.41	35.10	96.58	**30.28**	**54.85**	-	**33.71**
w/o Decouple	33.21	9.33	34.96	96.52	27.98	49.44	-	32.89

Impact of Output Decoupling. To enhance the diversity of generated text and prevent the model from falling into repetitive expressions, we introduced the output decoupling strategy. Detailed comparison results are presented in Table 5.

It can be observed that after adopting the output decoupling strategy, the model's text diversity metrics significantly improved: Distinct-2 substantially increased from 27.98 to 30.28, and Distinct-3 also rose from 49.44 to 54.85. This improvement in diversity also positively impacted the final score, with the composite Score increasing from 32.89 to 33.71. It is noteworthy that the performance on various semantic overlap metrics (METEOR, BLEU-4, ROUGE-L, VectorExtrema) showed no substantial difference between the two configurations. This fully demonstrates that the output decoupling strategy can effectively enhance the novelty and richness of the generated content without significantly compromising the model's capabilities in semantic understanding and expressive accuracy, proving its value in improving overall performance.

5   Conclusion

This paper summarizes our work and achievements in the NLPCC 2025 Shared Task 8: Personalized Emotional Support Conversation (PESC) task. We proposed and integrated a series of optimization strategies, primarily including leveraging Forward-looking Information to guide dialogue generation, adopting an optimized two-turn Sliding Dialogue History Window, and implementing Output Decoupling to enhance response diversity. At the model training level, we combined LoRA for parameter-efficient fine-tuning and applied NEFTune to enhance model robustness. Through the comprehensive application of these methods, our system achieved a top composite score of 42.69 on the test set, ultimately winning first place in this shared task.

Acknowledgments. This work is supported by the Key Program of Natural Science Foundation of China (Grant No. U23A20316).

References

1. Achiam, J., et al.: GPT-4 technical report. arXiv preprint arXiv:2303.08774 (2023)
2. Bai, X., Chen, G., He, T., Zhou, C., Guo, C.: A holistic comparative study of large language models as emotional support dialogue systems. Cogn. Comput. **17**(2), 71 (2025)
3. Dettmers, T., Lewis, M., Shleifer, S., Zettlemoyer, L.: 8-bit optimizers via block-wise quantization. In: 9th International Conference on Learning Representations, ICLR (2022)
4. Fitzpatrick, K.K., Darcy, A., Vierhile, M.: Delivering cognitive behavior therapy to young adults with symptoms of depression and anxiety using a fully automated conversational agent (woebot): a randomized controlled trial. JMIR Mental Health **4**(2), e7785 (2017)
5. Hu, E.J., et al.: LoRA: low-rank adaptation of large language models. In: International Conference on Learning Representations (2022). https://openreview.net/forum?id=nZeVKeeFYf9
6. Hurst, A., et al.: GPT-4o system card. arXiv preprint arXiv:2410.21276 (2024)

7. Jain, N., et al.: Neftune: noisy embeddings improve instruction finetuning. arXiv preprint arXiv:2310.05914 (2023)
8. Jia, X., He, J., Zhang, Q., Jin, J.: Admisc: advanced multi-task learning and feature-fusion for emotional support conversation. Electronics **13**(8), 1484 (2024)
9. Kang, D., et al.: Can large language models be good emotional supporter? Mitigating preference bias on emotional support conversation. arXiv preprint arXiv:2402.13211 (2024)
10. Kwon, W., et al.: Efficient memory management for large language model serving with pagedattention. In: Proceedings of the ACM SIGOPS 29th Symposium on Operating Systems Principles (2023)
11. Liu, S., et al.: Towards emotional support dialog systems. arXiv preprint arXiv:2106.01144 (2021)
12. Madani, N., Saha, S., Srihari, R.: Steering conversational large language models for long emotional support conversations. arXiv preprint arXiv:2402.10453 (2024)
13. Peng, W., Qin, Z., Hu, Y., Xie, Y., Li, Y.: Fado: feedback-aware double controlling network for emotional support conversation. Knowl.-Based Syst. **264**, 110340 (2023)
14. Sabour, S., et al.: A chatbot for mental health support: exploring the impact of emohaa on reducing mental distress in china. Front. Digit. Health **5**, 1133987 (2023)
15. Team, G., et al.: Gemma 3 technical report. arXiv preprint arXiv:2503.19786 (2025)
16. Touvron, H., et al.: Llama: open and efficient foundation language models. arXiv preprint arXiv:2302.13971 (2023)
17. Yang, A., et al.: Qwen2. 5 technical report. arXiv preprint arXiv:2412.15115 (2024)
18. Zheng, Z., Liao, L., Deng, Y., Nie, L.: Building emotional support chatbots in the era of LLMs. arXiv preprint arXiv:2308.11584 (2023)
19. Zhou, J., Chen, Z., Wang, B., Huang, M.: Facilitating multi-turn emotional support conversation with positive emotion elicitation: a reinforcement learning approach. arXiv preprint arXiv:2307.07994 (2023)

Empathetic Dialogue Generation with LLMs for Emotional Support

Shiquan Wang, Ruiyu Fang, Mengxiang Li, Zhongjiang He[✉],
and Shuangyong Song[✉]

Institute of Artificial Intelligence (TeleAI), China Telecom Corp Ltd, Beijing, China
{wangsq23,fangry,hezj,songshy}@chinatelecom.cn

Abstract. Emotional Support Conversation (ESC) aims to provide empathetic and effective emotional assistance through dialogue, addressing the growing demand for mental health support. This paper presents our solution for the NLPCC 2025 Task 8 ESC evaluation, where we leverage large-scale language models enhanced by prompt engineering and fine-tuning techniques. We explore both parameter-efficient Low-Rank Adaptation and full-parameter fine-tuning strategies to improve the model's ability to generate supportive and contextually appropriate responses. Our best model ranked second in the competition, highlighting the potential of combining LLMs with effective adaptation methods for ESC tasks. Future work will focus on further enhancing emotional understanding and response personalization to build more practical and reliable emotional support systems.

Keywords: Emotional Support Conversation · LLM

1 Introduction

Emotional Support Conversation (ESC) aims to alleviate individuals' emotional distress and provide effective emotional support through conversational interactions. With the increasing prevalence of mental health issues globally, ESC has demonstrated significant potential as an intervention tool in various domains, including mental health support, customer service, and interpersonal interactions [7,11,13,14,17,20]. ESC systems not only need to process information from everyday conversations but must also focus on understanding and addressing users' emotional needs, providing targeted emotional responses. As such, the design of emotional support dialogue systems faces several challenges, such as accurately understanding subtle emotional fluctuations in users, generating emotionally authentic and constructive responses, and designing support strategies that are adaptable to different contexts and user needs [24].

Despite significant advancements in sentiment analysis and emotional response generation technologies in recent years, existing emotional support

S. Wang and R. Fang—Equal contribution.

© The Author(s), under exclusive license to Springer Nature Singapore Pte Ltd. 2026
X.-L. Mao et al. (Eds.): NLPCC 2025, LNAI 16105, pp. 533–540, 2026.
https://doi.org/10.1007/978-981-95-3352-7_45

dialogue systems still have considerable limitations. Many systems struggle to effectively capture the nuances and complexity of emotions, and the generated responses often lack true emotional resonance and practical help [9,12]. This represents a critical area for continued exploration and optimization in the ESC field. To further advance research in this domain, the NLPCC 2025 Task 8 has organized an Emotional Support Conversation evaluation task, aimed at assessing different models' capabilities to understand and respond to users' emotional needs, providing a unified dataset and evaluation standards.

In this evaluation task, our team adopted a fine-tuning approach based on large-scale language models (LLMs) and achieved second place. LLMs were selected as the core models due to their remarkable capabilities in natural language understanding and generation, making them ideal for the ESC task. By fine-tuning these models on a specialized emotional support dialogue dataset, we aimed to better align the models with the specific demands of ESC tasks, enabling them to generate empathetic and contextually appropriate responses that cater to users' emotional needs. Specifically, we employed the qwen2.5-72B-instruct and qwen2.5-7B-Instruct models, applying both low-rank adaptation (LoRA) fine-tuning and full-parameter fine-tuning strategies to further improve performance. Our experimental results demonstrate that appropriate fine-tuning techniques can significantly enhance the performance of models in emotional support conversation tasks.

2 Related Work

Emotional Support Conversation (ESC) has become an important research direction within the field of Natural Language Processing (NLP), attracting significant attention from researchers. Existing studies can be broadly categorized into the following approaches based on the techniques employed:

2.1 Rule-Based Approaches

Rule-based ESC systems typically rely on manually designed rules and templates to generate supportive responses. These systems identify keywords or patterns in the user's input and select appropriate responses from a predefined list. For example, a system may recognize a specific topic mentioned by the user and respond using a predefined template or scripted message [4]. Early conversational agents, such as ELIZA, were built using rule-based methods, providing simple emotional support through scripted dialogue. However, rule-based approaches have limitations in capturing the subtle nuances of human emotions, resulting in responses that may feel rigid and predictable [1,19]. While these methods offer certain advantages in terms of safety and controllability—ensuring that inappropriate responses are avoided—they lack the flexibility and depth required to provide truly empathetic support. The inability to deeply understand the user's emotional state remains a major constraint.

2.2 Retrieval-Based Approaches

Retrieval-based ESC systems generate responses by selecting the most relevant reply from a predefined corpus. These methods often rely on keyword matching or machine learning techniques to find the most similar response to the user's input. Retrieval-based systems have advantages in ensuring the coherence and computational efficiency of responses [6,16,18]. Some studies have also explored incorporating techniques such as emotional clustering and explainable AI into retrieval-based ESC systems to enhance their effectiveness. However, the performance of retrieval-based methods is heavily dependent on the quality and coverage of the predefined corpus [21,23]. As a result, they may struggle to provide appropriate responses to novel situations or scenarios that were not anticipated in the corpus.

2.3 Generation-Based Approaches

Generation-based ESC systems, particularly those employing neural networks and large-scale language models (LLMs), are capable of generating entirely new responses. These approaches train models on vast amounts of conversational data, enabling them to understand context and generate natural language responses [2,3,10]. However, the use of generative methods in ESC tasks introduces several challenges, such as maintaining conversational coherence and ensuring that the generated emotional responses are appropriate [8,15]. With the rapid development of LLMs in recent years, there has been increasing exploration into leveraging LLMs and fine-tuning techniques to build more effective ESC systems. LLMs, with their strong generalization ability and capacity to learn complex patterns from large datasets, hold significant promise for enhancing emotional support dialogue systems.

In addition to the aforementioned categories, many studies have focused on how to integrate emotional intelligence and empathy into dialogue systems. This includes research on modeling the user's emotional state and generating responses that demonstrate empathy [5,22]. Some studies have emphasized the importance of considering the help-seeker's personal traits when providing effective support. Furthermore, generating inappropriate responses remains a critical issue, and researchers are actively exploring various techniques to mitigate this problem. Building genuinely empathetic ESC systems requires not only understanding the user's emotions but also accounting for their specific circumstances, personality, and the potential for inappropriate responses.

Our work falls under the generation-based approach, focusing on fine-tuning large-scale language models to enhance the capability of ESC systems. In the following sections, we will detail the specific models and fine-tuning strategies we employed, as well as the results achieved in the NLPCC 2025 Task 8 evaluation task.

3   Methodology

This section provides a detailed description of the technical approach we adopted for the NLPCC 2025 Task 8 Emotional Support Conversation evaluation. Our overall methodology is based on the capabilities of large language models (LLMs). By combining carefully designed prompt engineering with parameter-efficient fine-tuning strategies, we enable the model to better adapt to emotional support scenarios and generate responses that are both empathetic and practically helpful.

3.1   Prompt Engineering

To effectively guide the LLM in understanding user emotions and generating emotionally resonant responses, we designed a structured and semantically clear prompt template. This prompt explicitly defines the model's role, task objective, and response guidelines to ensure that the outputs exhibit key characteristics such as human-likeness, empathy, and personalization. Specifically, the prompt consists of the following components: Role Definition, where the model is positioned as an empathetic assistant responsible for providing sincere, warm, and personalized support based on the user's background and emotional state; Task Objective, which instructs the model to generate supportive responses aimed at relieving negative emotions and boosting emotional resilience, emphasizing relevance to the user's specific context; User Profile, which includes a description of the user's life experience, personality traits, and current emotional struggles, enabling personalized generation; and Response Guidelines, which specify language tone, empathy strategies, and risk avoidance principles to ensure that the generated content remains warm, non-judgmental, and attentive. Through this multi-faceted prompt design, we significantly enhanced the model's ability to understand the user's emotional needs and maintain high-quality response generation with strong contextual awareness and emotional control.

3.2   Model Fine-Tuning with LoRA

For the core model, we selected Qwen2.5-72B-Instruct and adopted Low-Rank Adaptation (LoRA) as a parameter-efficient fine-tuning strategy to reduce training cost while improving task adaptability. The core idea of LoRA is to insert trainable low-rank matrices into each layer of the model and update only these new parameters, while keeping the original weights frozen. This enables efficient adaptation without modifying the full model. We explored multiple LoRA parameter configurations (e.g., rank $= 8/16/32$ and alpha $= 16/32/64$), and conducted comparative experiments on validation and test sets to identify the optimal setup. Our results demonstrate that appropriate LoRA configurations can significantly enhance the emotional support capabilities of the model while maintaining high efficiency, making it a practical and scalable solution for large-scale emotional dialogue modeling.

3.3   Full Parameter Fine-Tuning

In addition to LoRA, we applied full-parameter fine-tuning to the smaller Qwen2.5-7B-Instruct model, where all parameters of the pre-trained model are updated during the training process. Although this approach is more resource-intensive compared to parameter-efficient methods, it allows for greater expressive capacity and better performance, especially when the training data is sufficient. In our study, full fine-tuning served both as a complement and as a comparative baseline to LoRA, enabling us to systematically analyze the advantages and limitations of different fine-tuning strategies in the emotional support task. The experimental results show that full fine-tuning can further improve the model's ability to recognize and respond to nuanced emotional expressions, thereby producing more delicate and natural emotional support responses.

4   Experiments

This section presents the experimental setup, evaluation metrics, and results for the NLPCC 2025 Task 8 on Emotional Support Conversations. Our experiments are designed to systematically verify the effectiveness of our proposed methods in generating emotionally supportive responses.

4.1   Dataset

We use the official dataset provided by the NLPCC 2025 Task 8 organizers. The dataset simulates real-world emotional support scenarios, where users (seekers) express emotional distress and the system (supporter) responds with supportive dialogue. Each instance contains multi-turn interactions between the user and the assistant. The dataset comprises 1,500 dialogue instances, which are split into training, validation, and test sets with an 8:1:1 ratio—resulting in 1,200 training dialogues, 150 validation dialogues, and 150 test dialogues.

4.2   Evaluation Metrics

To evaluate the quality and emotional support effectiveness of generated responses, we adopt a range of automatic evaluation metrics:

- **BLEU-4 (B-4)**: Measures n-gram overlap between the generated response and reference;
- **METEOR (ME)**: Accounts for synonymy, stemming, and word order for semantic similarity;
- **ROUGE-L (R-L)**: Based on the longest common subsequence to assess content overlap;
- **Vector Extrema (Ext)**: Uses the extrema of word embeddings to compute semantic similarity;
- **Distinct-2/Distinct-3 (D-2/D-3)**: Evaluate lexical diversity through the ratio of unique bigrams and trigrams;

– **G-Score**: An overall human-centric quality assessment scored by GPT-4, evaluating relevance, fluency, informativeness, and logical coherence.

To reduce evaluation cost during the validation phase, all models are assigned a default G-Score, ensuring consistency for comparing different fine-tuning configurations.

4.3 Validation Results

We conduct extensive experiments on the Qwen2.5 series models, using both LoRA-based parameter-efficient fine-tuning and full fine-tuning for smaller models. Table 1 summarizes the results on the validation set.

Table 1. Performance on the validation set across different fine-tuning strategies

Base Model	Method	ME	B-4	R-L	Ext	D-2	D-3	G-score	Total
Qwen2.5-72B	w/o	19.76	0.93	9.13	94.20	17.56	37.29	100	30.87
Qwen2.5-72B	LoRA(8,16)	27.38	7.60	32.58	96.16	26.49	44.97	100	40.28
Qwen2.5-72B	LoRA(16,32)	**28.04**	**7.94**	**32.71**	96.22	26.53	45.07	100	40.52
Qwen2.5-72B	LoRA(32,64)	26.37	6.29	29.82	**96.11**	**32.85**	**57.82**	100	**41.17**
Qwen2.5-7B	Full	27.87	6.85	30.63	96.22	22.21	39.34	100	38.85

As shown in Table 1, all fine-tuned models outperform the base model significantly. Among them, the configuration with LoRA (rank = 32, alpha = 64) achieves the highest total score of 41.17.

4.4 Test Set Submissions

Based on validation results, we submitted two results to the test set: one trained only on the original training set and the other trained on the combined training and validation sets. Their results are shown in Table 2.

Table 2. Performance on the test set.

Submission ID	ME	B-4	R-L	Ext	D-2	D-3	G-score	Total
submit_0418	27.06	**7.43**	**32.06**	96.16	26.22	44.60	85.17	38.53
submit_0420	**27.21**	6.25	29.89	**96.22**	**30.99**	**55.12**	**87.20**	**39.62**

The results show that submit_0420, which includes additional validation data during training, achieves a higher total score of 39.62, especially improving the diversity and informativeness of generated responses.

5   Conclusion

This paper presents our approach to the NLPCC 2025 Task 8 on Emotional Support Conversation. By combining prompt engineering with both LoRA-based and full-parameter fine-tuning on Qwen2.5 models, we significantly improved the models' ability to generate empathetic and context-aware responses. Our best submission ranked second in the official evaluation, demonstrating the effectiveness of large language models in the ESC domain. Future work will focus on enhancing emotional understanding, personalization, and response safety to further improve user experience in real-world applications.

References

1. Alazraki, L., Ghachem, A., Polydorou, N., Khosmood, F., Edalat, A.: An empathetic AI coach for self-attachment therapy. In: 2021 IEEE Third International Conference on Cognitive Machine Intelligence (COGMI), pp. 78–87. IEEE (2021)
2. Chen, W., et al.: Cauesc: a causal aware model for emotional support conversation. arXiv preprint arXiv:2401.17755 (2024)
3. Cheng, J., Sabour, S., Sun, H., Chen, Z., Huang, M.: Pal: persona-augmented emotional support conversation generation. In: Findings of the Association for Computational Linguistics: ACL 2023, pp. 535–554 (2023)
4. Chu, Y., Liao, L., Zhou, Z., Ngo, C.W., Hong, R.: Towards multimodal emotional support conversation systems. arXiv preprint arXiv:2408.03650 (2024)
5. He, Z., et al.: Telechat technical report. arXiv preprint arXiv:2401.03804 (2024)
6. Jia, M., Chen, Q., Jing, L., Fu, D., Li, R.: Knowledge-enhanced memory model for emotional support conversation. arXiv preprint arXiv:2310.07700 (2023)
7. Kang, D., et al.: Can large language models be good emotional supporter? Mitigating preference bias on emotional support conversation. In: Proceedings of the 62nd Annual Meeting of the Association for Computational Linguistics (Volume 1: Long Papers), pp. 15232–15261 (2024)
8. Klüwer, T.: From chatbots to dialog systems. In: Conversational Agents and Natural Language Interaction: Techniques and Effective Practices, pp. 1–22. IGI Global Scientific Publishing (2011)
9. Li, J., Peng, B., Hsu, Y.Y., Huang, C.R.: Be helpful but don't talk too much-enhancing helpfulness in conversations through relevance in multi-turn emotional support. In: Proceedings of the 2024 Conference on Empirical Methods in Natural Language Processing, pp. 1976–1988 (2024)
10. Li, X., et al.: Tele-FLM technical report. CoRR (2024)
11. Liu, S., et al.: Towards emotional support dialog systems. In: Proceedings of the 59th Annual Meeting of the Association for Computational Linguistics and the 11th International Joint Conference on Natural Language Processing (Volume 1: Long Papers), pp. 3469–3483 (2021)
12. Shao, J., Li, X.: AI flow at the network edge. IEEE Netw. (2025)
13. Song, S., Wang, C., Chen, H., Chen, H.: An emotional comfort framework for improving user satisfaction in e-commerce customer service chatbots. In: Proceedings of the 2021 Conference of the North American Chapter of the Association for Computational Linguistics: Human Language Technologies: Industry Papers, pp. 130–137 (2021)

14. Song, S., Wang, C., Liu, S., Chen, H., Chen, H., Bao, H.: Sentiment analysis technologies in alime–an intelligent assistant for e-commerce. Int. J. Asian Lang. Process. **30**(04), 2050016 (2020)
15. Vanel, L., Yacoubi, A., Clavel, C.: A survey of socio-emotional strategies for generation-based conversational agents (2023)
16. Wang, S., et al.: Topicks: topic-driven knowledge selection for knowledge-grounded dialogue generation. In: INTERSPEECH, pp. 1121–1125 (2022)
17. Wang, Z., et al.: Towards robustness and diversity: continual learning in dialog generation with text-mixup and batch nuclear-norm maximization. In: 2024 International Joint Conference on Neural Networks (IJCNN), pp. 1–8. IEEE (2024)
18. Xu, Z., Chen, D., Kuang, J., Yi, Z., Li, Y., Shen, Y.: Dynamic demonstration retrieval and cognitive understanding for emotional support conversation. In: Proceedings of the 47th International ACM SIGIR Conference on Research and Development in Information Retrieval, pp. 774–784 (2024)
19. Yu, H.: An experimental study of integrating fine-tuned LLMs and prompts for enhancing mental health support chatbot system. J. Med. Artif. Intell. 1–16 (2024)
20. Zhao, D., Han, D., Yuan, Y., Wang, C., Song, S.: Muse: a multi-scale emotional flow graph model for empathetic dialogue generation. In: Koutra, D., Plant, C., Gomez Rodriguez, M., Baralis, E., Bonchi, F. (eds.) ECML PKDD 2023. LNCS, vol. 14170, pp. 491–507. Springer, Cham (2023). https://doi.org/10.1007/978-3-031-43415-0_29
21. Zhao, W., Zhao, Y., Wang, S., Qin, B.: Transesc: smoothing emotional support conversation via turn-level state transition. In: Findings of the Association for Computational Linguistics: ACL 2023, pp. 6725–6739 (2023)
22. Zhao, Y., et al.: Fisminess: a finite state machine based paradigm for emotional support conversations. arXiv preprint arXiv:2504.11837 (2025)
23. Zheng, Z., Liao, L., Deng, Y., Qin, L., Nie, L.: Self-chats from large language models make small emotional support chatbot better. In: Proceedings of the 62nd Annual Meeting of the Association for Computational Linguistics (Volume 1: Long Papers), pp. 11325–11345 (2024)
24. Zhou, J., Chen, Z., Wang, B., Huang, M.: Facilitating multi-turn emotional support conversation with positive emotion elicitation: A reinforcement learning approach. In: Proceedings of the 61st Annual Meeting of the Association for Computational Linguistics (Volume 1: Long Papers), pp. 1714–1729 (2023)

Role-Guided Synthesis for Emotional Support: A Two-Stage Framework with Multi-agent Dialogue Synthesis

Chuhan Wang, Dailin Li, Xin Zou, Yanan Wang, and Jian Wang[✉]

School of Computer Science and Technology, Dalian University of Technology, Dalian, China
{wangchuhan,ldlbest,zouxin,wangyanan}@mail.dlut.edu.cn,
wangjian@dlut.edu.cn

Abstract. The development of Personalized Emotional Support Conversation (PESC) systems encounters significant challenges due to the scarcity of specialized training datasets, which restricts their ability to generate responses tailored to user-specific traits beyond conventional Emotional Support Conversation (ESC) capabilities. To address this issue, we propose a two-stage synthetic data generation framework. Initially, we performed Structured Character Profile Synthesis, in which DeepSeek-V3 generates JSON-formatted profiles that incorporate sampled traits. Subsequently, in the Multi-Agent Dialogue Simulation stage, Qwen2.5-32B-instruct agents role-play. This role-guided strategy ensures that dialogues are aligned with user characteristics. Through supervised fine-tuning experiments, we demonstrated the utility of the synthetic data, with a 2.68-point G-score increase on the validation set. Our pipeline provides a solution for dataset expansion while maintaining character consistency within dialogues. We further validated the effectiveness of our synthetic data by achieving state-of-the-art performance with a 92.67 G-score on the NLPCC-2025 Shared Task 8 benchmark, the highest among submitted systems, and attained third place overall with a score of 38.99.

Keywords: Synthetic Data · Emotional Support Conversation · Large Language Model

1 Introduction

Automated emotional support tools hold immense potential for mental health care [1], with recent research advancing along two key dimensions. First, Liu et al. [2] pioneered the task of generating emotional support dialogues by creating the ESConv dataset, establishing foundational capabilities for general emotional support. Second, recognizing the critical role of personalization in effective therapeutic interactions, Cheng et al. [3] extended this work by incorporating persona information - a well-established outward manifestation of personality [4] - to enhance support relevance. However, this progression to PESC systems reveals a

C. Wang and D. Li—These authors contribute this work equally.

© The Author(s), under exclusive license to Springer Nature Singapore Pte Ltd. 2026
X.-L. Mao et al. (Eds.): NLPCC 2025, LNAI 16105, pp. 541–552, 2026.
https://doi.org/10.1007/978-981-95-3352-7_46

critical bottleneck: the scarcity of specialized training datasets containing sufficiently diverse user-specific interactions. This data limitation severely constrains PESC systems' ability to generate personalized responses.

To address these challenges, we propose a novel two-stage synthetic data generation framework that strategically employs large language models (LLMs) to create emotionally supportive dialogues with personalized contextualization. In the first stage, DeepSeek-V3 produced structured character information encoded in JSON format, generating diverse personality attributes through constrained schema sampling. These schema-enriched profiles then direct Qwen-32B-instruct agents in the second stage to simulate psychologically seeker-supporter interactions via multi-agent dialogue synthesis.

Our research systematically explores the practical advantages of synthetic data generation, utilizing visual analysis of synthesized dialogues and comparative SFT experiments. This methodology demonstrates a viable solution to expand datasets while ensuring alignment between dialogue content and individual characteristics, thus enhancing the personalization aspect of emotional support systems.

Our contributions include:

- Development of a novel role-based dialogue generation mechanism.
- Integration of multi-agent systems to enhance dialogue simulation.
- Demonstrated the effectiveness of synthetic data via SFT experiments, showing significant improvements in evaluation metrics.

2   Related Work

In recent years, the rapid advancement of natural language processing (NLP) technologies has driven comprehensive upgrades in intelligent dialogue systems. LLMs, particularly those employing decoder-only architectures and the "pre-training plus supervised fine-tuning" paradigm, have demonstrated remarkable learning capabilities, offering versatile solutions for various NLP tasks. Concurrently, the field of affective computing has achieved a significant breakthrough in transitioning from generic responses to personalized care. The emerging PESC technology enables the generation of more tailored emotional responses based on user characteristics, though it currently faces challenges due to limited training data.

2.1   Large Language Models

Recent advancements in decoder-only architecture large language models (LLMs) have established them as versatile solutions for diverse NLP tasks, achieving competitive performance through unified frameworks [5]. The paradigm typically involves two-phase adaptation: self-supervised pre-training on massive corpora followed by task-specific refinement. While traditional SFT remains prevalent, emerging prompting techniques offer alternative adaptation pathways.

This dual adaptation framework enables flexible deployment strategies. As demonstrated by [6], well-designed prompts provide intuitive human-AI interaction interfaces while offering essential contextual constraints, making prompt engineering particularly valuable for scenarios requiring controlled generation formats [7]. However, empirical studies reveal inconsistent adherence to prescribed output structures, suggesting the need for complementary approaches. The effectiveness of SFT emerges in such scenarios, where domain-specific fine-tuning enhances structural compliance through targeted parameter updates.

The interplay between these adaptation strategies inspires innovative methodologies. [8] pioneers cross-lingual persuasion detection through chain-of-thought (CoT) enhanced synthetic data, combining prompt-based reasoning with SFT-enhanced generation capabilities. In classification tasks, recent work synergizes both strategies: initial SFT on domain corpora establishes baseline competence, followed by prompt-driven arbitration mechanisms to resolve prediction conflicts. The approach proposed by [9] extended this paradigm by employing LLMs as discrepancy arbitrators, leveraging their contextual understanding beyond conventional classifiers through hybrid prompting and fine-tuning techniques.

2.2 Personalized Emotional Support Conversation

With the rapid advancement of artificial intelligence technology, the generation of emotional support conversations has become a major research frontier in affective computing [2]. However, traditional ESC systems often generate generic responses that do not address user-specific and personalized needs. To address this issue, Cheng et al. [3]proposed a new task called the PESC. This paradigm shift motivates our investigation into PESC systems that can effectively balance empathetic responsiveness with privacy preservation.

The primary objective of this research domain is to develop dialogue systems capable of delivering PESC through context-aware interaction mechanisms. Such systems aim to assist users in alleviating psychological stress and obtaining emotional comfort.

2.3 Multi Agent and Data Synthesis

Recent advances in personalized emotional dialogue generation have increasingly relied on the integration of multi-agent systems and synthetic data. Existing implementations of Multi-Agent Systems in conversational AI predominantly focus on two dimensions: enhancing collaborative task completion through agent specialization [10], and simulating social dynamics in human-like interactions [11]. While Zhao et al.'s Sirius system demonstrates remarkable adaptability to dynamic conversational contexts through its self-improving multi-agent architecture, their work remains constrained to dialogue generation optimization rather than addressing fundamental data scarcity issues.

This limitation becomes particularly salient when considering the data synthesis paradigm. Current synthetic data generation methodologies predominantly employ single-agent approaches with persona templates [12] or rule-based interaction patterns [13]. Although these methods improve dataset diversity to some extent, they fail to capture the nuanced emotional reciprocity inherent in authentic human dialogues - a critical gap identified by recent empirical studies [14].

Our work innovatively bridges these two research streams by introducing a role-playing Multi-Agent Systems framework specifically designed for empathetic data synthesis. Unlike previous Multi-Agent Systems implementations that emphasize system-level performance optimization, our architecture deploys specialized agents as synthetic interlocutors with configurable emotional personas. This paradigm shift enables the generation of dialogue trajectories that preserve emotional consistency while exhibiting organic conversational dynamics, surpassing the scripted nature of existing single-agent synthesis approaches [12].

3 Our System

PESC incorporates user-specific traits to generate tailored responses, extending traditional ESC systems.

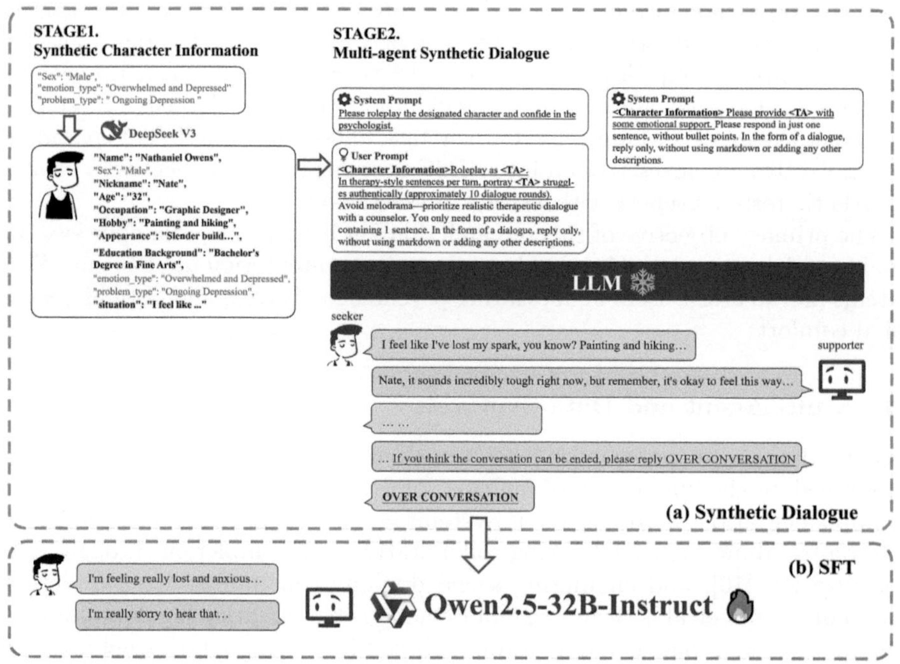

Fig. 1. The overall architecture of our system.

As shown in Fig. 1, our synthetic data framework uses a two-stage pipeline: the first stage generates structured character information, followed by the second stage that focuses on multi-agent dialogue synthesis. We then leverage the synthesized data to perform SFT for performance enhancement.

3.1 Synthetic Data

Synthetic Character Information. To ensure high relevance between emotional support dialogue content and personal characteristics, this study adopts a role-based dialogue generation approach utilizing large language models. The tight coupling between dialogue content and user background is achieved through structured character information, specifically by extracting three key feature dimensions from the character info field in the training dataset: sex, emotion type, and problem type. After randomly sampling and combining these feature dimensions, they are fed into the DeepSeek-V3 [15] model to generate JSON-structured outputs that conform to the training data format. These outputs encompass complete character background descriptions and personalized opening utterances matching the feature combinations, thereby ensuring the generated dialogues maintain both semantic coherence and individualized characteristics.

Multi-agent Synthetic Dialogue. The character information synthesized in Stage 1 guides the dialogue synthesis in Stage 2. We conducted experiments using two large language models: DeepSeek-V3 and Qwen2.5-32B-instruct [16]. In the experimental setup, we employed either two DeepSeek-V3 models or two Qwen2.5-32B-instruct models to assume the roles of seeker and supporter respectively. According to the character settings, the seeker initiates the conversation by sharing emotional issues with the supporter, who then provides emotional support in response.

To maintain conversational naturalness and avoid abrupt termination, we implemented two termination conditions: 1) When the total number of dialogue turns exceeds 6, the system adds an additional prompt "If you think the conversation can be ended, please reply OVER CONVERSATION", allowing the seeker to voluntarily terminate the conversation; 2) The maximum number of dialogue turns is set to 26, beyond which the conversation will be forcibly terminated. Furthermore, we found repetitive patterns in character name generation within DeepSeek-synthesized data, prompting the integration of randomized name substitution to enhance lexical diversity across dialogue samples.

The original dataset contains 1,500 dialogue instances, which are divided into training, validation, and test sets in an 8:1:1 ratio. To augment the original data, two sets of dialogue data were generated: DeepSeek-V3 produced 1,315 dialogues (7,074 sentences, 5.4 sentences/dialogue), while Qwen-32B generated 5,952 dialogues (41,584 sentences, 7.0 sentences/dialogue), all terminated by the voluntary actions of seekers, and representative samples were illustrated in the accompanying Fig. 2.

To compare the distributions of sentence vectors, we first utilized the BGE-base-en-v1.5 [17] embedding model to generate vector representations of the dialogue data, and then applied UMAP/t-SNE for dimensionality reduction, as illustrated in Fig. 3. This visualization highlights the difference between the sentence vectors synthesized by DeepSeek-V3 and those generated by Qwen-32B, where the latter exhibits significantly stronger consistency with the original data distribution. This observation was further corroborated in subsequent supervised fine-tuning experiments.

> **Qwen32b**
>
> "seeker:I've been feeling really down lately, like no matter what I do, I can't shake this sense of loneliness and it's starting to affect my work and my motivation.",
> "supporter:I'm really sorry that you're going through this, Eve; it sounds incredibly tough, but remember, it's okay to feel this way sometimes, and reaching out for support is a strong first step. Maybe trying a small creative project or reconnecting with a friend could help lift your spirits a bit?"
> … …

> **DeepsSeek**
>
> … …
> "seeker:I know you're right, but it's hard not to feel like a failure when I'm staring at my empty bank account and packing boxes.",
> "supporter:Your worth isn't measured by a job title or apartment - you're still the same creative, resilient person who turned blank canvases into magic.",
> "seeker:I miss that feeling of getting lost in a painting... lately I just sit staring at my brushes, paralyzed by all this uncertainty.",
> "supporter:That spark still lives in you, Len - maybe this difficult time is just your heart asking you to reconnect with art for the joy of it again."
> … …

> **Origin**
>
> "seeker:I just feel like everyone leaves me because I'm too strange, and I'm constantly messing things up in my life.",
> "supporter:It sounds really tough to feel that way, but many people experience those feelings of being different and struggling. You're not alone in this; it's okay to embrace your uniqueness.",
> "seeker: I appreciate the understanding, but it still feels like my weirdness drives everyone away. It's hard to feel good about myself when I keep failing to connect with others.",
> … …

Fig. 2. Example Dialogue Samples from DeepSeek-V3, Qwen-32B and Origin Data.

3.2 Supervised Fine-Tuning

We integrated the character information into a sentence and add it to the system prompt. The character information is integrated through natural language templates with `italicized variables`:

> *<Age>-year-old <Occupation> <Name> (friends call <TA> <Nickname>), <TA> has <Appearance>, and enjoys <Hobby>. <TA> educational background is <Education>. <TA> is currently feeling <EmotionType> and facing <ProblemType>, <TA> says <Situation>. Please provide <TA> with some emotional support.*

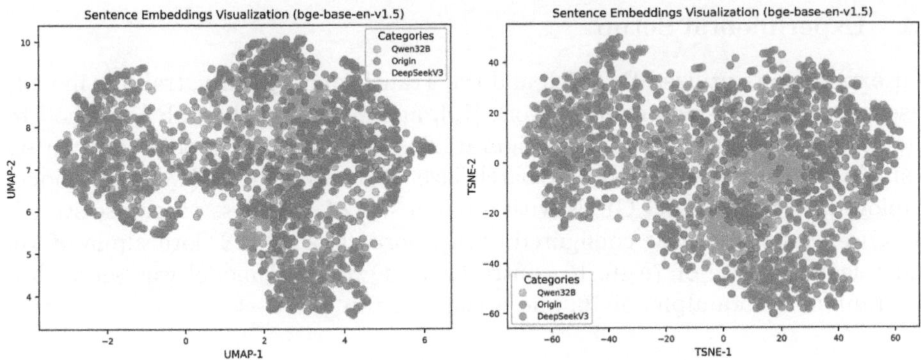

Fig. 3. UMAP/TSNE Visualization of Sentence Embeddings.

To efficiently fine-tune our sentiment dialogue generation model, we employ Low-Rank Adaptation (LoRA) [18]. LoRA reduces the number of trainable parameters in large language models while maintaining model capacity, resulting in significantly reduced resource consumption.

The method decomposes weight updates into low-rank matrices A and B , substantially lowering computational burden. The adaptation process can be formulated as:

$$W = W_0 + \Delta W \tag{1}$$

$$\Delta W = A \times B \tag{2}$$

where ΔW represents the low-rank update applied to the original weight matrix W_0, and W denotes the updated weight matrix after LoRA adaptation.

4   Experiment and Result

The shared task employs six automatic metrics: METEOR (ME), BLEU-4 (B-4), ROUGE-L (R-L), VectorExtrema (Ext), Distinct-2/3 (D-2/3), and GPT-4-based evaluation protocol (G-Score), which assesses response quality through four dimensions: relevance, fluency, informativeness, and logical coherence. The final score calculation is as follows.

$$\begin{aligned} score = {} & 0.2 \times \text{ME} + 0.2 \times \text{B-4} + 0.2 \times \text{R-L} + 0.1 \times \text{Ext} \\ & + 0.1 \times \text{D-2} + 0.1 \times \text{D-3} + 0.1 \times \text{G-Score} \end{aligned} \tag{3}$$

4.1   Experimental Setup

Our experiments utilized PyTorch and the Transformers library, training models based on the llama-factory framework [19], and employed the LoRA method to fine-tune the models. For our configurations, the Qwen-7B model was run on a single A100-80G GPU with a batch size of 1, while the Qwen-32B model employed four A100-80G GPUs with a batch size of 4. Unless otherwise stated, the Qwen-7B model was configured with a lora rank of 128, lora alpha of 16, and a learning rate of 7e−6. In contrast, the Qwen-32B model was set with a lora rank of 8, lora alpha of 16, and a learning rate of 1e−4.

4.2   Results and Analysis

In our parametric study involving the Qwen-7B model, we conducted LoRA fine-tuning on fundamental datasets to explore the effects of the alpha and rank ratio under specified hyperparameter constraints (alpha = 16, rank = 32). As illustrated in Fig. 4, the alpha-rank ratio exhibited relatively small influence on the experimental outcomes. Due to budget constraints, G-score evaluation was omitted for this experiment—all reported scores in Fig. 4 were calculated with G-score weighted at zero in Eq. 3. Notably, the model reached peak performance at ratio settings of 1 and 3, with its most optimal configuration being alpha = 48 and rank = 16.

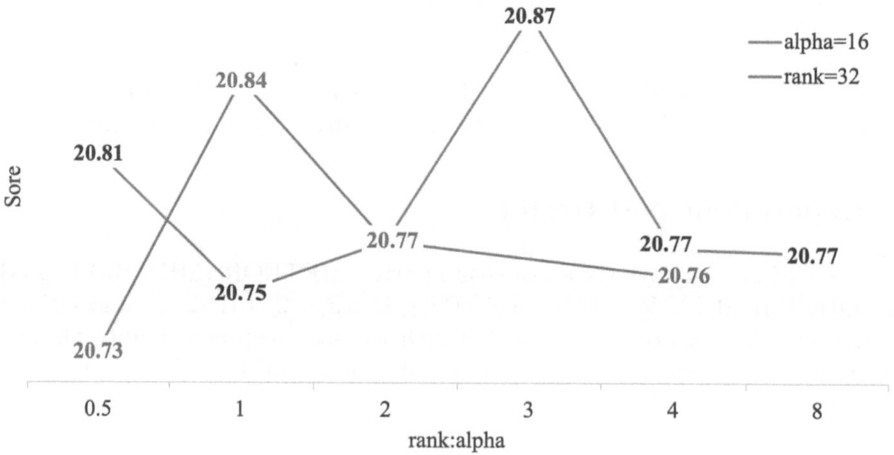

Fig. 4. Alpha-Rank Ratio Analysis.

As demonstrated in Table 1, baseline evaluations reveal significant performance differences between pre-trained models, with DeepSeek-v3 achieving the highest untuned score of 35.42 compared to Qwen32B's 29.05. The overall superiority of DeepSeek-v3 seems to be driven by its exceptional output diversity, as indicated by Distinct-2 and Distinct-3 scores of 44.69 and 70.93, respectively. However, Qwen32B exhibits stronger performance when excluding diversity metrics. This performance gap in diversity metrics can be largely attributed to a key behavioral difference: DeepSeek-V3 tends to incorporate user names more frequently in its responses, a characteristic that significantly enhances its Distinct-n score. Specifically, 19.8% of DeepSeek-V3's generated replies contain user names, whereas only 0.3% of Qwen32B's replies include such references. Notably, user names never appear in the validation set's original responses. As illustrated in the following example.

> *Seeker:*
> *I like the idea of keeping it simple; I really need something I can follow without feeling overwhelmed. If it feels manageable, it might actually help me regain some control.*
> *Supporter:*
> *Origin: It sounds like keeping things simple really resonates with you! Together, we can create a plan that feels light and manageable, so you can start feeling that sense of control again.*
> *DeepSeek-V3: Exactly—small wins build confidence! Let's celebrate every step, even the tiny ones, because each one is proof you're moving forward. You've got this, Sam.*

As shown in Table 1, SFT consistently improves performance across all model architectures. And our ablation study highlights the critical role of character information integration: removing character information from Qwen7B+SFT results in a score decline of 7.67 points.

In our experiments with Qwen7B, we incorporated additional datasets: EmpatheticDialogues [20] (abbreviated as ED) and DeepSeek synthetic data (abbreviated as DS). As shown in Table 1, our results indicated that integrating ED data led to a decline in performance metrics. This decline is attributed to the fact that ED stems from an open-domain conversational setting where two individuals discuss a situation related to a specific emotion, which does not align with the help-seeking scenarios targeted by our task. Although the inclusion of DeepSeek synthetic data increased the overall score, these improvements were primarily driven by Distinct metrics, while other scores showed a decrease.

In our study, we utilized Qwen32B to synthesize 3,431 dialogues, forming the dataset SDsmall. Applying the same methodology, we expanded it to 5,925 dialogues, resulting in the dataset SDplus. With the introduction of our synthetic data, certain scores were improved, particularly the G-score. The model trained on SDplus achieved a G-score of 84.35, which is 2.68 higher than that trained on the basic dataset. Furthermore, as shown in Table 2, the model demonstrated superior performance in the test phase, achieving the highest G-score of 92.67.

Table 2 lists our submitted results and the top scores from competing teams on the test set. Our experimental results underscore the profound effect of temperature tuning and data augmentation on model performance. Initially, applying Qwen2.5-7B with SFT on the original dataset at an inference temperature

Table 1. Our Result on Val Set.

model	Ext Data	Score	ME	B-4	R-L	Ext	D-2	D-3	G-Score
Qwen7B		25.47	16.56	0.58	7.17	93.54	15.49	32.89	64.17
+*SFT - Character Info*		36.85	26.69	6.11	29.85	96.25	24.70	44.25	77.96
+*SFT*		37.40	27.03	6.29	**30.33**	96.26	26.19	46.59	79.41
+*SFT*	ED	36.72	26.26	5.76	29.61	96.23	24.34	43.90	77.68
+*SFT*	DS	37.51	25.76	5.77	29.50	96.08	27.77	49.36	79.80
Qwen32B		29.05	19.37	0.82	8.82	93.93	21.17	45.09	72.31
+*SFT*		38.46	27.73	5.77	29.42	96.27	28.58	52.31	81.67
+*SFT*	SD*small*	**38.93**	28.31	**6.57**	30.06	95.83	28.96	52.55	82.11
+*SFT*	SD*plus*	38.34	**29.16**	5.29	26.90	**96.34**	27.88	52.18	**84.35**
Qwen72B		26.59	16.80	0.66	7.45	93.66	16.91	36.76	68.72
DeepSeek-v3		35.42	13.78	1.49	18.07	95.05	**44.69**	**70.93**	76.84

Table 2. Our Results and Other Teamsn' Results on Test Set.

model/team	temp	Score	ME	B-4	R-L	Ext	D-2	D-3	G-Score
Qwen7B*SFT*	0.7/1.0	38.84	27.4	**6.32**	**30.08**	96.36	27.80	50.16	86.55
Qwen7B*SFT*+DeepSeek	0.7/1.0	38.91	25.05	5.50	27.95	96.09	32.9	56.70	86.37
Qwen7B*SFT*	1.0	**38.99**	25.85	5.04	27.84	96.22	31.58	57.77	86.84
Qwen32B*SDsmall+SFT*	1.3	38.48	20.94	2.30	19.56	95.21	**53.94**	**81.48**	68.59
Qwen32B*SDplus+SFT*	0.7	38.97	**28.82**	5.05	26.77	**96.38**	27.79	51.57	**92.67**
ZZUNLP_Adventure		**42.69**	**32.83**	**8.90**	**34.70**	**96.48**	30.57	55.35	91.60
TeleAI		39.62	27.21	6.25	29.89	96.22	30.99	55.12	87.20

of 0.7 led to substantial content repetition in the generated outputs. To mitigate this issue, we implemented two distinct refinements: first, replacing repetitive content with responses regenerated at a temperature of 1.0 (as shown in Row 1 results), and second, enhancing output diversity by substituting high-similarity sentences (TF-IDF cosine similarity > 0.8) with DeepSeek-V3 responses, thereby significantly improving the distinctness score (as demonstrated in Row 2 results).

The configuration utilizing Qwen2.5-7B SFT with a temperature of 1.0 yielded the highest overall score, reflecting an optimal balance between response quality and diversity. Experiments involving synthetic data augmentation showed that enriching the original dataset with 1,315 Qwen-32B synthetic dialogue samples at a temperature of 1.3 maximized the distinctness score, albeit with less coherent outputs that negatively impacted the G-score and other evaluation metrics. Our final and most successful configuration continued this augmentation strategy, increasing the synthetic data scale to 5,952 dialogues and lowering the temperature to 0.7, resulting in the highest G-score of 92.67.

Ultimately, our model achieved a final score of 38.99 on the leaderboard, securing the third place ranking.

5   Conclusion

In this paper, we propose a two-stage synthetic data generation framework to address data scarcity in PESC systems. The framework comprises a Synthetic Character Information stage where DeepSeek-V3 generates JSON-formatted character information, followed by a Role-Guided Dialogue Simulation stage where conversational agents produce 5,952 synthetic interactions. Our synthetic data significantly enhances model performance. Experimental results demonstrate that Qwen-32B-based synthetic data exhibits superior semantic alignment with the shared task dataset compared to DeepSeek-V3 outputs. Supervised fine-tuning with synthesized dialogues achieves substantial performance gains, particularly evidenced by significant G-score improvements from 81.67 to 84.35 on the validation set.

Our system attained the highest G-score (92.67) on the NLPCC-2025 Shared Task 8 dataset, ultimately ranking third with an overall score of 38.99.

References

1. Cameron, G., et al.: Assessing the usability of a chatbot for mental health care. In: Bodrunova, S.S., et al. (eds.) INSCI 2018. LNCS, vol. 11551, pp. 121–132. Springer, Cham (2019). https://doi.org/10.1007/978-3-030-17705-8_11
2. Liu, S., et al.: Towards emotional support dialog systems. arXiv preprint arXiv:2106.01144 (2021)
3. Cheng, J., Sabour, S., Sun, H., Chen, Z., Huang, M.: Pal: persona-augmented emotional support conversation generation (2023). https://arxiv.org/abs/2212.09235
4. Leary, M.R., Allen, A.B.: Personality and persona: personality processes in self-presentation. J. Pers. **79**(6), 889–916 (2011)
5. Zhao, W.X., et al.: A survey of large language models. arXiv abs/2303.18223 (2023). https://api.semanticscholar.org/CorpusID:257900969
6. Zhou, Y., et al.: Large language models are human-level prompt engineers (2022)
7. Schick, T., Schütze, H.: Exploiting cloze questions for few shot text classification and natural language inference. arXiv preprint arXiv:2001.07676 (2020)
8. Li, D., et al.: CoT-based data augmentation strategy for persuasion techniques detection. In: Ojha, A.K., Doğruöz, A.S., Tayyar Madabushi, H., Da San Martino, G., Rosenthal, S., Rosá, A. (eds.) Proceedings of the 18th International Workshop on Semantic Evaluation (SemEval-2024), pp. 1315–1321. Association for Computational Linguistics, Mexico City, Mexico (2024). https://doi.org/10.18653/v1/2024.semeval-1.190, https://aclanthology.org/2024.semeval-1.190/
9. Wang, C., Li, D., Wang, Y., Qiao, X., Zhang, B., Wang, J.: Introducing structural information of argumentative essays into pre-trained models. In: CCF International Conference on Natural Language Processing and Chinese Computing (2025)
10. Du, Y., Leibo, J.Z., Islam, U., Willis, R., Sunehag, P.: A review of cooperation in multi-agent learning (2023). https://arxiv.org/abs/2312.05162
11. Zhao, W., Yuksekgonul, M., Wu, S., Zou, J.: Sirius: self-improving multi-agent systems via bootstrapped reasoning (2025). https://arxiv.org/abs/2502.04780
12. Ge, T., Chan, X., Wang, X., Yu, D., Mi, H., Yu, D.: Scaling synthetic data creation with 1,000,000,000 personas (2025). https://arxiv.org/abs/2406.20094

13. Liu, R., et al.: Best practices and lessons learned on synthetic data (2024). https://arxiv.org/abs/2404.07503
14. Wu, C., Wang, Z.: The dynamic features of emotion dysregulation in major depressive disorder: an emotion dynamics perspective. Adv. Psychol. Sci. **32**(2), 364 (2024)
15. DeepSeek-AI: Deepseek-v3 technical report (2024). https://arxiv.org/abs/2412.19437
16. Team, Q.: Qwen2.5: A party of foundation models (2024). https://qwenlm.github.io/blog/qwen2.5/
17. Xiao, S., Liu, Z., Zhang, P., Muennighoff, N.: C-pack: packaged resources to advance general Chinese embedding (2023)
18. Hu, E.J., et al.: LoRA: low-rank adaptation of large language models (2021). https://arxiv.org/abs/2106.09685
19. Zheng, Y., et al.: Llamafactory: unified efficient fine-tuning of 100+ language models. In: Proceedings of the 62nd Annual Meeting of the Association for Computational Linguistics (Volume 3: System Demonstrations). Association for Computational Linguistics, Bangkok, Thailand (2024). http://arxiv.org/abs/2403.13372
20. Rashkin, H., Smith, E.M., Li, M., Boureau, Y.L.: Towards empathetic open-domain conversation models: a new benchmark and dataset. In: Korhonen, A., Traum, D., Màrquez, L. (eds.) Proceedings of the 57th Annual Meeting of the Association for Computational Linguistics, pp. 5370–5381. Association for Computational Linguistics, Florence, Italy (2019). https://doi.org/10.18653/v1/P19-1534, https://aclanthology.org/P19-1534/

Author Index

© The Editor(s) (if applicable) and The Author(s), under exclusive license
to Springer Nature Singapore Pte Ltd. 2026
X.-L. Mao et al. (Eds.): NLPCC 2025, LNAI 16105, pp. 553–555, 2026.
https://doi.org/10.1007/978-981-95-3352-7

MIX
Papier aus verantwortungsvollen Quellen
Paper from responsible sources
FSC® C105338

If you have any concerns about our products,
you can contact us on
ProductSafety@springernature.com

In case Publisher is established outside the EU,
the EU authorized representative is:
**Springer Nature Customer Service Center GmbH
Europaplatz 3, 69115 Heidelberg, Germany**

Printed by Libri Plureos GmbH
in Hamburg, Germany